CHILDREN –
THE MODERN LAW

Second edition

CHILDREN –
THE MODERN LAW

Second edition

ANDREW BAINHAM
Fellow of Christ's College, Cambridge
Lecturer in Law, University of Cambridge

Family Law
1998

Published by Family Law
an imprint of Jordan Publishing Limited
21 St Thomas Street
Bristol
BS1 6JS

British Library Cataloguing-in-Publication Data
A catalogue record for this book is available from the British Library.

ISBN 0 85308 501 3

Front cover drawing by Victoria May, aged 10.
Back cover drawing by Helen Moreland, aged 7½.

Typeset by Mendip Communications Ltd, Frome, Somerset
Printed by MPG Books Ltd, Bodmin, Cornwall

TO MY CHILDREN, SAMI AND RHYS

PREFACE

Since the first edition of this book was published in 1993, there have been many substantial changes to the law affecting children. There has been major legislation including the Child Support Act 1995, the Education Acts of 1996 and 1997, the Family Law Act 1996 and, as the book was going to press, the Labour Government's School Standards and Framework Act 1998 and the Crime and Disorder Act 1998. The last five years have also seen an explosion of case-law under the Children Act 1989 which has included three important decisions of the House of Lords in the area of public family proceedings.

The aim of this second edition is to take account of these developments and to provide students of children law and family law with an overview of the principal areas of law and the central policy issues which affect children. I hope that the book can serve as a textbook for the growing number of self-contained courses in children law, which have resulted in part from semesterisation and modularisation, and also as a text for the children sections of those family law courses which, like the one in Cambridge, continue to occupy the whole academic year.

The traditional division of family law courses into sections dealing with children and sections covering so-called 'adult issues' such as divorce, family property and domestic violence is, I believe, a somewhat artificial one. There is no better illustration of this than the Family Law Act 1996. This deals primarily with divorce and mediation, domestic violence and occupation of the family home – matters which have been seen as raising predominantly 'adult' questions. Yet it cannot be doubted that there are also important 'children' issues involved. Does it, for example, make any sense to regard domestic violence and the new 'exclusion requirements' which can be imposed under Part IV of the Act as distinct from the issues surrounding child abuse and care proceedings? The Family Law Act 1996 therefore posed something of a dilemma. I decided to concentrate on those aspects of the legislation which affect children most directly. However, it would not have made sense to attempt to do this without at least sketching the principal features of the new law as it applies to divorce and to domestic violence and occupation of the family home. This I have tried to do in Chapters 4 and 12 respectively.

More than one review of the first edition made the point that it would have been desirable for the section dealing with the United Nations Convention on the Rights of the Child to appear earlier in the book and not to have been relegated to the final chapter dealing with Children in the International Community. I felt the force of this criticism and I have, accordingly, brought this discussion forward to Chapter 2.

Chapter 2 now looks at the Children Act 1989 and the United Nations Convention in juxtaposition as the two major sources of children law domestically and internationally. The reader should bear in mind that Part II of Chapter 2 could usefully be read with Chapter 17, which considers other international Conventions protecting children. Chapter 17 now concludes with a brief examination of the European Convention on Human Rights, which is expected to be incorporated into English law before the end of 1998 under the Human Rights Bill currently before Parliament. There is no doubt in my mind that one of the effects of such incorporation will be the necessity to confront, more openly than before, clashes between the fundamental rights and interests of children and those of adult society.

Something else which has changed since 1993 is my own view of the subject. The production of a second edition provides the opportunity for a re-evaluation of earlier work and the accommodation of the writings of other commentators. In the case of children law, commentaries have been very extensive indeed and show no sign of abating. Three matters perhaps stand out as worthy of mention. First, it is my view that with the growing emphasis and concentration on the concept of children's rights there has been a tendency to neglect the whole question of children's duties or responsibilities. I try to address this issue briefly in Chapter 3. Secondly, unlike many commentators, I no longer believe (if I ever did) that the Children Act is all about 'non-intervention', whatever that may mean. The legislation is too complex and the product of too many influences that it can be said to embrace a single philosophy about the State's relationship with the family. It is, I now think, dangerously misleading to refer to the principle in s 1(5) of the Children Act as the 'non-intervention principle' because of these wider connotations. I do not like 'no order principle' either but I have adopted it because I can think of no better way of describing it. Thirdly, I make no apology for expressing the strongly held opinion that it is unacceptable as we approach the twenty-first century, to continue to refer to 'illegitimate' children. I have, therefore, to an appreciable extent, expunged this terminology from the book, although it has not been possible to do so when referring to the historical position of children born outside marriage.

I have now assumed responsibility for the whole book. Chapters 1 and 9 in the first edition were written by Dr Stephen Cretney, and it is only right that I should acknowledge that they remain substantially the chapters which he wrote, updated to take account of recent developments. Dr Cretney was kind enough to read and comment on my alterations to these chapters but he is not to be held responsible for the final versions. In Chapter 9, in particular, I have concluded with some observations of my own about the policy issues surrounding child support. I remain very grateful to Stephen Cretney both for his recent comments and for his initial involvement with the first edition.

I am indebted also to all those friends and colleagues who have so willingly given of their time to assist, some in small ways and some in major ways, with the writing of this second edition. I would especially like to thank Caroline Bridge, Simon Deakin, Loraine Gelsthorpe, Neville Harris, Steve Hedley, Bridget Lindley, Rosemary Pattenden, John Spencer and Tony Weir. I am also very grateful to Carol Dowling who provided valuable assistance in producing the manuscript. The staff of Jordans, and Jo Morton in particular, were, as always, friendly and supportive throughout and committed to the quality of the finished product in a way which one does not always find or perhaps have a right to demand from a publisher. I also want to recognise the unusually stimulating experience of being involved with the teaching of the Family Law Tripos, the Family in Society seminar course and the Masters course in Family Law and Policy at the University of Cambridge. I hope that this second edition will be of use to the students of the

Cambridge Law Faculty with whom it has been my privilege and pleasure to be associated over the last five years. I have no doubt that they will be the first to tell me if I have got anything wrong!

If I were to be asked what was the most enjoyable aspect of producing this edition I would be able to reply that it was no contest. It was undoubtedly my visit with the publishers to St Joseph's and St Theresa's RCVA School in Wells, Somerset, to judge the children's competition for the cover design. I would like to thank the headteacher, Teresa Dicker, for her hospitality, and the children for entertaining us with their singing. Such was the standard of the children's paintings and drawings that we were able to choose not one, but two, for the front and back covers respectively. My special thanks are therefore due to Victoria May and Helen Moreland who produced the winning entries. Those who study the cover illustrations on books will see that on this one there is a baby in a pram, a toddler at the foot of the tree, a child of perhaps nine or ten sliding down the branch and what looks like an adolescent on the right. We sometimes forget that the expression 'children' embraces everyone from birth to majority and I felt that this drawing encapsulated the stages of childhood rather well.

Finally, my greatest debt is to my partner Christina who has lived through this second edition with me and without whose support this task would have been a good deal harder.

ANDREW BAINHAM
Christ's College, Cambridge
August 1998

CONTENTS

PART III   CHILDREN AND LOCAL AUTHORITIES

TABLE OF CASES

TABLE OF STATUTES

TABLE OF STATUTORY INSTRUMENTS, STATUTORY GUIDANCE, ETC

TABLE OF EC LEGISLATION, INTERNATIONAL CONVENTIONS, FOREIGN ENACTMENTS, ETC

Table of foreign enactments

PART I
BACKGROUND AND SOURCES OF CHILDREN LAW

Part I of the book aims to introduce the student to the historical evolution, sources and fundamental principles of the law affecting children. Chapter 1 sketches the profound historical and demographic changes which have influenced the attitude of society towards children and which provide the context in which legal change has occurred. Chapter 2 is concerned with the two most important sources of children law domestically and internationally. Section 1 of the chapter focuses on the immediate background to the Children Act 1989, its basic principles and underlying philosophies. There is now no question that the Act constitutes the single most important source of children law. Even where it does not have direct application, its influence is, nonetheless, likely to be pervasive. Section 2 of the chapter examines some of the more important articles and principles set out in the United Nations Convention on the Rights of the Child. This is, equally clearly, the most important international source. Chapter 3 attempts to identify some central issues which recur throughout the book. These relate to basic questions about the nature of childhood, parenthood and the interaction of children's rights with parents' rights and responsibilities.

Some understanding of these fundamentals is essential before embarking upon an examination of the substantive areas of law which are covered in the remainder of the book.

Chapter 1

CHILDREN AND THE LAW: A DEMOGRAPHIC AND HISTORICAL SKETCH

INTRODUCTION

The law reflects changing social and cultural attitudes and assumptions, and this is particularly true of family law. The history of those changes is a fascinating subject of study which, in recent years, has attracted much scholarly writing[1]. Considerations of space make it impossible to give even a brief summary of this research in this book, but it may be helpful for the reader to have a sketch of a number of key areas, such as the rules governing legal decision-taking within the family, the role of the State from the Elizabethan Poor Law through the child protection measures of the late nineteenth century down to the development of child-centred services as part of the post-Second World War Welfare State, and the development of legal procedures designed to shield children from the worst consequences of the

---

1   The most useful introduction is now to be found in WR Cornish and G de N Clark *Law and Society in England 1750–1950* (Sweet & Maxwell, 1989) (particularly chs 5 and 6); and both AH Manchester *A Modern Legal History of England and Wales 1750–1950* (Butterworths, 1980) and RH Graveson and FR Crane (eds) *A Century of Family Law 1857–1957* (Sweet & Maxwell, 1957) are valuable. RA Houlbrooke *The English Family 1450–1700* (Longman, 1984) is a study from a modern perspective, as is L Stone *The Family, Sex and Marriage in England, 1500–1800* (Weidenfeld & Nicolson, 1977). Reference may also usefully be made to the standard, if now dated, general legal history texts: F Pollock and FW Maitland *The History of English Law before the Time of Edward I* (Cambridge University Press, 1898); and Sir William Holdsworth *A History of English Law* (Methuen, 1966).

    The most accessible general social history is probably I Pinchbeck and M Hewitt *Children in English Society* Vol I (Routledge, 1969) and Vol II (1973) – although this work is not universally admired: see PEH Hair 'Children in Society 1850–1980' in T Barker and M Drake (eds) *Population and Society in Britain 1850–1980* (Batsford, 1982) at p 57. The evolution of public policy is traced in J Packman *The Child's Generation: Child Care Policy in Britain* (2nd edn) (Blackwell, 1981). For a recent authoritative study of the history of social policies for children, see H Hendrick *Child Welfare: England 1872–1989* (Routledge, 1994). A more discursive and international approach is taken in P Aries *Centuries of Childhood* (Jonathan Cape, 1962). Demographic factors are addressed in P Laslett and R Wall (eds) *Household and Family in Past Time: Comparative Studies in the Size and Structure of the Domestic Group over the Last Three Centuries in England, France, Serbia, Japan and Colonial North America, with further materials from Western Europe* (Cambridge University Press, 1972); EA Wrigley and RS Schofield *The Population History of England 1541–1871, A Reconstruction* (Cambridge University Press, 1989), and in J Eekelaar and D Pearl (eds) *An Aging World – Dilemmas and Challenges for Law and Social Policy* (Clarendon Press, 1989). For more specialist works, see L deMause (ed) *The History of Childhood* (Harper & Row, 1975); and L Pollock *A Lasting Relationship: Parents and Children over Three Centuries* (Fourth Estate, 1987). Useful comparative demographic material is to be found in the *Proceedings* of the *Seminar on present demographic trends and lifestyles in Europe* (Council of Europe, 1991).

    Stimulating general works include J Weeks *Sex Politics and Society: The Regulation of Sexuality Since 1800* (Longman, 1981); J Donzelot *The Policing of Families* (Hutchinson, 1980); JE Goldthorpe *Family Life in Western Societies: a Historical Sociology of Family Relationships in Britain and North America* (1987).

breakdown of their parents' relationships. These historical developments must be seen in the context of rapidly changing demographic factors, and a brief account of the most relevant data therefore follows.

Demographic factors: children and families

The first issue relates to the proportion of children in the population and to the size of the family units in which they are reared. There are two conflicting trends to note: on the one hand the number of live births[1] has fallen sharply since the early twentieth century[2], but on the other hand there has been a dramatic improvement (paradoxically most marked in the Second World War[3]) in infant mortality rates. The proportion of the population represented by children aged under 16 years in the UK fell from a quarter in 1961 to a fifth in 1995 and it is assumed that this trend will continue to at least 2031[4].

An ageing population, and its impact[5]

The life expectancy of a boy born in 1901 was 45 years; the life expectancy of a boy born in 2001 is estimated to be 74.5 years. By 1992 it had already risen to 73.7 years[6]. This significant improvement means that young people form a much smaller proportion of the population. The proportion of the population which is of pensionable age has risen sharply and can be expected to continue to rise: in 1961, 4% of the people in the UK were aged 75 and over; by 1995 the figure was 7%, by which year those aged over 65 represented around 16% of the population. Whereas in recent years the rate of increase in the number of elderly has slowed, it is expected to increase rapidly in 2007 when the post-war 'baby boomers' reach their sixties[7].

These changes have had (and will continue to have) a dramatic effect on the composition and size of kinship groups. Whereas the modern child expects to know both his parents throughout his childhood and some at least of his grandparents, eighteenth-century children often knew none of their grandparents,

---

1   The number of children in Britain probably increased decade by decade from the mid-eighteenth century to the early twentieth century: see PEH Hair 'Children in Society 1950–1980' in T Barker and M Drake (eds) *Population and Society in Britain 1850–1980* (Batsford, 1982); and, generally, EA Wrigley and RS Schofield *The Population History of England, 1541–1871, A Reconstruction* (Cambridge University Press, 1989).

2   In the first decade of the twentieth century the average number of live births was approximately 1.1 million each year, but – after the 'baby-boomer' years of the 1960s when, once again, more than a million live births were recorded – the number in the 1980s and 1990s seems to have stabilised at a figure below 800,000 annually and a slow decline is expected to continue. There were 732,000 births in 1995 and, on provisional figures, just over 733,000 in 1996: See *Social Trends 27* (1997) Table 1.12 and *Population Trends 90* (1997) Table 8.

3   In 1901 the rate of infant mortality approached 160 for every 1,000 live births, but by 1961 it had fallen to 22.1 for every 1,000 live births. In 1991 the rate had fallen to 7.4: *Population Trends 70* (1992) Table 8. By 1996 it had fallen yet further to 6.1: *Population Trends 90* (1997) Table 8.

4   *Social Trends 27* (1997) Table 1.5.

5   See, generally, J Eekelaar and D Pearl (eds) *An Aging World – Dilemmas and Challenges for Law and Social Policy* (Clarendon Press, 1989).

6   *Social Trends 23* (1993) Table 7.4 and *Social Trends 27* (1997) Table 7.5. The expectation of life of females is approximately five to six years longer.

7   *Social Trends 27* (1997) Table 1.5.

frequently knew only one of their parents, and not uncommonly knew neither of their parents[1].

So the modern child is much more likely to have at least the possibility of knowing his or her parents, grandparents and siblings. But, in fact, the family unit has become much smaller. Whereas the typical mid-Victorian family contained four or more children (and it was not uncommon to find families with up to 10 children), by 1991 only 5% of households had three or more dependent children and by 1995/96 this had fallen further to just 4%[2]. This trend towards a much smaller functioning family unit is reinforced by the increase in the number of single-parent families. The percentage of all dependent children living in lone-parent families has more than doubled since 1972 to reach 20% by 1995/96[3]; with the great majority of the parents being lone mothers rather than lone fathers[4].

Remarriage and step-children

There are just over 150,000 divorces each year in England and Wales, and there has been a very large increase in the number of children who experience the divorce of their parents: it has been estimated[5] that one in five children will experience a parental divorce by the time the child is 16 years of age. Many divorcing parents remarry[6] and in 1990 there were more than 40,000 births within marriage to women who had remarried. This figure had, however, sharply declined to 32,600 by 1996[7]. Such children will have kinship links with more than one family. The law's response to this phenomenon has not been consistent[8], while concern has also been expressed about the difficulties which children and parents encounter in keeping in contact after the breakdown of the parents' relationship[9].

Births outside marriage

Perhaps the most striking of all the demographic changes which has occurred since the end of the Second World War is the dramatic increase in the proportion of births which take place outside marriage. In 1961 there were 48,500 live births in England and Wales outside marriage (ie some 6% of all births)[10]; but by 1996

---

1 Hair 'Children in Society 1850–1980' in Barker and Drake (above) at p 44.
2 *Social Trends 27* (1997) Table 2.3.
3 Ibid, Table 2.10.
4 Ibid. But the majority – approximately 80% – of dependent children still live in a household headed by a couple.
5 J Haskey 'Children of Divorcing Couples' (1983); *Population Trends 31* (1983).
6 In 1990 there were more than 80,000 marriages in which one or both parties had been divorced; and 69.9 divorced persons per 1,000 divorced persons aged 16 and over remarried in that year: *Population Trends 70* (1992) Table 22. Recent provisional figures show a slight decline. In 1995 there were 77,000 such marriages and 56.1 per 1,000 divorced persons aged 16 or over remarried that year: *Population Trends 90* (1997) Table 23.
7 *Population Trends 70* (1992) Table 11 and *Population Trends 90* (1997) Table 11.
8 The Children Act 1975 introduced provisions intended to discourage the use of legal adoption by couples wishing to integrate children of a previous relationship into their family, while the Children Act 1989 is more neutral on the issue: see Chapter 7 below, and generally J Masson et al *Mine, Yours or Ours?* (1983).
9 See, generally, MPM Richards and M Dyson *Separation, Divorce and the Development of Children: a Review* (1983).
10 *Population Trends 70* (1992) Table 10.

there were 232,700, representing well over one-third (35.8%) of all births[1]. These figures are all the more remarkable in the light of the fact that a large number of pregnancies are now legally terminated by abortion. In 1991 over 167,000 legal abortions were carried out on residents in England and Wales (the great majority on unmarried women) and in 1996 the figure was just under 167,000[2].

Although a high proportion of lone-parent families are headed by a single woman[3], it should not be assumed that the child born outside marriage is likely to be brought up in a one-parent household: around four-fifths of all births outside marriage are registered jointly by both parents, and four-fifths of these parents are parents living at the same address[4]. It seems, therefore, that to some extent social reality and legal institutions are no longer so closely correlated as is often assumed. In particular, it is noteworthy that a significant number[5] of parents enter into parental responsibility agreements[6] which put them into a legal relationship with the child which is similar to that of married parents.

THE CHILD AS A LEGAL PERSON

All legal systems give parents or other adults powers in respect of the upbringing of children, but the extent of those powers differs from time to time and from place to place. In England, Blackstone (writing in the eighteenth century) accepted that the power of parents over their children was derived from the need to enable a parent more effectually to perform his duty to the child (although he also saw parental rights as being, to some extent, a recompense for the care and trouble taken by the parent in the faithful discharge of his duties)[7]. Blackstone also pointed out that the assessment of the scope of parental power varied from time to time and from nation to nation:

'the ancient Roman laws gave the father a power of life and death over his children; upon this principle, that he who gave has also the power of taking away. Moreover a son could not acquire any property of his own during the life of his father, but all his acquisitions belonged to the father, or at least the profits of them for his life.'

Parental power in English law was still 'sufficient to keep the child in order and obedience'[8]; and Blackstone's description of the eighteenth-century parent's right bears extended citation. The parent (he said):

'. . . may lawfully correct his child, being under age, in a reasonable manner: for this is for the benefit of his education. The consent or concurrence of the parent to the marriage of his child under age, was also directed by our ancient law to be obtained . . . and this is also another means, which the law has put into the parent's hands, in order the better to discharge his duty; first, of

---

1   *Population Trends 90* (1997) Table 10.
2   *Population Trends 70* (1992) Table 16 and *Population Trends 90* (1997) Table 17.
3   *Social Trends 27* (1997) Table 2.9.
4   Ibid at p 50.
5   Between October 1991 and the end of June 1992, 1,510 parental responsibility agreements had been registered. See *Children Act Advisory Committee Annual Report 1991/92*, Table 8, Appendix 1. The number registered reached what appears to be a peak of over 5,000 in 1994 but by 1996 had fallen away to 3,590. This was a slight (4%) increase on 1995. See *Children Act Advisory Committee Final Report June 1997*, Table 4, Appendix 2.
6   See Chapter 5.
7   Blackstone *Commentaries on the Laws of England* (4th edn) (1770) Book 1, ch 15, section 2.
8   Ibid.

protecting his children from the snares of artful and designing persons; and, next, of settling properly in life, by preventing the ill consequences of too early and precipitate marriages. A father has no other power over his son's estate, than as his trustee or guardian; for, though he may receive the profits during the child's minority, yet he must account for them when he comes of age. He may indeed have the benefit of his children's labour while they live with him, and are maintained by him: but this is no more than he is entitled to from his apprentices or servants. The legal power of a father (for a mother, as such, is entitled to no power, but only to reverence and respect) over the persons of his children ceases at the age of 21: for they are then enfranchised by arriving at years of discretion, or that point which the law has established (as some must necessarily be established) when the empire of the father, or other guardian, gives place to the empire of reason. Yet, until that age arrives, this empire of the father continues even after his death; for he may by his will appoint a guardian to his children. He may also delegate part of his parental authority during his life, to the tutor or schoolmaster of his child; who is then *in loco parentis*, and has such a portion of the power the parent committed to his charge, viz. that of restraint and correction, as may be necessary to answer the purposes for which he is employed.'

Legal power and social reality

Although it is difficult to make any confident assessment of the way in which parental authority was exercised in times past[1], there is ample evidence that the right to a child's services was widely regarded as being an economically valuable asset. As recently as 1921[2], it was said to be 'no uncommon thing, when a child has reached an age at which it can work and earn wages, for parents who have habitually neglected it and left it to be brought up by a relative or even a stranger, to claim it back simply in order to take its earnings'; and there is some evidence that child stealing – not a crime until 1814 – was sometimes practised by those who wanted a cheap supply of labourers for trades such as chimney sweeping and prostitution[3].

At the upper end of the socio-economic scale, it appears that parents and guardians did not hesitate to exercise parental rights in respect of matters such as education. In one of the (comparatively few) reported cases[4], a young man of 16 was told by the court that the guardian was the best judge of his education, and that, since the boy had no reasonable complaint against the master at Eton, he would be compelled to return there if he did not go voluntarily. And even in the latter part of the nineteenth century the courts were reluctant to give any real weight to a child's views. In *Re Agar-Ellis*[5], the parents of a 16-year-old girl were separated. The father exercised his legal right[6] to take his daughter away from her mother, to send her to boarding school and to have her looked after by clergymen and others during the holidays, moving from one lodging to another. The court refused an application for the daughter to spend the holiday with her mother and, indeed, for the mother to have any access to her. It was said that in the absence of any fault on the father's part the court had no jurisdiction to interfere with the father's legal right to control the custody and education of his daughter.

---

1   See, generally, I Pinchbeck and M Hewitt *Children in English Society* (Routledge, 1973) Vol 2 at chs 12 and 13.
2   See *Report of the Committee on Child Adoption* (1921) (Cmnd 1254) at para 13.
3   I Pinchbeck and M Hewitt (above) at p 360.
4   *Hall v Hall* (1749) 3 Att 721.
5   (1883) 23 ChD 317.
6   On parental 'rights' in the modern law, see Chapter 3 below.

The father's exclusive entitlement to parental authority

As already seen, in Blackstone's time, parental authority was vested exclusively in a child's father: the mother was not entitled to any power with respect to the child, but 'only to reverence and respect'[1]. One of the most remarkable features of the development of English law is that this remained the underlying principle of the law until 1973. Only in that year did Parliament enact that, in relation to the legal custody or upbringing of a minor and in relation to his property or the application of income therefrom, a mother was to have the same rights and authority as the law had previously allowed to a father[2]. The fact that, for so long, a mother had no legal rights in respect of a legitimate[3] child may prompt the reader to ask how far the law is, in reality, relevant in practical terms. How many mothers, fathers, or children born before 1973, were aware of the legal position which denied the mother any parental authority? How far did this rule of law affect their behaviour? Perhaps the reality is that the denial of parental authority to a mother was rarely noticed in the functioning family, but this is not to say that the 1973 reform was irrelevant. Although such things may be difficult to measure, the law presumably has some impact on attitudes and, in any event, it is, no doubt, important that the law should reflect a position which is defensible, both socially and morally.

Erosion of the father's legal rights

The evolution of the law is of more pressing practical significance in cases in which the parental relationship is no longer harmonious, and very slowly – but then at an increasing pace – nineteenth-century parliaments began to allow the courts to intervene between father and mother in such cases. It was no longer regarded as acceptable that mothers who had separated from adulterous or cruel husbands should be deprived of the care of their children, and even denied any form of contact with them; or for the children to be handed over to complete strangers or perhaps even to the father's mistress[4].

Talfourd's Act

The first legislative interference with the father's virtually absolute right to have the possession of his children and to deny the mother any contact with them was the Custody of Infants Act 1839 which empowered the court to make orders giving

---

1   Blackstone *Commentaries on the Laws of England* (4th edn) (1770) at p 453.
2   Guardianship Act 1973, s 1(1).
3   The position in respect of an illegitimate child was different: see Chapter 5 below.
4   See *R v de Manneville* (1804) 5 East 221 and *de Manneville v de Manneville* (1804) 10 Ves 52 in which a father forcibly took an eight-month-old unweaned baby from the house in which it was living with the mother; and see *R v Greenhill* (1836) 4 Ad&E 624 where the Court of King's Bench ordered Mrs Greenhill to hand over her three small daughters (all under six years of age) to their father, notwithstanding the fact that he had been guilty of considerable cruelty to the wife and children and intended to hand the children over to the care of his mistress. When Mrs Greenhill refused to comply with the order she was committed to prison for contempt of court.

custody of any child up to the age of seven to the mother and to make orders giving her access to her children during their infancy[1].

The Matrimonial Causes Act 1857

The introduction of judicial divorce by the Matrimonial Causes Act 1857 required the legislature to consider the consequences of granting a decree of divorce both in respect of financial matters and in respect of the upbringing of the parties' children; and the Act gave the court a wide discretion in judicial separation, nullity or divorce proceedings to make such orders with respect to the custody, maintenance and education of the children of the marriage 'as it may deem just and proper'[2]. The Act also empowered the divorce court to direct that proper proceedings be taken for placing such children under the protection of the Court of Chancery[3]. The Act thus accepted – for the first time – the important principle that, whenever there were matrimonial proceedings, a father's rights might be overridden by the court, and it also gave effect to the view that the child of divorced (or legally separated) parents might need the ongoing supervision, available in wardship, of all important steps in his or her life[4].

Later Victorian legislation[5]

The extensive discretion conferred on the court by the divorce legislation was not easy to reconcile with the restrictive approach underlying the Custody of Children Act 1839: on divorce or judicial separation, the court had a complete discretion, but in other cases its discretion was greatly circumscribed. Not without difficulty and hesitation it came to be accepted that a wide discretion vested in the courts was necessary in cases relating to the upbringing of children; and the Custody of Infants Act 1873 empowered the court[6] to give custody of a child up to the age of 16 (rather than seven) to the mother. That Act also removed the bar established by the Custody of Children Act 1839 against access or custody petitions by an adulterous mother; and it provided that no agreement contained in a separation deed should be held to be invalid by reason only of its providing that the father of an infant should give up the custody or control of the infant to the mother. But the parties were not to be allowed to oust the court's powers, since the Custody of Infants Act 1873 provided that the court should not enforce any agreement if it

---

1   The Act, known as Talfourd's Act, was promoted by Serjeant Talfourd, a lawyer with experience of some remarkable cases, and the parliamentary proceedings were protracted and bitter: see I Pinchbeck and M Hewitt *Children in English Society* Vol 2 at pp 371–375 and, generally, as to the scope and objects of the Act, see *Warde v Warde* (1849) 2 Ph 786. The Act was restrictively interpreted: see *Re Halliday* (1853) 17 Jur 56; *Shillito v Collett* (1860) 8 WR 683; *Re Winscom* (1865) 2 H&M 540.
2   Matrimonial Causes Act 1857, s 33.
3   Ibid.
4   For the wardship jurisdiction, see pp 12 et seq below.
5   The text deals only with legislation conferring powers on the superior courts, but the last quarter of the nineteenth century also saw the creation of the magistrates' jurisdiction – for long particularly significant in the case of the working classes. The Matrimonial Causes Act 1878, s 4, provided that when a husband was convicted of assault the court might order that the legal custody of any children of the marriage under the age of 10 years be given to the wife (although no order was to be made in favour of a wife proved to have committed adultery). The Summary Jurisdiction (Married Women) Act 1895 greatly extended the magistrates' powers.
6   The Court of Chancery.

was of the opinion that it would not be for the benefit of the infant to give effect thereto[1].

Father rules from beyond the grave: guardianship

At common law, a father's parental authority survived his death: a father could appoint a testamentary guardian[2] for his child, and the guardian then, effectively, stepped into the position of the father on the father's death. The mother had no right to interfere with the exercise of the testamentary guardian's authority[3]. But the principles underlying the statutes passed in 1839, 1857 and 1873 made it 'difficult to accept that in a free country a widowed mother might be robbed of her young children, even if they were babes in arms, by a stranger appointed guardian by her late husband against her wishes or by her late husband's distant relative whom she had never seen'[4]. A vigorous public campaign eventually lead to the enactment of the Guardianship of Infants Act 1886 which provided[5] that on the death of the father of an infant, the mother, if surviving, should be the infant's guardian, either alone (when no guardian had been appointed by the father) or jointly with any guardian appointed by the father. The 1886 Act also empowered the court to appoint a guardian or guardians to act jointly with the mother where no guardian had been appointed by the father, or where the guardians or guardian appointed by him had died or refused to act.

Freestanding custody applications

The problem of guardianship and abuse of paternal power were the matters which precipitated the enactment of the Guardianship of Infants Act 1886, but in conceptual terms that Act can today be seen as having a far greater significance. The reality is that the Act destroyed the concept of the family as a domestic kingdom ruled by the father. This was done by conferring on the court – which for this purpose included the county court as well as the High Court[6] – an unrestricted power on the mother's application to make such order as it thought fit regarding the custody of an infant and the right of access, thereto, of either parent, 'having regard to the welfare of the infant, and to the conduct of the parents, and to the wishes as well of the mother as of the father'[7]. It was no longer necessary to bring any other issue (such as the termination of the partners' marriage) before the court if either parent wanted the court to assume jurisdiction to deal with the

---

1   See, for example, the notorious case of *Re Besant* (1878) 11 ChD 508, in which the court overrode a provision in a deed of separation made between a Church of England clergyman and his wife. The mother (the founder of the ethical code known as theosophy) had written works which the Court of Appeal considered 'disgusting to decent English men and women, a violation of morality, decency and womanly propriety', and had proselytised on behalf of her atheistical beliefs, and the court directed that custody of the daughter be given to the father. For the background, see R Dinnage *Annie Besant* (1986).

2   Under the Tenures Abolition Act 1660, as amended by the Wills Act 1837.

3   *Talbot v Earl of Shrewsbury* (1840) 4 My&Cr 672 at 683.

4   See I Pinchbeck and M Hewitt *Children in English Society* Vol 2 at p 381.

5   Section 2.

6   Section 9.

7   The Act also provided that the court could alter, vary or discharge such orders on the application of either parent or, after the death of either parent, on the application of a guardian appointed under the Act.

upbringing of children; it was sufficient that either parent wanted the court to deal with the questions of custody and access.

The unfit parent

The Guardianship of Infants Act 1886 also[1] gave the divorce court power to include, in decrees of divorce and judicial separation, a declaration that one spouse was unfit to have the custody of the children. The person declared unfit lost the right to custody or guardianship of the child which he or she would otherwise have had on the death of the other parent; but, in theory at least, a declaration of unfitness did not mean that the parent was to be deprived of all contact with the child, nor did it debar the unfit parent from seeking and being given custody or access[2].

The family and outsiders

The 1886 legislation – the substance of which remained on the statute book until the enactment of the Children Act 1989 – gave effect to the principle that the child's welfare should be the determining factor in disputes between parents over their child's upbringing, but the position was very different when the dispute was between the parents and an outsider – typically a foster-parent who had provided a home for a destitute child. In particular, parents often sought to reclaim a boy or girl of an age to earn wages from one of the children's homes established by the philanthropist Dr Barnardo[3] in an attempt to provide vagrant and destitute children with care, training and a sound upbringing, according to the tenets of evangelical protestantism; and these parents were not deterred by the fact that Barnardo required the parents of those whom he 'rescued' to renounce all claim to the child[4]. On a number of occasions, Barnardo was ordered to return children to the legal parents[5]; but, in due course, Parliament responded to what was seen to be a scandalous situation. In the words of Lord Herschell:

> 'When a parent has abandoned or deserted his child, has cared nothing for it, and has left it to be cared for by others, it is outrageous that he should be allowed to go before a Court and say, although I have neglected every duty which I owed my child, and although to deliver up to me now would be most disastrous for the child, still I have a legal right to the custody of the child, that custody I will have, and you must give it to me ... All that this legislation proposes to do so is that where the court is satisfied that a parent has so behaved as to disentitle him to the custody of the child it shall have power to refuse its writ to procure the delivery of that child back to the parent.'

The Custody of Children Act 1891 (which remained on the statute book until repealed by the Children Act 1989) empowered the court in its discretion to decline to issue a writ of habeas corpus or make an order for the production of a child if the court considered that the parent had abandoned or deserted the child or that he had otherwise so conducted himself that the court should refuse to enforce his right to the custody of the child. More generally, the Act provided[6] that

---

1 Section 7.
2 *Re A & B* [1897] 1 Ch 786 at 795.
3 For a comprehensive account, see G Wagner *Barnardo* (Weidenfeld & Nicolson, 1979) at ch 13. See also J Rose *For the Sake of the Children: Inside Dr Barnardo's* (1988).
4 Such an agreement was without legal effect: see Chapter 4.
5 See *R v Barnardo* (1889) 23 QBD 305, (1890) 24 QBD 283, [1891] 1 QB 194; *Barnardo v McHugh* [1891] AC 388; *Barnardo v Ford* [1892] AC 326.
6 Section 3.

the court should not make an order for the delivery of a child to a parent who had abandoned or deserted the child or who had allowed the child to be brought up by another person at that person's expense (or by the poor law guardians) for such a length of time and under such circumstances as to satisfy the court that the parent was 'unmindful of his parental duties', unless the parent had satisfied the court that 'having regard to the welfare of the child' the parent was a fit person to have the custody of the child.

Religion: the first recognition of children's rights

Perhaps the most remarkable provision of the Custody of Children Act 1891, however, was that dealing with religious education. Some, at least, of the *Barnardo* cases were prompted by parents being brought to believe that the child's spiritual health was at risk by reason of the religious teaching given in the Barnardo homes; and, in an attempt to allay fears on this score, the Act provided[1] that a court denying a parent custody of his child might, nevertheless, take such steps as it thought fit to secure that the child be brought up 'in the religion in which the parent had a legal right to require that the child should be brought up'. To this extent, the parental right to control the child's spiritual upbringing was firmly reasserted, even though the parental right to have the physical care of the child was removed; but – remarkably for legislation of the period – it was also provided that nothing in the legislation should interfere with or affect the power of the court to consult the *wishes of the child* in considering what order ought to be made, or diminish the right which the child possessed to the exercise of the child's own free choice. It can plausibly be argued that this – little noted – provision marks the first statutory recognition of the child's legal right to autonomy.

The role of the Court of Chancery: wardship

The Court of Chancery exercised the prerogative jurisdiction of the Crown over infants; and it would, in so doing, apply the principle that the primary consideration was the child's welfare. However, the court was reluctant to override the wishes of the father[2]; and, in practice[3], it would at this time only act in cases in which it had the means of applying property for the use and maintenance of the children concerned[4]. Indeed, the promoters of the Custody of Children Act 1891

---

1 Section 4.
2 'It is not the benefit of the infant as conceived by the court, but it must be the benefit to the infant having regard to the natural law which points out that the father knows far better as a rule what is good for his children than a Court of Justice can': see *Re Agar-Ellis* (1883) 24 ChD 317 at 337–338, per Bowen LJ. A similar approach was taken nearly a century later by Lord Templeman in *Re KD (A Minor) (Access: Principles)* [1988] 2 FLR 139 at 141, HL: 'The best person to bring up a child is the natural parent. It matters not whether the parent is wise or foolish, rich or poor, educated or illiterate, provided the child's moral and physical health are not endangered'. An even more recent example is provided by Waite LJ in *Re T (Wardship: Medical Treatment)* [1997] 1 FLR 502 at 514: '. . . in the last analysis the best interests of every child include an expectation that difficult decisions affecting the length and quality of its life will be taken for it by the parent to whom its care has been entrusted by nature'. See further Chapter 8.
3 Although not in theory: see generally NV Lowe and RAH White *Wards of Court* (2nd edn) (Barry Rose/Kluwer, 1986) at p 3.
4 See *Wellesley v Duke of Beaufort* (1827) 2 Russ 1 at 21, per Lord Eldon.

sought to explain the necessity for legislation by arguing that legislation would give to the poorer child the same protection as that traditionally given by the Court of Chancery to wealthier children who had had property bestowed upon them[1].

Principles on which the court would exercise its discretion: the paramountcy of the child's welfare

Much of the late nineteenth-century legislation was influenced by the movement for achieving legal equality for women[2], particularly in relation to property and, although the child custody legislation gave the court a wide discretion, it did not give any specific guidance in respect of the *principles* upon which this discretion should be exercised. In practice, the courts seem often to have regarded the welfare of the child as identical to the father's wishes.

The Guardianship of Infants Act 1925[3] made its objectives clear in the preamble:

'... whereas Parliament by the Sex Disqualification (Removal) Act 1919, and various other enactments, has sought to establish equality in law between the sexes, and it is expedient that this principle should obtain with respect to the guardianship of infants and the rights and responsibilities conferred thereby.'

The Act provided that where, in any proceedings before any court[4], the custody or upbringing of an infant, or the administration of any property belonging to or held on trust for an infant, or the application of the income thereof, was in question, the court, in deciding that question, should regard the welfare of the infant as the first and paramount consideration, and should not take into consideration, whether from any other point of view the claim of the father, in respect of such custody, upbringing, administration or application was superior to that of the mother, or the claim of the mother was superior to that of the father.

There would seem to be little room for doubt that this legislation was designed to secure equality of rights *as between father and mother* in relation to their children, and to make the welfare of those children paramount in relation to the two, henceforth equal, interests of their parents[5]. The Act did not, in terms, apply to cases in which the dispute was between a parent and an outsider; and for many years it seems to have been thought that a parent – certainly an 'unimpeachable' parent – still had 'rights' in respect of a child's upbringing, which would prevail as against a stranger. For example, in *Re Thain*[6]:

... a father who on his wife's death had no means of looking after his eight month old daughter, accepted an offer by the child's uncle and aunt to look after her. Six years later he had re-married and was in a position to provide the child with a permanent and suitable home. He applied for

---

1 See Lord Thring *Hansard* 3rd series (1891) Vol 349, cols 1508–10.
2 Culminating in the Married Women's Property Act 1882.
3 For a detailed examination of the legislative history of the Act, see SM Cretney ' "What Will the Women Want Next?": The Struggle for Power Within the Family 1925–1975' (1996) 112 LQR 110.
4 The Act thus extended the principles applied by the Chancery Division of the High Court to the magistrates' court.
5 *A v Liverpool City Council* [1982] AC 363 at 377, per Lord Roskill; see also *Richards v Richards* [1984] 1 AC 174 at 203, per Lord Hailsham of St Marylebone.
6 [1926] Ch 676.

and obtained an order that she be handed back to him. The trial judge said[1] that he could quite understand that the little girl would be 'greatly distressed and upset' at the parting from her foster parents, but 'at her tender age, one knows from experience how mercifully transient are the effects of partings and other sorrows, and how soon the novelty of fresh surroundings and new associations effaces the recollection of former days and kind friends' ...

It was only in the landmark case of *J v C*[2], more than 40 years later, that the House of Lords unequivocally ruled that the principles of the 1925 legislation were applicable whether the dispute was between parents, or between parents and outsiders. In *J v C*:

> ... the question was whether a 10 year old boy should be returned to his natural parents (Spanish nationals resident in Spain) or whether he should continue to be in the care of English foster parents who had looked after him for all save some 18 months of his life. The House of Lords upheld the decision of the trial judge and Court of Appeal that the boy should stay in the care of the foster parents in England. The consequences of returning a boy who scarcely knew his natural parents and had been brought up as an English boy with English ways to a foreign country might have been disastrous, the more so since the parents would have been unable to cope with the problems of adjustment and consequent maladjustment and suffering. The fact that the parents were 'unimpeachable' could not prevail. The legislation required the child's welfare to be treated as the paramount consideration.

Child still not entitled to access to courts

This clear acceptance of the paramountcy of the child's welfare establishes a principle which is comprehensible, however difficult it may be to apply it in practice[3]. But for many years it was an inflexible rule that a child could not, directly, bring or participate in legal proceedings in the superior civil courts, and that a guardian ad litem or next friend must act on the child's behalf[4]. The child's father was, in principle, entitled to act in that capacity, and would only be removed if it could be shown that he was acting improperly. The difficulties to which this rule gave rise – as well as the difficulty of deciding what precisely is in a child's best interests, even in the context of legal and financial matters – was vividly demonstrated in *Re Taylor's Application*[5]:

> The defendants in actions brought on behalf of children claiming to have been damaged by the drug Thalidomide made an offer of settlement on terms that all the 365 plaintiffs accepted. The parents of five children refused to do so; and the defendants sought to remove the father from his position as next friend with a view to a person being appointed who would accept the proposed settlement. The court rejected the application: the only impropriety alleged against the father was that he was in a small minority in believing that the settlement was not in his child's best interests; but (as Lord Denning MR remarked) being in a minority is not itself evidence of unreasonableness.

---

1 Eve J at p 684.
2 [1970] AC 668.
3 See Chapters 2 and 4 below.
4 In certain circumstances, a child may now participate in family proceedings without it being necessary for a guardian or next friend to act: see Chapter 13 below.
5 [1972] 2 QB 369, CA. For the situation today, see Chapter 13 below.

The age of majority

A child is not entitled to full legal capacity[1] until he or she attains the age of majority. For many years, this was fixed at 21 years of age, but the Family Law Reform Act 1969 reduced the age of majority to 18 years[2].

THE ROLE OF THE STATE

The Poor Law

Lord Scarman has said that the historic base from which Parliament advanced to meet the needs of the orphans, the deserted, and the abandoned child was the Poor Law[3]; and it is certainly true that, for centuries, the problems associated with poverty, and particularly the problems of fatherless children begging and vagrancy, have been a major concern of Government. The statute which established the Elizabethan Poor Law in 1601 put legal sanctions, for the first time, behind the observance of what had formerly been regarded as the ordinary obligations of kinship[4]. Parents, grandparents and children were statutorily obliged to support their relatives, and this general principle survives in the obligation imposed on 'liable relatives' for income support purposes and in the provisions of the Child Support Act 1991 imposing maintenance obligations on absent parents. It should, however, be noted that the scope of the obligation has now greatly narrowed since the days of the Poor Law (which was abolished by the National Assistance Act 1948). The obligation is now restricted to husbands and wives and to parents and children; and the National Assistance Act 1948 also limited the extent of the liability to the recovery of sums paid out by way of supplementary benefit or income support[5].

The impact of the Poor Law was not confined to financial obligations; and two, often related, developments of practice in relation to the care of children can, in retrospect, be seen to have played a major part in the development of child care law and practice.

Boarding-out: assumption of parental rights

In the latter part of the nineteenth century, it increasingly became the practice for pauper children to be 'boarded out' under the authority of the Poor Law Board

---

1 Until the *Gillick* decision (*Gillick v West Norfolk and Wisbech Area Health Authority* [1986] 1 AC 112), it was widely assumed that a child was legally incapable for all purposes (except where capacity was specifically conferred on the child by statute) until he or she attained full age, but that case held that this view was erroneous: see particularly, Chapters 3 and 8 below.
2 Following the *Report of the Committee on the Age of Majority* (the 'Latey Report') (1967) (Cmnd 3342). The position is the same in Scotland but it should be noted that under the Age of Legal Capacity (Scotland) Act 1991 children over the age of 16 enjoy a large measure of active legal capacity to enter into civil transactions. See JM Thomson *Family Law in Scotland* (3rd edn) (Butterworths, 1996), ch 9, and see Chapter 15 below.
3 *Leeds City Council v West Yorkshire Metropolitan Police* [1983] 1 AC 29 at 41.
4 *Report of the Finer Committee on One-Parent Families* (1974) (Cmnd 5629) Vol 2, Appendix 5, para 51.
5 The Child Support Act 1991 imposes a much more extensive obligation: see Chapter 9 below.

with foster-parents[1]; and the Poor Law Act 1889 empowered the Poor Law
guardians to assume all the powers and rights in respect of a child deserted by his
parents and maintained by the Poor Law guardians[2]. The Poor Law Act 1899
extended the grounds on which such action could be taken – it sufficed if the
parent (for example) was thought to be unfit to have control of the child 'by
reason of mental deficiency, or of vicious habits or mode of life'[3]. These
procedures were seen to provide a means of caring for poor children without
institutionalising them in a workhouse or other Poor Law institution, and a
further stimulus to the practice of boarding-out was provided by the Poor Law
Institutions Order of 1913, which made it illegal to retain a healthy child over the
age of three years in a workhouse for more than six weeks.

Local authorities' responsibilities for child care

In some ways, the most significant step in the evolution of modern child care
practice[4] came in 1929, when the responsibilities of the Poor Law guardians were
taken over by local authorities[5]. The Second World War impeded any comprehensive reforms, but also provided a stimulus for further reform. A growing sense of
dissatisfaction[6] led to the appointment of a committee 'to enquire into existing
methods of providing for children who, from loss of parent or from any cause
whatever, are deprived of a normal home life with their own parents or relatives;
and to consider what further measures should be taken to ensure that these
children are brought up under conditions best calculated to compensate them for
parental care'.

---

1 See I Pinchbeck and M Hewitt *Children in English Society* (Routledge, 1973) Vol 2 at p 522. For
   further discussion of the powers of the Poor Law authorities in the context of the social and
   legal background to the introduction of legal, as opposed to informal, adoption in 1926, see
   S Cretney 'From Status to Contract?' in FD Rose (ed) *Consensus Ad Idem: Essays in the Law of
   Contract in honour of Guenther Treitel* (Sweet & Maxwell, 1996) pp 251 et seq, especially at
   pp 252–255.
2 Poor Law Act 1889, s 1(1).
3 Ibid, s 1. The Poor Law Act 1889 is commonly described as the Poor Law Adoption Act; and
   informal adoption was statutorily recognised by the Poor Law Act 1899, s 3, which dealt with the
   case where a child had been adopted notwithstanding the fact that at the time there was no
   legal machinery for adoption.
4 See the Literature Surveys by RA Parker in 'Residential Care, The Research Reviewed',
   commissioned by the *Independent Review of Residential Care Chaired by Gillian Wagner OBE PhD*
   (I Sinclair, ed) (HMSO, 1988).
5 Local authorities could also be appointed as 'fit persons' to whom the care of children removed
   from their parents under the child protection legislation could be committed.
6 For an account of practice, see *Report of the Care of Children Committee* ('the Curtis Report')
   (1946) (Cmnd 6922).

The Curtis Report

In 1946, the Committee (under the Chairmanship of Miss Myra Curtis) published its report[1] which led directly[2] to the enactment of the Children Act 1948. That Act sought to give effect to a policy that, so far as possible, all children deprived of a normal home life should have the advantages of which they had been deprived, and to that end the Act required local authorities to provide care for extended categories of children. The Act remained the cornerstone of the structure of children's social services for more than 40 years; and marked a significant step away from the traditional reliance on voluntary organisations, family doctors, the clergy and neighbours for dealing with welfare problems, and towards reliance on paid, trained, professional social workers employed by local authorities.

Caring involves paying

Although the Children Act 1948 imposed a duty on local authorities to provide care for children deprived of a normal home life, it soon came to be recognised that prevention was better than cure, and children's departments tried to forestall the need for children to come into care by working, in co-operation with the other community services, to keep the family in being whenever this was in the best interests of the children. But the legal basis on which such help could be given was often obscure; and in 1960 the Ingleby Committee[3] pointed out that authorities had no power to give help in cash or kind to the families of children in care or of children who might have to be received into care because of their home circumstances. The Children and Young Persons Act 1963 sought to deal with this problem by imposing on local authorities a duty 'to make available such advice, guidance and assistance as may promote the welfare of children by diminishing the need to receive children into or keep them in care' or to bring children before a juvenile court under the provisions then in force.

The range of services which could be provided under the Act was wide: authorities would provide general social work support, and also specific facilities such as the relief of overburdened mothers by admitting young children to day care and older children to after-school play schemes, and assistance with housekeeping and budgeting; while there was power for a local authority to provide housing for a family if the children would otherwise stand in peril of being received into care[4]. The Act[5] also empowered local authorities to make provision 'in kind or, in exceptional circumstances, in cash', and this power enabled local

---

1   *Report of the Care of Children Committee* (above). See, generally, J Packman *The Child's Generation* (2nd edn) (Blackwell, 1981). For a brief account of the background, see the speech of the Lord Chancellor moving the second reading *Hansard* (HL) Vol 153, cols 913–925.

2   The death of two children while in the care of foster-parents and the subsequent inquiry by Sir Walter Monckton, *Report on the circumstances which led to the boarding out of Dennis and Terence O'Neill . . .* ('the Monckton Report') (1945) (Cmnd 6636) highlighted some of the issues and may have contributed to the creation of a climate of opinion favouring change; but it seems that the Monckton Report did not directly influence the legislation: R Parker in Bean and MacPherson *Approaches to Welfare* (Routledge, 1983). For a more detailed examination of the legislative history and influences which contributed to the enactment of the Children Act 1948, see S Cretney 'The Children Act 1948 – lessons for today?' [1997] CFLQ 359 and 'The State as a Parent: The Children Act 1948 in Retrospect' (1998) 114 LQR 419.

3   *Committee on Children and Young Persons* (1960) (Cmnd 1191).

4   See *Attorney-General, ex rel Tilley v Wandsworth London Borough Council* [1981] 1 WLR 854, CA.

5   Child Care Act 1980 (a consolidating measure), s 1(1).

authorities to pay off rent arrears in order to keep a roof over the family's head, and to give help with fuel debts.

Child care: a subject for specialists?

The Children Act 1948 accepted the need for specialisation in the provision of the child care service. Each local authority had to have a children's committee, and each local authority was obliged to appoint a specialist children's officer and adequate staff. However, the Local Authority Social Services Act 1970 gave effect to the view that family needs were best integrated with all other relevant social services; and Directors of Social Services were thenceforth to manage integrated social services departments. The Children Act 1989 (as will be seen[1]) gives further impetus to the concept that services for families and children in need should be developed on the basis of a collaborative and inter-disciplinary approach.

The voluntary principle and its erosion

The emphasis of the Children Act 1948 was on the need to return children to their parents; and the main purpose of so-called voluntary care was to cater for short-term difficulties without overriding the rights and duties of a parent and without recourse to the courts[2]. The legislation imposed a duty on local authorities to receive children into their care in certain circumstances; it did not give the local authorities any right to compel a parent to place a child in care. Parents needed to be confident that, in using the child care service, they would not run any greater risk of losing their child than if they had made private fostering arrangements; and the 1948 Act provided that a local authority was not to keep a child in its care if any parent or guardian desired to take over the care of the child. It also imposed a duty on local authorities, in all cases where it appeared to them consistent with the welfare of the child so to do, to endeavour to secure that the care of the child would be taken over by a parent or guardian or by a relative or friend. It is true that local authorities could, in certain conditions – mostly involving parental culpability[3] – pass a resolution vesting the parental rights and duties in the local authority, but this could only be done[4] if the child was already in care. Moreover, the decision could be tested in the courts. The principle was thus clearly established that a child was not to be 'removed from his home or family against the will of his parent save by the order of the court, where the parent will have the opportunity to be heard before the order is made'[5].

---

1   See particularly Chapter 10 below.
2   See, per Lord Scarman, *Lewisham London Borough Council v Lewisham Juvenile Court Justices* [1980] AC 273 at 306, HL: 'No court proceedings are required for action under these subsections. The Act provides for social casework to relieve a child's distress and anger: it is not concerned to vindicate rights or to set a scene for litigation. The rescue of a lost or abandoned child, advice and help to a parent in difficulty are the objectives of the legislation. An emergency must be met, and the child protected. This is the world of social administration, not a legal battlefield. The purpose of the Act is to help in an emergency which will at best be only temporary but may be prolonged'.
3   See *O'D v South Glamorgan County Council* (1980) LGR 522 at 526, per Sir J Arnold P.
4   A court could, in certain circumstances, make a care order in favour of a local authority: see the Children and Young Persons Act 1969, s 1; see also Chapter 11 below.
5   See *Lewisham London Borough Council v Lewisham Juvenile Court Justices* [1980] AC 273 at 307, per Lord Scarman.

However, it came to be thought that the voluntary principle sometimes led to the long-term future of children who were in voluntary care being neglected, since it was difficult to make plans for them. The Children Act 1975 was much influenced by the perceived dangers of allowing children to 'drift' in care; and that Act, accordingly, contained provisions which may be thought significantly to have undermined the parents' rights over a child who had been received into voluntary care. First, once a child had been in care for a period of six months, a parent or guardian would be guilty of a criminal offence if he removed the child from the accommodation provided for him by the authority unless the parent or guardian had given the authority not less than 28 days' notice in writing of his intention or had the authority's consent; and, if a parent did give such a notice, the local authority would no doubt consider whether to take other action – for example, making the child a ward of court[1] – to enable it to protect the child's interests. Secondly, it was provided that the foster-parents of a child who had been boarded out with them for three years were to be entitled to seek a custodianship order[2] giving them legal custody of the child. Finally, the fact that a child had been in the care of a local authority for three years was made a ground on which the authority could pass a parental rights resolution assuming the parental rights and duties over a child in their care. Taking these three provisions of the 1975 Children Act together, it was clear that the rights of parents whose children had been in care for any length of time had been significantly eroded: consideration of the parents' rights should no longer be allowed to inhibit proper long-term planning for the welfare of children. As will be seen, the Children Act 1989 marks a decisive swing away from the philosophy of the 1975 Act, whilst still seeking to protect children from the dangers of drift.

Adoption

Background
It has already been mentioned that the Poor Law Act 1889 empowered poor law guardians to assume parental rights in respect of children who had been deserted, and legislation[3] sometimes referred to this procedure as 'adoption'. In fact – in marked contrast to other systems of law, which had long accepted the possibility of transferring a child from one family unit to another – English law made no provision for legal adoption until 1926, but it appears that the practice of informal adoption grew considerably in the first part of the twentieth century[4]. There were a number of reasons for this[5]. First, the 1914–18 war led to the increase in the numbers of orphans who were available for adoption. In addition, it may have led to an increase in the number of those who were unable or unwilling to look after their own children. Secondly, growing knowledge of child psychology led to a preference in informed circles for bringing up children as a member of a family in

---

1 See Chapter 11 below.
2 See Chapter 6 below.
3 For example, the Poor Law Act 1899.
4 On the history of legal adoption in England, see S Cretney 'From Status to Contract?' in
   FD Rose (ed) *Consensus Ad Idem: Essays in the Law of Contract in honour of Guenther Treitel* (Sweet & Maxwell, 1996) at pp 251–268.
5 See *Report of the Committee on Child Adoption* (1921) (Cmnd 1254) and *Report of the Child Adoption Committee* (1925) (Cmnd 2401).

a normal home surrounding rather than in an institution. Thirdly, there was an increasing tendency on the part of those who had no children of their own, or desired another child, to value a child's life and to desire association with and companionship with children. Finally, societies formed to encourage adoption gave publicity to the practice.

Not surprisingly, there was considerable dissatisfaction about the lack of any legal framework to regulate the practice of adoption. This dissatisfaction came from two main sources. First, there were those who were primarily concerned to provide security for the adopters: the law forbade a parent to bargain away his parental rights, and a parent might at any time seek to reclaim his child from the 'adopters'; conversely, a parent who had placed her child with adopters might then, at any time, be forced to take the child back. Secondly, there were those who were primarily concerned with the evils of child trafficking. Under the law as it stood before 1926, children could be handed from one person to another, with or without payment, or sent out of the country without any record being kept; intermediaries could accept children for adoption, and dispose of them as and when they chose; and 'homes' and institutions for the reception of children existed which were not subject to any system of inspection or control. A particularly obtrusive feature was the use of newspaper advertisements, often inserted by professional agents who would charge, both the natural parent and the adopters, large fees. For example, one individual was found to have inserted advertisements in these terms:

'Good refined home required for an army officer's twin boy and girl, fortnight old.'

'Adoption – beautiful blue-eyed boy wishes to be adopted where he would give love in return for parents and home.'

Pressure led to the appointment of the Hopkinson Committee on Adoption, in 1921. This Committee was favourably disposed to the introduction of legislation legalising adoption; and it considered that adoption was the next best thing to a stable home with natural parents. It thought that it was a proper object of the law to satisfy the natural desire of the childless to have the care and upbringing of the child, and it considered that this was often, in itself, the best guarantee of an adopted child's welfare. The Committee recognised that legal adoption would never be more than one link in the chain and proposed measures to prevent abuse of long-term child care arrangements.

There was still a reluctance, however, to legislate. Ultimately, the Government appointed a second committee under the chairmanship of Mr Justice Tomlin. That Committee was unenthusiastic about the validity of the arguments for legal adoption, but concluded that a case had been made for giving some legal recognition to the link between the adopter and the adopted child, and for creating a procedure for the transfer of parental rights and duties. The Adoption Act 1926, which laid the foundation for the modern law, followed.

The changing nature of adoption

The picture so far presented of adoption corresponds with its popular image; it is a legal procedure enabling those who are unable to have children to adopt a baby whom the adopters will thenceforth treat in all respects as if the child had been born to them. But, in fact, adoption increasingly came to be seen as an appropriate legal technique to be employed by local authorities concerned to provide a secure home for children in their care – often older children (who might have been in care for some years) and handicapped children. In recent years, the nature and purposes of adoption and adoption law have been the subject of an extensive review and there has been much speculation that the law will be changed to create a more 'open' adoption process. At the time of writing, it is not clear whether, and, if so, when, an Adoption Bill will be presented to Parliament or what the precise shape of adoption reform will be[1]. These developments are considered in Chapter 7.

Child protection legislation

What part does the criminal law have to play in promoting the welfare of children? One technique which has been increasingly used is to prohibit activities, such as caring for children for reward, unless certain formalities, for example registration, are met. The first example of such legislation is the Infant Life Protection Act 1872[2], which was concerned to eradicate the worst evils of baby farming – then, often described as adoption. It seems that a pregnant unmarried woman would arrange for her child to be delivered in a private lying-in house, and pay the owner a lump sum (perhaps as little as £5) in exchange for the owner agreeing to arrange the baby's adoption. The baby was soon removed to the 'worst class of baby farming house', where children were 'so culpably neglected, so ill-treated, and so badly nurtured' (for example on a diet consisting of a mixture of laudanum, lime, corn flour, water, milk and washing powder) 'that with rare exceptions they all of them die within a very short time'. In response to a number of notorious cases, the Infant Life Protection Act 1872 required registration of persons who, for payment, took charge of two or more infants under one year of age for more than 24 hours. As will be seen[3], legislation now requires registration and supervision of a wide range of activities, including the provision of private fostering, day care, residential care, and so on.

Punishment for ill-treatment of children
The Prevention of Cruelty to, and Protection of, Children Act 1889 was the first of many statutes seeking by the imposition of criminal penalties to deter mistreatment of children. Thus, it is an offence for a person over the age of 16 to assault, ill-treat, neglect or abandon any child for whom he has responsibility[4]. Over the years, criminal offences have often been created in the wake of particular well-publicised scandals – for example, it was made an offence to allow a child to be in a room containing an unguarded heating appliance if this resulted in serious injury to the child, and it was made an offence to cause the death of a child under the age of three by overlaying it in bed if the defendant was under the influence of

---

1 The Labour Government indicated in March 1998 that it was unable to find legislative time in the immediate future for the comprehensive reform of adoption suggested in 1996, but that it had signed the Hague Convention on Inter-Country Adoption and intended to ratify this as soon as the necessary legislation was in place. See Baroness Jay of Paddington *Hansard* (HL) col 1336 (26 March 1998).
2 Following the *Report of the Select Committee on Protection of Infant Life* (1871).
3 See Chapter 10 below.
4 The legislation is now embodied in the Children and Young Persons Act 1933, s 1, as amended (most recently by the Children Act 1989, Sch 13, para 1).

drink when the defendant went to bed[1]. Legislation also criminalises conduct which is thought to expose children to danger – it is, for example, an offence under the Crossbows Act 1987 to sell or hire a crossbow to a person under 17; the Children and Young Persons (Protection from Tobacco) Act 1991 creates offences intended to prevent children having access to that drug; while the Tattooing of Minors Act 1969 made it an offence to tattoo a person under 18 except for medical reasons. It is not always clear that such legislation serves any long-term need.

Preventing the economic exploitation of children

The Act to regulate the labour of children and young persons in the mills and factories of the UK enacted in 1883 was the first of many legislative attempts to prevent the economic exploitation of children, and the statute book contains general rules (for example, that no child be employed so long as he is under 14, or before 7 am and after 7 pm[2]) as well as specific prohibitions or regulations in respect of certain kinds of activity – such as acrobatics[3].

Compulsory child care measures

As discussed earlier, the Poor Law allowed the Poor Law guardians to assume parental rights in respect of pauper children in some circumstances and, latterly, juvenile courts were allowed to commit children who were found to be in danger to the care of a local authority. The juvenile courts were primarily concerned with children who were accused of criminal offences, but in the 1960s it was asked increasingly whether the social control of harmful behaviour by the young on the one hand, and social measures designed to protect and help the young on the other, should remain distinct and separate processes. The view that the aim of protecting society from juvenile delinquency and the aim of helping children in trouble to grow up into mature and law-abiding persons were essentially complementary[4] became increasingly accepted, and with it came a reluctance to classify children in need into two distinct groups – the deprived and the depraved.

The Children and Young Persons Act 1969 was influenced by these views. The court was given power to make orders – including a care order committing a child to the care of a specified local authority – if any one of a number of primary conditions was proved, but the court was only to make an order if the so-called 'care and control' test was satisfied – that is to say, if the court considered that the child was in need of care and control which he was unlikely to receive unless the court made an order[5]. The primary conditions included[6] the condition that the child was guilty of an offence[7], and it is fundamental to an understanding of the 1969 legislation that a primary focus of its concern was the delinquent child and

---

1   Children and Young Persons Act 1933, s 1(2)(b).
2   Ibid, s 18(1), as amended.
3   Ibid, ss 23, 30; and see Chapter 15 below.
4   *Children in Trouble* (1968) (Cmnd 3601) para 7.
5   Children and Young Persons Act 1969, s 1(2). On the evolution of policy, see generally
     JM Eekelaar, R Dingwall and T Murray 'Victims or Threats? Children in Care Proceedings'
     (1982) JSWL 67.
6   Children and Young Persons Act 1969, s 1(2)(f).
7   Excluding homicide: ibid, s 1(2)(f). Homicides continued to be dealt with under the provisions
     of the Children and Young Persons Act 1933, s 53.

that it was intended that care proceedings under the Act should routinely be used instead of prosecution in cases of delinquency.

This policy was always controversial; and it was abandoned by a Conservative government. Although the 'offence' condition remained in force, it was rarely used: the great majority of delinquent children against whom legal proceedings were taken continued to be prosecuted. Care proceedings were, in practice, taken by local authorities who considered that a child was being ill-treated or that his health or development was being avoidably impaired or neglected[1]. But the legislation was drafted to deal with both the delinquent and the needy, and this duality of function led to considerable ambivalence about the nature of the proceedings. For example, it seemed reasonable that the child accused of delinquency should be protected by strict rules of evidence, and that a high standard of proof be required if a finding of guilt was to be made. However, it increasingly came to be seen that these considerations sometimes prevented appropriate action being taken to protect a child who was suffering neglect. This ambivalence was only resolved by the provisions of the Children Act 1989 which impose a strict division between the prosecution of child offenders – now to be dealt with in special youth courts[2] – and taking measures for the care and protection of children at risk of significant harm[3].

SPECIAL PROTECTION FOR CHILDREN ON PARENTAL DIVORCE

Background

Since judicial divorce become available in the UK in 1858, there has been a substantial upward trend in the divorce rate. In 1858 there were only 244 divorce petitions. In 1914, for the first time, the number exceeded 1,000, and in 1942 the number of petitions rose above 100,000[4]. These figures may seem small by comparison with the 150,000 or so divorces which, it seems likely, will be the annual average in the last decade of the twentieth century, but there was grave concern about the impact of divorce on children, and there was also widespread agreement that the divorce process should do everything possible to mitigate any adverse effects. In the 1950s, divorce was not necessarily available to all who sought it: a matrimonial offence had to be proved, amongst other conditions[5], and there were those who thought that the interests of the children might be regarded as being of secondary importance. In particular, if the divorce was not opposed and there was no dispute about the custody of the children, the court would have no way of knowing whether the parties had done what was really best for the children, or whether (perhaps) one party had only agreed to the divorce in return for an assurance that he or she would be allowed custody. The traditional adversarial procedures of the courts – albeit, theoretically, not governing the practice of the

1 Children and Young Persons Act 1969, s 1(2)(a).
2 See the Criminal Justice Act 1991; and see Chapter 14 below.
3 See Chapter 11 below.
4 See the *Royal Commission on Marriage and Divorce* (1956) (Cmnd 9678) Appendix 2, Table 1.
5 See the brief summary in SM Cretney and JM Masson *Principles of Family Law* (6th edn) (Sweet & Maxwell, 1997) at ch 12.

divorce courts – did not enable the court to look behind the evidence which the parties chose to put before it, or to make orders which neither party had sought. There was, thus, a significant risk that the interests of the children would not be adequately safeguarded on divorce and, indeed, in 1947 the Denning Committee[1] expressed the view that, in divorce proceedings, the welfare of children was wrongly subordinated to the interest of the divorcing parents.

This concern weighed heavily with the Royal Commission on Marriage and Divorce in 1956 and the Commission concluded[2] that a procedure was needed to ensure that parents themselves had given full consideration to the question of their children's future welfare, and that the court had an effective control over the children's welfare.

Legislation

The scheme which was adopted was to enact that a decree nisi of divorce should not normally be made absolute unless, and until, the court had satisfied itself that the arrangements proposed for the care and upbringing of children were the best that could be devised in the circumstances. Legislation to give effect to this proposal was first enacted in 1958[3], and was re-enacted with modifications in 1970[4].

When this legislation was enacted, it was assumed that the divorce court would always hold a hearing but, in 1977, the 'special procedure' – under which undefended divorces are granted without the parties' attendance – was extended to cases involving children[5]. It was evidently thought important to ensure that the extension of the special procedure did not jeopardise the protection of children, and the Lord Chancellor said that he 'attached considerable importance' to the duty of the judges to protect children involved in divorce, and to the judges' ability to discuss the proposed arrangements with petitioners[6]. It was, accordingly, provided that if children were involved in divorce, a judge would hold a special children's appointment and would look into the arrangements to be made for the children's upbringing.

It was hoped that this procedure would be more effective than that available under the old system for the trial of undefended divorces in open court (which usually involved no more than the making of a formal enquiry to the petitioner as to whether there was anything to be added to the details already given in the papers). It was said that the greater informality of the children's appointment procedure would make for easier communication between parents and judge; and this would, in turn, help to uncover problems, as well as enabling judges to offer parents advice and encouragement. However, a major research project[7] demonstrated many imperfections in the system and, influenced by these considerations,

---

1   *Final Report of the Committee on Procedure and Matrimonial Causes* (Cmnd 7024) at para 31.
2   Ibid, para 372.
3   Matrimonial Proceedings (Children) Act 1958, s 2.
4   The legislation was consolidated in the Matrimonial Causes Act 1973, s 41.
5   In 1973 (when it was first introduced) the special procedure had been confined to undefended cases, based on living apart for two years, in which there were no children of the family: Matrimonial Causes Rules 1977, SI 1977/334, rr 33(3), 48.
6   *Hansard* Vol 371, col 1218.
7   Elston, Fuller and Murch (1975) 38 MLR 609.

Parliament amended the relevant statutory provisions. As explained below[1], the parties now have to give extended details about the arrangements which are proposed for their children, but these will be considered privately by a district judge sitting in his chambers. There is no necessity for a hearing or for any further investigation unless the district judge believes that there is ground for concern or further enquiry, and the circumstances in which a decree of divorce can be held up have been greatly restricted[2].

The Family Law Act 1996, when fully implemented, will radically reform the law of divorce[3]. The divorce aspects of the legislation as they affect children are considered further in Chapter 4. From an historical perspective there are perhaps two features of the new legislation which ought to be highlighted.The first is that, by generally requiring the new statutory period for 'reflection and consideration' to be extended by six months in cases where there are minor children[4], the Act represents something of a departure from the philosophy hitherto accepted by law reform bodies that divorce ought not to be made more difficult where there are children than where there are none[5]. Secondly, and most unusually for English legislation[6], the Act sets out a list of 'general principles' which are to be given effect by the court and 'any person, in exercising functions under or in consequence' of those parts of the legislation which deal with divorce and mediation. These principles refer, inter alia, to the need when bringing a marriage to an end to do so in a way which minimises distress or the risk of violence to children and which promotes 'as good a continuing relationship between the parties and any children affected as is possible in the circumstances'[7]. The legislation may be viewed by some as a bold attempt to adjust the existing balance by giving greater emphasis to the interests of children, as opposed to those of adults, on divorce. Whether the substance will match the rhetoric and how indeed the law *should* seek to balance the interests of children and parents on divorce are issues considered further in later chapters[8].

---

1 See Chapter 4.
2 Ibid.
3 This will certainly not be before 1999, and 2000 seems more likely at the time of writing. Part IV of the Act has already radically reformed the law relating to domestic violence and occupation of the family home, as to which see Chapter 12 below. On the Act generally, see Michael Freeman *The Family Law Act 1996* (Sweet & Maxwell, 1996), and on the divorce aspects specifically, see Roger Bird and Stephen Cretney *Divorce: The New Law* (Family Law, 1996). A more academic analysis is to be found in SM Cretney and J Masson *Principles of Family Law* (6th edn) (Sweet & Maxwell, 1997) at pp 317–383.
4 Section 7(11) and (13).
5 A principle accepted by the Law Commission in its report of 1990. See Law Com No 192 *Family Law: The Ground for Divorce* (1990) at para 5.28.
6 But not for Continental civil codes, as to which see Mary Ann Glendon *The Transformation of Family Law* (University of Chicago Press, 1987) at ch 3.
7 Section 1(c) and (d). See also s 11(3)(c).
8 Chapters 3 and 4.

Chapter 2

FUNDAMENTAL PRINCIPLES:
THE CHILDREN ACT 1989 AND THE UNITED
NATIONS CONVENTION ON THE RIGHTS
OF THE CHILD

Coincidentally, the United Nations Convention on the Rights of the Child was adopted by the General Assembly in November 1989 – the same month that the Children Act reached the statute book in England. Together, these two basic sources of children law represented a fresh beginning for children in domestic and international law. A key question for the student to consider is how far English law may be thought to be in conformity with the Convention and, for this and other reasons, the Children Act and the UN Convention are examined in juxtaposition in this chapter.

I THE CHILDREN ACT 1989

THE SCOPE OF THE LEGISLATION

General

The Children Act 1989 ('the Children Act') is now, undoubtedly, the most important single source of children law[1]. It was described by the then Lord Chancellor as 'the most comprehensive and far-reaching reform of child law which has come before Parliament in living memory'[2]. It constituted a completely new statutory code governing the 'public' and 'private' law affecting children and

---

1   The Children Act has been the subject of extensive commentary and generated an
     unprecedented number of books within a short time of Royal Assent. These include: A
     Bainham *Children: The New Law* (Jordans, 1990); R White, P Carr and N Lowe *A Guide to the
     Children Act 1989* (2nd edn) (Butterworths, 1995); J Eekelaar and R Dingwall *The Reform of Child
     Care Law* (Routledge, 1990); J Masson *The Children Act 1989, Current Law Statutes Annotated*
     (Sweet & Maxwell, 1990); N Allen *Making Sense of the Children Act 1989* (Longman, 1990);
     J Bridge, S Bridge and S Luke *Blackstone's Guide to the Children Act 1989* (Blackstone Press, 1990);
     L Feldman and B Mitchels *The Children Act 1989: A Practical Guide* (Longman, 1990); and S Bell
     MP *Shaw's Annotated Acts: Children Act 1989* (Shaw & Sons, 1990). The Department of Health
     also issued its official guidance on the 1989 Act under the title *An Introduction to the Children Act
     1989* (HMSO). Other commentaries on the legislation, which take account of the regulations
     and rules of court made under it, are: MDA Freeman *Children, Their Families and the Law*
     (Macmillan, 1992); and J Masson and M Morris *Children Act Manual* (Sweet & Maxwell, 1992).
     For more recent commentaries which take account of the extensive case-law under the Act, see
     SM Cretney and JM Masson *Principles of Family Law* (6th edn) (Sweet & Maxwell, 1997) Part V;
     M Hayes and C Williams *Family Law: Principles, Policy and Practice* (Butterworths, 1995) chs 1–4,
     and K Standley *Family Law* (2nd edn) (Macmillan, 1997) Part IV. For a very succinct, yet
     scholarly, commentary, see SM Cretney *Family Law* (3rd edn) (Sweet & Maxwell, 1997) Part III.
2   *Hansard* (HL) Vol 502, col 488.

drew those two branches much closer together[1]. It removed, in one fell swoop, much of the complex and technical statutory law which had grown up in characteristically English, piecemeal fashion over several decades. It was, in every sense, a fresh start. As if to emphasise this break with the past, the legislation was brought into force in its entirety on 14 October 1991, thereby avoiding the delay and disjointed implementation which had previously bedevilled this area of law[2].

The Children Act established parenthood as the primary legal status in relation to children and reformed the law of guardianship to reflect this. It introduced 'parental responsibility' as the central organising concept in children law and reasserted the significance of children's welfare as the paramount consideration in disputes concerning their upbringing. It gave to the courts wide-ranging and flexible powers to regulate the exercise of parental responsibility and introduced sweeping procedural and jurisdictional changes. In the public law, the legislation made fundamental adjustments to the powers and duties of local authorities regarding the family and to the relationship between local authorities and the courts in fulfilling their complementary child care functions. It established a wholly new basis for compulsory care or supervision and, while leaving intact the ancient wardship jurisdiction, imposed severe limitations on its use. New procedures for protecting children in emergencies were introduced and major changes made to the legal regulation of substitute care arrangements.

Much of the detail of the reformed law is contained in the Act's 15 Schedules, including the code now governing the courts' powers to make financial provision for children[3], the specific duties of local authorities to children looked after by them and, more controversially, the radically reformulated supervisory role of the divorce court. The law and procedure applying to children on divorce will be further amended when the Family Law Act 1996 is fully implemented. A vast amount of practical detail is consigned to the many regulations, rules of court and guidances issued under the Children Act's enabling provisions[4].

The legislation substantially replaced all the existing private law governing the custody and upbringing of children and the public law applying to social services for families, voluntary and compulsory care and supervision. This was no small feat. It entailed the repeal of eight post-war statutes, namely, the Nurseries and Child Minders Regulation Act 1948, the Guardianship of Minors Act 1971, the Guardianship Act 1973, the Children Act 1975, the Child Care Act 1980, the Foster Children Act 1980, the Children's Homes Act 1982 and the Children and Young Persons (Amendment) Act 1986. The Children and Young Persons Act 1969 and the Domestic Proceedings and Magistrates' Courts Act 1978 were significantly amended.

---

1 The expressions 'public' and 'private' law are used extensively throughout this book to indicate, respectively, the law governing care and related proceedings and family proceedings involving disputes between private individuals such as divorce, guardianship, wardship or adoption.

2 The staggered implementation of the Children Act 1975 was a notorious example of this. While that Act, inter alia, introduced the concept of custodianship, it was a decade before this was eventually brought into force. See Part II of the 1975 Act; and the Children Act 1975 and the Domestic Proceedings and Magistrates' Courts Act 1978 (Commencement) Order 1985, SI 1985/779.

3 The legislation largely consolidated the existing law on this, although major changes, which have severely restricted the jurisdiction of the courts, were subsequently introduced by the Child Support Act 1991, as to which see Chapter 9 below.

4 The principal enabling provisions are contained in ss 92 and 93 and Sch 11.

Children issues in adult litigation: beyond the Children Act 1989

Despite this extensive coverage, the Children Act still represents only one source of children law. The interests of children are affected, directly or indirectly, by a mass of statutory provisions and common law rules, many of which were left quite untouched by the Act. While, for example, the Children Act brought about some minor changes to adoption law, adoption continues to be governed by an essentially separate code[1]. This may be something of an oversimplification, since the fundamental principles and underlying philosophies which inform the Children Act have had an influence in *every* area of law in which issues concerning children's interests have arisen. Adoption is, indeed, a good example of this since the ideology of 'partnership' and 'inclusive' parenting, which the Children Act appears to support, perhaps made it inevitable that there would be an early reappraisal of the traditional English concept of adoption[2].

Yet it is clear that the student will need to look well beyond the Children Act for a proper understanding of the many and varied legal issues which concern children and young people. Thus, there are many matters which are conceptualised as 'adult issues' because it is thought that they relate *predominantly* to the competing interests of two or more adults. The interests of any children are not considered the central concern. This is evidently so in the case of divorce. The Family Law Act 1996, as noted above, does attempt to give greater prominence to children's interests on divorce[3] but does not go so far as to allow the interests or wishes of children to influence the essential basis or 'grounds' for divorce[4]. The welfare principle, which makes the best interests of children paramount, has no application. Adult interests are also deemed to be relevant in varying degrees on other questions which clearly affect children. The interests of children are the 'first' but not paramount consideration where a court is considering what financial and housing provision to make for a parent and dependent children on divorce[5]. Since the issue does not directly relate to the upbringing of the child, this is a question which falls outside the provisions of the Children Act and continues to be governed by the Matrimonial Causes Act 1973.

Likewise, where the issue is whether an order should be made excluding a husband or partner from the family home, the interests of children (while relevant) are neither the 'first' nor the 'paramount' consideration. The Matrimonial Homes Act 1983, s 1(3) specified as a factor the needs of the children alongside the conduct of the adult parties and their needs and resources. It is fair to say that the Family Law Act 1996 does attempt to give greater weight to the interests of children on applications for occupation orders since, in the case of 'entitled applicants' and former spouses, there is in effect a *presumption* that an order be made where 'the applicant or any relevant child is likely to suffer significant harm attributable to conduct of the respondent' unless at least as much, or more, harm is likely to be suffered if the order is made. The position is complex, however, in that no such presumption applies in the case of 'non-

---

1   The Adoption Act 1976.
2   See Chapter 7 below.
3   See Chapters 1 and 4.
4   For a full discussion of the ground for divorce, see Law Com Report No 192 *The Ground for Divorce* (1990) and Chapter 4 below.
5   Matrimonial Causes Act 1973, s 25(1). For a recent case in which the interests of a child had a significant influence on the outcome, see *C v C (Financial Relief: Short Marriage)* [1997] 2 FLR 26.

entitled' cohabitants or former cohabitants, although the court must still have regard to the 'balance of harm' criterion[1].

In all these instances, the welfare of children is bound to be affected by the various outcomes and, to the uninitiated, the way in which the law ascribes more or less relevance to this may appear somewhat arbitrary. Yet this may simply be a reflection of the relative importance which society is prepared to attach to the often competing claims of children and adults. It is not really surprising that this should vary depending on the question which is being asked or that a different answer to the same question may be given at different times. It must, moreover, be acknowledged that, notwithstanding the current trend to deny the existence of indepedent 'rights' for parents, the reality is that the law does not always give precedence to children's interests. The difficult question of balancing the claims of children with those of parents and other adults is considered below[2].

Impact of the Children Act 1989 on other legislation

Broadly, the Children Act incorporates those jurisdictions and those issues which can conveniently be termed 'children jurisdictions' and 'children issues'. 'Adult jurisdictions' and 'adult issues' are governed by separate pieces of legislation. At the same time, proceedings under certain other enactments are 'family proceedings' for the purposes of the Children Act[3]. Where this is so, and a 'children issue' arises in family proceedings, that issue will fall to be determined by applying the welfare principle and the other principles in the Children Act which apply to all family proceedings. To that extent the Children Act has a direct impact on other legislation.

Take the example of an application for an occupation order, a matter involving the criteria in Part IV of the Family Law Act 1996. The ouster issue itself must be determined by the criteria in that legislation. But the proceedings are 'family proceedings' and the question of the residential arrangements for any children is, clearly, highly relevant. This latter issue relates to the upbringing of children, falling directly within s 1 of the Children Act, and is governed by the welfare principle. The child's welfare is only one of several factors relevant to the occupation issue but is the sole consideration on the residence issue. The beauty of the Children Act was that it enabled the court, for the first time, to hear these obviously related issues together in the same proceedings. This can, of course, give rise to further difficulties concerning the proper balance to be struck between the interests of children and adults in this context.

The Law Commission considered whether it might be possible to collect, in a single statute, all the courts' powers over upbringing and financial provision for children. But it concluded that it was 'convenient for the statutes dealing principally with the affairs of adults to contain those of the provisions relating to children which cannot readily be separated from those relating to adults'. Where these powers related exclusively to children, the Law Commission felt that they

---

1   See Family Law Act 1996, ss 33(6) and (7), 35(6)–(8) and 38(4) and (5).
2   See Chapter 3 below.
3   Section 8(3) and (4). Section 8(4) has been amended to include proceedings under the Family Law Act 1996 and a new s 8(5) has been added to clarify precisely when children orders may be made under the new divorce procedures when they come into effect. See further Chapter 4.

could be conveniently collected in one place and the Children Act gave effect to this[1].

Other children issues

The Children Act does not provide the answer to certain other fundamental questions regarding the legal position of children. The very nature of the legal relationship between parents and children still largely falls to be determined at common law. The Children Act did little more than repeat the open-ended and imprecise definition of 'parental rights and duties' in its definition of 'parental responsibility'[2]. Certain aspects of upbringing, notably education, are substantially regulated by separate statutory regimes[3]. The principles of child support are now substantially contained in the Child Support Acts 1991 and 1995 and cannot be properly understood without some knowledge of social security legislation[4]. In fact, a host of issues concerning the position of children in society, and their involvement with individuals and institutions outside the family, are governed by a mixture of common law and statutory rules[5]. This is true of employment, contractual capacity, tortious liability and criminal responsibility. There is also a plethora of ad hoc statutory provisions reflecting society's concern to protect children from harmful activities and influences which arise from time to time[6]. Increasingly, also, it is necessary to take account of the international dimension. There is, in particular, a burgeoning growth in domestic and international law dealing with the problem of child abduction[7]; and there is now strong international recognition of the 'rights' of children as an aspect of human rights, most obviously reflected in the United Nations Convention on the Rights of the Child and the European Convention for the Protection of Human Rights and Fundamental Freedoms, and, increasingly, under other Conventions[8].

The student of children in the modern law must therefore be prepared to search well beyond the confines of the Children Act, but it would be idle to deny the key significance of the Act. A good part of this book is thus concerned with the application of the Children Act in particular contexts. This can only be properly understood in the light of the central principles which are expressly enunciated by the Children Act and some of the underlying philosophies which those principles may be thought to encapsulate.

THE HISTORY OF THE LEGISLATION

The Children Act is not the product of one single influence. It rather emerged in its final form as a result of the happy coincidence of two independent reviews, and

---

1 Law Com Report No 172 *Review of Child Law: Guardianship and Custody* (1988) at para 1.8.
2 Children Act 1975, s 85(1) and Children Act 1989, s 3(1).
3 The various Education Acts from 1944 to 1997 are discussed in Chapter 16 below.
4 See Chapter 9 below.
5 Part IV of this book is largely concerned with the law affecting the position of children in wider society.
6 Examples are the Tattooing of Minors Act 1969 and the Protection of Children Act 1978.
7 See Chapter 17 below.
8 See, generally, G Van Bueren *The International Law on the Rights of the Child* (Martinus Nijhoff, 1995) and Chapter 17 below.

a general climate of opinion in which there was impatience to rectify what were seen as intolerable deficiencies in existing law and practice.

The public law review

In 1982, the House of Commons Social Services Select Committee began an inquiry into aspects of the practice relating to children in care. Its report ('the *Short Report*') produced in 1984, concluded that a thorough-going review of the whole body of child care law was overdue. The Department of Health and Social Security (as it then was) set up an interdepartmental working party comprising civil servants from relevant government departments and representatives from the Law Commission. This Committee produced a lengthy consultation paper in October 1985, entitled the *Review of Child Care Law* ('the *Review*'). Most, but not all, of the recommendations were accepted by the Government in its White Paper entitled *The Law on Child Care and Family Services*[1] ('the White Paper') published in January 1987. It is important to appreciate that the bulk of the reforms to the public law, now embodied in the Children Act, derive from these two sources. The former document is the more significant since it sets out, in some considerable detail, the reasoning behind the reforms. The White Paper needs to be taken together with the *Review*, not least because it rejected certain of the *Review*'s recommendations, including the original proposal to retain the concept of 'voluntary care' and to sub-divide it into 'respite' care and 'shared' care[2]. In the event, the very idea of voluntary care was abandoned in favour of a new concept of 'looking after' or 'accommodating' children on a voluntary basis[3].

It is a popular misconception that the legislation in general, and the reforms to care procedures in particular, were a reaction to the crisis concerning the investigation of child sexual abuse which occurred in Cleveland in June 1987 and was the subject of a subsequent report by Lady Justice Butler-Sloss[4]. It is quite evident that this was not the case since, chronologically, the *Review* and the White Paper pre-date even the first murmurings of the crisis. Yet it is probably fair to say that, more than any other single influence, what happened in Cleveland contributed to the gathering impetus for early reform. Just as Cleveland had alerted public opinion to the dangers of 'over-reaction' to the problems of child abuse, so a succession of public inquiries into the domestic homicide of individual children exposed the opposite danger of 'under-reaction'. Among these, the more influential were probably those relating to Jasmine Beckford, Tyra Henry and Kimberley Carlile[5]. Other major influences on the legislation were several

---

1 Cmnd 62.
2 The *Review*, at chs 6 and 7. Cf the White Paper, at para 26.
3 See Chapter 10 below.
4 *Report of the Inquiry into Child Abuse in Cleveland 1987* (1988) (Cmnd 412). See also Chapters 11 and 12 below.
5 *A Child in Trust: The Report of the Panel of Inquiry into the Circumstances surrounding the death of Jasmine Beckford* (London Borough of Brent, 1985); *Whose Child? The Report of the Public Inquiry into the death of Tyra Henry* (London Borough of Lambeth, 1987), and *A Child in Mind: Protection of Children in a Responsible Society: Report of the Commission of Inquiry into the Circumstances surrounding the death of Kimberley Carlile* (London Borough of Greenwich, 1987). For academic assessments of the role of public inquiries in children cases, see R Dingwall 'The Jasmine Beckford Affair' (1986) 49 MLR 489 and N Parton and N Martin 'Public Inquiries, legalism and child care in England and Wales' (1989) 3 IJLF 21.

decisions of the European Court of Human Rights[1] (which found aspects of English child care procedures incompatible with the European Convention) and the House of Lords decision in the *Gillick* case[2] (which highlighted children's claims to have their views heard as an aspect of children's rights)[3]. Other provisions in the Children Act are the result of the many amendments to the Children Bill during its passage through Parliament, of which the most significant was probably the introduction of the 'child assessment order'[4]. This was not mentioned in the *Review* or the White Paper, was rejected by the Butler-Sloss report and only emerged at the eleventh hour following lengthy debate in Parliament.

The private law review

Contemporaneously with the review of child care law, the Law Commission had been conducting its own review of child law which was concerned with the 'private' law of custody, guardianship and wardship. Between 1985 and 1987 it produced four working papers on, respectively, *Guardianship*[5], *Custody*[6], *Care, Supervision and Interim Orders in Custody Proceedings*[7] and *Wards of Court*[8]. After consultation, the Commission unveiled its final report on *Guardianship and Custody*[9] in July 1988. It is this report which is the foundation for the private law reforms and the central principles which appear in Parts I and II of the Children Act. The content of the first three working papers was largely subsumed in the 1988 report but the fourth, on wardship, remains an important source of reference in its own right. This is because the Commission, after consultation, decided not to make final recommendations on the future of the wardship jurisdiction. Despite this, the Children Act (to the surprise of many) imposed drastic restrictions on the hitherto liberal use of wardship and the inherent jurisdiction by local authorities. In future, the procedure would be largely confined to the private sphere and there was some speculation on whether it could, or should, survive at all the radical remodelling of legal procedures effected by the Children Act[10].

The position in 1988, when the Law Commission reported, was that the Government had already announced its proposals for the reform of child care law. This convenient conclusion of the two reviews presented, as the former Lord Chancellor, Lord Mackay, put it, 'an historic opportunity to reform the English

1 *R v UK, O v UK, W v UK* [1988] 2 FLR 445, ECHR.
2 *Gillick v West Norfolk and Wisbech Area Health Authority* [1986] 1 AC 112. See Chapter 8 below.
3 For discussion of the provisions in the Children Act which reflect this aspect of children's rights see A Bainham 'The Children Act 1989: Adolescence and Children's Rights' [1990] Fam Law 311.
4 Section 43. See Chapter 12 below.
5 Law Com Working Paper No 91 *Review of Child Law: Guardianship* (1985).
6 Law Com Working Paper No 96 *Review of Child Law: Custody* (1986). See also Law Com Supplement to Working Paper No 96 *Custody Law in Practice in the Divorce and Domestic Courts* (1986).
7 Law Com Working Paper No 100 *Review of Child Law: Care, Supervision and Interim Orders in Custody Proceedings* (1987).
8 Law Com Working Paper No 101 *Review of Child Law: Wards of Court* (1987).
9 Law Com Report No 172 *Review of Child Law: Guardianship and Custody* (1988).
10 See, for example, N Lowe 'Caring for Children' (1989) 139 NLJ 87 and A Bainham 'The Children Act 1989: The Future of Wardship' [1990] Fam Law 270. Cf J Eekelaar and R Dingwall 'The Role of the Courts under the Children Bill' (1989) 139 NLJ 217.

Law into a single rationalised system as it applies to the care and upbringing of children'[1]. The draft Bill, which the Commission annexed to its report, reflected and incorporated the results of both reviews. This not only enabled all the public and private law to be gathered together in one place, it also presented the Commission with a unique chance to formulate common principles and establish common remedies which would apply, as far as possible, in both the public and private spheres[2]. Therefore, while the private law and public law remain distinct in certain important respects, the Children Act brought about a partial fusion of what were previously seen as two substantially distinctive codes.

CENTRAL PRINCIPLES

Part I of the Children Act contains a number of fundamental principles which apply throughout the legislation and are common to the public and private law. It also introduces and defines the key concept of 'parental responsibility' which, again, has application in the public and private spheres. In the following pages, the principles themselves as they appear in the Children Act are considered, after which the philosophies and ideologies which may be reflected in those principles are explored.

The welfare principle

Paramount or sole consideration
Section 1(1) of the Children Act re-enacted, in slightly modified form, what is the cardinal principle in children law. It provides:

> 'When a court determines any question with respect to:
> (a)   the upbringing of a child, or
> (b)   the administration of a child's property or the application of any income arising from it,
> the child's welfare shall be the court's paramount consideration.'

The former provision in the Guardianship of Minors Act 1971 made the welfare of the child the 'first and paramount' consideration, but, in 1970, the House of Lords in *J v C*[3] interpreted similar wording in the Guardianship of Infants Act 1925 to mean that the child's welfare should be the court's *sole* concern. All other considerations were to be excluded, except insofar as they had a bearing on the determination of the child's best interests. The principle, as Lord MacDermott put it, means:

> '... more than that the child's welfare is to be treated as the top item in a list of items relevant to the matter in question. [The words] connote a process whereby, when all the relevant facts, relationships, claims and wishes of parents, risks, choices and other circumstances are taken into account and weighed, the course to be followed will be that which is most in the interests of the child's welfare as that term is now to be understood. That is the first consideration because it is of first importance and the paramount consideration because it rules upon or determines the course to be followed.'[4]

---

1   Child and Co Lecture, April 1988.
2   For a succinct explanation of the general aims of the legislation, see B Hoggett 'The Children Bill: The Aim' [1989] Fam Law 217.
3   [1970] AC 668.
4   Ibid at 710–711.

Since, according to this interpretation, welfare is the *only* consideration, the Law Commission took the view that to describe it also as the 'first' consideration would be otiose[1]. Hence, this is the preferred formulation, but it should be noted that no change of substance was intended, and Lord MacDermott's settled interpretation applies as much today as it did in 1970.

Welfare 'checklist' introduced

Lord MacDermott referred, in his now famous dictum, to welfare 'as that term is now to be understood'. This begs the question of how precisely the term *is* understood at any given time. The truth is that the 'welfare' or 'best interests' of children are notoriously indeterminate concepts, so much so that it has been argued that the really crucial issue is not the concept of welfare itself but the choice of decision-maker[2]. What is or is not in children's interests depends largely on who is asked the question. Thus, there are those who have asserted that the psychological well-being of children following divorce is best protected by 'exclusive' custodial arrangements which provide them with the security of one 'psychological parent'[3]. But, equally, there are others who have taken the very different position that children fare best where contact with *both* divorcing parents is maximised and maintained[4]. It is, perhaps, inevitable that individual value judgments must intrude to some extent into the determination of a child's best interests. However, in an effort to structure judicial discretion, the Children Act broke new ground and incorporated a statutory 'checklist' of factors for courts applying the welfare principle.

The court must have regard in particular to:

'(a) the ascertainable wishes and feelings of the child concerned (considered in the light of his age and understanding);
(b) his physical, emotional and educational needs;
(c) the likely effect on him of any change in his circumstances;
(d) his age, sex, background and any characteristics of his which the court considers relevant;
(e) any harm which he has suffered or is at risk of suffering;
(f) how capable each of his parents, and any other person in relation to whom the court considers the question to be relevant, is of meeting his needs;
(g) the range of powers available to the court under this Act in the proceedings in question.'

The application of these factors in individual cases is discussed below[5]. At this stage, it is sufficient to note that the checklist applies only in *contested* private proceedings, whereas it applies to all public proceedings under Part IV of the Act whether or not they are opposed[6]. The absence of a duty to apply the checklist in

---

1 Law Com Report No 172 *Review of Child Law: Guardianship and Custody* (1988) at paras 3.12–3.16. In fact the Commission proposed that the welfare of the child should be the court's 'only concern' and this form of wording appeared in its draft Bill. In the event, the word 'first' was dropped while the 'paramount consideration' formula was retained.
2 RH Mnookin 'Child Custody Adjudication: Judicial Functions in the Face of Indeterminacy' (1975) 39 *Law and Contemporary Problems* 226 and 'Thinking about Children's Rights – Beyond Kiddie Libbers and Child Savers' (1981) 16 *Stanford Lawyer* 24.
3 J Goldstein, A Freud and AJ Solnit *Beyond the Best Interests of the Child* (The Free Press, New York, 1973).
4 J Wallerstein and JB Kelly *Surviving the Breakup* (Grant McIntyre, 1980). This certainly seems to be the thinking which informs some of the so-called 'general principles' in the new divorce law under the Family Law Act 1996. See Chapter 4 below.
5 See Chapter 4 below.
6 Section 1(4).

unopposed private proceedings is consistent with what some may see as an essentially 'non-interventionist' role for the courts. The implication appears to be that where all parties are in agreement about what should happen to children, the court's role may be limited to sanctioning officially that agreement. It has been suggested that the presence in the checklist of the final factor might also 'be taken as a tacit warning that too much should not be expected of court intervention'[1].

No premium is attached to any of the factors in the list. They are all apparently to be accorded equal weight, along with any others which the court may think relevant[2]. A considerable amount of discretion must, accordingly, remain vested in individual judges. There would appear to be nothing to prevent one judge from attaching greater importance to a child's wishes (factor (a)) than to considerations of the relative capabilities of the two parents (factor (f)). Another judge might, equally legitimately, place greater emphasis on the latter. While such differences might be put down to the distinctive features of individual cases, they might also be explained by divergent judicial attitudes on the value of children's views.

The problem of checklists

The problem (if it is a problem) of largely unfettered discretion in family law is not a new one. This particular checklist was not a revolutionary experiment, since similar devices had operated for some years to structure judicial discretion in relation to property and financial adjustments on divorce and ouster orders, now replaced by 'occupation' orders under Part IV of the Family Law Act 1996[3].

The experience under the Matrimonial Homes Act 1983 is instructive. For a considerable number of years it was not appreciated that the statutory criteria (previously enshrined in the Matrimonial Homes Act 1967) applied at all in ouster applications brought under the Domestic Violence and Matrimonial Proceedings Act 1976. During this period, individual judges and differently constituted divisions of the Court of Appeal had taken widely differing positions on the relative importance of children's welfare (especially housing needs) and the conduct of the adults[4].

In 1984 the House of Lords in *Richards v Richards*[5] held that all ouster applications were governed by the criteria in the Matrimonial Homes Act 1983. Ostensibly, this meant that the needs of children should, in principle, be given equal weight to the conduct of the adults, their own needs and financial resources, and all other circumstances of the case. Yet this ruling did nothing to preclude individual judges from taking the view that one or other of these factors should predominate in an individual case and there is plenty of evidence that they did just that[6]. Thus, while checklists or statutory criteria may serve the limited function of

---

1   SM Cretney 'Defining the Limits of State Intervention' in D Freestone (ed) *Children and the Law* (Hull University Press, 1990) at p 65.
2   Unlike other statutory checklists, this one does not contain a 'sweeping-up clause' but the clear implication, since the court must have regard to the specified factors 'in particular', is that the court may consider all other relevant circumstances not enumerated in the list.
3   Matrimonial Causes Act 1973, s 25(1); Matrimonial Homes Act 1983, s 1(3); and Family Law Act 1996, ss 33(6) and (7), 35(6)–(8) and 38(4) and (5).
4   *Samson v Samson* [1982] 1 All ER 780. Cf *Myers v Myers* [1982] 1 All ER 776.
5   [1984] AC 174.
6   Contrast, for example, *Lee v Lee* [1984] FLR 243 and *Summers v Summers* [1986] 1 FLR 343.

trying to ensure that all relevant factors are taken into account[1] they cannot affect the fundamentally indeterminate nature of concepts like 'welfare', 'best interests', 'significant harm'[2], 'children in need'[3], and so on.

Application of the welfare principle: public and private

Notwithstanding these practical limitations of the welfare principle, there is widespread agreement that the welfare of children should be an important priority in any civilised society. It may also be argued that the extent to which a legal system can offer effective protection of the rights of its most vulnerable members is a reasonable litmus test of the efficacy of that system. Perhaps it is these aspirations which have led to the bold assertion that the welfare principle has general application in English law and that parents and others who deal with children are legally bound by it[4]. Is there any substance in this contention?

It can certainly be said that the welfare principle in s 1(1) of the Children Act, as interpreted in Lord MacDermott's technical sense, applies only in certain well-defined and restricted circumstances. It has already been noted that it does not apply in relation to issues deemed to be 'adult issues', even where children's interests are liable to be affected. The principle also applies in quite different ways in public and private proceedings. Only in the latter does it function in Lord MacDermott's sense. In public proceedings there is no question of care or supervision orders being made on the sole basis of a broad welfare criterion and, indeed, this was specifically rejected as a ground for State intervention in both the *Review* and the White Paper[5]. The welfare principle only comes into play if the minimum 'threshold' condition relating to 'significant harm' has been established to the court's satisfaction so that there is, in effect, a 'threshold stage' and a 'welfare stage'[6]. It would, therefore, be fundamentally misleading to imply that the welfare principle has *equal* application in public and private law. This is not to deny that its application in care proceedings is a significant feature in the court's final determination at the 'welfare stage'.

What is the situation where no court is involved at all? Are local authorities bound by the welfare principle in performing their statutory functions? The answer to this must be an unequivocal 'no'. It is true that social services departments have a general legal duty 'to safeguard and promote the welfare of

---

1 Failure to take one of the statutory criteria into account, such as a failure to explore the child's own views, ought to be a ground of appeal. See, for example, the pre-Children Act decision in *M v M (Minor: Custody Appeal)* [1987] 1 WLR 404. But in *H v H (Residence Order: Leave to Remove)* [1995] 1 FLR 529 at 532, Staughton LJ said that the checklist was not 'like the list of checks which an airline pilot has to make with his co-pilot, aloud one to the other before he takes off'. It is sufficient if the judge takes all the statutory factors into account.

2 This is the key concept in care and emergency proceedings. See particularly ss 31, 43 and 44, and Chapters 11 and 12 below.

3 This is now the principal concept in preventive work and family support. See Part III of the Children Act, and Chapter 10 below.

4 See, for example, S Sedley 'Child's welfare limits parents' rights to punish or restrain' (1986) 26 *Childright* 18.

5 The *Review*, at para 15.10, and the White Paper, at paras 59 and 60. The welfare principle will apply, however, where a local authority succeeds in obtaining leave to invoke the inherent jurisdiction of the High Court but the principle does not itself govern the question of whether leave should be granted. See ss 8(4) and 100(3). There have been a number of recent controversial uses of this jurisdiction which are discussed in Chapter 11 below.

6 Section 31(2).

children within their area who are in need'[1]. But they are not obliged to regard the welfare of those children as their paramount or sole consideration. Indeed, their former statutory duty to give 'first consideration' to their welfare was removed by the Children Act [2]. Clearly, local authorities must have regard to factors other than the welfare of individual children when discharging their statutory obligations of which one (expressly mentioned in the legislation) is the need to protect members of the public from serious injury[3]. The Court of Appeal has now held that the issue of the use of secure accommodation in relation to children in care is governed by the criteria in s 25 of the Act and *not* by the welfare principle. The court went on to say that the welfare principle, significantly, did not apply to *any* of the decisions taken by local authorities under Part III of the Act[4].

What if there is more than one child?
The courts have also had to grapple with the problem of conflicting interests between two or more children. The answer they have given in each case is that it is the child who is the subject of the application whose interests are paramount. Thus, where care proceedings relate to the child of a mother who is herself a minor, it is the baby's and not the minor mother's interests which are paramount. This applies both to the question of contact with the child who has been taken into care[5] and on the initial application for the care order[6]. The same logic has been applied where the interests of siblings are thought to conflict[7]. Whether the interests of one child *should* as a matter of policy be preferred over the interests of another merely because the first child is technically the subject of the application and the other is not is open to doubt[8]. A better approach, as the Law Commission had suggested[9], might have been for the court to have regard in an even-handed way 'to the welfare of any child likely to be affected'.

Are parents and others bound by the welfare principle?
It can hardly be argued that parents, in taking family decisions affecting a child, are bound to ignore completely their own interests, the interests of other members of the family and, possibly, outsiders. This would be a wholly undesirable, as well as unrealistic, objective. Again, it is sometimes said that third parties dealing with children and young people are legally obliged to act consistently with their best interests. There is more than a suggestion of this in Lord Fraser's speech in *Gillick* where he stated that a doctor should not provide contraceptive advice or treatment to a girl under 16 unless, inter alia, he regarded it as in her best interests to do so. But he did not say that this was to be the doctor's *sole* concern. In fact, he made it clear that he was obliged also to have regard to the

---

1   Sections 17(1)(a) and 22(3)(a).
2   Formerly contained in the Child Care Act 1980, s 18(1) which was repealed by the Children Act.
3   Section 22(6).
4   *Re M (Secure Accommodation Order)* [1995] 1 FLR 418.
5   *Birmingham City Council v H (No 3)* [1994] 1 FLR 224.
6   *F v Leeds City Council* [1994] 2 FLR 60.
7   *Re F (Contact: Child in Care)* [1995] 1 FLR 510 and *Re T and E (Proceedings: Conflicting Interests)* [1995] 1 FLR 581.
8   For a critique of these decisions, see A Bainham 'The Nuances of Welfare' [1995] CLJ 512.
9   Law Com Report No 172 *Review of Child Law: Guardianship and Custody* (1988) at para 3.13 and Working Paper No 96 *Custody* (1986) at para 6.16.

interests of the girl's parents (by seeking to persuade the girl to involve them), and to her own *views* (as opposed to interests), judged in the light of her maturity and understanding. Lord Fraser clearly had in mind the application of a different kind of welfare test than that applied by the courts under Lord MacDermott's formulation. It is submitted that it would be a distortion to say that outsiders dealing with children are legally bound by the welfare principle.

Those who imply that the welfare principle has this much wider application are really expressing the hope that society in general, and individual adults, will, in their decisions, feel it appropriate to act in the best interests of children, as they see them. This hope appears to be behind many of the provisions in the Children Act as they affect parents. The Act reposes a great deal of trust in parents that they will know what is best for their children and act accordingly. Whether this level of trust is justified by the historical record is something which at least one commentator was quick to question[1].

The no order principle

The welfare principle must be read in conjunction with another fundamental principle which has come to be widely known as the 'no order' or 'non-intervention' principle. This states:

> 'Where a court is considering whether or not to make one or more orders under this Act with respect to a child, it shall not make the order or any of the orders unless it considers that doing so would be better for the child than making no order at all.'

The express purpose of this provision is to emphasise that there should be a demonstrable benefit to the child in any order which the court is contemplating. The Law Commission was concerned, specifically in the context of divorce, that orders for custody and access were routinely made, notwithstanding that a very high percentage were uncontested. They had, in reality, become 'part of the package' of divorce. The Commission's position was that the law should not intrude unnecessarily into the divorce process. Where divorcing parents were able to reach amicable and workable arrangements concerning children it was not desirable for these to be embodied in court orders. It was concerned also to avert the danger of polarising parents who were already co-operating with each other[2]. This view of the role of court orders also accorded with the notion of parenthood as a continuing responsibility. Thus, the responsibility of *both* parents should survive the process of divorce, and court orders should be reserved for those cases in which there was a clear need to regulate the exercise of that responsibility. Most, if not all, of those instances, it was thought, would be situations in which the parties themselves failed to reach agreement. The principle again applies equally to public orders. Before making a care or supervision order the court should be satisfied not only that this would be in the child's best interests but also that the order can achieve something which is unlikely to be achieved without it. This requires consideration of the other ways, falling short of compulsory action, in which social services might assist a family in difficulty[3].

---

1 J Eekelaar 'Parental Responsibility: State of Nature or Nature of the State?' (1991) JSWFL 37.
2 Law Com Report No 172 *Review of Child Law: Guardianship and Custody* (1988) at paras 3.2 et seq.
3 These services are discussed in Chapter 10 below. The principle does not, however, govern applications for financial provision (see *K v H (Child Maintenance)* [1993] 2 FLR 61).

The no order principle may, on one view, be seen as complementary to the welfare principle, since it cannot be in the best interests of children to be the subject of unnecessary court orders. If it is not better for a child that an order should be made, than that it should not, then the welfare of the child is ex hypothesi not furthered by the order. Looked at in this way, the principle might almost be regarded as superfluous, since it appears to add little to the welfare principle itself. Yet the intention is clear enough. It is to emphasise the need for courts to apply their minds specifically to the various options open to them, and not to assume that any order is better than none. The onus is on the applicant, whether a private individual or institution, to convince the court of the alleged benefits of the order sought. While it can be argued that this was always the case under the former law there is an undoubted shift of emphasis which has led to suggestions that there is now a *presumption* against court orders. This interpretation is open to doubt. It should be noted that the statute does not contain express language which presumes orders to be unnecessary. It merely says that they ought not to be made *if they are unnecessary*. It is also clear that the Law Commission's Report which is the source of the principle did not presume court orders to be unnecessary either[1]. And whether the principle may accurately be described as 'the non-intervention principle' or properly thought to embody a wider 'non-interventionist philosophy' about the relationship between the State and the family, as many commentators have been inclined to assert, is highly questionable[2].

Delay is prejudicial

Section 1(2) of the Children Act enshrines another central and innovative principle applying equally in public and private proceedings. It states:

> 'In any proceedings in which any question with respect to the upbringing of a child arises, the court shall have regard to the general principle that any delay in determining the question is likely to prejudice the welfare of the child.'

It has been known for a long time that delays in residence and related proceedings can have an adverse effect on children as well as prejudice the legitimate interests of the adult parties. Such delays have regrettably often occurred and have frequently been the subject of judicial censure[3]. The major concerns have been the uncertainty which delay engenders in the lives of children, and the prejudice which it can cause to the party who is not living with the children. Delay reinforces the status quo and makes it more difficult to argue effectively for a change of residential arrangements. This so-called 'status quo principle' is indirectly acknowledged in the statutory checklist which refers to 'the likely effect on [the child] of any change in his circumstances'[4].

---

1   Law Com Report No 172, para 3.2.
2   See A Bainham 'Changing Families and Changing Concepts: Reforming the Language of Family Law' [1998] CFLQ 1 at pp 2–4.
3   See, for example, Ewbank J in *Stockport Metropolitan Borough Council v B; Stockport Metropolitan Borough Council v L* [1986] 2 FLR 80. More recently, see *Re S (Contact: Grandparents)* [1996] 1 FLR 158, in which there had been 17 hearings between 1992 and the end of 1994, and in which the Court of Appeal said that there had been an inappropriate use of the 'no order principle' in s 1(5).
4   Section 1(3)(c).

It is, of course, one thing to bemoan delay in resolving disputes over children and quite another to do anything about it, but the Children Act attempted to underscore the principled objection to delay by giving the courts new powers and duties to ensure the expeditious disposal of cases. Thus, in both public[1] and private[2] cases the court is required to draw up a timetable with a view to determining the questions before it without delay and to give appropriate directions to ensure, as far as possible, that the timetable is followed. Rules of court spell out in greater detail the procedural requirements which may be imposed[3]. The wording in the Children Act concedes that there may be some instances (perhaps many) in which *some* delay is readily justifiable. There is only a *presumption* that delay is prejudicial and the Law Commission thought that this could be rebutted where, for example, the benefit to be derived from a full welfare report could outweigh the delay of having to wait for it[4]. Clearly this is a relative matter, and much will turn on the extent of the delay. The enactment of this principle injected into what might have been thought a hitherto largely adversarial system an inquisitorial feature, since it envisages that the court, and not the parties, should dictate the pace of children proceedings.

PHILOSOPHIES AND IDEOLOGIES

It would be surprising if a statute which was the product of such disparate influences embodied a single philosophy throughout. What exactly the values are which inform the legislation must, of necessity, be a matter of opinion. Different commentators have read different things into the Act[5] and it should be borne in mind that what follows is only one view of the Act. One commonly held view is that the Children Act has attempted to bring about a substantial shift in the relationship between the State and the family. By emphasising that the *primary*

---

1 Section 32.
2 Section 11.
3 See, particularly, Part IV of the Family Proceedings Rules 1991, SI 1991/1247.
4 Law Com Report No 172 *Review of Child Law: Guardianship and Custody* (1988) at para 4.57. For some early empirical findings on the operation of these provisions, see I Butler et al 'The Children Act and the Issue of Delay' [1993] Fam Law 412. *The Children Act Advisory Committee Final Report June 1997* (Lord Chancellor's Department, 1997) Appendix 2, Table 5 contains statistics on the time taken for the disposal of care and supervision cases. These reveal a considerable regional variation, but show that on average it takes almost a year (48.3 weeks) from the date of application to the final hearing in the High Court; and 43.7 weeks in the county court. The time-lag, as might be expected, is significantly shorter in the magistrates' (family proceedings) courts, being in the region of 30 weeks.
5 These include LM Fox Harding 'The Children Act 1989 in Context: Four Perspectives in Child Care Law and Policy' (1991) JSWFL 179 and 285; SM Cretney 'Defining the Limits of State Intervention' in D Freestone (ed) *Children and the Law* (Hull University Press, 1990) at p 58; SM Cretney 'Privatising the Family: The Reform of Child Law' (1988) *Denning Law Journal* 15; A Bainham 'The Privatisation of the Public Interest in Children' (1990) 53 MLR 206; G Douglas 'Family Law under the Thatcher Government' (1990) 17 *Journal of Law and Society* 411; J Eekelaar 'Parental Responsibility: State of Nature or Nature of the State?' (1991) JSWFL 37; M Ryan 'The Children Bill 1988 – The Philosophy and the Reality' (1989) 1 JCL 102; and M Freeman 'In the Child's Best Interests? Reading the Children Act Critically' in *The Moral Status of Children* (Martinus Nijhoff, 1997). For a recent re-evaluation of the Act's ideologies in the light of the experience since it came into force, see M Freeman 'The Next Children's Act?' [1998] Fam Law 341.

responsibility for raising children rests with parents the law might be thought to be 'in retreat from the private realm of family life'[1]. This change of direction was thought by some to be consistent with, if not positively inspired by, the neo-conservative political ideology of the 1980s, which in Britain has often been referred to as 'Thatcherism'[2]. An analogy has been drawn with the privatisation programme of the Thatcher administration, such that the Children Act might be seen as a move (perhaps a substantial move) towards 'privatising' the family. Others have noted the same phenomenon but prefer the term 'de-regulation'[3]. The issue is a complex one, not least because there is no unitary concept of the 'the State'. It is not clear how precisely the interaction between the State and the family is to be measured. Should we, for example, concentrate on the policies of central government as they affect families and, if so, should an attempt be made to evaluate their specific impact on children and young people[4]? Should we, perhaps, look more closely at adjustments to the powers and duties of local authorities in view of their primary functions regarding family support and child protection? And how significant are changes to the role of the courts, as an organ of the State, in upholding the interests of parents, children and others, vis-à-vis each other and defending them against unwarranted action by other public agencies? All of these questions need to be explored if any meaningful attempt can be made to evaluate the effect of the legislation on the balance between the State and the family.

There can be no doubt that the legislation has also affected the balance of other relationships. It redrew the division of responsibility for child welfare between the courts and local authorities, it altered the relative legal positions of men and women (in their respective roles as fathers and mothers), and it redefined the relationship in law between children and adults. Below, some views are offered on how the legislation may have impacted on these various relations.

One arguably consistent theme throughout the legislation is that of 'partnership'[5]. The concept of a 'voluntary partnership' between parents and the State was crucial to the thinking behind the public law reforms. This implies public support for parents in discharging their primary responsibilities, social work assistance where families experience difficulty, and continuing co-operation with parents in

1   An expression originating in the decision of the US Supreme Court in *Prince v Massachussetts* 321 US 158 (1944) and borrowed by SM Cretney in 'Defining the Limits of State Intervention' (above).
2   SM Cretney 'Defining the Limits of State Intervention' (above) at pp 67–68. For a discussion of the influence of neo-conservative philosophies on family law developments in North America, see B Dickens 'The Modern Function and Limits of Parental Rights' (1981) 97 LQR 462.
3   See, for example, G Douglas (above), and K O'Donovan *Sexual Divisions in Law* (Weidenfeld & Nicolson, 1985) at ch 1.
4   The need to consider the impact of national policies on children has led to some calls for the creation of a Children's Rights Commissioner such as exists in certain other countries, notably in Scandinavia. See M Rosenbaum and P Newell *Taking Children Seriously – A Proposal for a Children's Rights Commissioner* (Gulbenkian-Foundation, 1991) and critique by A Bainham (1992) JSWFL 552.
5   The White Paper, at para 5. It should be said that this idea of partnership between parents and the State is not a new one. Sir William Beveridge, in producing his report which laid the foundations for the post-war Welfare State, clearly proceeded on the assumption that the financial responsibility for the cost of raising children should be shared between parents and the wider community through a system of family allowances. See *Report of the Committee on Social Insurance and Allied Services* (1942) (Cmnd 6404).

the more extreme circumstances where it has proved necessary to remove a child from the family.

This was the classic use of the partnership notion in the debates leading up to the reforms but it is by no means the only sense in which the legislation underscores the essential nature of partnerships. The persistence of parental responsibility means that, increasingly, it will be shared between two (or conceivably more) individuals. It has been seen that divorced parents will, in law, each retain parental responsibility. If this is to be taken at all seriously it must imply that the law expects a degree of co-operation between them. Similarly, where a foster-parent obtains parental responsibility through a residence order, this will be shared with the current holder or holders (usually parents) of parental responsibility. This must surely give rise to a similar implication of co-operation between all those who now hold parental responsibility. It is equally clear that courts and local authorities are expected to work together to secure the welfare of children. Thus, for example, the court in family proceedings may direct an authority to investigate the circumstances of a child[1]. The same may also be said of the various statutory and voluntary agencies having particular responsibilities which may affect children. The urgent need to improve inter-agency co-operation was a significant feature of various public inquiry reports[2], and the legislation sought to give effect to this in a number of ways. Local education, housing and health authorities were thus placed under new statutory duties to assist social services departments where a request for help is made[3]. And the increased importance which the legislation attaches to children's views means that parents, social workers, judges and others now have to bring them into deliberations about their future more than has traditionally been the case[4].

The general thrust of all these developments may be seen as consistent with the partnership ideal. People and institutions having the care of children or dealings with them are apparently expected to work together to promote their welfare. In so doing they are expected to take account of what children want for themselves. This must surely mean that there is bound to be much more of what used to be described as the 'fragmentation' of parental rights[5]. This conveys the idea that the legal powers and responsibilities for children are not centralised in one carer but shared or allocated between two or more individuals or institutions.

The likely impact of the Children Act on these various 'partnerships' will now be addressed briefly.

The State and the family

Strengthening of the parental position
Most commentators agreed that the Children Act strengthened considerably the legal standing of parents (and others with parental responsibility) vis-à-vis social

---

1 Section 37(1).
2 See, particularly, *A Child in Trust: The Report of the Panel of Inquiry into the Circumstances surrounding the death of Jasmine Beckford* (London Borough of Brent, 1985).
3 Section 27.
4 See Chapter 3 below.
5 An expression originally coined by J Eekelaar in 'What are Parental Rights?' (1973) 89 LQR 210 at p 229 and taken up by S Maidment in 'The Fragmentation of Parental Rights' [1981] CLJ 135.

services[1]. Foremost among those changes was the abolition of the 'parental rights resolution', an administrative mechanism for retaining compulsory control of a child originally placed voluntarily in the care of social services[2]. Although susceptible to a subsequent judicial challenge, the resolution procedure failed to extend to parents the minimum participatory rights mandated by the European Convention[3]. In the same vein, the Children Act placed important restrictions on the length of time for which a child might be kept away from home without an opportunity for challenge under emergency procedures[4].

Other provisions which entail a distinct shift of power away from local authorities have been criticised as emanting from an ideological stance which takes insufficient account of the practicalities involved. These include the abolition of the notice requirement where parents wish to resume the care of a child voluntarily 'accommodated' by social services[5]. Here, there was an obvious unwillingness to allow any period of notice, however short, to detract (even in theory) from the apparently strict demarcation of voluntary services and compulsory care which the Children Act establishes[6]. Other provisions which involve a distinct loss of control by local authorities are those which were designed to ensure that parents are allowed to participate fully in decision-making[7]. These new 'participatory' rights can be viewed merely as the logical accompaniments of the statutory commitment to reuniting children with their families[8]. But, equally, some may see in them the potential for inhibiting local authorities in the discharge of their statutory functions, for no better reason than an ideological commitment to the primacy of natural parenthood[9].

Despite these apparent shifts of power away from local authorities, it should be said that in several important respects the Children Act strengthened their powers to take protective action. These include the re-casting of the grounds for care and supervision orders to embrace prospective harm[10], and the introduction of child

---

1 See SM Cretney 'Defining the Limits of State Intervention' (above); J Eekelaar 'Parental Responsibility: State of Nature or Nature of the State?' (1991) JSWFL 37; and A Bainham 'The Children Act 1989: The State and the Family' [1990] Fam Law 231.

2 For a critique of the resolution procedure, see M Adcock, R White and O Rowlands *The Administrative Parent* (BAAF, 1983) and LM Harding 'The Hundred Year Resolution' (1989) 2 JCL 12.

3 See the cases cited at fn 1 at p 33.

4 Section 45, and see Chapter 12 below.

5 Formerly parents were required to give 28 days' notice. Failure to do so constituted a criminal offence under s 13 of the Child Care Act 1980.

6 There was great concern that voluntary arrangements should not be allowed to slip into compulsion, as had frequently happened under the existing law, since this was thought to discourage some families in difficulty from seeking voluntary assistance. See the discussion of the 'voluntary principle' in BM Hoggett *Parents and Children: The Law of Parental Responsibility* (3rd edn) (Sweet & Maxwell, 1987) at pp 130 et seq.

7 These participatory rights are, to some extent, implicit in the very notion of continuing parental responsibility, but the Children Act also confers on parents specific rights to be consulted. See particularly s 22, and Chapter 10 below.

8 See s 23(6) and Sch 2, para 15, discussed by M Ryan 'The Children Bill 1988 – The Philosophy and the Reality' (1989) 1 JCL 102 at p 104.

9 See the views of J Eekelaar 'Parental Responsibility: State of Nature or Nature of the State?' (1991) JSWFL 37 at pp 48 et seq.

10 Section 31(2) overcoming the technical difficulties exposed in *D (A Minor) v Berkshire County Council* [1987] 1 All ER 33, discussed in Chapter 11 below.

assessment orders alongside emergency protection orders, thereby increasing the short-term options for protective action[1].

Restriction of court intervention in divorce

In the private sphere, there is an equally strong affirmation of the parental role and the need to restrict public intervention through the courts. Nowhere is this thinking more strikingly obvious than in the reforms to the court's supervisory role on divorce. These changes, together with the new procedures introduced by the Family Law Act 1996, are considered in Chapter 4.

Agents of the State: the courts and local authorities

Former use of wardship by and against local authorities

Courts and local authorities may be seen as partners in upholding the public interest in child welfare[2]. While local authorities are given primary responsibility for the protection of children, they may take compulsory action only with the sanction of the courts. More importantly, perhaps, the courts have long performed an independent role in safeguarding the welfare of children in a variety of family proceedings. The archetypal protective jurisdiction has been wardship, where the courts have traditionally exercised wide and flexible powers to deal with any serious issues affecting individual children[3]. The existence of this potentially unlimited jurisdiction alongside the statutory powers and duties of local authorities gave rise to much litigation in the decade or so preceding the 1989 legislation[4]. The result which had appeared to emerge was that, whereas local authorities were at liberty to seek the 'supplementary assistance' of the courts in discharging their child care functions, it was not open to parents and others to invoke wardship to question the merits of decisions taken by social services[5]. A clear disparity had therefore grown up in the treatment of local authorities and other applicants.

The Children Act addressed this disparity in dramatic fashion by curtailing drastically the circumstances in which local authorities might have access to the inherent jurisdiction of the High Court[6]. The broad effect is that neither social services nor anyone else may act outside the statutory regime. The authority must prove the statutory ground for care and supervision orders if it wishes to take compulsory action, and it cannot resort to wardship or the inherent jurisdiction as an extra-statutory alternative. Similarly, any judicial challenges to the actions of the authority must be based on an alleged failure to satisfy the criteria in the

---

1 Sections 43 and 44. See Chapter 12 below.
2 See A Bainham *Children, Parents and the State* (Sweet & Maxwell, 1988) at p 103.
3 On the nature of the wardship jurisdiction, see particularly NV Lowe and RAH White *Wards of Court* (2nd edn) (Barry Rose/Kluwer, 1986) at ch 1; and Cross 'Wards of Court' (1967) 83 LQR 200.
4 The leading cases were *A v Liverpool City Council* [1982] AC 363 and *Re W (A Minor) (Wardship: Jurisdiction)* [1985] AC 791.
5 An example of the former type of case was *Re CB* [1981] 1 All ER 16, where the local authority had insufficient grounds for passing a parental rights resolution. Examples of the latter type of case are the two cases cited above in fn 4.
6 Section 100. On the distinction between wardship and the other uses of the inherent jurisdiction of the High Court, see R White, P Carr and N Lowe *A Guide to the Children Act 1989* (2nd edn) (Butterworths, 1995) at paras 12.1–12.4.

legislation. By way of exception, where impropriety or ultra vires action is alleged against the authority this may be challenged through the judicial review procedure but no longer in wardship proceedings.

Parliament and the courts

The restriction on the use of wardship, outlined above, proved controversial from the start and the arguments will be discussed later[1]. The main concern here is to explore the essential thinking in the legislation about the proper relationship between the different organs of the State. The first point concerns Parliament and the courts and here the reasoning is patently clear. Where Parliament has through legislation defined with particularity the basis for State intervention in the family, it is not for the courts to gainsay this by allowing a 'back-door' entry into care. Authorities must operate within the statutory framework either by proving the grounds for compulsory action or by securing the voluntary co-operation of the family concerned. By the same token, it is improper for the courts to countenance extra-statutory challenges to the legitimate exercise of statutory discretions. To allow them to do so on the strength of some broad or open-ended welfare criterion would make a complete nonsense of that which Parliament has ordained. As a matter of pure logic this is impeccable, despite the practical ramifications of removing from local authorities what some regarded at the time as the crucially important safety net of wardship[2]. If it is illegitimate for the courts to ignore Parliament's scheme at the behest of parents and relatives then, logically, it must be improper for them to do so at the behest of local authorities.

Relationship between local authorities and the courts

It is more difficult to discern a consistent philosophical position regarding the appropriate relationship between local authorities and the courts[3]. The limitations imposed on wardship are characteristic of a number of provisions which assert the primary responsibility of local authorities (rather than the courts) for children falling within their statutory functions. It is for the authority to determine what level of social work involvement is appropriate to safeguard the well-being of children in families experiencing difficulties. It is not for the courts to act unilaterally of their own volition. Thus, it is no longer possible for a court, in family proceedings, to direct that a child be taken into care or put under supervision, unless the authority itself seeks such an order in those proceedings. All the court may do, where it is concerned about the welfare of a child before it, is to direct the authority to investigate his circumstances with a view to determining what level of intervention (if any) is necessary[4].

This represents a significant re-casting of the respective roles of the courts and social services. Before the reforms, the court might, of its own motion in wardship and certain other family proceedings, commit a child to care[5]. It could, thereafter,

---

1   See Chapter 11 below.
2   N Lowe 'Caring for Children' (1989) 139 NLJ 87.
3   See SM Cretney 'Defining the Limits of State Intervention' in D Freestone (ed) *Children and the Law* (Hull University Press, 1990) at pp 71–74; J Dewar 'The Courts and Local Authority Autonomy' [1995] 7 JCL 15; and M Hayes 'The proper role of the courts in child care cases' [1996] CFLQ 201.
4   Section 37.
5   Under, for example, the Guardianship Act 1973, s 2(2)(b) or the Matrimonial Causes Act 1973, s 43(1).

give directions to the authority about aspects of upbringing and, in wardship, it preserved for itself an on-going supervisory role[1]. The reasoning now is that the courts are not equipped to perform this kind of 'managerial' role and that the local authority should be firmly in control of case management provided only that it does not exceed its statutory powers[2]. This reasoning is apparent in the decision to improve the review procedures within authorities and the requirement that every authority establish an internal procedure to deal with representations or complaints[3]. Here, again, it was thought inappropriate that the detailed matters concerning the treatment of children 'looked after' by social services should be subject to external review by the ordinary courts. Instead, the concentration should be on trying to ensure good practice through a better system of internal reviews[4].

The courts' role: adjudicative or managerial?

These developments suggest strongly that the courts' role in children cases is conceptualised as an adjudicative rather than managerial one. Yet it has been observed that the legislation may not be entirely consistent on this since, in certain respects, the courts are now required to involve themselves much more with the substance of case management[5]. Nowhere is this more obvious than in relation to the vexed issue of contact (formerly access) with children in care[6]. Local authorities are now required to justify to the courts, to a greater extent than ever before, decisions to terminate or restrict contact between the child and prescribed individuals[7]. The impact of this greater level of scrutiny should not be underestimated given the crucial significance of the issue for the prospects of the child returning to the family and longer-term management of the child's case. It is also, without doubt, the single issue which generated the greatest number of wardship applications by parents and others[8]. Alongside this, the more inquisitorial role expected of the courts has been noted, with regard to the progress of proceedings. More recently, the House of Lords has held in effect that the courts remain in control of the interim stage of care proceedings, namely after making an interim care order but before the final hearing[9].

---

1   For a good example of the implications of this ongoing role, see *Re E (SA) (A Minor) (Wardship)* [1984] 1 All ER 289.
2   Where it does exceed its statutory powers the appropriate procedure is now judicial review rather than wardship. See *Re DM (A Minor) (Wardship: Jurisdiction)* [1986] 2 FLR 122.
3   Section 26.
4   See the White Paper at para 31.
5   See SM Cretney 'Defining the Limits of State Intervention' in D Freestone (ed) *Children and the Law* (Hull University Press, 1990) at p 68.
6   This is governed by a modified statutory code contained in s 34 and the regulations made under that section.
7   Under the former law, the courts had jurisdiction over decisions to 'refuse' or 'terminate' access but not over decisions regulating the amount or frequency of access; see the Child Care Act 1980, ss 12A–12G. It has been emphasised that the courts now have the final say on the whole question of contact. See, particularly, the remarks of Hale J in *Berkshire County Council v B* [1997] 1 FLR 171.
8   The leading wardship case of *A v Liverpool City Council* [1982] AC 363 was such a case in which a mother's access had been curtailed by the local authority to one hour per month under supervision at a day nursery.
9   See *Re C (Interim Care Order: Assessment)* [1997] 1 FLR 1 discussed in Chapter 11 below.

It may, therefore, be that there is some ambiguity in the way that the role of the courts is perceived. But it is fair to say that, in general, while the courts exercise significant control over entry into, and discharge from, care, most issues concerned with the treatment of children once in care (with the exception of the sensitive questions concerning contact, the use of secure accommodation and issues arising at the interim stage) are seen as internal matters for the local authority. Whether this is the appropriate distribution of functions is, naturally, debatable[1].

Children and adult society

The Children Act, more than any legislation before it, gives recognition to the views of children and young people. As such, it can be argued that it marks a distinct movement away from the perception of children as recipients of welfare and towards the view that they are juristic persons with distinctive rights. While it would be absurd to equate simplistically a multi-faceted concept like 'children's rights' with autonomy claims, there is a close association between the two ideas exemplified by the *Gillick* saga[2].

In several different instances, the legislation requires the wishes of children to be taken into account, to an extent appropriate to the individual child's age and understanding. This is a requirement which binds courts[3], local authorities, voluntary organisations and private children's homes[4] and, arguably (following *Gillick*), school authorities, medical personnel and other outsiders[5]. Curiously, there is no corresponding legal duty placed on parents and others with parental responsibility, but the Scottish Law Commission proposed that such an obligation should be introduced into Scots Law[6]. This has now been achieved by s 6(1) of the Children (Scotland) Act 1995, under which the parent, when reaching any major decision in fulfilling parental responsibilities or exercising parental rights, must have regard so far as practicable to the views of the child if he or she wishes to express them. The Children Act also gives greater autonomy to young people aged over 16 by providing that court orders should not generally be made or extended beyond that age[7], that they should be able to seek a 'self-referral' into 'care'[8] and that those leaving substitute care should be given more assistance in making the transition to independent living in the community.[9]

The Children Act does not go so far as to confer complete independence on adolescents. It should be appreciated that parental responsibility continues right

1   Discussed in Chapter 11 below.
2   See Chapter 3 below.
3   Section 1(3)(a).
4   Sections 22(4) and (5), 61(2) and (3) and 64(2) and (3).
5   Since *Gillick* decides that it is lawful for outsiders to have direct dealings with mature adolescents this might arguably imply an obligation to consult with them on major matters rather than to deal exclusively with their parents or other carers. Later Court of Appeal decisions have, however, cast doubt on this analysis. See Chapters 3 and 8 below.
6   Scottish Law Com Discussion Paper No 88 *Parental Responsibilities and Rights: Guardianship and the Administration of Children's Property* (1990) at paras 2.41–2.42, and Law Com Report No 135 *Report on Family Law* (1992) at paras 2.64–2.65.
7   Sections 9(6) and (7) and 91(10).
8   'Care' is used here in the non-technical sense since, by definition, a child who asks voluntarily to be accommodated is not in 'care' in the technical sense in which that term is now used in the legislation. See s 20, and Chapter 10 below.
9   Section 24.

up to the age of majority, but the degree of control exercised by parents gradually diminishes as the child grows older[1]. There is, however, a more radical view that parental powers (responsibility if this is preferred) should terminate completely when a child has sufficient level of competence to be able to make his own decisions[2]. There is little in the Children Act to support this theory except, perhaps, the mature child's right to refuse a medical or psychiatric examination or other assessment[3]. Instead, the Children Act generally supports the notion of participatory decision-making which gives to young people a degree of self-determination. This general principle to have regard to children's views[4] marked an important adjustment in the balance of power between children and adult society.

Fathers and mothers

It is not difficult to discover in the Children Act provisions which adjust the relative positions of men and women in their role as parents. The Act does not openly differentiate between men and women but perpetuates significant distinctions between parents inside and outside marriage. The courts, too, have abandoned in theory their former practice of applying presumptions to the effect that young children should be with their mothers or that older boys should be with their fathers. Nonetheless, the House of Lords has recently (in a case from Scotland) reasserted the value of mothers to young children in a way which some may think goes close to applying a presumption. In *Brixey v Lynas* Lord Jauncey of Tullichettle (who gave the only speech) said:

> '... the advantage to a very young child of being with its mother is a consideration which must be taken into account in deciding where lie its best interests in custody proceedings in which the mother is involved. It is neither a presumption nor a principle but rather recognition of a widely held belief based on practical experience and the workings of nature. ...'

He went on:

> 'Where a very young child has been with its mother since birth and there is no criticism of her ability to care for the child only the strongest competing advantages are likely to prevail.'[5]

The abolition of parental guardianship, primarily to distinguish parenthood from guardianship, removed the anachronistic rule that the married father was the sole guardian of his child. When the Guardianship Act 1973 gave to the married mother equal parental rights and authority, it left untouched the sole guardian-ship of the father[6]. The Children Act thus completed the process of conferring on married parents equal parenthood (by giving to each of them parental responsi-bility)[7]. More significantly, the Children Act adjusted the legal position of

---

1 This was the classic view of the relationship between parents and adolescents expressed by Lord Denning MR in *Hewer v Bryant* [1970] 1 QB 357 at 369 and apparently accepted by the House of Lords in *Gillick*.
2 J Eekelaar 'The Eclipse of Parental Rights' (1986) 102 LQR 4.
3 Sections 38(6), 43(8), 44(7) and Sch 3, para 4(4). See Chapter 8 below. The courts, however, have controversially taken the view that a child's objections, even under these provisions, may be overridden where his or her best interests require it by invoking the jurisdiction of the High Court. See, particularly, *South Glamorgan County Council v W and B* [1993] 1 FLR 574, and Chapter 11 below.
4 See, particularly, ss 1(3)(a) and 22(4) and (5).
5 [1996] 2 FLR 499 at 505.
6 See Law Com Working Paper No 91 *Review of Child Law: Guardianship* (1985) at paras 2.7–2.8.
7 Section 2(1), and see Chapter 4 below.

unmarried parents and strengthened, in a number of respects, the legal position of the father. While the unmarried mother remains exclusively entitled to automatic parental responsibility[1], the Children Act widened the mechanisms whereby the father might acquire it by agreement with the mother or by court order[2]. The legislation does not confer on the unmarried man automatic parental responsibility, although it does bring him within the definition of 'parent' for most other purposes[3]. Thus, although the legislation attaches greater significance to unmarried fatherhood, especially in the context of stable cohabitation, it still preserves the essential inequality of motherhood and fatherhood outside marriage while supporting equality within marriage[4].

Where parental responsibility is shared between father and mother, either in marriage or where an unmarried father has acquired it by legal process, the law takes a gender-neutral view of parenthood. The father or mother may exercise parental responsibility independently and each has an equal say in upbringing[5]. There has, nonetheless, been some speculation concerning the possible effect of the legislation on the respective child-rearing roles of men and women. One viewpoint is that the statutory framework was grounded in the notion of 'time-sharing' and a legal presumption of co-parenting which disguises and perpetuates substantial inequalities of power and responsibilities between men and women[6]. Some feminists have long argued that the concept of joint custody enables 'absent' men to exercise control over their ex-wives without shouldering the responsibility of child care[7]. The idea of continuing parental responsibility could be viewed as a variant on this theme. A further recent manifestation of this argument is perhaps the backlash against what is said to be too rigorous an enforcement of contact post-divorce[8].

Against this, it has been argued that the legislation, if anything, further strengthens the relative position of women by placing so much weight on parental agreements[9]. There is overwhelming evidence that a very high percentage of these agreements result in women obtaining the primary, if not exclusive, child care role[10]. The legislation does not attempt to redress this, as it might have done, by creating a legal presumption in favour of joint residence or time-sharing[11].

It is unclear whether the Children Act has had any significant impact on the way in which society perceives the parenting responsibilities of men and women. But

---

1 Section 2(2).

2 Section 4, and see Chapter 5 below.

3 This arises by virtue of the incorporation of s 1 of the Family Law Reform Act 1987 by s 2(3) of the Children Act.

4 These issues are discussed further in Chapter 5 below.

5 Section 2(7).

6 See, particularly, J Brophy 'Custody Law, Child Care, and Inequality in Britain' in C Smart and S Sevenhuijsen (eds) *Child Custody and the Politics of Gender* (Routledge, 1989) at p 217.

7 See, for example, A Bottomley 'Resolving Family Disputes: a critical view' in MDA Freeman (ed) *The State, the Law and the Family* (Tavistock, 1984) at p 293.

8 See, particularly, C Smart and B Neale 'Arguments Against Virtue – Must Contact be Enforced?' [1997] Fam Law 332, and Chapter 4 below.

9 A Bainham 'The Privatisation of the Public Interest in Children' (1990) 53 MLR 206 at pp 216–219.

10 The empirical evidence of the Law Commission testifies to this. See Priest and Whybrow, Law Com Supplement to Working Paper No 96 *Custody Law in Practice in the Divorce and Domestic Courts* (1986).

11 As in certain other jurisdictions. See Chapter 4 below.

in asserting parenthood as a primary and gender-neutral status and in making it so difficult for either parent to divest himself or herself of parental responsibility, the Children Act has given tacit encouragement to the notion of equal co-parenting, and the principles enunciated in the Family Law Act 1996 would appear to take this notion further, as discussed in Chapter 4 below[1].

THE STATUTORY SCHEME

This section describes the essential framework established by the Children Act. Before considering the application of the Children Act in distinctive contexts it is necessary to have an initial grasp of the function of parental responsibility, the way in which court orders relate to it, and the new jurisdictional arrangements under which these orders are made.

One important effect of the legislation has been to render less important the distinctions previously drawn between parents and non-parents and different categories of non-parent. Under the old law, the kind of proceedings and the kind of orders available to interested individuals varied considerably and were largely governed by technical rules on standing[2]. Thus, for example, it could make a difference whether a step-parent had married a divorced parent, a previously unmarried parent or a widowed parent[3]. The fact that access to the courts should depend on such technicalities reflected no credit on the legal system and most have been swept away to be replaced by a new 'open-door' policy. In general, *anyone* with a genuine interest in a child's well-being may apply to the court (albeit that in some cases they may need leave) in family proceedings although some important distinctions, especially between parents and non-parents, remain[4].

Another salient feature of the statutory scheme is its flexibility and the attempt to achieve a degree of uniformity in the orders available in different kinds of proceedings. 'Family proceedings' are defined expansively, with the result that, subject to certain qualifications, the same orders are available to the court whatever the nature of the particular proceedings. This has the added advantage of making available common remedies in public and private proceedings in accordance with the common principles discussed earlier.

The function of parental responsibility

Parental responsibility is now the central legal concept which establishes the link between a child and the person or persons who have authority to care for him, or

---

1   This objective is certainly implicit in much of the Law Commission's work leading up to the reforms. Thus, when discussing the need for court orders the Commission offered the view that 'anything which can be done to help parents to keep separate the issues of being a spouse and being a parent will ultimately give the children the best chance of retaining them both': Law Com Report No 172 *Review of Child Law: Guardianship and Custody* (1988) at para 3.3.
2   The general position can best be appreciated by referring to the relevant chapters of leading family law texts published before the Children Act, such as SM Cretney *Principles of Family Law* (4th edn) (Sweet & Maxwell, 1984) Part IV, particularly chs 13–18, or PM Bromley and NV Lowe *Bromley's Family Law* (7th edn) (Butterworths, 1987), particularly ch 9.
3   The step-parent who married a divorced parent had the advantage of recourse to the matrimonial and divorce jurisdictions under the Domestic Proceedings and Magistrates' Courts Act 1978 and the Matrimonial Causes Act 1973. These jurisdictions were not open to other step-parents.
4   See Chapter 6 below.

take decisions concerning his upbringing. It replaces the former concept of 'parental rights and duties' which performed a similar function. The change in terminology is intended to reflect changes in the way that the relationship between parents and children is perceived. The objective is to move away from the proprietorial connotations of 'rights' towards a more enlightened view which emphasises that children are persons rather than possessions[1]. According to this, parental powers and authority exist only to enable parents to discharge their responsibilities. In fact, the Children Act defines parental responsibility to include, inter alia, 'rights', and the new definition is remarkably similar to the old definition of parental rights and duties[2]. Thus, the unitary concept of parental responsibility includes within it 'all the rights, duties, powers, responsibilities and authority which by law a parent of a child has in relation to the child and his property'[3].

It should be appreciated that, as a legal concept, parental responsibility performs two distinct but interrelated functions[4]. First, it encapsulates all the legal duties and powers concerning upbringing which exist to enable a parent to care for a child and to act on his behalf. These duties and powers relate to all the obvious concerns such as the child's material needs and health care, the manner of his education and religious upbringing, legal representation, and administration of his property. There are many difficult questions about the extent of these powers and duties and how they relate to the capacities and responsibilities of children themselves[5].

Secondly, the concept of parental responsibility exists not only to determine the way in which the law expects a parent to behave towards his child, but also to determine that *someone* (usually, but not necessarily, a parent) is entitled to bring up a child without interference from others who do not have parental responsibility. It has been said that the focus here is *not* on the nature of the duties owed to a child 'but rather upon the distance between the parent and others in making provision for the child; indeed, on the degree of *freedom* given to parents in bringing up their children'[6]. The acquisition of parental responsibility thus becomes crucial in determining which individuals or institutions have decision-making authority concerning a child. It is this legal status which is all-important, however close or distant the de facto relationship with the child may be. A grandparent physically caring for a child may have less power and authority in law than an absent parent who scarcely ever sees the child. And it is for this reason that court orders are available, to regulate the acquisition and exercise of parental

---

1   On the view of children as property, see MDA Freeman *The Rights and Wrongs of Children* (Frances Pinter, 1983) at pp 13–18, and J Montgomery 'Children as Property?' (1988) 51 MLR 323.
2   Children Act 1975, s 85(1) which provided that the expression 'the parental rights and duties' meant 'all the rights and duties which by law the mother and father have in relation to a legitimate child and his property'.
3   Section 3(1).
4   These two senses in which the term 'parental responsibility' is used are brought out very helpfully by J Eekelaar in 'Parental Responsibility: State of Nature or Nature of the State?' (1991) JSWFL 37 at pp 38–39.
5   See Chapter 3 below.
6   J Eekelaar (above) at p 39.

responsibility[1]. The blanket statement that parental responsibility confers a legal status which others do not have, to act in relation to a child, requires qualification. First, it should always be remembered that parental responsibility may be vested in more than one person[2]. But, even where it is, the 'sharers' each have a status in relation to the child which distinguishes them from everyone else who does not have parental responsibility for that child. Secondly, it can be important to distinguish between the rights which parental responsibility confers, and the *enforcement* of the rights. For, while parental responsibility clearly implies freedom from external interference, it is by no means clear what legal action (if any) may be taken to prevent this interference[3].

The effect of court orders on parental responsibility

The general thinking in the legislation has already been noted: that the primary responsibility of parents for raising children should not be unnecessarily disrupted by court orders. Accordingly, the intention is that court orders should be confined to those instances in which it is necessary to resolve specific disputes about upbringing or to pre-empt such disputes by regulating in advance possible areas of disagreement. The courts were therefore given flexible new powers modelled on those which were traditionally available in wardship. These included a new range of orders and a general power to attach conditions and give directions[4]. The principal 'private' orders (s 8 orders) comprise the residence order, the contact order, the prohibited steps order, and the specific issue order[5]. The main 'public' orders are the care order and the supervision order[6]. Although private orders will usually be made in private proceedings and public orders in care proceedings, it should be remembered that both are, in principle, available in either type of 'family proceedings'. Thus, s 8 orders may be made in care proceedings as an alternative option to a care or supervision order. Likewise, a local authority may intervene in private proceedings and seek a care or supervision order. There is much more interchangeability and flexibility than

---

1   Thus, in this example the grandparent could seek a residence order or one of the other 's 8 orders' in order to prevent the parent from trying to exercise parental responsibility against the child's best interests as she (the grandparent) sees them. The parent, although retaining parental responsibility, would then be precluded from exercising it in a way which was incompatible with the court order: s 2(8).
2   Section 2(5) and (7).
3   See A Bainham 'Interfering with parental responsibility: a new challenge for the law of torts?' (1990) 3 JCL 3, commenting on *F v Wirral MBC* [1991] 2 WLR 1132.
4   These powers are largely contained in ss 10 and 11.
5   These orders are not exhaustive of the 'private' orders which can be made. The Children Act also introduced a new 'family assistance order' (s 16) and the unmarried father may obtain a 'parental responsibility order' (s 4(1)). It should also be noted that the court has power to attach conditions or make directions regarding any of the s 8 orders (s 11(7)) and this may have the effect of giving the court very wide-ranging powers of regulation going well beyond the straightforward effect of the order itself.
6   Section 31(1). Again, these are not exhaustive of 'public' orders. Others include the new 'education supervision order' (s 36 and Part III, Sch 3), the 'child assessment order' (s 43) and the 'emergency protection order' (s 44) and the various orders relating to the regulation of substitute care arrangements for children (see Chapter 11 below). Part IV of the Family Law Act 1996 has also amended the Children Act to enable the courts in specified circumstances to include 'exclusion requirements' in interim care orders and emergency protection orders (Children Act 1989, ss 38A, 44A; and see Chapter 12 below).

existed under the old law where there was a more rigid demarcation between public and private proceedings.

It is vital to appreciate that no order (with the exception of an adoption order or an order under s 30 of the Human Fertilisation and Embryology Act 1990)[1] actually *removes* parental responsibility from parents. A residence order *does* vest parental responsibility in the person in whose favour it is made (assuming he or she does not already have it), but it does not transfer it *from* anyone else.[2] The effect of the order is simply to regulate the child's residence[3]. In practical terms, this means that the 'non-residential' parent is simply precluded from exercising that aspect of parental responsibility which relates to the question of where the child is to live. This is because parental responsibility must not be exercised in a way which is incompatible with a court order[4]. But parental responsibility itself remains intact, unaffected by the order, and may be exercised to the full extent that is compatible with the order.

Exactly the same reasoning applies to the other s 8 orders. Again, these orders simply regulate contact or other specific matters, such as religious upbringing or medical treatment, but do not otherwise affect parental responsibility or its exercise. Remarkably, these principles also apply to care orders. Hence, even where a child has been compulsorily removed from home on account of some parental failing, the parental responsibility of the parent concerned is preserved and is shared with the local authority which acquires it by virtue of the care order[5]. This was a considerable departure from the effect of a care order under the old law which was to *transfer* the bulk of parental rights exclusively to the local authority[6]. Similarly, despite some contrary dicta in the Court of Appeal[7], it was widely thought that the effect of a custody order was to transfer to the custodial parent exclusively most of the major decision-making powers over the child. Now the theory in all of these instances is that court orders are strictly limited in their effect to the specific issues they purport to govern on their face. A note of caution should perhaps be sounded. While, in theory, there will be many situations in which someone living physically apart from a child will retain parental responsibility, the extent to which this can be effectively exercised must be a matter of some doubt[8]. It is not clear how far theory and practice coincide on this issue.

---

1 See Chapter 7 below.
2 Section 12(2).
3 Section 8(1) provides quite simply that a residence order 'means an order settling the arrangements to be made as to the person with whom a child is to live'.
4 Section 2(8).
5 Sections 2(5) and (6) and 33(3). For an extreme example, see *Re M (Care Order: Threshold Conditions)* [1994] 2 AC 424, where the father retained parental responsibility despite serving a life sentence for killing the mother in the presence of the children. (The case is discussed in Chapter 11 below.)
6 Section 10(2) of the Child Care Act 1980. For an analysis of the legal effect of the various routes into care under the old law, see S Maidment 'The Fragmentation of Parental Rights and Children in Care' [1981] JSWL 21.
7 *Dipper v Dipper* [1981] Fam 31; and, on the confusion surrounding the term 'custody', see M Parry 'The Custody Conundrum' (1981) Fam Law 213.
8 In the public context it is specifically provided that the local authority has the power 'to determine the extent to which a parent or guardian of the child may meet his parental responsibility for him': s 33(3)(b), discussed in Chapter 11 below. In the private context, it is not wholly clear how far the 'non-residential' parent has a right to be consulted by the 'residential' parent. See Chapter 4.

Jurisdictional arrangements[1]

There have been many calls for the establishment of a 'family court' in England[2]. The Children Act did not create a family court, in the sense in which that expression is normally used, but it was the Government's view that the new jurisdictional arrangements brought about by the reforms constituted a substantial move in that direction[3]. The Government felt that the substantive law affecting children should be rationalised before fundamental reforms to the court system were introduced. At the same time, it hoped that the jurisdictional and procedural reforms could incorporate some of the more desirable features associated with the concept of a family court[4].

The Children Act created a concurrent jurisdiction in 'family proceedings' to be exercised by magistrates' 'family proceedings courts', county courts and the High Court[5]. The definition of 'family proceedings' is drawn sufficiently wide to cover virtually all proceedings, public and private, in which issues affecting a child's upbringing might be raised. Thus, the definition[6] includes:

(i)   proceedings under the inherent jurisdiction of the High Court (these include, but are not synonymous with, wardship); and
(ii) proceedings under:
    (a)   Parts I, II and IV of the Children Act;
    (b)   the Matrimonial Causes Act 1973;
    (c)   ...
    (d)   the Adoption Act 1976;
    (e)   the Domestic Proceedings and Magistrates' Courts Act 1978;
    (f)   ...
    (g)   Part III of the Matrimonial and Family Proceedings Act 1984; and
    (h)   the Family Law Act 1996.

Although expansive, the definition is not quite all-embracing. In particular, it does not include proceedings under Part V of the Children Act which are concerned with the short-term protection of children, often emergency protection. There is, in effect, a special code governing these cases and it would have been inappropriate to make available the whole range of orders under the Children Act in that context. Also, it hardly needs saying that many proceedings which can affect the interests of children in some way are not in the nature of family proceedings and consequently fall outside the definition. The obvious examples are criminal proceedings and ordinary civil actions such as contractual or tortious claims[7].

---

1   See also Chapter 13 below where the position of the child in court is discussed.
2   See, particularly, B Hoggett 'Family Courts or Family Law Reform – which should come first?' (1986) 6 *Legal Studies* 1. Family courts have been operating in Australia since the mid-1970s. For a full evaluation of the Australian model, see A Dickey *Family Law* (2nd edn) (The Law Book Co, 1990) at ch 4, and S Parker, P Parkinson and J Behrens *Australian Family Law in Context* (The Law Book Co, 1994) at ch 7.
3   This at least was the view expressed by the Solicitor General, *Hansard* (HC) Vol 158 col 547.
4   It should not be thought, however, that the concept of family court, or informal justice in family matters, commands universal support. The Australian experience revealed remarkable public hostility, initially, to such matters as the derobing of the judiciary. See A Dickey (above).
5   Section 92(7).
6   In s 8(3) and (4), as amended.
7   See Chapter 15 below.

The broad objective of creating a concurrent jurisdiction is to achieve, as far as possible, uniformity of orders, flexibility and consistency in the procedure and remedies applying in different levels of court. This end is also promoted by rules of court which regulate the allocation of cases between the different courts and facilitate the transfer of cases either vertically between the various levels or horizontally within tiers. Thus, cases may be transferred sideways from one magistrates' court to another; upwards from the magistrates' to the county court or from the county court to the High Court; or downwards from the High Court to the county court or from the county court to the magistrates' court[1]. *The Children Act Advisory Committee Final Report June 1997*[2] contains statistics on upward transfers of public law cases from the magistrates' court which reveal that gravity of the case is the most important reason for such transfers (accounting for approximately 70%). While, in principle, concurrent jurisdiction means that a case could be heard at any of the three levels, in practice, cases are directed to the most appropriate court, depending on such factors as the complexity or gravity of the issues, the need to consolidate proceedings and the degree of urgency.

It has already been observed that the Children Act attempts to incorporate the more valuable features of the wardship jurisdiction. An aspect of this is the procedural changes designed to emphasise the non-adversarial nature of family proceedings. It has long been regarded as a distinguishing feature of wardship that the proceedings are essentially inquisitorial rather than adversarial[3]. The legislation seeks to emulate this (and thereby reduce the need to resort to wardship) by promoting a non-adversarial style of proceedings. The increased role for the court was noted in controlling the progress of cases. In addition, the rules require all family proceedings to be commenced by application (rather than complaint or summons), to have preliminary hearings, and to require advance disclosure of the nature of the case, the orders sought and proposed plans for the child's future. Full rights of appeal are conferred on all parties to care proceedings and appeals now lie to the High Court rather than the Crown Court to emphasise the civil nature of the proceedings[4]. The appointment of guardians ad litem to represent the independent interests of children in public proceedings has become the normal course, and further adds to the inquisitorial flavour of public family proceedings[5].

Whether or not the courts are fully equipped to respond to the new challenges posed by this radical change of approach has been questioned. While informal or participatory justice has an undoubted appeal, it has been said that 'the danger of adjudicators who have the responsibility of deploying the coercive power of the

---

1 Schedule 11 and the Children (Allocation of Proceedings) Order 1991, SI 1991/1677.
2 (Lord Chancellor's Department, 1997) Appendix 2, Table IB.
3 See NV Lowe and RAH White *Wards of Court* (2nd edn) (Barry Rose/Kluwer, 1986). Whether other children cases could really be described as 'adversarial' is debatable since the judges were often reluctant to insist on such matters as adherence to the strict rules of evidence. This is discussed further in Chapter 13 below.
4 Section 94(1). Under the old law, only the child had a right of appeal and this was to the Crown Court, an unlikely situation which arose from the 'criminal' model of care proceedings established by the Children and Young Persons Act 1969.
5 Section 41. It should be noted that the Family Law Act 1996, s 64 empowers the Lord Chancellor to make regulations providing for the separate representation of children in certain classes of 'private' proceedings under that Act and other legislation. See further Chapter 13 below.

State appearing to "descend into the arena" is a real one'[1]. That said, these fundamental procedural reforms are consistent with the general aim of encouraging a thorough investigation of a child's welfare, untrammelled by technicalities, which may be thought not only desirable but essential if the paramountcy of children's welfare is to be more than rhetoric.

II   THE UNITED NATIONS CONVENTION ON THE RIGHTS OF THE CHILD

The United Nations Convention on the Rights of the Child ('the UN Convention') now constitutes the most authoritative and comprehensive statement of the fundamental rights of children covering civil and political, social, economic, cultural, recreational and humanitarian rights[2]. The expression 'rights' must be treated with some caution, since many of the aspirations for children set out in the UN Convention could arguably never be enforced as *legal* rights by *individual* children in the courts[3]. They are of a progressive and programmatic nature and, thus, dependent on political will and the availability and commitment of resources in individual countries. Others are more specific, and many of these were arguably already implemented in English law before the advent of the UN Convention.

The legal effect of the UN Convention

The UK ratified the UN Convention on 16 December 1991, but this does not mean that its substantive provisions form part of English domestic law[4]. In broad terms, the UK government is legally bound to follow policies which are in conformity with the general and specific obligations set forth in the UN Convention. It is not, however, open to individual children to bring proceedings before the national courts, based solely on alleged violations of the UN Convention which affect them[5]. In order to achieve this result it would be necessary to *incorporate* the UN

---

1   SM Cretney 'Defining the Limits of State Intervention' in D Freestone (ed) *Children and the Law* at p 74.
2   See, generally: D McGoldrick 'The United Nations Convention on the Rights of the Child' (1991) 5 IJLF 132; B Walsh 'The United Nations Convention on the Rights of the Child: A British View' (1991) 5 IJLF 170; and see also (1992) 6 IJLF at Part I which issue is devoted entirely to a re-evaluation of the concept of children's rights in the light of the UN Convention. It is also published as a separate volume: see P Alston, S Parker and J Seymour *Children, Rights and the Law* (Oxford University Press, 1992). For more detailed treatment, see LJ LeBlanc *The Convention on the Rights of the Child* (University of Nebraska Press, 1995), and G Van Bueren *The International Law on the Rights of the Child* (Martinus Nijhoff, 1995). For a critical evaluation of how far English law complies with the Convention, see M Freeman *The Moral Status of Children* (Martinus Nijhoff, 1997) at ch 6.
3   Nonetheless, it can be persuasively argued that it is important to ascribe 'rights' to children even if some are unenforceable. See J Eekelaar 'The Importance of Thinking that Children have Rights' (1992) 6 IJLF 221, and Freeman (above), especially ch 2.
4   For a general discussion of the enforceability of the UN Convention, see G Van Bueren 'The United Nations Convention on the Rights of the Child: The Necessity of Incorporation into United Kingdom Law' [1992] Fam Law 373.
5   It is not, however, improbable that the spirit if not the letter of the UN Convention will increasingly be used in legal arguments in future. For a good example, see Ward LJ's judgment

Convention into English law. Some countries, for example the Netherlands and Spain, have a tradition of incorporating human rights treaties such as this directly into national law, but this is not the case in the UK[1].

It should not be concluded from this that the UN Convention is of no use to British children, but it does mean that the accountability of the Government is likely to be achieved more through political than legal means. Quite apart from legal redress, Van Bueren has noted that human rights treaties may be utilised as educational instruments and as evidence of the need for reform of national laws. So far as education is concerned, there is a specific obligation on States, under Article 42, to make the UN Convention's provisions and principles, by appropriate and active means, widely known to adults and children.

Political accountability leading to reform of national laws and practices is perhaps the key to enforcement of the UN Convention at the national level. In this respect, the Committee on the Rights of the Child, established under Article 43, has a vital role. This Committee consists of 'ten experts of high moral standing and recognized competence in the field covered by [the] Convention'[2], elected by the States parties. The main function of the Committee is to produce periodic reports on the operation of the UN Convention under Articles 44 and 45. States have undertaken to report on the 'measures they have adopted which give effect to the rights recognized ... and on the progress made on the enjoyment of those rights'[3]. These 'Reports' must indicate factors and difficulties affecting the degree of fulfilment of the obligations in individual countries[4]. The Reports are to be made public, and the Committee must report biennially to the General Assembly through the Economic and Social Council[5]. More significantly, the Committee may make suggestions and general recommendations on the strength of the information which it receives under Articles 44 and 45. These are then transmitted to the General Assembly and the State concerned, together with any comments made by that State[6].

A poor track record of implementation by individual States may, through these procedures, become a matter of public record and accountability within the international community. It is conceivable that this may have a potentially greater impact than recourse to an international tribunal might have done. The

---

in *Re H (Paternity: Blood Test)* [1996] 2 FLR 65 which was clearly influenced by Article 7 of the Convention. See further Chapter 5 below. The principles of the UN Declaration of the Rights of the Child 1959 are, however, now likely to be of less assistance, especially where they may be thought to conflict with, or at least be superseded by, the 1989 UN Convention. Thus, in *Re A (Children: 1959 UN Declaration)* [1998] 1 FLR 354, the Court of Appeal held that the judge had erred in granting residence to the mother in relation to a toddler and rejecting the welfare officer's recommendations for a residence order to be made in favour of the father. The mother had relied in part on Principle 6 of the 1959 Declaration to the effect that a child of tender years should not, save in exceptional circumstances, be separated from its mother. The court said that the relevance and value of the 1959 Declaration, now being 40 years old, was most doubtful. Moreover, the UN Convention of 1989 was gender-neutral. See also *Brixey v Lynas* [1996] 2 FLR 499.

1   See Van Bueren (above) for further discussion. It is, however, anticipated that the European Convention on Human Rights will shortly be incorporated into English law under the Human Rights Bill 1998.
2   UN Convention Article 43(2).
3   Ibid, Article 44(1).
4   Ibid, Article 44(2).
5   Ibid, Article 44(5).
6   Ibid, Article 45.

Committee's first report on the UK was less than glowing about the Government's record under the Convention. Among the matters it criticised were the extent of child poverty, the law permitting corporal punishment of children, the low age of criminal responsibility and the lack of children's rights in the educational sphere.[1] It has been suggested, in the English context, that an office of 'Commissioner for children's rights' is required, inter alia, to monitor the effective implementation of the UN Convention here[2]. In particular, the point is made that responsibility for different pieces of legislation and areas of policy affecting children is fragmented between a number of different government departments. No single department has responsibility for children. One of the Commissioner's functions would be to require all these separate departments to consider specifically the impact of legislation and policies on the rights and interests of children. Children's 'ombudsmen' exist in certain other countries, notably in Scandinavia and New Zealand, and it is argued that the ratification of the UN Convention highlights the need for a similar office to be established in the UK.

General aims and general obligations

The general aims of the UN Convention have been referred to as the '4 P's' – *Prevention, Protection, Provision,* and *Participation*[3]. As to *prevention*, there are articles relating to preventive health care[4] preventing child abduction[5] and prohibiting discrimination against children[6]. As to *protection*, the UN Convention seeks to protect children from all forms of torture, cruel, inhuman and degrading treatment and punishment, abuse and exploitation[7]. As to *provision*, there are articles creating rights of recipience in education[8] and social security[9], the right to rest and leisure[10], as well as the more general right to an adequate standard of living[11]. Rights of *participation* are recognised in articles which provide for access to information[12], freedom of expression[13] and the right of the child to express his views[14].

The UN Convention applies to 'every human being below the age of eighteen years unless, under the law applicable to the child, majority is attained earlier'[15]. Parties to the Convention are required to 'respect and ensure' that the rights in the UN Convention are extended to all children within their jurisdiction 'without

1 See United Nations *Concluding Observations of the Committee on the Rights of the Child: United Kingdom of Great Britain and Northern Ireland* CRC/C/15Add34 (1995), and see U Kilkelly, 'The UN Committee on the Rights of the Child – an evaluation in the light of recent UK experience' [1996] CFLQ 105.
2 M Rosenbaum and P Newell *Taking Children Seriously* (Gulbenkian Foundation, 1991).
3 See the discussion in G Van Bueren 'The UN Convention on the Rights of the Child' (1991) 3 JCL 63.
4 UN Convention Article 24.
5 Ibid, Article 11.
6 Ibid, Article 2.
7 Ibid, Article 37.
8 Ibid, Article 28.
9 Ibid, Article 29.
10 Ibid, Article 31.
11 Ibid, Article 27.
12 Ibid, Article 17.
13 Ibid, Article 13.
14 Ibid, Article 12.
15 Ibid, Article 1.

discrimination of any kind, irrespective of the child's or his or her parents' or legal guardian's race, colour, sex, language, religion, political or other opinion, national, ethnic or social origin, property, disability, birth or other status'[1].

Article 3 arguably contains the most important principle in the UN Convention, since it is the general standard which must be applied throughout the Convention to the more specific rights guaranteed by it. The Declaration of Geneva 1924 and the Declaration of the Rights of the Child 1959 had both embodied the general principle that 'mankind owes the child the best it has to give'. The UN Convention provides:

> 'In all actions concerning children, whether undertaken by public or private social welfare institutions, courts of law, administrative authorities or legislative bodies, the best interests of the child shall be a primary consideration.'[2]

Family lawyers will immediately detect echoes of the 'welfare principle' in English law but will also be struck by the difference in wording between the two provisions. First, the best interests of the child are expressed to be *primary*, but not paramount, and secondly, they are only *a* primary consideration and not *the* primary consideration. On the other hand, the domestic welfare principle applies only to courts and only in those instances in which the upbringing of the child is the central issue. The UN principle, in contrast, applies to a much wider range of public and private institutions, courts, authorities and bodies[3]. Quite apart from all the difficulties of interpretation of 'welfare'[4], it is plain that States may, under the UN Convention, have regard to other factors in discharging their obligations and may, conceivably, find that these outweigh the interests of the children in issue. Article 3[5] goes on to provide:

> 'States parties undertake to ensure the child such protection and care as is necessary for his or her well-being, taking into account the rights and duties of his or her parents, legal guardians, or other individuals legally responsible for him or her, and, to this end, shall take all appropriate legislative and administrative measures.'

Reading this with the preamble, which talks of taking due account of 'the importance of the traditions and cultural values of each people for the protection and harmonious development of the child', Eekelaar has commented that, prima facie, 'the way seems open for almost unrestricted welfarism by the injection of adult values into a conception of what constitutes the "best interests" of the child', but he notes that this must be read 'in the context of the series of explicit rights which the Convention protects'[6]. Thus, the apparently open-ended discretion which States have in promoting the best interests of children is circumscribed by a whole range of specific duties. This is not unlike the position of parents themselves, exercising parental responsibility[7]. Difficult questions can undoubtedly arise concerning the application of the best interests doctrine in very different cultural contexts[8].

---

1   UN Convention, Article 2(1).
2   Ibid, Article 3(1).
3   See Part I of this chapter for a discussion of the nuances of the welfare principle.
4   Ibid.
5   UN Convention Article 3(2).
6   J Eekelaar 'The Importance of Thinking that Children have Rights' (1992) 6 IJLF 221 at p 231.
7   See Chapter 3 below.
8   This question is explored in depth in P Alston (ed) *The Best Interests of the Child* (Clarendon, 1994).

The obligations of States to children are also in a sense qualified by specific duties owed to parents and other carers. The UN Convention assumes that many of the child's welfare needs will be met by his primary carers[1] but also requires States to respect the rights and duties of these adults. Article 5 provides:

> 'State parties shall respect the responsibilities, rights and duties of parents or, where applicable, the members of the extended family or community as provided for by the local custom, legal guardians or other persons legally responsible for the child, to provide, in a manner consistent with the evolving capacities of the child, appropriate direction and guidance in the exercise by the child of the rights recognised in the present Convention.'[2]

One way of looking at this provision is to regard it as merely reflecting the realities of life. Children do not exist in a vacuum and 'the Convention is not simply an exercise in abstraction'[3]. The rights of children must inevitably be secured in large measure by the actions of adults, usually those with their primary care, but in exercising these adult rights and duties in relation to children, the UN Convention requires those concerned to provide direction and guidance which is *consistent* with the rights set out in the Convention and not inconsistently with them[4]. Another way of viewing the Article is that it imports into the international arena all the uncertainties and difficulties which surround the interaction of children's rights and parental rights and responsibilities in domestic law[5]. The fact is that there may be a conflict between adults' and children's rights, and the UN Convention acknowledges this. As McGoldrick has astutely observed, 'those charged with providing "appropriate direction and guidance" to the child on the exercise of its rights may well have an interest, personal or institutional, in ensuring that the child does not exercise its rights'[6]. The practical application of the concept of evolving capacities of the child may, therefore, be no less fraught than it is in English domestic law.

Specific rights

It is not possible here to provide a comprehensive analysis of each and every article of the UN Convention or of what the various rights may mean for children in English law[7]. Instead, an attempt will be made to identify some of the more significant articles commenting, where appropriate, on the current state of English law.

The right to life and development

Article 6 requires States to recognise that every child has the inherent right to life and to ensure, to the maximum extent possible, the survival and development of the child. This provision clearly has implications for medical decision-making but,

---

1   UN Convention Article 3(2).
2   See also Article 14(2) which similarly recognises the parental role in the context of the child's right to 'freedom of thought, conscience and religion'.
3   J Eekelaar (above) at p 233.
4   Ibid.
5   As to which, see particularly Chapter 8 below.
6   D McGoldrick 'The United Nations Convention on the Rights of the Child' (1991) 5 IJLF 132 at pp 138–139.
7   See, generally, the sources cited at fn 2 at p 57 above.

as discussed later, the right to life and survival may have to be qualified in those instances in which a minimal quality of life is not sustainable[1].

The right to an identity

Two Articles are concerned with this. Article 7(1) requires that the child 'shall be registered immediately after birth and shall have the right from birth to a name, the right to acquire a nationality, and, as far as possible, the right to know and be cared for by his or her parents'. This is fast becoming one of the most significant and frequently cited provisions in the Convention since it is closely associated with recent claims that children have a right to knowledge of their biological origins[2]. It will be noted here that the UN Convention does not distinguish between married and unmarried parents and also that Article 2, the anti-discrimination provision, prohibits discrimination on the basis of status. The implications for English law, and for the laws of many other countries, may be that procedures for establishing paternity and giving recognition to the parental responsibility of unmarried fathers may need to be improved[3].

Under Article 8, States undertake to 'respect the right of the child to *preserve* his or her identity, including nationality, name and family relations as recognised by law without unlawful interference'. This article was an Argentinian initiative inspired by the 'disappearance' of an estimated 150–170 children in Argentina between 1975 and 1983[4].

The English reforms providing for the continuity of parental responsibility, especially post-divorce, may be viewed as an aspect of preserving the child's identity, as may the proposals for more open adoption[5].

Separation from parents

Article 9 requires States to 'ensure that a child shall not be separated from his or her parents against their will, except when competent authorities subject to judicial review determine, in accordance with applicable law and procedures, that such separation is necessary for the best interests of the child'[6]. Where the child *is* separated, the State must respect the right of the child 'to maintain personal relations and direct contact with both parents on a regular basis, except if it is contrary to the child's best interests'[7].

The reforms in the Children Act would appear to be in conformity with these obligations[8].

The right of the child to express views

Article 12(1) is another of the Convention's most important articles. It requires States to 'assure to the child who is capable of forming his or her own views the right to express those views freely in all matters affecting the child, the views of the

1 See Chapter 8 below.
2 This is an issue in many different contexts such as where there is a dispute over paternity (see Chapter 5), where the child has been conceived with the use of donated gametes (see Chapters 3 and 6) and following the adoption of a child (see Chapter 7).
3 See Chapter 5 below.
4 See Van Bueren (above) at pp 118–120.
5 See Chapters 4 and 7 below.
6 United Nations Convention Article 9(1).
7 Ibid, Article 9(3).
8 See particularly Chapters 10 and 11 below.

child being given due weight in accordance with the age and maturity of the child'.

This is close to the formulation which appears in several places in the Children Act[1] but its ambit extends well beyond those specific instances. Rather more troubling from an English perspective is Article 12(2) which states that 'the child shall in particular be provided the opportunity to be heard in any judicial and administrative proceedings affecting the child, either directly, or through a representative or an appropriate body, in a manner consistent with the procedural rules of national law'. Although it has been doubted that this necessarily entails separate representation of the child[2] it is the case[3] that representation in England is patchy, and there must also be doubt about whether the lack of independent representation of children's views in the educational sphere conforms with the spirit, if not the letter, of this Article[4]. Article 12(2) should now be considered alongside the new European Convention on the Exercise of Children's Rights 1996, which has as its essential aim to grant *procedural* rights to children in family proceedings and to improve their rights of participation in such proceedings[5].

Civil rights

Articles 13 to 17 deal with some of the classic civil liberties recognised by liberal democracies and expressly apply these to children. Thus, subject to certain qualifications, Article 13 recognises the child's right to 'freedom of expression'. Article 14 requires States to respect the right of the child to 'freedom of thought, conscience and religion' but this is qualified by the rights and duties of parents to give direction to the child[6]. Article 15 upholds the right of the child to 'freedom of association and to freedom of peaceful assembly'. Article 16 protects the child against interference with 'his or her privacy, family, home or correspondence', while Article 17 requires States to ensure that the child has 'access to information' on a range of material, especially that aimed at the promotion of his or her social, spiritual and moral well-being and physical and mental health.

Parental responsibilities

Under Article 18(1), States must 'use their best efforts to ensure recognition of the principle that both parents have common responsibilities for the upbringing and development of the child'. They must also recognise that parents or guardians 'have the primary responsibility for the upbringing and development of the child'.

This would, again, appear to have implications for the law applying to unmarried fathers. The Scottish Law Commission was clearly of the view that it required *automatic* rights for parents whether they were married or not and proposed changes to Scots law to give effect to this. These proposals were not accepted by the Westminster Parliament and did not find their way into the Children (Scotland) Act 1995[7]. The reference to the *primary* responsibility of

---

1   Especially that in s 1(3)(a).
2   D McGoldrick 'The United Nations Convention on the Rights of the Child' (1991) 5 IJLF 132 at p 141.
3   See Chapter 13 below.
4   See Chapter 16 below.
5   This Convention is examined in Chapter 17 below.
6   See text and fn 2 at p 61.
7   See Chapter 5 below.

parents implies a *secondary* responsibility in the State. This is borne out by Article 18(2) which requires States to 'render appropriate assistance to parents and legal guardians in the performance of their child-rearing responsibilities and [to] ensure the development of institutions, facilities and services for the care of children'. Article 18(3) also requires them to 'take all appropriate measures to ensure that children of working parents have the right to benefit from child-care services and facilities for which they are eligible'. It is arguable that English law, in failing to provide comprehensive nursery provision, is in breach of the spirit, if not the letter, of this provision[1].

Child protection

Articles 19 to 24 can all be said to relate to aspects of the protection of children, either generally, or specifically, to such groups of children as refugees[2] or disabled children[3]. Article 19 requires States to 'take all appropriate legislative, administrative, social and educational measures to protect the child from all forms of physical or mental violence, injury or abuse, neglect or negligent treatment, maltreatment or exploitation, including sexual abuse, while in the care of parent(s), legal guardian(s) or any other person who has the care of the child'. Article 20 provides that a child 'temporarily or permanently deprived of his or her family environment ... shall be entitled to special protection and assistance provided by the State'. It also states that, when considering solutions, 'due regard shall be paid to the desirability of continuity in a child's upbringing and to the child's ethnic, religious, cultural and linguistic background'. As discussed later[4], these considerations are now incorporated in the Children Act, and the adequacy of Part IV, regulating care and supervision, should be evaluated in the light of the above articles.

Article 21 regulates various aspects of adoption. Of particular interest is the requirement that States which 'recognize and/or permit the system of adoption shall ensure that the best interests of the child shall be the paramount consideration'. In English adoption law as it currently stands, at least in theory, the child's welfare is the 'first' but not 'paramount' consideration but, as discussed later, the whole of adoption law is liable to be reformed in the foreseeable future[5]. Article 24 deals with protection of the child's health, and requires States to 'recognize the right of the child to the enjoyment of the highest attainable standard of health and to facilities for the treatment of illness and rehabilitation of health'[6]. This and several other articles have major resource implications and the State's obligations must be viewed as programmatic or progressive.

Recipience of social welfare

Articles 26 to 31 are a cluster of articles dealing with the right of the child to receive various forms of social welfare. Article 26 protects the child's right to social

---

1   See Chapter 10 below.
2   UN Convention Article 22.
3   Ibid, Article 23.
4   See Chapters 10 and 11 below.
5   The Draft Adoption Bill 1996 would indeed make the child's welfare paramount, but this would itself be controversial, especially regarding the decision to dispense with parental consent. See Chapter 7 below.
6   UN Convention Article 24(2) also importantly requires States to take appropriate measures in relation to various forms of preventive medicine.

security while taking into account in particular 'the resources and the circum-stances of the child and persons having responsibility for the maintenance of the child'. Article 27(1) requires States to recognise 'the right of every child to a standard of living adequate for the child's physical, mental, spiritual, moral and social development'. However, this is then qualified by references to the 'abilities and financial capacities' of the child's carers[1] and the national conditions and means of States[2]. Subject to this, States are required to assist carers to implement the child's right by providing material assistance and support programmes directed, in particular, towards nutrition, clothing and housing. Article 27(4) is an interesting provision from the English perspective since it would seem to provide some justification for the controversial principles of the Child Support legis-lation[3]. It requires States to 'take all appropriate measures to secure the recovery of maintenance for the child from the parents or other persons having financial responsibility for the child ...'. While the motivation behind this provision is undoubtedly to benefit the child rather than the exchequer (as contrasted with that of the English Child Support Acts), this must be seen in the light of the principle that the *primary* responsibility for the child's financial support under the UN Convention is the *parent's*, and the State's responsibility, through social security, is *secondary*. This is, to say the least, contentious in the English context, since there are some who would argue that the *primary* responsibility for the casualties of family breakdown is the State's, and that parental responsibility is secondary. This is especially so where the parent concerned now has other responsibilities towards the children in his reconstituted household.

Articles 28 and 29 relate to education and are considered later[4]. Article 30 deals with rights of minority groups and provides that, in those States 'in which ethnic, religious and linguistic minorities or persons of indigenous origin exist, a child belonging to such a minority or who is indigenous shall not be denied the right, in community with other members of his or her group, to enjoy his or her own culture, to profess and practise his or her own religion, or to use his or her own language'[5]. Article 31(1) upholds the child's recreational rights. It requires States to recognise 'the right of the child to rest and leisure, to engage in play and recreational activities appropriate to the age of the child and to participate freely in cultural life and the arts'.

Protection against exploitation
Articles 32 to 35 recognise the child's right to protection from various forms of exploitation, including economic exploitation[6], protection against narcotics[7], sexual exploitation and sexual abuse[8], and trafficking in children[9]. Other articles:

---

1   UN Convention Article 27(2).
2   Ibid, Article 27(3).
3   See Chapter 9 below.
4   See Chapter 16 below.
5   For an excellent discussion of children's rights and cultural issues, which addresses the rival philosophical positions of monism, cultural relativism and cultural pluralism, see M Freeman *The Moral Status of Children* (Martinus Nijhoff, 1997) ch 7.
6   UN Convention Article 32.
7   Ibid, Article 33.
8   Ibid, Article 34.
9   Ibid, Article 35.

protect the child against torture or other cruel, inhuman or degrading treatment or punishment[1]; require States to abide by the rules of international humanitarian law regarding children and armed conflicts[2]; place States under rehabilitative duties towards child victims of the kinds of harm contemplated by the UN Convention[3]; and regulate the treatment of children under the criminal law[4].

Evaluation of the UN Convention

Critics of international law often question its value and whether it is truly law at all, in view of the difficulties of enforcement. It is fair to say that there is much in the UN Convention which can only be achieved with political will and a massive commitment of resources. Yet the UN Convention, like domestic law, should not be evaluated solely on the basis of its legal enforceability. Arguably more important is the educative and symbolic effect of internationally agreed norms against which domestic standards may be measured. McGoldrick has pointed out that the UN Convention is evidence that the international community has adopted a broad consensus on what rights children have and on what the obligations of the family, society and the international community should be[5]. The UN Convention also has a distinctive place in applying or extending to children, many of the human rights incontestably possessed by adults. The hope is that this will enable a more child-orientated or child-centred jurisprudence of human rights to develop. A possible criticism is that it fails to go far enough in the direction of empowerment rights and is over-concerned with protection. It is certainly true that the majority of its articles are protectionist in nature. One commentator's view is that it is a decidedly conservative instrument, built on compromise and concession, which is largely confined to reiterating existing human rights norms in their application to children[6].

It has been seen that the UN Convention gives explicit expression to the primary duties of parents but, importantly, it reaffirms the secondary role of the State. At the same time, it goes beyond merely listing a range of duties owed by adults to children and underlines the importance of recognising children as persons capable of possessing rights. It is, moreover, the possession of these rights which has the potential for transforming, not simply childhood, but adulthood as well. The point has been eloquently made by Eekelaar:

> 'The strength of the rights formulation is its recognition of humans as individuals worthy of development and fulfilment. This is not an appeal to narrow self-interest. On the contrary it recognizes the insight that people can contribute positively to others only when they are respected and fulfilled. And to recognize people as having rights from the moment of their birth continuously into adulthood could turn out, politically, to be the most radical step of all. If all *young people* are secured all the physical, social and economic rights proclaimed in the Convention, the lives of millions of adults of the next generation would be transformed. It would

---

1   UN Convention Article 37.
2   Ibid, Article 38.
3   Ibid, Article 39.
4   Ibid, Article 40.
5   D McGoldrick 'The United Nations Convention on the Rights of the Child' (1991) IJLF 132 at p 158.
6   LJ LeBlanc (above). See also M Freeman (above), especially ch 4.

be a grievous mistake to see the Convention applying to childhood alone. Childhood is not an end in itself, but part of the process of forming the adults of the next generation. The Convention is for all *people*. It could influence their entire lives. If its aims can be realised, the Convention can truly be said to be laying the foundations for a better world.'[1]

---

1   J Eekelaar 'The Importance of Thinking that Children have Rights' (1992) 6 IJLF 221 at p 234.

Chapter 3
THE CENTRAL ISSUES

What is a 'child' and what is a 'parent'? Do children have 'rights' and do parents have 'rights' or only 'responsibilities'? What duties or responsibilities (if any) may legitimately be expected of children? And if both children and parents have rights, how is the law to resolve a conflict between them? All of these questions attract simplistic answers, but on closer examination it is quickly apparent that each is an issue of considerable sophistication.

CHILDHOOD AND PARENTHOOD

The concepts of 'childhood' and 'parenthood' are both social and legal constructs. They are not immutable classifications and who may be regarded as a 'child' or a 'parent' by a society, or under the law of that society, is liable to revision and re-evaluation[1]. This most obviously occurred in England in 1969 when the status of childhood, or more accurately 'minority'[2], was redefined with the reduction in the age of majority from 21 to 18[3]. The effect of this was to regard as adults many young people previously denied this status. Yet the position is more complex than this. It has already been noted that children of various ages below majority nonetheless have legal capacity to take certain actions and decisions so that, to that limited extent, they might be viewed as 'adults' for some purposes and 'children' for other purposes[4]. It should also be remembered that although the expression 'child' is apposite to include all those aged from one day to 17 years and 364 days, there is a great deal of practical difference, in terms of the kinds of problems the law has to resolve, between the position of a newborn baby and that of a 17-year-old.

WHAT IS A CHILD?

A 'child' is normally defined as a 'person' below the age of majority, and this is the position taken in the Children Act 1989 and in the UN Convention on the Rights

---

1 On the changing historical conceptions of childhood, see P Aries *Centuries of Childhood* (Jonathan Cape, 1979) and I Pinchbeck and M Hewitt *Children in English Society* Vol I (Routledge and Kegan Paul, 1969) and Vol II (1973). See also MDA Freeman *The Rights and Wrongs of Children* (Frances Pinter, 1983) at ch 1, and *The Moral Status of Children* (Martinus Nijhoff, 1997) at ch 2.
2 The term 'minor' includes both 'children' and 'young persons', who are distinguished for certain purposes, especially in connection with juvenile justice, in English Law. Scots Law, until fairly recently, drew a distinction between 'minors' and 'pupils'.
3 Family Law Reform Act 1969, s 1, following the recommendations of the Latey Committee. See the *Report of the Committee on the Age of Majority* (1967) (Cmnd 3342).
4 The age of 16 years is particularly important in this respect, since children who have attained this age have a significant number of legal capacities in common with adults.

of the Child[1]. This inevitably gives rise to definitional difficulties at either end of the spectrum since there may be legitimate disagreement about when precisely personhood (and hence childhood) begins and when childhood ends.

The beginning of childhood

The beginning of childhood raises directly the status of the foetus or unborn child. English law generally takes the position that personhood is established at birth and not before[2]. Much the same view is taken in the United States, where the unborn child is not regarded as a person under the constitution[3]. It does not follow that no legal protections should be extended to the foetus but merely that, if they are, they are not based on the status of childhood or personhood[4]. The issue has caused particular difficulty where social services wish to take early action to protect a newly born baby from potentially inadequate or irresponsible parents. Here, it has been held that an authority may not take a pre-emptive strike by making the foetus a ward of court since a foetus is not a 'child', however well-developed or close to birth[5]. On the other hand, it was held that the authority

1   A child is defined, subject to limited qualifications relating to financial support, as 'a person under the age of eighteen' (s 105(1) of the Children Act). In the UN Convention, 'a child means every human being below the age of eighteen years unless, under the law applicable to the child, majority is attained earlier' (Article 1).
2   This is the assumption underlying much of the criminal law governing offences against the person, which depends on the child having achieved a separate existence from the mother. See, generally, JC Smith and B Hogan *Criminal Law* (8th edn) (Butterworths, 1996), especially at pp 338–340, and Chapter 14 below. The criminal law and the law of tort do offer certain protection to the foetus or unborn child but not on the basis that it is a 'child'. A good example is the case of *Attorney-General's Reference (No 3 of 1994)* [1996] 2 WLR 412 (CA) and [1997] 3 WLR 421 (HL) in which the Court of Appeal held that the doctrine of transferred malice could in principle apply where a defendant stabbed a pregnant woman causing the premature birth and subsequent death of her child. The defendant could be liable for the murder or manslaughter of the child on the basis of his intention to cause injury to the mother since, before birth, the foetus might be taken to be *part* of the mother. The House of Lords has now rejected the Court of Appeal's analysis on the basis that a foetus is 'neither a distinct person separate from its mother nor merely an adjunct of the mother' but 'a unique organism'. While holding that the doctrine of transferred malice could not be invoked so as to found a conviction for murder the House contrived to find a basis for liability in manslaughter. It held that it was a sufficient mens rea for constructive manslaughter that the defendant had intended to commit an act which was unlawful and which all sober and reasonable people would have recognised as creating a risk of harm to some other person. It was unnecessary to show that the person who died was the intended victim. Although a foetus was not a living person, the possibility of a dangerous act directed at a pregnant woman causing harm to the child to whom she subsequently gave birth made it permissible on public policy grounds to regard that child as within the scope of the defendant's mens rea when committing the unlawful act. For commentary, see J Keown 'Homicide by Prenatal Assault Revisited' [1998] CLJ 240.
3   *Roe v Wade* 410 US 113 (1973). For a discussion of some of the Canadian cases, see Alison Diduck 'Child Protection and Foetal Rights in Canada' (1993) 5 JCL 133. See also the decision of the Scottish Court of Session in *Kelly v Kelly* [1997] 2 FLR 828.
4   A useful and well-balanced discussion of the role of the law in regulating pregnancy is to be found in E Sutherland 'Regulating Pregnancy; Should We and Can We?' in E Sutherland and A McCall Smith (eds) *Family Rights: Family Law and Medical Advance* (Edinburgh University Press, 1990) at p 100. For a detailed examination of parental responsibility towards a child before birth, see M Brazier 'Parental responsibilities, foetal welfare and children's health' in C Bridge (ed) *Family Law Towards the Millennium: Essays for PM Bromley* (Butterworths, 1997) at ch 8.
5   *Re F (In Utero)* [1988] Fam 122.

might intervene immediately following birth, and might found its intervention largely, if not exclusively, on the mother's behaviour towards her unborn child while pregnant[1].

Under the Children Act 1989, it is now more likely that intervention would be based on the new prospective element in the threshold test of 'significant harm' which applies in care proceedings. An alternative would be, with leave, to use the inherent jurisdiction of the High Court. In one recent case this was used to authorise a Caesarean section to be performed on a 17-year-old crack cocaine addict, and thereafter to detain her for medical treatment, using reasonable force if necessary, in a maternity ward[2].

Another effect of drawing the line for childhood at birth, is to prevent the status of parenthood, and the legal responsibilities which go with it, from coming into being until that point. Thus, the prospective father of an unborn child has no legal standing to prevent the mother from undergoing an abortion[3].

The end of childhood

The end of childhood can also be problematic. The existence of an age of majority and the attainment of adulthood suggests, prima facie, a termination of the legal significance of the parent–child relationship and the disabilities of minority. Yet it is undeniably true that many young adults remain in the parental home, and some degree of factual dependency will often continue to exist[4]. This can cause acute difficulties in the case of mentally disabled young adults who, in reality, are as dependent on their parents as are young children. Thus, the cessation of parental responsibility and the wardship jurisdiction at majority, has left the courts struggling to find a legal basis for protective action where, for example, a sterilisation operation is thought necessary[5]. In certain limited respects, the relationship of parent and child endures for life, particularly for the purposes of succession. It is also the case that a few legal disabilities endure beyond majority, such as that relating to the holding of public offices, which is dependent on attaining the age of 21[6]. This was, until 1994, also true of private acts of buggery between consenting males, but the requisite age was reduced to 18 in that year[7] and the House of Commons recently voted to lower the age further to 16 to bring it in line with the age of consent for heterosexual intercourse. The attempt to

1   *D (A Minor) v Berkshire County Council* [1987] 1 All ER 33. Whether such early intervention is justified as a matter of policy is a contentious issue. See Chapter 11 below.
2   *A Metropolitan Borough Council v DB* [1997] 1 FLR 767. See further Chapters 8 and 11.
3   *Paton v British Pregnancy Advisory Service Trustees* [1979] QB 276, upheld by the European Court of Human Rights in *Paton v United Kingdom* (1980) 3 EHRR 408 and *C v S* [1987] 1 All ER 1230.
4   Legal liability can sometimes remain with parents to provide financial support for adult children who have left home and are in advanced education. See *B v B (Adult Student: Liability to Support)* [1998] 1 FLR 373, and Chapter 9 below.
5   See *T v T* [1988] Fam 52 and *Re F (Mental Patient: Sterilisation)* [1990] AC 1, discussed in Chapter 8 below. See also on the contact issue *Re C (Mental Patient: Contact)* [1993] 1 FLR 940. Recent cases involving judicially authorised Caesarean sections raise at the same time issues about the protection of the foetus and paternalistic interventions in relation to adults. See *Norfolk and Norwich Healthcare (NHS) Trust v W* [1997] 2 FLR 613 and *Re MB (Medical Treatment)* [1997] 2 FLR 426. But see now *St George's Healthcare National Health Service Trust v S* (1998) *The Times,* May 8, and Chapter 8 below.
6   Representation of the People Act 1949.
7   Criminal Justice and Public Order Act 1994, s 143, amending Sexual Offences Act 1967, s 12(1).

change the law has been, at least temporarily, defeated by the House of Lords, which voted against the proposed amendment to the Crime and Disorder Bill[1]. It is also generally the case that applicants for adoption should have attained the age of 21, subject to certain qualifications which apply to married couples adopting together[2].

WHAT IS A PARENT?

The concept of 'parenthood' is just as elusive. Many people would instinctively identify the natural mother and father of a child as his parents and, of course, this presents no problems in perhaps the majority of cases. The difficulty is that the notion of parenthood has been traditionally located in the conventional family centred on marriage. In recent decades there has been a gradual erosion in the relative significance of this form of family arrangement, and modern ideas of parenthood have to accommodate the many different forms which the 'new family' may take[3]. The growth in the divorce rate, remarriage and cohabitation outside marriage have meant that large numbers of children spend much of their childhood either in single-parent households or with at least one 'social' or 'psychological' parent who is not biologically connected to them[4]. Moreover, even the issue of who is a biological parent may now be unclear with the advent of the new reproductive technologies[5].

An initial point relates to terminology or language[6]. Many people may be known socially as 'parents' usually because they are performing what is thought to be the social role of parents by looking after and raising a child. These could include step-parents, foster-parents, grandparents or other relatives, cohabitants of parents, and so on. There is nothing, for example, to prevent a step-father or the mother's cohabitant from being known locally as the child's 'father' despite the absence of a genetic connection. But this will not make him the *legal* father. This raises two key questions. The first is whether it matters to social carers, like the man in this example, to be *called* a 'parent' or a 'father' or whether 'step-father' will do. The second is whether, if it does matter, it is appropriate for the law to confer on the social parent the *legal* status of parenthood. Here, matters are complicated further by the distinction which English law draws between the status of *parenthood* and the status of possessing *parental responsibility*. To return to the example, it may be that to give to the man in question the status of *parent* would be inappropriate, but to give him *parental responsibility*, and with it most of the powers and duties which parents possess in raising children, would be appropriate and desirable. This raises yet another question which is whether there is something special about the full legal status of *parent* or *parenthood* which suggests that it should be largely (if not exclusively) withheld from those who lack a genetic connection with the child.

---

1 See further Chapter 14.
2 See Chapter 7.
3 See, for example, the discussion in B Dickens 'Reproductive Technology and the "New Family" ' in E Sutherland and A McCall Smith (above).
4 'Social' or non-biological parenthood may take many forms. The issues surrounding social parenthood are discussed in Chapter 6, while adoption is discussed in Chapter 7.
5 See pp 74 et seq below.
6 See further p 81 below.

John Eekelaar has said that the concept of parenthood can in reality be broken down into three distinguishable elements[1]. The first is *biological parenthood*. This is the question of whose sperm as a matter of biological truth led to the conception of the child, and which woman gave birth to the child. The question of the child's biological mother has, however, become more complex since it is now possible, in some cases of surrogacy, for there to be a genetic mother and a gestational mother. In these instances the biological process of becoming a 'mother' is divided between two women and it is not so easy to give a straightforward answer to the question of who is the 'biological mother'. The law does, however, give a very clear answer to the question of who is the 'legal mother' in these cases[2]. This initial biological inquiry, it is submitted, is what is ordinarily understood by the concept of *parentage*, although many writers use the terms *parentage* and *parenthood* interchangeably and do not distinguish between the two. If we say, in ordinary language, 'there is a dispute over A's parentage' what we mean is that there is uncertainty about who is the *biological* parent (usually the father). So *parentage*, arguably, is the term used to describe the establishment of the initial connection between a child and a parent. Indeed, the *Concise Oxford Dictionary* defines *parentage* as 'descent from parents, lineage'. *Parenthood* on the other hand perhaps implies, in ordinary parlance, an ongoing status and role in relation to a child. John Eekelaar's second element is *legal parenthood*, which gives rise to certain legal incidents. But it is distinct from biological parenthood in that there are clear instances, mainly in the context of assisted reproduction and adoption, in which the biological parent is not initially, or is no longer, the legal parent[3]. Eekelaar's third element of parenthood is *parental responsibility*. This is distinct from both biological and legal parenthood in that, while it confers extensive powers and duties normally exercised by parents, it does not create the status of legal parenthood and it can be vested in many categories of carers who are not biologically connected with children. What makes this scheme so complex is that all three elements, biological parenthood, legal parenthood and parental responsibility, may be vested in the same person (as is the case with the parents of a child born to their marriage) but they may also be split up between individuals or between individuals and institutions (in the case of care and adoption)[4].

In *Law and Parenthood*[5], Barton and Douglas present a stimulating and challenging thesis about parenthood which they call 'a doctrine of intention'[6]. They describe a continuum of State regulation of parenthood, from minimal

---

1 J Eekelaar 'Parenthood, Social Engineering and Rights' in D Morgan and G Douglas (eds) *Constituting Families: A Study in Governance* (Franz Steiner Verlag, Stuttgart, 1994), especially at pp 85–89.
2 See p 74 below.
3 For the 'status provisions' which apply in cases of assisted reproduction, see pp 74 et seq below. For adoption, see Chapter 7.
4 Eekelaar (above) at p 87 gives an example of how convoluted the situation can become: 'Suppose a child is born from sperm donated by A to an unmarried couple (a woman, W, and a man, B) who jointly underwent treatment from a licensed facility. If the couple subsequently separate and the mother marries another man (C), in whose favour a Residence Order is made, then, while W is the biological and legal mother, and has parental responsibility, A is the biological father, B the legal father (without parental responsibility) and C shares parental responsibility with W'.
5 (Butterworths, 1995).
6 At pp 50 et seq.

regulation, as for example in the case of birth by an unmarried mother, to lengthy State investigation in the case of adoption. A second dimension to the analysis is a second continuum with biological parenthood at one end and social parenthood at the other. Their central argument is that 'the extent to which legal recognition is given to a person's intention or desire to be regarded as a parent, and to fulfil the functions of a parent, has increased over time, so that it is now the *primary* test of legal parentage'[1]. One response which can be offered to this thesis is that it fails to distinguish sufficiently between the different elements of parenthood outlined above. It may well be that the law has given increased recognition to the parental role of social parents but, more often than not, this has been by conferring on them *parental responsibility*. Whether it should go further and confer the full legal status of *parent* is a very different matter and this question has been given added significance by the growing acceptance of the child's right to knowledge of his biological origins. It may be that in future the law will need a clear concept through which to recognise and preserve the biological link. It is certainly arguable that this should be the concept of *parenthood*, leaving *parental responsibility* as the status-conferring concept for non-biological carers[2].

Who is the mother?

In general, the question of who is a child's mother will be straightforward and a self-evident fact of childbirth. The biological mother will also be the legal mother, whether the child is born in or out of wedlock, and the mother will also automatically acquire parental responsibility[3]. It has, of course, long been the case that the parental status of the mother may be terminated and transferred through the process of adoption[4]. But in recent years the question of who is the biological and legal mother has caused greater difficulty in the context of surrogacy arrangements which rely on techniques of assisted reproduction.

Where the surrogate mother has merely been inseminated with the sperm of the commissioning father (or that of a donor) she will be both the genetic and gestational mother and there is no question that she is appropriately described as the 'biological' mother. Where, on the other hand, she is implanted with an embryo created by in vitro fertilisation and involving the ova of the commissioning mother or donated ova, she will be the gestational or carrying mother but *not* the genetic mother. In these cases of 'full surrogacy', the concept of biological parenthood is difficult to apply. Is the biological link primarily about genetics or is it more to do with the process of gestation and childbirth? Whatever the biological position, the legal position is clear. For policy reasons[5], the law deems the woman who gives birth to the child, whether or not she is genetically related to the child, to be the child's *legal* mother with all that this implies for parental status and the acquisition of parental responsibility[6].

---

1   Barton and Douglas (above) at p 51.
2   It is conceded, of course, that this is not the direction in which the law has consistently moved thus far.
3   See Chapters 4 and 5 below for the allocation of parental responsibility between parents within and outside marriage respectively.
4   See Chapter 7 below.
5   Explored in Chapter 6 below.
6   Human Fertilisation and Embryology Act 1990, s 27(1) provides:
    'The woman who is carrying or has carried a child as a result of the placing in her of an

Who is the father?

The question of who is the 'father' of a child has always been a matter of proof since paternity, unlike maternity, is not biologically obvious in the process of parturition. Certain legal presumptions as to paternity apply where the mother is married. These usually result in her husband being presumed to be the biological father and, from that, the legal father, whatever may be the biological truth of the situation[1]. Where the mother is unmarried no such automatic presumptions apply. The determination of paternity depends primarily on birth registration and, failing that, on scientific tests which may or may not be directed in the event of a dispute. Important questions are raised by the development of the DNA testing technique which, unlike conventional blood-testing, now enables paternity to be determined with some certainty. We explore some of these issues when we look at the position of children born to two parents who are not, or may not be, married to one another[2].

At this stage, we address only the question of who is the father in cases of assisted reproduction under the so-called 'status provisions' of the Human Fertilisation and Embryology Act 1990. These techniques which enable the artificial transfer of gametes have been considered by Dickens to have comparable implications for family life to:

'. . . modern developments in social lifestyle that accommodate unmarried and serial married reproduction, in that they contribute to the creation of families in which children may be genetically unrelated to their social or psychological parents, and in which children in the same households may not genetically have both or either such parents in common.'[3]

In coming to the complex rules which determine who is the *legal* father in these cases it should be noted at the outset that they result in a situation in which English law is now prepared to treat quite openly, as the legal father, a man who is manifestly *not* the genetic father. While it is true that many married men have long been treated as the legal fathers of children to whom they may not in fact be genetically connected, it should be remembered that this is on the basis of a *presumed genetic link* arising from the fact of marriage to the mother. That said, the starting point, and indeed the conclusion if the status provisions do not result in another man being treated in law as the father, is that the man whose sperm leads to the conception of the child will be the legal father. In other words, all other things being equal, the genetic father of a child will also be the legal father[4]. He will not, however, necessarily have parental responsibility for the child, which will depend essentially on whether he is married to the child's mother. This is of

---

embryo or of sperm and eggs, and no other woman, is to be treated as the mother of the child.'

1   See Chapter 4.
2   See Chapter 5.
3   B Dickens 'Reproductive Technology and the "New" Family' in E Sutherland and A McCall Smith (eds) *Family Rights: Family Law and Medical Advance* (Edinburgh University Press, 1990) at p 28.
4   For a particularly good illustration of this principle, see the judgment of Bracewell J in *Re B (Parentage)* [1996] 2 FLR 15. See also *Re M (Child Support Act: Parentage)* [1997] 2 FLR 90. In this case, although the mother's husband had consented to her artificial insemination by donor, the resulting child had been born prior to 4 April 1988 and hence before the provisions of the

course an excellent illustration of the severance of genetic and legal parenthood from the independent concept of parental responsibility[1].

What then are the exceptions to the general rule? The first is that where a married woman is artificially inseminated or has infertility treatment involving the placing in her of an embryo, sperm or eggs but this does *not* involve the use of her husband's sperm, the husband will nonetheless be deemed to be the *legal* father of the child 'unless it is shown that he did not consent' to the treatment which took place[2]. A second exception clearly has in mind the situation of an unmarried couple in a stable relationship but has been drafted in such a way that difficult questions have arisen about its possible application outside that context. The rule is that, where no man is treated as the father under the first provision above, if a woman is artificially inseminated or receives infertility treatment 'in the course of treatment services provided for her and a man together' that man is treated as the father of the child[3]. Where a man is deemed to be the father under either of these provisions, the legislation goes on to provide that 'no other person is to be treated as the father of the child'[4]. Neither of the rules operate to rebut the normal presumption of legitimacy which arises in the context of a birth to a married woman[5]. Finally, it is expressly provided that sperm donors are *not* to be treated as the legal fathers of any resulting children, nor is a deceased man whose sperm was used after his death[6].

These provisions are exceptionally convoluted and have given rise to serious difficulties of interpretation, perhaps because they have been invoked in situations to which they were not really designed to apply. In essence, the policy of the law is clear enough – where a married or unmarried couple together undergo licensed fertility treatment involving donated gametes, *they* should be regarded together as the child's legal parents, thus excluding the gamete donor. But difficulties have arisen where the couple in question become estranged following the treatment and in the context of surrogacy arrangements.

In *Re CH (Contact: Parentage)*[7], a child was born to a married couple with the assistance of donated sperm. The husband had consented to the procedure. Following the birth of the child, the parties separated and the mother sought to deny the husband contact with the child on the basis that he was not the child's *genetic* father. He was of course the *legal* father under the above provisions, and Judge Callman held that he should not be denied contact unless there was a compelling reason against it. The presence or absence of the genetic link was not the crucial factor in a contact determination.

Human Fertilisation and Embryology Act 1990 and its predecessor, s 27 of the Family Law Act 1987, came into effect. The legislation was held not to have retrospective effect. Hence, the husband was not to be regarded as the legal father and was not liable for child support.

1   See Chapter 5.
2   Section 28(2).
3   Section 28(3).
4   Section 28(4).
5   Section 28(5).
6   Section 28(6). The problems associated with the posthumous use of sperm sprang to the attention of the public with the 'Diane Blood' saga, although the legal difficulties here concerned the absence of the late Mr Blood's consent to the use of his sperm to inseminate his wife after his death. See *R v Human Fertilisation and Embryology Authority ex parte Blood* [1997] 2 All ER 687.
7   [1996] 1 FLR 569.

Three decisions have considered the proper interpretation of the notoriously vague s 28(3). *Re Q (Parental Order)*[1] involved a surrogacy arrangement and an application for a parental order under s 30 of the Human Fertilisation and Embryology Act 1990. We consider the decision more closely when we examine the law applying to surrogacy arrangements[2]. The central question was whether the commissioning father and surrogate mother should be regarded as a man and woman who were 'together' provided with licensed treatment services. Crucially, the commissioning father's own sperm had not been used. Johnson J, in a restrictive interpretation, held that Parliament must have intended that *the man himself* should be provided with treatment services in order to trigger the provision. That was thought not to be the case here. The commissioning father was therefore *not* the legal father and his consent to a s 30 order was not required. In *Re B (Parentage)*[3] (a case which did not directly involve s 28(3)) Bracewell J took a less restrictive view suggesting that providing sperm and attending a hospital together with the mother might be sufficient although she agreed with Johnson J in *Re Q* that the provision would not apply merely because a man was living with the woman who received treatment. Finally, in *U v W (Attorney-General Intervening)*[4], an unmarried couple together received infertility treatment in Rome. IVF treatment took place using both the male partner's sperm and donor sperm. The resulting embryos were known to be created by the donor sperm and in due course twins were born. When the parties returned to England and their relationship broke down, the question arose as to whether the man was the legal father and thus liable for child support. Wilson J held that he was not the father since the provision had no application to unlicensed treatment. The treatment in Italy fell outside the licensing system and the safeguards established under it which would have applied if the treatment had been provided in England. But he did take the view that the parties had received treatment services together as envisaged by s 28(3) since the doctor had been 'responding to a request for that form of treatment by the woman and the man as a couple, notwithstanding the absence in the man of any physical role in such treatment'.

This case reveals the legal pitfalls of fertility treatment which takes place outside the licensing system established by the 1990 legislation. Difficulties may also arise where the extra-territorial complications of *U v W* are not present. The rule that a sperm donor is not to be treated as the father will only apply to licensed sperm donation so that those who operate outside the statutory scheme will be caught by the primary rule that the genetic parent is also the legal parent. Thus, failure to follow licensed procedures could have major disadvantages for both the mother and sperm donor. The former will run the risk that the donor might seek parental responsibility in relation to the child as he would be entitled to do as a 'parent'. The latter will risk being pursued for child support.

Fatherless children
The effect of the above provisions, illustrated by some of the cases, is to create in certain circumstances a category of 'fatherless' children. This can also arise where

---

1   [1996] 1 FLR 369.
2   See Chapter 6.
3   [1996] 2 FLR 15.
4   [1997] 2 FLR 282.

a single woman, without a partner and without any intention of having an involvement with any man, gives birth following licensed sperm donation. Inevitably, this raises questions about whether children can be conceptualised as possessing a 'right' to two parents or whether women have a superior right to produce a child without the physical and emotional involvement of a man[1]. Whatever view is taken of this potential clash of interests, it is fair to say that there are already very many instances in which children are effectively 'fatherless', either because paternity has never been established or because they are being brought up in single-parent households headed by mothers. There must also have been many instances of what has been termed 'genetic passing off' where a person regarded in law as the father is not in fact the genetic father[2]. Seen in this light, the 1990 provisions, which openly recognise as legal fathers social or non-genetic fathers, were not perhaps such a remarkable or contentious development.

THE CONCEPT OF CHILDREN'S RIGHTS

There is an initial difficulty in seeking to pin down the concept of children's rights. This is that whatever rights or interests children may have, they do not exist in a vacuum. It is quite impossible to evaluate the claims of children without considering their interaction with the claims of others, whether parents or others in the community. The very notion of children possessing rights implies the existence of legal or moral duties in *someone*, or indeed everyone, and this raises immediately the issue of the interests of the adult world which can often clash with children's interests. This should be borne in mind throughout this discussion.

'Welfare' versus 'rights'

An obvious question is whether there is any difference of substance between protecting the 'welfare' of children and protecting their 'rights'. English law has a strong theoretical commitment to the welfare or best interests of children, but is this the same as upholding their rights? Some liberationist writers are inclined to draw a sharp distinction between the two ideas, expressed most graphically by Farson, who differentiated between protecting *children* and protecting their *rights*[3]. For Farson, the critical birthright which children possess is self-determination and this overrides all other rights.

The extreme liberationist school represented by Farson and others would treat children as adults and extend to them all the liberties normally associated with adulthood. A child of *any* age would, in principle, have contractual freedom, sexual freedom, the right to work, the right to vote and so on. These 'kiddie

---

1   For the arguments from a children's rights perspective, see L Neilsen 'The Right to a Child versus the Right of a Child' in J Eekelaar and P Sarcevic (eds) *Parenthood in Modern Society: Legal and Social Issues for the Twenty-First Century* (Martinus Nijhoff, 1993). Related issues can arise in connection with the controversial question of the adoption of children by homosexuals, as to which see Chapter 7.

2   D Morgan and RG Lee *Blackstone's Guide to the Human Fertilisation and Embryology Act 1990* (Blackstone Press, 1991). This can arise most obviously where no one takes steps to rebut the presumption that the husband of a married woman is the father of any child born to her.

3   R Farson *Birthrights* (Harmondsworth, 1978). See also J Holt *Escape from Childhood* (Penguin, 1975).

libbers', as Mnookin has called them, stand in stark contrast to the 'child savers'[1]. The latter stress the vulnerability of children and the need to protect them from others and indeed from themselves[2]. According to this position, restrictions on contractual capacity, the prohibition of certain forms of sexual activity with minors, restrictions on child labour, and the disenfranchisement of children may all be justified. The very status of minority, with its attendant disabilities, has, as its raison d'être, children's assumed inability to act in their own best interests. Child protectionism is thus a highly paternalistic notion[3] for it supports the right of adults to take decisions for children and not the right of children to act for themselves[4].

There can be no doubt that the English law affecting children, although historically dominated by such influences as the devolution of property and preservation of the social order rather than the protection of children for their own sake[5], has had a strongly protectionist orientation[6]. It is certainly arguable that it has been the concentration on safeguarding the welfare of children which has obscured the issue of their rights and which explains, at least until recently, the absence of a generally accepted theory of children's rights.

Children's rights in the USA

Meanwhile, in the USA, the issue of rights had to be directly confronted because of the written constitution and bill of rights enshrined within it[7]. In the 1960s, the Supreme Court firmly grasped the nettle by holding that children were persons under the constitution and thus capable of possessing fundamental rights[8]. This did not mean that *all* those rights enjoyed by adults would automatically be extended to children[9], but it did mean that apparent infringements of those rights in the case of children would have to be justified by some other legitimate interest protected by the constitution[10]. Children's rights accordingly have a strong theoretical foundation in the USA since there is, in effect, a presumption that they

1　RH Mnookin 'Thinking About Children's Rights – Beyond Kiddie Libbers and Child Savers' (1981) *Stanford Lawyer* 24.

2　These protectionist concerns can clearly justify interferences with the civil liberties of children which would be unacceptable if imposed on adults. In the USA, certain forms of intervention, such as the prohibition of the sale of obscene materials to minors, may be constitutional as they apply to children, but would be unconstitutional if imposed on adults. See *Ginsberg v New York* 390 US 629 (1968).

3　On the philosophical justifications of paternalism in the writings of Hobbes, Locke and Mill, see MDA Freeman *The Rights and Wrongs of Children* (Frances Pinter, 1983) at pp 52–54.

4　This is why it is argued that the choice of decision-maker is crucial. See RH Mnookin (above).

5　See, particularly, JM Eekelaar and T Murray 'Childhood as a Social Problem: A Survey of the History of Legal Regulation' (1984) *Journal of Law and Society* 207 and J Eekelaar, R Dingwall and T Murray 'Victims or Threats? Children in Care Proceedings' (1982) JSWL 68.

6　Perhaps epitomised by the all-embracing wardship jurisdiction in which a 'ring of protection' is thrown around a ward of court.

7　The earlier developments of the constitutional guidelines affecting children's rights are discussed and extracted in W Wadlington, CH Whitebread and SM Davis *Children in the Legal System* (Foundation Press, 1983) at ch II. There were also calls there for a bill of rights for children. See Foster and Freed 'A Bill of Rights for Children' (1972) 6 Fam LQ 343.

8　*Re Gault* 387 US 1 (1967).

9　See RH Mnookin (above).

10　In the case of children, the standard is a 'significant state interest' – a somewhat lower standard than the 'compelling state interest' required in the case of adults.

are entitled to all the normal civil liberties possessed by adults. The onus is firmly on those who would withhold them to find a legal justification for doing so. Parents are also self-evidently persons under the constitution, and have rights both as individuals and in their capacity as parents[1]. This can give rise to a clash of constitutional rights between parents and children which the courts have occasionally had to resolve[2]. These conflicts of interest have been confronted less openly and more subtly in England[3].

Development of children's rights in England

Despite the absence of a written constitution or bill of rights in England, the rights of children have been firmly on the agenda since the early 1980s, and the cause received major boosts from the *Gillick* decision in 1985 and the Children Act 1989[4]. The debate has tended to focus on the autonomy claims of adolescents and there has been a strong inclination to associate, if not equate, the concept of children's rights with the claim to self-determination[5]. Yet, in reality, the notion of children's rights is a multi-faceted idea, far too complex to be looked at in a one-dimensional way. At the very least, any serious theory must acknowledge and admit elements of both protection and self-determination, and most do.

The concept of children's rights, although distinct from welfare, therefore includes within it welfarist or protectionist concerns. We should, moreover, question the assumption, sometimes made, that welfare as an idea is antithetical to self-determination. It can be cogently argued that the welfare of children dictates that they be allowed a *degree* of self-determination or qualified autonomy. Ronald Dworkin brings this out rather well in his philosophical analysis of distributional equality[6]. Dworkin discusses the various theories of welfare, one species of which is the 'success theories' which suppose that 'a person's welfare is a matter of his success in fulfilling his preferences, goals and ambitions'[7]. Although Dworkin is talking specifically about the distribution of resources, the welfare of children can be similarly viewed as a matter of individual self-fulfilment which must, by its nature, imply an element of independence from adult control. It was also noted that, under the statutory checklist governing the application of the welfare principle, the wishes of children must, in principle, be taken into account[8].

In one respect, the concept of rights performs a valuable function for which the concept of welfare is ill-adapted. It draws attention to the *universality* of children's claims. The concept of welfare, as interpreted in English case-law, is a highly

---

1   See, for example, *Prince v Massachusetts* 321 US 158 (1944).
2   See H Wingo and SN Freytag 'Decisions Within the Family: A Clash of Constitutional Rights' 67 (1982) *Iowa Law Rev* 401.
3   Chapter 2 above discussed the different weightings given to children's welfare which may be seen as one manifestation of this.
4   Other significant developments were the International Year of the Child in 1979 and the establishment of the Children's Legal Centre in London. Children's rights may well receive a further boost when the European Convention on Human Rights is incorporated into English law.
5   This might well have been a reaction to what might have been seen as the over-paternalistic attitude of English law before the *Gillick* ruling.
6   R Dworkin 'What is Equality Part I: Equality of Welfare' (1981) 10 *Philosophy and Public Affairs* 185.
7   Ibid at 191.
8   Children Act 1989, s 1(3)(a).

individualistic notion which is inadequate to embrace the multifarious legal and moral claims which children may be thought to have as a matter of social justice. The concentration is wholly on doing what is best for an individual child in an individual set of circumstances and it is often said that each case must turn on its own facts. Rights, on the other hand, although clearly capable of assertion in individual cases, are designed to safeguard the interests of *all* children as a class. Indeed, it has been said that 'a necessary feature of children's rights is that they be genuinely universal, appropriate for children everywhere'[1]. It is this aspect which has, at least until recent decades, been neglected in England.

The significance of language and terminology

Does it really matter whether the law's protection of children's interests is analysed in terms of 'rights' or 'welfare', or that parents are described as having 'rights' or 'responsibility', or whether someone is described as a 'parent' or in some other way? There is some truth in the assertion that playing with conceptual labels will not necessarily have any effect on the substance of family relations[2]. Perhaps there ought to be some healthy scepticism about the limits of what the law can achieve for children[3]. There are dangers in indulging in 'rights-talk' too loosely since it has been said that this can be a reductionist device for lawyers, reducing the complexity of human relationships (with which the law is ill-equipped to deal) to manageable concepts[4]. Against this, it can be argued that the use of certain expressions can have an influence on society. If this is correct, the modernisation of terminology *is* an important issue because it may have a symbolic or educative effect on social attitudes. There is no question that one of the most striking features of the reform of family law over the last decade has been the reformulating of concepts and that behind this reformulation lies shifting values[5]. Seen in this light, it becomes important to assert and defend rights for children, but it should be acknowledged that the *substance* of the relationships between children and the adult world are, in the final analysis, of greater significance than any theoretical description applied to them.

SOME THEORIES OF CHILDREN'S RIGHTS

Before attempting to explore the substantive rights which children have, the initial question of what is a 'right' arises and this is a matter of considerable

---

1 V Worsfold 'A Philosophical Justification for Children's Rights' (1974) 44 *Harvard Educational Review* 142 at 149.
2 See A Bainham *Children, Parents and the State* (Sweet & Maxwell, 1988) at pp 57–61.
3 See M King 'Playing the Symbols – Custody and the Law Commission' [1987] Fam Law 186. See also M King *A Better World for Children?* (Routledge, 1997) for a wide-ranging critique of decision-making, policy formulation and moral campaigns designed to improve the lot of children from the perspective of autopoietic theory – a social theory of self-regulation systems in 'society' of which law is said to be one.
4 M King and C Piper *How the Law Thinks About Children* (Gower, 1990) particularly at pp 68–70.
5 See A Bainham 'Changing Families and Changing Concepts: Reforming the Language of Family Law' [1998] CFLQ 1.

controversy[1]. Yet it is of crucial significance since someone who denies, for example, that children have a right to 'love and affection' may be saying one of two things. Either he may be saying that children have no claim or interest of any kind, whether legal or moral, in receiving love and affection or, alternatively, he may be saying that any such claim or interest is not properly classified as a 'right'. The second is the more likely interpretation since almost everyone would recognise the moral claims of children in this respect while there may be substantial doubt about whether they could ever be elevated to the status of legal rights, far less enforceable ones.

This general difficulty should always be kept in mind since there are many statements, particularly in international instruments[2], about the alleged rights of children which go well beyond what is normally understood by lawyers to constitute rights. It may be that much of this can be accounted for by distinguishing between legal rights and moral claims. The issue of children's rights is further complicated by the uncertainties surrounding the *content* of individual substantive claims. While it may be possible to conclude that children have rights to adequate food, medical care and education, the content of these rights may be uncertain. Thus, it may be fairly obvious what is adequate care and nourishment for a new born baby, but far less clear what is an adequate education for an older child. How far the child's basic right to an education extends may well be something on which there is no consensus.

With these initial difficulties in mind, a brief examination will now be made of three of the more influential British theories of children's rights, put forward by MacCormick, Eekelaar and Freeman respectively. This is followed by a short section summarising the views of Onora O'Neill, whose distinctive contribution to the debate is to argue that a concentration on children's rights is misplaced and that the emphasis should rather be on the duties or responsibilities of adults towards children. This leads neatly on to the following section which asks the question whether children themselves have, or ought to have, any duties.

MacCormick's test case

In an article, first published in 1976[3], Neil MacCormick used the claim that children have rights as a test case for theories of rights in general. MacCormick pointed out that before substantive theories of particular rights of children could be constructed it was necessary to address the fundamental issue of whether they have rights at all.

The 'will theory' and the 'interest theory'
There are broadly two competing theories of the nature of rights – the 'will theory' and the 'interest theory'. MacCormick sought to demonstrate that the former could not accommodate the rights of children and was accordingly suspect as a

---

1   For a discussion of the problem of children's rights in the context of the general dispute about rights, see WNR Lucy 'Controversy About Children's Rights' in D Freestone (ed) *Children and the Law* (Hull University Press, 1990) at p 213.
2   See, particularly, the United Nations Declaration of the Rights of the Child 1959, the United Nations Convention on the Rights of the Child 1989, and Chapter 17 below.
3   N MacCormick 'Children's Rights: A Test-Case for Theories of Right' (1976) 62 *Archiv für Rechts und Sozialphilosophie* 305; also published as ch 8 in *Legal Right and Social Democracy* (1982).

general theory. However, in his view, it was possible to make sense of the claim that children have rights by formulating a variant of the interest theory. The will theory is based on the notion that to have a legal or moral right is to be able to exercise individual choice over the enforcement or waiver of duties imposed on someone else. The essence of the theory is the pre-eminence of the right-holder's will over the will of others with respect to the subject-matter of the right. The interest theory concentrates on the protection of an individual's interests by the imposition of duties on others – what MacCormick refers to as 'the imposition of (legal or moral) normative constraints on the acts and activities of other people with respect to the object of one's interests'. Therefore, an important element in both theories is the existence of duties in others, correlative to the rights asserted[1]. The critical difference is that the will theory regards as crucial the capacity for individual autonomy, ie the ability to waive or enforce the duty in question, whereas under the interest theory it is sufficient for the existence of a right that there is an identifiable interest and a corresponding duty.

The will theory

MacCormick drew attention to the difficulty (in his view impossibility) of accommodating the concept of children's rights within the will theory. He took as an example the right of a baby to care, nurture and love[2]. The will theory is inept as a foundation for this, essentially for two reasons. First, a baby clearly lacks the physical and mental capacity to exercise any will or choice about whether to relieve his parents from their duty to provide him with these things. Secondly, and more importantly, it was MacCormick's contention that neither the baby, nor anyone acting on the baby's behalf, should be allowed to waive the parents' duty or acquiesce in its non-performance. For MacCormick it is the fundamental interest and moral claim of the infant to care and nurture which justifies the imposition of the duty on the parent. The duty is not constitutive of the right but rather a means of securing that right. When outside agencies, such as social services, intervene where parents have failed to provide adequate care, this does not remove the duty placed on parents. Rather, such action constitutes substituted performance of the duty as opposed to a waiver or release for parents. MacCormick concludes that to see such powers as constitutive of the child's right is to confuse the substantive right with ancillary remedial provisions.

The interest theory

MacCormick, instead, saw the rights of children as being located somewhere in the interest theory and grounded in the basic jural precept of respect for persons. Thus, to argue[3]:

'. . . that each and every child is a being whose needs and capacities command our respect, so that denial to any child of the wherewithal to meet his or her needs and to develop his or her capacities would be wrong in itself (at least in so far as it is physically possible to provide the wherewithal) and would be wrong regardless of the ulterior disadvantages or advantages to anyone else – so to argue, would be to put a case which is intelligible as a justification of the opinion that children have such rights.'

---

1 Correlativity was crucial to Hohfeld – see *Fundamental Legal Conceptions* (Yale University Press, 1919).
2 N MacCormick 'Children's Rights: A Test-Case for Theories of Right' (above).
3 Ibid at p 310 et seq.

Although MacCormick conceded that rights require the imposition of duties, for him the existence of a right preceded the imposition of a duty. It is *because* children have a right to care and nurture that parents have a duty to care for them[1].

If this is correct, it means that it may be possible to recognise that children have rights even where there is uncertainty about who is to bear the corresponding duty. MacCormick gives the example of education. While there may be a wide measure of agreement that children have a right to be educated to the limits of their abilities, it is far less clear who has the duty or power to provide it as between parents, local authorities, central government, a church or the children themselves[2]. MacCormick attempted to fit this reasoning into a general interest theory. His thesis was that to ascribe to all members of a class C (for present purposes, children) a right to treatment T (in the above examples, care and nurture or education) is to presuppose that T is, in all normal circumstances, a good for every member of C and that T is a good which it would be wrong to withhold from any member of C.

It should be noted that MacCormick's theory, as applied to children (especially young children) incorporates a measure of paternalism. Whereas in a liberal democracy it is generally accepted that a right-holder should be allowed the liberty to determine when to enforce his rights, this is not so, according to MacCormick, in the case of children – an exception acknowledged by the exponents of classical liberalism including JS Mill[3]. This is based on a contentious argument which will be discussed later: 'Children are not always or even usually the best judges of what is good for them'.

The emergence of children's rights according to Eekelaar

In a seminal article, published in 1986[4], John Eekelaar assessed the current status of the concept of children's rights in English law in the context of an historical overview and two (then) recent decisions of the House of Lords[5]. Like MacCormick, Eekelaar relied on the interest theory of rights, especially that version propounded by Joseph Raz that 'a law creates a right if it is based on and expresses the view that someone has an interest which is sufficient ground for holding another to be subject to a duty'[6].

Historical background

Eekelaar was at pains to demonstrate that, historically, the earliest legal duties towards children emerged not to protect the interests of children themselves but to further other interests, usually the interests of fathers or the wider community. Thus, the legal enforcement of parental support obligations in the sixteenth century arose primarily from the threat to social stability posed by the growth of mass unemployment and labour mobility. Insofar as this advanced the interests of children it did so only incidentally and was not its aim or purpose[7]. The same, he

---

1   N MacCormick 'Children's Rights: A Test-Case for Theories of Right' (above) at p 313.
2   Ibid.
3   JS Mill *Essay on Liberty* (1859).
4   J Eekelaar 'The Emergence of Children's Rights' (1986) 6 *Oxford Journal of Legal Studies* 161.
5   *Richards v Richards* [1984] AC 174 and the *Gillick* case.
6   J Raz 'Legal Rights' (1984) 4 *Oxford Journal of Legal Studies* 1 at p 13.
7   J Eekelaar 'The Emergence of Children's Rights' (above) at pp 166–169.

argues, may be said of the limited incursions into the father's right to custody of his legitimate children during the nineteenth century. Although, apparently, conceived as protective of the child's independent interests, the reality was that the father's interests were seen as paramount unless his behaviour posed a severe threat to the child's well-being. But the courts would only hold this to be so where it consisted of such matters as 'immorality, profligacy, impiety and radical social views, all of which might undermine the child's commitment to the dominant social values'[1]. For Eekelaar these judicial interventions had the effect of equating the welfare of children with the transmission of conventional social norms. In other words, their thrust was to uphold the prevailing community interest rather than the independent interests of children.

Isolation of interests

The key precondition for rights in Eekelaar's theory is the social perception that an individual or class of individuals has certain interests. Crucial to this is that the interests in question must be capable of isolation from the interests of others. Thus, to assert the existence of a particular right for children is to identify an independent interest which they have in the subject-matter or, as Eekelaar puts it, 'those benefits which the subject himself or herself might plausibly claim in themselves'. He gives the example of a parent's power to take decisions concerning his daughter's medical welfare. Although the parent might claim that this power is in the child's interests, the parental interest is not identical with the child's interest. Her interest or right is that only the *best* medical decisions are taken for her. Accordingly, it cannot per se be enough to see the child's interests as synonymous with those of the parent, despite the force of parental autonomy claims. Eekelaar's thesis is that no child would plausibly claim parental independence as an end in itself. If it is claimed at all it must be because it is perceived to advance other ends such as material or emotional stability[2]. He acknowledged, however, that children might lack the information or ability to evaluate their own best interests and, accordingly, the construction of a theory of children's rights involves 'some kind of imaginative leap and guess what a child might retrospectively have wanted once it reaches a position of maturity'.

Eekelaar identified three separate kinds of interest which might form the foundation of these retrospective claims. These he described as 'the basic interests', 'the developmental interests' and 'the autonomy interests'.

Basic interests

The 'basic interests' relate to what might be described as the essentials of healthy living, including physical, emotional and intellectual care[3]. The duty to secure these interests is placed initially on the child's parents but, where this is abused or neglected, the State may intervene in care proceedings[4]. These interests are 'basic' because they require compliance with minimally acceptable standards of upbringing. The parents' duty is 'to refrain from the actual prevention or neglect of

---

1 See, for example, *Shelley v Westbrooke* (1817) Jac 266 and *Symington v Symington* (1875) LR 2 SC and Div 415.
2 J Eekelaar 'The Emergence of Children's Rights' (above) at p 170.
3 Ibid at pp 171–172.
4 Under s 31(2) of the Children Act 1989, discussed in Chapter 11 (below).

proper development or natural health rather than the maximum promotion of these qualities'.

Developmental interests

The 'developmental interests' are wider and may be asserted not just against parents but against the wider community. They are more nebulous than the basic interests and, hence, more difficult to categorise as legal rights. The developmental interest, according to Eekelaar, is that, subject to the socio-economic constraints in a particular society, 'all children should have an equal opportunity to maximise the resources available to them during their childhood (including their own inherent abilities) so as to minimise the degree to which they enter adult life affected by avoidable prejudices incurred during childhood'. Eekelaar doubted that these interests, while the subject of moral claims, could legitimately be classified as legal rights since, beyond education, the law imposes no duty on parents to fulfil children's developmental interests, which depend rather on 'the natural workings of the economies of families which are themselves dependent on the wider social and economic mechanisms of the community'[1].

Autonomy interest

The 'autonomy interest', which a child might retrospectively claim, is 'the freedom to choose his own lifestyle and to enter social relations according to his own inclinations uncontrolled by the authority of the adult world, whether parents or institutions'. This is, of course, the classic claim of the child liberationists which was alluded to above. Eekelaar argued that this could be interpreted as a version of the developmental interest, no doubt on the basis that healthy development implies a measure of self-determination or autonomy. The justification for adopting a separate categorisation is that the autonomy interest has the potential for conflicting with the developmental interest or the basic interest. It is, for example, likely that the removal of age restrictions on drinking or driving would further the autonomy interest but would also result in more deaths or injury among children from road accidents, thereby infringing their developmental and basic interests. Eekelaar, agreeing with Freeman[2], would rank the autonomy interest as subordinate to the other two interests, since it is likely that the majority of adults would not give their retrospective approval to exercises of autonomy while children, which damaged their life chances in adulthood when compared with other children.

The value of Eekelaar's thesis is that it alerts us to potential conflicts both between the distinctive interests or rights which children may claim and between those interests and rights and the competing claims of the adult world, especially those of parents. Eekelaar has subsequently attempted to build on his earlier theory by suggesting a way in which furthering the best interests of children may be reconciled with treating them as possessors of rights. His theory, which is based on the concept of 'dynamic self-determinism', relies on the argument that the welfare principle, or best interests principle, should be properly understood to accommodate an opportunity for the child to determine what those best interests are[3]. He proposes, subject to two limitations, that a competent child's decision

---

1   J Eekelaar (above) at p 173.
2   MDA Freeman *The Rights and Wrongs of Children* (Frances Pinter, 1983).
3   J Eekelaar 'The Interests of the Child and the Child's Wishes: The Role of Dynamic Self-
    Determinism' in P Alston (ed) *The Best Interests of the Child* (Clarendon, 1994) at p 42.

should determine the outcome of the issue in question. These are 'compatibility with the general law and the interests of others' and, more controversially, situations in which a child might take a decision which is 'contrary to his or her *self-interest*, . . . narrowly defined in terms of physical or mental well-being and integrity'[1]. This, of course, raises again the central question of precisely what are the acceptable limits of paternalism.

Freeman's liberal paternalism

The most extensive study of children's rights in England is probably *The Rights and Wrongs of Children* by Michael Freeman[2]. This has now, to a degree, been superseded by his new collection of essays, *The Moral Status of Children*[3], which in some respects is intended by Freeman to serve as a second edition to his earlier work. The principal change is a shift of emphasis. He is now inclined to believe that he underestimated the importance of giving children participatory rights in *The Rights and Wrongs of Children*. Freeman stressed the importance of rights for children against benevolence towards children, or other morally significant values such as love, friendship or compassion. Rights enable, at least in theory, the right-holder to stand with dignity and demand or insist on certain treatment without embarrassment or shame. They represent entitlements and avoid the need to grovel, beg or show gratitude for favours. At the same time, Freeman was quick to warn that the enactment of legal rights could become merely an abstract affirmation of principle if the will was lacking to put it into practice. He pointed to examples from juvenile justice in which well-intentioned measures, designed to enhance the rights of children, back-fired and had the opposite effect of eroding them[4].

Freeman's distinctive contribution to the children's rights debate was to demonstrate the extremely diverse nature of the substantive rights which children might claim and to fit a categorisation of these rights into an over-arching theory of liberal paternalism. His theory adapts Rawls' influential 'Theory of Justice'[5] to apply to children. Freeman produced a fourfold classification of children's rights, comprising rights to welfare, rights of protection, rights to be treated like adults and rights against parents[6].

Rights to welfare

Freeman's first category, welfare rights, was located in the more general notion of human rights and he drew freely on the statements on children's rights in the

---

1   J Eekelaar (above).
2   (Frances Pinter, 1983).
3   (Martinus Nijhoff, 1997).
4   *The Rights and Wrongs of Children* (above) at pp 32–34. Freeman's attacks were levelled particularly at the system of juvenile justice and the juvenile court where well-intentioned measures designed to decriminalise juvenile misbehaviour, particularly those embodied in the Children and Young Persons Act 1969, had the unintended effect of establishing, inter alia, a 'criminal model' in care proceedings.
5   J Rawls *A Theory of Justice* (Harvard University Press, 1972). A similar adaptation of the theory to children was put forward by V Worsfold in 'A Philosophical Justification for Children's Rights' (1974) 44 *Harvard Educational Review* 142.
6   MDA Freeman *The Rights and Wrongs of Children* (above) at pp 40–54.

United Nations Declaration of the Rights of the Child[1]. Freeman regarded this as politically important because, by expressing children's rights as human rights, 'the United Nations was not saying that children ought to have these rights but, since children are undoubtedly human beings . . . they already have them'.

The rights in question are wide-ranging and include: entitlement to a name and nationality; freedom from discrimination based on, for example, race, colour or religion; social security extending to adequate nutrition, housing, recreation and medical care; entitlement to free education and equal opportunities; protection from all forms of cruelty, neglect and exploitation; and special treatment for the handicapped. These rights are not, as Freeman acknowledged, easily formulated against anyone in particular. They are, in essence, 'manifestos' of the rights which children *ought* to have against everyone. Typically, these types of 'rights against the world' are vague, perhaps deliberately so, to reflect cultural and economic differences between societies. Some, such as the provision of adequate nutrition and medical care, are clearly fundamental since they relate to survival and fall within what Eekelaar termed the 'basic interests'. The rights listed are essentially protectionist rather than liberationist and, to that extent, there is an overlap with Freeman's second category, rights of protection. But 'welfare rights' is a wide enough idea to include within it rights of *recipience*, ie rights to receive *positive* welfare benefits such as education, social security or (perhaps more controversially in rights analysis) love, understanding and affection.

Rights of protection

Freeman's second category, protective rights, was more overtly concerned with protection from *negative* behaviour and activities[2] such as inadequate care, abuse or neglect by parents, exploitation by employers or environmental dangers. Whereas welfare rights are pitched at a high level and are grounded in the assumption that society owes children the best it has to offer, protective rights are concerned that minimally acceptable standards of treatment are observed and, as such, are largely, although not exclusively, the province of the criminal law[3].

The first two categories of rights have a common paternalistic approach. They are rights which the adult world would deem to be appropriate for children whether or not they would be claimed by children for themselves. They contrast sharply with Freeman's third and fourth categories, both of which belong more to the liberationist school.

The right to be treated like adults

Freeman's third category was the right of children to be treated like adults. This right is grounded in social justice and egalitarianism. It is essentially that the rights and liberties extended to adults should also be extended to children as fellow human beings, unless there is a good reason for differentiating between them. Comment has already been made on this in the context of the USA. Although the UK does not have a bill of rights, there is, nonetheless, a strong tradition of respect

---

1   Adopted by the General Assembly on 20 November 1959. See also the United Nations Convention on the Rights of the Child, adopted on the thirtieth anniversary of the Declaration, both discussed in Chapter 2 above.
2   MDA Freeman *The Rights and Wrongs of Children* (above) at pp 43–45.
3   As to which see Chapter 14 below. Civil care proceedings are also, of course, concerned directly with protection.

for civil liberties and this must pose the question of how far the civil liberties enjoyed by adults are, or should be, extended to children and young people[1]. Freeman regarded the claim that children should be treated as adults with some scepticism. While distinctions between children and adults are social and legal constructs which may appear arbitrary, Freeman's view was that respect for children as persons requires that society provides 'a childhood for every child'[2] and not an adulthood for every child. Yet Freeman also questioned the double standard involved in the differential treatment of children and adults[3]. He pointed out that the basis for this was the supposed incapacity or lack of maturity which would prevent children from taking sound decisions on their own behalf. He nonetheless rejected the removal of all age-related disabilities since to do so would ignore the evidence about the cognitive abilities of children provided by developmental psychology. But he argued that children's rights at least required that age-related restrictions be kept under review in the light of this evidence. His own preference was for legal capacity to be determined on a case-by-case basis, by assessing the *actual* capacity for particular activities of individual children. This, he argued, could be achieved by employing an objective test of rationality determined in accordance with a neutral theory of what is 'good' for children.

Rights against parents

Freeman's fourth category was rights against parents[4]. This is also concerned primarily with self-determination or autonomy but, whereas the third category is concerned with the justification of civil liberties and the child's position under the general law, this fourth category is concerned with the claim for independence from parental control[5]. Claims in this category range from the trivial (eg length of hair, choice of clothes, bedtimes, etc) to serious matters (eg consent to abortion or provision of contraceptives). Freeman noted two variants of this claim. The first is the claim that the child should be able to act entirely independently. The second is the claim that the child should be able to act independently but with the sanction of an outside agency, usually a court[6]. Freeman's general position on parent–child conflicts was to view the parental role as a representative one. Where parents' and children's views accord with one another there is no problem. Where they do not, Freeman would uphold parental decisions insofar as they are consistent with an objective evaluation of what Rawls called 'primary social goods'. These include liberty, health and opportunity and are, in short, the things which any rational person would want to pursue. Where parents purport to take decisions not in accordance with this objective, Freeman would hold that parental representation ceases at that point and that the intervention of an outside agency is justified, his own preference being a court.

---

1   This is clearly going to become an even more relevant question as and when the European Convention on Human Rights is incorporated into English law. See further Chapter 17 below.
2   MDA Freeman *The Rights and Wrongs of Children* (above) at p 3. Freeman borrowed the quotation from M Gerzon *A Childhood for Every Child – Politics of Parenthood* (Outerbridge and Lazard, New York, 1973).
3   The legal capacities of children and young people are considered in Chapter 15 below.
4   MDA Freeman (above) at pp 48–52.
5   There is a discussion in the next section of the interrelationship between children's capacities and parental control.
6   This solution has often been adopted in the USA. See Chapter 8 below.

Rawls' fundamentals of justice

It is clear from this analysis that Freeman favoured a degree of paternalism as a feature of children's rights[1]. The critical requirement of respect for persons was, he thought, that the potential capacity of children for taking responsibility as free and rational agents should be recognised. But, since in the case of children we are often talking about *potential* rather than actual capacity, a limited amount of intervention could be justified to protect them against irrational actions. The obvious question is, what kind of actions are to be considered irrational for these purposes? What test of rationality can be employed? Here, Freeman found that it was Rawls' idea of equality at the stage of a hypothetical social contract which best captured the idea of treating people as equals with regard to their capacity for autonomy.

Rawls was concerned with the principles which individuals would hypothetically choose in a just society in order to secure fair treatment for everyone[2]. Everyone in society would participate in choosing these principles in a hypothetical state ('the original position') and in ignorance of their own specific interest and circumstances (behind 'the veil of ignorance'). Since they would be hypothetically unaware of what would be to their own advantage or disadvantage, all individuals would choose principles of justice impartially and with a view to equality. According to Rawls, individuals in this state of ignorance, but acting in self-interest, would choose two fundamental principles of justice. These were, first, that each person should have as much personal liberty as was compatible with similar liberty for everyone else and, secondly, that social and economic inequalities should be tolerated only to the extent that they were to the greatest benefit of the least advantaged and attached to offices and positions open to everyone under conditions of fair equality of opportunity.

Rawls included children in the initial social contract when they reached the 'age of reason'. Freeman interpreted this as meaning participation to the extent that they were capable. Justice required, therefore, that children be brought to a capacity whereby they were able to take responsibility as free and rational agents. In order to achieve this, Freeman argued that they required two types of right. The first was equal opportunity extending to such matters as good parenting and good teaching. The second was liberal paternalism. This would allow intervention to protect the child's potential for development. The test propounded by Freeman is 'what sorts of action or conduct would we wish, as children, to be shielded against on the assumption that we would want to mature to a rationally autonomous adulthood and be capable of deciding our own system of ends as free and rational beings'[3]? Within this framework, protection from death or injury and compulsory education could be readily justified. While there was no guarantee that every individual would consent to these principles, Freeman's thesis was that they were the ones which were most consistent with a neutral theory of the good and which would appeal to those in the 'original position'.

---

1 His theory of liberal paternalism is set out at pp 54–60 of his book.
2 See the explanation of Rawls' theory by V Worsfold in 'A Philosophical Justification for
   Children's Rights' (1974) 44 *Harvard Educational Review* 142 at pp 151 et seq.
3 MDA Freeman *The Rights and Wrongs of Children* (above) at p 57.

Common ground between the theories

This analysis has touched briefly on just three of the many theories of children's rights which have been advanced, and doubtless many more will emerge in the years to come[1]. There is much common ground between the three theories discussed above which, at the risk of over-simplification, might be summarised in the following propositions:

(1) Children have rights which arise from the fundamental moral requirement of respect for persons which underlies all human rights.

(2) The particular rights which children have are grounded in the interests which society recognises they possess and which justify the imposition of duties on others.

(3) 'Children's rights' is not a unitary concept but a catch-all expression for a range of legal and moral claims.

(4) The imposition of a duty on *someone* (perhaps unspecified) is a necessary concomitant of any right asserted for children. Where this is imposed on an identifiable entity, especially a parent, it may be possible to recognise the existence of a legal right stricto sensu – a 'claim right' in the Hohfeldian sense[2]. Where, conversely, the right is asserted against the world, it is less clear that it can be regarded as a legal right but may have the status of a moral right. The existence of such a moral claim may itself justify the creation of a legal right and, but for potential difficulties of enforcement, many such claims probably would be.

(5) Children's rights must embrace elements of both qualified self-determination and limited paternalism.

(6) Rights, although asserted by individual children, must have a general or universal character such that they can be applied to all children as a class.

Perhaps the most controversial issue arising from these theories is the basis upon which paternalistic interventions are justified. Broadly, there would appear to be two schools of thought on this. The first, accepted by Eekelaar and Freeman, entails a hypothetical enquiry by adult decision-makers into what children would ideally want for themselves. The judgment of adult society is, as it were, substituted for that of the child who is (as yet) unable to exercise it for himself. This can only be made on the basis of a projection of what rational persons would have wished for themselves as children. The second, adopted by Ruth Adler in her study of juvenile justice in Scotland[3], is that adult decision-making reflects the value judgments of the decision-maker about what is good for children and not the decision-maker's projection of what children would want for themselves. Adler would, accordingly, allow a form of modified protectionism based on external assessments of what is good or necessary for children. Whatever may be the

---

1 Many of these theories, particularly those put forward in North America, are cited by Freeman. For a Scottish perspective on children's rights, see R Adler *Taking Juvenile Justice Seriously* (Scottish Academic Press, 1985); and the review by J Eekelaar at (1986) 6 *Oxford Journal of Legal Studies* 439. For other significant collections of essays on the general subject of children's rights, see M Freeman and P Veerman (eds) *The Ideologies of Children's Rights* (Martinus Nijhoff, 1992) and P Alston, S Parker and J Seymour (eds) *Children, Rights and the Law* (Clarendon, 1992).

2 Hohfeld regarded these 'claim rights' as the only true legal rights: see Hohfeld *Fundamental Legal Conceptions* (Yale University Press, 1919).

3 R Adler *Taking Juvenile Justice Seriously* (above).

theoretical merits of the former school of thought, it is likely that the latter is a more realistic reflection of what actually happens in practice. We will return to this issue in the context of medical decision-making, where the 'substituted judgment test' has a certain following, especially in North America[1].

Onora O'Neill: Children's rights or adults' duties?

Onora O'Neill has made a distinctive contribution to the children's rights debate by questioning whether 'children's positive rights are best grounded by appeals to fundamental (moral, natural, human) rights'. Instead, she argues they are 'best grounded by embedding them in a wider account of fundamental obligations'[2]. In essence, her thesis is that regarding 'rights as fundamental in ethical deliberation about children has neither theoretical nor political advantages'. Instead, she thinks that the best way to achieve rights for children is to shift the concentration on to the fundamental *obligations* of adult society.

O'Neill does not deny the force of the rhetoric of rights in the claims of those who lack power but she is concerned that such rhetoric can lead to claims of 'spurious rights even when no corresponding obligations can be justified'. She warns that:

> 'many of the rights promulgated in international documents are not perhaps spurious, but they are patently no more than "manifesto" rights . . . that cannot be claimed unless or until practices and institutions are established that determine against whom claims on behalf of a particular child may be lodged. Mere insistence that certain ideals or goals are rights cannot make them into rights . . .'[3]

Thus, the rhetoric of rights cannot, according to O'Neill, establish positive rights for children. She goes on to consider whether the use of the language of children's rights might have a *political* usefulness contributing to the 'realisation of fundamental imperfect obligations'. Here, she rejects the analogy between children and other (formerly) oppressed groups such as colonial peoples, the working classes, religious or racial minorities and women, all of which 'have sought recognition and respect for capacities for rational and independent life and action that are demonstrably there and thwarted by the denial of rights'[4]. For O'Neill, the 'crucial difference between (early) childhood dependence and the dependence of oppressed social groups is that childhood is a stage of life, from which children normally emerge and are helped and urged to emerge from by those who have most power over them'. She concludes:

> 'Those who urge respect for children's rights must address not children but those whose action may affect children; they have reason to prefer the rhetoric of obligations to that of rights, both because its scope is wider and because it addresses the relevant audience more directly.'[5]

O'Neill's thesis has provoked considerable disagreement as it was bound to do[6]. Its value is to remind us that where any 'right' is being asserted for children we

---

1 See Chapter 8 below.
2 O O'Neill 'Children's Rights and Children's Lives' (1988) 98 *Ethics* 445, also reproduced in Alston, Parker and Seymour *Children, Rights and the Law* (Clarendon, 1992) at p 24.
3 Ibid at p 37.
4 Ibid.
5 Ibid at p 39.
6 For a particularly readable critique, see M Freeman *The Moral Status of Children* (Martinus Nijhoff, 1997) at pp 25–29.

ought to pause to consider on whom there is, or might be, a correlative obligation and whether such obligation is enforceable.

Do children have duties?

The whole children's rights debate raises one other important question. This is whether children *themselves* have any duties or responsibilities. Those rights which aim to protect children or secure positive welfare benefits for them largely entail, as perhaps O'Neill's thesis reminds us, the exercise of responsibility by others. But those rights which are autonomy based and would extend to children greater liberties, by treating them like adults or by giving them freedom from parental control, do invite consideration of how much responsibility children have for their own actions. It is striking how rarely the advocates of children's rights even mention, let alone deal with, this issue.

The short answer is that, whereas many jurisdictions do explicitly recognise the existence of certain obligations upon children and set them out in civil codes or legislation, English law is largely silent on the question[1]. Historically, the common law did enable a parent to sue for the loss of his child's services but this was only actionable where the child *in fact* performed some service for the parent – even if it was only making the tea![2] The action fell into disuse and was eventually abolished in 1982[3]. A more modern approach to the general obligation which children might be thought to have is a duty of respect for parents and this is acknowledged expressly in a number of jurisdictions[4]. In South East Asia, certain States provide expressly for the financial obligations of children (for these purposes including 'adult children') towards parents who are unable to support themselves[5].

In English law such legal obligations as children have really arise, if at all, by implication. These include criminal responsibility from the age of ten and limited tortious liability[6]. There is no direct statutory obligation on the child to attend school, although this arguably arises by implication from the parental duty to ensure the child receives a proper education and from the very existence of the compulsory education system[7]. It can be argued that the express imposition of certain duties on children would be desirable, or is even a necessary concomitant, of the acquisition of limited autonomy. The younger the child the less actual and

---

1   For a general discussion, see A Bainham, ' "Honour Thy Father and Thy Mother": Children's Rights and Children's Duties' in G Douglas and L Sebba (eds) *Children's Rights and Traditional Values* (Dartmouth, 1998).

2   So where a two-year-old was run down by the defendant's carriage no action would lie. See *Hall v Hollander* (1825) 4 B&C 660 and for a more detailed discussion PM Bromley, *Bromley's Family Law* (6th edn) (Butterworths, 1981) at pp 329–332.

3   Administration of Justice Act 1982, s 2(b).

4   Perhaps not surprisingly in Israel, given its traditions, but less obviously in Indonesia and the new family code of Croatia. See further Bainham (above) and the sources cited at fn 28 to that article.

5   This is so in Indonesia. See Wila Chandrawila Supriadi 'Indonesia: Indonesian Marriage Law' in A Bainham (ed) *The International Survey of Family Law 1995* (Martinus Nijhoff, 1997). More strikingly, Singapore has recently passed the Maintenance of Parents Act 1995 which gives to parents, in specified circumstances, the right to obtain maintenance from their children. See P de Cruz 'Singapore: Maintenance, Marital Property and Legislative Innovation' in A Bainham (ed) *The International Survey of Family Law 1996* (Martinus Nijhoff, 1998).

6   See Chapters 14 and 15 respectively.

7   See Chapter 16.

legal capacity that child will possess and the less justification there is for imposing duties or responsibilities on that child. As the child gets older and gradually acquires greater actual and legal independence so the case gets stronger for requiring increased actual and legal responsibility on the part of the child, or perhaps more accurately, young person. This might appear to justify, inter alia, a specific duty on the child to attend school and, it will be suggested later, a duty to remain in contact with parents – albeit one which would be qualified by the operation of the welfare principle[1]. Finally, it is noteworthy that the United Nations Convention on the Rights of the Child gives all manner of *rights* to children but nowhere addresses this question of responsibility.

PARENTS: RIGHTS, RESPONSIBILITIES AND DISCRETIONS

The change in terminology from 'parental rights' to 'parental responsibility' has already been noted, and the function performed by these two concepts described. But does this reformulation of the parent's position represent any real change in the substance of the legal relationship between parents and children? Over the last decade or so there has been a marked reluctance to accept that parents have 'rights', and one commentator more or less coupled the 'eclipse of parental rights' with the 'emergence of children's rights'[2]. It has been stressed frequently that any rights which parents do have exist only to enable them to discharge their duties to their children[3]. The law is apparently seeking to express parenthood in a different way which plays up the responsibility of parents and plays down any legal rights which may arise from the relationship[4].

The best-restatement of the parental position is perhaps that of the Law Commission in its first report on illegitimacy in 1982, taken up in its working paper on custody in 1986 in which it put it thus:

> 'Parenthood would entail a primary claim and a primary responsibility to bring up the child. It would not, however, entail parental "rights" as such. The House of Lords in *Gillick v West Norfolk and Wisbech Area Health Authority* has held that the powers which parents have to control or make decisions for their children are simply the necessary concomitant of their parental duties. This confirms our view that "to talk of parental 'rights' " is not only inaccurate as a matter of juristic analysis but also a misleading use of ordinary language.'[5]

This view of parenthood as embracing powers in order to discharge responsibilities accords with what has been termed the 'exchange view'. Parents have rights *because* they have responsibilities and they have responsibilities *because* they have rights[6]. On this view, the correct way of looking at parenthood is one which implies reciprocity.

---

1   See Chapter 4.
2   J Eekelaar 'The Eclipse of Parental Rights' (1986) 102 LQR 4 and 'The Emergence of Children's Rights' (1986) 6 *Oxford Journal of Legal Studies* 161.
3   For a post-*Gillick* re-statement of this position, see the views of the Scottish Law Commission, in its Discussion Paper No 88 *Parental Responsibilities and Rights* at paras 2.1 et seq.
4   On the similar trend in North America, see KT Bartlett 'Re-Expressing Parenthood' (1988) 98 *Yale Law Journal* 293.
5   Law Com Working Paper No 96 *Custody* (1986) at para 7.16 and Law Com Report No 118 *Illegitimacy* (1982) at para 4.18.
6   See KT Bartlett (above) at pp 297 et seq.

The new emphasis on responsibility raises a fundamental issue. Whether or not it is jurisprudentially accurate to say that parents have 'rights', can it at least be said that they have *independent interests* which can be asserted in law? After a period in which it was fashionable to deny that they do, there is now evidence in judicial decisions[1] and in academic commentaries[2] that not everyone is happy with this formulation.

The following section examines the substance of the parent's position in law. This revolves around the issue of the *control* which parents are required or allowed to exert over the lives of their children. Although there are many angles to this, the discussion can usefully be reduced to three distinct but interrelated questions.

(1) What are the legal incidents of parenthood and, in particular, over which areas of upbringing does the law charge parents with responsibility or allow them to exert control?
(2) What are the limits of parents' responsibilities and powers?
(3) How do these responsibilities and powers relate to the legal capacities and responsibilities of children themselves?

The legal incidents of parenthood

It has never been possible to state with complete confidence the legal incidents of parenthood. This is because they have never been set out in statutory form. The statutory definitions of 'parental rights and duties' and now 'parental responsibility' simply refer back to the general law. Therefore, in order to appreciate the full legal implications of the parent–child relationship, it has been necessary to piece this together by taking into account the legal effects recognised at common law and under various statutory provisions. A number of commentators attempted to do this[3] before the Children Act 1989, although the Law Commission eschewed the opportunity to do so in its report on guardianship and custody. The Commission argued that although it would be superficially attractive to provide a list, this would be a practical impossibility given the need for change periodically to meet different needs and circumstances[4]. It is nonetheless possible to collate with some accuracy the major incidents of parenthood. The following list is taken from one leading text on family law:[5]

(a) providing a home for the child;
(b) having contact with the child;
(c) determining and providing for the child's education;
(d) determining the child's religion;

1 See, for example, *Re K (A Minor) (Custody)* [1990] 2 FLR 64; and *Re K (A Minor) (Wardship; Adoption)* [1991] 1 FLR 57, discussed in J Eekelaar 'The Wardship Jurisdiction, Children's Welfare and Parents' Rights' (1991) 107 LQR 386. See also the decision of the European Court of Human Rights in *Hokkanen v Finland* (1995) 19 EHRR 134 which can surely only be explained on the basis that a parent has a right and an independent interest in contact with his child. See further Chapter 4 below.
2 J Eekelaar (above), and A Bainham 'Growing Up in Britain: Adolescence in the post-*Gillick* Era' (1992) *Juridical Review* 155.
3 See, for example, J Eekelaar 'What are Parental Rights?' (1973) 89 LQR 210 and S Maidment 'The Fragmentation of Parental Rights' (1981) CLJ 135.
4 Law Com Report No 172 *Review of Child Law: Guardianship and Custody* (1988) at para 2.6.
5 PM Bromley and NV Lowe *Bromley's Family Law* (8th edn) (Butterworths, 1992) at p 301.

(e) disciplining the child;
(f) consenting to the child's medical treatment;
(g) consenting to the child's marriage;
(h) agreeing to the child's adoption;
(i) vetoing the issue of a child's passport;
(j) taking the child outside the UK and consenting to the child's emigration;
(k) administering the child's property;
(l) protecting and maintaining the child;
(m) agreeing to change the child's surname;
(n) representing the child in legal proceedings;
(o) burying or cremating a deceased child.

Each of these requires qualification and there is considerable debate about their content and extent, but they do at least convey, in general terms, the areas of control which fall within parenthood. There is little cause for surprise since they relate to all the most important matters which can affect a child's upbringing and it would be expected that parents would exercise *primary* control over them.

The approach in Scotland

The Scottish Law Commission took a slightly different view of the nature of the parental position in law from that of the English Commission[1]. It agreed that it was correct to emphasise the *responsibility* of parents but recommended that parental *rights* should also be expressly recognised in legislation accepting that such rights would be subordinate to the child's best interests. The Commission also felt that it was helpful to set out the principal responsibilities and rights of parents in legislation, and the new Scottish legislation does just that[2]. Section 1 of the Children (Scotland) Act 1995 sets out the following *responsibilities* of parents:

(a) to safeguard and promote the child's health, development and welfare;
(b) to provide direction and guidance to the child in a manner appropriate to the stage of the child's development;
(c) if the child is not living with the parent, to maintain personal relations and direct contact with the child on a regular basis; and
(d) to act as the child's legal representative.

These responsibilities together with the rights set out below (which replace common-law, but not specific statutory, duties) must be exercised to the extent that it is practicable and in the interests of the child to do so.

Section 2 of the Act sets out a corresponding list of parental *rights* which a parent has in order to fulfil these responsibilities. They are:

(a) to have the child living with him or her or otherwise to regulate the child's residence;
(b) to control, direct or guide the child's upbringing in a manner consistent with the child's stage of development;

---

1 See Scot Law Com No 135 *Report on Family Law* (Edinburgh HMSO, 1992) especially at paras 2.1–2.35.
2 See generally JM Thomson *Family Law in Scotland* (3rd edn) (Butterworths, 1996) at pp 193 et seq, and E Sutherland 'Scotland: Child Law Reform – At Last!' in A Bainham (ed) *The International Survey of Family Law 1995* (Martinus Nijhoff, 1997).

(c) if the child is not living with the parent, to maintain personal relations and direct contact with the child on a regular basis; and

(d) to act as the child's legal representative.

It will be noted that there is a close correspondence, almost direct correlation, between the above responsibilities and rights, emphasising the reciprocal nature of rights and responsibilities which essentially conforms with the 'exchange view' of parenthood discussed earlier.

Parenthood or parental responsibility?

It is important to appreciate that there is a distinction between the effects of 'parenthood' and the effects of being vested with 'parental responsibility'. In most instances, of course, it will be the parents who have parental responsibility, so that their relationship with the child will be partly the result of being parents and partly the result of having parental responsibility. But where parental responsibility is vested in a non-parent, or where a parent does not have parental responsibility[1], the distinction is more significant. The essential point is that certain legal effects relate exclusively to parenthood[2] since they are dependent on being *related* to someone else in a particular way. As such, these incidents are not incorporated in the concept of parental responsibility in the sense that they are not acquired by a non-parent who obtains this by court order[3].

The clearest example is rights of succession. Neither the child nor the non-parent with parental responsibility will have any claim on the other's estate in the event of intestacy[4]. The acquisition of 'parental responsibility' does not make the child in the fullest legal sense a member of the family of the person acquiring it in the way that an adoption order does. The latter transplants *parenthood* and not merely parental responsibility. Thus, holding parental responsibility will not create a legally recognised relationship between the child and the wider kin of the holder. These wider kin (children, parents, siblings, uncles and aunts, etc) will not, for example, fall within the definition of 'relative' vis-à-vis the child under the Children Act 1989[5]. The Children Act 1989 also provides that certain powers which are considered fundamental to the status of parenthood or guardianship are not to pass to a non-parent who obtains parental responsibility through a residence order[6], or to a local authority which obtains it under a care order[7]. These are the right to consent or refuse to consent to an application to free the child for adoption, to agree or refuse to agree to the adoption order itself, and the right to appoint a guardian[8]. The right to change the child's name and the right to remove the child from the jurisdiction may also be restricted where a residence

---

1   This can only be the case regarding the unmarried father who has not acquired parental responsibility by agreement with the mother or by court order.

2   Although some also apply to guardianship in view of the assimilation of the legal effects of guardianship and parenthood. See Chapter 6 below.

3   A residence order in the case of an individual, and a care order in the case of a local authority.

4   This can, of course, be overcome by making a will.

5   See s 105(1) which defines 'relative' as 'a grandparent, brother, sister, uncle or aunt (whether of the full blood or half blood or by affinity) or step-parent'.

6   Children Act 1989, s 12(3).

7   Ibid, s 33(6)(b).

8   Additionally, a local authority may not 'cause the child to be brought up in any religious persuasion other than that in which he would have been brought up if the order had not been made' – ibid, s 33(6)(a).

order is in force[1]. Thus, while parental responsibility includes within it the bulk of powers over upbringing which parents and guardians enjoy, it is a somewhat more limited notion than either parenthood or guardianship.

This explanation does not adequately convey the peculiar status of the unmarried father which is essentially the converse of the non-parent with parental responsibility. Although he undoubtedly has the status of parenthood[2] (and with it, for example, succession rights), the unmarried father does not possess any of the powers included in parental responsibility which arguably constitute, in reality, the most important features of being a parent[3]. Despite this, he *is* liable to support the child financially. This gives rise to the rather incongruous result that a lawyer or other adviser may have to explain to such a man how it is that he does not possess parental responsibility but is still obliged to support his child[4]. Is, then, the notion of parental responsibility jurisprudentially accurate in conveying the legal position of parents and others having control over children?

The nature and extent of parental responsibility

Bernard Dickens, in a seminal article published in 1981 on the modern function and limits of parental rights[5] (and which has not been bettered by anything written on the subject in the intervening 17 years), attempted to apply to parents Hohfeld's analysis of legal rights[6]. Hohfeld's thesis was centred on correlative relations so that, for a right to exist, it was necessary to establish the existence of a correlative duty. Applying Hohfeld's analysis, Dickens described the parental 'right' as 'a parental discretion to act regarding a child in a way others have a co-relative duty to permit, or a duty to forbear from preventing'[7]. Yet Dickens recognised that certain powers which parents possess are more a question of duties than of rights. Parents have clear legal duties to provide their children with essential health care, food, shelter and clothing[8] and education[9]. These are absolute duties in the sense that failure to secure these minimal provisions for children may result in legal action against the parents.[10] It is therefore possible to say that children have correlative rights to be provided with these essentials of life. Insofar as parents have rights or powers over these matters, such rights or powers appear to exist only to enable parents to discharge their duties and 'the function of parenthood may appear to be the protection of children against physical, psychological, social and moral harm'[11].

---

1   Children Act 1989, s 13.
2   This was not always the position under the old law since the unmarried father fell outside the definition of 'parent' or 'guardian' for several purposes including care proceedings and adoption.
3   He can only acquire these by agreement with the mother or court order. See Chapter 5 below.
4   Social Security Administration Act 1992, ss 78(6)–(9) and 105 and Children Act 1989, s 3(4)(a). See the comments of SM Cretney 'Defining the Limits of State Intervention: The Child and the Courts' in D Freestone (ed) *Children and the Law* (Hull University Press, 1990) at pp 66–67.
5   BM Dickens 'The Modern Function and Limits of Parental Rights' (1981) 97 LQR 462.
6   Hohfeld *Fundamental Legal Conceptions* (Yale University Press, 1919).
7   BM Dickens (above).
8   Children and Young Persons Act 1933, s 1.
9   Education Act 1996, s 7, formerly Education Act 1944, s 36.
10 This could be in the form of criminal or care proceedings or, in the case of education, proceedings for an education supervision order, discussed in Chapter 16 below.
11 BM Dickens (above) at p 464.

   Dickens moved on to consider the area of discretion which parents have once they have complied with these minimal duties. He noted that 'parental duties and related rights appear to be defined by reference not to the positive standard of achieving good for children, but by reference to the negative standard of protecting children from harm'. He concluded that this leaves open 'a parental discretion to employ control over children for purposes not violating children's interests, but equally not advancing their welfare or best interests'[1].

   Many examples could be given of this area of parental discretion which is left open once basic obligations to children are met. Thus, while parents cannot elect not to educate their children at all, the *manner* of that education is left largely to parents themselves and parental choice has become an increasingly significant feature of education law[2]. Parents have a completely free hand over religious education. They may bring up their children in any religion or none at all[3]. In the medical sphere, while parents clearly do not have the sole say in matters of life and death[4], they have considerable influence over what non life-saving treatment or elective surgery a child should receive[5]. Whether a baby should be immunised against whooping cough is, for example, an issue which is left entirely to parents.

   The concept of 'discretion' conveys the realities of parenthood very well, perhaps better than the notions of 'rights' or 'responsibility'. Ronald Dworkin has used the image of a ring doughnut in analysing the nature of legal discretion. For Dworkin, discretion is a relative concept which can exist meaningfully only 'when someone is in general charged with making decisions subject to standards set by a particular authority'. Accordingly, discretion 'like the hole in a doughnut does not exist except as an area left open by a surrounding belt of restriction'[6]. Dworkin was concerned primarily with the discretions exercised by judges, officials or others charged with public duties, but the imagery of the Dworkinian doughnut may usefully be borrowed. It is not a distortion to describe parents as discharging a public function in the sense that there is an undoubted public interest in the well-being of children[7]. Even if the private law model of the trust is used, as some commentators have done[8], it will be evident that trustees have certain basic duties to the beneficiaries of the trust, but, beyond that, they enjoy significant discretion in the administration of trust funds. Likewise, parents have a large area of discretion to determine all manner of issues related to the upbringing of their children, but they are surrounded by a belt of restriction which requires them to

---

1 BM Dickens (above) at p 464.
2 This was very much the hallmark of the policy of the former Conservative administration embodied particularly in the Education Act 1980 and the Education Reform Act 1988.
3 Discussed in Chapter 16 below.
4 See *Custody of a Minor* 379 NE 2d 1053 (1978) in which the Supreme Court of Massachusetts stated that parental rights 'do not clothe parents with life and death authority over their children'. But they do, it appears, have a significant say. See *Re T (Wardship: Medical Treatment)* [1997] 1 FLR 502, and Chapter 8 below.
5 See Chapter 8 below.
6 RM Dworkin 'Is Law a System of Rules?' in RM Dworkin (ed) *The Philosophy of Law* (Oxford University Press, 1977) at p 52 et seq.
7 As to which, see J Eekelaar 'What is Critical Family Law?' (1989) 105 LQR 244 at pp 254–258.
8 C Beck, G Glavis, S Glover, M Jenkins and R Nardi 'The Rights of Children: A Trust Model' (1978) 46 *Fordham Law Review* 669; and R Dingwall, J Eekelaar and T Murray *The Protection of Children: State Intervention and Family Life* (Basil Blackwell, 1983) at p 224.

ensure that children are given certain basic protections to meet the necessities of life.

Returning to Dickens' view of parental discretion as a 'right', was he correct to assert that others have a correlative duty to permit, or forbear from preventing, parents from exercising that duty as they see fit? It may be that the answer to this question depends to some extent on who the 'others' are. Dickens had in mind those public and quasi-public officials, who are charged with child protection, which in England would largely refer to social services and other welfare agencies[1]. It is fair to say that such agencies cannot intervene, certainly not compulsorily, in family life unless and until parents have failed to achieve the minimum standard of upbringing required by law[2]. It is debatable whether this is also true of the courts since it is, in principle, open to anyone to challenge the exercise of a parental discretion on the basis that it is not in the best interests of the child[3]. But, in practice, a court would be reluctant to entertain such an application unless it thought that what was proposed by a parent would be likely to have a seriously detrimental effect on the child[4]. Dickens himself conceded that it could not be said, even in 1981, that children themselves would necessarily be bound by a duty of tolerance or compliance with parents' wishes, and this is most definitely the case today.

The most problematic category of 'others' are those who might be termed 'outsiders', which could include members of the extended family, other interested private individuals, and institutional authorities such as schools or hospitals. How far are such outsiders bound by a legal duty not to interfere with the exercise of parental discretions? There is currently considerable uncertainty about this. Few would disagree with the straightforward statement that parents have a primary claim to raise their children as they wish[5] and it is superficially attractive to conclude from this that external interference is, prima facie, unlawful. Yet the Court of Appeal has held that parents have no independent 'rights' capable of founding an action in tort for interference with parental rights[6]. Parents may be able to bring an action against outsiders for interferences which are tortious invasions of the child's own rights,[7] but they have no independent avenue of redress. Their former right to sue for loss of a child's services was thought to be based on outmoded proprietorial conceptions of parenthood and was finally abolished in 1982[8]. While it is true that parents can invoke the wardship

---

1   Particularly the National Society for the Prevention of Cruelty to Children.
2   Now defined in s 31(2) of the Children Act 1989.
3   Traditionally such 'single issues' have been heard in wardship proceedings but may now be the subject of an application in family proceedings for prohibited steps or specific issue orders.
4   Such as an irreversible procedure like sterilisation. See Chapter 8 below.
5   This was clearly the view of the Law Commission: see fn 5 at p 94 above.
6   *F v Wirral Metropolitan Borough Council* discussed in A Bainham 'Interfering with Parental Responsibility: A New Challenge for the Law of Torts?' (1990) 3 JCL 3. In limited circumstances, the crime of child abduction under the Child Abduction Act 1984, s 2 might be committed by an outsider removing a child from the lawful control of parents.
7   These will usually be physical interferences which constitute trespass to the child's person in the form of assault, battery or false imprisonment. Parents may also commit torts, or crimes, against their own children where they indulge in physical interferences with them which exceed the bounds of reasonable parental control. See *R v D* [1984] AC 778 and *R v Rahman* [1985] 81 Cr App R 349.
8   Law Reform (Miscellaneous Provisions) Act 1970, s 5 and Administration of Justice Act 1982, s 2.

jurisdiction, or now seek a s 8 order, to prevent unwelcome activities or undesirable associations between a child and a third party, they may only obtain relief on the discretionary (and therefore uncertain) basis that these involvements are not in the best interests of the child[1]. This is not at all the same as saying that the third party concerned is in breach of a duty of non-interference with parental rights or discretion. Quite apart from anything else, the court might, in its discretion, uphold the view of the outsider and not that of the parent[2].

We might wish to conclude from this that parental discretions do not give rise to 'rights', at least in the sense of claim rights[3] giving rise to correlative duties – except perhaps against the State. Parental discretion is really a 'privilege' or 'liberty' in the Hohfeldian sense. In Hohfeld's scheme of jural relations, a privilege is the opposite of a duty and the correlative of the inelegantly phrased 'no-right'. In simple language, what this means in the case of parents is that when they are exercising their discretions, they are not subject to legal duties, but, equally, outsiders have no right to require parents not to exercise them as they choose. While parents may have difficulty founding a legal action to prevent dealings between their children and third parties, it can at least be said with confidence that outsiders have no legal claim to prevent parents from determining issues of upbringing[4].

These principles must now be qualified by the added complication that the child himself may well have a view on what is proposed.

Parent–child conflicts

It is now clear, both at common law and under a variety of statutory provisions, that children have the capacity to perform certain acts and take certain decisions[5]. Sometimes this is dependent upon them having attained a certain age and sometimes it falls to be determined by the test of maturity propounded by the House of Lords in the *Gillick* case. That case will be discussed in depth later when medical issues are considered[6]. The present concern is to explore the interaction between children's capacity for decision-making and parental discretion[7].

The critical question is whether the child's acquisition of capacity, whether through age or maturity, *terminates* any parental claim to involvement, or whether the child's capacity and parental discretion co-exist in some form until the child reaches maturity. The traditional view was that parental rights 'dwindle' as the child approaches majority but at least survive until then. The older the child, the less likely it has been that a court would enforce parental control against his wishes[8]. But, although it was not always enforceable, it was thought that parental

---

1   See NV Lowe and RAH White *Wards of Court* (2nd edn) (Barry Rose/Kluwer, 1986) at ch 12.
2   As happened in *Re D (Sterilisation)* [1976] Fam 185 where the view of an educational psychologist was upheld.
3   See fn 2 at p 91 above.
4   Anyone wishing to do so would have the onus of bringing a legal action and seeking to persuade the court to overrule the parental view applying the welfare principle.
5   See Chapter 15 below for a further discussion.
6   Chapter 8 below.
7   For these purposes it is assumed that the ratio of *Gillick* is sufficiently wide to govern a range of issues other than contraception or medical issues.
8   See *Krishnan v Sutton London Borough Council* [1970] Ch 181 and the views of Lord Denning MR in *Hewer v Bryant* [1970] 1 QB 357 at 369.

control continued to exist even where it amounted, in the case of older teenagers, to no more than a right to give guidance or advice[1].

A radical interpretation of *Gillick* would suggest that any right of parental control is completely eclipsed by the child's ability to act for himself[2]. Such a view relies heavily on the speech of Lord Scarman in which he said that 'the parental right yields to the child's right to make his own decisions when he reaches a sufficient understanding and intelligence to be capable of making up his own mind on the matter requiring decision'[3]. But Lord Scarman himself appeared to acknowledge that parental rights would *survive* until majority and he was in general agreement with Lord Fraser. Lord Fraser adopted a noticeably more cautious approach to the interrelationship of adolescent capabilities and parental control. He evidently took the view that maturity alone should not be enough to justify the provision of contraceptives to 'under-age' girls without parental knowledge or consent[4]. Lord Fraser was especially concerned that, in every case, the medical personnel should attempt to persuade the girl to allow parental involvement in the decision, although it has been suggested that failure to do so might be merely a breach of professional ethics rather than unlawful[5]. Taken as a whole, the majority opinion in *Gillick* did appear to recognise the potential value of parents' participation in adolescent decision-making but accorded *priority* to the views of a competent adolescent. On this interpretation, the decision could be viewed as supportive of a form of participatory or inclusive decision-making which involves parents, children and third parties (in the *Gillick* case, the medical profession). Further, it might be concluded that the final decision rests with neither parents nor children but with the third party with whom they are dealing and that they each have only consultative rights[6]. This might provide a way of reconciling the continuing responsibilities and discretions of parents, particularly to provide advice and guidance, with the gradual legal emancipation of children although later Court of Appeal decisions represent something of a retreat from *Gillick* in that they appear to support the right of outsiders to act on parental authority in the face of objection by the competent child[7].

PARENTS AND CHILDREN: BALANCING RIGHTS AND INTERESTS

A case can certainly be made for saying that both children and parents possess rights and that the task for any legal system is to achieve an equitable and proper balance between them. If the notion of 'rights' is not thought to be appropriate, it can at least be acknowledged that children and parents have separate or

---

1   It could be argued that the adolescent child has a right of recipience to this parental guidance and advice. See A Bainham 'Growing Up in Britain: Adolescence in the post-*Gillick* Era' (1992) *Juridical Review* 155.
2   See J Eekelaar 'The Eclipse of Parental Rights' (1986) 102 LQR 4.
3   [1986] 1 AC 112 at 186.
4   In all, he laid down five preconditions. See Chapter 8 below.
5   J Eekelaar (above).
6   A Bainham (above) at p 172 et seq.
7   See *Re R (A Minor) (Wardship: Consent to Treatment)* [1992] Fam 11, *Re W (A Minor) (Medical Treatment: Court's Jurisdiction)* [1993] Fam 64, and Chapter 8 below.

independent interests which ought to be recognised in law. At the heart of the jurisprudential debate is the issue of when the interests of children and parents can truly be regarded as distinct and when they ought to be conflated. This is a problem deeply embedded in the welfare principle itself. For if the welfare of children is paramount and the sole consideration, the separate interests of parents (if they exist at all) are not only subordinate, they are actually irrelevant. This apparent denial of an independent parental interest is open to question.

Alexander McCall Smith has produced an ingenious analysis which attempts to establish two independent categories of parental rights, namely 'child-centred parental rights' and 'parent-centred parental rights'[1]. McCall Smith's thesis is that certain powers which parents have are 'child-centred' in that their sole or principal purpose is to advance the welfare of their child. Other powers which parents have are 'parent-centred' since they are exercised predominantly for the benefit of the parent, although they may incidentally benefit the child. Into the first category McCall Smith would put parental restrictions on the hours when a child is allowed out of the home since these are intended to safeguard the child from harm[2]. Into the second category he would put the rights to determine the manner of the child's religious upbringing and secular education since these relate to the basic moral issue of the sort of child the parents wish to have. Thus, for McCall Smith, the parent-centred right is an area of control in which 'the parent has a wide range of discretion to pursue goals which society as a whole might find undesirable, but which it will tolerate'. He also includes within this, the right to the 'society' of the child, by which he is presumably referring to the former right of access (now contact). While he accepts that there is also a right of children to parental society, he sees this as a distinct and independent right. The key to identifying independent rights is, according to this argument, to focus on the beneficiary of the alleged right.

There is considerable force in what McCall Smith has to say. The right of access (now contact), although often regarded as a right of the child[3], is equally a crucial benefit to the parent concerned – evidenced by the mass of litigation which the issue has generated. Parents and children might therefore be regarded as having mutual rights to their mutual society. And it is in precisely this area that the courts, in recent years, have been edging cautiously away from the exclusivity of the welfare principle towards the recognition of independent parental rights or interests[4]. They have, to some extent, been obliged to do so since an open denial of their existence, especially vis-à-vis the State, would not conform with the UK's obligations under the European Convention on Human Rights[5].

Increasingly, it is likely that the trend will be to admit the co-existence of independent rights and interests for children and parents whilst emphasising the

1   A McCall Smith 'Is Anything Left of Parental Rights?' in E Sutherland and A McCall Smith
    (eds) *Family Rights: Family Law and Medical Advance* (Edinburgh University Press, 1990) at p 4.
2   In fact it could be argued that this is not a good example since the restrictions imposed by
    parents may reflect their own value judgments about such matters as the kind of company they
    wish their children to keep.
3   The change in emphasis from access as a parental right to access as a child's right is usually
    traced back to the view of Wrangham J in *M v M (Child: Access)* [1973] All ER 81.
4   See fn 1 at p 95 above.
5   As to which see *Re KD (A Minor) (Ward: Termination of Access)* [1988] AC 806, discussed by
    J Eekelaar 'The Wardship Jurisdiction, Children's Welfare and Parents Rights' (1991) 107 LQR
    368 at pp 387–388, and *Hokkanen v Finland* (1995) 19 EHRR 134.

primacy of the rights and interests of children[1]. This has led to the suggestion that the welfare principle should itself be reformulated as a principle 'giving *priority* to children's rights over those of parents (or others) in cases where they cannot be reconciled'[2]. In the final analysis this would probably represent a more realistic and theoretically accurate approach than that which attempts to subsume everything within the notion of parental responsibility and the welfare role of the courts.

This does rather make the assumption that children's interests *should* always be given precedence over adult interests and this is certainly open to question. An alternative approach might be to devise criteria for determining in specific instances whether the interests of children or parents (or other adults) should be preferred[3]. The conclusion would not be automatic that children's interests come first and others' second, or vice versa. Instead, there would be an exploration of which interest should be regarded as the more significant or serious. That interest might then be designated as the primary interest and given priority[4]. Matters can become yet further complicated when the wider family interest is thrown into the balance since children and parents are not merely individuals with independent interests but members of a family unit. It may be that the family as a whole has a collective interest which in some cases should outweigh the interests of its individual constituent members[5]. It is this position of the child in various family contexts which is the subject of Part II of the book.

---

1   But see *Re R (A Minor)* [1992] Fam 11 and *Re W* [1992] 3 WLR 758 discussed in Chapter 8 below which are rather against this trend.
2   J Eekelaar (above) at p 389.
3   See generally A Bainham 'Non-Intervention and Judicial Paternalism' in P Birks (ed) *The Frontiers of Liability*, Vol 1 (Oxford University Press, 1994), pp 161, 173–174.
4   Ibid.
5   Discussed further in A Bainham in ' "Honour Thy Father and Thy Mother": Children's Rights and Children's Duties' in G Douglas and L Sebba (eds) *Children's Rights and Traditional Values* (Dartmouth, 1998).

PART II
CHILDREN AND FAMILIES

The chapters in Part II are all concerned primarily with legal questions which relate to children's relationships with their families or carers. While a large number of children continue to experience childhood within the conventional family based on marriage, increasing numbers of children spend all or part of their childhood in households in which they are unrelated genetically to one or more of their carers. Many children also spend a substantial part of their childhood in single-parent households. Part II considers the legal issues surrounding the various kinds of family arrangements in which children may be raised.

Chapter 4 begins by looking at what might have been considered the 'typical' family centred on marriage and addresses the issues for children which arise on marriage breakdown and divorce. Chapter 5 examines the law's reaction to the growing phenomenon of children born to parents who are not married to each other. Chapter 6 looks at the different family arrangements in which children may live where one or both natural parents are, for whatever reason, not raising their children. The expression 'social family' is used as an umbrella term including within it guardians, step-parents, foster-parents and certain other familial arrangements. Adoption is not considered in this chapter since the subject is of sufficient importance to merit a separate chapter (Chapter 7). The remaining two chapters in Part II deal with two of the most significant spheres of parental responsibility which have, particularly in recent years, been fertile areas of dispute. Chapter 8 considers medical decision-making which has often been the site of the most difficult questions concerning the interrelationship of children's rights and parents' rights and responsibilities. Chapter 9 discusses the principles which govern the ownership and management of children's property and responsibility for their financial support. It is in relation to the latter that the child support legislation radically adjusted the balance between the State and the family.

Chapter 4
THE MARRIED FAMILY AND DIVORCE

INTRODUCTION

Married parents

Biological parenthood within marriage gives rise to an automatic legal status for both father and mother. Historically, the married father was the sole guardian of his children to the exclusion of the mother, and it was not until the Guardianship Act 1973 that the mother became automatically entitled to equal rights and authority over the children. The Children Act 1989 now provides that, where a child's father and mother were married to each other at the time of the child's birth, each has parental responsibility for the child[1]. Being married to each other at the time of the birth is given an extended meaning for these purposes in accordance with the Family Law Reform Act 1987[2]. The broad effect of that legislation is that certain children will be *regarded* as being born to married parents. These include some children of void marriages, legitimated and adopted children, and children who are treated as legitimate. The legal significance of being born to parents who are not married to each other is explored later.

Proof of parentage

Proof of parentage within marriage is usually established by the fact of birth and by applying legal presumptions. Maternity is invariably established by the fact of parturition[3], although it has already been noted that the definition of biological motherhood may have to be re-evaluated in certain cases of assisted reproduction[4]. The determination of paternity within marriage is usually just a matter of applying the legal presumption that any child born to the wife is the child of her husband[5]. But this may be rebutted under s 26 of the Family Law Reform Act 1969 by evidence which establishes, on the balance of probabilities, that the husband is not the father. The test is less exacting than the former common law requirement that the matter be established beyond reasonable doubt. The courts have wavered in their attitudes to the amount of evidence required to rebut the presumption[6], but the availability of the DNA technique now means that paternity may be established virtually conclusively, thus overcoming the limitations of conventional blood tests. It is now provided that 'scientific tests' are to be made available to determine parentage[7]. The reality is that, where the husband does not deny

---

1 Section 2(1).
2 Section 2(3), incorporating, by reference, s 1 of the Family Law Reform Act 1987.
3 *The Ampthill Peerage* [1977] AC 547.
4 See Chapter 3 above.
5 Encapsulated in the maxim *Pater est quem nuptiae demonstrant.*
6 *S v S; W v Official Solicitor* [1972] AC 24. Cf *Serio v Serio* (1983) FLR 756 and *W v K (Proof of Paternity)* [1988] 1 FLR 86.
7 Family Law Reform Act 1987, s 23(1), amending the Family Law Reform Act 1969, s 20(1) and (2).

paternity, and no other man asserts that *he* is the father, the husband will be treated in law as the father whatever may be the true biological position. Whether this is consistent with the increasingly recognised right of the child to knowledge of his or her biological origins is a matter to which we return in Chapter 5.

What happens where a married woman, while pregnant, divorces? At common law, it appears that the courts will continue to apply the *pater est* presumption, provided that the child is born within the normal period of gestation. They have also done so where the mother has remarried before the birth of the child[1]. In this situation, there may be a *clash* of presumptions. The child would be presumed the child of the first husband (H1), but birth after the second marriage would also trigger a presumption of paternity of the second husband (H2). It seems likely that if the mother and H2 jointly register the birth with H2 named as the father, and if H1 does not dispute this, then the presumption arising from registration of the birth will prevail. If H1 should dispute the paternity of H2, the matter would nowadays be likely to be settled by a direction for DNA or blood testing[2].

Parental responsibility

The general philosophy has been observed that the primary responsibility for raising children rests with parents. And, despite the apparent neutrality of the welfare principle as between the competing claims of parents and non-parents, the courts have, from time to time, appeared to attach a premium to the natural blood tie[3]. The assumption is often made that the responsibility of parenthood is a natural phenomenon and that the very fact of biological parenthood gives rise to moral obligations which are then translated into legal obligations. Whilst it is evident that most legal systems do place automatic legal obligations on parents to care for their children, the pre-existing moral basis for such obligations is elusive.

Eekelaar has convincingly demonstrated that contractarian theories of moral obligation (which rely heavily on the principle that the participants in a social contact are motivated at least in part by self-interest) cannot adequately account for parental obligations to children[4]. Eekelaar found the true basis for these moral obligations to children in the non-contractarian theory of human flourishing propounded by John Finnis[5]. According to this, there are moral obligations on *everyone* to respect the well-being of others, including children. This background moral duty may, according to Eekelaar, give rise to *special* obligations by reason of the social roles in which certain individuals are cast. Thus, the duty to care for children arises from the 'conjunction' of the general duty to promote human

1   *Re Overbury (deceased)* [1954] Ch 122. It should be noted, however, that this remarkable case arose from a birth which took place in 1869 and which occurred some eight months after the death of H1 and just two months after the mother's second marriage to H2. The case for allowing the first presumption to apply in such circumstances was a strong one especially in the social conditions which prevailed in the mid-nineteenth century. Whether the preference for the first presumption would be appropriate in the very changed social circumstances of the late twentieth century and in the context of divorce is questionable.

2   See Chapter 5.

3   For a modern example see, particularly, the views of Fox LJ and Waite J in *Re K (A Minor) (Ward: Care and Control)* [1990] 1 WLR 431.

4   J Eekelaar 'Are Parents Morally Obliged to Care for Their Children?' (1991) 11 *Oxford Journal of Legal Studies* 340. The most well-known of modern contractarian theories is J Rawls *A Theory of Justice* (Harvard University Press, 1972).

5   J Finnis *Natural Law and Natural Rights* (1980) discussed by Eekelaar (above) at pp 348–349.

flourishing and the independent moral duty to comply with the social practice of particular societies – in this case the social practice that a *particular* responsibility for children should be placed on biological parents[1].

Responsibility is automatic

This automatic imposition of responsibility, which carries considerable powers of control over children, is not accompanied by any attempt to discover in the first instance whether individual parents are able and/or willing to perform the task. Whilst it is generally accepted that raising a child is no easy matter, there is no regulatory system for biological parents such as applies to adoption and, to a lesser extent, certain other substitute care arrangements[2]. The State assumes that the natural family will properly discharge the obligation of child-rearing unless and until there is clear evidence to the contrary. It is therefore tempting to agree with the sentiments expressed by a Washington court that 'fortunately for the preservation of the human species . . . a lot of people who would rate poorly on any scale of parental prospects have done rather well at it when confronted by the reality of a baby, in a crib, in the home . . .'[3]. It has, nonetheless, been suggested that a system of licensing for parents would at least be feasible, using a variety of predictive screening techniques, the purpose of which would be to pre-empt the worst cases of child abuse or neglect by identifying in advance 'very bad' parents[4]. It has even been argued that it might be possible to formulate a concept of 'responsible parenthood' which might generate an obligation not to have children or not to continue a pregnancy in certain circumstances[5]. Whilst no such approach exists in England, or would be likely to command much support, it has been the case for some years that legal powers have been utilised to remove certain babies from their parents at birth[6]. But such cases are exceptional and do not detract from the central principle that the status of parenthood gives rise to a legal right and duty to care for the child.

Parenthood is for life

It is important to appreciate that parenthood is a legal status. As such, *all* the incidents of parental responsibility devolve automatically on the married parent. It has been said that parenthood is a package deal[7]. It is not open to a parent to pick and choose between the various responsibilities attaching to his status. Parenthood is, in this respect, like marriage itself, the condition of belonging to a class of persons in relation to whom the law assigns particular rights and

---

1 Eekelaar (above), at p 351.
2 See Chapters 6, 7 and 10 below.
3 In *Re Welfare of May* 14 Wash App 765 (1976) at pp 768–769, 545 P.2d 25 (1976).
4 H La Follette 'Licensing Parents' (1980) 9 *Philosophy and Public Affairs* 182 and C Pap Mangel 'Licensing Parents: How Feasible?' (1988) 22 Fam LQ 17. Cf Sandmire and Wald 'Licensing Parents – A Response to Claudia Mangel's proposal' (1990) 24 Fam LQ 53.
5 M Freeman 'Do Children Have the Right not to be Born?' in *The Moral Status of Children* (Martinus Nijhoff, 1997), ch 9.
6 As to which, see MDA Freeman 'Removing Babies at Birth: A Questionable Practice' (1980) Fam Law 131 and, generally, Chapter 11 below.
7 A McCall Smith 'Is Anything Left of Parental Rights?' in Sutherland and McCall Smith (eds) *Family Rights* (Edinburgh University Press, 1990) 4 at p 7.

obligations[1]. This status is not lost except through the ultimate step of adoption (or a 'parental order' under s 30 of the HFEA 1990) – a position neatly encapsulated in the catchphrase 'parenthood is for life'.

Parental responsibility cannot be transferred

An aspect of the lifelong nature of parenthood is that the legal status of parenthood and the parental responsibility which goes with it is 'non-transferable'. While parents may delegate the exercise of parental responsibility, they may not surrender or transfer it[2]. Thus, they may arrange for someone to take temporary care of their children, or meet some aspect of parental responsibility, but this does not result in the temporary carer acquiring parental responsibility or in the parent losing it. Such an arrangement may be made with someone who already has parental responsibility as well as with someone who does not[3]. The former situation could cover married parents who might agree that one of them should take all the decisions on some aspect of upbringing, for example, education. It might be particularly appropriate to come to some definite arrangement where, for example, one parent is frequently absent from the home, perhaps for employment reasons. Where the delegate is a person without parental responsibility, that person will have the legal power (and arguably the duty) to 'do what is reasonable in all the circumstances of the case for the purpose of safeguarding or promoting the child's welfare'[4]. Yet even in these temporary arrangements the parent retains parental responsibility and may be held liable for 'any failure to meet any part of his parental responsibility for the child concerned'[5]. The natural parent could thus be civilly or criminally liable for any harm caused to the child arising from his failure to ensure satisfactory care.

SHARING PARENTAL RESPONSIBILITY IN MARRIAGE

Potential for sharing

Since both married parents have parental responsibility, they must share it. The Children Act 1989 confirms that parental responsibility may be held contemporaneously by more than one person[6]. Whilst this is self-evident in the case of married parents, it should be remembered that responsibility may also be shared between parents and non-parents, such as foster-parents or guardians. Indeed, it may be shared in a triangular relationship as where a mother and step-father obtain a joint residence order but the divorced father retains his own parental responsibility. Since parental responsibility is not lost because someone else acquires it[7], the potential for a multiplication of sharing arrangements is

---

1   See Sir C Allen 'Status and Capacity' (1930) 46 LQR 277, especially at p 288.
2   Section 2(9). This was also the case at common law. See *Vansittart v Vansittart* (1858) 2 De G&J 249. The unmarried mother may, however, agree to share parental responsibility with the father, and clause 85 of the draft Adoption Bill 1996 would also amend s 4 of the Children Act 1989 to allow a natural parent to share parental responsibility by agreement with a step-parent.
3   Section 2(9) and (10).
4   Section 3(5).
5   Section 2(11).
6   Section 2(5).
7   Section 2(6).

considerable. The precise legal effect of sharing parental responsibility is, therefore, a matter of some theoretical and practical importance. In particular, the regime which applies during marriage will be carried over into the post-divorce situation unless it is specifically altered by a court order.

What is involved in sharing?

In simple terms, the statutory scheme provides for *joint* and *several* parental responsibility. While both parents have equal powers and responsibilities, they may act independently as well as jointly in exercising them, and they are not obliged to consult each other before doing so. No doubt in a functioning marriage, all serious issues affecting the children will be discussed and real attempts will be made to reach agreement. This is not a legal requirement, but whether there is a legal right of consultation where parents separate or divorce is not wholly clear. This issue is discussed below.

The Children Act provides that where parental responsibility is shared between two or more people 'each of them may act alone and without the other (or others) in meeting that responsibility'[1]. There are just two limitations on this right of independent action. The first is where statute requires the consent of more than one person[2]. The second is that parental responsibility may never be exercised in a way which is incompatible with a court order[3]. The best example of the first limitation is adoption and the procedure of freeing for adoption, both of which require the consent of all parents or guardians[4]. The consent of others with parental responsibility[5] and local authorities who have a care order[6] is not required. Statute also imposes certain automatic restraints on changing a child's surname unilaterally or taking him out of the country. In both of these instances, the consent of all those with parental responsibility is normally required, unless the court orders otherwise[7].

Both of these restraints on independent action continue to cause difficulty in the modern law. So far as changing the child's surname is concerned there has long been an *automatic* restraint on unilateral action arising from the concept of the residual rights of the natural guardian. While the courts have vacillated to some extent in their views of the importance of children's names, they have been consistent in upholding the prohibition[8]. Recently, they have done so in a case in which three older children were all in favour of the change[9]. There was apparently some doubt following the Children Act about whether the automatic prohibition continued to apply otherwise than in the context specifically envisaged by the

---

1   Section 2(7).
2   Ibid.
3   Section 2(8).
4   Adoption Act 1976, s 16(1)(b). This is subject to the court's power to dispense with consent on specified grounds. See Chapter 7 below.
5   Section 12(3).
6   Section 33(6).
7   Section 13; Child Abduction Act 1984, s 1, discussed in Chapter 17 below.
8   The leading authority before the Children Act was *W v A (Child: Surname)* [1981] Fam 114.
9   *Re B (Change of Surname)* [1996] 1 FLR 791. Cf *Re C (Change of Surname)* [1998] 1 FLR 549 where the children were younger (aged 7 and 8) and where the 'non-residential' mother failed to prevent an order that the 'residential' father be allowed to give his surname to the children along with the other members of his household.

legislation, namely where a residence order has been made[1]. The suggestion was bizarre since, if correct, it would have meant that the mother without a residence order in her favour would have been in a stronger legal position in this respect than the mother who had one! The argument was rightly scotched by Holman J in *Re PC (Change of Surname)*[2], who held that where two or more persons have parental responsibility for a child, one of them may lawfully effect a change of surname only if everyone with parental responsibility consents. Thus, where the parents are unmarried it is only the mother who holds parental responsibility (unless the father has taken steps to acquire it) and she alone is entitled to choose or change the name of the child[3]. *Re PC* (above) also illustrates that where there has been an unlawful change of name it does not necessarily follow that a reversion to the previous name will be in the children's best interests. The result in this case, applying the welfare principle, was to preserve the status quo. Orders were made allowing the children to continue to be known by their new name but prohibiting the mother from taking steps to 'cause, encourage or permit any person or body to use the new surname without the prior consent of the father or the court'.

The question of leave to take the children out of the jurisdiction has been the subject of a great deal of litigation both before and after the Children Act. We return to this issue in the context of the law governing child abduction[4].

The right of independent action represents something of a change from the position before the Children Act. Under the old law it was provided that parents might exercise parental rights alone but this was thought to be qualified by a separate provision which restricted unilateral action where another joint holder of parental rights had signified prior disapproval of the proposed action[5]. There was some doubt whether this encompassed the situation of married parents or was confined to non-parental holders of parental rights. What is clear is that there was never any statutory duty of consultation between parents. The Law Commission was concerned with the practicalities of daily living and thought it would be unworkable to require parents to consult with each other[6]. There is evidently force in this argument with respect to the myriad of trivial actions parents perform on a daily basis, but its wisdom may be doubted where major or irreversible decisions are concerned. It is also questionable whether the scheme can work where parental responsibility is shared by two or more persons who do not live in the same household[7].

Disputes over children during marriage

It is unlikely that serious disagreements over children between married partners will as such lead to litigation. The former provision in the Guardianship Act 1973,

---

1   Section 13(1)(a).
2   [1997] 2 FLR 730. But for a very different perspective, see J Eekelaar 'Do Parents Have a Duty to Consult?' (1998) 114 LQR 337. See also A Bond 'Reconstructing families – changing children's surnames' [1998] CFLQ 17 and M Ogle 'What's in a Name?' [1998] Fam Law 80.
3   *Dawson v Wearmouth* [1997] 2 FLR 629.
4   See Chapter 17.
5   Guardianship Act 1973, s 1(1); and the Children Act 1975, s 85(3).
6   Law Com Report No 172 *Guardianship and Custody* (1988) at para 2.10.
7   Such as, for example, a surviving parent and an appointed guardian, a natural parent and a foster-parent or two divorced parents.

which enabled a parent to bring such disagreements before the courts, was seldom, if ever, utilised[1]. The reason is obvious. Where disputes over children reach the point of litigation, it is a virtual certainty that the parents will be seeking divorce or some other more limited matrimonial relief, or a more comprehensive order relating to the care of the children[2]. This remains the case under the Children Act. Most s 8 orders are likely to be made in the context of divorce, but it should be noted that the court has jurisdiction to regulate any aspect of a child's upbringing during the marriage. It could do so, for example, on a freestanding application for such an order, where one of the spouses is seeking financial relief under the Domestic Proceedings and Magistrates' Courts Act 1978 or in wardship proceedings, all of which are 'family proceedings'[3].

The position of third parties

The effect of independent exercises of parental responsibility on third parties is an important practical matter. Since a single holder of parental responsibility may act alone, it follows that an outside entity such as a school, hospital or church may safely deal with him or her alone without risking any legal liability. It would seem that this applies even where the third party is aware of a disagreement between those with parental responsibility, although the prudence of going ahead with a course of action in these circumstances is questionable[4]. But, in principle, the third party is free to choose between two equally valid yet discordant views and is, indeed, *obliged* to choose between them even if this involves inactivity. An added complication in the case of an older child is that the child may be '*Gillick*-competent' so that a third party could lawfully choose to comply with the wishes of a competent child rather than those of one or both parents[5].

Preventative court orders

In theory, at least, no *legal* (as opposed to practical) advantage is derived from having the physical care of the child. The so-called 'absent' parent has just as much authority and responsibility as the one with day-to-day care, but will inevitably have less opportunity of exercising it. This may well be an area in which theory and practice diverge[6]. Where one parent wishes to assert superior control over any particular area of a child's upbringing, it will be necessary for that parent to seek a court order. The other parent will then be precluded from exercising

---

1   Section 1(3).
2   Under the old law, this might have been under the Matrimonial Causes Act 1973, the Domestic Proceedings and Magistrates' Courts Act 1978 or the Guardianship of Minors Act 1971.
3   'Family proceedings' are defined in s 8(3) and (4) of the Children Act, discussed in Chapter 2 above.
4   Technically, for example, a doctor would be acting lawfully in performing an abortion on a minor which was supported by one parent but opposed by the other; but the more sensible course in this situation would be to seek the authority of the court. For further discussion, see J Herring 'Children's Abortion Rights' (1997) 5 *Medical Law Review* 257.
5   Although this proposition is more doubtful following the Court of Appeal decisions in *Re R (A Minor) (Wardship: Consent to Treatment)* [1992] 1 FLR 190 and *Re W (A Minor) (Medical Treatment: Court's Jurisdiction)* [1993] Fam 64, discussed in Chapter 8 below.
6   Especially, perhaps, in the context of divorce.

responsibility inconsistently with the order, although this may lead to some awkward questions of interpretation[1].

DIVORCE AND CHILDREN

The problem

The United Kingdom is the divorce capital of Europe with, as noted in Chapter 1, something of the order of 150,000 divorces plus per annum. These figures are bound to give rise to concern about the interests of the very large numbers of children involved and the possible adverse effects on them. It is frequently said, particularly in the media, that divorce has a harmful effect on children. Is this true and, if so, what (if anything) can the legal system do about it?

There is now clear evidence from a large number of research projects that there are negative associations between parental separation or divorce and the development of children and young adults[2]. No summary can do justice to this extensive body of research, but Martin Richards has described these associations as follows:

> 'Compared with those of similar social backgrounds whose parents remain married, children whose parents divorce show consistent, but small differences in their behaviour throughout childhood and adolescence and somewhat different life courses as they move into adulthood. More specifically, the research indicates on average lower levels of academic achievement and self-esteem and a higher incidence of conduct and other problems of psychological adjustment during childhood. Also during childhood a somewhat earlier social maturity has been recorded. A number of transitions to adulthood are typically reached at earlier ages; these include leaving home, beginning heterosexual relationships and entering cohabitation, marriage and child bearing. In young adulthood there is a tendency toward more changes of job, lower socio economic status, a greater propensity to divorce and there are some indications of a higher frequency of depression and lower measures of psychological well-being. The relationships (in adulthood) with parents and other kin relationships may be more distant.'[3]

This all sounds rather drastic and might be thought to justify the popular catchphrase 'divorce is bad for children'. It is clear, however, that these findings must be treated with very great caution and are subject to significant qualifications.

The first and most important point is that there has frequently been a tendency on the part of the public, the media and, it must be said, the former Conservative

---

1   Thus, it will be important for the court to spell out these matters with particularity by attaching conditions to its orders or giving directions as to how they are to be carried into effect. The statutory scheme is quite flexible enough for this to be done. See s 11(7).

2   The published research is extensive and includes PR Amato and B Keith 'Parental divorce and adult well being: a meta-analysis' (1991) 53 *Journal of Marriage and the Family* 26; PR Amato and B Keith 'Parental divorce and the well being of children: a meta-analysis' (1991) 110 *Psychological Bulletin* 16; PR Amato 'Children's adjustment to divorce: theories, hypotheses and empirical support' (1993) 55 *Journal of Marriage and the Family* 23; KE Kiernan 'The impact of family disruption in childhood on transition in young adulthood' 46 *Population Studies* 213; and BJ Elliott and MPM Richards 'Children and Divorce: educational performance and behaviour, before and after parental separation' (1991) 5 IJLF 258. For an accessible and brief review of some of the research in the context of the changes to English divorce law, see C Piper ' "Looking to the Future" for Children' (1994) 6 JCL 98.

3   M Richards 'The Interests of Children at Divorce' in M-T Meulders-Klein (ed) *Familles et Justice* (Bruylant, Bruxelles, 1997) at p 543.

Government to make the rather naïve assumption that *association* is to be equated with *cause*. It does not follow in the least that because an *association* can be established between the fact of divorce or parental separation and certain developmental disadvantages for children and young people, that the divorce or separation was actually the *cause* of those disadvantages. As Richards puts it:

'... while it is relatively easy to establish associations, it is a great deal more difficult to unravel the processes that may produce them ... Simple cause and effect models of divorce are not very helpful.'[1]

Other factors which may have a bearing on outcomes for children are economic factors, 'welfare provision, housing policies, availability of child care, minimum wage legislation, as well as attitudes to divorce and marriage'.[2]

The second qualification is that there is a great deal of variation in outcomes for individual children and between children of different social class or gender. The research findings are based on *averages* between groups of children whose parents stay together and those whose parents divorce. But this disguises the fact that 'some children whose parents divorce will do very well at school with excellent psychological well-being while others whose parents remain together will have unhappy or traumatic childhoods and do poorly at school'[3]. Allied to this is the third qualification that, in a sense, to compare the position of children whose parents divorce with those whose parents stay together is almost bound to be a flawed operation from a policy perspective since it is making the wrong comparison. What policy-makers might wish to know is whether there is evidence to show that the children of *unhappy* marriages do better if the parents stay together rather than separate, but the research does not, and probably cannot, isolate happy from unhappy marriages in the samples of parents who stay together. In other words, there is a qualitative element which is missing and which would be difficult, if not impossible, to pin down. What *is* beginning to be realised is that 'some (but not all) of the attributes in children which have been associated with divorce can be seen *before* a couple separate', but 'pre-divorce effects cannot account for all the differences which have been described after divorce'[4]. This again suggests that there should be greater emphasis placed on the *quality* of relationships between parents and children both pre- and post-separation.

A key aim of policy ought therefore to be to encourage and preserve a better *quality* of relationships between parents and children rather than to preserve marriages at all cost. We consider below what the Family Law Act 1996 has to say about this. At this stage, it is sufficient to note that, in the light of available research, two policy conclusions do seem to have been drawn. The first is that parental *conflict* is bad for children, and the legal system should do what it can to minimise this. The second is that children are likely to do better if they can preserve a good ongoing relationship with *both* parents following divorce[5]. The first of these is relatively uncontroversial but the second represents a considerable shift in thinking over the last couple of decades and continues to provoke some

1   Richards (above) at p 545.
2   Ibid at p 544.
3   Ibid.
4   Ibid at p 545, and Elliott and Richards 'Children and Divorce: educational performance and behaviour, before and after parental separation' (above).
5   The most influential research was probably JS Wallerstein and JB Kelly *Surviving the Breakup* (Grant McIntyre, 1980) and JS Wallerstein and S Blakeslee *Second Chances* (Bantam, 1989).

disagreement. For some years, the dominant philosophy favoured sole custodial arrangements and a central role for the so-called 'psychological parent'[1]. This was, in part, reflected in England and Wales by the overwhelming number of sole custody orders in favour of mothers and an apparent preference for maternal care and control even where 'joint custody' orders were made[2].

This view was, in the 1980s and 1990s, largely supplanted by empirical evidence suggesting that the childen who suffer least from the breakdown of parental relationships tend to be those who are able to maintain good ongoing relationships with *both* parents. Conversely, those who suffer most are those whose parents carry on the conflict which was apparent during the marriage and at divorce[3]. This thinking originally manifested itself in the growth of 'joint custody' especially in the United States, but also in England[4]. It undoubtedly also influenced the principles established by the Children Act, although the concept of 'custody' itself was abandoned in favour of the new idea of minimal interference with the joint parental responsibility which exists during marriage.

The legal background

Chapter One considered the origins of the post-war principle that divorce is an occasion for some form of public scrutiny of the interests of children. We saw that the former 'children's appointments' system was ultimately discredited as a perfunctory process. We must now turn to the changes brought about by the Children Act 1989 and the further adjustments which will be made when the Family Law Act 1996 is implemented.

The effect of the Children Act 1989

The no order principle

The essential regime of the Children Act, as has been seen, is that the responsibility of parents should not be unnecessarily disturbed and that orders should not be made unless they can positively achieve something for the child. This applies both during the marriage and on divorce. The technical distinctions between orders under the old law were swept away by the Children Act. The new law applies in all 'family proceedings', including divorce[5]. Thus, in a large number of cases, no order relating to children will be made on divorce, and the effect of this will be to preserve joint and several parental responsibility. It is *joint* in the sense that both parents retain it equally, and *several* in that it may be exercised independently and arguably without consultation.

---

1   J Goldstein, A Freud and AJ Solnit *Beyond the Best Interests of the Child* (The Free Press, New York, 1980) was the classic exposition of this view.
2   Research conducted for the Law Commission, based on the statistical returns of 174 divorce registries, found, for example, that in 1985 sole custody orders were made in 86% of cases, 77.4% being in favour of the mother and 9.2% in favour of the father. See JF Priest and JC Whybrow *Custody Law in Practice in the Divorce and Domestic Courts*, Supplement to Law Com Working Paper No 96 (1986) at para 4.21.
3   See fn 5 at p 115 above.
4   JA Priest and JC Whybrow (above), at paras 5.2–5.6, found that joint custody orders were made in 12.9% of cases in 1985 but there were marked regional variations.
5   Defined in s 8(3) and (4). For an academic analysis of the no order principle, see R Ingleby *The Presumption of No Order* (Faculty of Law, University of Manchester, 1993).

The requirement to act if necessary

Under the Children Act, the court was no longer required to declare itself satisfied with the arrangements proposed for the children. It was given the more limited duty of considering whether it should exercise any of its powers in relation to any child of the family[1]. This was analogous to the duty placed on the magistrates' court under the old law[2]. Parents were, however, required to file a more detailed statement of arrangements in the hope that this would alert the court to problem cases and facilitate reference to mediation services[3]. The court retained the power to direct that the decree of divorce or nullity should not be made absolute, or a decree of judicial separation not granted, in restricted circumstances, but such cases were rare[4]. The former rule that a decree absolute which was made without the necessary declaration was void was abolished along with the declaration requirement itself. Where the court was concerned about the proposed arrangements it might order a welfare report and, in disputed cases, would need to consider making one or more s 8 orders. But there was thought to be no reason why the decree itself should be delayed where the court made appropriate directions regarding the resolution of the children issues[5]. There was, thus, no requirement of judicial approval or, indeed, scrutiny in any real sense of the existing and proposed arrangements.

The impact of the Family Law Act 1996

The Family Law Act 1996 largely adopts the procedures of the Children Act for the investigation of children's interests at divorce. In theory, an attempt has been made to give more weight to these interests and there is no doubt that the former Conservative Government took the position that divorce, an evil to be avoided if

---

1 Schedule 12, para 31, amending s 41 of the Matrimonial Causes Act 1973. By s 105, 'child of the family' means in relation to the parties to a marriage:
  '(a) a child of both of those parties; and
  (b) any other child, not being a child who is placed with those parties as foster parents by a local authority or voluntary organisation, who has been treated by both of those parties as a child of their family.'
The Family Law Act 1996, s 24 retains the meaning of 'child of the family' as used in the 1973 Act. The most important category of children (who are not the children of both parties) to be included in the expression are step-children. Other children, however, may also be regarded as children of the family, for example the grandchild in *Re A (Child of the Family)* [1998] 1 FLR 347. See further Chapter 6.
2 Domestic Proceedings and Magistrates' Courts Act 1978, s 8(1), now amended by the Children Act 1989, Sch 13, para 36.
3 Law Com No 172 *Guardianship and Custody* (1988) at para 3.10, and *The Children Act 1989 Guidance and Regulations Vol 1 Court Orders* (HMSO, 1991) at paras 2.54 et seq.
4 Schedule 12, para 31(2), amending s 41(2) of the Matrimonial Causes Act 1973, provides:
  'Where ... it appears to the court that –
  (a) the circumstances of the case require it, or are likely to require it, to exercise any of its powers under the Act ... with respect to any such child;
  (b) it is not in a position to exercise that power (or as the case may be) those powers without giving further consideration to the case; and
  (c) there are exceptional circumstances which make it desirable in the interests of the child that the court should give a direction under this section,
  it may direct that the decree of divorce or nullity is not to be made absolute, or that the decree of judicial separation is not to be granted, until the court orders otherwise.'
5 The court has a duty to set a timetable in this respect under s 11.

possible, was even more of an evil where the children were concerned. Thus, in the Foreword to the Government's consultation paper on Mediation and the Ground for Divorce[1], the former Lord Chancellor, Lord Mackay, said:

'... Almost inevitably the breakdown of a marriage is hard for one or both of the parties and especially for the children. I believe that a good divorce law will support the institution of marriage ... it should seek to eliminate unnecessary distress for the parties and particularly for the children in those cases where a marriage has broken down irretrievably ...'

It is important to appreciate that the legislation, like all legislation, is the product of different influences both before and during the Parliamentary process. Yet the Family Law Act 1996 is more overtly ideological than most statutes, setting out in s 1 a list of *general principles* behind which, as Freeman has pointed out, lie values[2]. It is not possible to gain a proper appreciation of the specific provisions which relate to children without a realisation that some of these have, controversially, been grounded in the notion that divorce is per se bad. Freeman has rightly described the legislation as 'anti-divorce' and there is no question that one way in which it is seeking, rightly or wrongly, to protect the interests of children is by attempting to *prevent* the divorce itself from happening. And even where it is clear under the new procedures that one or both parties intend to go ahead with divorce, the Act still attempts to make this more difficult to achieve where there are minor children by extending by six months the period of time which must elapse before a divorce order can be made. How well this sits with the other central feature of the new divorce law – the abandonment of fault and the matrimonial offences of adultery, desertion and 'unreasonable behaviour' – is open to doubt. There is indeed a curious ambivalence about a law which in substance makes divorce available as of right and without proof of grounds but, at the same time, procedurally makes divorce more difficult to obtain[3].

The 'general principles' in s 1 referred to above do, however, to a limited extent and for the first time in English legislation, articulate an official view of what is good or bad for children in the context of divorce and they are reinforced later in s 11 of the Act. This section substantially re-enacts the procedures of the Children Act, with modifications, and it is not clear whether it will bring about any real change of substance. The final feature to note about the legislation is its emphasis on *mediation* (previously usually referred to as 'conciliation' in children cases) and this raises questions about the implications for children and their part (if any) in the mediation process. We now consider briefly the general principles, the new process for obtaining a divorce, the court's role where there are children and, finally, the question of children and mediation.

The general principles

These are set out in s 1 of the Act and must be applied by 'the Court and any person, in exercising functions under or in consequence of Parts II and III' which

---

1   Lord Chancellor's Department *Looking to the Future: Mediation and the Ground for Divorce* (1993, Cm 2424).

2   See the annotations to s 1 in M Freeman *The Family Law Act 1996* (Sweet & Maxwell, 1996), in which he identifies these values as 'pro-marriage, pro-children and anti-violence'.

3   For critiques, see M Freeman 'England: family justice and family values in 1995' in A Bainham (ed) *The International Survey of Family Law 1995* (Martinus Nijhoff, 1997), and G Douglas 'England and Wales: "family values" to the fore?' in *The International Survey of Family Law 1996* (Martinus Nijhoff, 1998).

are the parts of the Act dealing with divorce and mediation. We set out below the principles as they stand but with emphasis added to highlight those which directly refer to children. We then return to these principles in the final section of the chapter which considers some of the policy issues for the future.

The principles are:

'(a)   that the institution of marriage is to be supported;

(b)   that the parties to a marriage which may have broken down are to be encouraged to take all practicable steps, whether by marriage counselling or otherwise, to save the marriage;

(c)   that a marriage which has irretrievably broken down and is being brought to an end should be brought to an end –

(i)   *with minimum distress* to the parties and *to the children affected;*

(ii)   *with questions dealt with in a manner designed to promote as good a continuing relationship between the parties and any children affected as is possible in the circumstances;* and

(iii)   without costs being unreasonably incurred in connection with the procedures to be followed in bringing the marriage to an end; and

(d)   *that any risk to one of the parties to a marriage, and to any children, of violence from the other party should, so far as reasonably practicable, be removed or diminished.'*

The basis for divorce

This is a book about children and the intricacies of the new divorce law are beyond the scope of the present discussion[1]. It is, however, necessary to sketch the main features of the process for a basic understanding of the framework within which the divorce court's powers over children operate[2].

There are essentially five stages, although it should be borne in mind that there are a number of opportunities for the process to be halted or extended. Stage 1 is the so-called 'information meeting'[3]. Before the actual process of divorce can be commenced at all, it is now a statutory requirement that the spouse or spouses intending to initiate the process should have attended an information meeting not less than three months before doing so. These meetings are designed to provide information on a range of matters, some of which relate directly to children. Thus, it is provided that regulations made under the Act must, in particular, 'make provision with respect to the giving of information about . . . the importance to be attached to the welfare, wishes and feelings of children' and 'how the parties may acquire a better understanding of the ways in which children can be helped to cope with the breakdown of a marriage'.

Stage 2 involves the filing in court of a 'statement of marital breakdown'[4] in prescribed form. This constitutes the commencement of proceedings and will ultimately be the basis upon which a divorce order is granted. The statement, which may not be made before the first anniversary of the date of the marriage, is a neutral declaration of belief by one or both parties that the marriage has broken down, that he or she is aware of the purpose of the new statutory period for

---

1   For detailed treatment, see R Bird and S Cretney *Divorce: The New Law* (Family Law, 1996). For a succinct and readable account, see SM Cretney *Family Law* (3rd edn) (Sweet & Maxwell, 1997) ch 3.

2   For the best account of the main features of the new divorce process in the context of the historical reform of English divorce law, see SM Cretney 'Divorce Reform in England: Humbug and Hypocrisy or a Smooth Transition?' in M Freeman (ed) *Divorce Where Next?* (Dartmouth, 1996).

3   Family Law Act 1996, s 8.

4   Ibid, s 6.

'reflection and consideration', and that he or she wishes to make arrangements for the future.

Stage 3 is the passage of the 'period for reflection and consideration'[1]. The prescribed period must elapse before a divorce order can be made, but the precise length of this period will depend on a number of factors[2]. It will usually be nine months beginning with the fourteenth day after the statement of marital breakdown has been received by the court[3]. This will, however, be extended by a period of six months 'where there is a child of the family who is under the age of sixteen when the application is made'[4]. So, leaving aside the complications which can arise where one or both of the parties seek to halt the process, the earliest period of time within which a divorce involving minor children may be obtained will normally be over 18 months from the date of attendance at the initial information meeting. This is about one year longer than the time it took under the old divorce law to obtain a fault-based 'quickie' divorce where the median time was about six months from presentation of the petition – hence the claim that the Family Law Act makes divorce more difficult for the majority of people since the majority of divorcing couples (about three-quarters) relied on the fault-based facts under the old law. This is especially the case where there are minor children, although this must be qualified in two respects. First, the six-month extension will not apply if, at the time when the application for the divorce order is made, 'there is an occupation order or a non-molestation order in force in favour of the applicant, or of a child of the family, made against the other party or . . . the court is satisfied that delaying the making of a divorce order would be significantly detrimental to the welfare of any child of the family'. Secondly, it is now a precondition of obtaining a divorce order that the parties have settled their arrangements for the future. Therefore, issues which have traditionally been resolved after the granting of a divorce decree will now to a large extent have to be settled before the making of the divorce order. Hence, the overall length of the divorce process, conceived more broadly, may not be increased by quite as much as might appear at first sight.

Stage 4 is indeed concerned with *arrangements for the future*[5]. The intention in the legislation is that the period for reflection and consideration should be used constructively, if not to attempt to effect a reconciliation, 'to consider what arrangements should be made for the future'[6]. Before a divorce (or separation) order may be made, the requirements of the Act about such arrangements must be satisfied[7]. Some of these relate to financial arrangements. So far as children are concerned, the requirements of the legislation are set out in s 11, which we consider below.

Stage 5 involves the application for the divorce order[8]. The court, subject to limited cases of hardship, *must* grant the divorce order on the application of either

1 Family Law Act 1996, s 7.
2 As, for example, where the parties jointly give notice to the court that they are attempting a reconciliation but require additional time (ibid, s 7(7), (8)).
3 Ibid, s 7(3).
4 Ibid, s 7(11).
5 Ibid, s 9.
6 Ibid, s 7(1).
7 Ibid, s 3(1).
8 Ibid.

party if all the above requirements are satisfied and a declaration is made by that party that he or she believes that the marriage cannot be saved. From this declaration and the satisfaction of the other statutory requirements, the court is entitled to assume that the marriage has irretrievably broken down and is not required to look for proof of any 'ground' as such. The Act preserves, with modifications, the court's existing power to refuse a divorce in cases of hardship. An order can be made preventing divorce where the court is satisfied 'that dissolution of the marriage would result in substantial financial or other hardship to the other party or to a child of the family and that it would be wrong, in all the circumstances (including the conduct of the parties and the interests of any child of the family), for the marriage to be dissolved'. The principal change is the new concept of 'substantial' rather than 'grave' hardship but it is unlikely that this provision will result in the prevention of more than a few, if any, divorces[1].

The court's role in relation to children

As indicated ealier, the court's role within this very different framework of divorce, has not been much affected by the 1996 legislation. It is still the case that the court's duty will be the limited one of considering whether there are any relevant 'children of the family' and, if so, 'whether (in the light of the arrangements which have been, or are proposed to be, made for their upbringing and welfare) it should exercise any of its powers under the Children Act 1989 with respect to any of them'[2].

This duty will almost certainly continue to be exercised by the district judge on the strength of written statements about the arrangements for children filed with the court. The court has power 'in exceptional circumstances which make it desirable in the interests of the child that the court should give a direction' to direct that the divorce (or separation) order should not be granted until the court orders otherwise[3]. It is unlikely that this provision will be much used but there are likely to be a significant number of cases in which the district judge will exercise his power to call for further evidence or for the attendance of the parties at a hearing in chambers, or to direct welfare reports in cases where it may be necessary to exercise the court's powers – usually but not invariably because the parties are not in agreement. Where a hearing is held it would be usual for a court welfare officer to be present and to attempt 'in-court conciliation' between the parties.

The court is required to regard the welfare of the child as the paramount consideration, and the 1996 Act does introduce the important modification that it must now have particular regard to a checklist of factors in deciding whether it needs to exercise its powers[4]. These are:

'(a)   the wishes and feelings of the child considered in the light of his age and understanding and the circumstances in which those wishes were expressed;

(b)   the conduct of the parties in relation to the upbringing of the child;

(c)   the general principle that, in the absence of evidence to the contrary, the welfare of the child will be best served by –

---

1   Family Law Act 1996, s 10.
2   Ibid, s 11(1).
3   Ibid, s 11(2).
4   Ibid, s 11(3), (4).

> (i) his having regular contact with those who have parental responsibility for him and
>   with other members of his family; and
> (ii) the maintenance of as good a continuing relationship with his parents as is possible;
>   and
> (d) any risk to the child attributable to –
>   (i)   where the person with whom the child will reside is living or proposes to live;
>   (ii) any person with whom that person is living or with whom he proposes to live; or
>   (iii) any other arrangements for his care and upbringing.'

These requirements apply to children of the family who are under 16 at the relevant time but the court has power to direct that they should also apply to a child over that age[1].

The reality is that, as under the previous divorce law, what parents agree about the children will be followed, and the cases in which the court seeks to intervene in any way are likely to be only a small minority of the total. Cretney, commenting on the provisions of s 11, sees something of a philosophical inconsistency between the principles of the Children Act and those of the Family Law Act:

> 'The truth is that the provisions of the Children Act in general are based on a philosophy of
> non-intervention which does not sit easily with the more interventionist philosophy of the 1996
> Act.'[2]

Children and mediation

One of the central features of the new divorce process under the Family Law Act 1996 is the much increased role envisaged for mediaton vis-à-vis the more traditional processes of negotiation by lawyers and adjudication[3]. Mediation is a process whereby the parties are assisted by an impartial third person, the mediator, to reach their own agreements on separation or divorce. Mediation, often referred to in the past as 'conciliation', has tended to be confined to children issues but, in recent years, there has been a growth in the idea of 'comprehensive' or 'all-issues' mediation[4]. After many years in which the former Conservative Government had shown an unwillingness to fund properly the existing mediation services, it then underwent what appeared to many to be a dramatic conversion[5]. The result is that the Family Law Act contains a whole range of provisions designed to bring to the attention of the divorcing parties the supposed benefits of mediation to enable them to take advantage of mediation services and, in those cases in which they are eligible for legal aid, to have the costs of mediation borne by public funds[6]. The precise relationship between mediation and legal advice or adjudication will not become totally clear until the Act is in

---

1 Family Law Act 1996, s 1(5).
2 SM Cretney *Family Law* (3rd edn) (Sweet & Maxwell, 1997) at p 53.
3 On the nature of family mediation, see J Haynes *Alternative Dispute Resolution: The Fundamentals of Family Mediation* (Old Bailey Press, 1993), and L Parkinson *Family Mediation* (Sweet & Maxwell, 1997).
4 For a discussion of mediation in the context of the interests of children at divorce, see M Richards 'The Interests of Children at Divorce' in M-T Meulders-Klein (ed) *Familles et Justice* (Bruylant, Bruxelles, 1997) especially at pp 554–557.
5 This change of heart was signalled in the Green Paper *Looking to the Future: Mediation and the Ground for Divorce* (1993) (Cm 2424) and was followed by a White Paper, *Looking to the Future* (1995) (Cm 2799).
6 See particularly s 13, dealing with the court's power to give directions with respect to mediation.

operation. What is clear is that to some extent this is a false dichotomy since many lawyers have trained as mediators and it is, in any event, necessary for mediation to operate in conjunction with legal advice, particularly in relation to the drawing up in legal form of agreements arrived at in mediation.

Where do children fit into all of this? While this also will not be clear until the Act is in operation, several points can be made with some confidence at the time of writing. The first is that hitherto only a tiny minority of divorcing couples have used mediation services at all[1]. While it can be predicted that the number is almost certainly bound to increase sharply with the implementation of the legislation, it is equally clear that a high proportion of divorcing couples will not be in dispute about children and that, in many cases, the arrangements for the children, as now, will be worked out by agreement under the procedures outlined above. Secondly, while the official assumption has been made that mediation is somehow 'better' in terms of outcomes for children there is scant evidence to support this beyond the intuitive feeling that it may enhance communication and assist in avoiding prolonged conflict where conflict is known to be bad for children[2]. Thirdly, it is not at all clear what part, if any, children themselves are expected to play in the mediation process but, in most cases at present, children play no direct role. Any benefits of mediation for them are therefore likely to be of an indirect nature. Recently, there have been some examples of children's views being obtained in separate sessions as an adjunct to the mediation itself. The question of how a conflict of interest between the parents and the children arising in mediation ought to be resolved is also uncertain[3].

The issue of the participation of children in mediation and the most appropriate way of ascertaining and accommodating their views is part of a much wider issue about the representation of children in legal processes, and we return to this in Chapter 13.

Private orders and the exercise of the court's discretion

Where it appears to the divorce court that it *should* exercise its powers, it may make one or more s 8 orders, the effect of which is to regulate the *exercise* of particular aspects of parental responsibility whilst leaving parental responsibility itself intact. Since divorce is by far the most numerically significant occasion when s 8 orders are made, consideration is given here to the circumstances under which these orders may be appropriate, their legal effect and the criteria which the courts must apply in deciding whether to make them. We look briefly at the court's flexible powers to attach conditions and give directions when making the orders. We also consider the powers which the courts have to make a 'family assistance order' or to direct a local authority to investigate the circumstances of a child which could lead

---

1   Cretney notes, for example, that National Family Mediation had, before the enactment of the 1996 legislation, been providing out-of-court mediation to some 6,500 families per annum while the equivalent figure for the Family Mediators Association was about 1,500 families. Set against the annual divorce rate of more than 150,000 divorces per year, it is readily apparent that mediation has been very much a minority interest up to now. See SM Cretney 'Divorce Reform in England: Humbug and Hypocrisy or a Smooth Transition?' in M Freeman *Divorce Where Next?* (Dartmouth, 1996) at p 49 and the sources cited there.

2   See M Richards 'The Interests of Children at Divorce' (above) at pp 554–557.

3   Ibid.

to the making of a supervision or care order. It should be remembered that these powers are available generally in 'family proceedings', subject to certain restrictions, and that much of what is said here can be applied to litigation involving social parents[1]. Parents, unlike certain categories of social parents, may always apply in family proceedings for any s 8 order as of right and do not require the leave of the court[2]. *Any* child whose welfare arises in family proceedings may be the subject of an order and not simply a 'child of the family'[3]. Orders will not normally be made after the child has attained 16 years of age but may be made, in exceptional circumstances, such as those of a mentally disabled young person[4].

The range of orders

The residence order
Arguably, the most significant of the orders is the 'residence order'. This is defined as 'an order settling the arrangements to be made as to the person with whom the child is to live'[5]. In contested cases, it is important that the court should give adequate reasons for making a residence order[6].

Statistically, there are fewer residence orders made than contact orders. In 1996, an estimated 27,600 residence orders were made, an increase of 8% on the 1995 figures. This compared with 40,330 contact orders in 1996, a 14% increase from 1995[7]. In many divorces, therefore, no residence order will be made, and the expressions 'residential' and 'non-residential' parent might be thought somewhat ambiguous. They may be used where a residence order has been made, but they may just reflect the fact that there is a primary carer looking after the child with or without an order.

The effect of the order
In the case of married parents, who already possess parental responsibility, the order simply regulates where the child is to live and no more. This contrasts with the position of non-parents who *acquire* parental responsibility by virtue of the order and retain it as long as the order remains in force[8]. Divorcing parents will therefore retain, to the full, all aspects of parental responsibility which they exercised during the marriage, save only that the 'non-residential' parent will lose his right physically to look after the child except insofar as this is compatible with

---

1   See Chapter 6 below.
2   Section 10(1) and (4).
3   Sections 10(1) and 105(1) defining a 'child', subject to certain qualifications regarding financial support, as 'a person under the age of eighteen'.
4   Section 9(7). For the reasoning behind the change in the law (the age limit under the old law generally being 18) see Law Com Report No 172 (above) at para 3.25.
5   Section 8(1). It was held in *Re B (A Minor) (Residence Order: Ex Parte)* [1992] 2 FLR 1 that the court has jurisdiction to make an ex parte interim residence order. See also *Re W (A Minor) (Residence Order)* [1992] 2 FLR 332. The Court of Appeal in *Re P (A Minor) (Ex Parte Interim Residence Order)* [1993] 1 FLR 915 has, however, stated that such orders will rarely be appropriate except, for example, to thwart abduction. Another decision to similar effect is *Re G (Minors) (Ex Parte Interim Residence Order)* [1993] 1 FLR 910. The latest case emphasising caution in the use and interpretation of ex parte residence orders is *Re J (Children: Ex Parte Orders)* [1997] 1 FLR 606.
6   *B v B (Reasons for Decision)* [1997] 2 FLR 602.
7   *The Children Act Advisory Committee Final Report June 1997* (Lord Chancellor's Department, 1997), Appendix 2.
8   Section 12(2).

the residence order and any other order, condition or direction which the court may make[1]. In practical terms, the non-residential parent will be able to take all decisions on upbringing while the child is with him but it may be difficult to participate in the child's upbringing in the more common situation of the child being in the care of the residential parent. The Law Commission recognised this when it suggested that the reality of parental responsibility is that it 'runs with the child'[2]. But, technically at least, the non-residential parent is entitled to exercise parental responsibility even where the child is not physically with him. Whether this is more than a merely symbolic retention of parental responsibility may depend, to a large extent, on how far the non-residential parent wishes to assert his potential contribution to the upbringing of his child.

No express rights of consultation, even on major matters, were written into the legislation but judicial remarks have cast doubt on this analysis. In *Re G (Parental Responsibility: Education)*[3], Glidewell LJ said obiter that the non-residential mother should have been consulted by the residential father on the matter of changing the child's school from a day school to a boarding school. On the other hand, in *Re P (A Minor) (Parental Responsibility)*[4], Wilson J made remarks suggesting that the acquisition of parental responsibility by an unmarried father would not give him the right to question everyday decisions taken by the mother if she had a residence order in her favour. This rather suggests that the non-residential parent does not have an automatic right of consultation. The matter is in need of clarification by the higher courts. The factual superiority of the residential parent's position, if such it is, may be preserved on his or her death where the residential parent has appointed a guardian[5].

In most cases, therefore, despite theoretical equality and the ethos of continuing parental responsibility, it is the residential parent who, for practical purposes, will exercise parental powers. The legislation may, notwithstanding, have some influence on the way in which the role of parents is perceived following divorce. It might even be viewed as an attempt at social engineering. It is statutory recognition that ex-spouses remain parents and are expected to be able to distinguish between termination of their own legal and factual relationship and their continuing moral and legal obligations to their children. There is a clear expectation in the legislation that these obligations should not simply be off-loaded onto the other parent or the State[6].

Joint residence orders
There is no restriction in the Act which prevents a residence order being made in favour of more than one person. Since the Act was implemented, two separate and

---

1   Just what is incompatible with a residence order may prove contentious in practice. It seems that the concept of residence is a more restricted idea than the notion of physical possession or control associated with the old idea of custody. The order simply settles where the child is to live. Does this mean that the residential parent has the right to control the physical movements of the child and the non-residential parent would be acting unlawfully, for example, in taking the child away for an afternoon without the residential parent's consent? Clearly, it would be desirable for this kind of situation to be regulated by a contact order.
2   Law Com Working Paper No 96 (1986) at paras 4.51 et seq.
3   [1994] 2 FLR 694.
4   [1994] 1 FLR 578.
5   Section 5(7)(b), discussed in Chapter 6 below.
6   These expectations are reflected most obviously in the child support legislation and are reinforced by the general principles in the Family Law Act 1996.

distinct uses of the joint residence order have emerged. The first is to give effect to what might be termed 'time-sharing' arrangements. The second is a status-conferring device to give parental responsibility to a social parent.

Time-sharing

The Children Act enables an order to be made 'in favour of two or more persons who do not themselves all live together' and it 'may specify the periods during which the child is to live in the different households concerned'[1]. The Law Commission considered that a joint residence order would be more realistic than a sole residence order coupled with a contact order where it is proposed that the child should spend substantial periods in the care of each parent. The effect is to introduce the possibility of 'time-sharing', a feature of some joint custodial arrangements elsewhere[2]. It marks a shift away from the attitude expressed judicially which was antagonistic to the idea of joint custody orders which included joint physical care and control on the basis that a child needs a settled home and such arrangements could be disruptive[3].

It is unlikely that orders like this will be made except where there is already a very high level of co-operation. One instance will be where a child spends school holidays with one parent and term-time with the other. A joint order may also be appropriate where the parties continue to reside geographically close to one another, thereby increasing the practicability of the arrangement and minimising the risk that the child will be 'shunted about'. It should be noted that the Children Act creates no presumption of joint physical care. Several reported cases have made it plain that joint residence orders contemplating shared physical care may be appropriate in some situations such as, for example, to accommodate the working patterns of a shift worker[4]. The leading case is *Re A (A Minor) (Shared Residence Orders)*[5]. The Court of Appeal held that the pre-Children Act decision in *Riley v Riley* could not stand in the light of the new statutory framework. In many cases, it would be confusing for children to have two homes but joint residence orders were not to be confined to 'exceptional circumstances'. Sole residence orders would be more usual and it would need to be shown that there was some positive benefit to the child in making the unconventional order. Butler-Sloss LJ warned that such an order would be inappropriate where there were still concrete issues which required resolution, such as a dispute concerning the amount of contact. In *Re R (Residence Order: Finance)*[6], the Court of Appeal upheld a joint residence order where both parents worked full-time. The three-year-old son lived during the week with his father (although the care was actually provided by the paternal grandmother) and with his mother at most weekends and during holiday periods. The mother then declared her intention to give up work and sought a sole residence order. The court held that the judge had been entitled to have regard to the consequences of the mother giving up work and having to rely on State benefits. He could not be criticised for taking the view that the existing arrangement was the best of the alternatives on offer.

---

1   Section 11(4).
2   The American concept of joint custody, for example, envisages joint physical and legal custody.
3   *Riley v Riley* [1986] 2 FLR 429.
4   *G v G (Joint Residence Order)* [1993] Fam Law 570.
5   [1994] 1 FLR 669.
6   [1995] 2 FLR 612.

It should be remembered that in the great majority of divorces no order at all will be needed, or made, in relation to the children. In these cases, the parties will themselves work out informally the most practicable arrangements for themselves. It seems entirely likely that in some of these cases there will be a kind of *de facto* shared residence[1]. With or without residence orders, there will be in practice a very wide range of caring arrangements, from equal time-sharing at one end, to sole and exclusive residential arrangements at the other. Between these two extremes, there will be many variations, but the real change brought about by the Children Act was the demise of the stereotypical sole custody order which was so much a feature of the old law. The great variation in arrangements for the care of children merely reflects the rich kaleidoscope of family arrangements which are characteristic of late twentieth-century Britain.

Joint residence and parental responsibility

It has been noted that one effect of a residence order is to confer parental responsibility on the holder if he or she does not already have it, although this will only be for as long as the residence order itself lasts[2]. Two reported cases have shown an ingenious use of the joint residence order as a device for conferring this legal status on a social parent.

In *Re H (Shared Residence: Parental Responsibility)*[3], the mother's husband was the father of her younger child but not of her elder son. He was therefore step-father to the older boy and had accepted him as his own. After separation there had been a joint residence order by consent and both children continued to see a lot of the father with the mother's full co-operation. The mother sought to vary the order to a sole residence order but the court upheld the original order on the basis that it had value in giving the father parental responsibility in relation to the elder boy. In this way, the law could give its stamp of approval to the factual position that the boy was accepted by the man as his own.

An even more imaginative use of the joint residence order occurred in *Re AB (Adoption: Shared Residence Order)*[4]. An unmarried couple were foster-parents to a five-year-old child. They wanted to adopt the child but were precluded from doing so since the adoption legislation requires that all *joint* adoptions be made by a *married* couple[5]. Cazalet J granted the foster-father an adoption order[6] (one effect of which was that the child could bear his surname) and made a shared residence order in favour of both of them. This had the effect of giving the foster-mother parental responsibility during the child's minority and was the next best thing to adoption.

---

1 For critiques of the use of the joint residence order, see C Bridge 'Shared residence in England and New Zealand – a comparative analysis' [1996] CFLQ 12 and Baker and Townsend 'Post-divorce parenting – rethinking shared residence' [1996] CFLQ 217. For an analysis of the essential scheme for joint parenting under the Children Act, see B Hoggett 'Joint parenting systems: the English experiment' (1994) 6 JCL 8.

2 Children Act 1989, s 12(2).

3 [1995] 2 FLR 883.

4 [1995] Fam Law 663.

5 Adoption Act 1976, s 14. See further Chapter 7.

6 Adoptions by single unmarried persons are allowed in some circumstances. See Adoption Act 1976, s 15, and Chapter 7 below.

The contact order

The contact order is 'an order requiring the person with whom a child lives, or is to live, to allow the child to visit or stay with the person named in the order, or for that person and the child otherwise to have contact with each other'[1]. There has been some difference of opinion about whether contact is the right of the parent or the right of the child[2]. We saw in Chapter 3 that the Scottish approach is to accept that parents have both responsibilities and rights and that contact falls into both categories. The view in Scotland must therefore be that contact is a right of *both* parent and child. The new order (replacing the former access order) is certainly 'child-centred' in form, providing for *the child* to visit or stay with a named individual. This is a deliberate change of emphasis from the old law, under which access orders were 'adult-centred' and allowed a named adult to visit the child. While it is now generally accepted in England that contact with parents is a fundamental right of children, it remains a matter of controversy whether it may also legitimately be regarded as a right of parents. It was suggested earlier that it is perhaps best regarded as a mutual interest (and possibly right) of both parent and child[3].

What is clear, beyond doubt, is that if it is a right, it is a qualified one. While parents may be thought to have a prima facie right to contact as an aspect of respect for their family life, protected by the European Convention, this is subject to the welfare principle and the courts' power of intervention[4].

Yet the power to deprive a parent and child of contact is not one which will be exercised lightly, and the courts will require a sound justification for doing so[5]. The mere fact that contact arrangements are difficult to operate, or that a parent or child would prefer not to have contact with the other parent, is not of itself a sufficient justification for refusing it. The leading case on the principles applicable to contact under the Children Act is the Court of Appeal decision in

1   Section 8(1). For an analysis of the contact question in the private and public contexts, see I Weyland 'Contact within different legal contexts' [1992] Fam Law 138.
2   It was first described judicially as a right of the child by Wrangham J in *M v M (Child: Access)* [1973] 2 All ER 81. For the view that it is *both* the child's and the parent's right, see A Bainham 'Changing Families and Changing Concepts: Reforming the Language of Family Law' [1998] CFLQ 1, 5–8.
3   A particularly helpful discussion on the nature of the right to the 'society' of parents and child is to be found in A McCall Smith 'Is Anything Left of Parental Rights?' in McCall Smith and Sutherland (eds) *Family Rights* (Edinburgh University Press, 1990) at p 10.
4   Article 8(1) of the European Convention on Human Rights and Fundamental Freedoms provides that 'Everyone has the right to respect for his private and family life, his home and his correspondence'. See also *Re KD (A Minor)* [1988] AC 806. In *Hokkanen v Finland* [1996] Fam 22, the European Court of Human Rights found that the State of Finland had breached Mr Hokkanen's right to respect for family life under Article 8 of the Convention by the failure of the Finnish authorities over a long period of time to enforce effectively his right of access to his daughter.
5   See, for example, *Re C (Minors) (Access)* [1985] FLR 804, *Williams v Williams* [1985] FLR 509 and *Wright v Wright* (1981) FLR 276. See also, more recently, *Re B (Minors: Access)* [1992] 1 FLR 142 in which the Court of Appeal held that 'eccentric, bizarre behaviour' ought not to deprive a father of defined access (now contact) provided that there was no suggestion of violence or verbal aggression in his personality or any suggested risk that he might use access to undermine the children's feelings of love and loyalty towards their mother. In this case the father had, inter alia, allegedly attempted to set fire to some of the grass on which the children were sitting. On another occasion it was alleged that he had walked down the street with a plastic bag over his head. See also *Re H (Minors) (Access)* [1992] 1 FLR 148 in similar vein.

Re M (Contact: Welfare Test)[1]. It was a comparatively unusual case in that it involved denial of contact to a *mother*. The children were living with their father and had exhibited 'extreme distress' on previous attempts at contact. The mother argued that contact was a fundamental right of the child only to be displaced in 'wholly exceptional circumstances'. The Court of Appeal thought that this was going too far. There was a strong presumption in favour of contact but each case had to be examined on its merits. Wilson J said that the applicable principles now had to be cast in terms of the statutory checklist of factors in s 1(3) of the Children Act. Thus, the test would now be:

> '... whether the fundamental emotional need of every child to have an enduring relationship with both his parents [s 1(3)(b)] is outweighed by the depth of harm which in the light, inter alia, of his wishes and feelings [s 1(3)(a)] this child would be at risk of suffering [s 1(3)(e)] by virtue of a contact order.'

The new public law governing contact is constituted by a separate code in Part IV of the Children Act[2]. This creates, inter alia, a *presumption* of reasonable contact in favour of parents and certain other individuals, and local authorities are placed under a statutory duty to promote contact between the child, his relatives and friends[3]. There are no corresponding provisions in the private law, although a presumption of contact with parents is implicit in what was said above and it was probably felt unnecessary to put it into statutory form. Although the hallmark of the scheme is flexibility, it would seem likely that orders for 'reasonable contact', which leave the parties to work out the precise arrangements, will become the norm where a residence order is made. Indeed, without a contact order, the non-residential parent's right to see the child would be in doubt, notwithstanding his retention of parental responsibility, since to take physical control of the child for however short a period would arguably contravene the terms of the residence order[4]. Where, on the other hand, there is no residence order, parents will each have rights of contact as an aspect of parental responsibility and, provided they can work out an arrangement which is acceptable to both of them, a contact order would not appear necessary[5]. A parent, while exercising contact, will also exercise parental responsibility to the full, but this arises quite independently of any order.

The experience over many years has been that contact (formerly access) was at best difficult, and at worst impossible, to enforce[6]. Children, especially older children, cannot be forced to see parents, 'absent' parents cannot be forced to be actively involved in parenting, and residential parents cannot be forced to be welcoming and co-operative towards an ex-spouse. Various enforcement mechanisms have been resorted to, including defining and varying the terms of contact,

---

1 [1995] 1 FLR 274, discussed alongside the European Court of Human Rights decision in *Hokkanen v Finland*, in A Bainham, 'Contact as a Fundamental Right' (1995) CLJ 255.
2 Section 34 and Sch 2, para 15, which require local authorities to promote contact between children looked after by them and their families and friends. See also the Contact with Children Regulations 1991, SI 1991/891.
3 Ibid.
4 Although, as discussed earlier, this is a contentious issue.
5 This follows automatically from the no order principle in s 1(5).
6 See, for example, *Churchard v Churchard* [1984] FLR 635 and *I v D (Access Order: Enforcement)* [1988] 2 FLR 286.

changing the residence of the child[1] making supervision or care orders[2] and imposing penal sanctions on the recalcitrant parent[3]. There has been some debate about how far the courts should go in their endeavours to enforce contact, much of which centres on the concept of 'implacable hostility'[4]. Recently the notion that contact is a fundamental right which the courts should attempt to enforce in the absence of a very good reason to the contrary has been challenged. It has been said that 'the public and judicial treatment of contact has taken on an increasingly rigid and dogmatic form, which is becoming a harmful trend in family law'[5]. Against this it has been argued that the *attempt* to enforce needs to be made not least for ideological reasons. Unless the courts are seen to be taking the contact issue seriously, the message of the law that contact is an important right of the child may be lost. And caution needs to be exercised in equating too readily the interests of women (usually the so-called 'primary carers') and children in this matter[6].

Two recent decisions illustrate the approach of the courts. In *A v N (Committal: Refusal of Contact)*[7], it was held that where the mother had justification for refusing contact with the father it should not be regarded as a case of so-called 'implacable hostility'. In this case, the mother genuinely feared violence from the father. These fears were found to be justified as was the judge's refusal to make a contact order.

Despite attempts at enforcement, it remains the case that many 'non-residential' parents (usually, but not invariably, fathers) lose all substantial contact with their children within a few years of divorce[8]. A major challenge is to discover why it is that so many contact arrangements break down with the passage of time. Certainly there is a philosophical commitment in both the Children Act and the Family Law Act 1996 to continued dual parenting following divorce, but

---

1   But see *Re B (Residence Order: Status Quo)* [1998] 1 FLR 368 for an inappropriate change in the child's residential arrangements precipitated by contact difficulties.
2   A drastic example under the old law being *R v G (Surrey County Council Intervening)* [1984] Fam 100, where the child was eventually committed to care.
3   But see *Re F (Contact: Enforcement: Representation of Child)* [1998] 1 FLR 691 where the child in question was disabled, having been born with cerebral palsy, and where the Court of Appeal held that the judge had rightly not attached a penal notice to the contact order made in favour of the father.
4   See particularly Parker and Eaton 'Opposing Contact' [1994] Fam Law 636; Jolly 'Implacable Hostility, Contact and the Limits' [1995] CFLQ 228; and Conway 'Implacable Hostility – Seeking a Breakthrough' [1997] Fam Law 109.
5   Smart and Neale 'Arguments against virtue – must contact be enforced?' [1997] Fam Law 332.
6   A Bainham 'Changing Families and Changing Concepts: Reforming the Language of Family Law' [1998] CFLQ 1 at 7.
7   [1997] 1 FLR 533. See also *Re B (Contact: Stepfather's Opposition)* [1997] 2 FLR 579, in which the Court of Appeal made it plain that the mere fact of a stepfather's opposition to contact between the child and the natural father would not prevent the court making a contact order if the best interests of the child required it. On the facts, however, the stepfather's position was justifiable since the child had had virtually no contact with the natural father since birth. On the problems of contact and residence orders where there has been a background of domestic violence, see M Kaye 'Domestic Violence, Residence and Contact' [1996] CFLQ 285. In *Re H (Contact: Domestic Violence)* [1998] 2 FLR 42, the Court of Appeal held that, as a matter of principle, domestic violence was not of itself a bar to contact but was simply one factor in a very complex question. For a case which illustrates the problems involved in dealing with breaches of s 8 orders see *G v C (Residence Order: Committal)* [1998] 1 FLR 43.
8   See J Bradshaw and J Millar *Lone Parent Families in the UK* (HMSO, 1991).

the question of whether the legal system can do much, or indeed anything, to achieve this remains unresolved.

Prohibited steps and specific issue orders

These orders are designed to resolve what might be described as 'single issues' affecting children and are modelled on the powers of the court in wardship. It was an express aim of the Children Act to emulate and incorporate the better features of the wardship jurisdiction[1]. Both orders may be made in conjunction with other s 8 orders or on freestanding applications. They are intended to be subsidiary to residence and contact orders (which are the principal orders governing the exercise of parental responsibility) and they must not therefore be made with a view to achieving a result which could be achieved by the main orders[2] or in a way which is denied to the High Court in the exercise of its inherent jurisdiction[3]. The court in wardship exercises a degree of continuing control over a child's situation and retains parental responsibility (formerly 'custody') in the wider sense of the decision-making powers. The new statutory powers are narrower (at least conceptually) than this all-embracing 'custodial' control. In wardship, every major issue affecting the ward must be referred back to the court for its determination[4]. The statutory orders do not vest parental responsibility in the court but do enable it to exercise control over particular areas of difficulty.

These orders should be considered alongside the court's wide powers to attach conditions and give directions in relation to residence and contact orders. These respective powers are two alternative ways of addressing problem areas. The orders may be pre-emptive or reactive in nature. Where it appears to the court, on making a residence or contact order, that there is likely to be a potential area of dispute, for example over education, it may wish to address the difficulty in advance. On the other hand, such difficulties may only manifest themselves sometime later, at which point it will be open to a parent to return to court for those difficulties to be resolved.

A prohibited steps order is an order 'that no step which could be taken by a parent in meeting his parental responsibility for a child, and which is of a kind specified in the order, shall be taken by any person without the consent of the court'[5]. Around 8,730 applications and 5,780 orders were made for prohibited steps in 1996, approximately the same numbers as in 1995[6]. The order is entirely prohibitive or negative in substance as its name suggests. The kinds of involvements with children which might be prohibited are infinitely various but, most obviously, contact between the child and an 'undesirable adult' could be

---

1 Law Com Report No 172 *Guardianship and Custody* (1988), Part IV.
2 Section 9(5)(a). See *Nottinghamshire County Council v P* [1994] Fam 18, cf *Re H (Prohibited Steps Order)* [1995] 1 FLR 638, and Chapter 12 below.
3 Section 9(5)(b), and Law Com Report No 172 (above) at paras 4.18–4.20.
4 There were several good examples under the old law of a failure to refer issues back to the court. See, particularly, *Re GU (A Minor) (Wardship)* [1984] FLR 811 where a local authority was criticised by the High Court for arranging an abortion for an adolescent girl in their care, who was also a ward of court, without first referring the issue to the High Court. The ongoing control exercised by the court in wardship is best illustrated by the House of Lords decision in *Re E (SA) (A Minor) (Wardship)* [1984] 1 All ER 289.
5 Section 8(1).
6 *The Children Act Advisory Committee Final Report June 1997* (Lord Chancellor's Department, 1997).

restrained[1]. This example highlights one of the limitations of the order. In view of the reference to the exercise of parental responsibility, the order cannot be used to prohibit a mature child herself from having such contact. It may be that this is one instance in which the wardship jurisdiction will continue to have a special usefulness, especially in view of the Court of Appeal's ruling that the court in wardship or under the inherent jurisdiction has power to override the wishes of a mature minor[2].

An interesting use of the prohibited steps order occurred in *Re Z (A Minor) (Freedom of Publication)*[3] which concerned a child of famous parents who was receiving treatment at a special unit for her special educational needs. The courts had previously granted an injunction under the inherent jurisdiction restraining the media from publishing information which could lead to revelation of the child's identity. The mother then wished her daughter to take part in a television programme about the unit. It was held by the Court of Appeal that the child had a right of confidentiality concerning her attendance at the unit. The mother could, prima facie, waive this right of confidentiality on the child's behalf but to do so would amount to an exercise of parental responsibility. A prohibited steps order could therefore be made to control the exercise of this aspect of parental responsibility. Here, the child's welfare prevailed over the freedom of publication and the order should be made.

A specific issue order is an order 'giving direction for the purpose of determining a specific question which has arisen, or which may arise, in connection with any aspect of parental responsibility for a child'[4]. As such, the order may be positive or negative, and its function is to *regulate* a sphere of upbringing. The order may be especially useful where a sole residence order is *not* made. Where the court makes a joint residence order, or no order at all, both parents will exercise full responsibility. However, it is possible that there may be an area of disagreement which could jeopardise the whole arrangement if it is not resolved. Here, the court might use the specific issue order in a variety of ways which, it has been suggested, could include imposing its own view, referring the issue to an appropriate third party such as a welfare officer or doctor, or reserving this one area of upbringing to one parent[5].

Two cases illustrate the diverse uses of the specific issue order. In *Re HG (Specific Issue Order: Sterilisation)*[6], a specific issue order was used to authorise the sterilisation of a severely epileptic young woman with a chromosomal deficiency.

---

1   The so-called 'teenage wardship' cases would fall within this category – as to which, see
    NV Lowe and RAH White *Wards of Court* (2nd edn) (Barry Rose/Kluwer, 1986) at ch 12.
    Another use of the order, the subject of much recent litigation, is to restrain the removal of a
    child from the country, as to which see Chapter 17 below.
2   *Re R (A Minor) (Wardship: Medical Treatment)* [1992] 1 FLR 190, discussed in Chapter 8 below.
3   [1996] 1 FLR 191. For an analysis of the decision in the wider context of protecting children's
    privacy, see J Moriarty 'Children, Privacy and the Press' [1997] CFLQ 217, especially at pp 226
    et seq.
4   Section 8(1).
5   SM Cretney and JM Masson *Principles of Family Law* (6th edn) (Sweet & Maxwell, 1997) at
    pp 681–682. It is of course fair to point out that too liberal a use of the order would jeopardise
    the principle of continuing parental responsibility, but the non-intervention principle in s 1(5)
    ought to operate as a check on this.
6   [1993] 1 FLR 587. On sterilisation generally, see further Chapter 8 below. On the capacity of
    children to seek court orders, see Chapter 13 below.

Since she was under a legal disability, her father was allowed to apply for the order on her behalf as next friend. In *Re F (Specific Issue: Child Interview)*[1], the father to two boys was due to stand trial for assaulting the mother. The father's defence lawyers succeeded in obtaining a specific issue order to authorise them to interview the boys in order to prepare the father's defence. It was held that interviewing children involved an aspect of parental responsibility which could be controlled through s 8 orders.

In contrast, in *Re J (Specific Issue Order: Leave to Apply)*[2], it was held by Wall J that the determination of 'children in need' for the purposes of Part III of the Children Act was not intended by Parliament to be susceptible to adjudication by the courts through s 8 orders. Accordingly, a 17-year-old boy failed in his attempt to obtain leave to apply for a specific issue order requiring the local authority to deem him to be a child in need.

The power to attach conditions and give directions

The court has a general power when making a s 8 order to give directions or attach conditions to the order. These conditions may be imposed on the person in whose favour the order is made, a parent or a non-parent with parental responsibility, and anyone with whom the child is living. The court may also make 'such incidental, supplemental or consequential provision as the court thinks fit'[3]. The former distinction between interim and final orders has been abolished and all s 8 orders may be limited to a specific period and individual provisions in the orders may be subject to time-limits. There is also a general power to vary all orders which cease when the child reaches 16 years of age, other than in exceptional circumstances[4].

The width and flexibility of these powers should enable the court to tailor its orders to the individual circumstances of the case. Where appropriate, the court may go into considerable detail about the future upbringing of the child, although to attempt to regulate this too closely might actually generate opportunities for dispute. Moreover, an extensive use of detailed orders would run counter to the ethos of continuing parental responsibility. The court has the power to dilute considerably the input of a non-residential parent by preventing the exercise of parental responsibility or by making it subject to extensive restrictions. It will, however, be bound by the welfare and no order principles in deciding whether or not to make directions or conditions and this should operate as a restraint on the use of these powers.

Re E (Residence: Imposition of Conditions)[5] provides a recent illustration of an inappropriate use of conditions. Here, the judge made a residence order in favour of the mother but sought to impose a requirement that she should continue to reside at a named address. The Court of Appeal held that this was an unwarranted

---

1   [1995] 1 FLR 819.
2   [1995] 1 FLR 669.
3   Section 11(7).
4   Section 9(7).
5   [1997] 2 FLR 638. For other illustrations, see *Re D (Residence: Imposition of Conditions)* [1996] 2 FLR 281 and *D v N (Contact Order: Conditions)* [1997] 2 FLR 797, both of which establish the principle that the court ought not to make orders, which are injunctive in nature, dressed up as conditions under s 11(7).

imposition on the right of a parent to choose where she would live within the UK and with whom.

Orders restricting applications

Under s 91(14) of the Children Act it is possible for the court to prevent any further applications in relation to a particular child when it disposes of an application for any order under the Act. There have now been several reported examples of the use of these restrictions which are designed to prevent the unsettling effect of successive and potentially endless applications to the court[1]. Where such a restriction has been enforced the party affected will be required to apply to the court for leave to lift it and allow a further application. It has been held by the Court of Appeal that the criteria in s 10(9) of the Act (which generally govern applications for leave to seek s 8 orders) are inappropriate in these circumstances[2]. The test is rather the simple one of whether the application for leave demonstrates that there is a need for renewed judicial investigations. It appears that the matter is not governed by the welfare principle[3].

Orders in problem cases

In a small minority of cases, the court may be positively unhappy, or at least concerned, about what is proposed for children on divorce. Whether problem cases will come to light at all, given the court's more limited duty, must be a matter of doubt[4]. Under the old law, the court might, of its own volition, make a supervision or care order on the basis that there were 'exceptional circumstances making it desirable that the child should be under the supervision of an independent person'[5]. These orders were, by definition, not extensively used and, where they were, they were used in two quite different kinds of circumstances[6]. The Law Commission was concerned that a clear distinction should be drawn between those cases in which the court simply wished to assist with difficulties which might occur following relationship breakdown and those in which it was concerned to protect the child from possible harm[7]. The choice for the court under the Children Act is now between making a 'family assistance order' (intended to cover the first situation) and a 's 37 direction' to the local authority (intended to cover the second situation). It might also, in appropriate cases, seek to meet its concerns by making one or more s 8 orders with or without attaching conditions, or by giving directions. In practice, it is likely that the distinction between family assistance orders and s 37 directions may be less than clear cut and that the court's choice of order will be determined by the level of concern it feels for the child's situation.

---

1   See, particularly, *B v B (Residence Order: Restricting Applications)* [1997] 1 FLR 139, *Re G (Child Care: Parental Involvement)* [1996] 1 FLR 857 and *Re N (Section 91(14) Order)* [1996] 1 FLR 356. For an inappropriate use of the restricting order, see *Re M (Contact: Restrictive Order: Supervision)* [1998] 1 FLR 721.
2   *Re A (Application for Leave)* [1998] 1 FLR 1.
3   *Re R (Residence: Contact: Restricting Applications)* [1998] 1 FLR 749.
4   It may be that the combined effect of the no order principle and the court's reformulated duty on divorce will be to make the court's role in practice a more reactive rather than proactive one. Unless a party before the court raises a problem, it is possible that it may go unnoticed.
5   Such orders could be made in a range of family proceedings including guardianship, divorce and adoption.
6   Discussed in Law Com Report No 172 *Guardianship and Custody* (1988) at paras 5.10 et seq.
7   Ibid.

The family assistance order

The family assistance order ('FAO') was an innovation of the Children Act[1]. It is, in essence, a form of short-term voluntary assistance to the parties, usually in the immediate transitional period following breakdown of their relationship. It contrasts with the traditional form of supervision order which is now confined to cases in which the protection of the child is in issue. The FAO may be made, in principle, wherever family proceedings take place and the court has power to make it whether or not it makes any other order. Its effect is to require either a probation officer or an officer of the local authority to be made available 'to advise, assist and (where appropriate) befriend anyone named in the order'[2]. This could be a parent or guardian, any person with whom the child is living or in whose favour a contact order has been made, or the child himself[3].

The order may only be made in 'exceptional circumstances' and requires the consent of every person named in it other than the child[4]. The consent requirement underlines the voluntary nature of the order but it is noticeable that there is no obligation to obtain the child's consent or, it would appear, to ascertain or take into account his wishes[5]. Those persons named in the order must keep the specified officer informed of their addresses and must permit visits by that officer. The order will last for a maximum of six months or such shorter period as the court specifies[6]. The officer's powers are limited to referring to the court the question of whether an existing s 8 order should be varied or discharged[7]. He has no power to seek a supervision or care order but, where he expresses concern for the child's situation, this may prompt the court to direct an investigation by the local authority.

Re C (Family Assistance Order)[8] shows the potential limitations of the order in practice. In this case, a boy of 10, who had left home to live with his uncle and aunt, succeeded, with leave, in obtaining a residence order in their favour. The court also made a family assistance order directed to the local authority with a view to repairing the damaged relationship between the boy and his mother. The local authority complained that it lacked the resources to carry out the order and Johnson J, noting the limited options for enforcement of the order, felt that it was not in the child's best interests to attempt to force the authority to carry it out.

Section 37 directions

Prior to the Children Act, the courts had powers in a variety of family proceedings to take the initiative and make a supervision order or, in cases of more serious

---

1   Section 16 and Law Com Report No 172 (above) at paras 5.19–5.20.
2   Section 16(1).
3   Section 16(2). In *Leeds City Council v C* [1993] 1 FLR 269, Booth J held that the FAO was the correct order to achieve local authority supervision of contact between a mother and her three children. The court should not try to achieve this result by making directions under s 11(7).
4   Section 16(3).
5   The statutory checklist, which applies to s 8 orders and care and supervision orders, does not apply to family assistance orders. Nonetheless, it is suggested that, as a matter of good practice, the wishes of the child concerned should be explored.
6   Section 16(4) and (5).
7   Section 16(6).
8   [1996] 1 FLR 424. See also *S v P (Contact Application: Family Assistance Order)* [1997] 2 FLR 277, in which the court refused to make the order, the effect of which would have been to provide an 'escort service' for the children to visit their father in prison.

concern, to commit a child to care[1]. While the local authority might itself have been intervening in the proceedings and seeking an order, there was nothing to preclude the court from, in effect, over-ruling the authority and imposing an order on it. A major objective of the reforms in the public sphere was to spell out and standardise the basis upon which a child might be placed compulsorily under supervision or committed to care. There was concern that the courts in private proceedings, particularly but not exclusively wardship, could reserve to themselves a wider power of compulsory intervention based not on the criteria laid down by Parliament but on some more open-ended criterion such as 'best interests' or 'exceptional circumstances'[2]. The Children Act removed this power to act independently, except the power to make interim care orders[3]. The new principle is that the local authority, which has primary statutory responsibility for child protection, must seek care or supervision orders which must only be made where the statutory threshold is crossed[4].

The court is, however, given a more limited power of independent action. It may, in any family proceedings, direct an authority to investigate a child's circumstances[5]. In this way, the court can still take the lead in the sense of triggering action by the authority. The power to make the direction exists wherever 'a question arises with respect to the welfare of any child' and 'it appears to the court that it may be appropriate for a care or supervision order to be made with respect to him'. This power is additional to the authority's right to intervene in family proceedings to seek such orders[6]. Where a direction is made, the authority must investigate and consider whether any action is required and, if so, what this should be[7]. It must then report back to the court within eight weeks but, significantly, where it decides to take no action, the court may not overrule it by imposing a care or supervision order. This is one area in which the Children Act effected a clear shift in the balance of power for child protection away from the courts and towards local authorities.

The remarkable case of *Re H (A Minor) (Section 37 Direction)* illustrates the use of the s 37 direction[8]. Here, a child was born to a couple who already had one child and did not want a second. They agreed to hand the baby over to a lesbian couple (A and B) who lived nearby and wanted to bring up the child as their own. In fact, the birth had taken place at their home. A and B wished to adopt or foster the child but were not permitted to do so. Scott Baker J made an interim residence order in A and B's favour, coupled with an interim supervision order and a s 37 direction to the local authority. While he made no criticism of the care offered by A and B, he thought that there were long-term concerns which justified investigation by the local authority.

---

1 Law Com Report No 172 (above) at paras 5.2–5.9.
2 See the DHSS *Review of Child Care Law* (1985) at paras 8.20–8.23 and 15.35–15.38, and the White Paper *The Law on Child Care and Family Services* (1987) (Cmnd 62) at para 36.
3 Section 38(3).
4 Section 31(2), and see Chapter 11 below.
5 Section 37(1).
6 Thus, under s 31(4) an application for a care or supervision order may be made 'on its own or in any other family proceedings'.
7 Section 37(2).
8 [1993] 2 FLR 541. For another illustration, see *Re CE (Section 37 Direction)* [1995] 1 FLR 26.

Applying the welfare principle: the court's discretion

It was noted that the court, in applying the welfare principle, is obliged in contested private proceedings, to have regard to a checklist of factors[1]. While it is not required to do so in uncontested private cases, it remains bound in those cases by the welfare principle and the no order principle and, in applying these, it is likely to take into account factors similar to those in the checklist. These factors represent, for the most part, those which were habitually taken into account by the courts under the old law[2].

Factors taken into consideration by the courts

Under the old law, the court had a largely unfettered discretion. Athough certain principles did emerge from appellate decisions it was probably incorrect to see them as creating hard precedents in view of the infinite number of variables which had to be taken into account and the court's overriding duty to do what it considered best for the *individual* child. It was also held by the House of Lords[3] that the Court of Appeal should not interfere with the order of the judge unless satisfied that his decision was plainly wrong. It was, nonetheless, possible to discern the kind of factors which the courts took into account and the sort of reasoning which formed the basis of their decisions[4]. Thus, for example, it was generally thought desirable that siblings be kept together where possible[5], that matrimonial 'misconduct' should be ignored except where it was directly relevant to parenting capacity[6], that disparities in material circumstances should not generally be decisive except in extreme cases[7], that existing arrangements for the

---

1 See Chapter 2 above.
2 The reasoning behind the introduction of a statutory checklist is to be found in Law Com Report No 172 *Guardianship and Custody* (1988) at paras 3.17–3.21.
3 *G v G (Minors) (Custody Appeal)* [1985] 1 WLR 647.
4 See, particularly, SM Cretney and JM Masson *Principles of Family Law* (6th edn) (Sweet & Maxwell, 1997) at pp 733–745.
5 See, for example, *C v C (Minors: Custody)* [1988] 2 FLR 291. The principle, however, has never been an inflexible one. For a recent case in which the Court of Appeal upheld the judge's decision to keep siblings apart, see *B v B (Residence Order: Restricting Applications)* [1997] 1 FLR 139.
6 Thus, a matrimonial 'offence', such as adultery, would certainly not per se affect the custody issue – see, particularly, *Re K (Minor) (Children: Care and Control)* [1977] Fam 179. Neither would other sexual proclivities of a parent such as lesbianism – see *C v C (A Minor) (Custody Appeal)* [1991] 1 FLR 223 and *B v B (Minors) (Custody, Care and Control)* [1991] 1 FLR 402. On the other hand, sexual abuse of the child could be decisive but, even here, contact might be allowed in appropriate cases – see, for example, *H v H (Child Abuse: Access)* [1989] 1 FLR 212 and *L v L (Child Abuse: Access)* [1989] 2 FLR 16. And see *Re H (Minor: Custody Appeal)* [1991] Fam Law 422, in which the Court of Appeal held that 'reprehensible' behaviour towards a spouse or former spouse did not of itself disentitle either or both spouses from being good or adequate caretakers of the children. Thus, the judge had not erred in failing to make findings concerning the father's allegations that the mother had, inter alia, committed perjury, theft, blackmail, assault and battery, as well as adultery.
7 Thus, in *Richards v Richards* [1984] AC 174 at 205, Lord Hailsham said that 'the court ought not to confine itself to a consideration of purely material requirements or immediate comforts'. But the courts would, nonetheless, wish to satisfy themselves that a parent had the practical resources to ensure that the child's material needs were adequately looked after, as to which see *D v M (Minor) (Custody Appeal)* [1983] Fam 33.

child's care should not be unnecessarily disturbed[1], and that the courts should remain neutral as between different religious persuasions except where they were thought to have a clearly deleterious effect on their adherents[2]. Although the Children Act ushered in a completely new set of principles and orders, well-established principles like those above are, to an extent, still applied under the new law.

We will now consider briefly some of the principles which have emerged from previous decisions of the higher courts and which are likely to carry weight when applying the statutory criteria[3]. In view of the infinite number of variables which are inevitably present in individual cases, these should be treated with caution – the more so, since the scheme introduced by the Children Act has no precise equivalence with what existed before[4].

The ascertainable wishes and feelings of the child concerned (considered in the light of his age and understanding)
The increased importance attached to the views of children in the legislation has already been noted[5]. In this context, despite the argument (following *Gillick*) that the courts might be obliged to follow the wishes of mature children[6], the Children Act merely requires the court to ascertain those wishes and to take them into account. Its overriding duty is to do what is *best* for the child and that may not always coincide with what the child wants[7].

Precisely how old or how mature an individual child has to be before the court's duty bites must, inevitably, be rather uncertain. But it would appear that the onus is on the court to justify its failure to seek out and consider the wishes of an older child. Even before the Children Act, the Court of Appeal had held that failure to

---

1   Whether or not it ought to be disturbed would, of course, depend, to some extent, on how satisfactory was the existing arrangement. As Ormrod LJ said in *S v W* (1981) Fam Law 81 at 82, 'the status quo argument depends for its strength wholly and entirely on whether the status quo is satisfactory or not. The more satisfactory the status quo, the stronger the argument for not interfering. The less satisfactory the status quo, the less one requires before deciding to change'.

2   The most striking example of judicial disapproval of a religious sect and the effect of this on custody arrangements is probably the Court of Appeal's diatribe against Scientology in *Re B and G (Minors) (Custody)* [1985] FLR 493. Discrimination based purely on a parent's religion (as opposed to its effects on the child) might indeed amount to a breach of that parent's rights under the European Convention on Human Rights. See *Hoffmann v Austria* (1993) Series A, No 255C, and Chapter 16 below.

3   These are discussed in greater depth in SM Cretney and JM Masson *Principles of Family Law* (6th edn) (Sweet & Maxwell, 1997) at pp 733–745. For a concise trawl through the checklist, see SM Cretney *Family Law* (3rd edn) (Sweet & Maxwell, 1997) at pp 252–259.

4   While there may, for example, be similarities between custody and residence orders or between access and contact orders, there are also important differences.

5   See Chapter 2 above. On the practical problems involved in ascertaining and conveying the views of children in family proceedings, see C Piper 'Ascertaining the Wishes and Feelings of the Child' [1997] Fam Law 796.

6   J Eekelaar 'Gillick in the Divorce Court' (1986) 136 NLJ 184. In *Re P (Minors) (Wardship)* (1992) *The Times*, May 11, Butler-Sloss LJ emphasised that the court was not *bound* by the wishes of the children, in this case brothers aged 13 and 11 years respectively, and should depart from them when their future welfare required it.

7   For a striking example of the court's refusal to follow children's wishes, see *Re B (Change of Surname)* [1996] 1 FLR 791. For a case in which the child's views proved decisive, see *Re P (A Minor) (Education)* [1992] 1 FLR 316, discussed in Chapter 16 below.

accord proper weight to the strongly held views of a 12-year-old girl was a good ground of appeal[1]. Now, it is quite clear that a demonstrable failure to have regard to *any* factor in the checklist would sustain an appeal. How much weight individual courts may give to the views of particular children must be speculative. Traditionally, there has been some inconsistency among the judiciary on this. The message of the modern law is that the capacity of children of all ages to express a valid opinion on matters affecting them must not be underestimated but must be taken seriously. This is also a striking feature of developments in the public law and the law governing children's evidence[2]. The Children Act makes no express provision for the court to take into account the wishes of parents or other interested adults in private proceedings, although this is required of local authorities looking after children[3]. In practice, the court will, of necessity, be presented with these views and it is implicit in the legislation that it should take them into account.

How, then, should the court discover children's views? The answer to this will depend to some extent on the kind of proceedings in question and the ages of the children. In public proceedings, the child will usually be represented by a guardian ad litem whose duties include conveying the child's views to the court[4]. In private proceedings, children will usually be unrepresented. The judge may decide to interview older children in private[5] or may rely on the report of a welfare officer. In wardship, the official solicitor has traditionally acted as the child's representative. Representation of children is one area in which a major distinction still exists between the public and private law. In public cases, representation of the child is the norm, whereas in private proceedings it is exceptional. It must, at least, be questioned whether this dichotomy is wholly justifiable[6]. On the other hand, there would be massive resource implications in any proposal for the routine representation of children in, for example, divorce proceedings and it can certainly be argued that this degree of intervention would be contrary to the philosophy of the legislation[7].

The physical, emotional and educational needs of the child
The court's task is to take a broad and wide-ranging view of the various needs of the child. Needs other than those specifically mentioned may be taken into account. It is well-established that the court will not allow itself to be unduly swayed by considerations of the child's material needs[8]. The fact that one parent can offer a higher standard of living than the other should not weigh heavily unless the standard of living which one of the parents is able to provide is wholly

---

1   *M v M (Transfer of Custody: Appeal)* [1987] 2 FLR 146.
2   See Chapter 13 below.
3   Section 22(4) and (5).
4   Section 41, Family Proceedings Rules 1991, SI 1991/1247, r 4.11(4) and Family Proceedings Courts (Children Act 1989) Rules 1991, SI 1991/1395, r 11(4).
5   See, for example, *H v H (Child: Judicial Interview)* [1974] 1 WLR 595.
6   See, for example, M Richards 'But what about the children? Some reflections on the Divorce White Paper' [1995] CFLQ 223.
7   As has been noted, the Family Law Act 1996 does provide for the possibility of increased representation of children in certain private proceedings. See Chapter 13 below.
8   As Griffiths LJ put it in *Re P (Adoption: Parental Agreement)* [1985] FLR 635 at 637: 'Anyone with experience of life knows that affluence and happiness are not necessarily synonymous'.

inadequate. The court is much more likely to be influenced by the quality of the relationship which the child has with each parent[1].

Educational needs ought not to be decisive in determining who has the care of a child, since they can usually be met by attaching conditions to the court's principal orders or by accepting undertakings from the primary carer, for example to preserve the existing religious education of the child[2]. Whilst the assessment of needs is supposed to be wholly objective, the value judgments and prejudices of the judiciary have occasionally appeared to intrude[3]. This is perhaps an inevitable hazard with indeterminate welfare tests[4].

The likely effect on the child of any change in his circumstances
We have already alluded to the status quo principle. There is a wealth of empirical evidence that courts, applying the old law, made orders which preserved the existing child care arrangements predominantly involving sole care by mothers[5]. It has been said that this was much more a reflection of what parents agreed themselves than any conscious maternal preference on the part of the judges[6]. The application of this factor should be seen alongside the new principle that delay is prejudicial and the court's proactive role is to eliminate it. There is, in any event, some evidence that, in certain contexts, especially 'snatching' cases, the weight being attached to this factor had already diminished[7]. More fundamentally, the courts are increasingly likely to explore a variety of ways in which parental responsibility may effectively be shared. Hence, the stereotypical notion of

---

1 The spirit of the court's approach to ascertaining welfare is captured particularly well in the following passage from the judgment of Hardie Boys J, in the New Zealand case of *Walker v Walker and Harrison* noted in [1981] *NZ Recent Law* 257:
    ' "Welfare" is an all-encompassing word. It includes material welfare, both in the sense of an adequacy of resources to provide a pleasant home and a comfortable standard of living and in the sense of an adequacy of care to ensure that good health and due personal pride are maintained. However, while material considerations have their place, they are secondary matters. More important are the stability and the security, the loving and understanding care and guidance, the warm and compassionate relationships, that are essential for the full development of the child's own character, personality and talents.'
2 For a case which did apparently turn on the relative capacities of the parents to provide educational stimulus and discipline, especially in the periods immediately before and after the school day, see *May v May* [1986] 1 FLR 325.
3 An example is, perhaps, *B v B (Custody of Children)* [1985] FLR 166 where the judge's decision to deny custody to the father had been influenced by his alleged moral duty to find work and not to take advantage of welfare benefits.
4 Indeed, the view has been put forward that 'the heavily subjective nature of the power granted to the judge means that, so long as he does not claim to be applying it as a conclusive rule of law, a judge can consider almost any factor which could possibly have a bearing on the child's welfare and assign to it whatever weight he or she chooses'. See J Eekelaar *Regulating Divorce* (Clarendon Press, 1991) at p 125. It should also be recalled that no one factor in the checklist is accorded more weight than any other. See Chapter 2 above.
5 See the discussion in SM Cretney and JM Masson *Principles of Family Law* (6th edn) (Sweet & Maxwell, 1997) at p 728 and the studies cited there. For a recent case which reaffirms the status quo principle, see *Re B (Residence Order: Status Quo)* [1998] 1 FLR 520. Here, the father had cared for the child since he was aged two. There were major difficulties concerning contact which culminated in the judge making a residence order in favour of the mother. By that time the boy was aged eight and the Court of Appeal took the view that the decision to transfer residence was plainly wrong and could not possibly be justified on the evidence.
6 J Eekelaar *Family Law and Social Policy* (2nd edn) (Weidenfeld & Nicolson, 1984) at pp 79–80.
7 See Chapter 17.

'winners and losers' reflected in exclusive child care arrangements is fast becoming a thing of the past. The legislation appears to provide at least tacit encouragement for the exploration of a range of possible caring arrangements and it does not support any kind of presumption that existing arrangements should be preserved. Having said that, it remains true that the courts will wish to avoid unnecessary disruption to children where it cannot be demonstrated that a modification of present arrangements would positively advance their interests.

The child's age, sex, background and any characteristics of his which the court considers relevant

While the age or sex of a child has never determined conclusively which parent should have care of the child, the courts have traditionally applied certain rules of thumb which would normally be followed unless there was a good reason for not doing so. These embodied the view that young children, and girls of any age, were generally better off with their mothers, while older boys were more appropriately looked after by their fathers[1]. The House of Lords, as we have seen, has now held that there is no such legal *presumption* but that, in practice, there would still be advantages to a very young child in being with his mother[2]. There was also a well-established principle that siblings should be kept together where possible[3].

The Children Act now requires local authorities in their decision-making to give due consideration to children's 'religious persuasion, racial origin and cultural and linguistic background'[4]. These factors are likely to be especially relevant to the child's placement[5]. Whether or not cultural factors ought to be taken into account by a court which is considering whether the ground for care or supervision is made out, is the subject of some dispute[6]. In the present context it ought to be the case that religious, racial and linguistic factors are relevant to the choice of home for the child although some concerns might be met by conditions or directions[7]. The courts maintain that they take a neutral stance on religious beliefs except where the practices associated with a particular sect are thought to be potentially harmful to the welfare of children[8].

---

1   See, for example, *Bowley v Bowley* [1984] FLR 791; *Allington v Allington* [1985] FLR 586; and *W v W and C* [1968] 3 All ER 408. In *Re W (A Minor) (Residence Order)* [1992] 2 FLR 332, the Court of Appeal held that there was a rebuttable presumption that a baby's best interests were served by being with its mother. But cf *Re S (A Minor) (Custody)* [1991] 2 FLR 388, in which the Court of Appeal held that there was no presumption that one parent should be preferred to another parent for the purpose of looking after a child at a particular age. In this case the judge had erred by substituting his own discretion for that of the justices who had decided that a girl aged two years should live with her father rather than her mother. See also *Re A (A Minor) (Custody)* [1991] 2 FLR 394, another Court of Appeal decision in similar vein.
2   *Brixey v Lynas* [1996] 2 FLR 499.
3   See, for example, *C v C (Minors: Custody)* [1988] 2 FLR 291.
4   Section 22(5)(c).
5   See Chapter 10 below.
6   See Chapter 11 below.
7   See particularly the Court of Appeal decision in *Re M (Child's Upbringing)* [1996] 2 FLR 441, in which the court ordered that a Zulu boy should return to his natural parent in South Africa despite his being cared for in England for some years by a white Afrikaner woman. Cf *Re B (Residence Order: Leave to Appeal)* [1998] 1 FLR 520.
8   See Chapter 16 below.

Any harm which the child has suffered or is at risk of suffering
Exposure of the child to a risk of physical or sexual abuse will be a strong reason
for denying a residence order but not necessarily for refusing contact where this
can be adequately supervised. Where the court considers the child to have
suffered or be at risk of suffering harm, it may wish to direct the local authority to
investigate that child's circumstances. Whether or not the court makes such a
direction, may be a question of degree, since only 'significant' harm is sufficient to
found a care or supervision order. In other cases, the court might wish to give
consideration to short-term protective remedies under the legislation governing
domestic violence and occupation of the family home[1]. Where the court's concern
is of a lesser degree, a family assistance order may be appropriate.

*How capable each of the child's parents (and any other person in relation to whom the
court considers the question to be relevant) is of meeting the child's needs*
The most obvious 'other person' contemplated in the legislation will be any
step-parent or partner of a former spouse. Where a parent has remarried, the
court may see advantages, especially material advantages, to the child living in a
two-parent household rather than a one-parent household[2]. But where a new
partner is thought 'undesirable' or likely to have a seriously negative impact on
the child, the court may be reluctant to reinforce the position with a residence
order[3]. The high incidence of step-parenthood and unmarried cohabitation
following divorce has generated a significant number of applications for either
adoption or joint residence orders in favour of a parent and the new married or
unmarried partner. Under the old law there was, in effect, a legal presumption
against step-parent adoption and in favour of what was then joint custody. The
Children Act abandoned any form of statutory directive against adoption and the
court now has an unfettered choice between adoption and alternative orders.
Much is likely to turn, in individual cases, on the perceived value of the existing
relationship between the child and the parent who does not have primary care[4].
Where a spouse is in full-time employment, his or her capacity to undertake the
day-to-day care of the child will be limited and the court will want to be satisfied
that adequate arrangements for day care have been proposed. This may be a
problem for fathers more than for mothers, given prevailing employment
patterns[5].

*The range of powers available to the court under the Children Act in the proceedings in
question[6]*
It should be remembered that the court is not confined to making those orders
specifically sought by the parties. It has power to make orders of its own volition[7]. A
rather obvious example is that it might, in making a residence order in favour of a

---

1   Part IV of the Family Law Act 1996.
2   As in *Re DW (A Minor) (Custody)* [1984] Fam Law 17.
3   Cohabitation in a lesbian household, for example, has proved a cause of concern, as in *Re P (A
    Minor) (Custody)* (1983) FLR 401.
4   The abolition of the former statutory directives is discussed in A Bainham 'The Privatisation of
    the Public Interest in Children' (1990) 53 MLR 206 at pp 214–216.
5   The fact that a father may have to give up employment or remain unemployed will not
    necessarily prevent an order in his favour. See *B v B (Custody of Children)* [1985] FLR 166.
6   This provision was discussed in Chapter 2 above.
7   Section 10(1)(b).

mother, wish to couple this with a contact order in favour of the father – even if this were not specifically sought. The critical question will be which order, if any, from the range of orders at the court's disposal, would best advance the welfare of the child.

The above factors are not exhaustive since the court is merely required to have regard 'in particular' to them. At the same time the Court of Appeal has held[1] that the checklist represents an extremely useful and important discipline in ensuring that all relevant factors are considered and balanced. Where the factors are finely balanced it is, moreover, important for the judge to give reasons for his decision.

In contested cases the court will pay particular regard to any recommendations in welfare reports and, indeed, must give reasons where it decides not to follow them[2]. The court's power to order a welfare report in family proceedings is a general one whenever it is considering a question with respect to a child under the Children Act[3]. The report may be requested from a probation officer or local authority social worker. Although the court may direct that the report should deal with specific matters relevant to the welfare of the child, it may be more wide-ranging[4]. Welfare reports are ordered much more frequently in contested than in uncontested cases[5]. The Law Commission resisted the suggestion that the court should be obliged to order a report in every case, partly because it was mindful of the need to target limited resources, and partly because of the delays which might otherwise be engendered[6].

The welfare report may be oral or in writing[7]. Where it is in writing, rules of court require its disclosure to the parties in advance of the hearing[8]. The court is entitled to have regard to any statement in the report, or any evidence in it insofar as the court thinks it is relevant to what it is considering[9]. There can, thus, in children cases, be a relaxation in the normal rules of evidence and, in particular, hearsay evidence may be permitted. Evidential issues involving children are discussed in greater depth later[10].

---

1 *B v B (Residence Order: Reasons for Decision)* [1997] 2 FLR 602.
2 *Stephenson v Stephenson* [1985] FLR 1140. Failure to do so may be a ground of appeal: see *W v W (A Minor: Custody Appeal)* [1988] 2 FLR 505 and *Re CB (Access: Attendance of Court Welfare Officer)* [1995] 1 FLR 622.
3 Section 7(1). The court is not confined to ordering one report if it thinks a second report would be useful. See *Re W (Welfare Reports)* [1995] 2 FLR 142.
4 Section 7(2).
5 See the discussion in SM Cretney and JM Masson *Principles of Family Law* (6th edn) (Sweet & Maxwell, 1997) at pp 668–670.
6 Law Com Report No 172 *Guardianship and Custody* (1988) at para 6.15.
7 Section 7(3).
8 Family Proceedings Rules 1991, SI 1991/1247, r 4.17(1) and Family Proceedings Courts (Children Act 1989) Rules 1991, SI 1991/1395, r 17(1). In *Re C (A Minor: Irregularity of Practice)* [1991] 2 FLR 438, the Court of Appeal held that while it was permissible for a judge to see a court welfare officer privately in his chambers during the course of a trial he should only do so in exceptional circumstances, which did not exist in this case.
9 Section 7(4).
10 See Chapter 13 below.

THE CHILDREN ACT AND THE FAMILY LAW ACT: A PHILOSOPHICAL INCONSISTENCY?

It might be thought that there is something of a philosophical inconsistency between the Children Act, which may appear to some to embody a non-interventionist philosophy, and the Family Law Act, which attempts through the enunciation of substantive principles and the manipulation of procedures to give effect to an official policy of discouraging divorce and upholding the institution of marriage. Yet this is only part of the picture. Where the Children Act and the Family Law Act may be seen to be ideologically at one is in their support for, and encouragement of, agreements between parents.

The Family Law Act takes English law a long way towards consensual divorce and is the logical conclusion of a move away from fault-based divorce which began with the Divorce Reform Act 1969. The cumulative effect of consensual divorce, the reform of s 41 of the Matrimonial Causes Act 1973 and the substantial removal of judicial scrutiny of the arrangements for children brought about by the Children Act arguably attaches supreme importance to parents' agreements concerning their children[1]. The reasoning in each case appears to be that the reforms ought to encourage parents to exercise more responsibility, but it has been pointed out that they may just as easily have the opposite effect and encourage a lack of responsibility[2]. This is because the empirical evidence over a long period of time is that, given the choice, men and women are likely to agree, overwhelmingly, that children should remain in the sole, or at least primary, care of their mothers[3]. There is still much uncertainty surrounding the role expected of 'absent' parents, usually, but not invariably, fathers[4]. Thus, it has been said that 'the question is whether legal ideology typifies women as care-givers and men as providers and, if it does, whether this is detrimental to women, or to men, or to both'[5].

The two pieces of legislation do, however, diverge, in one important respect. The Children Act fell short of expressly declaring any official policy on what was best for children when parents part. Eekelaar referred to the position taken in that legislation as 'legal agnosticism'[6]. No attempt was made to influence the *content* of parental agreements by creating legal presumptions in favour, for example, of time-sharing or even of contact as such. Insofar as any particular policy was embodied in the Children Act, this was implicit rather than explicit. There *appeared* to be an ideological commitment to *dual* parenting both during the marriage and following separation or divorce by the preservation of joint parental responsibility. Whether this joint parenting (which carries with it the power of

---

1   See A Bainham 'The Children Act 1989: Welfare and Non-Interventionism' [1990] Fam Law 143.
2   See J Eekelaar *Regulating Divorce* (Clarendon Press, 1991) at ch 6.
3   Discussed by Eekelaar (above) at pp 121–122.
4   Ibid at pp 134–138.
5   Ibid at p 122. For two contrasting perspectives on this question, see J Brophy 'Custody Law, Child Care and Inequality in Britain' in C Smart and S Sevenhuijsen (eds) *Child Custody and the Politics of Gender* (Routledge, 1989); and A Bainham 'The Privatisation of the Public Interest in Children' (1990) 53 MLR 206 at pp 216–219.
6   J Eekelaar *Regulating Divorce* (Clarendon Press, 1991) at pp 123 et seq.

independent action) is the same thing as *co-operative* parenting is open to doubt as we saw with the uncertainty surrounding rights of consultation.

The Family Law Act, in contrast, strikes out and declares an official view of what is best for children in the context of divorce. In the very first section it sets out, inter alia, the general principle that questions should be 'dealt with in a manner designed to promote as good a continuing relationship between the parties and any children affected as is possible in the circumstances' and this is reinforced in s 11. In deciding whether it needs to exercise its powers over children the court is to have particular regard, inter alia, to:

> 'the general principle that, in the absence of evidence to the contrary, the welfare of the child will be best served by –
> (i)   his having regular contact with those who have parental responsibility for him and with other members of his family; and
> (ii) the maintenance of as good a continuing relationship with his parents as is possible.'[1]

It might therefore be said that the Family Law Act builds on the Children Act by making explicit that which was previously only implicit. Whether it will succeed in its aim of preserving better relationships between children and parents remains to be seen.

---

1   Section 11(3)(c).

Chapter 5

THE UNMARRIED FAMILY

INTRODUCTION

The assumption that natural parents have moral obligations, reinforced by legal obligations, to care for their children has not as readily been made in the case of parentage outside marriage. Historically, the child born out of wedlock was a social outcast, 'filius nullius'. When the law first began to impose obligations on unmarried parents through the Poor Law, this was motivated primarily by the desire to avoid unwanted children becoming a pubic burden[1]. In due course, it was recognised that the rights and obligations of unmarried mothers extended beyond purely financial concerns to the responsibility for safeguarding the welfare of their children, but the historical attitude to unmarried fathers persists to some extent today.

Nowadays, the remaining legal distinctions between children born in or out of wedlock, and the underlying policy issues behind these distinctions, revolve around the connection between children and fathers. For this reason, most of this chapter is concerned with how paternity is established and to what extent, and in what circumstances, a man who is found to be the genetic father of a child acquires the benefits and burdens of parenthood. It is again crucial in this context to bear in mind the distinction which the law makes between *parenthood* and possessing *parental responsibility*[2]. A further point which should be made at the outset is that this is not primarily (as some readers might be inclined to think) a chapter about 'father's rights' although, inevitably, this dimension surfaces. The position taken here is rather that there is a *reciprocity* about the relationship between the child and the father so that legal distinctions or discrimination between fathers necessarily amounts to distinctions or discrimination between children[3]. It is, moreover, obvious that the position the law takes on the presence or absence of a legal parental relationship between fathers and children has important legal and practical implications for the mothers of those children.

The law generally does not recognise the parental responsibility of unmarried fathers, except for limited purposes such as financial support and succession[4]. The expression 'unmarried father' is chosen throughout this chapter to describe the father of a child who is not married to the child's mother. Strictly speaking, it can be something of a misnomer since, as Stephen Cretney has pointed out, many such men are in fact *married* – but to someone other than the mother:

---

1   Useful materials tracing the development of illegitimacy laws in their historical context can be found in B Hoggett, D Pearl, E Cooke and P Bates *The Family, Law and Society* (4th edn) (Butterworths, 1996) at pp 488 et seq. See also M Maclean and J Eekelaar *The Parental Obligation* (Hart Publishing, 1997) at ch 3, especially at pp 33 et seq.
2   See Chapter 3.
3   This is not something which has, thus far, been accepted by the English Law Commission or by the Lord Chancellor's Department. See below.
4   This has, however, assumed a greater significance with the enactment of the Child Support legislation, as to which see Chapter 9 below.

'... Charles II, King of England, enjoys a certain notoriety as the father of a number of illegitimate children; yet it would be absurd to describe him, in defiance of the facts, as "unmarried".'[1]

The use of the expression 'unmarried father' is for reasons of convenience and because it is extremely difficult to think of a satisfactory alternative. Some people view the unmarried father as an unnecessary figure in the life of the child, except for his part in the reproductive process and his continuing financial obligation. In recent years, debate concerning the use of so-called 'virgin birth' techniques, where a single woman elects to have a child on her own, has even called into question the first of these functions[2]. It is, of course, possible for a child to be conceived without sexual involvement or any semblance of a relationship between the mother and the genetic father. Ruth Deech has described this rather extreme view of unmarried fatherhood thus:

'Men are nothing more than mobile sperm banks ... their rôle over as soon as conception has been achieved. They fulfil only decorative purposes. It could even be said that in England and in a number of other scientifically advanced countries, the unmarried father has come to be seen as sexually and socially unnecessary, merely a man who pays, or should pay: nicknamed in German a "Zahlvater", expressing the idea that the duties of paternity are a form of perpetual payment for sinful and stolen pleasures, the act of insemination as the occasion for a lifetime of financial obligation. Of the positive and familial aspects of fatherhood we hear little in law.'[3]

In recent years, rather more has been heard of the positive aspects of fatherhood outside marriage. The reasons for this are undoubtedly complex but may be thought to include a heightened awareness of children's rights, the growing numbers of children born into stable cohabitations and the more assertive claims of unmarried fathers themselves. Some of these concerns were expressed by Sir George Baker P, as long ago as 1982, when he said that 'children, whether born in wedlock or not, need fathers. If there is a father then he should have the opportunity of developing the relationship'[4]. Perhaps most importantly, it can be argued that there are international obligations which require the State to create the conditions in which these extra-marital familial relationships can develop[5]. The difficulty with such a policy is that it might be thought to detract from the support which a society wishes to give to the institution of marriage. Hence, the existence of a discriminatory status of illegitimacy can be explained on the basis that the family within marriage was considered to be the only acceptable social grouping in which to raise children.

1 SM Cretney *Family Law* (3rd edn) (Sweet & Maxwell, 1997) at p 176.
2 The matter came to public attention in 1991. See, for example, 'The Inviolate Conception' [1991] Fam Law 204 and 'Virgin birth or filius nullius?' (1991) NLJ 433. The Human Fertilisation and Embryology Act 1990, s 13(5) does attempt to address this issue as follows:
   'A woman shall not be provided with treatment services unless account has been taken of the welfare of any child who may be born as a result of the treatment (including the need of that child for a father), and of any other child who may be affected by the birth.'
   For commentary on this provision, see G Douglas 'Assisted Reproduction and the Welfare of the Child' [1993] *Current Legal Problems* 53.
3 R Deech 'The Unmarried Father and Human Rights' (1992) 4 JCL 3.
4 *S v O (Illegitimate Child: Access)* (1982) 3 FLR 15 at 18.
5 See, for example, A Bainham 'When is a Parent not a Parent? Reflections on the Unmarried Father and his Child in English Law' (1989) 3 IJLF 208, and NV Lowe 'The Meaning and Allocation of Parental Responsibility – A Common Lawyer's Perspective' (1997) 11 *International Journal of Law, Policy and the Family* 192, especially at pp 201–205.

The complementary concepts of legitimacy and illegitimacy also played a crucial role in achieving the orderly devolution of property. The modern law is much less concerned with this latter consideration and much more with the assertion of *parenthood* as the primary legal status in relation to children – perhaps now outstripping marriage as the central organising concept in family law.

Illegitimacy: before 1987

The history of the gradual reform of the illegitimacy laws in England is the story of an attempt to equalise the positions of children born in and out of wedlock by removing the legal disadvantages suffered by the latter but to do so in a way which did not unnecessarily weaken the institution of marriage. This was a piecemeal and incremental process over many years, culminating in the Family Law Reform Act 1987 which at least came close to removing the concept of illegitimacy[1].

The 'illegitimate' child suffered significant legal disadvantages and a considerable social stigma. The disadvantages at common law were principally the absence of succession rights, rights of financial support and the lack of a legal nexus with the father. These legal distinctions were slowly whittled away by widening the categories of those children who were regarded as legitimate[2] and by removing some of the specific disadvantages attaching to illegitimacy more directly by legislation[3]. When, at the end of the 1970s, the Law Commission came to examine the whole question of illegitimacy, a fundamental issue had to be addressed. This was whether the removal of the residual legal discrimination could be achieved simply by sweeping away the few legal distinctions which were left, or whether the status of illegitimacy itself would have to be removed. The Law Commission provisionally preferred the more radical alternative[4] but later resiled from this position[5]. It concluded that the advantages of removing the status of illegitimacy were outweighed by the disadvantages which would flow from conferring automatic parental rights on unmarried fathers[6].

Meanwhile, the Scottish Law Commission was also considering this issue. It, too, concluded that it would be undesirable to give automatic parental rights to unmarried fathers but that all remaining legal distinctions between *children* could, nonetheless, be removed. Insofar as it was necessary to distinguish between fathers, this could be done by reference to the marital status of the parents and not by attaching labels to the children[7]. The English Commission subsequently produced a second report which substantially adopted the Scottish solution[8]. Consequently, s 1 of the Family Law Reform Act 1987 embodies a general rule of

---

1   The Family Law Reform Act 1987 removed most of the remaining legal disadvantages suffered by children born out of wedlock and it became a matter of some doubt whether the distinctions which remained were enough to add up to a discriminatory status.
2   Particularly through the process of legitimation under the Legitimacy Acts of 1926, 1959 and 1976.
3   Thus, under the Family Law Reform Act 1969, ss 14 and 16, an illegitimate child could claim under his father's intestacy or under his will.
4   Law Com Working Paper No 74 *Illegitimacy* (1979).
5   Law Com Report No 118 *Illegitimacy* (1982).
6   Ibid, particularly at paras 4.29–4.36.
7   Scot Law Com No 82 *Illegitimacy* (1984).
8   Law Com Report No 157 *Illegitimacy* (Second Report) (1986).

construction which applies to all legislation and instruments made after 4 April 1988. This is that:

> 'references (however expressed) to any relationship between two persons shall, unless the contrary intention appears, be construed without regard to whether or not the father and mother of either of them, or the father and mother of any person through whom the relationship is deduced, have or had been married to each other at any time.'

The position after 1987

The position, following the 1987 legislation, was that all but a few legal distinctions between children born in and out of wedlock had been removed, along with an attempt to remove the stigmatising language and terminology of illegitimacy. The only remaining differences (apart from the relationship with the father) relate to titles of honour and citizenship. In the light of this, it is an unresolved question whether it is still accurate to talk of a status of legitimacy and illegitimacy[1]. In 1992 the Scottish Law Commission recommended the complete abolition of the concepts of legitimacy, illegitimacy and legitimation in Scotland. The Commission's view was that a separate status could only be justified where the person possessing it was in a significantly different legal position from other people. Since this would no longer be so if the Commission's proposals were accepted, these concepts would be unnecessary, anachronistic and regarded by some as offensive. Thus, the Commission recommended that they all ought to be removed from Scots Law, subject to certain savings relating to hereditary titles and existing deeds and enactments. As the Commission put it, 'In the new Scottish Family Law children should just be children, and people should just be people, whether their parents were married to each other or not'[2]. These proposals were not, however, accepted by the Westminster Parliament and Scots law thus continues to distinguish between married and unmarried fathers[3].

What, then, is the current position in English law? There is no doubt that legal distinctions of substance do remain between children born in and out of wedlock and that the concepts of legitimacy and illegitimacy remain on the statute book, albeit in pre-1987 legislation not repealed by the 1987 Act. On the other hand, it is equally clear that it was an express purpose of the Family Law Reform Act to remove the discriminatory labelling of children and in this way to lessen any social stigma there might be attaching to birth outside marriage. As long ago as 1979 the English Law Commission recognised the force of the language used by the law. It said:

> 'We believe that the law can help to lessen social prejudices by setting an example clearly based upon the principle that the parents' marital relationship is irrelevant to the child's legal position. Changes in the law cannot give the illegitimate child the benefits of a secure, caring, family background. They cannot even ensure that he does not suffer financially ... But they can at least remove the *additional* hardship of attaching an opprobrious description to him.'[4]

---

1   The Scottish Law Commission concluded in 1992 that, at least in Scotland, the equivalent legislation (the Law Reform (Parent and Child) (Scotland) Act 1986) had not removed the status of legitimacy or illegitimacy; Scot Law Com No 135 *Report on Family Law* (1992) at para 17.3.

2   Ibid at para 17.4.

3   For a critique, see E Sutherland 'Scotland: Child Law Reform – At Last!' in A Bainham (ed) *The International Survey of Family Law 1995* (Martinus Nijhoff, 1997) 435 at pp 438–439.

4   Law Com Working Paper No 74 *Illegitimacy* (HMSO, 1979) at para 3.15.

Hence the policy of the 1987 legislation was to distinguish only between *parents* and not between children where it was still thought necessary to perpetuate legal distinctions. A reasonable question, therefore, if 'illegitimacy' is considered to have survived the 1987 reforms, is whether we should be talking about *illegitimate parents* rather than *illegitimate children*[1]. Rightly or wrongly, the evidence is that the media, judges, academics and society in general continue to use the language of illegitimacy in some cases apparently oblivious of the policy of the law over the last decade. Many illustrations could be given from post-1987 case-law[2], but a recent one is the Court of Appeal decision in *Dawson v Wearmouth*[3] where the judgment (given by Hirst and Thorpe LJJ) is riddled with references to 'an illegitimate child'. Is this use of language perhaps justifiable? If there are still distinctions of substance, and if the concepts of legitimacy and illegitimacy remain on the statute book, perhaps differentiating language is still required. Perhaps to refrain from using the language of legitimacy/illegitimacy in relation to children is to prefer 'political correctness' to accuracy[4]. An opposing view is that the spirit, if not the letter, of the 1987 legislation together with international obligations require that the language of illegitimacy be expunged from the law[5] even if certain substantive legal distinctions survive. The essence of this argument is that in the real world the question of status is going to be bound up to a large extent with the use of language. If those most involved with applying and interpreting the law continue to use the language of illegitimacy, it is not really surprising that it remains in common usage in society[6].

The rest of this chapter is devoted to these issues. The initial question of how paternity is established outside marriage is considered first. The nature of the legal relationship between the father and the child is then examined. The legal effects of establishing paternity are looked at and consideration is given to the initial allocation of parental responsibility and legal procedures which may be invoked by the unmarried man who wishes to acquire full parental responsibility. The chapter concludes by reviewing some of the very different perspectives on the future direction of the law.

---

1   See B Hoggett, D Pearl, E Cooke and P Bates *The Family, Law and Society* (4th edn) (Butterworths, 1996) where there is a section headed 'Illegitimate children or illegitimate parents?'.
2   For illustrations of the use of the language of illegitimacy post-1987 in the press, by judges and by academics, see A Bainham 'Changing families and changing concepts: reforming the language of family law' [1998] CFLQ 1, at pp 8–11.
3   [1997] 2 FLR 629.
4   This is certainly Cretney's view. See SM Cretney *Family Law* (3rd edn) (Sweet & Maxwell, 1997) at p 176.
5   Mary Ann Glendon, writing in 1989, clearly thought that the Family Law Reform Act had succeeded in expunging the terminology of illegitimacy from English law. See MA Glendon *The Transformation of Family Law* (University of Chicago Press, 1989) at p 269.
6   A Bainham (above) at p 11.

ESTABLISHING PATERNITY

The automatic position

Where a child is born to an unmarried woman, there is no presumption of paternity equivalent to that which applies where a child is born to a married woman[1], and this is so whether or not she is in a stable relationship or cohabiting. The above statement requires some qualification where a child is born following assisted reproduction[2]. We considered the issue of the determination of legal fatherhood in cases of assisted reproduction in Chapter 3 and are concerned here only with children conceived in the ordinary way by sexual intercourse.

Proving paternity

Births outside marriage take place in a wide variety of circumstances, ranging from stable cohabitations equivalent to marriage in all but name, to the casual encounter, or even rape. In some instances the mother will have had intercourse with more than one man around the time of conception so that there may be doubt, even in her own mind, about who is the father. Hence, the law has to provide mechanisms for determining paternity, although in many cases paternity will in fact remain a matter of doubt. These are the system of birth registration and the use of blood tests or other scientific tests, often, but not necessarily, in the context of legal proceedings. It should be noted that the Labour Government has issued a Consultation Paper which is seeking views, inter alia, on whether it would be possible to establish a single procedure for obtaining a declaration of paternity which would be valid for all purposes[3].

Birth registration

The effect of registration of the name of a man as father of a child is to create a rebuttable presumption that he is the father[4]. Accordingly, where registration takes place, the onus will shift to anyone wishing to dispute paternity. The circumstances under which registration may be effected are, therefore, all-important.

Where parents are married, there is for both parents a statutory obligation to register particulars of the birth within 42 days of its occurrence[5]. Where the child is born to an unmarried mother, only the mother is under this obligation[6]. The father is neither under a duty, nor does he have an unqualified independent right, to register his paternity. The circumstances under which his name may be registered were significantly extended by the Family Law Reform Act 1987 and the

---

1 See Chapter 4 above and, generally, G Douglas and NV Lowe 'Becoming a Parent in English Law' (1992) 108 LQR 414.
2 As to which see Douglas and Lowe (above) at pp 418–422; G Douglas *Law, Fertility and Reproduction* (Sweet & Maxwell, 1992) at pp 127–132; and D Morgan and RG Lee *Blackstone's Guide to the Human Fertilisation and Embryology Act 1990* (Blackstone Press, 1991), especially ch 6.
3 See Consultation Paper *1. Court Procedures for the Determination of Paternity*; and *2. The Law on Parental Responsibility for Unmarried Fathers* (Lord Chancellor's Department, March 1998).
4 Births and Deaths Registration Act 1953, s 34(2).
5 Ibid, s 2.
6 Ibid, s 10(1), which provides that the unmarried father is not required to give information concerning the birth.

Children Act 1989[1]. These circumstances are set out below. In essence, their cumulative effect is to prevent independent registration by a man claiming to be the father, viz without the mother's co-operation in recognising his paternity, or a court order.

The circumstances are:

(1) at the joint request of the mother and father by personal attendance;
(2) at the request of either the father or mother where statutory declarations of paternity and the mother's acknowledgment of it are produced;
(3) at the request of either on production of a copy of a parental responsibility agreement under s 4 of the Children Act and a declaration that the agreement has not been terminated by the court; and
(4) at the request of either on the production of certain orders which entail a determination of paternity together with a declaration that the order has not been terminated by a court. The relevant orders are parental responsibility orders under s 4 of the Children Act, and orders that the father make financial provision for the child[2].

Where none of the above circumstances apply, the father's name will be left blank but may subsequently be added to the register by re-registration, subject to the same conditions set out above[3], where a declaration of parentage has been obtained under the Family Law Act 1986[4], or where the parents have married following the birth[5]. It is clearly the case that many men registered as fathers under these procedures will not in fact be the genetic fathers. As with the *pater est* presumption at common law, registration of paternity provides a means of *attributing* legal parentage which may or may not coincide with the biological reality. It is usually only in the event of a dispute that there will be an occasion to look behind the attribution of parentage arising from the fact of registration. Yet, although a man seeking registration as father will not have to establish an actual genetic link with the child he will, it seems, have to establish that he is himself a biological *male*. Such is the result of the decision of the European Court of Human Rights in the remarkable case of *X, Y and Z v The United Kingdom*[6].

Here, a female-to-male transsexual (X) sought to be registered as the father of a child (Z) with the co-operation of his female partner (Y) who was the mother of the child. The child had been conceived through artificial insemination by donor after X and Y had successfully obtained licensed fertility treatment together. The Registrar-General refused to register X as the father taking the position that only a biological male could be so registered. For these purposes English law still takes the line that a person's sex is determined at birth, applying biological criteria, and

---

1 Births and Deaths Registration Act 1953, s 10(1), as amended.
2 A maintenance order under the Children Act 1989, Sch 1 qualifies. A declaration of parentage under the Child Support Act 1991, s 27 does not, of itself, have effect for these purposes (s 27(3)) but is admissible in evidence in other civil proceedings concerning paternity under the Civil Evidence Act 1968, s 12(5).
3 Births and Deaths Registration Act 1953, s 10A(1).
4 Ibid, s 14A.
5 Ibid, s 14.
6 (1997) 24 EHRR 143. For a commentary on the case, see A Bainham 'Sex, Gender and Fatherhood: Does Biology Really Matter?' (1997) CLJ 512.

does not recognise the 'psychological' sex of a post-operative transsexual[1]. The European Commission had found by 13 votes to 5 that the refusal of registration violated X's rights under the Convention but the Court (with six dissenting opinions) found that there had been no violation of Article 8 taking into account the wide margin of appreciation enjoyed by States. In particular, it regarded as crucial the fact that there was, as yet, no common European standard about granting rights to transsexuals or about the manner in which the social relationship between a child conceived by donor sperm and the person performing the social role of the father should be reflected in law. It was not thought to be clearly demonstrated that to register X would be of benefit to the child Z and it was pointed out that X and Y could together apply for a joint residence order, the effect of which would be to give X parental responsibility over Z.

Findings of paternity in legal proceedings

Questions of paternity may fall to be determined in many kinds of legal proceedings. They may arise as a secondary, yet necessary, issue in proceedings the primary purpose of which is something else. A child's upbringing or welfare may be in issue, for example where an alleged father is seeking a parental responsibility order or a s 8 order. To establish standing to seek these orders, he will need to prove that he is indeed the father of the child[2]. The principal issue may relate to property or financial claims. Thus, rights of inheritance may depend on being able to establish a biological connection[3]. Most obviously, the issue will often arise where a man is denying financial responsibility for a child under the child support legislation[4]. Alternatively, paternity may be the only question where, for example, a person is seeking a declaration of parentage or legitimacy. Under the Family Law Reform Act 1987[5], an application may be made by someone for a declaration that a named person is or was his parent, that he is the legitimate child of his parents, or that he has or has not become a legitimated person. The procedure may only be invoked by the 'child' and not by an alleged parent and it is not possible to obtain a negative declaration of paternity or a declaration of illegitimacy. The court may refuse a declaration only if to grant it would be manifestly contrary to public policy. A finding of paternity in any of the above proceedings binds the parties and is prima facie evidence of paternity in any other proceedings. As such, the onus is on anyone seeking to challenge this to rebut the presumption[6].

---

1   *Corbett v Corbett (otherwise Ashley)* [1971] P 83. The European Court has twice held that this approach does not itself violate the rights of transsexuals under the Convention in *Rees v The United Kingdom* (1986) 9 EHRR 56 and *Cossey v The United Kingdom* (1990) 13 EHRR 622.
2   Otherwise he would require leave to seek a s 8 order. See s 10 of the Children Act.
3   As we saw in Chapter 4, this was the case in *Re Overbury (deceased)* [1954] Ch 122.
4   See, for example, *T v Child Support Agency and Another* [1997] 2 FLR 875, and Chapter 9 below.
5   Section 22 of the Family Law Reform Act 1987 and s 56 of the Family Law Act 1986, which followed Law Com Report No 132 *Declarations in Family Matters* (1984).
6   Civil Evidence Act 1968, s 12, as amended by the Family Law Reform Act 1987, s 29.

Blood tests and other scientific tests

The most effective way of proving paternity in legal proceedings is through the use of tests, although other evidence may also be valuable[1]. Whilst tests will usually be court directed, there is no reason why they should not be undertaken voluntarily.

Traditionally, the best available evidence has been the conventional blood test. This entails a comparison of the blood of the mother, the child and the alleged father. Since blood has certain inherited characteristics it is possible to identify those which have been derived from the father. Such a test cannot identify conclusively who is the father, since the blood of more than one man may exhibit the relevant characteristics. Yet where these characteristics are absent, it is possible to *exclude* conclusively the man in question. Where the alleged father is not excluded by the test, his blood group characteristics are examined as a percentage of the general population. If the incidence of men in the group is small, this will be strong evidence that he is the father, especially if supported by other evidence concerning, for example, the mother's sexual relationships at the relevant time.

The Family Law Reform Act 1987[2] extended the court's powers to order 'scientific tests' based on samples of genetic material other than blood, but this power has not as yet been implemented. The DNA profiling technique, however, now enables paternity to be established conclusively, thus overcoming the limitations of the conventional blood test. The technique entails the analysis of genetic samples such as blood specimens, semen, saliva or hair roots. It examines the deoxyribonucleic acid in chromosomes which contains an individual's unique genetic pattern of characteristics transmitted by that individual's parents[3].

The court has a general power to direct such tests[4], but may not order a party to undergo them without that party's consent[5]. The consent of a person with care and control of a child under 16 years of age is also required[6]. Where someone refuses to comply with a direction, the court may, however, draw adverse inferences from this[7]. This will often result in a finding of paternity against him and the very fact of refusal may amount to corroboration of the mother's evidence[8]. Refusal by a certain man to undergo a test may result in an adverse

---

1 Such as evidence of the mother's sexual relationships during the relevant period or the physical absence of her husband.

2 Family Law Reform Act 1987, s 23(1).

3 See, particularly, R White and J Greenwood 'DNA Fingerprinting and the Law' (1988) 51 MLR 145, and K Kelly, J Rankin and R Wink 'Method and Applications of DNA Fingerprinting: A Guide for the Non-Scientist' (1987) Crim LR 105.

4 Family Law Reform Act 1969, s 20(1), as amended.

5 Ibid, s 21(1).

6 Ibid, s 21(3). In *Re R (Blood Test: Constraint)* [1998] 1 FLR 745, Hale J held that since a parent had a right to compel a child to submit to a blood test, the court had power also, in the exercise of its inherent jurisdiction, to authorise the use of physical constraints against a child if satisfied that it was the right course of action. In this case the child, aged 22 months, was ordered to be delivered into the care and control of the Official Solicitor for the purpose of compliance with the court's direction. Cretney comments (at [1998] Fam Law 256) that this was a controversial use of the inherent jurisdiction since it appears to be contrary to the principle in the Family Law Reform Act 1969 that blood tests are not to be administered compulsorily. It is not clear from the report whether the mother was objecting to the child being tested but this seems likely to have been the case. On other controversial uses of the inherent jurisdiction, see Chapter 11 below.

7 Ibid, s 23(1).

8 *McVeigh v Beattie* [1988] Fam 69.

inference that he is the father[1]. Conversely, where a man believes he is the father and does not want to put his paternity to the test, he may have an adverse inference drawn against him that he is *not* the father[2]. The court has a discretion to direct tests and is not bound by the welfare principle in exercising this, since the child's welfare is not directly in issue[3]. It is clear that the court should have regard to the interests of the child in arriving at its decision, although it may not always be easy to determine where these lie. Undoubtedly, there is a case for saying that the child himself (in addition to the other parties) has an interest in discovering the truth about his identity[4], but this may have to be weighed against a possible risk to the disruption of existing relationships. Two Court of Appeal decisions illustrate the dilemmas with which the courts have had to wrestle in these cases. They also reveal how the courts have wavered in the weight which they have attached to ascertaining the biological truth as opposed to considerations of family stability.

Re F (A Minor: Paternity Test)[5] shows the traditional preference of the courts for leaving the status quo undisturbed and refusing to direct tests where the child is being raised in an ongoing marriage. Here, the mother had had sexual relations with her husband and another man claiming to be the father at around the time of conception. This man's relationship with the mother had ceased but he nonetheless applied for a parental responsibility order and contact order in relation to the child. The Court of Appeal upheld the judge's refusal to direct blood tests. It was held that the child's welfare depended primarily for the foreseeable future on her relationship with her mother and the stability of the family unit and that this need was not outweighed by any advantage to the child which could accrue from knowledge of the biological truth.

A very different view was taken in *Re H (Paternity: Blood Test)*[6], but here there was a crucial distinguishing feature in that the mother's husband had had a vasectomy well before the birth of the child. Again, the child was being raised as a child of the marriage – the mother having become reconciled to her husband following an affair. Her former lover sought contact with the child and a parental responsibility order. Here, the Court of Appeal upheld the judge's decision to direct tests notwithstanding the mother's opposition to tests on her child. Ward LJ said that it was in the child's best interests to be told 'the truth' unless the child's welfare justified a 'cover up'. The mother ought not to be 'living a lie' but ought to be following the maxim which she should be teaching her children 'at her knee' that

---

1   See *Re A (A Minor) (Paternity: Refusal of Blood Test)* [1994] 2 FLR 463, in which it was held that since a DNA test could have conclusively established who the father was, a man could put the issue beyond doubt by submitting to the test.

2   *Re G (Parentage: Blood Sample)* [1997] 1 FLR 360.

3   *S v McC* [1972] AC 24. Such a test should not be directed where the court is satisfied that it would be *against* the best interests of the child concerned, but a direction can be made despite the opposition of a parent if it is consistent with the child's welfare. See *Re H (Paternity: Blood Test)* [1996] 2 FLR 65.

4   Discussed in K O'Donovan 'A Right to Know One's Parentage?' (1988) 2 IJLF 27, E Haimes '"Secrecy": What Can Artificial Reproduction Learn from Adoption?' (1988) 2 IJLF 46, and S Maclean and M Maclean 'Keeping secrets in assisted reproduction – the tension between donor anonymity and the need of the child for information' [1996] CFLQ 243.

5   [1993] 1 FLR 598.

6   [1996] 2 FLR 65. For comments, see A Bainham, 'Vasectomies, Lovers and Disputed Offspring: Honesty is the Best Policy (Sometimes)' (1996) CLJ 444 and B Gilbert 'Paternity, truth and the interests of the child' [1996] CFLQ 361.

'honesty is the best policy'. Moreover, the sooner the child was told the truth, the better. Importantly, the court did not see any necessary inconsistency between upholding the *social* fatherhood of the husband while possibly establishing the *biological* parentage of the former lover.

It may be that increasingly in the future it will not be assumed that a choice necessarily has to be made between stability and truth or between potential fathers. With the very high incidence of social parenting and a growing emphasis on the child's right to knowledge of biological origins, the way forward may be to acknowledge the child's interests in *both* potential fathers albeit performing different roles. Certainly, the courts do not regard the genetic link as crucial to the contact question and have openly recognised in this context the importance to the child of the social father[1]. Part of the problem may be thought to arise from the legal position that there can only be *two* parents which in turn can create a mindset that the child can have only two significant adults in his life. This is a view which is likely to be increasingly questioned.

A compulsory or voluntary process?

The process of establishing paternity outside marriage is still largely a voluntary one in the sense that neither the mother nor the father is under any automatic legal obligation to disclose or register paternity. Also, there is no public agency in England charged with the responsibility of establishing the parentage of *all* children[2]. Yet it is possible to identify certain features of the existing legal process which, while falling short of compulsion, do exert pressure on individuals to co-operate. The power of the court to draw adverse inferences in the course of legal proceedings for non-compliance with a blood test direction is one such feature. A rather unusual example of pressure on mothers occurred in *Re J (A Minor) (Wardship)*[3] where the court restrained, by injunction, a mother from leaving the country until a DNA test could be carried out. Sheldon J held that since the test could establish paternity with virtual certainty, it was in the interests of the alleged father and the child that it be carried out and that these interests outweighed the mother's interest in freedom to travel.

---

1   See, for example, *O v L (Blood Tests)* [1995] 2 FLR 930.
2   In some jurisdictions, notably in the countries of Scandinavia and the former West Germany, the State has assumed a much more proactive role on the principle that, wherever possible, paternity should be established in every case of birth outside marriage. For an illuminating account of the position in the former West and East German States and the problems caused by reunification, see R Frank, 'Germany: The Need for Reform in Parentage Law' in A Bainham (ed) *The International Survey of Family Law 1995* (Martinus Nijhoff, 1997). The policy in the Scandinavian countries reflects in part the notion of the child's right to knowledge of biological origins. For the position in Sweden, see Å Saldeen 'The Rights of Children to Speak for Themselves and Obtain Access to Information Concerning their Biological Origins' in A Bainham (ed) *The International Survey of Family Law 1994* (Martinus Nijhoff, 1996) at pp 443–444.
3   [1988] 1 FLR 65. See also *Re R (Blood Test: Constraint)* [1998] 1 FLR 745 discussed above.

The whole emphasis in the 1990s has shifted with the enactment of the Child Support Act 1991[1]. Where an unmarried mother is in receipt of State benefits, the Child Support Agency is charged with the responsibility of pursuing an alleged father for child support maintenance calculated in accordance with a statutory formula. In fulfilling these functions, the Secretary of State may, subject to certain qualifications, require the mother to authorise action to recover maintenance[2]. Where the mother fails to co-operate, the Secretary of State may give a 'reduced benefit direction'[3]. Moreover, once action has been taken by the Agency, the mother is required to co-operate with the Agency by providing information relating to the father[4].

Thus, in this context at least, there is an element of compulsion in establishing paternity. Whether similar pressure should be applied where considerations of public expenditure savings do not intrude is no less controversial. The issue involves examination of a wide spectrum of interests including those of the child, the mother, the alleged father, the State, and third parties such as other members of the mother's family.

PARENTAL RESPONSIBILITY IN THE UNMARRIED FAMILY

The automatic position

A *parent without parental responsibility*
Where a child's parents were unmarried at the time of his birth[5], the mother has sole parental responsibility[6]. The father is, however, within the definition of 'parent' in the Children Act and is thus in the unique position of being a 'parent without parental responsibility'. In order to become a legal parent in the fullest sense, the unmarried father must take steps to acquire parental responsibility through legal process. There are now several alternative options open to him, depending on the circumstances, which include an agreement with the mother, a parental responsibility order, a residence order or (in the event of the mother's death) guardianship. All of these mechanisms must be considered but, before doing so, it is important to have an appreciation of what it means, in law and in practice, to be a parent without parental responsibility. This is the position which arises by operation of law and it is, certainly for the foreseeable future, likely to be the legal position which applies to the majority of unmarried fathers. Only the very small minority who take positive action acquire the increased benefits and burdens which go with having parental responsibility.

---

1   For a detailed analysis of the Act, see R Bird *Child Maintenance: The New Law* (2nd edn) (Family Law, 1993) and E Jacobs and G Douglas *Child Support: The Legislation* (Sweet & Maxwell, 1997). For critiques of the objectives of the legislation, see J Eekelaar 'A Child Support Scheme for the United Kingdom' [1991] Fam Law 15 and M Hayes 'Making and Enforcing Child Maintenance Obligations: Will the Proposed Scheme Cause More Harm than Good?' [1991] Fam Law 105.
2   Child Support Act 1991, s 6(1).
3   Ibid, s 46.
4   Ibid, s 6(9).
5   This has a restricted meaning in accordance with the Children Act, s 2(3). In essence, the expression excludes those regarded as legitimate under various enactments, and adopted children.
6   Children Act 1989, s 2(2).

As we have seen, certain legal consequences flow automatically from the legal status of *parenthood* and are not dependent on the possession of parental responsibility. The unmarried father is thus in the same position as all other parents for the purposes of succession. He may succeed to his child's estate, or the child may succeed to his, in the event of either of them dying intestate[1]; he has an obligation to maintain the child financially[2]; there is a presumption of reasonable contact in his favour where the child is in care and he has a right to be consulted by a local authority about decisions taken in relation to the child, where the authority is accommodating the child[3], and, finally, he has standing to commence or participate in certain kinds of legal proceedings. Thus, as a parent, the unmarried father may apply without leave for any s 8 order[4]; he ought to be entitled to participate in care proceedings[5]; and, although his consent is not required for adoption[6], and he is not entitled to be party to the adoption hearing[7], the court must satisfy itself in certain respects about his intentions[8] where it is considering an application to free a child for adoption[9].

On the other hand, those legal effects which arise from holding parental responsibility do not accrue to the unmarried father despite his being a parent. He has no right to look after the child physically and no right to take or participate in decisions regarding upbringing[10]. Third parties have no duty to deal with him or to take his views into account. For these purposes, it must be appreciated that no distinction is made between the unmarried man in a stable cohabitation and the unmarried man who is living separately from the mother. There will, of course, be practical distinctions since the cohabitant, unlike the non-cohabitant, is likely to be performing the role of social father. Indeed, it is probable that at least some unmarried cohabitants are unaware of the male partner's lack of legal responsibility for the child. While they are living together amicably it is unlikely that much will turn on the strict legal position between the parents and, of course, the father will, in any event, have the powers and responsibilities which devolve on any de facto carer[11].

---

1 Family Law Reform Act 1987, s 18.
2 Child Support Act 1991, ss 1(1) and 54. This obligation applies notwithstanding that the father has not acquired parental responsibility. See the Children Act, s 3(4).
3 Children Act, ss 34(1) and 22(4) respectively.
4 Ibid, s 10(4) and *M v C and Calderdale Metropolitan Borough Council* [1993] 1 FLR 505.
5 He is not automatically a party unless he has acquired parental responsibility but may apply to be joined. In any event, he is entitled to receive notice of the proceedings. See Family Proceedings Rules 1991, SI 1991/1247, r 4.7 and Appendix 3.
6 Adoption Act 1976, ss 16(1), 72, as amended by FLRA 1987, s 7(2) and interpreted in *Re L (A Minor) (Adoption: Procedure)* [1991] 1 FLR 171.
7 The court may join him at its discretion. See *Re B (A Minor) (Adoption)* [1991] Fam Law 136.
8 Adoption Act 1976, s 18(7) and see Chapter 7 below.
9 In *Re L (A Minor) (Adoption: Procedure)* [1991] 1 FLR 171, the Court of Appeal said that the effect of the rules was to require an adoption agency to take into account the views of the father where these were known to it, but not to seek him out especially where his views might not be in the child's best interests. See also *Re P (Adoption) (Natural Father's Rights)* [1994] 1 FLR 771.
10 A good example is *Dawson v Wearmouth* [1997] 2 FLR 629, where an unmarried father tried unsuccessfully to persuade the courts that the child should be known by his surname rather than the surname of the mother's ex husband which she had chosen. The initial choice of name is the mother's alone (as the person with sole parental responsibility) and the father's claims are limited to a possible legal challenge based on the child's best interests.
11 Section 3(5) of the Children Act. In some ways his position is analogous to that of a step-father.

Reasons for withholding automatic parental responsibility

It is the range of circumstances in which parentage can arise outside marriage which best explains the reluctance to confer full parental responsibility on all unmarried fathers. As Balcombe LJ has put it:

> 'the position of the natural father can be infinitely variable; at one end of the spectrum his connection with the child may be only the single act of intercourse (possibly even rape) which led to conception: at the other end of the spectrum he may have played a full part in the child's life from birth onwards, only the formality of marriage to the mother being absent. Considerable social evils might have resulted if the father at the bottom end of the spectrum had been automatically granted full parental right and duties ...'[1]

These considerations carried some weight with the Law Commission. In particular, the Commission was impressed by fears that unmarried mothers, who undoubtedly bear primary responsibility for the care of their children, might be subjected to interference and harassment by 'unmeritorious' men and might suffer stress or insecurity where they had formed subsequent relationships[2].

The father's lack of parental responsibility not only affects his relationship vis-à-vis the mother, but also, significantly, his standing in relation to the State[3]. He has no right to object to a voluntary arrangement between the mother and social services for the local authority to look after the child. This was a problem which surfaced in several reported cases under the old law[4]. Although the father does have standing to apply for a residence or contact order in these circumstances, the reality is that this may prove a difficult hurdle where the child has, in the meantime, been placed in substitute care. It is certainly not as effective, from the father's point of view, as an initial right of objection would be.

It has been noted that the unmarried father has no right to veto adoption[5]. Neither does he have the right to appoint a guardian[6]. All of these limitations on the father's parental status will, however, be overcome if he succeeds, through one route or another, in obtaining parental responsibility.

Acquiring parental responsibility

The unmarried father may obtain parental responsibility by agreement with the mother, by obtaining a residence order or parental responsibility order or, possibly, where the mother has died, by being appointed guardian. Where he is only concerned to establish or preserve contact with the child, or question some aspect of upbringing, the appropriate course will be to apply for a s 8 order.

1　*Re H (Illegitimate Child: Father: Parental Rights) (No 2)* [1991] 1 FLR 214 at 218.
2　Law Com Report No 118 *Illegitimacy* (1982) especially at para 4.50.
3　For a particularly good example of this under the old law see the House of Lords decision in *M v H* [1988] 3 All ER 5.
4　The right of objection extends only to those with parental responsibility, as does the subsequent right of removal of the child. See s 20(7) and (8) of the Children Act.
5　But see the decision of the European Court of Human Rights in *Keegan v Ireland* (1994) 18 EHRR 342 which effectively holds (in the context of Irish Law) that a secret adoption deliberately concealed from the father is a breach of his rights under the European Convention.
6　The right extends only to parents with parental responsibility and guardians. See s 5(3) and (4) of the Children Act.

Parental responsibility agreements

The Family Law Reform Act 1987 stopped short of allowing unmarried parents to share parental responsibility by agreement without the necessity of going to court. The Law Commission originally rejected the idea on the basis that it had the potential for eroding the institution of marriage by 'blurring the legal distinction between marriage and other relationships'[1]. This view was criticised by some commentators who felt that to recognise private agreements could be a means of allowing 'meritorious' fathers in stable relationships to acquire full parental status while excluding 'unmeritorious' men from parental participation[2]. The Law Commission was, in due course, persuaded of this view[3] and the Children Act 1989 gave effect to its recommendations. The Children Act provides that 'the father and mother may by agreement ... provide for the father to have parental responsibility for the child'[4]. The agreement must be made in prescribed form and recorded in the Principal Registry of the Family Division[5]. The purpose of these formalities is to warn parents that the agreement will seriously affect their legal position, to advise them to seek legal advice and to inform them about the ways in which the agreement can be brought to an end. The court's function is a purely administrative one and it has no power to question the desirability of the agreement for the welfare of the child. The agreement is, however, revocable by the court on the application of anyone with parental responsibility, or on the application of the child himself where the court has given the child leave on being satisfied that he has sufficient understanding to make the application[6].

The parental responsibility agreement is primarily designed for unmarried couples in stable relationships who wish to bring the legal situation into line with the factual position in which they are effectively raising a child together. It also seems highly likely that at least some agreements are made to head off applications to the courts for parental responsibility orders. Given the apparently liberal attitude of the courts to the making of such orders, in many instances the mother will be advised to share parental responsibility voluntarily rather than go to court. Under the old law, this sharing of parental status was not possible, even by court order[7]. Yet it was questionable from the outset how far these agreements would be used in practice. Parents living together amicably may see no advantage in formalising their arrangements, especially since some people choose to cohabit precisely because of their dislike of the formalities which attach to marriage. They may also be unaware of the disparity in their respective legal positions or of the provision for agreements[8]. There is yet a further possibility that the mother may not be sufficiently confident about the relationship, or the father's parenting role,

---

1 Law Com Report No 118 (above) at para 4.8.
2 See, in particular, J Eekelaar 'Second Thoughts on Illegitimacy Reform' [1985] Fam Law 261.
3 Law Com Report No 172 *Guardianship and Custody* (1988) at para 2.18.
4 Section 4(1)(b).
5 Section 4(2) and the Parental Responsibility Agreement Regulations 1991, SI 1991/1478.
6 Section 4(3) and (4).
7 It was possible for a legal custody order to be obtained by the father but this was unenforceable where he was cohabiting with the mother and lapsed after three months' cohabitation. See Guardianship of Minors Act 1971, s 9(3). In effect, an order for joint legal custody was not possible.
8 The Scottish Law Commission thought that these agreements were only a 'second best solution' and that an automatic status was preferable. See Scot Law Com Report No 135 at para 2.51.

that she would wish to dilute her own legal control by sharing parental responsibility.

The statistics for the registration of parental responsibility agreements reveal rather strikingly that these misgivings about the extent of the use of these agreements were warranted. After an initial surge of interest which lead to the registration of over 5,000 agreements in 1994, the figure for 1996 had fallen back to an estimated 3,590, although this was a slight increase of 4% on 1995. Interestingly, in the same period, indeed since 1992, there has been a slow but steady increase in parental responsibility *orders* which rose by over 27% between 1995 and 1996 to around 5,680[1]. Yet, even taken together, agreements and orders made in 1996 total less than 10,000 and clearly account for only a tiny minority of births outside marriage[2]. It therefore remains the case that the overwhelming majority of unmarried fathers do not acquire parental responsibility.

A final matter is guardianship. The mother might be prepared to appoint the father as guardian, in which case he would only acquire parental responsibility if she should die. In this event, if she had not appointed the father as a guardian, he might himself apply to the court to be appointed guardian[3].

Court orders

If the mother is unwilling to share responsibility voluntarily, the father may apply to the court for a parental responsibility order or, if he wishes to take over the physical care of the child, a residence order. Clearly, this will most commonly arise where the father and mother are living apart and do not have an ongoing relationship.

The parental responsibility order is a reincarnation of the former 'parental rights order' introduced by the Family Law Reform Act 1987[4], and reflects the conceptual changes wrought by the Children Act. The order, if granted, has the same effect as the parental responsibility agreement and may be similarly terminated by the court[5]. Its effect is to give the father an equal say in all matters of upbringing but it will not give him any superior claim vis-à-vis the mother to look after the child. If the father wishes to have the child in his care, he will need to apply for a residence order.

The parental responsibility order: a status-conferring device?

It was quickly established, even before the Children Act came into force, that the primary purpose of the former 'parental rights order' was to confer on the father the full status of legal parent and that the order was appropriately used even where it was not contemplated that the man in question would be actively involved in the child's upbringing. Thus, the order could be of value even where the child was in the care of the local authority since it could give him the standing to challenge the authority's plans for the child[6] or to resist a proposed adoption of the child[7]. It was

---

1   *Children Act Advisory Committee Final Report, June 1997* (Lord Chancellor's Department, 1997) Appendix 2 and Table 4.
2   See Chapter 1 above.
3   On the appointment of guardians generally, see Chapter 6 below.
4   Section 4.
5   Section 4(3).
6   *D v Hereford and Worcester County Council* [1991] 1 FLR 205.
7   *Re H (Illegitimate Child: Father: Parental Rights) (No 2)* [1991] 1 FLR 214.

not therefore fatal to an application that the father would not in practice be in a position to exercise parental rights or responsibilities[1].

These principles have now been carried forward and reinforced by the jurisprudence of the courts dealing with applications for parental responsibility orders[2]. The leading authority is *Re S (Parental Responsibility)*[3]. Here, the unmarried parents had intended to marry. The birth of their daughter was jointly registered and the child took her father's surname. The relationship between the parents broke down when the father was convicted of possessing obscene literature. The mother suspected that he might be involved in paedophiliac activities and became reluctant to allow him contact with the girl. The father applied for contact (which ceased to be an issue) but also for a parental responsibility order which was refused by the judge. Allowing the father's appeal, the Court of Appeal set out the principles applicable to the use of these orders. The court emphasised that the purpose of the order was to give the father the full status 'for which nature had already ordained that he must bear responsibility'[4]. The order would not, however, entitle the father to interfere in matters concerned with the management of the child's life[5]. Any abuse of the order or any interference with upbringing which was inconsistent with the child's welfare could be controlled by the court through s 8 orders. The court went on to say that expert psychological evidence regarded it as important that a child should grow up with good self-esteem and have a 'favourable positive image' of the 'absent' parent. Ward LJ emphasised that, wherever possible, the law should confer the stamp of its approval on a committed father lest the child should grow up with a belief that the father was in some way disqualified from fulfilling his parental role. Butler-Sloss LJ emphasised the significance of the conceptual and linguistic change from the notion of parental 'rights' to that of 'responsibility':

> 'It is important for parents to remember the emphasis placed by Parliament on the order which is applied for. It is that of duties and responsibilities as well as rights and powers. Indeed the order itself is entitled "parental responsibility". A father who has shown real commitment to the child concerned and to whom there is a positive attachment . . . ought . . . to assume the weight of those duties and cement that commitment and attachment by sharing the responsibilities for the child with the mother.'

The reported cases and judicial statistics do indicate a readiness on the part of the courts to make parental responsibility orders[6]. It should not, however, be assumed that such orders will be routinely granted simply because fathers ask for them. The court will want to make an evaluation of the individual father's

---

1   *Re C (Minors) (Parental Rights)* [1992] 1 FLR 1.
2   See, for example, *Re H (A Minor: Parental Responsibility)* [1993] 1 FLR 484; *Re CB (A Minor) (Parental Responsibility Order)* [1993] 1 FLR 920; *Re G (A Minor) (Parental Responsibility Order)* [1994] 1 FLR 504 and *Re E (A Minor) (Parental Responsibility)* [1995] 1 FLR 392.
3   [1995] 2 FLR 648. See also now *Re C and V (Contact and Parental Responsibility)* [1998] 1 FLR 392.
4   On the 'natural' rights of parents, see Chapter 3 above.
5   As indicated in Chapter 4, this interpretation of the Children Act is open to question since, unless a s 8 order has been made, all holders of parental responsibility at least in theory have an equal and independent say in the child's upbringing.
6   Not even a failure to pay maintenance for the benefit of the child should by itself be enough to deprive a father of the order if he is otherwise devoted to the children. It was held in *Re H (Parental Responsibility: Maintenance)* [1996] 1 FLR 867 that withholding the order should not be used as a weapon to extract money from the applicant father even where the court was critical of his failure to contribute financially.

potential contribution to the child's life. Adverse conduct may also lead to an order being refused. In *Re P (Parental Responsibility)*[1] an order was refused where the father was serving a long prison sentence for several offences of robbery. The Court of Appeal upheld the judge's decision which had properly taken into account the nature of the offence committed by the father and the effect of his incarceration as a restriction on his ability to exercise parental responsibility.

If a father should wish to go beyond merely acquiring the full status of parenthood and actually seek primary care of the child, this would necessitate an application for a residence order[2]. If successful, the court is obliged to make a parental responsibility order at the same time[3] and this must not be terminated while the residence order remains in force[4]. Clearly, if the child is to live with the father, the father must be given the necessary legal authority to take decisions on upbringing.

The termination of parental responsibility

Parental responsibility orders and agreements terminate automatically when the child attains the age of 18[5], or by earlier order of the court[6]. Although a parental responsibility order cannot be terminated while a residence order is in force, the converse is not true. Thus, when a residence order is terminated, the father will continue to have parental responsibility unless the court specifically decides to terminate it, which it may do where it considers that the welfare of the child requires it[7]. Applications to remove a father's parental responsibility are most likely to arise where, following an agreement, the relationship between the father and mother breaks down. In *Re P (Terminating Parental Responsibility)*[8], the child had suffered very severe non-accidental injuries when nine weeks old which were later attributed to the father. The father was convicted and sent to prison but

---

1   [1997] 2 FLR 722. See also *Re H (Parental Responsibility)* [1998] 1 FLR 855 where the judge had found that the father had previously injured the child and the child of a former partner and had displayed cruel behaviour with an element of sadism. The Court of Appeal upheld the decision not to make a parental responsibility order (although the judge had allowed supervised contact) emphasising that the court was obliged to decide whether the order was in the best interests of the child. In this case the judge was entitled to conclude that the father posed a future risk to his son and that his previous behaviour rendered him unfit to have parental responsibility. The case also perhaps reveals that a parental responsibility order is not exclusively (even if primarily) a status-conferring device. Cf *Re C and V (Contact and Parental Responsibility)* [1998] 1 FLR 392 discussed below. The latest reported decision is *Re P (Parental Responsibility)* [1998] 2 FLR 96, where the Court of Appeal again upheld the judge's decision not to make a parental responsibility order on the basis that there was clear evidence that the father would use it inappropriately to interfere with and undermine the mother's care for the child.
2   See Chapter 4 above for the legal effect of residence orders.
3   Children Act 1989, s 12(1).
4   Ibid, s 12(4).
5   Ibid, s 91(7) and (8).
6   Ibid, s 4(3).
7   This is in contrast to the position in marriage where the parental responsibility of a married or divorced parent cannot be terminated through any legal mechanism short of adoption. For a particularly striking example, see *Re M (A Minor) (Care Order: Threshold Conditions)* [1994] 2 AC 424, where the father retained parental responsibility despite murdering the mother in the presence of the children. Ironically, he was one of several fathers of the mother's children but the only one who happened to be married to her. See further Chapter 11.
8   [1995] 1 FLR 1048.

sought contact with the girl, who by this time was in the care of foster-parents. The mother, unaware of the father's guilt, had previously entered into a parental responsibility agreement with him. She succeeded in having this revoked and in obtaining an order under s 91(14) preventing further applications by the father without the leave of the court. The court emphasised that, once obtained, parental responsibility ought not to be terminated except on solid grounds and there was a strong presumption in favour of its continuance. It was relevant to consider whether in the circumstances now obtaining the court would have made a parental responsibility order which required evidence of attachment and commitment to the child. These requirements were clearly not met in the circumstances of this case.

It should be noted that whether or not the father acquired parental responsibility while the parents' relationship lasted, there is no automatic judicial scrutiny of the arrangements for the child following relationship breakdown, approximating to those which apply on divorce[1]. Since the issue of the parties' relationship (as opposed to marriage) is not itself before the court, the question of any child's welfare will not get there either unless someone takes steps to bring it there.

Section 8 orders: the court's discretion

What is the position where an unmarried father is seeking a residence or contact order in relation to the child? Is there any evidence that unmarried fathers are likely to find it more difficult than their married counterparts to obtain residence or contact orders? Can distinctions readily be drawn between the man who has, at some point, cohabited with the mother and the man who has not?

The reported cases do not give a clear message but it is evident that the unmarried man starts from a weaker position than the married man who has parental responsibility from the outset. There is a perceptible feeling that the unmarried man wishing to secure a residence, or perhaps even a contact, order is likely to experience an uphill struggle in convincing the court of his case. This is an area in which, in recent years, there has been some judicial disagreement.

On the one hand, there have been cases in which the judges have gone out of their way to emphasise the importance of the blood tie and have not distinguished in this respect between married and unmarried parents. A striking example is *Re K (A Minor) (Custody)*[2]. Here, a boy aged four years went to live with his uncle and aunt following the suicide of his mother. The natural father had had regular contact at weekends and on Wednesday evenings. He applied for care and control of the child and was supported by the welfare officer and a psychiatric social worker. The judge found that the standard of care which would be provided by the uncle and aunt was far superior to that which the father would be able to offer since he was in full-time employment and would have to rely, to a large extent, on the back-up services of his own mother. Her long-term commitment was in some doubt and the judge concluded that the child's best interests would be served by

1   The question of whether there should be is a fascinating one, touched upon briefly in
    J Eekelaar *Regulating Divorce* (Clarendon Press, 1991), discussed below, and in M Richards
    'Private Worlds and Public Intentions – The Role of the State at Divorce' in A Bainham,
    DS Pearl and R Pickford (eds) *Frontiers of Family Law* (2nd edn) (John Wiley & Sons, 1995).
2   [1990] 2 FLR 64.

giving care and control to the uncle and aunt. The Court of Appeal disagreed, taking the view that the best person to bring up a child was the natural parent. It mattered not whether the parent was wise or foolish, rich or poor, educated or illiterate, provided that the child's moral and physical health were not in danger. The court referred to the 'prima facie right' of the natural parent to raise his child which would require 'compelling factors' to be overridden. What the father could offer was considered adequate and his commitment to the child was not in doubt so that to make comparisons with someone who could provide a better home was an erroneous approach.

A similar view of the value of natural parenthood was expressed in *Re O (A Minor) (Custody: Adoption)*[1]. Here, the child was aged 15 months, the product of a brief relationship between a married woman and a divorced man whose relationship had ceased before the child's birth. The mother returned to her husband and placed the child, at birth, with an adoption society, who in turn placed him with short-term foster-parents where his welfare blossomed. The father had had a number of short-lived relationships with women but no settled home with any of them for any length of time. The Court of Appeal upheld the judge's decision granting custody to the father, coupled with a one-year supervision order in favour of the local authority. The court held that, where the natural mother could not look after the child for whatever reason, and the father desired to do so, he should be given first consideration as the long-term carer. It was not just a balancing exercise between the father and an unknown adoptive family. The issue was whether the father, despite the criticisms made of him, was fit to care for the child. Only if he was considered unfit should other options be looked at outside the family circle. The court went on to say, specifically, that no distinction should be drawn between those fathers who had not applied for parental responsibility, those who had parental responsibility and those who were married to the mother.

These were both cases in which an unmarried father was seeking to assert his claims against individuals other than the mother and this may have been the crucial factor in the decisions. Even so, they are difficult to reconcile with the traditional approach of integrating any parental or other adult claims into the general examination of the child's welfare and giving it no further weight than as an element in determining the child's best interests[2]. The position will almost certainly be very different where the contest is between the father and mother, since here it is *the mother* who has the initial advantage of possessing parental responsibility. *Re SM (A Minor) (Natural Father: Access)*[3] provides a striking contrast to the above decisions. It reveals that the father may face a considerable hurdle in securing even contact where the mother is opposed to this. Here again, the relationship between the parents broke down before the child's birth. The father subsequently had regular monthly access for 22 months. At that point the mother

1   [1992] 1 FLR 77.
2   See, particularly, *Re KD (A Minor)* [1988] AC 806 where the House of Lords made it clear that any claims parents may have against third parties are liable to be displaced where the welfare of the child requires it.
3   [1991] 2 FLR 333 at p 339. See also *Re F (A Minor) (Access)* [1992] Fam Law 484 which is in similar vein. See also *Re D (A Minor) (Contact: Mother's Hostility)* [1993] 2 FLR 1 in which the Court of Appeal stated that the principles regarding contact between unmarried fathers and children had not changed since the Children Act.

remarried her former husband and denied further access to the father. The magistrates awarded the father monthly access but their decision was overturned by Sir Stephen Brown P. What weighed with him was that the decision was largely founded on the 'theoretical general principle of access being maintained between a child and his or her natural parent'. The justices had taken insufficient account of the particular facts and the very strong reasons for denying access here. Insufficient account had been taken of the absence of a bond between the father and the child and the risk of destabilising the mother's new family unit in which there was a bond between the child, herself and the stepfather.

It might seem from this case that any prima facie claim which an unmarried man, as a natural parent, might have against 'outsiders' is not effective vis-à-vis the mother – not even to the extent of a presumption of contact[1]. The unmarried father, certainly in this context, will have to show that he is responsible and has some practical benefit to offer to the child through contact. He will also have to show much more than this if he is to succeed in securing the physical care of the child. There is no question that the courts are likely to be heavily influenced by the history of the father's interest or lack of interest in the child from birth onwards. They are likely to view unfavourably an application by a father who never lived with the mother, had no previous involvement with the child's upbringing, and limited or no contact with the child. On the other hand, the father who has cohabited with the mother for some time following the child's birth is likely to be in a much stronger position, especially regarding contact with the child.

Several recently reported cases have been concerned with the question of contact between children and unmarried fathers. In *Re C and V (Contact and Parental Responsibility)*[2] the Court of Appeal upheld the judge's decision to refuse contact where the child concerned had severe medical problems which required constant attention by the mother. The mother's ability to provide the necessary care might have been impeded if contact, which she strongly opposed, had been allowed. In contrast, in *Re M (Contact: Supervision)*[3] the Court of Appeal allowed the father's appeal against the judge's refusal to order supervised contact. The father had a background of drug and alcohol abuse and an unstable lifestyle but was gaining some control over his problems. The Court of Appeal reiterated the importance of contact between the child and his natural parent and took the view that the judge had been over-concerned with short-term considerations. The medium and long-term pointed inexorably to the benefits of the child having meaningful, effective contact with her father. The importance of establishing contact as soon as possible was also the basis of the decision of Holman J in *A v L*

---

1   This is a principle which certainly seems to have been affirmed by the House of Lords in a recent appeal from Scotland. In *S v M (Access Order)* [1997] 1 FLR 980, it was held that there was no *presumption* that the courts should seek to preserve the link between the child and the natural parent unless there were strong reasons to the contrary. The onus was on the parent to show on the balance of probabilities that an order (in this case for contact) was in the child's best interests. On the facts, the order denying contact to the father who had on occasions been violent and aggressive was justified. It has been pointed out that the onus on the unmarried father will be that much more difficult to discharge since he lacks automatic parental rights and responsibilities. See E Sutherland 'Scotland: From Birth to Death' in A Bainham (ed) *The International Survey of Family Law 1996* (Martinus Nijhoff, 1998) at p 383, especially pp 391–393.
2   [1998] 1 FLR 392.
3   [1998] 1 FLR 727.

(Contact)[1]. Here, the father had had a short-lived and violent relationship with the mother and now found himself in prison with an earliest release date in 2000. He had, however, applied for contact before his incarceration and was now pursuing indirect contact with the child. The magistrates refused this on the basis that the mother and her family would not co-operate in any arrangements. Allowing the father's appeal, Holman J emphasised the importance of introducing the child to the fact that he had had two fathers (the mother's partner acting as social father). It was appropriate, given the young age of the child, to introduce him gently so that he could assimilate the biological facts about his parentage. An order for indirect contact at this early stage would enable the nettle to be grasped. He therefore ordered indirect contact through letters and modest presents, with the mother's solicitors acting as a conduit.

Perhaps the key policy issue is whether distinctions can, or should, be drawn between fathers who have a record of cohabitation with the mother and those who do not but who are, nonetheless, interested in having an involvement with the child. The next section attempts to address this and other controversial policy issues.

PUBLIC POLICY AND UNMARRIED PARENTHOOD

Introduction

Despite the reform of the illegitimacy laws and the removal of most forms of discrimination against children born out of wedlock, the question of the relationship of such children with their fathers remains a controversial one for policy-makers. At its most basic, the central issue has been identified as how far mothers should be able to control the extent to which fathers may become legally involved in the lives of their children. In a seminal article considering the position of fathers (married and unmarried) in the legislation of Western European States, Marie-Thérèse Meulders-Klein observes that recent scientific and cultural developments have had the effect of reversing the historical dominance of men in relation to children[2]. It is now *women* who substantially control the conception, birth and upbringing of children. In England, for example, it is still impossible for the unmarried man to make a voluntary acknowledgment of paternity without either the mother's co-operation or a relevant court order[3]. Acquisition of full parental responsibility is, likewise, dependent on the father persuading either the mother or the court that he is deserving of this level of involvement. Automatic legal effects of paternity are limited to such matters as financial obligations and succession rights. Yet there is an ongoing debate about whether the father's moral and legal obligations ought to be only financial or whether they should be the

---

1   [1998] 1 FLR 361.
2   M-T Meulders-Klein 'The Position of the Father in European Legislation' (1990) 4 IJLF 131.
3   This is not the case, for example, in France where the French Civil code imposes no checks on voluntary acknowledgment of paternity. See Meulders-Klein (above) at pp 140–141. For a particularly stimulating review of the procedures for establishing paternity in France, Belgium, Luxembourg and The Netherlands, see P Senaeve 'Reform of Affiliation Law in France and the Benelux Countries' in J Eekelaar and P Sarcevic (eds) *Parenthood in Modern Society* (Martinus Nijhoff, 1993) at ch 6.

more wide-ranging obligations which the law imposes on married fathers. The conceptual shift from parental 'rights' to parental 'responsibility' has led some to question why it is that unmarried men are not encouraged or required to accept more responsibility[1].

This debate is now taking place in the shadow of the international obligations of the UK under various international Conventions, most notably the European Convention on Human Rights and Fundamental Freedoms and the United Nations Conventions on the Rights of the Child[2]. The European Convention protects, inter alia, the right of every individual to 'respect for his private and family life, his home and his correspondence'[3]. It is clear that the protection offered by Article 8(1) has application outside marriage and the European Convention also contains provisions against discrimination which have been held to extend to discrimination based on marital status[4]. Likewise, the United Nations Convention prohibits discrimination of any kind against children including discrimination based on 'birth or other status', and requires 'recognition of the principle that both parents have common responsibilities for the upbringing and development of the child'. The key question is the *extent* of the State's obligations under these provisions and this is a matter of interpretation upon which opinion is divided.

Marckx v Belgium[5]: the case of unmarried mothers

This case concerned the status of unmarried mothers in Belgian law. Here, the European Court of Human Rights held that Belgian law violated the rights of mother and child under Article 8, both independently and in conjunction with Article 14, in failing to acknowledge the mother's maternity from the moment of birth. As Belgian law stood at the time, the unmarried mother was required to undertake a formal legal process of voluntary recognition. No legal bond was recognised by the mere fact of birth. Alternatively, maternity could be established in legal proceedings. These formal requirements were not imposed in relation to legitimate children. The court held that it was discriminatory to distinguish between legitimate and illegitimate children, since all such children had an equal interest in establishing the maternal bond. It found that there was no objective and reasonable justification for making this distinction. The most significant feature of the decision, however, was the interpretation of Article 8 as imposing *positive* obligations on the State and not merely the negative obligation not to interfere with family life. Thus, the State was obliged to act in a manner calculated

---

1 For the nature and effects of parental responsibility see Chapter 2 above.
2 See, particularly, JS Davidson 'The European Convention on Human Rights and the "Illegitimate" Child' in D Freestone (ed) *Children and the Law* (Hull University Press, 1990) at p 75; and NV Lowe 'The Meaning and Allocation of Parental Responsibility – A Common Lawyer's Perspective' (1997) 11 *International Journal of Law, Policy and the Family* 192, especially at pp 201–205.
3 Article 8(1).
4 Article 14 provides:
    'The enjoyment of the rights and freedoms set forth in this Convention shall be secured without discrimination on any ground such as sex, race, colour, language, religion, political or other opinion, national or social origin, association with a national minority, property, birth or other status.'
5 EUR Court HR Series A No 31. Discussed by JS Davidson (above) at pp 78–92 and in S Maidment 'The Marckx case' (1979) Fam Law 228.

to allow ties between near relatives to develop normally. In other words, the European Convention required States to promote the development of family life whether within or outside the institution of marriage[1].

Another important feature of this case, confirmed by the court's later decision in *Johnston v Republic of Ireland*[2], was the recognition by the court that the interests of mother and child were inextricably linked, so that discrimination against one was discrimination against the other. Thus, in the *Johnston* case it was said that 'the close and intimate relationship between the third applicant (the child) and her parents (a cohabiting unmarried couple) was such that there was of necessity also a resultant failure to respect the family life of each of the latter'. This approach, it can be argued, is inconsistent with the current position in English law. The basis of this is that any remaining distinctions between married and unmarried parent-hood are to be made by distinguishing between adults (fathers) and not between children. Yet the approach of the European Court has been to underline the mutuality or reciprocity inherent in the parent–child relationship. It is doubtful, therefore, whether the English appoach can be justified when looking to the spirit, if not the letter, of the Convention[3].

Unresolved questions: the international arena

An unresolved question is how far these international Conventions require the State to allow for such matters as the voluntary acknowledgment of paternity and the conferment of parental responsibilities and rights, merely from the fact of paternity. It is also unclear how far the positive obligations on the State to foster family relationships might require the State itself to take a proactive role in establishing paternity in the absence of voluntary acknowledgment[4]. These questions may all have to be addressed in the coming years and addressed not only in the context of the father's rights and interests but also the child's. As Meulders-Klein has said:

---

1 Davidson (above) pp 88–89.
2 EUR Court HR Series A No 112.
3 See A Bainham 'When is a Parent not a Parent? Reflections on the Unmarried Father and his Child in English Law' (1989) 3 IJLF 208 at pp 211–215. Cf R Deech 'The Unmarried Father and Human Rights' (1992) 4 JCL 3, and NV Lowe who, while arguing that the automatic allocation of parental responsibility to unmarried fathers would be desirable, does not believe that English law is 'yet' in breach of the Convention, see 'The Meaning and Allocation of Parental Responsibility – A Common Lawyer's Perspective' (1997) 11 *International Journal of Law, Policy and the Family* 192 at p 205. This view is shared by the Government. In its recent Consultation Paper *1. Court Procedures for the Determination of Paternity. 2. The Law on Parental Responsibility for Unmarried Fathers* (Lord Chancellor's Department, March 1998) the view is expressed (at para 62) that 'the current law which does not give responsibility automatically to unmarried fathers on the birth of the child complies with Articles 8 and 14 of the Convention. The wide range of types of relationship outside marriage means that the interests of the child and mother have to be protected. The law gives this protection while still permitting the unmarried father to acquire parental responsibility by agreement or court order. Nevertheless, it is not easy to find a rule of law which strikes the right balance in this respect between the interests of the unmarried father, the mother and the child.'
4 The State actively seeks to establish paternity in all cases in most of the Scandinavian countries, albeit largely for financial reasons, as to which see Meulders-Klein (above) at pp 141–142. See also A Eriksson and Å Saldeen 'Parenthood and Science – Establishing and Contesting Parentage' in J Eekelaar and P Sarcevic (eds) *Parenthood in Modern Society* (Martinus Nijhoff, 1993) at ch 5.

'When we seek to regulate the problems of parents, we should look to the apex of the triangle: to the child, for we have all been children, and children are the bearers of our future. The fundamental rule, therefore, which was made clear in the *Marckx* and *Johnston* judgments, is that every child has the fundamental right to have a normal family life, that is to say, a father and mother with whom he has a personal relationship. . . . The child needs a father and a mother in order to develop normally, and, as has been said, if possible he should have a father and a mother who love each other. However, if the parents no longer love each other, it remains true that the child needs *both* parents, and that one parent is *not* the other.'[1]

Not everyone agrees with this interpretation of international obligations, nor, indeed, with the view that children necessarily need fathers. In 1991, Ruth Deech launched a frontal attack on the very idea that unmarried fathers have independent human rights qua fathers[2]. She pointed out that the relevant international treaties give no *paternal* rights as such since they are rooted in the concept of the family. For Deech, it is the fact of cohabitation between unmarried parents which is all-important in determining whether the father has any familial rights which are capable of protection[3]. And it is the lack of commitment demonstrated by the unmarried, non-cohabiting man which is the primary justification for discriminating between him and other fathers. Deech takes the position that, not only is the conferment of automatic parental responsibility not required by international Conventions, but also that as a matter of public policy it would be quite unwarranted. She argues that the man who wishes to have this superior status has the option of marrying the mother to acquire it. The essence of Deech's argument appears to be that so-called 'absent' fathers generally (married or not) have failed to undertake the kind of responsibilities which would justify the allocation of an equal parental status with the mother. She finds the idea of 'absent' fatherhood an empty egotistical concept since it does not encompass a fair share of the practical tasks of child-rearing, including 'feeding, washing and clothing the child, putting her to bed, housing her, educating and stimulating her, taking responsibility or arranging babysitting and day care, keeping the child in touch with the wider family circle, checking her medical condition, arranging schooling and transport to school, holidays and recreation, encouraging social and possibly religious or moral development'[4]. She does, however, concede that

1 M-T Meulders-Klein (above) at p 151. And see the remarks of Butler-Sloss LJ, albeit referring to an absent *married* father, in *Re R (A Minor) (Access)* (1993) *The Times*, March 29, in which she emphasised the urgent need for a child of five years old to be told the truth about her parentage and for urgent steps to be taken to re-introduce her to her natural father. The child was being brought up to believe that her mother's cohabitant was her natural father. In much the same vein are the remarks by Ward LJ in *Re H (Paternity: Blood Test)* [1996] 2 FLR 65 discussed above.

2 R Deech 'The Unmarried Father and Human Rights' (1992) 4 JCL 3.

3 She relies on the decision of the European Court of Human Rights in *Berrehab v The Netherlands* (1988) EUR Court HR Series A No 138 at p 7. Cf A Bainham 'When is a Parent not a Parent? Reflections on the Unmarried Father and his Child in English Law' (1989) 3 IJLF 208 at p 213 for a different interpretation of the decision. The decision in *Keegan v Ireland* (1994) 18 EHRR 342, where the parents had ceased to cohabit well before the birth of the child is also difficult to reconcile with the Deech view. See also *Kroon v The Netherlands* (1994) 19 EHRR 263. In this case, the unmarried father and mother *were* cohabiting at the time of the child's birth but the mother was married to someone else. The European Court found Dutch law to be in violation of Article 8 in failing to provide a procedure for recognition of the biological father's paternity unless the mother's husband chose to deny *his* paternity.

4 R Deech 'The Unmarried Father and Human Rights' (1992) 4 JCL 3 at p 8.

'criticism of absent fathers is to recognise, not to decry, the importance of a father's involvement'[1].

Parental responsibilities and rights: the view of the Scottish Law Commission

The Scottish Law Commission reported in 1992 on the whole question of parental responsibilities and rights[2]. As part of its review, it reopened the question of the allocation of rights and responsibilities within the unmarried family[3]. Its central recommendation was that Scots law should no longer maintain the distinction between the married and the unmarried in the matter of parental status. It identified many defects in the existing law. It pointed out the incongruity of giving an automatic parental relationship to the married man who abandons his pregnant wife, but denying this to the unmarried man who might be cohabiting with the mother and playing a full parental role[4]. It was concerned that, at a time when the parental position was being recast in terms of responsibility, the law might be seen as encouraging irresponsibility in unmarried men[5]. It felt that the arguments against automatic rights and responsibilities should be re-examined in view of the increasingly large category of fathers excluded from a full parental relationship. It further thought that the uninterested absent parent, who would not attempt to exercise responsibility, posed no realistic threat to the mother[6]. Even where the child was the product of a casual liaison, the Commission thought that rights and responsibilities ought to be conferred since they existed for the benefit of the *child* and not for the parent. Moreover, the mother's own parental status arose automatically where she too had been involved in a purely casual affair[7].

The Commission also rejected the argument, which had previously weighed with both the English and Scottish Law Commissions, that offence would be caused to women struggling to bring up children on their own. It drew an analogy with divorce where the policy is to encourage the father's involvement, and it questioned whether approaches by unmarried fathers should be viewed as 'interference' or 'harassment' as opposed to genuine manifestations of concern and interest. Where there was real interference or harassment, the Commission thought that the answer was for a court to remove parental rights and responsibilities[8]. The effect of the present law was, it thought, to create an unwarranted presumption that paternal involvement was against the child's best interests and to allow the feelings of one parent, viz the mother, to predominate. It concluded that Scots law currently discriminates against unmarried fathers both by treating them less favourably than married fathers and by treating them less favourably than unmarried mothers[9]. It also felt that there was at least an

---

1   R Deech 'The Unmarried Father and Human Rights' (1992) 4 JCL 3 at p 8.
2   Scot Law Com Report No 135 (1992). Many of the recommendations were subsequently
    enacted in the Children (Scotland) Act 1995, as to which see Chapter 3 above.
3   Scot Law Com Report No 135 (1992) at paras 2.36–2.51.
4   Ibid at para 2.36.
5   Ibid at para 2.37.
6   Ibid at para 2.38.
7   Ibid at para 2.39.
8   Ibid at para 2.48.
9   Ibid at para 2.43.

argument that the law also discriminated against the *children* by denying them a father with normal legal responsibilities and rights[1].

In the event, Parliament failed to act on these recommendations and Scots law, like English law, continues to withhold automatic parental rights and responsibilities from the unmarried man while introducing a procedure for acquiring them by agreement with the mother[2]. We may reasonably expect to see some challenges by unmarried fathers under the European Convention and further clarification of international obligations. But there is likely to remain some uncertainty and ambiguity in societal attitudes to the role of fatherhood generally and unmarried fatherhood in particular. One of these uncertainties surrounds the significance of the blood tie. Within marriage, presumed if not actual biological parenthood is enough, per se, to trigger wide-ranging moral and legal obligations for both mothers and fathers. It has been seen that the judiciary have occasionally recognised the importance of the blood tie, even outside marriage. Against this, cultural and medical changes have undoubtedly lessened the significance of biological parenthood and, instead, recognised the importance to the child of *social* parenthood[3]. Attitudes to the 'rights' of the child to a father are likely to be influenced by the position taken on this wider question of the importance of genetic versus social parenthood.

---

1 Scot Law Com Report No 135 (1992) at para 2.44.
2 Children (Scotland) Act 1995, s 4. See also E Sutherland 'The Unequal Struggle – Fathers and Children in Scots Law' [1997] CFLQ 191. The whole question of the law governing parental responsibility for unmarried fathers has, however, now been reopened by the Lord Chancellor's Department in its Consultation Paper *1. Court Procedures for the Determination of Paternity. 2. The Law on Parental Responsibility for Unmarried Fathers* (March 1998). At para 51 of this Consultation Paper, the following view is expressed:
    'Discrimination between married and unmarried fathers in respect of parental responsibility is increasingly seen as unacceptable, in view of the large numbers of children who are born to unmarried parents, many of whom are likely to be in stable relationships. It is clearly impossible to assume that most unmarried fathers are irresponsible or uninterested in their children, and do not deserve a legal role as parents.'
    The Consultation Paper moots a number of options for reform including the automatic allocation of parental responsibility to *all* fathers or to a more restricted category such as those who jointly register the child's birth with the mother or those who are cohabiting with the mother (see paras 57–61).
3 See Chapter 6 below for the various forms of social parenthood and their legal effects. For a fascinating case raising the question of the value which should be attached to the *absence* of a blood tie, see the decision of the Court of Appeal in *Re C (A Minor) (Access)* [1992] 1 FLR 309. In this case the mother's husband was seeking access to her child with whom he had had a social relationship for a number of years before serving a term of imprisonment. He was not the natural father but the child believed him to be her father for the first eight years of her life. The mother had two other children by different fathers neither of whom was her husband. The Court of Appeal, upholding the recorder's decision to exclude the husband from access, held that he had been entitled, indeed *bound*, to take the lack of blood tie into account. He had been correct, however, to make it clear that, because of the early long-standing de facto relationship of father and daughter, the absence of a blood tie was not *per se* a reason for refusing future contact between the husband and the child.

The unmarried father and the divorced father

A final issue is whether valid distinctions can be drawn between the unmarried father and the divorced father[1]? If the policy of the law is to foster the involvement of fathers following marriage breakdown, ought it not to do so where non-marital relationships break down? And, bearing in mind the central importance now attached to the status of parenthood, ought the breakdown of the relationship between unmarried parents to be the subject of any judicial scrutiny, as when married parents divorce[2]? As Eekelaar has put it:

> '... if the main worries about divorce now centre around its harmfulness to children and the unequal distribution of the risks of parenthood, these risks will arise also on the break-up of *unmarried* cohabitation if children have been born into the relationship.... If the bonds of parenthood are now assuming the degree of indissolubility once accorded to marriage, any significant readjustment in the relationship between the parents themselves and between parents and children is just as deserving of regulation as the dissolution of marriage itself'.[3]

Eekelaar's remarks question how far the State, through the courts or some other public agency, should actively support parental relationships outside marriage. The Child Support Act 1991 undoubtedly represented a shift in this direction, but for the limited purpose of enforcing the financial liability of absent fathers and, only then, where the mother was dependent on State support[4]. Beyond this, the question of the father's involvement with the child (assuming that this is not agreed between the parents) is fundamentally one of where the onus of undertaking legal proceedings should lie. At present, it falls on the father to take legal action to assert his full parental role. Perhaps the central question to be resolved is whether the combined interests or rights of father and child, together with any public interest, are such that the onus should shift to the mother to take steps to deprive the 'unmeritorious' man of parental responsibility.

---

1   This is a crucial question to which the English and Scottish Law Commissions, in effect, gave different answers. See A Bainham 'Reforming Scottish Children Law: Sense from North of the Border' (1993) 5 JCL 3.
2   J Eekelaar *Regulating Divorce* (Clarendon Press, 1991). See also M Maclean and J Eekelaar *The Parental Obligation* (Hart Publishing, 1997) especially at p 144. The authors' empirical study of children across households leads them to conclude that the children of broken unmarried cohabitations were likely to be in a more precarious position than the children of divorce. Yet 'legislation and policy hitherto has paid scant attention to the parenthood of unmarried cohabitants' and 'the position of children of broken unmarried cohabitations is entirely neglected in comparison to the attention given to the children of divorced parents'. Much the same point is also made in G Douglas, M Murch and A Perry 'Supporting children when parents separate – a neglected family justice or mental health issue?' [1996] CFLQ 121.
3   *Regulating Divorce* (above) at pp 172–173.
4   See Chapter 9 below.

Chapter 6
THE SOCIAL FAMILY

INTRODUCTION

This chapter considers the legal position of those persons who are not biological parents but who take care of children or are otherwise interested in their upbringing[1]. It is not easy to find a convenient generic term to describe the disparate categories involved but they have been variously described as 'social parents'[2], 'non-parents'[3], 'de facto carers' and 'substitute parents'. None of these labels does justice to the variety of circumstances which can arise. Here, the expression 'social family' is used to embrace any family unit in which a child is looked after wholly or partly by someone who is not his biological or legal parent. It includes, therefore, guardians, step-parents, foster-parents, relatives, and others such as the cohabitant of a parent.

This chapter does not discuss adoption, for two reasons. The first is that the effect of the legal process of adoption in England is to create the full legal relationship of parent and child – which is not true of the other arrangements under consideration here with the limited exception of 'parental orders' in surrogacy cases. The second reason is that adoption is a vast subject in its own right and has been the subject of a fundamental review and recent proposals for reform. Thus, the next chapter is devoted entirely to the subject of adoption.

The question of the legal controls on day care, foster-care and the different kinds of residential care are also discussed separately in another chapter, since it is convenient to deal with these when looking at the powers and duties of local authorities' social services departments[4].

Parental responsibility

There are two fundamental features of the law affecting social parents. The first is that they do not have parental responsibility simply by virtue of looking after a child. The second is that they may acquire parental responsibility by court order. Guardians, however, are an exception. When guardianship comes into being this automatically carries with it parental responsibility[5]. The lack of any automatic legal status places the social parent in a precarious position, especially when faced with claims by a natural parent or someone else who *does* have parental responsibility. This vulnerability is well illustrated by *Re N (Minors) (Parental Rights)*[6] decided nearly a quarter of a century ago. Here, the widowed step-father

---

1   For a useful general guide to the pre-Children Act law, see J Priest *In Place of a Parent* (Jordans, 1986).
2   See, for example, J Dewar *Law and the Family* (2nd edn) (Butterworths, 1992) at ch 11.
3   See, for example, A Bainham 'The Children Act 1989: The Standing of Non-Parents' [1990] Fam Law 362, and C Barton and G Douglas *Law and Parenthood* (Butterworths, 1995) at pp 99 et seq.
4   See Chapter 10 below.
5   Discussed at pp 181 et seq below.
6   [1974] Fam 40.

and maternal grandmother of orphaned children were in dispute over their upbringing. Without a court order neither of them had any parental right (now parental responsibility) and neither of them was in a stronger legal position than the other. In this case the matter had to be resolved in wardship proceedings.

In the absence of a court order, under the Children Act 1989, the social parent has the limited powers and duties of all de facto carers, namely to 'do what is reasonable in all the circumstances of the case for the purpose of safeguarding or promoting the child's welfare'[1]. While there is some doubt about the scope of this provision, it seems that it does not empower the carer to take 'major', as opposed to 'minor' or day-to-day, decisions and, more importantly, it does not give any legal right to retain the care of a child. These greater responsibilities and rights, as before the Children Act, can only be acquired by court order. The old law was full of technicalities about which proceedings and which types of order were available to persons other than parents. It is the policy under the Children Act to allow much more open access to the courts and greater consistency in the available orders[2]. The broad scheme of the legislation is to draw the various groups of social parents closer together by the elimination of the technical distinctions which the old law made between them and by substantially assimilating their legal position to that of parents where they acquire parental responsibility. It is, nonetheless, still necessary to differentiate between natural parents and social parents on the one hand and different kinds of social parents on the other. Accordingly, after discussing the general scheme, we explore some particular considerations which apply to different types of social parents.

THE GENERAL SCHEME

The nature and effect of court orders in family proceedings were discussed earlier. Our concern now is with the circumstances in which these orders may be sought by social parents.

The private law

Subject to limited qualifications, *anyone* may, in principle, apply for a s 8 order in *any* kind of family proceedings[3]. A clear and relatively uniform set of rules now governs the standing of social parents to make applications, whatever the specific nature of the proceedings. The Children Act divides applicants into two categories – those who are entitled to apply for orders as of right, and those who require the leave of the court[4].

---

1 Section 3(5), and see Chapter 2 above.
2 See Chapter 2 above. But for a critique of the way this policy may operate in practice, see SM Cretney 'Litigation may seriously endanger your welfare: Locus standi and the family' (1993) 109 LQR 177.
3 The expansive definition of 'family proceedings' was discussed in Chapter 2 above.
4 Section 10.

Applications without leave

Parents, guardians and persons in whose favour a residence order has been made may apply for *any* s 8 order as of right[1]. These are people whose interest in the child is self-evident since they already possess parental responsibility. The legislation then prescribes a further category of persons whose presumed closeness to the child entitles them to apply for residence or contact orders, but not for other orders, without leave[2]. The reasoning for this distinction is not obvious, but it probably reflects the view that prohibited steps and specific issue orders are sufficiently unusual and intrusive that a preliminary filter is appropriate to weed out unmeritorious applications. The reason why these orders might be thought intrusive is that their effect is to interfere with and curtail the normal exercise of parental responsibility by a person in whom it is vested.

Those persons who are entitled to apply for residence or contact orders without leave include parties to a marriage in relation to whom the child is a 'child of the family'[3], persons with whom the child has lived for at least three years[4], and persons who have the consent of those with parental responsibility[5]. The first group covers, primarily but not exclusively, step-parents, whose position is discussed below. The other two groups essentially embrace those who would have qualified to apply for an order under the former custodianship procedure[6]. Rules of Court may extend the categories of those entitled to apply without leave, of which grandparents are thought, by some, to be prime contenders given that under the old law some grandparents did have an automatic right to intervene in certain proceedings. This is a rare example, perhaps, of the Children Act tightening, rather than relaxing, the rules on standing[7]. The thinking behind these provisions is that, in all the above cases, the genuineness of the concern for the child would be so palpable that in most cases a requirement of leave would be an empty ritual.

---

1   Section 10(4). For these purposes, 'parent' does not include a former natural parent after the child has been adopted. In *Re C (A Minor) (Adopted Child: Contact)* [1995] 2 FLR 431, it was held that the natural mother of an adopted child had rightly applied for leave (in this case to seek contact and specific issue orders) since the effect of the child's adoption had been to terminate her parental relationship with the child.

2   Section 10(5).

3   Defined in s 105(1) as:
    'in relation to the parties to a marriage ...
    (a) a child of both of those parties;
    (b) any other child, not being a child who is placed with those parties as foster parents by a local authority or voluntary organisation, who has been treated by both of those parties as a child of their family.'
    See further Chapter 4 above.

4   It is provided by s 10(10) that the period of three years need not be continuous but must not have begun more than five years before, or ended more than three months before, the making of the application.

5   This includes the consent of those who have parental responsibility while a residence order is in force, the consent of the local authority where the child is in care and, in other cases, the consent of each person with parental responsibility.

6   Under the Children Act 1975, s 33, but not implemented until 1985. The most comprehensive treatment of the subject is to be found in MDA Freeman *The Law and Practice of Custodianship* (1986).

7   Section 10(7). No such rules have been made at the time of writing.

Applications with leave

Where interested persons are unable to bring themselves within any of the above categories they may, nonetheless, make applications with the leave of the court[1]. The purpose of leave is to provide a 'filter to protect the child and his family against unwarranted interference in their comfort and security'[2]. The statutory scheme is designed to be flexible enough to obviate the need to resort to the wardship jurisdiction. The leave requirement should thus be relatively easily satisfied, except where the motives of the applicant are improper or where there is a sound reason for regarding the application as inappropriate[3]. The Children Act prescribes a checklist of factors for the court considering leave applications[4], including the nature of the proposed application, the applicant's connection with the child, the risk of disruption to the child's life and, where the child is being looked after by a local authority, the authority's plans and the feelings of the child's parents.

The Court of Appeal has held that the initial application for leave is not governed by the welfare principle[5]. In *Re A and W (Minors) (Residence Order: Leave to Apply)*[6], the mother had had a colourful personal life in which she had accumulated three husbands (two she divorced and one committed suicide), a cohabitant and six children. The application for leave to apply for a residence order was by the foster-mother of the four younger children. The judge granted her leave on the basis that the children's welfare was paramount. The local authority (supported by the mother) appealed. Allowing the appeal, the Court of

---

1   Section 10(2)(b). The procedure governing applications for leave is set out in r 4.3 of the Family Proceedings Rules 1991, SI 1991/1247, and r 3 of the Family Proceedings Courts (Children Act 1989) Rules 1991, SI 1991/1395. See, generally, E Hamilton *Applications for Leave and Joinder in Children Act Cases* [1993] Fam Law 263. In an urgent case, an application for leave may be made ex parte. In *Re O (Minors) (Leave to Seek Residence Order)* [1994] 1 FLR 172, an ex parte application for leave to apply for a residence order was granted to a paternal cousin who had been looking after two boys while the mother was in hospital. The mother was demanding their immediate return and was proposing to return to her alcoholic husband. Leave was granted together with an interim residence order although the length of the latter was reduced on appeal.

2   Law Com Report No 172 *Guardianship and Custody* (1988) at para 4.41.

3   But it should be noted that this is, in some ways, more restrictive than the more traditional wardship proceedings in which there was never a leave requirement as such. The wardship could, of course, have been discontinued at the court's discretion. See also SM Cretney 'Litigation may seriously endanger your welfare: Locus standi and the family' (1993) 109 LQR 177.

4   Section 10(9). In *G v Kirklees Metropolitan Borough Council* [1993] 1 FLR 805, Booth J held that these guidelines are equally applicable where the applicant is seeking to be joined as a party to existing proceedings with a view to seeking a s 8 order. There is some common ground between this checklist and the checklist in s 1(3) but a notable distinction is that there is no mention of the wishes and feelings of the child among the leave criteria. However, in *Re A (A Minor) (Residence Order: Leave to Apply)* [1993] 1 FLR 425, Hollings J held that the factors in the checklist were not exhaustive and did not exclude consideration of the ascertainable wishes and feelings of the child concerned. In *Re M (Care: Contact: Grandmother's Application for Leave)* [1995] 2 FLR 86, the Court of Appeal held that, although the criteria in s 10(9) did not govern applications for contact to children in care, the court, in exercising its discretion in that context, should have in mind the factors in the checklist.

5   There has been some judicial inconsistency on this question where the application for leave is by a *child*. We consider this matter in Chapter 13.

6   [1992] Fam 182. For commentaries, see J Masson 'Leave, Local Authorities and Welfare' [1992] Fam Law 443 and R White 'Liverpool Revisited? *Re A and W (Minors)*' (1992) 4 JCL 190.

Appeal held that the leave application was governed by the particular statutory checklist in s 10(9), which included such matters as the local authority's plans for the children, the mother's wishes and feelings, any risk of disruption to the children's life, etc. The upbringing of the child was *not*, however, directly in issue. That would arise for determination on the substantive application if leave were granted. On the facts, the children were of an age where they could express a view, it was unlikely in the circumstances that a residence order would be made and leave should therefore be refused.

After considering the criteria in s 10(9), the crux of the matter will be whether the applicant has been able to establish an arguable case or whether the prospects of success on the substantive application are so remote that leave should be refused. But it has been said that the court should not approach the question of leave in a restrictive or inflexible manner[1].

The public law

The extent to which social parents are entitled to participate in public family proceedings (ie those relating to care and supervision) is discussed later[2]. It is sufficient to note here that the policy of the legislation is to increase the opportunities for their participation in these proceedings[3]. Moreover, local authorities have wider duties under the Children Act to seek out and take into account the views of 'outsiders' when taking decisions regarding children 'looked after' by them[4]. The Children Act, on the other hand, prohibits applications for s 8 orders, other than residence orders where a child is 'in care'[5] reflecting the general policy that outsiders ought not to be able to interfere with the proper discharge of local authority responsibilities to children in care. Local authority foster-parents are considered a special kind of social parent for much the same reason, and their position is examined below.

The nature and effect of orders obtained by social parents: parental responsibility not parenthood

It might be thought that the legal effect of the various s 8 orders is the same for a social parent as it is for a parent, but this would be misleading. The natural parent's legal position is constructed not simply by possessing parental responsibility but also by the status of being the legal parent. Thus, where a parent obtains a residence order, it has no effect beyond regulating where the child is to live. The parent already has parental responsibility and this is neither gained through the residence order nor lost if the order is revoked. The social parent, however, depends on the residence order for parental responsibility[6] and retains this only

---

1 See *Re M (Care: Contact: Grandmother's Application for Leave)* [1995] 2 FLR 86.
2 See Chapter 11 below.
3 See A Bainham 'The Children Act 1989: The Standing of Non-Parents' [1990] Fam Law 362, at pp 364–365.
4 Section 22(4) and (5).
5 Section 9(1). This restriction does not apply where the child is merely 'looked after' by the authority.
6 Section 12(2).

while the order subsists[1]. Further, the order does not pass on the wider rights attaching to the status of parenthood[2]. While a residence order remains in force, the holder will exercise parental responsibility (alongside the parent or other person already possessing it) and there may also be some important consequential implications of this enhanced status. Thus, a person with parental responsibility is automatically in a stronger position vis-à-vis the local authority[3] and has better standing in family proceedings[4].

Other s 8 orders will not give parental responsibility to the social parent but will merely regulate the exercise of parental responsibility by those having it. Most obviously, many social parents will be seeking contact orders. Prohibited steps and specific issue orders may prove especially useful where the social parent has a residence order but is in disagreement over the child's upbringing with someone else sharing parental responsibility. Alternatively, potential problems may be pre-empted by the court attaching conditions or giving directions when it makes a residence order in favour of a social parent[5]. The statutory regime is flexible enough to enable the court to regulate, in some detail, the complex relationships between parents, children and social parents[6].

A general underlying issue is how far it is desirable to support 'inclusive' networks of relationships or 'exclusive' substitute arrangements which are designed to centralise the child's existence in the social family and to shut out the natural family. While it is a truism that every case must turn on its own peculiar facts, there is little doubt that *inclusive* arrangements are more in keeping with the philosophy of the legislation and with the proposals for reform of adoption law[7]. Martin Richards has, perhaps, captured the mood of current thinking by criticising the 'very persistent prejudice that children should never have more than two parents and when a new one arrives, an old one has to go'[8]. We should, however, remember to take care to distinguish between an inclusive policy which contemplates relationships between children with more than two significant adults, perhaps by giving *parental responsibility* to more than two persons, and one which visualises more than two *parents* for a child. *Parenthood* is different from the possession of parental responsibility and the case has not been made out, it is submitted, for conferring *parenthood* on more than two adults.

---

1   In this respect it should be noted that the court has a general power to vary or discharge s 8 orders since the definition of a s 8 order in s 8(2) of the Children Act includes 'any order varying or discharging such an order'.

2   Section 12(3) provides that the order does not confer the right to consent to or refuse adoption, or to appoint a guardian. Neither does the order, for example, affect succession rights or, more generally, the child's kinship relations in the wider family.

3   He has, for example, the right to object to the child being accommodated by the authority (s 20(7)) and the subsequent right to remove the child (s 20(8)). He must be consulted by the authority (s 22(4)) and may invoke the complaints procedure (s 26(3)). He has a right in due course to apply for discharge of a care order (s 39(1)(a)).

4   He may, for example, apply for s 8 orders without leave.

5   Section 11(7) and see Chapter 2 above.

6   The key point here is that no one may exercise parental responsibility in a way which is incompatible with an order of the court (s 2(8)).

7   See Chapter 7 below.

8   MPM Richards 'Private Worlds and Public Intentions: The Role of the State at Divorce' in A Bainham, DS Pearl and R Pickford (eds) *Frontiers of Family Law* (2nd edn) (John Wiley & Sons, 1995) 13 at p 21.

In deciding whether to make an order (on the substantive application, as opposed to the initial application for leave), the court is bound by the welfare principle and the statutory checklist. It has been observed by Douglas and Lowe[1] that, whilst the court may order the preparation of a welfare report, there is no mandatory involvement of the local authority (as was the case under the former custodianship procedure)[2]. Douglas and Lowe characterise the procedure for obtaining parental responsibility by court order as embracing a degree of State regulation which is lower than that required for adoption but greater than that applying to guardianship which is largely a matter of private ordering. We now turn to the individual considerations which apply to different groups of social parents.

GUARDIANS

The nature of guardianship

The traditional concept of guardianship
Guardianship has a long history[3]. At common law, the father was the 'natural guardian' of his legitimate children. Thus, he exercised all parental rights, to the exclusion of the mother. When the mother was eventually given equal rights and authority by the Guardianship Act 1973, the father still remained, in theory, the sole guardian. Indeed, until comparatively recently, the father was, on losing custody, said to retain the 'residual rights of the natural guardian'. The concept was invoked by the courts as the basis for the father's right to object to a unilateral change of the child's surname by the mother, following divorce[4]. Alongside this natural or parental guardianship there was another kind of guardianship which arose where someone other than a parent took over legal responsibility for a child on the death of a parent[5]. Neither of these concepts of guardianship is to be confused with the office of *guardian ad litem* which is concerned with the representation of the child in certain kinds of legal proceedings. We consider this role in Chapter 13.

Abolition of parental guardianship
The policy of the Children Act, following the work of the Law Commission, was to abolish the notion of parental guardianship and replace it with the primary status of parenthood[6]. Henceforth, parents would just be parents and guardianship would be confined to non-parents who stepped into the shoes of deceased parents. Yet it was recognised that guardians who do take over in this way, in practice, take on all the responsibilities of parents and are accordingly in an

---

1 G Douglas and NV Lowe 'Becoming a Parent in English Law' (1992) 108 LQR 414 at p 429.
2 In every case, the custodianship applicant was required to notify the local authority which was, in turn, obliged to prepare a full report.
3 The best account of this is probably to be found in Law Com Working Paper No 91 *Guardianship* (1985), especially Part II.
4 The leading authority was *W v A* [1981] Fam 114 and see Chapter 4 above.
5 Guardianship was largely governed by the Guardianship of Minors Act 1971, and formerly by the Guardianship of Infants Act 1925.
6 This had the incidental advantage of finally equalising the legal position of the married mother and father.

analogous position. Hence, the second aspect of the reforms was to assimilate the legal position of parents and guardians. By conferring parental responsibility on guardians as a matter of status, it was possible to do this and also to remove the anachronistic distinctions which the old law made between guardianship of the person and guardianship of the estate[1].

The legal effects of guardianship

Guardianship differs significantly from all other forms of social parenthood. It is by far the least regulated, the appointment of guardians being largely a private matter not subject to public scrutiny, judicial or otherwise. It is also the most far-reaching in its legal effects since it carries some of the incidents which are normally associated with legal parenthood but which do not arise merely by possessing parental responsibility[2]. Yet the status of guardianship, although closely resembling parenthood, is not identical. For example, guardians are not liable for child support as parents are[3]. More importantly, they may voluntarily disclaim their appointment, whereas the obligations of parenthood are imposed by operation of law and may not be voluntarily relinquished or transferred. The status of guardianship may also be revoked by court order, whereas parenthood survives all court orders except adoption.

The view has been expressed that:

> 'Given the gamut of safeguards, or controls, ... existing to ensure that a transfer of parental responsibility to a non-parent is consistent with the child's welfare, their absence in the case of guardianship is striking.'[4]

This emphasis on private ordering may be accounted for partly by the principle of testamentary freedom. Just as testators enjoy a wide measure of independence from legal controls in disposing of their material wealth[5] on death, so also should they be able to plan appropriate arrangements for the care of their minor children should death be untimely. It is also, to some extent, consistent with the lack of legal controls on the acquisition of parenthood[6]. The Law Commission did consult on the question whether there ought to be restrictions on private appointments or the disqualification of certain individuals analogous to those applying to private foster-parents but rejected the idea[7]. Indeed, the Law Commission thought guardianship was such a desirable institution that it wanted to encourage more private appointments by relaxing the formalities governing appointment; and the Children Act gives effect to this policy.

The appointment of guardians

The Children Act preserves the two ways in which guardians might be appointed before it, ie by private appointment or by appointment by the court[8].

---

1   For an explanation of these distinct offices, see Law Com Working Paper No 91 (above) at paras 2.21–2.25.
2   See below.
3   See Chapter 9 below.
4   G Douglas and NV Lowe 'Becoming a Parent in English Law' (1992) 108 LQR 414 at p 428.
5   But less so since the Inheritance (Provision for Family and Dependants) Act 1975.
6   See Chapter 4 above.
7   Law Com Working Paper No 91 *Guardianship* (1985) at paras 3.27–3.29.
8   Sections 5 and 6 constitute the new statutory framework for guardianship.

Private appointments

Private appointments of guardians may be made by parents with parental responsibility or by guardians themselves[1], but not by anyone else, even where they hold parental responsibility. The unmarried father may not appoint a guardian unless he has acquired parental responsibility. The extension of the power of private appointment to guardians reflects the general legislative policy of assimilating their position to parenthood. Under the old law, appointments were valid only if made by will or deed, but the Children Act allows a simple appointment by any written document which is dated and signed[2]. The hope is that this will encourage more people, especially younger adults who may have a natural disinclination to contemplate death, to appoint guardians. Having said that, the more formal method of appointment by will is likely to remain the norm. The most common situation is probably joint appointments by parents who are fearful of sudden death together, most obviously in an accident. In many cases, they are likely to discuss together and agree upon a suitable individual or individuals. The Children Act confirms that such appointments may be made jointly by two or more persons[3].

Court appointments

The court may appoint a guardian where there is no parent with parental responsibility or where a deceased parent had a residence order in his or her favour at the time of death[4]. The appointment may be made on the application of the intended guardian or by the court of its own motion, during the course of family proceedings[5].

The first situation could arise where both parents have died, having failed to appoint guardians. The court's intervention might be necessary, for example, to avoid a family wrangle, where more than one relative is asserting the right to look after the children. It could also arise where an unmarried father survives an unmarried mother. The appointment of an unmarried father by either the mother or the court is the only remaining way in which a parent may also become a guardian, and this would also have the effect of conferring parental responsibility on him.

The second situation most obviously includes the case where a divorced parent with a residence order is survived by the non-residential parent. The implication of this power is that it is not automatically desirable that the latter should be entitled to take over the care of the children which he has not had during the subsistence of the residence order. There must be cases in which a former spouse would be the very last person the deceased parent would have wished to look after the child. Where the court makes an appointment in these circumstances, the guardian will share parental responsibility with the survivor. It may become apparent that the level of actual or potential disagreement between them is such that the court will need to back up the appointment with a s 8 order[6].

---

1 Section 5(3) and (4).
2 Section 5(5).
3 Section 5(1).
4 Section 5(1).
5 Section 5(2).
6 A residence order might, for example, be required to resolve the question of the child's home.

The legal effects of guardianship

Guardianship can only take effect on the death of a parent. Its express purpose is to provide a complete replacement for a deceased parent. Where it is thought in the best interests of a child that a living parent be replaced, this can be achieved through adoption or by a residence order. The Law Commission did float the idea of inter vivos guardianship but it did not attract much support and was not pursued[1]. Subsequently, the interdepartmental *Review of Adoption Law* took up the idea and proposed that it ought to be possible to make the social parent holding parental responsibility under a residence order the guardian of the child. This would enable parental responsibility to be extended to the child's majority, viz up to the child's eighteenth birthday[2]. This could be thought desirable since most court orders in relation to children generally cease at 16[3]. The Draft Adoption Bill presented in 1996 does not incorporate this proposal as such but does make provision for the extension of residence orders to the child's majority[4].

Before the Children Act, the appointment of a guardian always took effect immediately on the death of the appointing parent. The effect was that the guardian would share parental 'rights', if there was a surviving parent, with that parent. This was a peculiarly English phenomenon. No comparable rule existed in any member country of the Council of Europe. The Law Commission considered that the rule had the potential for creating unnecessary conflict between the guardian and surviving parent, and that a surviving parent should normally be protected from unwelcome interference by an outsider. The Law Commission thought that the general aim of guardianship law should be 'to balance the claims of the surviving parent and the wishes of the deceased in the way which will be best for the child'[5]. To this end, the Children Act established the general rule that a guardian should only take office on the death of the surviving parent[6]. But this rule is displaced where the deceased parent had a residence order at the date of death. Here, the guardianship takes effect immediately[7]. This exception will not apply where *both* parents had residence orders, ie where a joint residence order has been made[8].

The thinking behind these provisions can be called into question. The implication is that while a surviving parent, who was living with the deceased in a united household, can be trusted to assume the sole care of the children without assistance, the divorced survivor cannot. The primary rule is understandable enough. Few would disagree with the notion that the surviving parent, in what was a united family, should receive help only if this is requested informally and should not have it thrust upon him by unwelcome interference from inside or outside the family. The issue is why a non-residential parent should not be similarly protected. The thinking seems to be that the deceased parent should be able, through guardianship, to preserve the 'advantage' of the residence order after his death. It

---

1 Law Com Working Paper No 91 *Guardianship* (1985) at paras 4.4 et seq.
2 Department of Health and Welsh Office *Review of Adoption Law* (HMSO, 1992) at para 6.5, and the White Paper *Adoption: The Future* (1993) (Cm 2288) at para 5.24.
3 Section 9(6).
4 Clause 86.
5 Law Com Report No 172 *Guardianship and Custody* (1988) at para 2.27.
6 Section 5(8).
7 Section 5(7).
8 Section 5(9).

is questionable how far this can be squared with the central principle of continuing parental responsibility.

Apart from the residence issue, the non-residential parent is as much a parent as was the deceased residential parent[1]. To make him share parental responsibility with a guardian may seem inappropriate where he has continued, in fact, to be actively connected with the child. It would arguably have been more consistent with the general aims of the legislation to have placed the onus on the guardian to seek immediate appointment where it could be demonstrated that this was in the child's best interests[2]. On the other hand, the view has been expressed that where one person had responsibility for a child under a residence order, it is reasonable that he or she should be able to control the arrangements made for the child immediately following his or her death[3].

Another difficulty is that the rule appears to create uncertainty about who is entitled to take over the physical care of a child. Both the guardian and the surviving parent have parental responsibility and, with it, an equal claim to look after the child. An initial dispute over where the child is to live would, therefore, appear to require a residence order to resolve it. This could have been avoided if the survivor held sole parental responsibility unless and until challenged by the guardian. The rather unsatisfactory outcome at present is that the onus to commence proceedings will be on 'the person wishing to change the existing arrangements'[4].

Assuming the appointment is operative, what are the essential legal effects of guardianship? The most immediate and significant effect is that the guardian acquires parental responsibility[5]. But, as noted above, the incidents of guardianship extend beyond this. In fact, the guardian occupies a position somewhere between legal parents and social parents who merely have parental responsibility. Like a parent, the guardian is entitled to object to adoption and to appoint a guardian[6], but unlike a parent (and in common with other social parents with parental responsibility), the guardian is not a liable relative for the purposes of public[7] or private[8] financial responsibility for children. No succession rights arise on the death intestate of either the guardian or the child (although they may, of course, arise expressly by will) and the child cannot derive citizenship from his guardian.

---

1 It should also be recalled that there will be many instances of so-called 'absent' parents who survive the parent looking after the child but, because of the no order principle, no residence order will have been made. These 'non-residential' parents will in these cases have *sole* parental responsibility and the onus will be on the appointed guardian to challenge this position.

2 See A Bainham 'The Children Act 1989: Parenthood and Guardianship' [1990] Fam Law 192 at pp 194–195.

3 SM Cretney *Family Law* (3rd edn) (Sweet & Maxwell, 1997) at p 180.

4 Law Com Report No 172 *Guardianship and Custody* (1988) at para 2.28. This rather resembles the law of the jungle since it turns on whether the guardian or the survivor has managed to get to the child first. For other practical difficulties which may arise under the new regime, see R Oswald 'The Appointment of Testamentary Guardians and the Children Act 1989' [1992] Fam Law 519.

5 Section 5(6).

6 Adoption Act 1976, s 16(1), and s 5(4) of the Children Act respectively.

7 Social Security Administration Act 1992, s 78.

8 Section 15 of and Sch 1 to the Children Act.

Revocation, disclaimer and termination of guardianship

An appointed guardian may never take office because the appointment is revoked. He may disclaim his appointment or may be removed by order of the court.

Revocation

An appointment may be revoked in a number of ways[1]. This may be achieved expressly by a written and dated instrument, made by the appointing parent or guardian[2], or impliedly by the destruction of the written document[3], by the later appointment of a guardian unless there was a clear intention to appoint an additional guardian[4], or by subsequent revocation of a will or codicil in which the appointment was made[5]. Following a recent amendment, the appointment of a spouse as guardian will be automatically revoked by a subsequent divorce[6].

Disclaimer

The Children Act allowed, for the first time, a guardian to disclaim his appointment in writing within a reasonable time[7]. It is perhaps a surprising feature of the law relating to guardians that the consent of the intended guardian is not required before appointment. There is not even a requirement of notification. Common sense dictates that the appointing parent ought to approach the person concerned and discuss the matter before making the appointment. The right of disclaimer ought to cover the minority of cases in which this sensible approach has not been taken or where, perhaps, a change of circumstances has caused the guardian to change his mind about accepting responsibility.

Termination

Guardianship will automatically terminate on the death of the child[8] or the guardian, or on attainment of majority of the child[9]. It may also be brought to an

---

1 Section 6.
2 Section 6(2). The document must be signed by him, or at his direction, in his presence and in the presence of two witnesses who attest the signature.
3 Section 6(3). It has to be shown that the intention was to revoke the appointment but this may be implied from the destruction.
4 Section 6(1). The intention to appoint an additional guardian might be express or by necessary implication.
5 Section 6(4).
6 Section 6(3A), added by the Law Reform (Succession) Act 1995 and amended by the Family Law Act 1996, Sch 8, para 41.
7 Section 6(5). There is provision for the Lord Chancellor to prescribe the manner in which disclaimers are to be recorded. This is analogous to the similar provision for recording parental responsibility agreements. The objective in each case is to resolve any doubt about who has parental responsibility for a child at a given time. At the time of writing, no such regulations had been made.
8 Although it has been argued that a guardian would remain under a duty to bury or cremate the deceased child, unlike a local authority where the child was in care. See *R v Gwynedd County Council ex parte B* [1991] 2 FLR 365, and the evaluation of the decision in *Bromley's Family Law* (8th edn) (Butterworths, 1992) at pp 311 and 406.
9 Section 91(7) and (8). Cf parenthood which can, in effect, continue beyond majority for limited purposes such as succession and financial support, where the child is in further education or undergoing training for a trade, profession or vocation.

end by court order[1]. The court may act on the application of anyone with parental responsibility (including the guardian himself), the child (with the leave of the court), or of the court's own motion in family proceedings. In all cases, the court must apply the welfare principle. A termination is likely to be ordered where the guardian himself wishes to be released (and the allowable time for disclaimer has elapsed) or where the guardian's continued involvement with the child is considered undesirable for whatever reason. One example would be where there is suspicion of abuse. A more likely scenario would be where a guardian and surviving parent are at loggerheads, although such disputes could also be resolved in some cases by a lesser order such as a s 8 order, perhaps with directions or conditions attached. Where the court does remove a guardian, it may need to consider whether to appoint another guardian, especially where a sole guardian is involved, since there might otherwise be a hiatus in parental responsibility for the child.

It has been observed that, apart from the legal framework outlined above, little is known about the operation of private guardianship appointments in practice, despite their encouragement in the Children Act[2]. It has been suggested that research could usefully be carried out into the incidence of such appointments and disclaimers and to ascertain whether there is any evidence of abuse by guardians.

STEP-PARENTS

The nature of step-parenthood

Step-parents have not always had a good press. Successive generations of children have, through fairy-tales, been introduced at an early age to the genre of the wicked step-parent. The step-mothers of Cinderella, Snow-White and Hansel and Gretel all spring to mind, although, curiously, wicked step-fathers have not achieved the same degree of prominence. These absurdly unjust stereotypes do, nonetheless, contain an element of truth – that the step-parent/step-child relation can often be a difficult one. The step-parent is in a potentially awkward position from the start[3]. He (or she) is part of a family unit and has a regularised relationship with the natural parent through marriage, but lacks a regularised relationship with the children in the family. Thus, while the step-parent undoubtedly is in most cases in loco parentis and has de facto care of the children, he lacks in law the parental responsibility which would put him on an equal footing with his spouse and legitimise his standing to be fully involved in upbringing. Mention should perhaps be made at this point of the growing category of cohabitants of natural parents who are sometimes also (inaccurately) referred to as step-parents. While there is a high incidence of 'serial' marriage,

---

1   Section 6(7).
2   *Bromley's Family Law* (8th edn) (Butterworths, 1992) at p 407. This is arguably the best academic treatment of guardianship and the whole of chapter 12 repays attention. See also G Douglas and NV Lowe 'Becoming a Parent in English Law' (1992) 108 LQR 414 at pp 427–430.
3   On how step-families cope with the difficulties of not being a 'normal' family, see J Burgoyne and D Clark *Making a Go of it – A Study of Step-Families in Sheffield* (Routledge and Kegan Paul, 1984), and B Maddox *Step-Parenting* (Unwin Paperbacks, 1980).

equally there are many people who, following divorce, have become disenchanted with the institution of marriage and prefer, thereafter, the more informal relation of cohabitation. These cohabitants of legal parents are in an analogous, but not identical, position to step-parents since their access to the courts is slightly less assured under the regime of the Children Act.

The step-parent or cohabitant is in no better and no worse position than other de facto carers and has the same powers and obligations[1]. But he is in the unusual position of occupying the same household, potentially permanently, with a person (his spouse) in whom parental responsibility is vested. While the relationship between the adult partners may be viewed as a partnership of equals, the relationship between them and the child is clearly not equal in law. In the event of disagreement, the natural parent (by virtue of parental responsibility) has the sole authority on any issues affecting the children. This is a situation which has all the potential for conflict between the spouses and between the step-parent and the children. Douglas and Lowe have contrasted the strength of the guardian's position with the 'complete lack of legal recognition of step-parenthood'[2]. This weakness of step-parents' legal position has led to calls for an upgrading of their status. We now consider how this might be achieved under existing mechanisms and we examine the possibilities for further reform.

Acquiring a status

The options open to step-parents are broadly those which are available to other de facto carers. One option is to apply for a s 8 order. The residence order would give parental responsibility while other orders, especially the contact order, might prove useful if the step-family breaks down. Step-parents will usually qualify to apply, as of right, for residence or contact orders, as applications may be made by 'any party to a marriage (whether or not subsisting) in relation to whom the child is a child of the family'[3]. The effect of this provision is to place all step-parents, whether they are married to a widowed, divorced or formerly unmarried spouse, on an equal footing with that spouse, and also to enable an application to be made by him while his marriage is intact, as well as on its breakdown[4]. The child in question must be a 'child of the family'[5] which entails 'treatment' of the child by both parties to the marriage as a child of the family[6]. The test is an objective one which should not be difficult to satisfy in most cases of step-parenthood. Alternatively, a step-parent might qualify on the basis of having lived with the child for three years or having the relevant consents[7]. The cohabitant of a parent is in a less favourable position. He will not qualify as a party to a marriage and, if he does not qualify on the other grounds, he will require leave[8]. Whether or not this would

---

1   Section 3(5), and see Chapter 2 above.
2   See G Douglas and NV Lowe 'Becoming a Parent in English Law' (1992) 108 LQR 414 at p 430.
3   Section 10(5)(a).
4   Under the old law, only those who had married divorced parents could invoke the divorce jurisdiction.
5   Defined in s 105(1) of the Children Act.
6   See *Teeling v Teeling* [1984] FLR 808; *D v D (Child of the Family)* (1981) FLR 93; *W v W (Child of the Family)* [1984] FLR 796; *Carron v Carron* [1984] FLR 805; and *Re A (Child of the Family)* [1998] 1 FLR 347.
7   Discussed above.
8   See fn 4 at p 178 above and accompanying text.

be granted might turn on the duration of the cohabitation and the nature of the relationship which the cohabitant has established with the child.

An alternative which has, in the past, proved popular with step-parents is to apply to adopt the child. Adoption in this context is, however, controversial because of its traditionally 'exclusive' nature involving termination of the child's legal relationship with one side of his natural family. There has been a policy of discouraging step-parent adoption since the Children Act 1975[1], although the current position is that the court is free to choose between the alternatives of s 8 orders and adoption[2]. These adoption issues are considered in Chapter 7 below. The underlying issues about balancing the interests of the natural family and the step-family run through the whole debate about the status of step-parents and an attempt is made to address some of these in the next section.

Further reform?

A number of commentators have argued for greater recognition of the step-parent relationship[3]. In some ways, the debate about step-parents is reminiscent of that regarding unmarried fathers. Generally, the step-father will be part of a reconstituted family following the divorce of a 'residential' mother[4]. The available options for reform are, again, to create an automatic legal status by giving parental responsibility to all step-parents, to allow private arrangements for sharing it, or to continue to require an application to the court.

Judith Masson has advocated the first approach. This would involve giving, automatically, to a step-parent or parent's cohabitant, the same status which his spouse possesses[5]. Others have been less radical. Douglas and Lowe have argued that consideration ought to be given to the second alternative, which has been adopted for unmarried fathers, of allowing a private agreement by parent and step-parent to share parental responsibility[6]. This was also recommended in the *Review of Adoption Law* and found its way into the Draft Adoption Bill 1996[7]. If enacted, this would amend the Children Act 1989 to enable the natural parent (with parental responsibility)[8] to share parental responsibility with his or her spouse. Where the other natural parent also has parental responsibility, his or her agreement would be required to what would then amount to a tripartite sharing of parental responsibility. The court would also be empowered, failing agreement, to

---

1   The directives to the court in the Children Act 1975 followed the recommendations of the Houghton Committee in the *Report of the Departmental Committee on the Adoption of Children* (1972) (Cmnd 5107).

2   For a critique of the removal of the former statutory directives, see A Bainham 'The Privatisation of the Public Interest in Children' (1990) 53 MLR 206 at pp 214–216.

3   See, for example, J Masson, D Norbury and SG Chatterton *Mine, Yours or Ours? A Study of Step-Parent Adoption* (HMSO, 1983); J Masson 'Old Families into New: A Status for Step-Parents' in MDA Freeman (ed) *State, Law and Family* (Tavistock, 1984) at ch 14.

4   The expression 'residential mother' is used here in the non-technical sense of the parent with whom the child is living, perhaps with a residence order in her favour but, increasingly, under the new law, without one.

5   J Masson 'Old Families into New: A Status for Step-Parents' (above) at p 237.

6   G Douglas and NV Lowe 'Becoming a Parent in English Law' (1992) 108 LQR 414 at p 431.

7   See the White Paper, *Adoption: The Future* (1993) (Cm 2288) at para 5.21.

8   The new procedure would not be available to an unmarried father who has not himself already acquired parental responsibility.

make a parental responsibility order[1]. The Draft Bill also contains important proposals for the amendment of the law governing step-parent adoption which we consider later. Under these proposals, and where a step-parent obtains a residence order, parental responsibility would be shared with the parent. Would this be a sound policy? A distinction should perhaps be made between the different circumstances of step-parenthood. For, while the spouse of a widowed or formerly unmarried parent would be likely to share parental responsibility *only* with that parent, this is manifestly not the case where the marriage is with a divorced parent. The case for allowing automatic or informal sharing may be stronger where there is no third parental figure on the scene, since this would not entail a tripartite power-sharing arrangement.

There is room for argument about how consistent a tripartite power-sharing arrangement is with the philosophy of the Children Act. On the one hand, this undoubtedly favours an 'inclusive' model of child-rearing which might appear to support the regularisation of the step-parent's position. On the other hand, the principle of continuing parental responsibility might appear to militate against anything which would weaken or detract from the position of the non-residential father who remains, in all respects, a parent. The view expressed in one leading textbook that it is 'unclear why the agreement of the parent who is not living with the child is thought necessary' and that 'granting parental responsibility to a person does not involve the reduction of the power of others holding it'[2] is questionable. On the contrary, the policy is very clear. The essential philosophy of the Children Act is that parents remain parents and continue to exercise parental responsibility regardless of divorce. It would thus be quite improper to allow a voluntary sharing of parental responsibility by one parent without the other's concurrence or a court order. Moreover, to share decision-making for a child between three rather than two adults is equally clearly a weakening of the position of the parent who is not in the household.

The problem with an enhanced status for step-parents might therefore be that it could be seen as shutting out, or at least diluting, the parental contribution of the non-residential parent, contrary to the spirit of the legislation. There is plenty of evidence that this is precisely what *some* step-families have tried to do by attempting to change the child's surname and/or adopt the child[3]. While a triangular sharing of parental responsibility may work well where all parties have an interest in the child and wish to enter into a co-operative arrangement, it could be a recipe for conflict where this is not the case. It also questionable whether the proliferation of parental responsibility which could occur where children are caught up in serial marriages, would be in their best interests, or workable at all, on a practical level. There is, therefore, an argument for saying that any acquisition of parental responsibility by a step-parent should continue to be subject to judicial scrutiny. As Brenda Hale has observed, the step-relation is not

---

1 See *Adoption – A Service for Children* (Department of Health and Welsh Office, 1996), and cl 85 of the Draft Bill, amending Children Act 1989, s 4.
2 See SM Cretney and JM Masson *Principles of Family Law* (6th edn) (Sweet & Maxwell, 1997) at p 648.
3 This is part of the rationale for the former restrictions on step-parent adoptions. See p 189 above.

the same as the 'normal' family constituted within marriage and 'perhaps we should not pretend that it is'[1].

FOSTER-PARENTS

The nature of foster-parenthood

Broadly speaking, foster-parents are those who look after children on more than a purely temporary basis but who are not related to those children. Yet the expression 'foster-parent' covers a range of different child care arrangements[2]. The principal distinctions are between private and local authority foster-parents and between short-term and long-term fostering arrangements. What all these arrangements have in common is that foster-parenthood does not of itself confer parental responsibility. Thus, unless legal steps are taken to acquire it, foster-parents are in a similar position to other de facto carers. What distinguishes their position is that they are subject to certain legal controls and, in the case of local authority foster-parents, controls which do not apply to other categories of social parents. The controls on the making and conduct of fostering arrangements are considered later under the supervisory functions of local authorities[3]. The concern here is to get a sense of the nature of fostering as one form of social parenthood, and its legal status.

Private foster-parents
The Children Act[4] provides a technical definition of a 'privately fostered child' (and hence of private foster-parents) which is designed to distinguish, by a process of elimination, the private foster-parent from other carers. It is this definition which triggers the provisions of Part IX of the Children Act governing local authority control and support of private fostering[5]. A privately fostered child is under 16 years of age[6], is cared for or accommodated by someone who is *not* a parent, does *not* have parental responsibility, is *not* a 'relative'[7] of his, and is *not* accommodated for a period of less than 28 days where the carer has no intention of accommodating him for a longer period. This last part of the definition excludes temporary carers such as babysitters or day-carers, playgroups and nurseries, friends and others who provide a host of day-to-day child-minding activities[8].

Foster-parents have always been in a precarious legal position. Their principal problem has been, and still is, one of insecurity in the face of demands for the

---

1   BM Hoggett *Parents and Children: The Law of Parental Responsibility* (3rd edn) (Sweet & Maxwell, 1987) at p 126. This view does not appear to have been repeated in the fourth edition of the book.
2   For general discussions of fostering, and materials on it, see Hoggett (4th edn) (above) at chs 7 and 9, and Hoggett, Pearl, Cooke and Bates *The Family, Law and Society* (4th edn) (Butterworths, 1996) at pp 653–663.
3   See Chapter 10 below.
4   Section 66.
5   Also governed in greater detail by the Children (Private Arrangements for Fostering) Regulations 1991, SI 1991/2050.
6   Where the child is disabled, the age-limit is raised to 18 years (s 66(4)).
7   'Relative' is also defined in the legislation. See p 196 below.
8   Chapter 10 below discusses the controls on day-care arrangements.

return of the child, from the parents or, in the case of local authority foster-parents, from the authority itself. Their status as foster-parents gives them no right to retain the child where such a request is made, except perhaps for a very short time which is strictly necessary to safeguard the child's welfare[1]. Where the arrangement was always intended to be short-term, perhaps, for example, to provide respite care while a natural parent has a period of illness, the foster-parents may be happy to return the child. The difficulty arises where the arrangement has lasted long enough for an attachment to build up between the child and the foster-parents and a so-called 'tug of love' situation results. The longer the arrangement has lasted, the more likely it is that foster-parents may be able to demonstrate that it is in the best interests of the child to remain with them. This time factor is reflected in the rules which previously qualified foster-parents to apply under the custodianship procedure and in the current qualifications governing s 8 orders. The basis of these rules is, in part, that it is positively inconsistent with the nature of fostering that applications by foster-parents for parental responsibility should be made in the early years of an arrangement and this applies, a fortiori, to local authority fostering[2].

Foster-parents qualify to seek a residence or contact order without leave where they have been living with the child for three years or have the consent of those with parental responsibility, usually the natural parents[3]. Otherwise, they must seek leave and this is also required where they wish to apply for one of the other orders. Other alternatives are to apply for adoption[4], or to seek an order in wardship proceedings[5]. Whichever proceedings are invoked, the court will have to decide between the alternative claims, and this will always be a difficult and sensitive task. The court will, in particular, be faced with intractable problems about weighing the value of the blood tie to the child, against the emotional tie of the foster-parents and the disruption to a settled home[6].

These dilemmas and the uphill struggle faced by some foster-parents are well-illustrated by *Re K (A Minor) (Wardship: Adoption)*[7]. In this case, the natural parents handed over their third child at the age of six weeks to foster-parents, a much older childless couple. The parents' circumstances were far from ideal and there were serious question marks as to their suitability to look after the child. They nonetheless regretted their decision and wanted to resume the care of the baby and to reintroduce her to her two older siblings. The foster-parents sought to prevent this by making the child a ward of court and at first instance succeeded in obtaining care and control with a view to adoption, and an order terminating the mother's access (now contact).

The Court of Appeal allowed the parents' appeal and emphasised that the court was not justified in removing a child permanently from natural parents merely because the child might be better off with the foster-parents. As Butler-Sloss LJ put

---

1   They would appear to be empowered to do so under s 3(5) of the Children Act as where, for example, they refuse to hand the child over to a drunken parent who has turned up on the doorstep in the dead of night.
2   See below.
3   See p 177 above.
4   See Chapter 7 below.
5   Discussed at p 199 below.
6   The classic case was *J v C* [1970] AC 668.
7   [1991] 1 FLR 57.

it: 'The mother must be shown to be entirely unsuitable before another family can be considered, otherwise we are in grave danger of slipping into social engineering'.

While other decisions have been less strident in their support of the blood tie, the case does illustrate the difficulties which will inevitably be faced where private foster-parents, who are essentially conceived as short-term carers, are seeking to make the arrangement permanent against the parents' wishes and in the absence of grounds which would enable the statutory threshold for care proceedings to be crossed[1]. Another important point to emerge from this decision is that the law must not be seen to be allowing private fostering arrangements to slip into compulsion where, if there had been local authority involvement from the outset, it was unlikely that the foster-parents would have succeeded in retaining the child. We now turn to the position of local authority foster-parents.

Local authority foster-parents

Local authority foster-parents occupy a special position in substitute care arrangements and are singled out for peculiar treatment in the legislation[2]. Placement in a foster-family is one of the major options (perhaps the best option) for accommodating a child in the care of a local authority or 'looked after' by it[3]. This 'boarding-out' of children is part of the local authority's services to children and families and it is the involvement of social services which makes this a special kind of fostering. Part IX of the Children Act does not apply to these arrangements which are instead governed by their own set of regulations[4].

It was not thought that local authority foster-parents should have the same access to the courts as other social parents[5]. It was reasoned that to allow them open access might be to interfere unduly with the local authority's ability to make plans for the child and might undermine public confidence in child care services. Before the Children Act, there was a great deal of concern about the way in which children, originally placed in 'voluntary care', could become detained compulsorily under various procedures. It was a major objective of the legislation to remove the stigma of these public services and encourage a more positive attitude to local authority assistance. Early applications for s 8 orders by local authority foster-parents might discourage parents from seeking this assistance. Moreover, most foster-parents will have no legitimate expectation of acquiring parental responsibility, especially in the early years of a placement. Many are seen from the outset as short-term carers and not as long-term foster-parents or prospective adopters. Thus, even where social services do conclude that a return to the natural family is no longer in the child's best interests, there is no guarantee that the existing foster-home will be seen as the best, or even an acceptable, long-term prospect for the child[6]. Where, however, the local authority is seeking to remove the child from the foster-parents, and the foster-parents counter with notice of

---

1   As to which, see Chapter 11.
2   For the official reasoning, see Law Com Report No 172 *Guardianship and Custody* (1988) at para 4.43.
3   Chapter 10 below discusses the options available to authorities.
4   Foster Placement (Children) Regulations 1991, SI 1991/910.
5   See Law Com Report No 172 *Guardianship and Custody* (1988) at para 4.43.
6   These difficulties are particularly well illustrated by *Re JK (Adoption: Transracial Placement)* [1992] 2 FLR 340.

their intention to apply to adopt the child, the courts are liable to refuse leave to remove the child before there has been a proper investigation of the merits of the adoption application[1].

The legislation, accordingly, sets up additional hurdles, which local authority foster-parents must surmount[2]. These restrictions prevent them from seeking leave to apply for s 8 orders. They may only do so with the consent of the local authority if they are relatives of the child or if the child has lived with them for three years[3]. Most local authority foster-parents, in the early years of an arrangement, will require the consent of both the local authority and the court before an application can even get off the ground, let alone succeed[4]. After the child has had his home with foster-parents for several years, different consider-ations may apply, and greater weight may be attached to the claims of the foster-parents where these diverge from the plans of the local authority. Foster-parents' increased eligibility to apply for orders after three years reflects this.

Exclusive versus inclusive fostering

There has been a long-standing debate about whether foster-parenthood is best viewed as an exclusive or inclusive arrangement[5]. Exclusive parenting is the notion that children are better off if they relate to only one set of 'parents' who have their care. Outside involvement with other adults is conceived as undesirable and disruptive of the foster-family. Some foster-parents have evidently held this view and have not welcomed interaction with natural parents. Inclusive fostering, in contrast, recognises the value to foster-children of other family ties and seeks to preserve these through contact arrangements. Some foster-parents have appar-ently seen their role in this light. There is now no question that the inclusive model is in the ascendant and is the one which accords with the spirit of the Children Act.

Where foster-parents have not acquired parental responsibility through a residence order, they clearly have no authority whatsoever for refusing parental contact or participation in upbringing and are susceptible to an immediate request for the return of the child. Yet, even where they *have* managed to acquire a residence order, parental responsibility must be *shared* with the natural parents, who do not lose it. Foster-parents may, thus, have to accept the idea of greater parental involvement in upbringing, even where they have some security (through a residence order) against removal of the child. It should, of course, be said that the extent to which they will, in practice, have to accommodate parents'

---

1 See *Re C (A Minor) (Adoption)* [1994] 2 FLR 513.
2 A local authority foster-parent is defined in s 23 of the Children Act. Essentially, he or she is someone with whom a child has been boarded by the local authority, which can include a relative, but who is not a parent, someone with parental responsibility, or someone who held a residence order immediately before a care order was made.
3 Section 9(3). The period of three years in s 9(3) need not be continuous but must not have begun more than five years before the application (s 9(4)). These restrictions apply to anyone who has been a local authority foster-parent at any time within the previous six months.
4 For a case in which foster-parents succeeded in obtaining leave to seek a residence order, with the consent of the local authority, but in the face of parental opposition, see *C v Salford City Council* [1994] 2 FLR 926.
5 For an excellent discussion of these concepts, see R Holman 'The Place of Fostering in Social Work' (1975) 5 *British Journal of Social Work* 3.

views will depend in part on how enthusiastic parents are about being involved, and on the propensity of the courts to regulate the exercise of parental responsibility by the various orders at their disposal[1]. Local authority foster-parents are liable to find themselves in an even more inclusive situation, since they have to concern themselves with the managerial control of the local authority, as well as with the natural parents. Indeed, the greater threat to the security of local authority foster-parents will be from the authority itself if it should decide that the child's future lies elsewhere. Where the child is not in care but is 'looked after' by the local authority under a voluntary arrangement, the local authority will not formally have parental responsibility, but major aspects of its exercise will have been delegated to the authority under an agreement with the parents. Whether the local authority has the child voluntarily or compulsorily, it *must* involve the parents in the child's upbringing. Hence, local authority fostering is bound, at least in theory, to be inclusive in nature. If local authority foster-parents succeed in obtaining a residence order, this has the effect of discharging a care order but not terminating the parental responsibility of the parents[2] which continues to be shared with the foster-parents. How this more inclusive model of fostering will work out is something which will not be known until the legislation has been in operation for some time.

A reform proposal

The interdepartmental *Review of Adoption Law* expressed concern that residence orders 'are not perceived as being likely to offer a sufficient sense of permanence for a child and his carers'[3]. Accordingly, it proposed that where a court made a residence order in favour of, inter alia, a foster-parent and it considered that the foster-parent would be responsible for the child's upbringing until he grew up, the court should have a further power to appoint, where appropriate, the foster-parent as the child's inter vivos guardian[4]. The foster-parent obtaining such an order might regard it as giving him 'foster-plus' status but without having to go through the rigmarole of the adoption process[5]. The Draft Adoption Bill does not provide for inter vivos guardianship as such, but would amend the Children Act to enable the court to direct, with the consent of all those with parental responsibility, that a residence order in favour of a non-parent (including for present purposes a foster-parent) should continue in force until the child reaches the age of 18[6]. It would also be provided that where such a direction is made, the leave of the court would be required for an application to discharge or vary the order. If enacted, the hope would be that this would give greater legal security to long-term foster-parents without severing the legal relationship between the child and the birth family which adoption would entail.

---

1 It should be remembered that, in addition to s 8 orders themselves, courts have a wide power to give directions or attach conditions to their orders (s 11(7)).
2 Sections 91(1) and 2(6) respectively.
3 Department of Health and Welsh Office *Review of Adoption Law* (HMSO, 1992) at para 6.4.
4 Ibid at para 6.5.
5 See the White Paper *Adoption: The Future* (1993) (Cm 2288) at paras 5.24–5.25.
6 Clause 86, amending Children Act 1989, s 12.

RELATIVES

Definition and problems

The legislation also contains a technical definition of a 'relative'. The expression includes 'a grandparent, brother, sister, uncle or aunt (whether of the full blood or half blood or by affinity) or step-parent'[1]. Relatives are arguably distinguishable from other de facto carers in that the family tie which exists between them and the child creates a prima facie presumption that any interest they express in the child will be genuine and not flimsy or fanciful. In some cases, the relative in question may have been looking after the child (temporarily or over a long period), while in other cases, the relative's concern may be about some aspect of upbringing. Where the child has been looked after for a substantial time, perhaps by a grandparent, the caring relative has a claim for security analogous to that of other long-term carers, such as foster-parents. Yet the existence of a familial connection can also create special problems of its own which surface particularly where a relative wishes to adopt a child. The difficulty here is that to allow an adoption might be to distort existing family relationships. This issue is considered further in Chapter 7 below. Where a local authority is contemplating an application for a care order, exceptionally difficult questions can arise concerning whether it is, or should be, under a legal obligation to exhaust the resources of the wider, extended family before seeking to place the child in substitute arrangements outside the birth family. Also, wherever a local authority is 'looking after' a child, it is under a statutory obligation to promote contact between that child and the wider family. We consider these issues in Part III of the book.

Since adoption by relatives was discouraged, the more traditional course was to resort to wardship, which was often the *only* available procedure[2]. An exception was made specifically for grandparents who were first allowed to intervene to seek access in certain matrimonial proceedings[3] and, later, to participate in care proceedings[4]. Other relatives remained dependent on wardship or, in some circumstances, qualified to apply under the custodianship procedure when this was eventually implemented.

Improved rights of access to the court
It was the policy of the Law Commission[5] to improve the rights of interested persons, including relatives, to access to the courts and the *Review of Child Care*

---

1 Section 105(1). Cf the much wider definition of 'relative' in Part IV of the Family Law Act 1996 contained in s 63(1) of that Act.
2 One of the best examples under the old law was the failed attempt of an uncle, aunt and grandparent to challenge a local authority's plans for a child in care through wardship in *Re W (A Minor) (Wardship: Jurisdiction)* [1985] AC 791. Another example is *Re H (A Minor) (Custody: Interim Care and Control)* [1991] 2 FLR 109 where a maternal grandmother succeeded in gaining interim care and control of a nine-year-old girl as against her divorced natural father, in wardship proceedings. The grandmother and step-father had been appointed testamentary guardians by the deceased mother.
3 Domestic Proceedings and Magistrates' Courts Act 1978.
4 Children and Young Persons (Amendment) Act 1986.
5 Law Com Report No 172 *Guardianship and Custody* (1988), especially at paras 4.40 and 4.41.

Law and subsequent White Paper[1] also accepted that they should have greater rights of participation in public procedures relating to care and supervision. It was perhaps questionable whether grandparents ought to have been given preferential treatment. Whilst, undoubtedly, grandparents can often have close emotional ties with their grandchildren, the same may often be true of other relatives such as adult siblings. Moreover, as any parent will testify, grandparents can often have a capacity for interference which may strain relations not simply between grandparent and parent also between the parents themselves[2].

Relatives' rights: residence and contact orders

The Children Act did not maintain the preference for grandparents but placed all relatives on an equal footing[3], although most of the reported cases have in fact concerned grandparents. A relative may now apply for a residence or contact order without leave where the child has lived with him for three years or where he has obtained the relevant consents[4]. A few points should be made regarding the latter possibility. First, there is no question of a relative having to obtain the consent of the local authority as is required of local authority foster-parents[5]. Secondly, it is perhaps more likely that relatives (as opposed to outsiders) will have the consent of natural parents to their seeking residence orders, since many situations in which relatives look after children are family arrangements which are made with the full co-operation of the natural parents. A good example is the child of a young unmarried mother being raised by the maternal grandparents while the mother pursues her career or education or generally gets on with her own life. Thirdly, many of these family arrangements will, almost by definition, be inclusive in nature and this may be one situation in which it is realistic to talk about a genuine sharing of parental responsibility between parents and relatives. Obviously, there will be other situations in which there is a family dispute

1 DHSS, *Review of Child Care Law* (1985) and White Paper *The Law on Child Care and Family Services* (1987) (Cmnd 62). And see *R v Hereford and Worcester County Council ex parte D* [1992] 1 FLR 448 in which Scott Baker J, granting an application for judicial review by the aunt who was also the foster-mother of the child, held that a foster-parent had a legitimate expectation to be consulted by the local authority before the child was removed from her care.

2 As Lord Mackay LC put it, 'not all interest in a child's life is necessarily benign, even if well-intentioned. Arguably, at least until we have some experience of wider rights of application, the law should provide some protection to children and their parents against unwarranted applications by grandparents, when they occur' (503 HL Official Report, col 1342). And see *Re M (Minors)* [1993] Fam Law 161 in which the Court of Appeal took the view that it was unnecessary and unduly expensive for everyone that grandparents intervene as parties where they had no separate point to make or issue to ventilate.

3 Step-parents do, however, have an advantage in that they may qualify to bring proceedings as parties to a marriage in which the child is a child of the family. 'Child of the family' is defined in s 105(1) of the Children Act.

4 Any person may also apply for variation or discharge of a s 8 order where the order was made on his application or where, in the case of a contact order, he was named in the order (s 10(6)). In *B v B (A Minor) (Residence Order)* [1992] 2 FLR 327, a maternal grandmother succeeded in obtaining a residence order on appeal from the magistrates' decision not to make an order, applying s 1(5). Johnson J held that, although the child was already settled in the care of the grandmother, a residence order would confer parental responsibility on her and would reassure outsiders, such as education authorities, of her authority in relation to the child. Cf *B v B (Interim Contact with Grandparents)* [1993] Fam Law 393 where, unusually, an appeal was allowed against an interim order in favour of grandparents.

5 Section 9(3)(b).

requiring the court to regulate the exercise of parental responsibility by drawing on the panoply of orders at its disposal. The Children Act also provides that rules of court may prescribe other categories of those qualified to apply without leave for s 8 orders and there has been some speculation that this right might, in due course, be extended to grandparents.

Where a relative does not automatically qualify to apply under the above rules, an application may be made with leave. Several reported cases have, not surprisingly, concerned grandparents. Here, the problem may be that the input of grandparents may be important to the children following separation or divorce, but family relations between the various adults may be so strained that contact is denied. Such was the position in *Re A (Section 8 Order: Grandparent Application)*[1] where the paternal grandmother wanted contact with her young grandson following an acrimonious divorce. She did not, however, have a close or existing relationship with the child and the mother was fearful of her. In dismissing the grandmother's appeal against refusal of contact, the Court of Appeal rejected her submission that a member of the family should be allowed contact unless there were cogent reasons to the contrary. While there was such a presumption in favour of a parent there was no such presumption, even where a grandparent succeeded in obtaining leave, in favour of other members of the family.

This decision was followed by Hollis J in *Re W (Contact: Application by Grandparent)*[2], a case in which the hostility was between the mother and her own mother. Here, leave had been granted to the grandmother to apply for contact but she failed on the substantive application to obtain the order. It was held that there was no presumption of contact which arose by virtue of crossing the hurdle of leave. Except in the case of the natural parent, anyone applying for contact had to show grounds for it. It was said, however, that it would be nonsense in the long term for a child to be denied contact with his grandmother because of bitterness between her and the mother. Grandparents, it was said, play an important role in children's lives, especially for young children, and their influence could be extremely beneficial if exercised with care and not too frequently. In this case, there was no justification for preventing *indirect* contact between the grandmother and the child through birthday cards and the like.

The position of grandparents may perhaps be stronger where they are seeking contact with a child in care rather than contact which is opposed by parents. There is certainly more than a flavour of this in *Re M (Care: Contact: Grandmother's Application for Leave)*[3]. Here, the Court of Appeal, while noting that there is no presumption of reasonable contact in favour of a grandparent where a child is in care[4], said that grandparents should, however, have a special place in any child's affections. Any contact between a child and his natural family should be assumed to be beneficial and the local authority would be required to file evidence to justify why it was not thought to be consistent with the child's welfare to promote contact with relatives[5].

---

1   [1995] 2 FLR 153.
2   [1997] 1 FLR 793.
3   [1995] 2 FLR 86.
4   See Children Act 1989, s 34(1), and Chapter 11 below.
5   These remarks were made against the background of a statutory obligation under the Children Act, Sch 2, para 15 to promote such contact with relatives.

Applications by other relatives, in particular to be joined as parties to children proceedings, have not fared particularly well – at least in the reported cases[1], and there is a feeling that aunts and uncles and remoter kin would face an even more difficult task than grandparents face where their involvement with the child is opposed by the parents. Siblings have, however, enjoyed a degree of success in seeking orders to remain in contact with adopted children[2].

OTHER INTERESTED PERSONS

Introduction

There is a category of non-parents who, while not caring for children or related to them, may yet feel strongly about issues affecting them. Such cases have sometimes been referred to as 'single issue' cases and they have traditionally been resolved in wardship proceedings. The questions raised have often been so complex or sensitive that, quite apart from the applicant's lack of standing in other proceedings, wardship has been seen as the approprite forum[3]. Many examples could be cited but the most well known is *Re D (A Minor)*[4] in which an educational psychologist succeeded in preventing the sterilisation of an 11-year-old girl.

The option of wardship

The official policy of the legislature was to cut down reliance on wardship and, instead, to incorporate its most valuable features into the statutory code[5]. As will be seen, wardship has effectively been abolished where the child is in the care of the local authority[6] but it remains intact as one procedure within the definition of family proceedings[7], and may still be used to resolve 'private' disputes concerning children. How far it will be used is likely to depend on whether legal advisers feel that it still has advantages to offer over and above the more usual statutory procedures. It is also likely to depend on how far the courts will be prepared to continue a wardship where a statutory alternative exists. This might be to seek leave to apply for a prohibited steps or specific issue order, either during the course of family proceedings or, more likely, on a freestanding application. The policy is to allow *anyone* to seek leave, but it is in this context that the court is perhaps most likely to be restrictive in granting it. Because of the applicant's looser link with the child, the court will wish to be convinced that the applicant is not just interfering, that there is a real issue at stake, and that the court's intervention is justified. Where it is satisfied as to these matters, the leave

---

1 For two unsuccessful applications by aunts, see *G v Kirklees Metropolitan Borough Council* [1993] 1 FLR 805 and *Re A (A Minor) (Residence Order: Leave to Apply)* [1993] 1 FLR 425.
2 See Chapter 7.
3 On the general nature of the wardship jurisdiction, see Lowe and White *Wards of Court* (2nd edn) (Barry Rose/Kluwer, 1986), especially ch 1 and *Bromley's Family Law* (8th edn) (Butterworths, 1992) at ch 14.
4 *Re D (A Minor) (Wardship: Sterilisation)* [1976] Fam 185.
5 Law Com Working Paper No 100 *Wards of Court* (1987) and Law Com Report No 172 *Guardianship and Custody* (1988), especially at paras 4.18–4.20.
6 Section 100, and see Chapter 11 below.
7 Section 8(3)(a) includes, within the definition of family proceedings, those under the inherent jurisdiction of the High Court, which includes wardship.

requirement ought to be easily surmounted to enable matters to be resolved in accordance with the welfare principle.

A remaining issue is whether the court would entertain an application in wardship, or under its wider inherent jurisdiction, where leave has been refused. It is arguable that it would not, and should not, since to do so would be to frustrate the intention of Parliament in creating the hurdle of leave. The courts have usually refused to allow wardship to be used to circumvent restrictions in the statutory code governing child care[1], and this is the rationale of the restrictions on wardship where the child is in care. Hale J has made *obiter* remarks which suggest that an applicant who fails to obtain leave to seek a s 8 order will be unlikely to be allowed to proceed in wardship[2].

The more difficult question is how far it remains appropriate, or indeed proper, to use wardship as an *alternative* to seeking leave to apply for a s 8 order. This might be an attractive proposition where the applicant is not confident of getting leave. It might also be a desirable option where the sheer complexity or seriousness of the case suggests that the all-embracing 'ring of protection'[3], which is a feature of wardship, should be thrown around the child. This could arise where, for example, the child has a life-threatening medical condition or some irreversible medical procedure is under consideration[4]. It is most likely to continue to be used in cases with a foreign element such as child abductions, which we consider in Chapter 17. Ultimately, whether wardship continues to be used in the private sphere or withers away may depend on the level of success which practitioners feel they have with the statutory options.

Outsiders' rights where child is in the care of a local authority

Before leaving the question of outsiders, something should be said about their standing where a child is 'looked after' by a local authority. How far may outsiders question, by legal means, the actions of the authority in relation to the child? The answer is – not very far. The legislation leaves the management of the child's welfare largely to the local authority. Where the child is formally 'in care' no one may seek an s 8 order, other than a residence order; neither is it possible to invoke wardship[5]. The only recourse open to an outsider might be to make representations to the authority. The Children Act requires the authority to ascertain and take into account, before taking its decisions, the wishes and feelings of, inter alia, 'any other person whose wishes and feelings the authority consider to be relevant'[6], and it must also consider the representations, including complaints, of 'such other person as the authority consider has a sufficient interest in the child's welfare to warrant his representations being considered by them'[7]. The catch is

---

1 The so-called '*Liverpool* Principle' since it was firmly established in *A v Liverpool City Council* [1982] AC 363.
2 *C v Salford City Council* [1994] 2 FLR 926, where she said of foster-parents: 'Had I not granted them leave, it would have been a bold decision, to say the least, to say that although I was against them on the leave criteria I should nevertheless permit them to proceed in wardship proceedings'.
3 As described by Cross in 'Wards of Court' (1967) 83 LQR 200.
4 See Chapter 8.
5 Sections 9(1) and 100(2)(c) respectively.
6 Section 22(4)(d).
7 Section 26(3).

that it is for the authority itself to determine whether any particular individual falls within the qualifying categories. The only possible redress for an aggrieved individual would then be to apply for judicial review on the basis that the authority has improperly exercised its discretion, or possibly to seek to invoke the inherent jurisdiction of the High Court, but neither of these offers a very realistic prospect in most cases[1]. These procedures also apply where a child is voluntarily 'looked after' by the authority. But here there is no formal restriction on the use of wardship or on seeking (with leave) a prohibited steps or specific issue order. How enthusiastic the courts would be about entertaining such applications is, however, a matter of doubt, given the judicial tradition of support for local authorities in the discharge of their child care functions[2].

SURROGACY ARRANGEMENTS

The nature of surrogacy

Surrogacy is an arrangement whereby a woman agrees to bear a child for someone else and to hand over that child, on birth, to another person or persons (the 'commissioning parents') with a view to relinquishing parental responsibility in their favour[3]. Contrary to popular belief, the idea of surrogacy is not revolutionary or new but has ancient antecedents. Pinhas Shifman has described how the practice was not unusual in biblical times as a means of compliance with the religious duty to procreate[4]. Such births were, of course, achieved through ordinary sexual intercourse with a concubine or, as Shifman puts it, 'surrogate wife'[5]. Nowadays, while this may still be the method in a small minority of cases, the focus is on assisted reproduction in its various forms[6]. The carrying mother may have been inseminated artificially with the sperm of the commissioning 'father' or she may be genetically unrelated to the child where donated gametes from the commissioning parents or others may be used to create an embryo which is then carried to term by her. Either way, the carrying mother is deemed, in law, to be the

---

1   Judicial review, in particular, is a public law remedy and it is necessary to show that the local authority improperly exercised its powers and not simply that its decision was wrong on its merits.
2   In Chapter 2 above it was argued that the courts and local authorities may be seen as partners in discharging their respective child care functions.
3   On surrogacy generally, see: D Morgan 'Making Motherhood Male: Surrogacy and the Moral Economy of Women' (1985) 12 *Journal of Law and Society* 219; D Morgan 'Who to be or not to be: The Surrogacy Story' (1986) 49 MLR 358; and L Nielsen 'The Right to a Child versus the Rights of a Child' and M Field 'Surrogate Motherhood' in J Eekelaar and P Sarcevic (eds) *Parenthood in Modern Society* (Martinus Nijhoff, 1993) at chs 13 and 14 respectively.
4   P Shifman 'A Perspective on Surrogate Motherhood in Jewish and Israeli Law' in A Bainham, DS Pearl and R Pickford (eds) *Frontiers of Family Law* (2nd edn) (John Wiley & Sons, 1995) at pp 65–66.
5   The classic examples being the transaction between Abraham, his wife Sarah, and Hagar the Egyptian, which resulted in the birth of Ishmael (Genesis 16:1–3) and that between Jacob, his wife Rachel, and Bilhah her maid, which led to the births of Dan and Naphtali (Genesis 30:1,3).
6   For a readable and succinct description of the principal available methods of assisted conception, see B Dickens 'Reproductive Technology and the "new family"', in E Sutherland and A McCall Smith (eds) *Family Rights* (Edinburgh University Press, 1990) at p 21.

mother of the child[1]. The legal determination of paternity in these cases is much more complex, as discussed in Chapter 3.

Surrogacy arrangements, perhaps more than any other kind of familial arrangement, focus our attention on what is meant by being a parent. They might be thought to exemplify the case of the *intentional* parent having claims derived from intending to perform the social role of a parent[2]. Who could be more of an intentional parent than a man or woman who goes to the extreme length of commissioning another woman to bear a child for them? Yet, paradoxically, surrogacy will often be inspired by what is thought to be the value of *genetic* parenthood. More often than not, surrogacy will be triggered by a *man's* desire to have his own genetic child where his wife or partner is unable to conceive or bear a child. We shall see that in order to obtain a 'parental order' at least *one* of the commissioning parents must be genetically related to the child. The importance of *marriage* is also underlined by the requirements for this order – perhaps hinting that it is the family unit centred on marriage which really ought to be crucial to the acquisition of parenthood[3]. So in surrogacy we can perhaps observe the deep ambivalence in society, reflected in the law, about the true nature of parenthood. We discuss surrogacy in this chapter simply because it will usually (but not invariably) be the case that one or both commissioning parents will be unrelated to the child genetically. Hence it can be regarded as a situation of social parenthood.

The effectiveness of surrogacy arrangements

The current position in English law could be described as an official policy of discouraging surrogacy arrangements whilst providing some 'back-door' mechanisms for indirectly giving effect to them. The matter was considered in depth by the Warnock Committee[4]. The Committee did not recommend either the recognition or the outright prohibition of surrogacy but did propose a ban on commercial arrangements. This recommendation was implemented by the Surrogacy Arrangements Act 1985[5] which makes it an offence to be involved in prescribed ways with assisting, on a commercial basis, the making of surrogacy arrangements. The commissioning parents and surrogate mother are, however, specifically exempted from liability[6]. Following the Surrogacy Arrangements Act 1985, there was uncertainty, and a good deal of speculation, about the enforceability (as opposed to legality) of surrogacy arrangements. The majority view was that they were not enforceable and this was later confirmed by the Human Fertilisation and Embryology Act 1990[7].

Although a criminal offence may conceivably have been committed, and although an agreement may be unenforceable, there remains the question of the destiny of a child born into such an arrangement. Here, the courts and the legislature have shown some ingenuity in dealing pragmatically with the situation.

---

1   See Chapter 3 above.
2   On the doctrine of intention as it applies to parenthood, see C Barton and G Douglas *Law and Parenthood* (Butterworths, 1995), especially at pp 50–52.
3   See further Chapter 3 above.
4   *Report of the Committee of Inquiry into Human Fertilisation and Embryology* (1984) (Cmnd 9314).
5   Surrogacy Arrangements Act 1985, s 2(1).
6   Ibid, s 2(2).
7   Ibid, s 1A and HFEA 1990, s 36(1).

First, it has been the case since before the Surrogacy Arrangements Act that the courts have exercised jurisdiction to determine, in accordance with the welfare principle, who should have the care of the child[1]. This could lead to a decision in favour of the commissioning parents, thereby achieving indirectly the intended result of the agreement. Secondly, the same result might be brought about by allowing the commissioning parents to adopt the child, perhaps turning a blind eye to violation of the rules prohibiting payment for adoption by retrospectively authorising the payments[2]. Thirdly, and more significantly, the Human Fertilisation and Embryology Act 1990 provides a means of avoiding the need to resort to adoption or the unbridled discretion of the court. It is provided[3] that, where the commissioning parents are married, a so-called 'parental order' may be made 'providing for a child to be treated in law as the child of the parties to a marriage', provided certain conditions are met. These are that at least one of them must be genetically related to the child, the child must be resident with them, there must be no payment involved (although the court can authorise this and the surrogate's reasonable expenses are allowable), and the surrogate mother and the legal father must have agreed unconditionally to the order. The power to make this 'parental order' does not arise where the child was conceived as a result of intercourse between the surrogate and the commissioning father, or where the commissioning couple are unmarried. In these instances, if the parties are in dispute (most obviously where the surrogate mother is refusing to hand over the child), they will have to rely on the inherent jurisdiction or the court's more general discretion to make s 8 orders.

Re MW (Adoption: Surrogacy)[4] is an illustration of the use of adoption where a surrogacy arrangement has gone wrong and the parties are at loggerheads. Here, the initial agreement between the commissioning parents and the surrogate mother was that the former would apply to adopt the child following the birth. The handover took place and for a time there was continued contact between the baby and the surrogate mother. Relations then deteriorated, contact ceased and the mother began a media campaign to draw attention to her situation. She withheld her consent to the adoption and, alternatively, sought post-adoption contact with the child. The court applied the test of whether the advantages of adoption for the welfare of the child were sufficiently strong to justify overriding the views and interests of the objecting mother. It also took into account the fact that the mother had been independently advised and had previously given her consent to adoption. In these circumstances, the court dispensed with her consent and denied her contact with the child during the child's minority.

---

1 The first such case came before the courts as early as 1978 but was not reported until 1985. See *A v C* [1985] FLR 445. See also *Re C (A Minor) (Wardship: Surrogacy)* [1985] FLR 846 (the 'Baby Cotton' case).

2 *Re Adoption Application (Payment for Adoption)* [1987] Fam 81 and *Re An Adoption Application* [1992] 1 FLR 341.

3 Human Fertilisation and Embryology Act 1990, s 30 and see the helpful discussion of this provision in *Bromley's Family Law* (8th edn) (Butterworths, 1992) at p 266. See also *Re W (Minors) (Surrogacy)* [1991] 1 FLR 395, the case which inspired the introduction of 'parental orders' under s 30. Here, twins born under a surrogacy arrangement were allowed, in wardship proceedings, to remain under the care of the genetic (commissioning) parents on their undertaking to make an application for a parental order, within 28 days of the implementation of s 30 of the Human Fertilisation and Embryology Act 1990.

4 [1995] 2 FLR 789.

Where it is possible for the court to make a 'parental order', this avoids recourse to adoption but has substantially the same legal effect in treating the successful applicants as parents for all purposes. It is thus wider in its effect than a parental responsibility order[1].

Some policy considerations

Surrogacy cases continue to attract media attention both when there is a successful outcome and when they go drastically wrong. There have been periodic calls for the review of surrogacy legislation and suggestions for a more regulated system[2]. English law is frankly ambivalent about surrogacy. On the one hand it is seeking to discourage the making of agreements, whilst on the other it is providing mechanisms for giving effect to a proportion of them. This ambivalence can be explained as follows.

Whilst the initial agreement is not considered to be in the best interests of the *intended* child, when the *actual* child is born it may be, at that point, that it is in his best interests (perhaps as the lesser of two unsatisfactory alternatives) to be with the commissioning parents rather than the surrogate mother. The solutions adopted at this stage are not very different to other substitute care arrangements which the courts can sanction where the natural or 'normal' family fails. Douglas and Lowe, in drawing attention to the debate about whether assisted reproduction is more akin to 'normal' reproduction or adoption, refer to the view of Warnock, rejecting the adoption analogy[3]. According to Warnock:

> 'It is plausible to talk about the good of the child when the child exists and there are alternative futures before it, between which someone must choose. To choose whether or not a baby should be born in the first place is a different kind of choice altogether. The whole undertaking is *in fact* for the sake of the infertile would-be parents. It is *they* who want the baby.'[4]

Herein lies the initial objection to surrogacy. It sits ill with the law's general commitment to the welfare of children since it is predicated on the prioritisation of adult interests. It is difficult to see how it could be argued that surrogacy is designed *primarily* for the benefit of the intended child. But there are unresolved difficulties with this view. The fact is that many 'normal' births in 'normal' families are also the result of decisions by adults who *want* to have a child. These adults are distinguishable from commissioning parents only because their wants can be satisfied in the context of what society currently accepts as 'normal' while this is not so with surrogacy. The distinction can only be sustained if we think of the child having an interest in or, perhaps, a right to a 'normal' start to life. Yet, given the variety of social parenting arrangements examined in this chapter and elsewhere in this book,[5] it may be no easy matter to define what 'normality' is, if indeed it exists at all.

---

1 Parental responsibility confers on the non-parent most, but not all, parental powers and duties (not the right to object to adoption or the right to appoint a guardian) and does not make the holder of parental responsibility the child's 'parent'.
2 For a recent review, see M Hibbs 'Surrogacy Legislation – Time for Change?' [1997] Fam Law 564.
3 G Douglas and NV Lowe 'Becoming a Parent in English Law' (1992) 108 LQR 414 at p 416.
4 M Warnock 'The Good of the Child' (1987) 1 *Bioethics* 141 at p 144.
5 See also Chapter 7 below.

Chapter 7
ADOPTION

INTRODUCTION

Adoption has in recent years been the subject of a major interdepartmental *Review of Adoption Law* (hereafter 'the *Review*') which was published in 1992[1]. This was followed by a White Paper in 1993[2] and a subsequent consultative document which incorporated a draft Adoption Bill was presented in March 1996 by the former Conservative administration[3]. At one time it looked as though major adoption reform, along the lines proposed in the Bill, was imminent. Yet it soon became clear, after consultation with the various interested groups, that some aspects of the Bill were controversial. The result was that the Bill was not introduced into Parliament in the latter days of the former Conservative Government and there has been no indication, at the time of writing, that the new Labour Government sees adoption reform as a priority. Thus, there is considerable uncertainty about the precise shape of future adoption law but it seems likely that a major reform will take place in the foreseeable future. This chapter attempts to set out the salient features of current adoption law and to identify the core issues. We comment on the proposals for reform, distinguishing where necessary between the *Review* proposals and those in the draft Bill, as we come to the various key issues in the text. We conclude the chapter with some comments on the more general shape of reform. The two central features are perhaps the shift towards a more 'open' system of adoption and the perceived need to harmonise adoption law with the principles and scheme of the Children Act 1989[4].

A permanent solution

Adoption in English law is distinguishable from all other forms of social parenthood[5]. It is with limited exceptions the only legal mechanism for terminating the parental responsibility of a parent[6]. Adoption is, in effect, a 'legal

---

1   Department of Health and Welsh Office *Review of Adoption Law* (HMSO, 1992).
2   *Adoption: The Future* (Cm 2288) (Department of Health, Welsh Office, Home Office and Lord Chancellor's Department, 1993).
3   *Adoption – A Service for Children: Adoption Bill – A Consultative Document* (Department of Health and Welsh Office, 1996).
4   For commentaries on adoption reform and the shape of adoption in the future, see: JA Priest 'The Review of Adoption Law – a revival of diversionary tactics?' (1992) 5 JCL 56; C Bridge 'Changing the Nature of Adoption: Law Reform in England and New Zealand' (1993) 13 *Legal Studies* 81; B Lindley 'Open adoption – is the door ajar?' [1997] CFLQ 115; B Lindley and N Wyld 'The Children Act and the draft Adoption Bill – diverging principles' [1996] CFLQ 327; and N Lowe 'The changing face of adoption – The gift/donation model versus the contract/ services model' [1997] CFLQ 371.
5   On adoption law generally, see SM Cretney and JM Masson *Principles of Family Law* (6th edn) (Sweet & Maxwell, 1997) at ch 24, *Bromley's Family Law* (8th edn) (Butterworths, 1992) at ch 13, and M Richards *Adoption* (Jordans, 1989).
6   See Chapter 2 above. Parental responsibility of a legal parent may also be terminated by 'parental orders' under the Human Fertilisation and Embryology Act 1990, s 30 and revocation

transplant' involving the total replacement of one family with a new substitute family. The adoptive parents step into the shoes of the birth parents. Unlike the residence order under the Children Act 1989 (now the primary order affecting non-parents), adoption is permanent and with very restricted exceptions irrevocable, and it is precisely this permanence which has often been seen by adoption applicants as the chief advantage of adoption over other solutions.

In *Re B (Adoption: Jurisdiction to Set Aside)*[1], the Court of Appeal held that there was no general inherent power to set aside an adoption order on the basis of misapprehension or mistake. B was the child of an Arab father and Roman Catholic mother who had been adopted and raised in the Jewish faith by an orthodox Jewish couple. On investigating his background, B discovered the truth and, now an adult, sought to have the adoption order set aside. While expressing great sympathy for his position, the court thought that its ultimate imperative must be the inviolability of the adoption system. This case should be contrasted with *Re K (Adoption and Wardship)*[2] which provides a rare example of an adoption order being set aside.

In *Re K*, the English foster-parents had adopted a Muslim Bosnian baby found under a pile of bodies during the conflict in the former Yugoslavia. There had, however, been fatal flaws in the adoption process including failure to appoint a guardian ad litem, failure to contact the baby's appointed guardian in Bosnia, failure to serve notice of the proceedings on the Home Office and the provision of inadequate evidence of the death of the natural parents. The Court of Appeal held that this was a denial of natural justice to the Bosnian guardian and, through him, to the natural parents and the child. The adoption order was therefore set aside and remitted for rehearing. At the rehearing in wardship proceedings, care and control was given to the foster-parents, the child was to remain a ward of court and the foster-parents were required to cause the child to receive appropriate instruction in the Bosnian language and Muslim religion. They were also required to report every three months to the Official Solicitor as to the progress of contact with the natural family back in Bosnia.

The case is an excellent illustration of the problems which can arise from overseas adoptions[3]. It also shows the continuing value of wardship in some cases, particularly where ongoing judicial control of a situation is thought desirable, and the interrelationship of legal procedures affecting children – in this case wardship and adoption.

Policy and purposes

Although its general effect may be easily described, the policy and purposes of adoption are far from easy to state. First, it is clear that adoption has served different needs at different times and these have differed markedly from society to society. Thus, for example, Duncan[4] notes that in Roman Law and in the Code

---

of agreements or orders giving parental responsibility to the unmarried father, but these procedures account for only a small number of cases.
1   [1995] 2 FLR 1.
2   [1997] 2 FLR 221.
3   See below.
4   W Duncan 'Regulating Intercountry Adoption – an International Perspective' in A Bainham, DS Pearl and R Pickford (eds) *Frontiers of Family Law* (2nd edn) (John Wiley & Sons, 1995) at ch 3.

Napoleon of 1804, the primary purpose of adoption was to ensure the continuation of the family line. In the Hindu tradition, adoption was mandated by the need for a child to perform certain spiritual tasks for the parent. When adoption was first introduced in England[1], it served the dual purpose of offering a discreet way out of the stigma and economic hardship faced by unmarried mothers and of meeting the needs of childless couples. Historically, it can be said that the emphasis in adoption was on satisfying adult needs of one kind or another. The major shift in thinking which has occurred in recent years is that adoption is now more 'child centred' and is seen as a means of finding families for children and not children for families. Nonetheless, there remains considerable anxiety, especially in the context of intercountry adoption, that the process can still be used to prioritise adult needs without proper regard for the interests of the children involved[2].

Another reason why it is difficult to state the aims of adoption is that the circumstances in which applications are made differ widely. Some adoption applications involve babies who have never known their birth parents. Others involve older children who may have long-standing relationships of some sort with birth parents or other relatives. Some applicants are unrelated to the children, others are related in some way, the most obvious examples being grandparents and step-parents. In some cases, adoption is used by local authorities as one long-term option for children who are in their care[3]. It has become increasingly evident that a single, rigid model of adoption cannot be appropriate in all these different circumstances. In particular, there has been a growing realisation that the 'exclusivity' and secrecy of adoption, perhaps the cardinal features of English adoption law[4], may have to give way to a more flexible concept which admits of greater 'openness'[5].

---

1   By the Adoption of Children Act 1926. See also Chapter 1.
2   W Duncan (above).
3   The practice was heavily influenced by empirical evidence that many children in long-term care of local authorities had been allowed to 'drift' without the prospect of a permanent home. See J Rowe and L Lambert *Children Who Wait* (ABAFA, 1973).
4   For a recent illustration of the confidentiality of the English adoption process, admittedly dealing with unusually sensitive material, see *Re K (Adoption: Disclosure of Information)* [1997] 2 FLR 74. Here, Wall J granted an application to withhold information from the natural mother which concerned the conviction of one of the prospective adopters for a serious offence. The judgment contains a detailed analysis of the criteria to be applied and the correct procedure in relation to disclosure of material in adoption proceedings.
5   In fact, the English concept of adoption is by no means universal. Many countries already have more open concepts of adoption. Thus, for example, the 'clean-break' model of adoption does not operate in most of the countries of South America or in France. Under Nepalese law an intercountry adoption will be permitted only on condition that the child be allowed direct correspondence or contact with his birth parents and the opportunity of returning to his country of origin on attaining majority. See W Duncan 'Regulating Intercountry Adoption – an International Perspective' in A Bainham, DS Pearl and R Pickford (eds) *Frontiers of Family Law* (2nd edn) (John Wiley & Sons, 1995) at pp 44–45. For useful articles discussing the tradition of full and simple adoptions in Latin America, see CP Grosman 'Argentina: The Recent Reform of Argentine Adoption Law' and PA Monroy 'Colombia: Adoption Law in Colombia', both in

Factors contributing to statistical decline

In statistical terms, adoption has declined dramatially over the last few decades[1]. A number of factors have contributed to this. Among the more obvious are the greater effectiveness and availability of contraception and the decline in the birth rate, the increase in abortion, and the greater social acceptability of birth outside marriage. Alongside these social and demographic changes there have been some direct legislative attempts to restrict adoption in certain kinds of cases. The Houghton Committee, which reported in 1972[2], was concerned with the use of adoption by relatives and more especially with the major escalation in step-parent adoptions. The Children Act 1975, later consolidated in the Adoption Act 1976, introduced directives that the courts should give specific consideration to alternative legal solutions in these cases[3].

Effect of the Children Act 1989

The Children Act 1989, while reforming almost all the public and private law affecting children, made few direct changes to adoption law, which continues to be largely governed by its own separate legislation[4], but the impact of the Children Act cannot be measured solely in these terms. The Children Act, both as a general principle and as a matter of substantive law, supports the notion of sharing parental responsibility for children. The orthodox view of adoption law, that all contact and links with the birth family should be completely severed[5], could scarcely have survived unscathed the philosophical changes of the Children Act. As the law now stands, adoption proceedings are 'family proceedings' and, hence, the court, on an adoption application, will always have the option of making some other order instead, most obviously a residence order[6]. Thus, the Children Act

---

A Bainham (ed) *The International Survey of Family Law 1996* (Martinus Nijhoff, 1998) at pp 13 and 99 respectively.

1   Between 1968 and 1987 the number of adoption orders had declined from around 25,000 to just over 7,000. Dramatic changes have also occurred to the age structure of adopted children. In 1977, of approximately 13,000 children adopted, about 3,000 (23%) were babies. By 1991, the total number of adoptions had halved to just over 7,000 but only about 900 of these (just over 12%) were babies (White Paper *Adoption: The Future*, paras 3.2–3.3). For a discussion of the recent Scottish adoption statistics which confirm these trends, see R Hothers 'The Scottish Office Statistics on Adoption' [1998] Fam Law 86.

2   *Report of the Departmental Committee on the Adoption of Children* ('the *Houghton Report*') (1972) (Cmnd 5107).

3   Children Act 1975, s 10(3) and s 37(1).

4   Adoption Act 1976. On the direct effect of the Children Act on adoption law, see *The Children Act 1989 Guidance and Regulations Vol 9 Adoption Issues*. Note also that in *Re G (Adoption: Freeing Order)* [1997] 2 FLR 202, the House of Lords held that the adoption legislation operated as part of the general legislation regulating powers over children and that the court's powers under the Adoption Act 1976 could be used in conjunction with its powers under the Children Act. See further below for discussion of this decision in the context of the freeing procedure.

5   An approach epitomised by those decisions of the courts which set their face against attaching conditions for contact to adoption orders. See, for example, *Re M (A Minor) (Adoption Order: Access)* [1986] 1 FLR 51; *Re M (Adoption: Parental Agreement)* [1985] FLR 664; *Re C (A Minor) (Adoption: Contact with Siblings)* [1987] 2 FLR 383 and *Re R (A Minor) (Adoption: Access)* [1991] 2 FLR 78.

6   But the former statutory directives no longer apply. For a critique, see A Bainham 'The Privatisation of the Public Interest in Children' (1990) 53 MLR 206 at pp 214–216.

injects, to an extent, some of the flexibility needed to deal with the many different needs and aspirations of substitute parents and the children concerned.

LEGAL CONTROL OF ADOPTION SERVICES AND PLACEMENTS

If adoption is viewed as a process of providing children with the love and security of a family, it follows that great care needs to be taken to ensure the suitability of placements. The process of selection and matching of children with prospective adopters is, therefore, tightly controlled. This is achieved partly by prohibiting private placements and partly by providing a comprehensive adoption service by properly approved adoption agencies.

Prohibition of private placements

Under the Adoption Act 1976 ('the 1976 Act')[1], it is a criminal offence for anyone other than an adoption agency to make arrangements for the adoption of a child or to make a placement unless the individual concerned is a relative of the child or is acting with the authority of a High Court order. There is no such restriction on private foster placements[2] and it is possible that such a placement could ultimately result in adoption. However, if it can be shown that the fostering arrangement was intended as a 'back-door' route to adoption, the offence will still have been committed[3]. Whilst the prohibition on private placements is generally thought, in England, to be a necessary safeguard, this is not universally agreed, and the USA, in particular, has allowed widespread use of private placements by professionals such as lawyers and doctors[4]. The prohibition should be seen alongside the complementary offence relating to financial reward. The 1976 Act[5] makes it a criminal offence:

'to make or give to any person any payment or reward for or in consideration of –
(a) the adoption by that person of a child;
(b) the grant by that person of any agreement or consent required in connection with the adoption of a child;
(c) the handing over of a child by that person with a view to the adoption of the child or
(d) the making by that person of any arrangements for the adoption of a child.'

The court does, however, have power to authorise payments retrospectively in appropriate cases[6].

---

1 Section 11.
2 See Chapter 6 above.
3 *Gatehouse v Robinson* [1986] 1 WLR 18.
4 See W Duncan 'Regulating Intercountry Adoption – an International Perspective' in A Bainham, DS Pearl and R Pickford (eds) *Frontiers of Family Law* (2nd edn) (John Wiley & Sons, 1995) at pp 45–47.
5 Section 57.
6 The circumstances under which the court should retrospectively authorise illegal transactions in breach of either s 11 or s 57 of the 1976 Act have been the subject of considerable litigation. See *Re Adoption Application (Payment for Adoption)* [1987] Fam 81; *Re An Adoption Application* [1992] 1 FLR 341; *Re AW (Adoption Application)* [1993] 1 FLR 62; *Re ZHH (Adoption Application)* [1993] 1 FLR 83; and *Re C (A Minor) (Adoption Application)* [1993] 1 FLR 87. There has been a tendency to overlook illegal *payments* (under s 57) where to make an adoption order would promote the child's welfare. See, for example, *Re WM (Adoption: Non-Patrial)* [1997] 1 FLR 132.

The adoption service and adoption agencies

The corollary of the prohibition on private placements is the requirement in the 1976 Act[1], following the recommendations in the *Houghton Report,* that every local authority should provide a comprehensive adoption service designed to meet the needs of children who have been or may be adopted, their parents or guardians, and prospective adopters. Long before the partnership idea became entrenched in the Children Act, local authorities and voluntary adoption societies worked in partnership and co-operation to meet local needs in relation to adoption. Some of these societies, such as Barnardos, are national societies, while others operate only at local level.

All bodies wishing to act, or to continue to act, as adoption agencies must be centrally approved by the Secretary of State[2]. Approval will only be granted if the Secretary of State 'is satisfied that the applicant is likely to make, or ... is making, an effective contribution to the Adoption Service'[3]. The 1976 Act[4] prescribes the factors which must be taken into account and these include the applicant's adoption programme, the number and qualifications of its staff, its financial resources, and the organisation and control of its operations. Where the applicant is an existing adoption society, another factor will be its record and reputation in the adoption field[5]. Approval is given for three years[6] but the Secretary of State has power to withdraw this earlier if it appears to him that 'the body is not making an effective contribution to the Adoption Service'[7]. Detailed control of the functions of adoption agencies is provided under the Adoption Agencies Regulations 1983, which deal with such matters as the setting up of adoption panels and the duty of agencies to explain the adoption process to children (having regard to their age and understanding), and their parents or guardians[8].

The position is less clear where there has been an illegal *placement* (contrary to s 11). Here, the tendency has been to refuse an adoption, but in *Re Adoption Application (Non-Patrial: Breach of Procedures)* [1993] 1 FLR 947, Douglas-Brown J took the view that the court's inability to authorise, retrospectively, an illegal placement should not automatically result in a refusal of the later adoption application. It should merely go to the exercise of the court's discretion. For a review of all of these cases, see the note by SM Cretney at [1993] Fam Law 276 and K O'Donnell 'Illegal Placements in Adoption' (1994) 6 JCL 17.

1   Sections 1 and 2.
2   Ibid, s 3(1).
3   Ibid, s 3(2).
4   Ibid, s 3(3).
5   Ibid, s 3(5).
6   Ibid, s 3(7).
7   Ibid, s 4(1).
8   Other matters relate to such things as the provision of a counselling service and the confidential nature of the adoption process.

QUALIFICATIONS FOR ADOPTION

There are few restrictions on which children may be adopted. The 'child' must be under 18 years of age and must not have been married[1]. An adopted child may also be re-adopted[2].

There are, however, significant statutory restrictions on those persons who are eligible to adopt and, in practice, in view of the importance to children of finding suitable placements, adoption agencies impose wider restrictions.

The statutory rules

The rules governing qualification for adoption are contained in ss 14 and 15 of the 1976 Act and their effects are as follows.

An applicant must usually be 21 years of age[3]

The Children Act introduced a minor amendment to the statutory rules by allowing a joint application by a married couple where one of the spouses is a parent of the child and at least 18 years of age. The other applicant must still be at least 21 years of age[4].

Joint applications must be made by married couples but single persons may also apply

The statutory provisions prescribe that a joint application may only be made by a *married* couple[5] but that an application may also be made by a single person[6]. It has been held, perhaps surprisingly, that these rules do not prevent an adoption order being made in favour of a married couple who have separated following the application to adopt[7]. But where a *sole* applicant is also a married person, the court must be satisfied that his spouse cannot be found, that the two are living apart in what is likely to be a permanent separation, or that his spouse is, by reason of physical or mental ill-health, incapable of applying for an adoption order[8].

The effect of these statutory rules is to preclude *joint* applications by heterosexual cohabitants, gay and lesbian couples and other 'home sharers' such as, for example, adult siblings. But the rules do not positively prevent *single* applications by *one* member of such a couple, and the courts have ingeniously circumvented the statutory restrictions by allowing one member of a heterosexual

---

1 Section 12(5) of the 1976 Act. In *Re D (A Minor) (Adoption Order: Validity)* [1991] 2 FLR 66, the Court of Appeal upheld an adoption order which had been the subject of an application made only six days before the child (who suffered from a severe mental handicap) attained majority, although this case must be regarded as exceptional.
2 Ibid, s 12(7).
3 Ibid, s 14(1A) and s 15(1).
4 Ibid, s 14(1B), inserted by Sch 10, para 4 to the Children Act.
5 Ibid, s 14(1).
6 Ibid, s 15(1).
7 *Re WM (Adoption: Non-Patrial)* [1997] 1 FLR 132. But this case had peculiarities, in that it involved the adoption of a young child from El Salvador. The court, having taken the view that the adoption was now in the child's best interests and having decided to overlook certain irregularities in the process, held that there was no specific restriction in the legislation preventing the making of the adoption order. Cf *Re C and F (Adoption: Removal Notice)* [1997] 1 FLR 190.
8 Section 15(1) of the 1976 Act.

unmarried couple[1] and one member of a homosexual partnership[2] to proceed with an adoption application. These decisions can be supported on the basis of the welfare of the individual children concerned but they fly in the face of the policy underlying the adoption legislation. This has been to restrict adoption to the context of family relationships centred on marriage. The *Review*, while recognising the potential suitability of some unmarried couples to adopt, recommended that the current restriction be preserved. It argued in the final analysis 'that the security and stability which adopted children need are still more likely to be provided by parents who have made a publicly recognised commitment to their relationship and who have legal responsibilities towards each other'[3]. The restriction is preserved in the draft Adoption Bill[4].

Whether these statutory restrictions can continue to be justified as a matter of policy is open to doubt. In particular, it is illogical that one member of an unmarried couple, whether heterosexual or homosexual, should be allowed to achieve singly what that couple cannot achieve together. Now that the courts have admitted adoption through the back door in these cases, it would surely be better from the point of view of family solidarity to allow joint applications. It is also questionable how far what might be seen as discrimination based on sexual orientation can be legally defended in this context[5]. This is undoubtedly one area in which there needs to be some fundamental rethinking before any reformed adoption law reaches the statute book.

Non-statutory restrictions

Beyond these statutory restrictions, individual agencies have developed their own policies regarding the acceptability of applicants, and an important consideration in relation to infants is the age of the prospective adopters. Many jurisdictions prescribe a maximum age differential between the adopters and the child. While there is no maximum statutory age-limit or age differential in English law, almost all agencies have their own guidelines, which can range from early 30s to around 40 years of age. These guidelines 'reflect the view that it is better for very young children to be placed with adopters who are not older by too wide a margin than most couples starting a family'[6]. Older applicants may be considered suitable for older or special needs children or, perhaps more controversially, they may seek to

---

1   In *Re AB (Adoption: Joint Residence)* [1996] 1 FLR 27, Cazalet J made an adoption order in favour of the foster-father of a five-year-old child together with a joint residence order in favour of both foster-parents. This latter order had the effect of giving parental responsibility also to the foster-mother, although it was not of course as fundamental in its effect as a joint adoption order would have been.

2   In *Re W (Adoption: Homosexual Adopter)* [1997] 2 FLR 406, Singer J held that there was nothing in principle in the adoption legislation to prevent a single applicant for adoption being a homosexual. In this case the applicant was a 49-year-old lesbian woman in a stable long-standing cohabitation with a professional woman who was herself a grandmother. Significantly, the child had had a very disrupted life but had been well looked after for some time by the applicant. For a comment on the decision, see A Bainham 'Gay Survivors and Lesbian Parents' (1998) CLJ 42.

3   At paras 26.9 et seq.

4   Clause 44.

5   For an excellent critique of the position in Europe, Canada and the United States on legal differentiation based on sexual orientation, see R Wintermute *Sexual Orientation and Human Rights* (Clarendon Paperbacks, 1995).

6   *Review* at para 26.7.

adopt a child from overseas. In addition to satisfying the minimum requirements of eligibility, applicants can then expect to undergo a quite intrusive vetting procedure, involving medical examinations, lengthy home visits, the provision of references and so on. It has, however, been observed[1] that the modern emphasis in agency practice is moving away from the notion of vetting and towards education and self-selection. The adoption panel then makes recommendations on whether adoption is in the best interests of the child and as to the suitability of the prospective adopters. The agency must take account of the panel's recommendations in taking its decisions[2].

Probationary period

After placement, the applicants must serve a probationary period with the child before an order can be made. The requirement of a probationary period is, again, not universal and is an issue which caused difficulty at the Hague Conference on Intercountry Adoption[3]. The English position is that the minimum probationary period is 13 weeks in the case of agency and in-family adoptions. The child must also be at least 19 weeks old[4]. In other cases (usually where foster-parents apply to adopt) the period is 12 months, and the child must be at least 12 months old[5]. If these conditions are satisfied, it will then be a matter for the court to determine whether or not the order should be made. Where the necessary agreements are forthcoming, the court must appoint a reporting officer[6]. In contested cases, the court must appoint a guardian ad litem ('GAL') to investigate the case[7]. The *Review*[8], in keeping with reforms in the Children Act, recommended that a GAL should be appointed in *every* agency adoption. The draft Adoption Bill would extend to GALs the right to have access to the adoption records of adoption societies in line with a similar right which they have under the Children Act in relation to local authority records[9]. As noted above, before taking the final decision the court will need to consider all the possible options, especially the alternative of a residence order.

---

1 SM Cretney and JM Masson *Principles of Family Law* (6th edn) (Sweet & Maxwell, 1997) at p 903.
2 Adoption Agencies Regulations 1983, SI 1983/1964, regs 10 and 11.
3 W Duncan 'Regulatory Intercountry Adoption – an International Perspective' in A Bainham, DS Pearl and R Pickford (eds) *Frontiers of Family Law* (2nd edn) (John Wiley & Sons, 1995) at p 47.
4 Section 13(1) of the 1976 Act.
5 Ibid, s 13(2). It is now proposed under clause 36 of the draft Adoption Bill that in non-agency cases the probationary period should be reduced from 12 months to six months and that the child should be at least six months old.
6 Adoption Rules 1984, SI 1984/265, r 5.
7 Ibid, r 18.
8 *Review* at para 15.1.
9 See, on GALs generally, cls 74–76. On GALs in care and related proceedings, see Chapter 13 below.

ADOPTION AND THE RELEVANCE OF WELFARE

The United Nations Convention on the Rights of the Child[1] requires States parties that 'recognise and/or permit the system of adoption' to 'ensure that the best interests of the child shall be the paramount consideration'. This is, prima facie, contrary to the historical tradition and the current state of English law which acknowledges the child's welfare to be the 'first' but not 'paramount' consideration for courts and adoption agencies[2].

There is considerable scope for disagreement about whether this different weighting of welfare makes any practical difference, but the purpose at least is reasonably clear. It is that the total severance of the parent/child relationship (the orthodox English view of adoption) ought not to occur without a thorough examination of the parent's claims and interests as well as those of the child. The welfare principle, as interpreted by the English courts, subsumes any parental claim in the overall inquiry into the child's welfare. The appropriate weight which the court ought to attach to the child's welfare has exercised the courts many times in the context of applications to dispense with parental consent. Some of these cases are looked at below. Suffice it to say at this stage that the 'first but not paramount' formula would seem to imply that, whilst the child's welfare is the single most important consideration, it can conceivably be outweighed, in theory at least, by other factors.

The *Review*[3] recommended that the welfare principle should be extended to adoption to bring it in line with other family proceedings, but this was subject to the important qualification that the child's welfare should not be the paramount consideration in determining whether to make an adoption order *without* the consent of the child's parent.

At least as far as the current theory of the adoption legislation is concerned, the welfare of the child is not paramount. In *Re B (Adoption: Child's Welfare)*[4], Wall J went out of his way to reiterate this hitherto fundamental feature of English adoption law. In this case he refused an adoption application in relation to a Gambian child who had come to this country under an agreement between her parents and the applicants, an English couple. In ordering a phased return of the girl to Gambia, he held that there were good reasons why the child's welfare was not paramount in adoption proceedings and that s 6 of the 1976 legislation had not been affected by the passing of the Children Act. We must now focus rather more closely on how precisely the welfare of the child is relevant to the question whether an adoption order should be made. It should be said at the outset that this is an issue on which there has been considerable judicial disagreement and vacillation so that the current state of the authorities is far from easy to summarise.

---

1 Article 21.
2 Section 6 of the 1976 Act.
3 *Review* at para 7.1.
4 [1995] 1 FLR 895.

SHOULD ADOPTION BE GRANTED?

The welfare stage

At the final adoption hearing, the court has to consider two questions. First, it must decide whether adoption would be in the child's best interests and, secondly, whether the relevant consents have been obtained or can be dispensed with on one of the prescribed statutory grounds. There are thus two distinct stages to the court's approach in deciding whether an adoption order should be granted. It has been determined that the court should address the welfare question first. If the answer at the welfare stage is that adoption would *not* be in the child's best interests that will be the end of the matter. If adoption *is* thought to be the best course the court should then move on to the issue of consent[1]. Procedurally it has been held that the two issues should be heard together[2].

The question of consent

Parental consent

Before an adoption order can be made, it must be shown that each parent or guardian 'freely, and with full understanding of what is involved, agrees unconditionally' to the making of the order, or that agreement can be dispensed with on one of the statutory grounds[3]. For these purposes, a parent means a parent with parental responsibility, thus excluding the unmarried father unless he has acquired parental responsibility by legal process. The unmarried father without parental responsibility does have certain limited rights under the adoption process. He is entitled to be heard on the merits of the application where he is contributing to the child's maintenance[4] – an interesting illustration of the connection between financial support and the wider parental relationship which is not always acknowledged. Beyond this, the court may allow an unmarried father to participate at the court's discretion, which enables it to add anyone as a party[5]. An alternative course for the father, since the Children Act, may be to apply for a residence order, but this will only be appropriate if he is able and willing to provide a home for the child. Where he is concerned just to preserve his parental relationship, the father might seek a parental responsibility order instead[6]. If he is successful, his consent would then be required or would have to be dispensed with before an adoption order could be made. The consent of other persons who merely have parental responsibility, or look after the child, is not required.

The agreement of the child

The consent of the child who is the subject of an adoption application is not currently needed, although courts and adoption agencies must 'so far as

---

1   *Re R (A Minor) (Adoption: Parental Agreement)* [1987] 1 FLR 391 and *Re D (A Minor) (Adoption: Freeing Order)* [1991] 1 FLR 48.

2   *Re K (A Minor) (Adoption: Procedure)* [1986] 1 FLR 295.

3   Section 16(1) of the 1976 Act. For a discussion of the various options for reform of the criteria for dispensing with parental consent, see E Cooke 'Dispensing with parental consent to adoption – a choice of welfare tests' [1997] CFLQ 259.

4   He must be joined as a respondent under r 15(2)(h) of the Adoption Rules 1984, SI 1984/265.

5   Rule 4(3) of the Adoption Rules 1984, SI 1984/265.

6   Under s 4 of the Children Act, as to which see Chapter 5 above.

practicable ascertain the wishes and feelings of the child regarding the decision and give due consideration to them, having regard to his age and understanding'. This is now a familiar formula, but the *Review*[1] went further in recommending that the court should not be allowed to grant an adoption order in relation to a child of 12 years of age or over, unless the child has agreed to it or the court has dispensed with the child's agreement. The objective was to ensure that agencies and GALs properly consult and involve older children in adoption decision-making. The draft Adoption Bill would give effect to this recommendation[2]. In relation to the unmarried father, whose child is the subject of an adoption application, no change was proposed on the consent question but it was recommended[3] that agencies and GALs should be under a duty to make all reasonable efforts to inform an unmarried father of the adoption application and to ascertain his views and wishes. This would certainly appear to be required by the spirit, if not the letter, of the decision of the European Court of Human Rights in *Keegan v Ireland*[4] to the effect that a 'secret' adoption of a child born out of wedlock was in breach of the unmarried father's rights under the Convention.

Dispensing with consent

The court has power to dispense with parental consent but only on proof of one of the statutory grounds and, importantly at least under current law, not just on the basis that it considers it would be in the best interests of the child for it to do so. It is vital to appreciate that neither the welfare principle under s 1 of the Children Act nor the 'diluted welfare principle' (if such it may be termed) under s 6 of the 1976 Act[5], govern the question of dispensing with consent. Yet this bald statement needs to be qualified since the issue is one of considerable sophistication. The point is that, as will be seen, the child's welfare is bound to be relevant, to some extent, since the courts have held that a reasonable parent has regard to his child's welfare in deciding whether to agree to adoption[6]. The precise weight to be attached to the child's welfare in relation to parental claims is the real difficulty, and there has been considerable judicial disagreement on this question.

Statutory grounds for dispensing with consent

The statutory grounds for dispensing with consent will now be set out, but only the ground of parental unreasonableness will be examined[7]. This approach is taken for two reasons. The first reason is that, statistically, the other grounds are of negligible importance alongside the unreasonableness ground and would, in any

---

1   *Review* at para 9.5.
2   *Review* at para 9.5, and cl 41(7) of the draft Bill which provides that no adoption order may be made in relation to a child who has attained the age of 12 unless the court is satisfied that the child:
    '(a) freely and with full understanding of what is involved consents unconditionally to the making of the order; or
    (b) is incapable of giving such consent.'
3   Ibid, at para 9.3.
4   (1994) 18 EHRR 342.
5   See fn 2 at p 214 above and accompanying text.
6   See pp 217 et seq below.
7   For a discussion of the interpretation of the other grounds by the courts, see *Bromley's Family Law* (8th edn) (Butterworths, 1992) at pp 435–436, and SM Cretney and JM Masson *Principles of Family Law* (6th edn) (Sweet & Maxwell, 1997) at pp 923–930.

event (where established) almost certainly also amount to unreasonableness. The second reason is that the *Review* has proposed that all but one of the existing statutory grounds be swept away and replaced with a single, newly reformulated ground. The draft Bill would also remove all but one of the existing grounds for dispensing with consent but, as we discuss below, it departs significantly from the *Review* in relation to what should be the major ground for overriding parental opposition in the reformed adoption law.

However, for the sake of completeness, the existing statutory grounds are that the parent or guardian:

(a) cannot be found or is incapable of giving agreement[1];
(b) is withholding his agreement unreasonably[2];
(c) has persistently failed without reasonable cause to discharge his parental responsibilities for the child[3];
(d) has abandoned or neglected the child[4];
(e) has persistently ill-treated the child[5]; and
(f) has seriously ill-treated the child but only where (because of the ill-treatment or for other reasons) the rehabilitation of the child within the household of the parent or guardian is unlikely[6].

What is unreasonableness?

There has been much litigation on the question of when a parent is withholding consent unreasonably. The leading authority is still the House of Lords decision in *Re W (An Infant)*[7]. In this case, Lord Hailsham LC emphasised that unreasonableness was not synonymous with culpability. The test was an objective one and it would have to be shown that the parent was acting outside a band of reasonable decisions. In other words, the fact that *one* parent might consent to adoption does not lead to the automatic conclusion that it is unreasonable for *the parent in question* to withhold consent. But Lord Hailsham went on to say that a reasonable parent would have regard to the welfare of his child, and it is this portion of the speech which has led to nuances of interpretation in later cases. What Lord Hailsham said was[8]:

> 'But, although welfare *per se* is not the test, the fact that a reasonable parent does pay regard to the welfare of his child must enter into the question of reasonableness as a relevant factor. It is a relevant factor in all cases if and to the extent that a reasonable parent would take it into account. It is decisive in those cases where a reasonable parent must so regard it.'

Judicial vacillation

The tendency after *Re W* has been for the courts to attach more significance to the welfare of the child (and to dispense with consent more readily) such that it is questionable how much practical difference there is in the application of the approach in *Re W* and the welfare principle itself. One factor which appears to

---

1 Section 16(2)(a) of the 1976 Act.
2 Ibid, s 16(2)(b).
3 Ibid, s 16(2)(c).
4 Ibid, s 16(2)(d).
5 Ibid, s 16(2)(e).
6 Ibid, s 16(2)(f) and (5).
7 [1971] AC 682.
8 Ibid at 699.

have emerged from the case-law is the length of time during which the child has been settled with the applicants. The longer the arrangement has lasted, the more likely the court is to find that a parent is unreasonable in not recognising the importance to the child of that continuity and stability[1]. Allied to this, the courts are generally unsympathetic to changes of heart by parents who have previously agreed to adoption. Again, the longer the arrangement has lasted after consent has been indicated, the less likely it is that the court will find the parent to be acting reasonably in seeking to retract it[2]. The time factor, rightly or wrongly, has also proved crucial in local authority cases where social services are using adoption as a long-term solution for children looked after by them[3]. The concomitant of long-standing substitute care is often an absence of recent contact between the objecting parent and the child. It is the combination of this and the settled nature of the child's home life which often proves decisive[4].

The above developments, on the whole, pushed the question of the child's welfare to the fore but, in 1983, there was something of a backlash in *Re H; Re W (Adoption: Parental Agreement)*[5]. In that case, the Court of Appeal appeared to revert to an approach which emphasised that there was a distinction between the assessment of parental reasonableness and the professional assessment of a child's best interests. The court emphasised that a parent could be behaving reasonably in withholding consent, even where, for example, the social workers concerned thought adoption to be in the child's best interests, and the court thought that the critical factor in the assessment of reasonableness was the chance of a successful reintroduction of parent and child, or the continuation of meaningful contact.

In 1993, the Court of Appeal had another opportunity to clarify the issue in *Re C (A Minor) (Adoption: Parental Agreement)*[6] but, if anything, clouded it further. Balcombe LJ appeared to take what might be described as the more 'parent-centred' approach exhibited in *Re H; Re W*. He agreed with the view that the drift towards attaching greater weight to the child's welfare had meant that insufficient weight was now being given to the parents' lack of agreement. Neither was it the case, he thought, that, because a child had to remain in long-term substitute care, the parents' relationship with that child should be irrevocably terminated. This, in his view, had the flavour of 'social engineering'. On the other hand, Steyn and Hoffmann LJJ took what appeared to be a more 'child-centred' approach to the question which focused more closely on whether the advantages of adoption from the point of view of the child's welfare justified overriding the views and interests of the objecting parent.

Finally, in late 1997, the Court of Appeal was again divided over the issue in *Re M (Adoption or Residence Order)*[7]. The peculiarity in this case was that, although there was a strong professional view that a residence order in favour of the child's long-term carers was the preferred option, the adoption applicants appeared adamant that they would only continue to care for the child if an adoption order

---

1   See, for example, *Re F (A Minor) (Adoption: Parental Agreement)* [1982] 1 All ER 321.
2   See, for example, *Re H (Infants) (Adoption: Parental Consent)* [1977] 2 All ER 339.
3   See, for example, *Re El-G (Minors) (Wardship and Adoption)* (1983) FLR 589 and *Re H (Adoption: Parental Agreement)* (1982) FLR 386.
4   See, for example, *Re B (A Minor) (Adoption: Parental Agreement)* [1990] 2 FLR 383.
5   (1983) FLR 614 and see also *Re E (Minors) (Adoption: Parental Agreement)* [1990] 2 FLR 397.
6   [1993] 2 FLR 260.
7   [1998] 1 FLR 570.

were made. This was so despite the fact that the natural mother was willing to accept that a residence order should be made together with an order under s 91(14) of the Children Act in the interests of the security of the carers. The Court of Appeal held by majority that it could not be said that the mother was unreasonably withholding her consent to adoption in these circumstances. It was not merely a matter of where in the best interests of the child she should live. The majority (Ward and Judge LJJ) in fact differed on whether, in any event, adoption was shown to be in the girl's best interests. The adoption application was dismissed and a residence order made in favour of the applicants together with a s 91(14) restriction. The court expressed the hope that this would be accepted by the applicants. Dissenting, Simon Brown LJ, applying a welfare test, favoured adoption and thought that the making of a residence order would almost certainly cause the applicants to reject the child.

Reform

The reported cases thus continue to exhibit considerable ambivalence in the courts' attitude to the relative importance of children's welfare and parental interests in determining the consent issue. The *Review*[1] was scathing in its criticism of the current law. It expressed concern that insufficient weight is, at present, given to a parent's lack of agreement. It deplored the situation in which, because of the passage of time, the court might be presented with what it regards as a fait accompli arising from the length of the child's relationship with the prospective adopters[2], and it took the view that, in reality, the child's welfare had, de facto, become the court's paramount consideration on an application to dispense with consent. The *Review* regarded this as unsatisfactory 'when dealing with parental wishes and feelings in relation to so important a step as adoption'[3]. It also thought it unsatisfactory that a parent could acquire what might be perceived as a stigma of unreasonableness in these circumstances. The *Review*[4], therefore, recommended that only the first of the existing grounds (that the parent cannot be found or is incapable of giving agreement) be retained, and that the others be replaced by a single ground. This would, in essence, focus on the benefits to the child of adoption as opposed to alternative solutions. The new ground it proposed would have required the court to be satisfied that the advantages to the child of becoming part of a new family and having a new legal status were so significantly greater than the advantages to the child of any alternative option as to justify overriding the wishes of a parent or guardian[5]. The only other ground for dispensing with consent would have related to the problem of withdrawal of agreement. It was proposed[6] that it should, in itself, be a ground for dispensing with agreement that a parent who agreed to an adoption when a placement order was made[7] had withdrawn that agreement. This would only be so where the court considered that there had not been any significant changes since then to justify a different outcome. Finally, the *Review*[8] made it plain that the welfare of the child

---

1 *Review* at paras 12.1 et seq.
2 Ibid, para 12.2.
3 Ibid, paras 12.3–12.4.
4 Ibid, para 12.6.
5 Ibid.
6 Ibid, para 12.7.
7 On placement orders, see p 227 below.
8 *Review* at para 12.8.

ought *not* to be the paramount consideration in deciding whether or not to dispense with consent. Moreover, where adoption would only be marginally better than another option, the *Review* took the position that the parent's opposition to adoption should tip the balance in favour of the other option.

This, however, was not the last word on the matter. When the draft Adoption Bill was presented for consultation in March 1996 it soon became clear that a very different emphasis was being given to the place of welfare in the determination of the question of dispensing with parental consent[1]. Clause 1 of the draft Bill provides that 'the paramount consideration of the court or adoption agency must be the child's welfare, in childhood and later'[2]. Specifically in relation to consent it is provided that:

> 'The court cannot dispense with the consent of any parent or guardian of a child to the making of a placement order or adoption order in respect of that child unless –
> (a) the parent or guardian cannot be found or is incapable of giving consent;
> (b) the court is satisfied that the welfare of the child requires the consent to be dispensed with.'[3]

Under this proposal, gone would be the artificiality of the 'hypothetical reasonable parent' and few would regret his or her demise. But conferring and terminating *parenthood*, as opposed to parental responsibility, remains a very significant step in relation to which parents surely have some rights. At the time of writing, the matter remains controversial and there may yet be a further twist before a reformed adoption law reaches the statute book.

Special considerations in family adoptions

The law before the Children Act contained certain statutory directives, initially designed to discourage the use of adoption by step-parents and by relatives such as grandparents. These directives were incorporated in the Children Act 1975 (and then in the 1976 Act, which consolidated adoption legislation) following the recommendations in the *Houghton Report*[4].

Step-parent adoptions

The *Houghton Report* was concerned with the large increase in step-parent adoptions in the early 1970s, following the liberalisation of divorce and the consequential increase in remarriage[5]. It thought that this form of adoption could be inappropriate, since it would have the effect of terminating the child's legal relationship with one parent and, indeed, with one whole side of the child's wider family. It thought that, in many of these cases, a joint custody order in the divorce court would be more appropriate. This would offer security in looking after the child without terminating the child's links with the divorced, non-custodial parent. The courts were, therefore, directed to have regard to this alternative[6]. In

---

1   For commentary on these inconsistencies see E Cooke 'Dispensing with Parental Consent to Adoption – A Choice of Welfare Tests' [1997] CFLQ 259.
2   Clause 1(2).
3   Clause 46(2).
4   Children Act 1975, s 10(3), and ss 14(3) and 15(4) of the 1976 Act.
5   On the position of step-parents generally, see Chapter 6 above. See the *Houghton Report* (above) at paras 103–110.
6   It would offer security since it would give the parent a right to continue looking after the child and to participate in decisions on upbringing.

other step-parent cases, where the divorce jurisdiction was not available[1], an analogous provision required the court to consider the alternative of a 'custodianship' order[2]. These directives were inconsistently interpreted by the courts. At first, they appeared to place the onus on those persons seeking adoption, in keeping with the Houghton philosophy which sought to show that adoption would offer the child more than the custody alternative[3]. Later, the courts appeared to reverse this position, taking the view that, on their proper construction, the directives only required adoption orders to be refused where it could be shown that the child's welfare would be better secured by the alternative orders[4]. Whilst some uncertainties remained, it was clear, long before the Children Act, that the courts had abandoned any policy of actively discouraging step-parent adoption. At best, the courts considered the alternatives of adoption and custody/custodianship in a neutral way and it is at least arguable that they leant *towards* adoption.

The Children Act repealed the directives[5] and the current position is that the court *may* (but not must) consider alternative orders on an adoption application. Since adoption proceedings are 'family proceedings', the court may consider making any of the s 8 orders (particularly residence or contact orders) and may also exercise its powers to attach conditions or give directions. In some step-parent cases, it is therefore probable that the court will consider the matter can be adequately dealt with by means of a residence order.

A new type of adoption order

The *Review*[6] took the position that where the child had some sort of relationship with a parent or that parent's family, it would generally not be in the child's best interests for an adoption order to be made. Conversely, there would be instances in which one parent might never have acted in a parental capacity and the child might never have known anyone on one side of his birth family. In these circumstances, step-parent adoption could be appropriate. The *Review*[7], therefore, recommended the introduction of a new type of adoption order which could be granted to a step-parent but which would not, as at present, make the birth parent (the spouse of the step-parent) also the adoptive parent of the child. The consent of that parent to the step-parent's application would, of course, be required. It also recommended that there should be provision for revocation of a step-parent adoption order where the marriage in question ends by divorce or death[8]. The thinking here is that there may be instances in which the other birth parent and/or the child might wish to have their relationship restored. The draft

---

1   As where the step-parent had married a widow or widower or previously unmarried parent.
2   Children Act 1975, s 37.
3   *Re S (Infants) (Adoption by Parent)* [1977] Fam 173.
4   *Re D (Minors) (Adoption by Step-Parent)* (1980) FLR 102.
5   Schedule 15. See *Re EH and MH (Step-Parent Adoption)* [1993] Fam Law 187 and *Re PJ (Adoption: Practice on Appeal)* [1998] 2 FLR 252 for rare reported examples of court dispensation with parental consent in the case of step-parent applications.
6   *Review* at paras 19.1 et seq.
7   Ibid at para 19.3.
8   Ibid at para 19.4.

Adoption Bill would give effect to the central recommendation that the step-paent should be able to apply as a single applicant[1].

More controversially perhaps, the *Review* went on to recommend that a procedure for sharing parental responsibility between parent and step-parent, analogous to that introduced for unmarried natural parents[2], be introduced, and that the court should have power to make a parental responsibility order in favour of a step-parent. The *Review* did not favour the reintroduction of any statutory directives against step-parent adoption, but did offer the view that it was 'likely that in many circumstances a residence order would be a better way of confirming a step-parent's responsibility for a child, because it does not alter a child's legal relationship with his or her parents and family'[3].

Relatives

The Houghton Committee was also concerned about certain kinds of adoption within the natural family[4]. Here, the principal objection has been the possible distortion of family relationships. In the case, for example, of an application by a grandparent, the legal effect of adoption would be to make that grandparent a parent and, hence, the natural parent a sibling of the child. There was also concern about the effect which hiding the real situation from the child might have on the child's sense of identity in later life. The Children Act 1975[5] created a new procedure of custodianship, the purpose of which was to confer some legal security on carers such as grandparents but without the drastic effect of adoption. As has been seen[6], this procedure was abolished by the Children Act 1989, but it remains the case that the 'lesser' alternative of a residence order may be appropriate in the case of some, perhaps the majority, of adoption applications within the family. This is not to say that adoption should be ruled out in all cases involving relatives. The courts, over the years, have shown a willingness to grant adoption orders in some of these cases[7]. This is most likely to be thought appropriate where the relative has raised the child over a considerable period of time and the natural parents have effectively dropped out of the child's life.

The *Review*[8] noted the importance to children of being cared for in the wider family where a parent is unable to offer the child a suitable standard of care, but it thought that the security and stability required in this situation could usually be met by means of a residence order[9]. It did not, however, wish to rule out adoption by relatives, as where a parent was dead, but it considered it important that applicants for adoption should explore all other alternatives, particularly

---

1 Clause 45(2)(a) allows a single application to be made by a person 'married to a parent of the person to be adopted'. Clause 51(1)(b) goes on to provide that in such adoptions the child would be treated in law as if he had been born as a child of the marriage of the step-parent and the natural parent to whom the step-parent is married.
2 Under s 4 of the Children Act, as to which see Chapters 5 and 6 above.
3 *Review* at para 19.5.
4 Ibid at paras 111 et seq.
5 But this was not implemented until 1985.
6 See Chapter 6 above.
7 See, for example, *Re O (A Minor) (Adoption by Grandparents)* [1985] FLR 546, *Re S (A Minor) (Adoption or Custodianship)* [1987] Fam 98 and *Re W (A Minor) (Adoption: Custodianship)* [1992] Fam Law 64.
8 *Review* at para 20.1.
9 Ibid at para 20.2.

residence orders. The central recommendation was that relatives, together with other carers, should be at least allowed to apply for adoption at any time, with the agreement of those having parental responsibility or, without that agreement, after caring for the child for a cumulative period of at least three years within the last five years[1]. The draft Adoption Bill essentially gives effect to these recommendations[2].

PROTECTION OF CHILDREN PENDING ADOPTION APPLICATIONS

Provisions to protect children

The legislation contains a number of provisions designed to ensure that children who are placed for adoption, and those in relation to whom an adoption application is pending, are not unceremoniously removed, with a view to frustrating the adoption process and perhaps preventing fulfilment of the probationary period. The relevant circumstances are as follows:

(1) Where a parent has agreed to the making of an adoption order, he cannot then remove the child without the consent of the applicants or the leave of the court[3].

(2) An adoption agency may not remove a child it has placed for adoption without the leave of the court if an application is pending[4].

(3) Where the child has had his home with the applicants for at least five years, no one may remove the child while an adoption application is pending. Protection begins as soon as notice of intention to adopt is given to the local authority[5]. It should be appreciated that this provision protects the applicants from removal by the local authority as well as by a parent. However, adoption

---

1 *Review* at para 21.2.
2 Under cl 38, prospective adopters, where the child has not been placed by an agency, must satisfy one of three conditions:
  '(a) each parent or guardian of the child has consented to the adoption of the child by them and has not withdrawn the consent;
  (b) for not less than three years (whether continuously or not) during the period of five years ending with the application, the child's home has been with the prospective adopters or one of them; or
  (c) the court gives leave to make the application.'
3 Section 27(1) of the Adoption Act 1976.
4 Ibid, s 30(1)(b) and (2). Where an adoption application has *not* yet been made, the agency may give notice of its intention to remove the child, and the courts have no power to intervene by reviewing the *merits* of the agency's decision (*Re C and F (Adoption: Removal Notice)* [1997] 1 FLR 190). A decision to remove a child under these provisions is, however, susceptible to judicial review. It has been held that there was a duty to consult foster-parents who had been looking after a child for about two years, and to ascertain the child's own views, before a strategic decision to remove a child was taken (*R v Devon County Council ex parte O (Adoption)* [1997] 2 FLR 388).
5 Ibid, s 28.

cannot be used as a device to prevent a change in fostering arrangements which is in the best interests of the child[1].

(4) In relation to freeing applications[2], where the child is in the care of an adoption agency, the parents may not remove the child, even if they have not consented to the application[3].

Protection under the draft Adoption Bill

The draft Adoption Bill would substantially repeal the existing provisions relating to protected children and replace them with a new code relating to the removal of children[4]. Following the recommendations in the *Review*, the new provisions distinguish between agency and non-agency cases[5]. In agency cases, they also distinguish between cases in which the placement was by *consent* and those in which the child was placed under a *placement order*.

Where the placement was by consent, the parent, consistent with the philosophy of the Children Act which distinguishes sharply between consensual and compulsory substitute 'care'[6], may withdraw consent and require the return of the child (subject to prescribed procedures) at any time up to the time when an application to adopt is made but they may not themselves remove the child from accommodation[7]. Failure to comply with these provisions constitutes a criminal offence. Where, on the other hand, the child is placed under a placement order, the parent will not be allowed to reclaim the child unless the placement order is revoked and the court decides that the child should be returned to the parent[8]. In non-agency cases, there are restrictions on removal of children where the persons looking after the child have been looking after the child for a period of at least three years in the last five and have given notice of their intention to adopt the child, or they have been looking after the child for a shorter period and have actually made an adoption application which is pending[9]. In these cases, the child must not be removed without the leave of the court. Subject to these restrictions the general principle is that a parent or guardian may remove the child and the prospective adopters are under an obligation to return the child to them at once[10]. Removal of the child in contravention of the restrictions, or failure to return the child where there is a legal obligation to do so, will amount to a criminal offence[11].

---

1 *Re H (A Minor) (Adoption)* [1985] FLR 519.
2 See below.
3 Section 27(2) of the Adoption Act 1976.
4 Clauses 29–34.
5 See *Review*, paras 17.4–17.6.
6 See Chapters 10 and 11.
7 Clauses 29–31.
8 Clause 32.
9 Clause 34.
10 Clause 34(7).
11 Clause 34(8).

FREEING FOR ADOPTION

Relinquishing parental rights: the problem

One of the difficulties prior to the Children Act 1975 was that parents were unable to relinquish their parental rights (as they then were), even though they were in favour of adoption, until the final adoption order itself was made. This meant that there could be a substantial delay following a parent's decision to give up a child while a suitable placement was found and while the prospective adopters served out the necessary probationary period with the child. The delay could be a source of anxiety also to the prospective adopters and the agency, since natural parents could, and sometimes did, withdraw their consent to adoption at the eleventh hour.

The freeing procedure

The Houghton Committee sought to meet these difficulties by recommending the introduction of a two-stage procedure which could enable the question of parental agreement to be disposed of at a much earlier stage. The procedure, known as 'freeing for adoption', is incorporated in the 1976 Act[1] but it must be emphasised that it is only one of two alternative ways for adoption agencies to proceed. Many adoptions have continued to take place without use of the earlier freeing procedure. It should also be noted that the procedure can only apply in agency cases. Moreover, since the Children Act, unless a parent or guardian consents to the making of a freeing application, the agency may only apply for a freeing order if the child is in the care of a local authority under a care order[2]. The reasoning here is that, where the child is merely voluntarily accommodated, the local authority ought not to be able to take action which would prevent the parents from removing the child, other than by satisfaction of the statutory criteria for care or supervision[3].

Consent to a freeing order

As with an adoption order itself, a freeing order may not be made unless each parent (with parental responsibility) and guardian, freely, and with full understanding of what is involved, agrees unconditionally to the making of an adoption order, or his agreement can be dispensed with on one of the statutory grounds[4]. The effect is, therefore to confront the issue of parental agreement at an earlier stage in adoption proceedings rather than to postpone it to the final hearing. It has been suggested that it may be more difficult to show the ground of unreasonableness on the part of a parent before a placement has been made[5], and certainly there are reported freeing cases in which the court has refused to

---

1 Section 18.
2 Section 18(2) and (2A), as amended by Sch 10, para 6 to the Children Act 1989.
3 See Chapter 11 below.
4 Section 18(1) of the 1976 Act. On a freeing application the parent must be given a proper opportunity to put his case. See *Re B (Minors) (Freeing for Adoption)* [1992] 2 FLR 37.
5 *Bromley's Family Law* (8th edn) (Butterworths, 1992) at p 438.

dispense with parental consent[1], but the usual expectation is that consent will be dispensed with as it usually is in the case of final adoption orders. There are special provisions in the legislation to cater for the position of the unmarried father without parental responsibility. Before making a freeing order, the court must be satisfied that anyone claiming to be the father does not intend to apply for a parental responsibility order or a residence order or that, if he did make such an application, it would be likely to be refused[2]. In *Re H*[3], the court was prepared to make a parental responsibility order despite its acceptance that the father's agreement would, in all probability, be dispensed with on the basis that it was being withheld unreasonably.

Effects of a freeing order

Where the court makes a freeing order, the effect is to confer parental responsibility on the adoption agency and to terminate the parental responsibility of anyone else who held it before the order[4]. However, this is not necessarily a final transfer of parental responsibility, since a freeing order is revocable in certain circumstances. Each parent or guardian must be given the opportunity of making, if he so wishes, a declaration that he prefers not to be involved in future questions concerning the adoption of the child[5], but where such a declaration has not been made, the agency must[6], within 14 days following the date 12 months after the making of the freeing order, give notice to the 'former' parent informing him whether the child has been adopted or placed for adoption. It must then give him notice of any subsequent adoption order, placement or termination of placement[7]. Where at least 12 months after the freeing order was made the child has not been adopted and is not placed for adoption, the birth parent may apply for the order to be revoked[8] and while this application is pending the agency may not place the child without leave of the court[9]. If the court accedes to the request for revocation, the effect is to transfer parental responsibility back from the agency to the parent or guardian[10]. The court must decide the matter giving first consideration to the need to safeguard and promote the welfare of the child throughout his childhood[11]. If the order is refused, the parent or guardian is then precluded from making any further revocation application without the leave or the court, and the agency is relieved of the responsibility of keeping him informed of further progress[12].

---

1 See, for example, *Re C (Minors) (Adoption)* [1992] 1 FLR 115 and *Re E (Minors) (Adoption: Parental Agreement)* [1990] 2 FLR 397.
2 Section 18(7), inserted by Sch 10, para 6(3) to the Children Act 1989.
3 *Re H (Minors) (Local Authority Parental Rights) (No 3)* [1991] Fam 151.
4 Section 18(5) of the Adoption Act 1976. But since the Children Act 1989, it is possible for the court, on making a freeing order to make a contact order in favour of a parent. See *Re A (A Minor) (Adoption: Contact Order)* [1993] 2 FLR 645.
5 Ibid, s 18(6).
6 Ibid, s 19(2).
7 Ibid, s 19(3).
8 Ibid, s 20(1).
9 Ibid, s 20(2).
10 Ibid, s 20(3).
11 Ibid, s 20(4) applying s 6.
12 Ibid, s 20(4).

These provisions have not always worked smoothly and have been the subject of a recent appeal to the House of Lords in *Re G (Adoption: Freeing Order)*[1]. Here, a young mother had been unable to care for her child. A freeing order was made but the child's placement with prospective adopters broke down. The mother then applied to revoke the freeing order although she accepted that the child should stay at a special boarding school for disturbed children. The difficulty was that the effect of revocation of the freeing order would be to discharge the care order and revive the mother's sole parental responsibility which was not thought appropriate in the circumstances. The mother herself accepted that if the freeing order were revoked the local authority should obtain a care order, but the Court of Appeal had held that revocation could not be made conditional in this way. Disagreeing, the House of Lords held that it could not have been Parliament's intention to create a situation in which a child could be left in 'indefinite legal limbo'. This would be the case if the freeing order were not revoked but no other proposed adoption was on the horizon. The correct interpretation, it was said, was that the powers under the Adoption Act 1976 and the Children Act 1989 could be, and should be, exercised in conjunction. Accordingly, the court did have jurisdiction to revoke the freeing order conditional upon consequential orders under the Children Act or the court's inherent jurisdiction. In this case, since the local authority was prepared to apply for a care order and the mother to consent to one, this was the answer.

It is widely acknowledged that freeing for adoption has not worked in the way originally intended by the Houghton Committee. Far from facilitating adoption, it has usually had the opposite effect of delaying matters by adding a stage to the proceedings – something which sits ill with the principles of the Children Act against delay in children cases. Moreover, it has not tended to be used as a facility for parents to relinquish parental responsibility voluntarily, but rather as a mechanism by which local authorities may resolve the question of parental agreement at an early stage and prevent parents from contesting the later adoption application. The use of the procedure by different agencies has varied considerably.

The recommended abolition of freeing for adoption: placement agreements and orders

The *Review*[2] found the practice of freeing for adoption so unsatisfactory that it recommended its abolition. Concern was expressed that the current procedure involved the court taking decisions in a vacuum, ie before the *particular* placement of the child was known. This involved the rather artificial exercise of comparing what the birth parents had to offer the child with the care likely to be offered by 'hypothetically perfect adoptive parents', and there was no guarantee that thereafter the child would be found a suitable adoptive family, with the consequent risk that he might be left without a family at all[3]. The solution

---

1 [1997] 2 FLR 202. For commentary, see M Richards 'Relinquishment, freeing or abandonment' [1997] CFLQ 313.
2 *Review* at paras 14.3–14.8.
3 Ibid at para 14.4.

proposed in the *Review*[1] was that there should be a 'pre-placement hearing' in all contested agency cases. The suggested procedure was that, where an agency wished to place a child with prospective adopters, it should have to apply to the court for a 'placement order'.

These proposals proved controversial and a further consultation document was produced in 1994 following the Goverment's White Paper in 1993[2]. The result, thus far, is a remodelled scheme for placement agreements and placement orders under the draft Adoption Bill[3]. It seems fairly clear that the freeing procedure itself will be abolished and replaced by this scheme whatever its final shape is.

The central feature of the proposed scheme, and the major change to current law and practice, is that an adoption agency (which includes for these purposes a local authority) will require *either* the consent of the parent or guardian *or* a placement order from the court *before* placing a child for adoption. Other features of the scheme are as follows.

In relation to placement with parental consent[4], parents may give only *specific* consent to the child being placed with named prospective adopters or, alternatively, may give *general* consent to placement. But a distinction is to be made between consent to placement and consent to adoption which are considered to be two distinct stages and requirements. However, it will be possible to give consent to the making of a future adoption order either when consenting to placement or after an application to adopt has been made. Although a parent will not lose parental responsibility until an adoption order is made, he will be required to agree to parental responsibility being given to, and hence shared with, the prospective adopters or the adoption agency where there are as yet no prospective adopters.

With regard to placement orders[5], these will be required wherever the parent or guardian does not consent to placement but the adoption agency, having considered all the available options, is satisfied that adoption is in the child's best interests. The purpose of the order is to enable the court to be involved at an early stage when it too will need to consider all the alternative options. The effect of the placement order will be to authorise the adoption agency to place the child for adoption with suitable prospective adopters. This will not restrict the placement to named prospective adopters, the idea being that the agency should not have to go back to court for a fresh order if the initial placement breaks down. Under a placement order, prospective adopters will acquire parental responsibility which will revert to the agency in the event of the placement breaking down. In many cases, the adoption agency will be the local authority which will have a care order. The draft Bill provides that a placement order will nevertheless be required in these cases. If made, its effect will be to suspend the care order while it lasts. It is already the case that where an authority seeks a care order the majority of courts require the authority to submit a care plan for the child. The draft Bill would amend the Children Act to make care plans mandatory whenever an application is

---

1   *Review*, at para 14.6. For a critique of the original proposals, see NV Lowe 'Adoption Placement Orders – Freeing by another name?' (1993) 5 JCL 62.
2   *Placement for Adoption – A Consultative Document* (Department of Health, 1994).
3   Consultation Paper *Adoption – A Service for Children*, paras 4.2–4.13 and draft Adoption Bill, cls 19–28.
4   Ibid at paras 4.4–4.7 and cls 20–21, respectively.
5   Ibid at paras 4.8–4.10 and cls 22–25, respectively.

made on which a care order might be made[1]. In the context of adoption, the draft Bill provides that where there is a recommendation for adoption in the care plan, the authority must apply for a placement order at the same time as applying for a care order[2].

THE LEGAL EFFECTS OF ADOPTION

General effects

The broad effect of an adoption order is that the child's legal relationship with his birth family is irrevocably terminated and, in its place, the child is treated in law for almost all purposes as if he were a child of the adopters' marriage[3]. Thus, any parental responsibility of a parent or guardian, or held by someone under a court order, is extinguished[4], as is any existing liability to maintain the child[5]. An adoption order will also automatically terminate other court orders and will discharge any existing care order[6]. There are some limited exceptions to the general principle. Although, for example, the child is deemed to be within the prohibited degrees and is prevented from marrying his adoptive parent, he may nonetheless marry his adoptive sister or other adoptive relative[7]. Conversely, he may *not* marry anyone falling within the prohibited degrees on the assumption that the adoption order had not been made[8]. The reasoning is that the prohibited degrees are concerned primarily with perceived genetic objections to intermarriage, which clearly do not arise in the case of adoptive relationships. The *Review*[9] thought that the existing legal effects of adoption were appropriate and should continue to apply, subject to a minor reform relating to contingent interests arising on intestacy[10]. The draft Adoption Bill partially gives effect to this recommendation by giving the court a discretion to allow a child to retain a contingent interest (or part of it) in his birth family's property after adoption[11].

Adoption and contact

The traditional view of English adoption law has been that it is contrary to the very nature of adoption, which severs permanently and irrevocably the tie between the

---

1 Clause 87.
2 Paragraph 4.11 and cl 23(2).
3 Section 39 of the 1976 Act.
4 Ibid, s 12(3).
5 Ibid.
6 Ibid, s 12(3)(a), as inserted by Sch 10, para 3(3) to the Children Act.
7 Marriage Act 1949, Sch 1.
8 Section 47(1) of the 1976 Act.
9 *Review* at para 8.
10 Where a child's parents die intestate, the child is entitled to a contingent interest under the statutory trusts arising under the Administration of Estates Act 1925. The concern is that, at present, if the child is subsequently adopted the interest is forfeited. The *Review* (at para 8.2) proposed that the child should not lose this interest on adoption.
11 Clause 53(5). See also *Staffordshire County Council v B* [1998] 1 FLR 261 in which it was held that a child's contingent interest arising under his great-grandmother's will and derived from his mother's interest vested in possession before his adoption could, on the proper construction of the adoption legislation (ss 39(2) and 42(4)), survive his adoption.

natural parent and the child, that there should be continued contact between the child and the birth family. This was the view which largely prevailed in the courts before the passing of the Children Act[1]. Some relaxation in this position was evidenced by the House of Lords decision in *Re C (A Minor) (Adoption Order: Conditions)*[2]. Here, it was held that there was power under the adoption legislation, in appropriate circumstances, to attach conditions to an adoption order and one of these conditions could be to preserve contact between the child and the child's siblings. A feature of this decision was, however, that all parties were in agreement and this has become an important factor, perhaps even the decisive factor, in later cases which have considered post-adoption contact.

Under the Children Act, adoption proceedings are 'family proceedings' and the court has jurisdiction to make a s 8 contact order. There will undoubtedly still be many cases in which this will be inappropriate but the thrust of the *Review* was to advocate a more 'open' model of adoption in which it would not necessarily be assumed that contact with the birth family was incompatible with the nature of an adoption order. Where the court is minded to make a contact order this needs to be made contemporaneously with the adoption order, or after it, since the effect of the adoption order would be to terminate any pre-existing contact order[3].

The principle which perhaps emerges from the post-adoption contact cases decided under the Children Act is that contact can only really work with the full co-operation and agreement of the adoptive parents, but that if this is forth-coming there may be benefits to the child in such contact. Thus, in *Re T (Adoption: Contact)*[4] the Court of Appeal was at pains to emphasise, in a case in which the adoptive parents had agreed to allow the natural mother some contact, that the mother's security resided in the trust she had in the adopters and not in any court order. The onus should not be on the adoptive parents to go to court in the event of disagreement over contact but should be on the mother who could go back to court with leave[5].

The contact issue is just one manifestation or aspect of a much wider debate about the future role of adoption and what its legal effects should be. Another equally important aspect of this is the issue of the child's identity.

The issue of identity

Adoption has for some time been a secretive process. It has been usual to preserve the anonymity of adoptive parents and often to shield children from knowledge

---

1   For pre-Children Act cases, see fn 5 at p 208 above.
2   [1988] 2 FLR 259.
3   *Re A (A Minor) (Adoption: Contact Order)* [1993] 2 FLR 645. See also *Re O (Transracial Adoption: Contact)* [1995] 2 FLR 597.
4   [1995] 2 FLR 251. For a thorough examination of the issues involved in post-adoption contact from a social work perspective, see M Ryburn 'In whose best interests? – Post-adoption contact with the birth family' [1998] CFLQ 53.
5   Cf *Re T (Adopted Children: Contact)* [1995] 2 FLR 792 in which the adoptive parents resiled from an undertaking to provide annual reports to the adopted child's half-siblings via social services. The Court of Appeal allowed the child's half-sister's appeal against refusal to grant her leave to seek a contact order. The court took the view that if adoptive parents changed their minds about an informal agreement for contact they ought to give reasons for doing so and that their decision was open to challenge in the courts.

about, or contract with, their natural family[1]. This has gradually given way to recognition, acknowledged in the *Review*, that 'a child's knowledge of his or her background is crucial to the formation of positive self-identity, and that adoptive families should be encouraged to be open about the child's adoptive status and the special nature of the adoptive relationship'[2]. Certain provisions in existing adoption legislation enable adopted persons to investigate their origins and, perhaps, to re-establish some form of contact with their birth families.

Following the recommendation of the Houghton Committee[3], the 1976 Act enables an adopted person over the age of 18 years to obtain a copy of his birth certificate[4]. The duty of disclosure is not, however, absolute. Thus, in the remarkable case of *R v Registrar-General, ex parte Smith*[5], the Court of Appeal upheld the decision of the Registrar-General to refuse access to a Broadmoor patient who had killed his cellmate in Wormwood Scrubs in the mistaken belief that he was killing his adoptive mother. The court held that access to his original birth certificate could be refused on the grounds of public policy if there was evidence to suggest that the applicant might use the information to harm his natural mother. There is no right of access to birth records for those adopted persons under 18 years of age, except those intending to marry. Such persons may be given information about whether they are likely to be within the prohibited degrees vis-à-vis the intended spouse[6]. In this way, an adopted adult may discover the truth of his origins – at least where the records contain the necessary information. There is no right, as such, for an adopted person to be told that he is adopted, so that some adopted persons are bound to remain in ignorance of the true circumstances of their birth. Neither do these rights of access extend to birth parents wishing to trace children they have given up for adoption. In *D v Registrar-General*[7], a mother was seeking to trace her daughter. The Court of Appeal held that only in truly exceptional circumstances would confidential information held by the Registrar-General be ordered to be given to a birth parent. This is reinforced by clause 64(2) of the draft Adoption Bill.

The Children Act took the process of disclosure a stage further by establishing an Adoption Contact Register[8]. The purpose of this is to enable adopted children to discover whether attempts to contact relatives would be welcome and, where this is the case, to provide them with factual information which may enable them to do so.

The Register is in two Parts. Part I contains the names of adopted persons over 18 years of age who have obtained copies of their birth certificates and who wish to contact a relative. Part II contains details of the name and present address of any

---

1   In particular, adoption proceedings are private and adoption applicants may apply for a serial number so that the natural parents are prevented from discovering their identity (r 14 of the Adoption Rules 1984, SI 1984/265). All information collected during the adoption process is confidential, thus generally preventing anyone from linking the child's identity before and after adoption.

2   *Review* at para 4.1. See also Articles 7 and 8 of the UN Convention and Chapter 2 above.

3   *Houghton Report* (above) at para 303.

4   Section 51(1) of the 1976 Act.

5   [1991] 2 QB 393.

6   Section 51(2) of the 1976 Act.

7   [1997] 1 FLR 715.

8   Section 51A of the 1976 Act as inserted by Sch 10, para 21 to the Children Act; and see *The Children Act 1989 Guidance and Regulations Vol 9 Adoption* (HMSO, 1991) at ch 3.

relative who would like to contact an adopted person. Under this system of registration, the adopted person, but not the relative, may be given the necessary information where there is a 'match' on the register[1]. The procedure should satisfy the natural curiosity of those who feel the need to discover more about their origins, but it has been pointed out[2] that the increased use of adoption as an option in local authority care cases may mean that some people will have to come to terms with extremely difficult circumstances surrounding their early lives. Whilst counselling is available in relation to disclosure of birth records[3], there is, perhaps surprisingly, no special provision for counselling in relation to the use of the contact register.

The draft Adoption Bill builds on these provisions by requiring the adoption agency which prepared the report for the court to provide the adoptive parents with certain non-identifying information about the child's background and to lodge a copy of this information with the court. The adopted child would then have the right to obtain a copy of this information on attaining majority either from the agency or from the court[4]. In this way, the adopted person would be able to acquire more information about his origins than would be apparent from the basic details in the birth certificate. So far as the Adoption Contact Register is concerned, the draft Bill, following a recommendation in the *Review*, provides for adopted persons and relatives to be able to register their wish *not* to be contacted if that is the case[5]. At present, the register only contains the names of those who positively want to make contact. Although it was recognised that this might be deeply disappointing for the adopted person, it was acknowledged that some birth mothers have, in the past, suffered grave distress when traced by adopted children, or at the prospect of such an approach being made. Finally, the point should be made that none of these provisions will be of any use to a person who does not know, or even suspect, that he was adopted as a child. Although it is good adoption practice for a child to be told, the *Review* recommended that the child should have a statutory right to know that he is adopted[6]. It is to be hoped that this will be embodied in the reformed adoption legislation.

INTERCOUNTRY ADOPTION

Introductory background[7]

The significant decline in the number of babies available for adoption in developed countries has resulted in a situation in which demand from childless

---

1   Section 51A(9) and (11) of the 1976 Act.
2   SM Cretney and JM Masson *Principles of Family Law* (6th edn) (Sweet & Maxwell, 1997) at pp 886–887.
3   Section 51 of the 1976 Act.
4   Clause 48.
5   *Review* at para 31.5, and cl 65 of the draft Bill.
6   Paragraph 4.9.
7   See, generally: W Duncan 'Regulating Intercountry Adoption – an International Perspective' in A Bainham, DS Pearl and R Pickford (eds) *Frontiers of Family Law* (2nd edn) (John Wiley & Sons, 1995); C Bridge 'Reforming Intercountry Adoption' (1992) 4 JCL 116; White Paper *Adoption: The Future*, Part VI; Consultation Paper *Adoption: A Service for Children* at paras 4.27– 4.34; and draft Adoption Bill, cls 88 et seq.

couples vastly outstrips the supply. One consequence of this is that there has been an upsurge in applications for intercountry adoption, illustrated most dramatically in the aftermath of the Romanian revolution[1]. The figures for abandoned children across the world, particularly in Latin America, Asia and Africa, have reached staggering proportions[2]. As the *Review*[3] noted, it is scarcely surprising that some people, especially those unable to have children, should wish to combine the needs of destitute children with their own desire to have a family. Yet in recent years, fears have been expressed across the international community that many of these adoptions have not been child-centred but have had, instead, as their main objective, the satisfaction of adult needs. Often they have been arranged privately and without the professional supervision, support and safeguards which characterise many domestic adoption laws including English adoption law. At their worst, some unregulated adoptions have involved corruption, child-stealing and trafficking. Added to this, there is a further controversy about whether transracial adoptions are in children's best interests.

In an effort to meet these concerns, and to facilitate intercountry adoption only when it is in the best interests of the child concerned, the Hague Conference on Private International Law set up, in 1990, a Special Commission to develop an international Convention on intercountry adoption[4]. The Convention was finalised in May 1993. The principal aims and features of the Convention are considered below, but first we look briefly at the terms of the United Nations Convention on the Rights of the Child and the recommendations of the *Review* and draft Adoption Bill as they apply to intercountry adoption.

The United Nations Convention

The Hague Convention takes, as its starting point, the principles of the United Nations Convention on the Rights of the Child, and these must also be the yardstick for evaluating domestic law and practice. The all-important provison is Article 21, the relevant part of which requires Member States to:

'(b)   recognise that inter-country adoption may be considered as an alternative means of a child's care, if the child cannot be placed in a foster or an adoptive family or cannot in any suitable manner be cared for in the child's country of origin;

(c)   ensure that the child concerned by inter-country adoption enjoys safeguards and standards equivalent to those existing in the case of national adoption;

(d)   take all appropriate measures to ensure that, in inter-country adoption, the placement does not result in improper financial gain for those involved in it;

---

1   See W Duncan (above) at p 43. And for a review of the position in the former Soviet Union, see OA Dyuzheva 'Adoption and the Abandonment of Children in the former Soviet Union' [1992] Fam Law 389. For illustrations of the kinds of difficulties which can arise in practice concerning overseas adoptions, see *Re WM (Adoption: Non-Patrial)* [1997] 1 FLR 132 and *Re K (Adoption and Wardship)* [1997] 2 FLR 221. For the immigration difficulties which can occur, see *Re J (Adoption: Non-Patrial)* [1998] 1 FLR 225. Cf *Re B (Adoption Order: Nationality)* [1998] 1 FLR 965. The correct test appears to be whether the adoption is genuinely justified as in the best interests of the child as opposed to a 'status device' designed purely to confer British nationality and the right of abode on the child. The appellate decisions are, however, by no means easy to reconcile on their facts. See the comment by S Cretney at [1998] Fam Law 385.

2   See W Duncan (above).

3   *Review* at para 46.2.

4   See, generally, W Duncan (above).

(e) promote, where appropriate, the objectives of this article by concluding bilateral or
     multi-lateral arrangements or agreements and endeavour, within this framework, to
     ensure that the placement of the child in another country is carried out by competent
     authorities or organs.'

The *Review*

The *Review*[1] recognised that intercountry adoption, while not a solution to
problems arising from world poverty, might, in some cases, represent the *only*
opportunity for some children to have a stable home life. Accordingly, those
applicants who were assessed as being suitable to offer a home to a child from
overseas should be allowed to do so. At the same time, the *Review* took the view that
the practice of intercountry adoption should be regulated to ensure that it only
takes place where it is in the interests of the child concerned and with safeguards
to protect the welfare of the child and to eliminate corrupt practices[2]. The system,
it was said, should reflect certain fundamental principles accepted in international statutory instruments. In particular, intercountry adoption should
operate as a child-centred service and *not* a child-finding service for adults. It
should be allowed only in relation to those children who could not be suitably
cared for in their own countries[3]. Other significant recommendations were as
follows. It was proposed that children should be admitted to the UK only where
authorisation had been granted by the responsible authority in the UK that the
adoption proceed, subject to immigration requirements being met[4]. It was also
proposed that local authorities should have a duty to provide services in
connection with intercountry adoption, or arrange for them to be provided by
approved adoption societies. They should be responsible for supervising the
placement of children from overseas from the time of their arrival in the UK[5].
Once the new system had been properly developed, it was proposed that it should
be a criminal offence to bring a child to the UK for adoption without having
obtained the prior authorisation of the relevant authority to proceed[6].

The UK is a signatory to the Convention but, before it can be ratified, detailed
implementing legislation is necessary. Part III of the draft Adoption Bill would, if
enacted, enable ratification of the Convention and it embodies many of the
principles in the Convention for regulating adoption from overseas.

The Hague Convention

Objectives
The objects of the Convention[7] are threefold. They are:

(1) to establish safeguards to ensure that intercountry adoptions take place in the
     best interests of the child and with respect for his or her fundamental rights as
     recognised in international law;

---

1   *Review* at para 47.1.
2   Ibid.
3   Ibid at para 47.2.
4   Ibid at para 47.3.
5   Ibid at para 53.
6   Ibid at para 56.2.
7   Article 1.

(2) to establish a system of co-operation amongst Contracting States to ensure that those safeguards are respected and thereby prevent the abduction, the sale of, or traffic in children;

(3) to secure the recognition in Contracting States of adoptions made in accordance with the Convention.

Encouraging adoption of children within their country of origin

The Convention contains a number of fundamental provisions. One of these, which requires special mention, derives from the important principle of *subsidiarity* in Article 21(b) of the United Nations Convention on the Rights of the Child[1]. This is that an intercountry adoption should only take place after the competent authorities in the State of origin have determined, after possibilities for placement of the child within the State of origin have been given due consideration, that an intercountry adoption is in the child's best interests[2]. This is, in many ways, the crux of the matter. The chief concern of the international community is that priority should be given to the fostering of child care services in the developing countries and that, wherever possible, abandoned children should be placed with families in their own communities.

The purpose of the Hague Convention is, therefore, not simply to facilitate intercountry adoption but to regulate it so that it only takes place when the possibilities in the child's country of origin have been exhausted. The difficulty is that, in many developing countries, inadequate child care services exist. Duncan[3] has noted how difficult it is for the child-centred approach to be maintained when, on the international scene, the supply of children available for adoption vastly exceeds the demand. It is his view[4] that the success of the Convention may ultimately be measured 'as much by what it does to encourage and stimulate the growth of child care services in countries of origin as by the number of intercountry adoptions effected under it'.

Once intercountry adoption has been approved

Assuming that it is determined by the State of origin that an intercountry adoption *is* in the child's best interests, the Convention contains a number of other fundamental provisions including the following.

(1) The competent authorities of the State of origin must ensure that the child is adoptable, that all relevant consents (including the child's consent where appropriate) have been given freely and unconditionally after appropriate counselling, and that they have not been induced by payment or compensation[5].

(2) The competent authorities of the State of origin must also ensure, having regard to the age and degree of maturity of the child, that his or her consent has been given freely and unconditionally after appropriate counselling

---

1 Discussed above.
2 Article 4(b).
3 W Duncan 'Regulating Intercountry Adoption – an International Perspective' in A Bainham, DS Pearl and R Pickford (eds) *Frontiers of Family Law* (2nd edn) (John Wiley & Sons, 1995) at pp 42–43.
4 Ibid at p 51.
5 Article 4(a) and (c).

(where the child's consent is required) and that, where it is not, consideration has been given to the child's wishes and opinions[1].

(3) The competent authorities in the receiving State must determine that the prospective adopters are eligible and suited to adopt and that the child will be authorised to enter and reside permanently in that State[2]

(4) There should be no unsupervised contact between the prospective adopters and the natural parents until the fundamental requirements for intercountry adoption have been satisfied[3]. The purpose of this provision will be to prevent economic and other pressure being brought to bear on the birth parents.

(5) Transfer of the child to the receiving State is prohibited, until it has been verified by the competent authorities of both States that no bars exist to the adoption under the respective laws of those States and that a permanent placement has been agreed. This is to avoid the situation of 'legal limbo' in which some children arriving in another State currently find themselves[4].

Designation of a Central Authority

Another important feature of the Convention is the requirement that the Contracting States designate a Central Authority to discharge their obligations under the Convention[5]. These Central Authorities will be expected to co-operate with one another, especially in the exchange of information and in monitoring the operation of the Convention. Some of their functions may be delegated to 'accredited bodies' which are expected to be, for the most part, approved adoption agencies[6]. Finally, the Convention provides for the automatic recognition in all Contracting States of adoptions certified by the competent authority of the State in question as having been made in accordance with the Convention[7].

REFORM: THE FUTURE FOR ADOPTION

Reference has been made throughout this chapter to the recommendations of the *Review* and the proposals in the draft Adoption Bill as they affect specific aspects of adoption law. It remains for us to consider the wider vision of the *Review* for the future of adoption and to what extent this may have been affected by later consultations and other developments[8].

The *Review* recognised that adoption, as we know it, has a continuing role to play as a distinctive mechanism for making a child legally part of a new family, and

---

1 Article 4(d).
2 Article 5.
3 Article 29.
4 Articles 17–19.
5 Article 8. Cf the role of Central Authorities in relation to the International Conventions on Child Abduction, discussed in Chapter 17 below.
6 See Articles 6–13.
7 Article 23.
8 The *Review* was preceded by four consultation papers: *The Nature and Effect of Adoption* (September 1990); *Agreement and Freeing* (September 1991); *The Adoption Process* (November 1991); and *Intercountry Adoption* (January 1992). Three background papers were also issued dealing with international perspectives, research relating to adoption and intercountry adoption. For a critique of some of these papers, see C Bridge, 'Changing the nature and effect of adoption: comment on the first discussion paper published by the Interdepartmental Review

severing any legal relationship with the birth family. In this respect, it differs from all other court orders, particularly residence orders, which simply regulate aspects of the child's upbringing and where the child is to live. The central recommendation was, therefore, that the fundamental nature and effect of adoption should be preserved and that there should not be an alternative or 'simple' form of adoption having a lesser effect[1]. The draft Adoption Bill would give effect to this recommendation[2] but this does require a couple of qualifications. First, it should be recalled that the draft Bill, although not proposing a lesser form of adoption as such, certainly would create more opportunity for court orders to be made as *alternatives* to adoption[3]. These include parental agreements and parental responsibility orders for step-parents and the extension of residence orders to the child's majority in appropriate cases[4].

Secondly, it will not be possible to ignore 'simple' adoption completely since the effect of ratification of the Intercountry Adoption Convention will be that the UK will be obliged to recognise in some way 'simple' adoptions made overseas[5]. Where the UK is the 'receiving' State, it is proposed that a simple adoption made under the Convention in the child's State of origin will be automatically converted to full adoption in the UK provided that the UK is satisfied that the birth parents consented to the adoption in the full knowledge that this conversion would take place in the UK[6]. The position is much more complex where the UK is not the receiving State but will be obliged to recognise simple adoptions in a Convention country such as France. Here, there are a number of alternatives concerning what legal effect such a simple adoption should be given in the UK. The detailed arguments are beyond the scope of the present work, but suffice it to say that there is the potential for the UK perhaps having to recognise that the effect of certain overseas adoptions is to preserve some legal relationship between the child and *both* his birth parents and his adoptive parents, viz the child might have two sets of parents for different purposes[7].

In looking to the future for adoption, there are two other central features of the *Review* which stand out and which continue to excite controversy. The first relates to so-called 'open adoption' and the second to the changes designed to bring adoption law into line with the principles of the Children Act.

Open adoption

The *Review*[8] recognised the argument for a system which would allow more open adoption while preserving secrecy and confidentiality in those cases in which this

---

of Adoption Law' (1991) 3 JCL 37 and 'Reforming the adoption process: Inter-Departmental Reviews 2 and 3' (1992) 4 JCL 72. For research findings on the operation of the adoption process, see N Lowe, M Borkowski, R Copner, K Griew and M Murch 'The Pathways to Adoption' [1992] Fam Law 52. For a concise summary of the principal recommendations of the *Review*, see [1992] Fam Law 564.

1   Paragraph 3.6
2   Clause 51 and, more generally, Part IV of the draft Bill.
3   See White Paper *Adoption: The Future* at paras 5.18–5.27.
4   Clauses 45, 85 and 86 and see also Chapter 6 above.
5   See Consultation Paper *Adoption – A Service for Children* at paras 4.31–4.34.
6   Ibid at para 4.32.
7   Ibid at paras 4.33–4.34.
8   *Review* at para 4.2.

was thought appropriate. It was concerned that the existing law and procedure 'assumes a closed model of adoption where this is not always the case, nor always appropriate'. Accordingly, the *Review* made a cluster of recommendations designed to promote openness at different stages of the adoption process. We have already made reference to the proposal that the child should have a statutory right to know that he is adopted. Other relevant proposals were that the courts should continue to have power to make a contact order in conjunction with an adoption order[1]; that birth parents' wishes and feelings about such matters as race, religion, language and culture should be taken into account more than in the past[2]; and that adoption agencies should have the power to be proactive in contacting adopted adults and birth relatives to ask whether they would agree to identifying information being passed on to each other[3]. It was also proposed that it should be made plain in adoption legislation that the users of local authority adoption services should have access to the authority's statutory complaints procedure established under the Children Act and that approved adoption societies should be under an obligation to operate similar complaints procedures[4].

It has been said that open adoption 'has emerged as a buzz concept in adoption circles'[5]. There appears to be no clear definition of what it is and no clearly accepted view from research findings that it is desirable to promote it. But in its different variants it may mean preserving some level of contact with the birth family[6], involving the birth parents more in the selection of prospective adopters or the adoption agency passing on full, but non-identifying, information about the birth and adoptive families to each other. Or it might mean all of these things. It is not clear at the time of writing how much of a push, if any, will be given to the concept of open adoption in the reformed legislation. The former Conservative Government's White Paper and draft Adoption Bill appeared to some commentators to have 'gone cool' on the question as much for what is *not* included as for what *is* included[7]. It will certainly remain the case that the court will be able to make contact orders whether at the time of adoption or after making an adoption order, but how enthusiastic they will be about doing so, especially in the absence of the agreement of the adoptive parents, is open to doubt. In short, it is by no means certain that the new adoption legislation when it comes will embody any clear official directives in favour of openness.

Adoption and the Children Act

The *Review* contained a number of proposals designed to extend to adoption law some of the central principles of the Children Act and, to a large extent, the draft

---

1 *Review* at para 5.5.
2 Ibid at para 28.2.
3 Ibid at para 31.7.
4 Ibid at para 7.1.
5 B Lindley 'Open adoption – is the door ajar?' [1997] CFLQ 115.
6 It should be noted that the kind of post-adoption contact envisaged is a much more limited idea than the weekly or fortnightly contact we associate with divorce. In many cases, contact might be limited in the adoption context to indirect contact such as periodic progress reports about the child.
7 See Lindley (above) at pp 128–129.

Adoption Bill would give effect to these. They include the extension of the welfare principle to adoption generally although, as we have seen, the *Review* and draft Bill diverge significantly on its application to the question of dispensing with parental consent. The *Review* recommended and the draft Bill provides[1] that the 'no order' principle be extended to adoption and that the court should be required in adoption proceedings to have regard to the whole range of powers available to it. In other words, it would consider alternative orders such as residence orders. In making any decisions relating to adoption, agencies and courts will also be required to have regard to the principle that delay is likely to be prejudicial to the welfare of the child[2]. In applying the welfare principle, courts and adoption agencies will be required to apply a statutory checklist of factors similar to that in the Children Act but adapted to take account of the special considerations involved in adoption. The proposed checklist is as follows[3]:

(a) the child's ascertainable wishes and feelings regarding the decision (considered in the light of the child's age and understanding);
(b) the child's particular needs;
(c) the likely effect on the child (during childhood and later) of having ceased to be a member of the original family and become an adopted person;
(d) the child's age, sex, background and any of the child's characteristics which the court or agency considers relevant;
(e) any harm which the child has suffered or is at risk of suffering; and
(f) the relationship which the child has with relatives, and with any other person in relation to whom the court or agency considers the question to be relevant, including:
  (i) the value to the child of any such relationship continuing,
  (ii) the ability and willingness of any of the child's relatives, or of any such person, to provide the child with a secure environment in which the child can develop, and otherwise to meet the child's needs,
  (iii) the wishes and feelings of any of the child's relatives, or of any such person, about the child.

There is no doubt that the draft Bill, if enacted, would go a long way towards harmonising the fundamental principles of adoption law with those of the Children Act. At the same time, doubts remain about whether some of the details of the new law and procedure are consistent with the philosophy and procedures of the Children Act[4]. In particular, it has been questioned whether the early compulsion involved in the proposed placement orders is consistent with the ethos of continuing partnership under the public law provisions of the Children Act[5]. And there will undoubtedly continue to be arguments about whether the unbridled discretion associated with the welfare principle is really appropriate in the context of adoption.

---

1 Clause 1(5).
2 Clause 1(3).
3 Clause 1(4).
4 For an informative discussion, see B Lindley and N Wyld 'The Children Act and the draft Adoption Bill – diverging principles' [1996] CFLQ 327.
5 Ibid at pp 332–333, and see Chapters 10 and 11 below.

International pressure: the right to knowledge of biological origins

As we have seen, the alleged right of the child to knowledge of biological origins, apparently recognised implicitly under Articles 7 and 8 of the United Nations Convention on the Rights of the Child, has gathered considerable ground in recent years. Such a right, if indeed it exists, has wide-ranging implications in the contexts of establishing paternity, assisted reproduction[1] and, not least, adoption. It would certainly seem to favour a more open system of adoption and, indeed, it may be doubted how far the English 'transplant' model of adoption could continue to be defended where children have 'rights' to knowledge of, and continued involvement with, their birth families. The Children Act, in contrast, with its support for partnership and *inclusive* relationships between various adults and children seems more in harmony with the objectives of the UN Convention. It seems almost certain that the reformed adoption law will preserve the 'transplant' effect of adoption. But unless it also properly accommodates the child's 'right' or 'interest' in an ongoing link with the birth family, international obligations might well trigger further reform.

---

1   It is doubtful whether existing provisions (principally the Human Fertilisation and Embryology Act 1990, s 31) comply fully with the child's right to knowledge of biological origins where the child has been born following gamete donation. Information about donors, which can be provided to the child on attaining majority, is limited to non-identifying information – unlike the information which can be provided to *adopted* persons. For a full discussion, see S Maclean and M Maclean 'Keeping secrets in assisted reproduction – the tension between donor anonymity and the need of the child for information' [1996] CFLQ 243, and SM Cretney and JM Masson *Principles of Family Law* (6th edn) (Sweet & Maxwell, 1997) at pp 948–949.

Chapter 8

CHILDREN AND MEDICAL DECISIONS

INTRODUCTION

The principles which now govern the relationship between the legal capacities of children, the responsibilities of parents and the limits of State intervention have to a considerable extent been fashioned in the context of medical decision-making. This is not really surprising since the health of children is self-evidently the most basic and essential consideration in protecting their welfare. In this chapter we take a close look at some of the more important decisions of the courts which have determined whether medical procedures should, or should not, be carried out on individual children[1]. These decisions, important in their own right, have a significance which goes beyond this, since they are probably the best practical applications of the theoretical perspectives discussed in Chapter 3. They deal in a very practical way with the limits of parents' powers and duties, the extent of children's rights (whether to be protected or to exercise autonomy) and with the acceptable limits of State paternalism over children exercised through the courts. It is for this reason that in this chapter we go into the facts and reasoning of individual decisions in greater depth than we do elsewhere in the book. Although medical issues affecting children have been many and various, they may perhaps be reduced to two central questions:

(1) who decides what medical procedures or treatment are appropriate for a child?; and

(2) on what criteria ought such decisions to be based?

Who decides?

As to the first question, there are any number of possibilities. It would be possible to give parents (or others exercising parental responsibility) an unfettered discretion, although there might need to be a mechanism for resolving

---

1 There are now several established texts on medical law including: I Kennedy and A Grubb *Medical Law* (2nd edn) (Butterworths, 1994); JK Mason and RA McCall Smith *Law and Medical Ethics* (4th edn) (Butterworths, 1994); J Montgomery *Health Care Law* (Oxford University Press, 1997); and J McHale and M Fox with J Murphy *Health Care Law: Text and Materials* (Sweet & Maxwell, 1997). For a collection of essays focusing specifically on medical issues in the family, see E Sutherland and A McCall Smith *Family Rights: Family Law and Medical Advance* (Edinburgh University Press, 1990). For a detailed study of reproductive legal issues, see G Douglas *Law, Fertility and Reproduction* (Sweet & Maxwell, 1991). For an introduction to the central issues involving medical decisions and children, see MDA Freeman *The Rights and Wrongs of Children* (Frances Pinter, 1983) at ch 7. Also of use is M Freeman *The Moral Status of Children* (Martinus Nijhoff, 1997), especially ch 15 (which deals with adolescents' rights to take their own decisions) and ch 16 (which deals with sterilisation of the mentally handicapped). A major new text on medical law entitled *Principles of Medical Law* edited by I Kennedy and A Grubb is to be published by Oxford University Press in September 1998. Many useful articles may now be found in the *Medical Law Review* also published by Oxford University Press.

disagreements between parents[1]. Equally, decisions could be handed over entirely to children themselves, at least where they have acquired a certain age or level of understanding.

Another alternative might be to allow an outside agency, such as a court, to take the final decision. In that case, the circumstances under which the courts would become involved would need to be addressed. There could, for example, be a mandatory judicial procedure for certain operations[2]. Yet another possibility is that decisions could be left to the medical profession subject to a requirement that they be taken in accordance with accepted medical practice[3].

Yet the English case-law alerts us to the danger of assuming that there must necessarily be a single decision-maker. Whilst it is incontrovertibly true that *someone* has to have the final say, it is equally clear, in the family context, that the law has had to grapple with forms of participatory or inclusive decision-making which take at least some account of *all* the legitimate interests involved. The crucial question in any given situation therefore becomes one of determining precisely how this balance should be struck.

On what criteria?

As to the second question, there is an argument for saying that, since the facts of no two cases are ever identical, all medical decisions affecting individual children should be taken on an individualistic basis applying the welfare principle. Indeed, this largely represents current practice in England. Even the minority of cases which have reached the higher courts have, on the whole, failed to establish general criteria to determine with any precision such matters as when life-saving treatment should be given or withheld or when the sterilisation of mentally incompetent young women should be authorised or prohibited. Occasionally, the courts have appeared to go out of their way to deny that general principles of public policy are involved in such cases[4]. Moreover, they will often defer to the

---

1   For a review of the place that parental opinion has held in the reported decisions on medical treatment for children see J Loughrey 'Medical treatment – the status of parental opinion' [1998] Fam Law 146.

2   Such procedures, especially for abortions on minors without parental consent, have been adopted in the USA, but English law has so far stopped short of this, while accepting that for sterilisation of mentally handicapped minors judicial authorisation is required in virtually all cases. See *Practice Note* [1996] 2 FLR 111.

3   This would be in line with the general requirement imposed by the law of tort that doctors act in accordance with the practice accepted by a responsible body of medical men skilled in that particular art. See *Bolam v Friern Hospital Management Committee* [1957] 2 All ER 118. This duty has been the subject of a recent decision of the House of Lords in *Bolitho v City and Hackney Health Authority* [1997] 3 WLR 1151, a case in which a two-year-old child with acute respiratory difficulties died after a doctor negligently failed to attend him in hospital. Here, the House refined the *Bolam* test by holding that there could be *rare* cases in which it might be demonstrated that professional medical opinion was incapable of withstanding logical analysis. In these rare cases, a judge might be entitled to hold that the body of opinion concerned was not reasonable or responsible. On the facts, however, this was not such a case, since there was good reason to accept the defendant's expert opinion, and it had therefore not been proved that the doctor's failure to attend the child had caused the injuries which had led to his death. For commentary, see J Keown 'Reining in the Bolam test' [1998] CLJ 248.

4   A particularly striking example is the speech of Lord Hailsham in *Re B (A Minor) (Wardship: Sterilisation)* [1988] AC 199, in which he offered the view that no general issues of public policy were raised by the proposed sterilisation of a mentally handicapped teenager.

expertise of the medical profession on what are seen as clinical matters, preferring to confine themselves to giving broadly defined directions[1]. Indeed, it has been put more strongly by Montgomery (specifically in the context of selective treatment of the newborn) whose assessment is that it has become 'clear that the courts will respect the clinical freedom of doctors and refuse to force them to act against their clinical judgement'[2].

The practical value, therefore, of decisions (even those of the House of Lords) as precedents must inevitably be limited. This immediately provokes the question whether a more concerted attempt should be made to formulate, through legislation, legal standards for decision-making[3]. The difficulty with this is that any such attempt would be bound to raise awkward moral questions about the value and quality of life which are, in the end, dependent on individual beliefs and on which there is never likely to be a societal consensus. Yet the consequence of failing to establish reasonably clear criteria is that this can lead to widespread variations in the treatment or non-treatment of children with broadly similar medical conditions and this may be thought to offend principles of formal equality[4]. It is doubtful how far such an approach could be reconciled with a commitment to children's rights.

Who is a child?

The following discussion follows the definition of 'child' in the Children Act 1989 as a person below the age of 18 years. It has been noted that this can cause difficulties at either end of the spectrum, ie the problems of the status of the foetus and the mentally incompetent adult 'child'[5]. Even within this spectrum there is a world of difference between the sort of medical questions which can arise in relation to neonates or young children on the one hand and adolescents on the other. The latter have a capacity for self-help in seeking medical assistance, whilst the former are wholly dependent on the support of interested adults. The general question relating to young children, given that there must be a proxy decision-maker, is when precisely an outside party or agency should be able to challenge parental authority. The general issue regarding adolescents, on the assumption that they themselves have legal capacity, relates to the circumstances in which they may act in conjunction with medical advice and by-pass parental involvement or go ahead with a medical procedure in the face of parental opposition.

We begin by discussing the legal framework within which medical decisions are taken. We then examine the operation of these principles in two key areas which illustrate the particular problems affecting infants and young children and also the special considerations applying to adolescents.

---

1   See, for example, *Re C (A Minor) (Wardship: Medical Treatment)* [1989] 2 All ER 782.
2   J Montgomery *Health Care Law* (Oxford University Press, 1997) at p 420.
3   Such attempts were made in relation to the treatment or non-treatment of handicapped infants in the USA, as to which see RH Mnookin and DK Weisberg *Child, Family and State* (2nd edn) (Little, Brown and Co, 1989) at pp 509 et seq.
4   The principle entails treating like cases alike. A good theoretical discussion of what is involved in equal treatment is to be found in B Williams 'On Equality' in *Problems of the Self* (Cambridge University Press, 1976).
5   See Chapter 3 above.

GENERAL PRINCIPLES

The parental consent principle

The consent requirement

As a general proposition it is accepted that the consent of the patient is required for any medical examination or procedure. The principle is rooted in the idea of self-determination. The patient should be left alone to decide what is or is not done to his body[1]. Prima facie, any unauthorised 'touching', which for these purposes includes medical procedures, would constitute an assault or, more accurately, a battery. But provided that the patient has an essential understanding of what is proposed and consents to it, no assault will have been committed. It is possible that a doctor may be liable in negligence where the patient's consent was induced by his failure to disclose information which any prudent medical practitioner would have disclosed[2]. But beyond this there is no requirement in English law that the patient give an 'informed consent'[3]. The consent requirement throws up an immediate problem in the case of children. The very status of minority has, as its raison d'être, the assumed incapacity of children to act on their own behalf. Thus, as a general rule, the law allows parents (and others in loco parentis) to provide a proxy consent for medical treatment and procedures performed on children.

Who can give consent?

This power, recognised at common law, is now included in the concept of parental responsibility and thus devolves automatically on married parents, unmarried mothers and anyone else (including an unmarried father) who acquires parental responsibility by legal process[4]. The Children Act, as already discussed, allows anyone with de facto care of a child, for however short a time, to 'do what is reasonable in all the circumstances of the case for the purpose of safeguarding or promoting the child's welfare'[5]. The Law Commission specifically instanced the operation of this provision in relation to medical care. It offered the view that it would enable a temporary carer to arrange medical assistance following an accident to the child but would not allow a temporary carer to consent to major elective surgery for the child[6]. While there could be some difficult line-drawing,

---

1   The consent issue is discussed generally in JK Mason and RA McCall Smith *Law and Medical Ethics* (4th edn) (Butterworths, 1994) at ch 10, I Kennedy and A Grubb *Medical Law* (2nd edn) (Butterworths, 1994) at ch 4, and J Montgomery *Health Care Law* (Oxford University Press, 1997) at ch 10. J McHale and M Fox with J Murphy *Health Care Law: Text and Materials* (Sweet & Maxwell, 1997) deal with the consent issue in ch 6 and devote ch 7 specifically to issues involving children. For a view from the Official Solicitor's office, dealing particularly with the problems of incapacity, see M Nicholls 'Consent to Medical Treatment' [1993] Fam Law 30. See also J Montgomery 'Consent to health care for children' (1993) 5 JCL 117.
2   See Lord Bridge in *Sidaway v Board of Governors of the Bethlem Royal Hospital and Maudsley Hospital* [1985] 1 All ER 643 at 663.
3   But we discuss below the apparently high level of understanding required of minors wishing to provide their own consent to medical matters.
4   The general principles concerning acquisition of parental responsibility are discussed in Chapter 2 above.
5   Section 3(5).
6   Law Com Report No 172 *Guardianship and Custody* (1988) at para 2.16.

the essence of the distinction would appear to be that emergency or routine medical care would be covered, but procedures with long-term or irreversible implications would require the consent of a person with parental responsibility. It should also be said that anyone looking after a child might be criminally liable or liable in negligence for failing to secure essential medical aid for a child[1], although there is no wider legal, as opposed to moral, duty on members of the public at large to come to the aid of a distressed child[2].

Wilful neglect

The position of parents as proxies entails both a duty and a discretion, and the primary difficulty is to determine when duty ends and discretion begins. Anyone over the age of 16 years, with 'responsibility' for a child, who 'wilfully assaults, ill-treats, neglects, abandons, or exposes him ... in a manner likely to cause him unnecessary suffering or injury to health' commits a criminal offence[3]. The offence specifically includes failure to provide adequate medical aid or failure to take steps to secure it to be provided. This offence of 'wilful neglect' imposes certain minimum standards of medical care on anyone, most obviously a parent, who has the physical care of a child. It has been held that the test of 'wilfulness' is a subjective one, requiring actual appreciation of the risk to the child's health. Consequently, it can be a defence to show that parents of low intelligence did not have this appreciation at the relevant time[4]. On the other hand, the offence may be committed where there is failure to summon medical aid even though *in fact* there was no help which a doctor could have given[5].

When can a parent withhold medical care?

In addition to this special offence, parents and others are, of course, subject to the ordinary criminal law and may, for example, be liable for the death of the child where death was caused by their unwillingness to summon essential aid. Such refusals are sometimes influenced by religious considerations, but while parents may lawfully make martyrs of themselves, they may not make martyrs of their

---

1 Criminal liability arises primarily under the Children and Young Persons Act 1933, s 1.
2 Thus, no criminal offence is committed where an unconnected bystander watches a child drown in a shallow pool, however morally reprehensible this inactivity might be. For a discussion of these principles, see JC Smith and B Hogan *Criminal Law* (8th edn) (Butterworths, 1996) at p 51. In similar vein, there is no mandatory reporting law in England which would require a neighbour or anyone else to inform the relevant authorities of child abuse or neglect.
3 Children and Young Persons Act 1933, s 1(1). The statute makes it explicit that the suffering or injury to health is widely defined and includes 'injury to or loss of sight, or hearing, or limb, or organ of the body, and any mental derangement'.
4 *R v Sheppard* [1981] AC 394. Failure to satisfy an objective test of reasonableness might, however, give rise to tortious liability.
5 *R v S and M* [1995] Crim LR 486.

children[1]. Thus, in *R v Senior*[2], a parent's conviction for manslaughter by gross negligence was upheld where for religious reasons he failed to summon medical aid for his dangerously ill child who then died of diarrhoea and pneumonia[3]. It is clear then that parental rights or responsibility 'do not clothe parents with life and death authority over their children'[4]. However, it cannot be concluded from this that in no circumstances is it proper for parents, acting in conjunction with the medical profession, to withhold life-saving treatment from certain children[5]. A fortiori, the extent of the parent's duty to secure medical treatment in *non*-life-threatening situations requires careful examination in individual cases[6].

Therapeutic versus non-therapeutic treatment

Where parents are not under a positive duty to secure medical treatment they nevertheless, as a general principle, have a discretion to consent to or veto it[7]. Although the courts have been loathe to draw rigid distinctions between therapeutic and non-therapeutic procedures, it is generally accepted that parents have power to consent to treatment of a therapeutic nature, but their capacity to authorise non-therapeutic treatment is more doubtful[8]. It is thought that they *do* have power to consent to non-therapeutic procedures insofar as they are for the

---

1   *People (ex rel Wallace) v Labrenz* 104 NE 2d 769 (Ill, 1952). The principle has recently been illustrated by cases in which the courts have sanctioned blood transfusions for children in the face of religious objections by their parents. See *Re S (A Minor) (Medical Treatment)* [1993] 1 FLR 376 and *Re O (A Minor) (Medical Treatment)* [1993] 2 FLR 149. Moreover, the courts may be prepared to override the *combined* objections of the parents and an adolescent, as in *Re E (A Minor) (Wardship: Medical Treatment)* [1993] 1 FLR 386. In this case, Ward J, while giving full weight to the religious principles accepted by the patient (a boy aged 15) and his parents (all of whom were devout Jehovah's Witnesses), held that the welfare of the patient, objectively judged, led to the inevitable conclusion that blood transfusions should be authorised.
2   [1899] 1 QB 283.
3   The accused belonged to a sect known as the 'Peculiar People' who objected to the use of doctors because of their interpretation of verses 14 and 15 of the Epistle of St James – 'Is there any sick among you? Let him call for the elders of the church and let them pray over him, anointing him with oil in the name of the Lord; and the prayer of faith shall save the sick, and the Lord shall raise him up; and if he have committed sins, they shall be forgiven him'. Accepting evidence that proper medical aid could have prolonged and probably saved the child's life, the judge had pointed out that Christ himself had, according to biblical text, said: 'They that are whole need not a physician but they that are sick'.
4   *Custody of a Minor* 379 NE 2d 1053 (1978).
5   See particularly now *Re T (Wardship: Medical Treatment)* [1997] 1 FLR 502, discussed below. For a recent examination of the whole issue of parents' powers in relation to the medical treatment of children, see C Bridge 'Parental powers and the medical treatment of children' in C Bridge (ed) *Family Law Towards the Millennium: Essays for PM Bromley* (Butterworths, 1997) at ch 9.
6   This has received much closer examination in the United States than it has in England. See RH Mnookin and D Weisberg *Child, Family and State* (2nd edn) (Little, Brown and Co, 1989).
7   It should be noted, however, that a parent's objection to a blood test on a child for the purposes of establishing paternity may, it seems, be overridden by the court if the court considers this to be in the child's best interests: see *Re R (Blood Test: Constraint)* [1998] 1 FLR 745. On the question of consent to genetic screening and tests associated with this, see J McHale 'Genetic screening and testing the child patient' [1997] CF LQ 33.
8   An illustration of this principle is *Re E (A Minor) (Medical Treatment)* [1991] 2 FLR 585 where it was held that, contrary to normal requirements regarding the sterilisation of mentally handicapped minors, parents might provide a valid consent to a *therapeutic* hysterectomy without obtaining a judicial declaration.

benefit of the child[1]. Thus, they may consent to blood tests on the child for the purposes of establishing paternity, since it is usually thought to be in the child's best interests for this question to be determined[2]. The Court of Appeal has confirmed that such a direction should not be given where the court is satisfied that it would be *against* the child's interests[3].

Particularly difficult questions can arise where the benefits to the child are less obvious, as where it is proposed that a child should participate in non-therapeutic research or become an organ donor[4]. Such research may be justified on the altruistic basis that it benefits *other* children but may be of no direct benefit to the child undergoing the procedure, which might be hazardous and uncomfortable[5]. Here, the difficult legal issue is whether parents and others are bound by a legal duty to act *only* in the best interests of the child in question[6]. The point is uncertain but it appears to be accepted medical practice that, in *some* circumstances, research on individual children which is intended to benefit other children, may be justifiable. This is subject to significant qualifications concerning the older child's right to object and the need to obtain the consent of the parent or guardian. It is also accepted that parental consent per se should not justify participation in research.

Parents may not validly consent to a procedure which is to the obvious *detriment* of the child and, more generally, it is considered ethically unsound to proceed except where the risks to the child concerned are minimal[7].

Consequences of proceeding without parental consent

We discuss below the circumstances in which parental consent may not be required, but there is a preliminary question. On the assumption that the consent of a parent *is* necessary, what course of action is open to that parent if the doctor or other medical personnel go ahead without his or her consent? Here, it has been established by the Court of Appeal in *F v Wirral Metropolitan Borough Council*[8] that

---

1   It is non-medical benefits which are referred to here, since medical benefits to the child would render the procedure therapeutic in nature.

2   *S v S; W v Official Solicitor* [1972] AC 24.

3   *Re H (Paternity: Blood Test)* [1996] 2 FLR 65.

4   The issue is discussed in JK Mason and RA McCall Smith *Law and Medical Ethics* (4th edn) (Butterworths, 1994) at pp 369–374, and I Kennedy and A Grubb *Medical Law* (2nd edn) (Butterworths, 1994) at ch 14. See now *Re Y (Mental Incapacity: Bone Marrow Transplant)* [1996] 2 FLR 787. This case concerned organ donation between two adult sisters but there is no reason why the principles should not be extrapolated to children. Connell J held that the test to be applied was the best interests of the prospective donor. Here, there was a closely knit family and it was possible to conclude that it was in the best interests of a severely mentally and physically handicapped woman (who was unable to provide a valid consent) that she should donate bone marrow to her elder sister who suffered from leukaemia. For assessments of the decision, see D Feenan 'A good harvest?' [1997] CFLQ 305 and SE Mumford 'Bone marrow donation – the law in context' [1998] CFLQ 135.

5   JK Mason and RA McCall Smith (above) cite the example of a French project involving lumbar punctures on newborn infants. See also the discussion in J Montgomery *Health Care Law* (Oxford University Press, 1997) at pp 292–296.

6   This may be the implication of the welfare principle but it has already been noted that the application of this principle to parents is problematic. See Chapter 3 above.

7   The attitude of various medical professional bodies to the issue is discussed by JK Mason and RA McCall Smith (above) at p 369.

8   [1991] 2 FLR 114.

no civil action will lie for interference with parental 'rights' and this principle must surely apply equally to the new concept of 'parental responsibility'. Any tortious action a parent has must, therefore, be based on trespass to the *child's* person. The function of parental consent is thus to prevent a tort being committed against the *child* and not to protect any independent parental claim[1]. Where a 'touching' is involved (which would be the case with most medical examinations and procedures), it ought not to be difficult to establish the tort of battery. But the position is much less clear if all that is involved is the giving of advice or the prescription of medication since here there is no obvious physical contact. It is doubtful whether the doctor would be acting unlawfully in those situations although a parent, forewarned of these dealings, might seek to prevent them in wardship or by seeking a prohibited steps order[2].

Exceptions to the parental consent requirement

There are several well-established qualifications to the general rule that the consent of a parent is both a necessary and sufficient consent to treatment for a child. First, the State may, in certain circumstances, restrict the area of parental discretion, either directly through legislation or indirectly through the protective agency of local authorities or the courts. Secondly, the child's own view may prevail over that of a parent in some instances in which they are in conflict. Thirdly, there will be instances in which the medical profession may proceed lawfully without a parent's consent. Some of these instances will arise where no consent is either available or required, while in other cases it may be lawful for a doctor, in effect, to choose between the conflicting views of parents and children.

The State as decision-maker

As has been seen, the State may, through the criminal law, cut down the area of parental discretion by imposing duties to ensure certain minimum standards of health for children[3]. An alternative mechanism, used extensively in the USA, is to require compliance with a variety of screening procedures designed to detect particular diseases in children or to require certain immunisations against, for example, diphtheria, whooping cough, tetanus, measles and polio, as a condition of school admission. In the USA, some State legislation has made provision for parents' objections to these procedures, in some cases only on religious grounds,

---

1   The dangers of the medical profession proceeding with an operation on a child without obtaining parental consent were graphically illustrated in the tragic case of six-year-old Debbie Jenkins which received a great deal of media attention in March 1998. Dr James Taylor, a senior consultant heart surgeon at Great Ormond Street Hospital, was found guilty of professional misconduct by the General Medical Council. The child had died following irreparable brain damage which she sustained when Dr Taylor performed a procedure which involved using a balloon catheter to try to enlarge a narrowed artery. He was fully aware of the lack of the parents' consent to this procedure and had evidently informed them that he would not use it. He was found to have had insufficient medical grounds to undertake the procedure without parental consent. It was also reported that the parents were considering a civil action against the hospital following the ruling of the GMC. (See (1998) *The Times*, March 21.)
2   Section 8(1) of the Children Act. This issue is relevant to other professionals such as teachers, as to which see Chapter 16 below.
3   Children and Young Persons Act 1933, s 1.

but there has been no consistent pattern[1]. In England, the courts have occasionally exercised their powers to direct that children be tested for HIV infection, although the basis for exercising this jurisdiction is not wholly clear. Such tests should only be directed by the High Court[2]. Interventions like these represent restrictions on parental discretion grounded in the public interest in the prevention of disease.

The State may intervene through the local authority or the court (on the initiative of some interested party) to protect the health of *individual* children. Traditionally, this was achieved in wardship proceedings. While this jurisdiction may remain the appropriate one in sensitive or complex cases, the alternative of applying in family proceedings for a prohibited steps or specific issue order might now be used[3]. Any interested person may ward the child, whereas leave of the court may be required to seek a s 8 order[4]. The leave requirement might appear to give wardship proceedings an advantage but it is perhaps unlikely that the courts will allow wardship to be used to circumvent the normal statutory requirements. In any event, where it is a single medical issue which requires resolution, the continuing control of the court in wardship will not be required and it is likely that the inherent jurisdiction (but not wardship as such) will be invoked. A genuine applicant for a s 8 order should not experience difficulty in obtaining leave where a serious medical issue has arisen. Where there is more general concern about the ability of parents or other carers to safeguard the health of a child on an ongoing basis, this will usually be a matter for action by social services.

The court's protective role

The court's protecive role in relation to children is seen most obviously in life-saving cases involving perhaps newborn infants or the refusal of blood transfusions for children of any age on religious grounds. Yet the courts can also be involved other than in life-saving situations, of which the best example is arguably the sterilisation of the mentally handicapped. In this section we concentrate on this controversial issue[5].

There is no better illustration of the court's protective role in the medical arena than the reported cases on the proposed sterilisation of young, mentally handicapped women. The issue first came to the fore in *Re D (Sterilisation)*[6] where an educational psychologist invoked wardship in an attempt to prevent the sterilisation of an 11-year-old girl who suffered from an uncommon disorder

---

1 RH Mnookin and D Weisberg *Child, Family and State* (2nd edn) (Little, Brown and Co, 1989) at pp 472–475.
2 See, particularly, *Note: Re HIV Tests* [1994] 2 FLR 116, and *Re O (Minors) (Medical Examination)* [1993] 1 FLR 860.
3 The future of wardship in the private sphere is uncertain following the Children Act but it seems likely that it will continue to be used in sensitive or difficult medical cases. For a general discussion, see A Bainham 'The Children Act 1989: The Future of Wardship' [1990] Fam Law 270.
4 Section 10 of the Children Act.
5 For a scathing attack on the compulsory sterilisation of the mentally handicapped, see M Freeman 'Sterilising the Mentally Handicapped' in *The Moral Status of Children* (Martinus Nijhoff, 1997), ch 16. See also M Beaupré 'Decision-making and the sterilisation of incompetent children' in A Grubb (ed) *Decision-Making and Problems of Incompetence* (John Wiley & Sons, 1994) at p 89.
6 [1976] Fam 185.

known as 'Sotos syndrome'. While the principles governing sterilisation have been much refined in later cases, *Re D* arguably remains the classic example of judicial intervention in the medical sphere and repays close attention. The symptoms of the disease in this case included accelerated growth during infancy, epilepsy, generalised clumsiness, emotional instability, aggressive tendencies and the impairment of mental function. The girl's widowed mother, fearful that the girl might become pregnant and give birth to an abnormal child, proposed that she be sterilised. The mother had the support of a paediatrician and a gynaecologist who was prepared to perform the operation. Heilbron J held that it was an appropriate case for wardship and that the procedure should be prohibited. It was not in the girl's best interests, since it involved an irreversible procedure of a non-therapeutic nature, which would entail the deprivation of a 'basic human right to reproduce'. The girl's future role in society and subsequent development could not be accurately predicted but there was medical evidence that her condition was improving and that she might, at some future time, acquire the capacity to make an informed choice about the procedure. Thus, it was not a matter which fell within a doctor's sole, clinical judgment and the court should intervene.

The decision in this case was no more than a straightforward application of the welfare principle, ie that it was not in this particular girl's best interests to undergo a sterilisation. This is the characteristic approach of the English courts, and later cases have revealed a marked reluctance to lay down any general guidelines or standards[1]. Hence, it was not possible to extract from this decision any general principle against sterilisation of mentally handicapped minors. It is clear, both from evidence in the case itself, and from later reported cases[2], that sterilisation operations will often be sanctioned where the level of disability is greater than that which was suffered by the girl in *Re D*. Nevertheless, there was, in *Re D*, more than a suggestion that Heilbron J was influenced by what the girl's own view might be on attaining adulthood and making the discovery of what had happened to her whilst a child. This has a flavour of 'substituted judgment' about it, but this was only one element in the judge's thinking[3]. The decision was, in the final analysis for the court, based on what it thought best for the child and this is conceptually distinct

---

1   Thus in *Re B (A Minor) (Wardship: Sterilisation)* [1988] AC 199 the House of Lords rejected any distinction between therapeutic and non-therapeutic sterilisation on the basis that it would detract from the application of the welfare test.

2   See, particularly: *Re M (A Minor) (Wardship: Sterilisation)* [1988] 2 FLR 497; *Re P (A Minor) (Wardship: Sterilisation)* [1989] 1 FLR 182; *T v T* [1988] Fam 52; *Re F (Mental Patient: Sterilisation)* [1990] 2 AC 1; and *Re W (Mental Patient: Sterilisation)* [1993] 1 FLR 381 (young woman aged 20 suffering from severe epilepsy and minor degree of cerebral palsy). In *Re HG (Specific Issue Order: Sterilisation)* [1993] 1 FLR 587, Peter Singer QC (sitting as a deputy High Court judge) held that, in principle, it was possible for an issue such as sterilisation to be the subject of an application for a specific issue order under the Children Act. But he was of the view that such proceedings ought always to be commenced in a district registry of the High Court and that the Official Solicitor should always be involved. For a case in which leave to perform a sterilisation on a severely handicapped 21-year-old was *refused*, the arguments being fairly evenly balanced, see *Re LC (Medical Treatment: Sterilisation)* [1997] 2 FLR 258. See also *Re S (Medical Treatment: Adult Sterilisation)* [1998] 1 FLR 944 where sterilisation of a 22-year-old mentally handicapped young woman, with no understanding of sexuality, was emphatically refused by Johnson J. Here, the risk of sexual exploitation was found to be speculative and not identifiable.

3   Heilbron J clearly attached significance to the evidence that in later years the girl would be able to make her own choice and that 'the frustration and resentment of realising (as she would one day) what had happened, could be devastating'.

from a judicial process which attempts to project what a child would have wanted if she was not suffering from incapacity. The case was significant also from a procedural angle. It revealed that child protection can be dependent on the chance intervention of an interested third party. It thus paved the way for consideration in later cases of the need for a mandatory judicial procedure designed to ensure some consistency in the practice of sterilisation[1].

In *Re B (A Minor) (Wardship: Sterilisation)*[2] (popularly known as '*Jeanette's case*') the more serious case of mental disability, visualised in *Re D*, materialised.

Jeanette was 17 years of age and approaching majority. She had a mental age of five or six years. The evidence was that she was unable to appreciate the causal connection between sexual intercourse and childbirth and would be incapable of consenting to marriage. If she should carry a child to term it was predicted that she would need to be delivered by Caesarean section and that she would thereafter be likely to pick at the operational wound. It was also found that she had no maternal instincts and lacked the ability to care for a child. There was, however, evidence that she was becoming sexually aware and that there was a realistic danger of pregnancy resulting from casual sexual activity. Other methods of contraception were found not be feasible, apart from an oral contraceptive, progesterone. She would be required to take this for the remainder of her reproductive life, the success rate was only 40%, and the long-term side effects were speculative. Sunderland Borough Council, in whose care Jeanette had been since 1973, decided with the support of her mother, that sterilisation was the best course.

The House of Lords upheld the decision of the judge in wardship proceedings and the Court of Appeal that the operation be sanctioned. The reasoning was again based on the single consideration that the procedure was in her best interests. The House of Lords rejected all other criteria which were considered extraneous to the welfare test. Lord Hailsham stressed that the case involved no general issue of public policy and, in particular, had nothing to do with eugenics. Lord Oliver said that the operation was not sought for social purposes, the convenience of those taking care of Jeanette or to allay family anxieties. The House of Lords specifically rejected as unhelpful a Canadian distinction between therapeutic and non-therapeutic purposes, with only the former being regarded as a legitimate reason for sterilisation in Canada[3]. Lord Hailsham thought that any reference to a 'basic human right to reproduce' was meaningless where an individual lacked the mental capacity to make an informed choice in matters of pregnancy and childbirth. Lord Templeman alone expressed the view that sterilisation, as a procedure of last resort, should only be carried out with the leave of a High Court judge. The House was unanimous that the operation was the only way of averting the 'unmitigated disaster' of pregnancy. Since there was some

---

1 Discussed below.

2 [1988] AC 199.

3 *Re Eve* (1987) 31 DLR (4th) I; and see CAP Finch-Noyes 'Sterilisation of the Mentally Retarded Minor: The *Re K* Case' (1986) 5 Can J of FL 277. The matter has also exercised the higher courts in Australia a good deal in recent years, as to which see F Bates 'In the Shadow of Change – Australian Family Law in 1995' in A Bainham (ed) *The International Survey of Family Law 1995* (Martinus Nijhoff, 1997) at pp 29 et seq, and F Bates '"Disputes Do Not Always End Where They Begin": Australian Family Law in 1996' in A Bainham (ed) *The International Survey of Family Law 1996* (Martinus Nijhoff, 1998) at pp 33 et seq.

doubt about whether the court would have jurisdiction once Jeanette reached 18 years of age, it sanctioned performance of the operation without delay[1].

This case rejected the notion that there is any absolute right to reproduce. It showed that, in cases of severe mental handicap, the court's intervention might be required to protect the child's right *not* to reproduce. It was open to the court to determine that it was in the best interests of a minor not be denied medical care which would be available to a competent person and which could guarantee a better lifestyle[2]. At the same time, it is questionable whether the objection to sterilisation for contraceptive or social purposes, as opposed to medical purposes, is sustainable in the light of subsequent decisions[3]. The distinction between therapeutic and non-therapeutic sterilisation, rejected by the House of Lords, was specifically utilised in *Re E (A Minor) (Medical Treatment)*[4] where it was held that parents could consent (without the necessity of going to court) to a therapeutic sterilisation occasioned by the need for a hysterectomy.

There remains some doubt about the criteria which should be used in assessing when a sterilisation is justified in individual cases. These concerns have to some extent been met by a number of Practice Notes[5]. It is now clear that sterilisation, whether of a minor or of a mentally incompetent adult, requires 'in virtually all cases' the prior sanction of a High Court judge. Applications may be either under the inherent jurisdiction of the High Court (the preferred choice of the Official Solicitor) or for a specific issue order. The purpose of the proceedings must be to establish whether or not the proposed sterilisation is in the best interests of the patient. The court will, accordingly, 'require to be satisfied that those proposing sterilisation are seeking it in good faith and that their paramount concern is for the best interests of the patient rather than their own or the public's convenience'. The proceedings, it is said, 'will normally involve a thorough adversarial investigation of all possible viewpoints and any possible alternatives to sterilisation'. The court will require clear evidence establishing:

(1) the mental incapacity of the patient to take the particular decision regarding sterilisation;
(2) that there is a real need for contraception;
(3) that the patient would be likely, in the event of pregnancy or birth, to experience substantial trauma or psychological damage greater than that resulting from sterilisation; and
(4) that there is no appropriate reversible method of contraception available having regard to the most up-to-date medical knowledge in the field.

---

1   It has since been decided that the courts *do* have jurisdiction to grant declarations as to the lawfulness of sterilisations performed on mentally handicapped adults. See *Re F (Mental Patient: Sterilisation)* [1990] 2 AC 1.
2   This was a matter emphasised by Lord Jauncey at 83. It has more than a suggestion of a right to be sterilised which can conveniently be contrasted with Heilbron J's view of the alleged human right to reproduce in *Re D (Sterilisation)* [1976] Fam 185.
3   See fn 2 at p 250 above.
4   [1991] 2 FLR 585.
5   See *J v C (Note)* [1990] 3 All ER 375; *Practice Note: Official Solicitor: Sterilisation* [1993] 2 FLR 222 and *Practice Note: Official Solicitor: Sterilisation* [1996] 2 FLR 111.

The statutory role of the local authority

Where it has come to the attention of social services that a child's health may be jeopardised by potential parental abuse or neglect, or because of a parent's inability to cope, there will be a number of options[1]. As a starting point, the local authority will probably wish to explore the possibility of some form of voluntary social work assistance which could include the temporary accommodation of the child away from home. In *F v Wirral Metropolitan Borough Council*[2], for example, the children had been born with phenylketonuria (PKU), a metabolic disease which can lead to severe mental retardation and which calls for skilled dietary management. The parents were persuaded to allow the children to be cared for by social services and to be boarded out with foster-parents.

Where parents are unwilling to co-operate, the local authority may need to take compulsory action for a care or supervision order[3]. Where the authority is merely concerned to secure authorisation for a medical procedure (rather than to assume the overall care of a child), it may apply for leave to invoke the inherent jurisdiction of the High Court. There have been a number of controversial uses of this jurisdiction, which we discuss in Chapter 11. Where the local authority are refused access to a child whose health is suspected to be at risk, the local authority may apply for a child assessment order or emergency protection order and may obtain a direction that the child be produced for medical or psychiatric examination[4]. The grounds for these orders are considered later. Suffice it to note here that the definition of 'significant harm' includes within it the impairment of the child's health and, for these purposes, health includes physical or mental health[5]. It has been said that this is wide enough to include such matters as poor nutrition, low standards of hygiene, poor emotional care, and failure to seek treatment for an illness or condition[6]. The 'significant harm' test requires a comparison of the state of health of the particular child with that of a hypothetical child with similar attributes[7]. A disabled child, for example, requires a higher standard of care than a normal child. It is not clear how far cultural expectations would be taken into account in applying the test[8].

There was considerable uncertainty before the Children Act concerning the power of local authorities to assume compulsory control of newly born babies whose health was considered to be at risk if left under the control of inadequate or irresponsible parents. The House of Lords had held in *D (A Minor) v Berkshire County Council*[9] that a child requiring intensive care, having been born with

---

1   Public intervention is discussed in greater depth in Chapters 10–12 below.
2   [1991] 2 FLR 114.
3   Under s 31 of the Children Act, discussed in Chapter 11 below.
4   Sections 43 and 44 of the Children Act, discussed in Chapter 12 below. For a general discussion of the medical examination of children under the scheme of the Children Act, see G Brasse 'Examination of the Child' [1993] Fam Law 12.
5   Section 31(9) of the Children Act.
6   J Masson *The Children Act 1989 Current Law Statutes Annotated* (Sweet & Maxwell, 1990).
7   Section 31(10) of the Children Act, which provides: 'where the question of whether harm suffered by a child is significant turns on the child's health or development, his health or development shall be compared with that which could reasonably be expected of a similar child'.
8   Cultural considerations gave rise to difficulty under the old law, as to which see particularly *Alhaji Mohammed v Knott* [1969] 1 QB 1.
9   [1987] 1 All ER 33.

drug-withdrawal symptoms, could legitimately be the subject of a care order based, in part, on the mother's abuse of her own body while pregnant. Despite some academic commentary to the contrary[1], it is now reasonably clear that a care order may be made, if necessary, exclusively on the strength of an apprehended risk to the child's health, even where present harm cannot be established. This is subject to the limitation that the local authority not make a pre-emptive strike *before* the birth of the child. This is because a 'foetus' does not fall within the definition of 'child' in the legislation. The local authority cannot insist on supervision and management of the later stages of pregnancy and the birth itself, however concerned it may be about the mother's situation[2]. As soon as the child is born, protective action may be instigated. In *A Metropolitan Borough Council v DB*[3], for example, an emergency protection order was obtained at birth in relation to the child of a 17-year-old crack cocaine addict. The mother herself had undergone a Caesarean birth following an application to the High Court and was later detained in the maternity ward under judicial authorisation. For discussion of this case in the context of the use of the inherent jurisdiction, see Chapter 11 below.

The child as decision-maker

Another approach to the whole question of medical decision-making would be to allow older children independence of action. The obvious incapacity of young children for rational decision-making precludes this option in their case, but wholly different considerations apply to adolescents. Their factual capacity for self-help prompts the question of how far this should be legally recognised. If the law does recognise the ability of some children to provide or refuse a valid consent to medical treatment, how precisely should this relate to the powers of parents as proxies? Should parental consent be viewed simply as a *substitute* consent to be made available only where the child lacks capacity, or should it be viewed as an *alternative* consent remaining available *despite* the child's capacity? If so, there would then be *concurrent* capacities and this would raise the further issue of priority, in the event of a conflict of opinion. Should the law prioritise the view of the child or that of the parent, or should the medical profession be allowed to determine its own ranking order of consents?

These questions may become yet more complicated by ethical considerations of medical confidentiality[4]. Even if the requirement of parental consent is by-passed, it does not necessarily follow that a parent is not entitled to participate at all in the decision-making process. The issues of parental consent and notification have tended to be conflated in England[5] but have been treated as distinct, especially

---

1   MDA Freeman 'Care After 1991' in D Freestone (ed) *Children and the Law* (Hull University Press, 1990) at ch 6. Cf A Bainham 'Care After 1991 – a Reply' (1991) 3 JCL 99.
2   Neither may the unborn child be made a ward of court nor, presumably, otherwise the subject of the inherent jurisdiction of the High Court. See *Re F (In Utero) (Wardship)* [1988] 2 FLR 307.
3   [1997] 1 FLR 767.
4   The confidentiality issue is treated at length in JK Mason and RA McCall Smith *Law and Medical Ethics* (4th edn) (Butterworths, 1994) at ch 8, especially in relation to minors at pp 178–180.
5   This was so in *Gillick v West Norfolk and Wisbech Area Health Authority* [1986] 1 AC 112 where the issue was whether a doctor might lawfully provide contraceptives to an under-age girl without parental knowledge or consent. There was no direct discussion in the case about whether the issues of knowledge and consent could be separated, although Lord Fraser's requirement that the doctor should always seek to persuade the girl to allow him to involve her parents is perhaps some indication of what his thinking was.

with respect to abortion, in the USA. Certain decisions of the US Supreme Court are thus of considerable interest, provided that due allowance is made for the constitutional setting within which they were made. So far as English law is concerned, there has been no authoritative ruling on the question of when a minor is entitled to have information kept confidential from his parents. Academic commentators seem to be agreed that the *competent* child is entitled to confidentiality to the same extent as an adult patient but opinion is divided on the position of the *immature* or *incompetent* minor[1]. The better view, apparently now accepted by the British Medical Association, is that 'children are entitled to expect confidentiality, quite independently of their consent to treatment'[2]. Given the inherent uncertainties surrounding the evaluation of individual competence, this would seem to be a more practical solution than attempting to differentiate between children for the purposes of confidentiality. A final complication is the power of the State, through the courts, to override the wishes of a mature minor.

All these issues are examined in the context of medical problems arising from adolescent sexuality. A large number of the reported cases in England (with the notable exceptions of *Re R* and *Re W*[3]) have been concerned with either contraception, abortion, or sterilisation for young women, most of whom have been below the age of majority. There is, however, no obvious reason why the principles established in these cases should not be extrapolated to other medical questions.

Medical paternalism – the doctor as decision-maker

Under certain circumstances, the decisive say may be left to the medical personnel concerned; where a doctor declines to carry out a medical procedure which either a parent or child is requesting, this may be stating the obvious. The mere fact that a parent or a young woman wishes, for example, that an abortion or sterilisation be performed, does not lead to the automatic conclusion that a doctor is obliged to perform it. Any doctor would be acting lawfully in refusing to do so unless it would be negligent not to proceed[4].

These principles were graphically illustrated in *R v Cambridge District Health Authority ex parte B*[5]. Here a ten-year-old girl had received extensive treatment for acute myeloid leukaemia including two courses of chemotherapy, total body irradiation and a bone marrow transplant. Sadly, she suffered a further relapse and the doctors who had treated her and other experts concluded that she had a very short time to live and that no further treatment could usefully be

---

1 The arguments either way are rehearsed in J Montgomery *Health Care Law* (Oxford University Press, 1997) at pp 301–304.
2 Ibid at p 304.
3 *Re R (A Minor) (Wardship: Consent to Treatment)* [1992] Fam 11 and *Re W (A Minor) (Medical Treatment: Court's Jurisdiction)* [1992] 3 WLR 758.
4 There is more than a suggestion in *Re F (Mental Patient: Sterilisation)* [1990] 2 AC 1, however, that a doctor could be under a duty arising from the principle of necessity to perform a sterilisation on a mentally handicapped young woman in certain circumstances. Thus, Lord Brandon said that 'it will not only be lawful for doctors on the grounds of necessity to operate on or give other medical treatment to adult patients disabled from giving their consent: it will also be their common law duty to do so'. This was a view with which Lord Goff specifically concurred. On this point, there would seem to be no good reason for distinguishing between the handicapped adult and the handicapped minor.
5 [1995] 1 FLR 1055.

administered. Her father, unwilling to accept this, secured a further medical opinion which gave his daughter a 10% to 20% chance of life if further chemotherapy were carried out and successful, and a second transplant were then successfully performed. The initial cost was projected at £15,000, with the cost of the second transplant being £60,000.

The health authority refused to go ahead on the basis: (i) that the proposed treatment would cause considerable suffering and was not in the child's best interests; and (ii) that the substantial expenditure on treatment with such a small prospect of success and being of an experimental nature would not be an effective use of limited resources bearing in mind the present and future needs of other patients. The child applied, through her father as next friend, for this decision to be quashed in judicial review proceedings.

At first instance she succeeded. Laws J attached considerable importance to her right to life as a fundamental right. He held that the authority had not put forward a sufficiently substantial objective justification on public interest grounds for its decision which infringed this right. However, on appeal, the Court of Appeal emphasised that, in judicial review proceedings, the court's role was only to rule on the *lawfulness* of the authority's decision and not to substitute its own view of the merits. It could not be said here that the authority had exceeded its powers or acted unreasonably in the legal sense. It had been aware of the family's strongly held views but the treatment proposed was at the frontier of medical science and appropriately described as experimental. The authority was entitled also to have regard to the competing claims on its resources.

Much more difficult legal questions arise where the doctor wishes to go ahead and either no one is available to give the consent normally required or someone, be it the child or parent, objects.

The doctrine of necessity

Perhaps the easiest principle to state (although not the easiest to apply) is that, in limited circumstances, the doctrine of necessity will allow the doctor to proceed without any consent at all. The obvious example is an accident. The law allows not only the doctor, but *anyone*, to render first aid to the child, subject only to the requirement that what is done to the child must not exceed what is required by the exigencies of the situation. It is arguable that a doctor would have a legal duty to assist, as would anyone having the care of the child. The case of accidents is a relatively simple one yet, even here, it might become complicated where a conscious child, or a parent on the scene, is refusing emergency aid[1]. The doctrine is difficult to apply in those cases in which there is time to consult parents and, if necessary, obtain judicial authorisation. A difficult case is that of the opposition of parents to blood transfusions on religious grounds. In a succession of cases[2], the courts have been prepared to override the objections of Jehovah's Witnesses, both parents and children, to life-saving blood transfusions. But would the hospitals concerned have been covered by the doctrine of necessity if they had decided to go ahead *without* judicial authorisation and in the face of parental opposition? Given the uncertain application of the doctrine, the better view would seem to be

1   The better view is, however, that the doctor ought to be empowered to take all essential emergency action on the principle of necessity, whatever the parents' view.
2   *Re E (A Minor) (Wardship: Medical Treatment)* [1993] 1 FLR 386, *Re S (A Minor) (Medical Treatment)* [1993] 1 FLR 376, and *Re O (A Minor) (Medical Treatment)* [1993] 2 FLR 149.

that life-saving procedures should only be carried out without parental approval in cases of real emergency in which there is no time to bring the matter to court.

The extent of a doctor's power to act

What, then, is the extent of a doctor's power to act where what is proposed is *not* urgent or necessary but is considered by the doctor to be desirable, and in the best medical interests of the child? In *Re F (Mental Patient: Sterilisation)*[1], the House of Lords held that beneficial medical treatment might be performed on a mentally handicapped *adult* where to do so would save her life or ensure the improvement of, or prevent deterioration in, her mental or physical health. Provided that individual decisions and treatment conformed with medical practice which would be accepted by a responsible body of medical opinion skilled in the particular field, they would be lawful[2]. In earlier cases, it had been suggested that all 'touchings' by the medical profession which conformed to this standard could be lawful on the basis of a general principle that they were not 'hostile' (and therefore non-tortious) if they were 'acceptable in the ordinary conduct of everyday life'[3]. However, in *T v T*[4], Wood J rejected the view that all actions taken in accordance with good medical practice were non-tortious. In his opinion, medical procedures performed without consent were prima facie unlawful unless a justification could be found for them. This position was accepted by the House of Lords in *Re F*. A justification for sterilisation was nevertheless found in the twin concepts of necessity and the best interests of the patient, which appear to have been used interchangeably in this case[5].

---

1   [1990] 2 AC 1.
2   The *Bolam* test, see *Bolam v Friern Hospital Management Committee* [1957] 2 All ER 118 but see now *Bolitho v City and Hackney Health Authority* [1997] 3 WLR 1151 (fn 3 at p 242 above).
3   *Wilson v Pringle* [1987] QB 237 and *Collins v Wilcock* [1984] 3 All ER 374.
4   [1988] Fam 52.
5   Take, for example, the following passage from the speech of Lord Brandon:
    'In my opinion the solution to the problem which the common law provides is that a doctor can lawfully operate on, or give other treatment to, adult patients who are incapable, for one reason or another, of consenting to his doing so, provided that the operation or other treatment concerned is in the *best interests* of such patients. The operation or other treatment will be in their best interests if, but only if, it is carried out in order to save their lives or to ensure improvement or prevent deterioration in their physical or mental health ... the principle is that when persons lack the capacity for whatever reason to take decisions about the performance of operations on them, or the giving of other medical treatment to them, it is *necessary* that some other person or persons, with the appropriate qualifications, should take such decisions for them.' [Emphasis added.]
    It should, however, be noted that this justification can only be used, at least in the case of *adult* patients, where they are *incompetent* to take the particular decision involved. Thus, in *Re C (Refusal of Medical Treatment)* [1994] 1 FLR 31, the court held that it had not been established that a paranoid schizophrenic in Broadmoor lacked the competence to decide whether or not to have his gangrenous leg amputated. An order was therefore made prohibiting the operation without his consent. See also *Re JT (Adult: Refusal of Medical Treatment)* [1998] 1 FLR 48 in which a woman of 25, despite suffering from mental disability involving learning difficulties and extremely severe behavioural disturbances, was found to have the capacity to refuse dialysis for renal failure. As such, Wall J held that it would have been a criminal and tortious assault to perform physically invasive treatment without her consent.

Procedures performed on children without consent

It is not certain how far these principles could be used to justify procedures performed on children without parental consent[1]. It is clear from the *Gillick* case that the medical profession may act in cases of parental abandonment or abuse[2]. It is equally clear that they may obtain the court's authority to act against parents' wishes either in wardship or under the inherent jurisdiction or by seeking a specific issue order. But it has been pointed out by Lavery that a key objection to this process of obtaining judicial approval is that 'it should not be necessary to invoke the court's authority for medical treatment which is clearly in the child's best interests'[3]. Following *Gillick*, a doctor may be able to act against parental wishes where he has the agreement of the child who is herself competent to produce a valid consent. Even though, following *Re R* and *Re W*, the parent retains a concurrent right to consent, the doctor would appear to be acting lawfully in electing to give priority to the child's view[4]. But what of the immature child who would fail the test of *Gillick* competence? Here, the obvious implication of *Gillick* was that the parent's right to give or withhold consent would remain intact and this has been confirmed by the later Court of Appeal decisions. Are there, then, any circumstances under which a doctor may act against parental wishes, in non-urgent cases, because he judges it to be in the child's best interests to do so?

It must be said that, as the law stands, this would be a precarious course of action for the medical profession. Much may turn on how far the courts would be prepared to extend the concept of necessity or apply the reasoning in *Re F*, outside the rather special case of sterilisation. Alternatively, some support for such independent action might be found in those cases which have determined that parental responsibility must be exercised *reasonably* and that where parents exceed the bounds of reasonableness they themselves act unlawfully and may, indeed, commit a criminal offence[5]. The difficulty with relying on these principles is that, in the medical context at least, parents do appear to have been allowed considerable latitude in non-life-saving situations. Thus, a refusal to agree to treatment, even if adjudged undesirable, might still be regarded as falling within a band of reasonable decisions and within the scope of parental discretion.

Dispensing with parental consent

Ruth Lavery has argued convincingly that the concept of necessity should be redefined in its application to immature children. She has advocated the adoption of a principle which would enable a doctor to dispense with parental consent where there is a clear consensus within the medical profession that treatment is for a child's benefit in a given set of circumstances. This would ensure that particular children would not be denied the benefit of treatment, which is clearly in their best interests, because of parental prejudice, phobia or carelessness. On the other hand, the parent's right to consent, she argues, ought to be preserved where there

---

1 For an excellent analysis of the implications of *Re F* for the non-emergency treatment of children, see R Lavery 'Routine Medical Treatment of Children' [1990] JSWL 375.
2 *Gillick v West Norfolk and Wisbech Area Health Authority* [1986] 1 AC 112. Although this situation is not entirely unproblematic in practice: see Lavery (above) at pp 378–379.
3 Ibid at p 377.
4 Discussed further in A Bainham 'Non-Intervention and Judicial Paternalism' in P Birks (ed) *The Frontiers of Liability*, Vol 1 (Oxford University Press, 1994), especially at pp 162–166.
5 See, particularly, *R v D* [1984] AC 778 and *R v Rahman* (1985) 81 Cr App R 349.

is a difference of medical opinion as to what is in a child's best interests or where the decision is not a purely medical one but has other social, moral or long-term implications[1].

Lavery saw her proposal as a 'fairly modest inroad' into the parental right to consent. Once a procedure ranges beyond the routine, the prudent course for the doctor would be to seek the sanction of the court. Even where the doctor is dealing with an adolescent, the interaction of the child's competence and parental responsibility is now so uncertain that the doctor could not be confident about whose view should prevail in law, in the event of a clash – although it is perhaps debatable how far the courts would want to question retrospectively the clinical judgment of the medical profession. These doubts must arise, a fortiori, where the child himself is thought to be possibly incapable of providing a valid consent. The courts may have an increasingly important role in resolving these uncertainties.

THE PROBLEM OF INFANTS AND YOUNG CHILDREN: THE SELECTIVE TREATMENT OF THE NEWBORN

The issue of treating, or not treating, newly born infants with serious medical conditions, illustrates the operation of these principles in an extreme context, where life itself is at stake[2]. The reported cases in England have largely been concerned with neonates but there is no good reason why the principles which have emerged from these decisions should not also be applied to young children[3]. The giving or withholding of life-saving treatment for babies or young children, who are self-evidently incapable of expressing any view, gives rise to a multitude of legal and ethical issues[4].

When may a parent and/or a doctor be liable under the criminal or civil law for refusal to authorise or carry out life-saving treatment? Can the law realistically distinguish for these purposes between acts and omissions? Is, for example, the decision to withhold life-saving surgery or food to be equated with the positive act of administering a drug which has the effect of hastening death? And, in the case of the latter, does it matter that the primary purpose was to relieve pain and suffering and that the acceleration of death was an unavoidable effect of this? Is the duty of the medical profession towards defective newborns the same as it is to 'normal' babies and, if it is not, what are the implications of this for the treatment of handicapped adolescents or adults?

Leaving side the question of criminal liability, the civil law issues are no less complex. What is the extent of parental discretion in this area? How big a part should parents' views play in medical decisions – are doctors bound by them and, if not, how much value ought to be attached to them? When might the State

---

1   See R Lavery 'Routine Medical Treatment of Children' [1990] JSWL 375 at pp 383–384.
2   See JK Mason and RA McCall Smith *Law and Medical Ethics* (4th edn) (Butterworths, 1994) at ch 7, and J Montgomery *Health Care Law* (Oxford University Press, 1997) at ch 18.
3   In fact, two of the leading Canadian cases do involve young children rather than neonates and repay examination for this reason. See *Re Superintendent of Family and Child Service and Dawson* (1983) 145 DLR (3rd) 610 and *Couture-Jacquet v Montreal Children's Hospital* (1986) 28 DLR (4th) 22.
4   These issues were particularly well identified in M Mulholland 'Neo-Natal Care and Treatment – The Doctor's Dilemma' (1989) 5 *Professional Negligence* 109.

intervene, through the local authority or the court, to impose its own view, and on what basis should it do so? If such intervention does occur, whose responsibility does the child become? Do children have an absolute right to life or ought the quality of life to be taken into account – and who decides, and on which criteria, what *is* a worthwhile life? Ought we, for example, to differentiate between those infants who are terminally ill, those who have reasonable prospects of an appreciable life-span and those where the prognosis is uncertain? Finally, and perhaps most importantly, what is the correct allocation of decision-making responsibility where neither the court nor the local authority is involved? Are the prevailing standards and practices of the medical profession conclusive or are there moral and philosophical questions which ought to be outside the exclusive control of the profession?

English law has given a definite response to some of these questions while others remain shrouded in uncertainty.

The Baby Alexandra case

In *Re B*[1], a baby was born in July 1981 with the double disadvantage of Down's Syndrome[2] and duodenal atresia, an intestinal blockage. The latter condition is not uncommon in Down's Syndrome infants but, if not operated upon, death by starvation results. The baby's parents, acting with what was accepted to be the best of motives, thought it kinder to let her die in view of her condition. The doctors concerned contacted the local authority which made her a ward of court. Ewbank J gave care and control to the authority and initially authorised the surgery. But when the baby was transferred to another hospital, surgeons there declined to operate in the face of parental objection. The authority then returned to court but, after hearing the parents' views, Ewbank J refused to consent to the operation. The Court of Appeal heard evidence that other surgeons were available who were prepared to operate. There was a good prognosis for success of the surgery which was thought to give the child a life expectancy of 20 to 30 years – the normal life span of someone with the disorder.

The Court of Appeal, applying the welfare principle, authorised the surgery. Templeman LJ thought that the judge had attached too much weight to parental wishes and was wrong to conclude, in this case, that those wishes should be respected. The issue was what was in the best interests of the child and the test which ought to be applied was whether her life was demonstrably going to be so awful that she should be condemned to die, or whether it was so imponderable that she should be allowed to live. The evidence here was that the operation would give the child the normal life expectancy of a mongoloid child with the handicaps and defects of mongolism. He concluded that it was not for the court (on whom the decision devolved) to say that a life of that description ought to be extinguished. He did, however, visualise more serious cases where 'severe proved damage where the future is so certain and where the life of the child is so bound to

---

1   *Re B (A Minor) (Wardship: Medical Treatment)* (1982) FLR 117. This decision should now be compared closely with *Re T (Wardship: Medical Treatment)* [1997] 1 FLR 502 – see p 266 below.

2   Down's Syndrome, often referred to as 'Mongolism', is a chromosomal aberration occurring in an estimated 1 in 700 live births. It produces mental retardation and is often accompanied by other congenital abnormalities of which the most common are gastro-intestinal blockages and congenital heart defects. Corrective surgery is usually required in the first year of life.

be full of pain and suffering that the court might be driven to a different conclusion'.

Already in this case, several important principles had emerged. First, it confirmed that, in English law, there was no absolute principle that parents' wishes should be respected in life and death cases. The court in wardship had jurisdiction to override them in appropriate cases. Secondly, it was equally clear that the court rejected any absolute right to life in the child. The court had to make a qualitative assessment of the sort of life the child might lead and balance this with the risks involved in the operation. In this case, where the operation was considered to be relatively routine and where the prognosis was good, the balance was in favour of intervening unless the court was prepared to conclude (which it was not) that a life afflicted by Down's Syndrome was not worth living. Thirdly, it was accepted that the responsibility for, and cost of, substitute care for the child should fall on the local authority if the child should ultimately be rejected by the parents following corrective surgery. In this case, adoptive parents were available if necessary[1]. The case left open the question of what the *automatic* legal position might have been had the court not become involved. Since the court here decided that intervention was required by the child's welfare, does this mean that the parents and medical profession, acting in conjunction, would have behaved unlawfully if they had agreed to allow nature to take its course? That no such simple deduction can be made is implicit from the result in the next case.

The trial of Dr Arthur[2]

John Pearson was also born with Down's Syndrome, but without any additional complication. He died within three days of birth and Dr Arthur, a highly respected consultant paediatrician, was charged with his murder – a charge reduced to attempted murder during the course of his trial at Leicester Crown Court[3]. The baby was discovered at birth to have Down's Syndrome and was immediately rejected by the mother. After discussion with both parents, Dr Arthur wrote in the casenotes, 'Parents do not wish the baby to survive. Nursing care only'. On the treatment chart, he prescribed the drug dihydrocodeine (DF 118) to be given 'as required' at doses of 5mg every four hours by the nurse in charge. The baby died 57.25 hours after birth. The cause of death was stated to be broncho-pneumonia resulting from Down's Syndrome. A member of the 'Life' organisation alleged that the baby had been drugged and starved to death. The pathologist's evidence was that the cause of death was lung stasis produced by DF 118 poisoning. The prosecution case was that this was the result of the defendant's decision to cause the death of the child. The jury acquitted Dr Arthur.

---

1   It is understood that, in the event, adoptive parents were not required since the natural parents accepted the child.

2   The case never appeared in the official law reports but was reported in (1981) *The Times*, November 6. Passages from the judge's direction to the jury are extracted in I Kennedy and A Grubb *Medical Law* (2nd edn) (Butterworths, 1994) at pp 1247–1249 and there is a penetrating analysis of the case in MJ Gunn and JC Smith 'Arthur's Case and the Right to Life of a Down's Syndrome Child' [1985] Crim LR 705.

3   The child was found to have been suffering from certain inherent defects at birth so that the precise cause of death was uncertain. Nonetheless, the prosecution was relying in the murder charge on an intention to kill so that the reduction of the charge was of no relevance to the alleged mental state of the doctor. See *R v Whybrow* [1951] 35 Cr App R 141.

Academic opinion is divided on whether the case of Dr Arthur can be said to have established any principles at all. Since it did not reach the higher courts, what is left is a jury decision which can scarcely have value as a legal precedent. Nevertheless, it has been argued that inferential guidance on the principles of the criminal law, within which these decisions must be taken, can be drawn from the directions which Farquharson J gave to the jury[1]. In particular, the judge regarded the distinction between acts and omissions as crucial. He directed the jury to consider whether 'there was an act properly so-called on the part of Dr Arthur, as distinct from simply allowing the child to die'. The judge contrasted the administration of a deliberately lethal dose of a drug (a positive act) with a decision to decline to operate on an intestinal blockage (an omission). No one, he said, could regard the latter as an act of murder. At the same time, he directed that no one, doctors included, had the right to kill a handicapped child any more than they had a right to kill anyone else.

In a powerful critique of this reasoning, Gunn and Smith point out that the criminal law *does* impose liability for omissions where there is a duty to act. Such a duty arises in principle where *anyone*, including a doctor, has physical care of a child. It would include an obligation to provide proper sustenance and medical aid to a 'normal' child[2]. They conclude that the implication of the case is that the duty to an abnormal child must be different from, and lower than, that owed to a normal child. The duty appears to be limited to doing what is reasonable in all the circumstances, something acknowledged by Dunn LJ in the baby Alexandra case, where the parents' decision to allow the child to die was viewed as 'entirely responsible' and could not properly be regarded as an intention to kill.

It is difficult to regard the baby Alexandra case and the case of Dr Arthur as reconcilable. What is clear is that, simply because a court might have exercised *its* discretion in favour of life, it does not mean that parents and doctors exercising *their* discretion in favour of death would automatically commit an offence[3]. The issue of the limits of decision-making powers under the civil law is a quite separate question from that of criminal liability for homicide. But this leads to the unsatisfactory conclusion that neither case could truly be said to have established standards capable of determining, with any precision, the extent of legal duties owed to handicapped infants. And there is a stark incongruity between the life-saving decision for baby Alexandra and the decision to terminate the life of the Pearson baby, who had a comparatively less complicated condition. It is difficult to resist the conclusion that the decisive factor was that the parents and doctors were in agreement in one case but not in the other.

---

1   JK Mason and RA McCall Smith *Law and Medical Ethics* (4th edn) (Butterworths, 1994) at
    pp 151 et seq.
2   'Arthur's Case and the Right to Life of a Down's Syndrome Child' [1985] Crim LR 705 at
    pp 709–711.
3   Ibid.

The case of the hydrocephalic baby: *Re C (A Minor)*[1]

Re C (A Minor) concerned the situation of a terminally ill infant. The local authority had decided, before the child's birth, and without knowledge of her medical abnormality, that the parents would be unable to cope. When the child was born, she was found to be hydrocephalic – a condition involving a blockage of cerebral spinal fluid within the brain. In addition, her brain structure was poorly formed[2]. The issue was whether medical staff should seek to prolong her life and whether they should provide treatment appropriate to a child with her condition or appropriate for a child without this handicap. The Official Solicitor, acting as guardian ad litem, obtained a report from a foremost paediatrician which stated that the aim of treatment should be to ease suffering rather than achieve a short prolongation of life.

In wardship proceedings, Ward J gave leave to the hospital authorities 'to treat the ward to die; to die with the greatest dignity and the least of pain, suffering and distress'. He also gave specific directions that they should not be required to treat any serious infection or set up an intravenous feeding system. On the Official Solicitor's appeal against these directions, the Court of Appeal held that it was appropriate to authorise treatment for the purpose of alleviating suffering but it would accept the opinions of medical staff if they decided that the aim of nursing care should be limited to this and not to achieve a short prolongation of life. But it was not appropriate for the judge's directions to be worded in that way or to be that specific. The directions concerning infections and feeding were therefore removed and the general direction was amended to authorise the hospital authorities 'to treat the minor to allow her life to come to an end peacefully and with dignity'.

The facts of this case were clearly distinguishable from those in the baby Alexandra case. The child in this case was already dying and no treatment could enable her to have a significant future life. Moreover, the existing 'quality' of her life was far removed from that of the Down's Syndrome child. Her brain was incapable of even the most limited intellectual function and she suffered major physical handicaps which *would* render her life demonstrably awful and intolerable. These included a mixture of severe mental handicap, blindness, probably deafness and spastic cerebral palsy of all four limbs. She was already not absorbing food properly or growing. In these circumstances there was a prognosis of an extremely short life and any treatment could be no more than a temporary palliative.

This decision confirmed that there was no absolute right to life and it provided the classic illustration of the more serious case of handicap envisaged in the baby Alexandra case. There were, at the same time, strong echoes of the Dr Arthur case and the refusal of the law to countenance anything which smacks of positive killing.

---

1   *Re C (A Minor) (Wardship: Medical Treatment)* [1989] 2 All ER 782. See J Stone 'Re C – Any Nearer a Solution to the Problem of Severely Handicapped Newborns?' (1989) 1 JCL 1 and D Morgan 'Severely Handicapped Babies and the Courts' (1989) 139 NLJ 723.
2   The most extreme form of brain malformation occurs in anencephalic infants and this entails the absence of all or most of the higher brain. For an illuminating discussion of this condition, see I Kennedy and A Grubb *Medical Law* (2nd edn) (Butterworths, 1994) at pp 1402 et seq.

Hence, the judge's direction required amendment in form if not in substance. While it remains the case that the courts are the final arbiters of what kind of treatment is warranted for a child, the decision in *Re C* revealed that they will usually wish to confine themselves to giving broad directions about the general nature of treatment or non-treatment and will prefer to leave the detailed management of the case to the medical professionals. Beyond this, the case went no further than the baby Alexandra case in articulating, other than indirectly, the scope of parental and medical authority or the standards which should govern these cases.

What then of the child who is *not* terminally ill but whose medical condition is arguably far worse than that of the uncomplicated Down's Syndrome child?

The case of the premature baby: *Re J*[1]

Re J concerned a baby born very prematurely at 27 weeks' gestation. At birth, J weighed 1.1 kg. He was not breathing and was placed on a ventilator and given antibiotics on a drip to avoid infection. His pulse rate remained low for the next 10 days and it was touch and go whether he would survive. At three to four months old, he was taken off the ventilator but thereafter suffered repetitive fits and cessations of breathing requiring resuscitation by ventilation. The prognosis was severe brain damage arising from prematurity. The most optimistic neonatalogist thought that there would be serious spastic quadriplegia. It was likely that J would never be able to sit up or hold his head upright, he would probably be blind and deaf and would be most unlikely to develop even the most limited intellectual abilities. On the other hand, since pain was a very basic response, there was evidence that he would be able to feel pain to the same extent as a normal baby. Life expectancy at its highest was late teens and would probably be considerably shorter.

The issue concerned what should be done in the event of J suffering a further collapse which could occur at any time but was not inevitable. Scott Baker J, at first instance, directed that there should be no further ventilation. The Court of Appeal held that the court could, acting in a child's best interests, approve a medical course of action which failed to prevent death. There was *no* absolute rule that life-prolonging treatment should never be withheld except in the case of a terminally ill child. Nor was the 'demonstrably so awful' test propounded in the baby Alexandra case to be treated as a quasi-statutory yardstick. While there was a strong presumption in favour of life, the court had to have regard to the quality of life, and to any additional suffering which might be caused by the life-saving treatment itself. In assessing the quality of life if treatment were given, the correct approach was to assess whether such a life *judged from the child's viewpoint* would be intolerable to him. In this case, the court authorised treatment within the parameters of a medical report which advised that, in the event of J requiring further resuscitation, it would not be in his best interests for this to be done unless this seemed appropriate to the doctors caring for him in the prevailing clinical situation. Again, the court was at pains to emphasise that what was at issue was not the right to impose death, but rather the right to choose a course of action which would fail to avert it. Where a patient had full capacity, this choice fell to him, but

---

1　*Re J (A Minor) (Wardship: Medical Treatment)* [1990] 3 All ER 930.

where, as an infant, he lacked capacity, the choice had to be a co-operative effort between the parents and the doctors or, where a court was involved, between the court and the medical profession, taking into account the views of the parents. In the end, the conclusion might be legitimately reached that it would not be in the *best* interests of a child to subject him to treatment which would cause increased suffering and no commensurate benefit, while giving full weight to the child's desire to survive.

This case was significant for its apparent application of the 'substituted judgment' test. The court emphasised the need for assessments of the quality of life to be made from the *assumed view of the child patient* and not from that of the adult decision-maker. Thus, severely handicapped people might subjectively find a quality of life rewarding which to normal people would appear intolerable. The doctrine does not sit well with the traditional English approach which, applying the welfare principle, requires the decision-maker to arrive at his own view of what is best for the child[1]. The court here did, of course, have to apply this principle, but it did so in a way which appeared to equate the best interests of the child with a hypothetical projection of what that child would have wished if fully competent. This approach is, arguably, not merely contrary to the usual application of the welfare principle (which as has been seen does not require the actual wishes of competent children to be followed[2]) it also involves the use of a legal fiction. Handicapped neonates have never possessed the capacity to express a rational view on anything and there is, therefore, no basis upon which their supposed wishes can be predicted, except that of the individual judgment of the decision-maker. In reality, it is necessary to fall back on what the court itself thinks would be best for a particular child. The decision confirmed that the court must engage in a balancing exercise in determining the quality of life, if prolonged, against the pain and suffering involved in the treatment itself. It was also a further illustration of the court's preference for deferring to the medical profession's clinical judgment within broadly based guidelines.

Later decisions are further evidence of this approach[3].

---

1 Although it fits better with some theories of children's rights which involve retrospective inquiries about what adults would have wished for themselves while children. See Chapter 3.

2 For a critique of the use of the substituted judgment test in cases like this, see Wells, Alldridge and Morgan 'An Unsuitable Case for Treatment' (1990) 140 NLJ 1544.

3 See *Re J (A Minor) (Medical Treatment)* [1992] 2 FLR 165 (not to be confused with the earlier case under discussion). In this later case, the Court of Appeal held that it would be an abuse of judicial power for the court, in the exercise of its inherent jurisdiction, to require a medical practitioner to treat a minor in a manner contrary to his fundamental duty to exercise his best clinical judgment. In this case, the child aged 16 months suffered from severe cerebal palsy, epilepsy and cortical blindness following a fall. He required 24-hour attention and medical opinion was unanimous that his life expectation was short. The Court of Appeal refused, in these circumstances, to order the health authority to continue with artificial ventilation and other life-saving measures. See also *Re C (A Baby)* [1996] 2 FLR 3, in which Sir Stephen Brown P said that the courts were ready to assist the medical profession with taking responsibility in cases of grave anxiety. In this case, the baby suffered severe brain damage after developing meningitis. She could not survive without continuing artificial ventilation. This would involve her in increasing pain and distress, and the prognosis was hopeless. The medical experts were agreed that further artificial ventilation was not in her best interests and the court in wardship proceedings granted leave to discontinue it. More recently, it has been held, again by Sir Stephen Brown P, that the court may authorise the withdrawal of ventilation for a terminally ill baby where this is advised by the medical team but opposed by the parents. See *Re C (Medical*

The resurgence of parental rights: *Re T*

In October 1996, the Court of Appeal handed down its judgment in *Re T (Wardship: Medical Treatment)*[1]. The decision comes close to reasserting the concept of parental 'rights' in the medical context and has been the subject of critical academic comment[2]. The baby, C, suffered from a life-threatening liver defect known as biliary artresia. There was a unanimous medical prognosis that without a liver transplant C could not live beyond the age of two-and-a-half years, but the prospects of success were thought to be good if a donor liver became available. All the medical experts thought it was in C's best interests to undergo such an operation but the parents (who were unmarried[3]) were opposed to it. The case undoubtedly had special features. Both parents were health care professionals with experience of caring for sick children; C had previously undergone unsuccessful surgery which had caused him much pain and distress; and the parents had, albeit against medical advice, gone to a 'distant Commonwealth country'. The issue was whether the mother should be ordered to return to the jurisdiction with C and present him to hospital for liver transplantation assessment.

At first instance, Connell J held that she should, but he appeared to ground his decision on an assessment that the mother's opinion was unreasonable, rather than on a straightforward application of the welfare principle. Allowing the mother's appeal, the Court of Appeal emphasised that the matter was governed by the welfare principle. While there was a strong presumption in favour of life, prolonging life was not the court's sole objective. The judge, it was held, had failed to give adequate weight to certain factors which ought to have been fed into the welfare test. According to Butler-Sloss LJ, he had given insufficient emphasis to 'the enormous significance of the close attachment between the mother and baby' and 'whether it [was] in the best interests of C for [the court] in effect to direct the mother to take on this total commitment where she [did] not agree with the course proposed'. Roch LJ thought that there was a clinical aspect to the bond between mother and child 'because in the absence of parental belief that a transplant [was] the right procedure for the child, the prospects of a successful outcome [were] diminished'.

As we have seen, there is nothing unusual or unprincipled about a court refusing life-saving surgery to a child in an appropriate case. What makes the decision in *Re T* so controversial is the close association which the Court of Appeal was prepared to make between the interests of the mother and the child and this gives the case an importance which goes beyond the fate of the individual child. Here, the focus of the court's attention went beyond the child's best *medical* interests which had, it is submitted, been the decisive factor in the earlier cases. It was prepared to attach significance to the issues surrounding the care of the child

---

Treatment) [1998] 1 FLR 384, in which the parents were Orthodox Jews and did not believe that their religion permitted them to contemplate a course of action which would indirectly shorten life.

1   [1997] 1 FLR 502.
2   See particularly M Fox and J McHale 'In Whose Best Interests?' (1997) MLR 700, and A Bainham 'Do Babies Have Rights?' (1997) CLJ 48.
3   The significance of their being unmarried was that sole parental responsibility was with the mother although it was clear, in any event, that the father agreed with her.

in the event of a successful operation – yet nowhere was there the suggestion, as there was in the baby Alexandra case (above), that if necessary the State should be prepared to provide a substitute home. It was sufficient for Butler-Sloss LJ that C's future treatment 'should be left in the hands of his devoted parents'. Waite LJ thought it unhelpful to indulge in 'rights-talk'. This was 'not an occasion – even in an age preoccupied with "rights" – to talk of the rights of the child, or the rights of a parent, or the rights of the court'[1]. Whether or not it is jurisprudentially accurate to assert 'rights' for children or parents, the real criticism of this ruling is that it fails to differentiate sufficiently between the *interests* of the mother and the child which were assumed to coincide but which, it might be argued, were in conflict. In Waite LJ's opinion, 'in the last analysis the best interest of every child incudes an expectation that difficult decisions affecting the length and quality of its life will be taken for it by the parent to whom its care has been entrusted by nature'. Yet to take this literally would be to turn the clock back to the nineteenth century and ignore the advances made for children as persons over the last hundred years.

Quality of life over sanctity of life

These reported decisions have firmly rejected the sanctity of life approach in favour of a *quality* of life approach to the treatment of defective newborns. They establish, beyond question, that there is no absolute duty to save life, either on the part of parents, or the medical profession, and they draw a theoretical distinction between acts of positive killing and omissions which do not prevent natural death occurring. It is, of course, true that the medical profession has a certain duty to act in the interests of the patient so that the distinction between acts and omissions can be somewhat artificial in this context. It is also true that positive acts, such as the administration of drugs which are designed to alleviate pain and suffering, can have the 'double effect' of also hastening death. The most difficult question is the *extent* of the doctor's duty to act and it seems that this now turns on the notoriously vague notion of 'reasonableness'. The effect of the House of Lords decision in *Airedale NHS Trust v Bland*[2] is that a doctor would be acting lawfully in allowing a patient to die if a responsible body of medical opinion would support that course of action in the circumstances as being in the patient's best interests. This is effectively an application in life-saving cases of the *Bolam* test for medical negligence[3]. A principle of proportionality appears to have emerged whereby a qualitative assessment of the life of the child must be made and this must be balanced with an evaluation of the treatment required to sustain that quality of life.

Yet these principles are themselves problematic and there remain many unanswered questions. It is not obvious that a sensible distinction can really be drawn between acts and omissions. It is even less clear that, if such a distinction can indeed be made, there is a valid moral distinction between failing to keep a child alive and actively helping to hasten death. It may be that a more justifiable moral

---

1   On children's rights as a concept, see Chapter 3.
2   [1993] 2 WLR 316. For recent applications of the *Bland* decision in relation to adults, see *Re D (Medical Treatment)* [1998] 1 FLR 411, *Re D (Medical Treatment: Mentally Disabled Patient)* [1998] 2 FLR 22 and *Re H (A Patient)* [1998] 2 FLR 36.
3   But see now the refinement of the test in *Bolitho v City and Hackney Health Authority* [1997] 3 WLR 1151 (above).

distinction can be drawn between different kinds of acts and different kinds of omissions. Refusing surgical intervention is arguably of a quite different moral order than withholding food. But the greatest area of concern must be the absence of accepted standards or guidelines to regulate the decisions taken by parents, in conjunction with the medical profession, in the large number of cases which never reach the courts. There is substantial evidence that the decision about whether to treat or not to treat a child is significantly influenced by parental attitudes. A decision to withhold life-saving treatment is much more likely to be taken where parents desire it. Looking at the matter from a children's rights perspective, the question must be whether the unequal treatment of children with like disorders, for example two essentially similar cases of uncomplicated Down's Syndrome, can be justified largely, if not entirely, on the basis of parents' preferences[1]. It might be argued that children's rights demand like treatment for like cases, making due allowance for the fact that no two cases are wholly identical.

Children's rights to equality of treatment

The concern to try to ensure a measure of equality of treatment led to successive attempts in the USA, at both the federal and State levels, to formulate legal standards to govern the circumstances under which non-treatment is allowable[2]. It has also led to proposals in England for legislation to regulate, admittedly in a broad way, medical practice in this area[3]. What kind of standards then could be evolved? One possibility is that a relatively plain distinction could be drawn between purely *mental* defects and severe *physical* defects. Selective non-treatment of the latter could be justified, in certain circumstances, since the state of the physical disorder might mean that the child in question would die anyway and that nature should, therefore, take its course. On the other hand, children with purely mental disorders will not die unless 'encouraged and guided towards death' by some positive act and, for these purposes, an instruction to withhold food can be viewed as such[4]. A distinction like this may mean that the non-treatment of an uncomplicated Down's Syndrome child could *never* be justified, whereas clearly it could be justified in the case of a hydrocephalic or anencephalic child. Between these extremes there would, undoubtedly, be difficult judgments to be made. What view, for example, ought to be taken of spina bifida and how can the line be drawn between different levels of severity of particular disorders[5]? The formulation and application of statutory standards would inevitably be contentious but

---

1   For children's rights perspectives, see Chapter 3 above.
2   These were triggered by the *Baby Doe* case; as to which see J Dunsay Silver 'Baby Doe: The Incomplete Federal Response' (1986) 20 Fam LQ 173.
3   JK Mason and RA McCall Smith *Law and Medical Ethics* (4th edn) (Butterworths, 1994), propose, at p 162, the adoption of a single clause Bill and suggest the following draft clause:
      'In the event of positive treatment being necessary for a neonate's survival, it will not be an offence to withhold such treatment if two doctors, one of whom is a consultant paediatrician, acting in good faith and with the consent of both parents if available, decide against treatment in the light of a reasonably clear medical prognosis which indicates that the infant's further life would be intolerable by virtue of pain or suffering or because of severe cerebral incompetence.'
4   Ibid at pp 156–157.
5   Some of these difficulties are addressed ibid at pp 159–162.

would at least address the inescapable problem that, in numerical terms at least, what happens in the cases which do not reach court is of much greater practical significance than what happens in the few which do[1].

THE PROBLEM OF OLDER CHILDREN: MEDICAL ISSUES ARISING FROM ADOLESCENT SEXUALITY

Section 8(1) of the Family Law Reform Act 1969 provides that:

'... the consent of a minor who has attained the age of sixteen years to any surgical, medical or dental treatment ... shall be as effective as it would be if he were of full age; and where a minor has by virtue of this section given an effective consent to any treatment it shall not be necessary to obtain any consent for it from his parent or guardian.'

This provision clarified the position regarding young people of 16 and 17 years of age, by conferring on them legal capacity to provide a valid consent to treatment, and dispensing with the normal requirement of parental consent. The Family Law Reform Act 1969 did not deal directly with the question of a clash between the views of a 16-year-old and his parents, but the implication appeared to be that, at least where the minor was consenting, this could be effective to override any parental objection. The position was somewhat less clear in the converse situation, where the minor was *objecting* and the parent was purporting to consent. The better view seemed to be that the effect of the provision was to confer complete independence in medical decision-making on the 16-year-old – in effect to equate his position with that of an adult. On this interpretation, the objection of the minor would be conclusive. This view now cannot be sustained as a matter of law in the light of the Court of Appeal decisions in *Re R* and *Re W*[2].

Uncertainty surrounded the position of those under 16 years of age where perhaps four major issues are involved:

(1) Can the child under 16 years of age ever have legal capacity to take independent medical decisions?
(2) What are the limits of parental authority?
(3) What is the effect of the child's competence on the legal responsibility of parents? Does the child's view prevail and are parents entitled to be involved at all in the decision-making process?
(4) When may the courts intervene to override the wishes of parents and/or the views of a competent child?

The answer to these questions must now be gleaned from three leading cases – *Gillick v West Norfolk and Wisbech Area Health Authority*, *Re R* and *Re W*[3]. *Gillick* was concerned only with the first three questions, while *Re R* and *Re W* were directly concerned with the fourth but have reopened the debate about the other issues.

---

1 Mason and McCall Smith (above) on balance, prefer legislation to the alternative of hospital ethical committees.
2 [1992] Fam 11 and [1992] 3 WLR 758, respectively.
3 [1986] 1 AC 112, [1992] Fam 11, and [1992] 3 WLR 758, respectively.

The *Gillick* case

Background

In 1980, the then Department of Health and Social Security issued a notice[1] to the effect that, although it would be 'most unusual', a doctor could, in exceptional circumstances, lawfully give contraceptive advice or treatment to a girl under 16 years of age without prior parental consultation or consent. In so doing, he would be required to act in good faith to protect her against the harmful effects of sexual intercourse. Victoria Gillick, a Roman Catholic mother, with five daughters then under 16 years of age, objected to this advice and sought assurances from her area health authority that no minor daughter of hers would receive such advice or treatment without her permission. When she failed to receive a response acceptable to her, she applied for a declaration that the advice in the Circular was unlawful.

In what was arguably to become the most significant twentieth-century decision on the legal relationship between parents and children, Victoria Gillick lost at first instance, won unanimously in the Court of Appeal and eventually lost to a 3–2 majority in the House of Lords. Such was the measure of judicial disagreement at the time, and the analysis of the two principal majority speeches of Lord Scarman and Lord Fraser continues to provide a fertile source of argument both academic and judicial[2].

Doctor as secondary party to offence of unlawful sexual intercourse

Victoria Gillick advanced several arguments in support of her claim. The first of these is noted only briefly here, since it concerned the scope of the criminal law and is peripheral to the present discussion[3]. The argument that a doctor who provided contraceptives to a girl under 16 years of age would be a secondary party to the offence of unlawful sexual intercourse[4] was rejected by four of the five Law Lords, following the reasoning of Woolf J at first instance. This was, in essence, that, while the doctor who provided contraceptives *with the intention* of encouraging the commission of the offence would be liable, the doctor who acted in compliance with the DHSS advice would not necessarily commit the offence. His motives were much more likely to be to protect the girl from the possible adverse consequences of sexual intercourse, including unwanted pregnancy and/or abortion, and not to encourage the offence[5].

---

1   HN (80) 46.
2   The major academic commentaries include: J Eekelaar 'The Eclipse of Parental Rights' (1986) 102 LQR 4; G Williams 'The Gillick Saga' (1985) 135 NLJ 1156 and 1169; A Bainham 'The Balance of Power in Family Decisions' (1986) CLJ 262; and SM Cretney 'Gillick and the Concept of Legal Capacity' (1989) 105 LQR 356. For a more recent assessment of the issues surrounding adolescent autonomy in the medical arena, see M Brazier and C Bridge 'Coercion or Caring: Analysing Adolescent Autonomy' (1996) *Legal Studies* 84. Judicial disagreement is perhaps best illustrated by the apparent reluctance of Farquharson and Staughton LJJ to associate themselves with the more wide-ranging remarks of Lord Donaldson MR in *Re R* [1992] Fam 11.
3   Chapter 14 below considers the protective function of the criminal law in relation to children.
4   Offences Against the Person Act 1861, s 6. The girl herself does not commit an offence on the basis that the criminal law exists for her own protection: *R v Tyrell* [1894] 1 QB 710.
5   While this may have been a sound decision on policy grounds, it is rather more difficult to justify as a correct application of legal principle since the criminal law distinguishes between

Issue 1: capacity of child under 16 years to provide valid consent

The first issue was whether a girl under 16 years old could ever provide a valid consent and thus prevent the commission of the tort of battery by the doctor[1]. The Family Law Reform Act 1969 did not address the position of those under 16 years of age, but it did provide in s 8(3) that 'nothing in this section shall be construed as making ineffective any consent which would have been effective if this section had not been enacted'. The majority held that the cumulative effect of this provision and s 8(1) was simply to avoid doubt in relation to those *over* 16 years old. The child *under* 16 years did not lack capacity by virtue of age alone, but acquired it, according to Lord Scarman, when 'he reaches a sufficient understanding and intelligence to be capable of making up his own mind on the matter requiring decision'. The test propounded by Lord Scarman involves an individualistic assessment of a particular child's level of maturity and intellectual ability. The clear implication is that, if a child fails the test of competence, the doctor will need to look to a person with parental responsibility for a proxy consent and that to go ahead without this will be to risk committing a tort on the child. Further, to make an incorrect assessment of competence will likewise be to run the risk of committing a tort if the matter should subsequently be taken to court. *Gillick* was concerned with the child's capacity to *give* consent and not expressly with the child's capacity to *refuse* it, but many commentators at the time thought that the two must stand or fall together[2].

A key question is what precisely must be understood by the child in order to achieve '*Gillick* competence'? Lord Scarman envisaged that a high level of understanding would be required, extending beyond the purely medical issues. Dealing specifically with contraception, he said:

> 'It is not enough that she should understand the nature of the advice which she is being given: she must have sufficient maturity to understand what is involved. There are moral and family questions especially her relationship with her parents, long-term problems associated with the emotional impact of pregnancy and its termination and there are risks to health of sexual intercourse at her age, risks which contraception may diminish but cannot eliminate. It follows that a doctor will have to satisfy himself before he can safely proceed on the basis that she has at law capacity to consent to contraceptive treatment.'

It will be seen, following *Re R* and *Re W*, that a similarly high level of competence is evidently demanded where a child is *objecting* to a medical procedure.

Issue 2: the limits of parental authority

The second issue relates to the legal limits on parental authority and, here, the majority in the House of Lords was quite clear that parental power was not absolute. According to Lord Scarman 'parental rights are derived from parental duty and exist only so long as they are needed for the protection of the person or property of the child'. Lord Fraser emphasised that such rights existed for the benefit of the *child* and not for the benefit of the parent.

---

motive and intention, concerning itself only with the latter. See JC Smith and B Hogan *Criminal Law* (8th edn) (Butterworths, 1996) at pp 81 et seq.

1 It should be said that while a medical examination involving 'touching' would clearly be tortious without an appropriate consent it is difficult to see how the giving of advice about contraception or the prescription of contraceptive pills could have this tortious character.

2 But this has now been exploded by Lord Donaldson's remarks in *Re R* [1992] Fam 11 and by the decision in *Re W (A Minor) (Medical Treatment: Court's Jurisdiction)* [1992] 3 WLR 758 which drew a distinction between *consent* and *refusal*.

Issue 3: the clash of views – whose view prevails?

The third issue was the effect of a child achieving competence on the parental 'right' to give or withhold consent. Whose view should be decisive in the event of disagreement? Both Lord Scarman and Lord Fraser were of the opinion that a doctor could, in certain circumstances, proceed on the competent child's consent alone, but Lord Scarman appeared to take a more radical view than Lord Fraser of the effect of the child acquiring capacity[1]. According to Lord Scarman 'the parental right yields to the child's right to make his own decisions when he reaches a sufficient understanding and intelligence to be capable of making up his own mind on the matter requiring decision'[2]. This was interpreted by one commentator quite literally to mean that the attainment of competence by the child would *terminate* parental responsibility over the matter in question and would give to the child an *exclusive* right to decide[3]. Lord Fraser, on the other hand, adopted a more guarded approach. In his view, the mere acquisition of capacity would not, per se, enable a doctor to proceed without parental notification or consent. Lord Fraser laid down five further conditions which would have to be satisfied in order that the doctor could proceed without parental notification or consent:

'(1) that the girl will understand his advice;
(2) that he cannot persuade her to inform her parents or allow him to do so;
(3) that she is very likely to begin or to continue having sexual intercourse with or without contraceptive treatment;
(4) that unless she receives advice or treatment her physical or mental health or both are likely to suffer; and
(5) that her best interests require him to act without consent.'[4]

These extra requirements might have been explained away on the basis that they are not strict legal requirements but rather matters which pertain only to good professional practice[5]. But, equally, Lord Fraser's formulation might have been interpreted as one which supports a *participatory* decision-making process in which neither the parents nor the child would have the sole right to decide. The final decision would rather rest with the doctor who would take into account the girl's own capacity and wishes, if possible the views of the parents, and would then make an evaluation of her best medical and other interests before deciding whether to proceed. Such an interpretation would be in keeping with the tradition of medical paternalism in England[6]. Certainly, Lord Fraser did not appear to think that a competent girl was entitled to contraceptives on demand.

The precise inter-relationship of adolescent capacities and parental responsibility was thus the subject of considerable speculation and this has now been accentuated by obiter remarks of Lord Donaldson in the Court of Appeal and by the later decision in *Re W (A Minor) (Medical Treatment: Court's Jurisdiction)*.

Issue 4: extent of the courts' powers over adolescents

The *Gillick* case was not directly concerned with the extent of the courts' jurisdiction over adolescents. It has fallen to the Court of Appeal to define the

---

1 Lord Bridge, unhelpfully for present purposes, simply agreed with both of them.
2 [1986] 1 AC 112 at 186.
3 J Eekelaar 'The Eclipse of Parental Rights' (1986) 102 LQR 4.
4 [1986] 1 AC 112 at 174.
5 J Eekelaar (above).
6 This is the position taken by A Bainham in 'Growing Up in Britain: Adolescence in the

limits of their powers in *Re R* and *Re W*. While *Re R* was concerned with a young person *under* the age of 16, crucially *Re W* involved a young person *over* 16. This gave the court the opportunity of ruling upon the relationship between s 8 of the Family Law Reform Act 1969 and the courts' powers under the inherent jurisdiction.

Re R

Background

Re R[1] was not concerned with issues of adolescent sexuality but with the competence of an adolescent to *refuse* certain medical procedures – in this case the forcible administration of sedative drugs. The principles can nevertheless be applied to questions such as contraception, abortion or sterilisation.

R was a young woman aged 15 years and 10 months at the time of the hearing. Following a history of mental disturbances and a deterioration in her mental health, she entered the care of the local authority and was, in due course, placed in an adolescent psychiatric unit. She had a mental condition which fluctuated between periods of lucidity and rationality and times when she displayed 'florid psychotic symptoms'. In these latter periods, she was considered a serious suicide risk and 'sectionable' under the Mental Health Act 1983. As part of its regime, the unit used sedative drugs as a last resort. It indicated to the local authority (which had parental responsibility for R) that it was not prepared to retain her unless its whole regime, including medication where appropriate, was accepted by it. Initially, the local authority acceded to this, but later withdrew its consent following a long telephone conversation between R and one of its social workers. R indicated, during this conversation, that the unit were trying to give her drugs which she neither wanted nor needed. The social worker was of the opinion that R was lucid and rational during the conversation, and this view of her mental state was subsequently confirmed by a consultant child psychiatrist. The authority made R a ward of court to resolve the disagreement.

Gillick competence – can it be overridden?

In the proceedings, the unit sought leave to administer such medication as was medically necessary, including anti-psychotic drugs, without R's consent. The Official Solicitor, acting as guardian ad litem, opposed this. His principal argument was that, where a child had capacity to withhold consent to treatment (based on sufficient understanding and intelligence to comprehend fully what was proposed) any parental right to give or withhold consent terminated. He argued further that, since, in wardship, the court steps into the shoes of a parent, the court could have no greater power to give or withhold consent. The two main issues were, therefore, whether R was '*Gillick*-competent' and, if so, whether the court would have power to override her wishes. These were the only issues directly raised, but Lord Donaldson MR felt it necessary to reopen the whole question of the relationship between the capacity of a competent minor and a parent's right to consent on a minor's behalf.

---

post-*Gillick* Era' (1992) *Juridical Review* 155 and which, it is submitted, is reflected in the later Court of Appeal decisions in *Re R* and *Re W*.

1 *Re R (A Minor) (Wardship: Consent to Treatment)* [1992] Fam 11.

Competence as a developmental concept

The Court of Appeal upheld the decision of Waite J, that R failed the test of competence and that it was in her best interests for the treatment to be authorised. The court rejected the idea that competence could fluctuate from day to day or week to week. Competence was seen as a developmental concept, although it was acknowledged that a child could be competent for some purposes but not for others. But the *extent* of competence regarding any particular matter (in this case, medication) could not be variable. Farquharson LJ even doubted that *Gillick* could sensibly be applied at all to 'on/off' situations where the impact of a mental illness had to be taken into account. In his view, mental state and capacity could not be isolated from the medical history and background. Lord Donaldson emphasised, as Lord Scarman had in *Gillick*, that the acquisition of capacity was no easy matter. It required not only the ability to understand the procedure of compulsory medication but also 'a full understanding and appreciation of the consequences both of the treatment in terms of the intended and possible side effects and, equally important, the anticipated consequences of a failure to treat'[1]. She would particularly need to be aware of the risk that she might lapse into her former psychotic state, and of the possible harmful consequences of this to herself.

Determination and consent

Despite the court's decision that R was not *Gillick*-competent, Lord Donaldson alone made controversial obiter remarks about what the position would have been had she been adjudged competent. He used the metaphor of keys and locks to illustrate what he took to be the position. Consent was a key which could unlock a door. Both the competent child and the parent were keyholders but neither had a master key. Thus, *either* the child's key *or* the parent's key could unlock the door and open it for the doctor to proceed. He thus drew a distinction between *determination* and *consent*. The former, he said, was a wider concept than the latter since it implied a right of veto. He interpreted Lord Scarman's speech in *Gillick* to mean that it was this right of *determination* which terminated where the child achieved a state of competence. In other words, the parent would, at that point, lose the *exclusive* right to consent. But this did not mean that the parent's independent right to consent would be lost. The parent and child in these circumstances would enjoy *concurrent* rights to consent and it would be open to a doctor to act on either consent. Otherwise, said Lord Donaldson, a doctor would be faced with the 'intolerable dilemma' of having to choose between two potentially valid, but also potentially invalid, consents. An incorrect assessment of maturity might then expose the doctor to criminal or tortious liability. He was also of the opinion that the same principles applied to a young person over 16 years, notwithstanding s 8(1) of the Family Law Reform Act 1969. He adopted a literal interpretation of this provision to the effect that, whilst it was necessary for a doctor to secure parental consent in relation to a young person of 16 years of age, there was nothing to preclude him from acting on a parent's consent alone.

---

1   [1991] 4 All ER 177 at 187.

Power of the court to override consent

The most significant issue in this case, since it had not been addressed in *Gillick*, was whether the court, exercising its protective jurisdiction was empowered to override the wishes of a competent minor[1]. Here, the court held that such a power existed, since the *Gillick* reasoning had no application in wardship proceedings[2]. The court's powers, it was said, were not derived from parents but from the Crown's duties of protection[3]. The court had wider powers than those enjoyed by natural parents including, for example, the power to restrain the publication of information about a child or the power to grant injunctions restraining contact between the child and others. It was also beyond doubt that the court could override the wishes of parents in exercising its powers of protection[4]. By analogy, there was no reason why it should not override the wishes of a competent minor if this was thought to be in her best interests. In wardship, this was the court's sole objective and it was perfectly possible that the application of the welfare test and the *Gillick* test could lead to different results. Whilst the issue had not been directly raised before, there was ample previous authority which had assumed that the court was not obliged to follow the wishes of a mature child[5].

Re W

The principles governing the role of the courts in relation to adolescents and medical decision-making were further considered in the important decision of the Court of Appeal in *Re W (A Minor) (Medical Treatment: Court's Jurisdiction)*[6]. The decision proved no less controversial than that in *Re R*[7].

In this case, it was held that the High Court could properly exercise its inherent jurisdiction over children[8] to order a 16-year-old girl, suffering from anorexia nervosa, to be transferred, against her wishes, to a London unit specialising in the treatment of eating disorders. The court extended the reasoning in *Re R* to 'children' over 16 years having prima facie capacity to consent under s 8 of the Family Law Reform Act 1969. It held unanimously that that section had not been

---

1   The court's decision on this point was, strictly speaking, obiter since R was adjudged *incompetent*. Nevertheless, it was the principal point of law in the case and one which was unanimously answered by all three judges.

2   Although the court was specifically only concerned with wardship, there is no reason why the logic cannot be applied to other jurisdictions.

3   In fact, the analogy between natural and judicial parenthood was always a rather crude and imperfect one. See A Bainham 'Handicapped Girls and Judicial Parents' (1987) 103 LQR 334.

4   Many examples of this power might be cited, but one in the medical arena is *Re B (Wardship: Abortion)* [1991] 2 FLR 426 where the wish of a 12-year-old girl to have an abortion, supported by a grandparent, was upheld by the court in the face of objection by her mother. The court took the view that the operation was in her best medical interests.

5   See, particularly, the abortion cases of *Re P (A Minor)* [1986] 1 FLR 272 and *Re G-U (A Minor) (Wardship)*[1984] FLR 811.

6   [1992] 3 WLR 758.

7   It was the subject of extensive critical comment. See, for example, J Eekelaar 'White Coats or Flak Jackets? Doctors, Children and the Courts – Again' (1993) 109 LQR 182, and J Masson 'Re W: Appealing from the Golden Cage' (1993) 5 JCL 37. The decisions of *Re R* and *Re W* were followed in controversial circumstances by Thorpe J in *Re K, W and H (Minors) (Medical Treatment)* [1993] 1 FLR 854 (a case which also raised significant issues of representation of children, which we discuss in Chapter 13 below) and by Douglas Brown J in *South Glamorgan County Council v W and B* [1993] 1 FLR 574.

8   On the distinction between the inherent jurisdiction and wardship, see Chapter 11 below.

designed to confer absolute autonomy on 16-year-olds in medical matters but rather to enable them to provide a consent upon which the medical profession could safely act without incurring legal liability. The court's jurisdiction had not been excluded by the Act and, owing to the serious deterioration in W's health, this was a case in which the court should act. Lord Donaldson (now joined by Balcombe LJ) also reiterated his view in *Re R* that a parent might provide a *concurrent* consent in the case of a '*Gillick*-competent child', although he cast off the metaphor of the 'keyholder' which he had employed in *Re R*, for that of the legal 'flak jacket'. According to this, consent is a flak jacket which protects the doctor from legal actions. He can acquire it from a child over 16 years (under s 8), *or* a *Gillick*-competent child under 16 years, *or* someone with parental responsibility – but he only needs one consent. The decision is in much the same vein as *Re R*, and together the two cases compound the uncertainties about the inter-relationship of adolescent capacities and parental responsibility. The issue must surely return to the House of Lords.

The decisions in *Re R* and *Re W* should now also be read with other recent decisions of the higher courts evincing a greater willingness to make paternalistic interventions in the case of *adults*[1]. If the courts are willing to intervene in the case of adults, the objection to doing so in the case of children (at least if based on the unwarranted differential treatment of children and adults) rather falls apart. The issue of the proper limits of State paternalism in either case, of course, remains[2].

The recent decision of the Court of Appeal in *St George's Healthcare National Health Service Trust v S*[3] perhaps heralds a new era in which the courts may be less willing to intervene paternalistically in the case of adults. Here, the court held that a pregnant woman could not be forced to undergo a Caesarean section even where her objections were bizarre and irrational and contrary to the views of the overwhelming majority of the community at large. This was so even where her own

---

1   See particularly *Re S (Adult: Surgical Treatment)* [1993] 1 FLR 26 in which Sir Stephen Brown P granted a declaration that a health authority, through its medical staff, could lawfully perform an emergency Caesarean section on a 30-year-old woman on the grounds that it was in her best interests and those of her unborn child. She had refused her consent on religious grounds but the medical evidence was that the 'transverse lie' of the child constituted a grave threat to the lives of both mother and child which could only be saved by the operation. See also *Re T (An Adult) (Consent to Medical Treatment)* [1992] FLR 458 in which the Court of Appeal sanctioned a blood transfusion where the patient (who had been raised by her mother as a Jehovah's Witness) had apparently refused consent. In this case the decision was, however, based in part on the view that the patient's purported refusal may have been the product of external influence and thus not a genuine refusal. Nonetheless, the decision is perhaps evidence of a greater willingness to intervene in emergency situations in which the concept of necessity may apply. More recently, in *Re L (Patient: Non-Consensual Treatment)* [1997] 2 FLR 837, Kirkwood J granted a declaration that it would be lawful for a hospital trust to insert needles for the purposes of anaesthesia and intravenous infusion and to perform an emergency Caesarean section on a young woman in her twenties who had been in labour all day. She had agreed in principle to a Caesarean birth but had an extreme needle phobia. It was clear that anaesthesia by any other method was utterly contra-indicated and that in the absence of intervention the baby would die. The court held that her extreme phobia amounted to involuntary compulsion which prevented her from taking a balanced decision and that the treatment advocated was in her best interests.
2   For further discussion, see A Bainham 'Children, Parents and the Law: Non-Intervention and Judicial Paternalisation' in Peter Birks (ed) *The Frontiers of Liability* (Oxford University Press, 1993).
3   (1998) *The Times*, May 8.

life depended on receiving medical interventions and where failure to consent would result in the death of her unborn child. The court further held that a person detained under the Mental Health Act 1983 for mental disorder could not be forced into medical procedures unconnected with her mental condition unless her capacity to consent to such treatment was diminished. It is interesting to speculate on whether the result might have been different here if the person concerned had been an adolescent young woman of, say, 16 or 17. Would the court have been justified in intervening, and if so, on what basis?

Cumulative effect of the leading cases

What then is the cumulative effect of *Gillick*, *Re R* and *Re W*? The only principle which can be stated with any confidence, is that the court has jurisdiction to overrule the parents, the child, the medical profession or, indeed, all of them in performing its protective functions and, even here, there are arguments about whether it should do so. The distribution of decision-making power which arises by operation of law is now a matter of considerable uncertainty and it is extremely difficult to state the law with any precision. Perhaps this is an inevitable hazard of an appellate system, in which multiple opinions are delivered. Thus, in *Gillick* only three Law Lords were in the majority, two of whom said materially different things and the third of whom simply agreed with the other two. In *Re R*, the Master of the Rolls gave an opinion which incorporated an idiosyncratic interpretation of the majority decision in *Gillick* while the other two Lords Justices of Appeal appeared almost anxious to distance themselves from his views[1]. On the other hand, the decision in *Re R* has now been reinforced by that in *Re W* and must be taken to be the law in the absence of a further ruling by the House of Lords.

We will now attempt an evaluation of the present position.

Acquiring legal capacity

It seems reasonably uncontentious that the 16-year-old acquires capacity for taking medical decisions on attaining that age and that there is no question of having to engage in an evaluation of individual maturity or intelligence. The sole exception to this will be where the young person is mentally handicapped and therefore lacks the ability to give a real consent. Those under 16 years of age must pass the *Gillick* test and, in theory at least, the leading cases require a high level of understanding, extending beyond the mechanics of the medical procedure involved, to the wider medical, moral and family considerations surrounding what is proposed.

There are several features of this approach to capacity which may be considered unsatisfactory. First, the more that is required of the individual child, the greater is the opportunity for manipulation by adult decision-makers. Someone, whether it be a doctor or the court, has to determine whether an individual child is competent, and there is an obvious danger that the child will be deemed incompetent because his views happen to diverge from the adult assessment of his best interests[2] or that the child's views will simply be overridden under the

---

1 Staughton and Farquharson LJJ confined themselves to the questions of the girl's competence and the power of the court in wardship.
2 A point forcefully presented in J Eekelaar 'Parents' Rights to Punish – Further Limits after *Gillick*' (1986) 28 *Childright* 9.

inherent jurisdiction. Secondly, it is not obvious that the medical profession should be allowed to pass judgment on non-medical matters such as moral and family issues. A young woman's decision to have an abortion may, for example, be seen essentially as a *moral* choice and there may be no decisive medical reason pointing to termination or continuation of the pregnancy[1]. Thirdly, it is arguable that the law is demanding *more* of adolescents in the way of emotional or intellectual maturity than it requires of adults (or, in the case of medical treatment, those over 16 years of age)[2]. Adults, many of whom are not noted for their prudent and cautious approach to sexual involvements, are *not* required to demonstrate (but are rather assumed to have) the necessary maturity to make this all-round judgment of their interests. Many of them make mistakes and this must at least prompt the question, from a civil libertarian and children's rights standpoint, whether those under 16 years should not also have the right to make mistakes.

Finally, the extent of what has to be understood under the *Gillick* formulation has led to some speculation that, in the case of minors, the doctrine of informed consent has been admitted through the back door. This might prompt further speculation about the extent of a doctor's duty of disclosure in the case of young people[3].

Reconciling adolescent capacity, parental responsibility and medical paternalism

There is now considerable uncertainty about when a doctor ought to proceed on either a parent's or a child's consent alone[4]. *Gillick* had ostensibly supported the view that the wishes of a competent child should have priority over those of a parent, at least after suitable attempts had been made to persuade the child to involve her parents. It was apparent from the terms of the original departmental Circular, and from the majority speeches, that it would be seen as unusual for a doctor to deal with a child without parental participation. There was evidently concern that any positive contribution which parents might make in the context of the particular family situation should be explored[5]. It is, however, beyond doubt

---

1 A similar view of the decision whether or not to make contraceptives available was expressed in the US Supreme Court by Brennan J in *Carey v Population Services International* 431 US 678, 699 (1977).

2 It may be argued that the purpose of the test of understanding in both *Gillick* and *Re R* is simply to ensure that minors measure up to adult levels of understanding. Against this it may be argued that the reality is that they are being required to demonstrate more than is demanded of adults. The assessment of the capacity of adolescents also arises in relation to their ability to initiate legal proceedings without a next friend or participate in them without a guardian ad litem. We discuss these issues and the relevant case-law in Chapter 13.

3 The point is raised in B Hoggett 'Parents, Children and Medical Treatment: The Legal Issues' in Peter Byrne (ed) *Rights and Wrongs in Medicine* (1986) 165 at p 173.

4 Although Montgomery *Health Care Law* (Oxford University Press, 1997) (above) at p 292 makes a telling point relying on the decision of the Court of Appeal in *Northampton Health Authority v The Official Solicitor and the Governors of St Andrews Hospital* [1994] 1 FLR 162. This is that a health authority may find costs awarded against it if it takes a case to court when presented with a child's refusal to consent but where parental consent is forthcoming. In fact, in this case, on appeal, the hospital rather than the health authority was ordered to pay half the Official Solicitor's costs.

5 In *Re R* itself it was the possible contribution of the local authority, which had parental

that both Lord Scarman and Lord Fraser took the position that a doctor would be acting lawfully in dealing exclusively with the child in appropriately defined circumstances. There was no suggestion that a parent's view should be allowed to trump the view of a competent minor.

The decisions in *Re R* and *Re W* have now cast doubt on this analysis. It appears to be envisaged that a doctor would be acting lawfully in relying on parental consent in the face of express objection by a competent child. It could, of course, be argued that whilst *Gillick* was concerned with the child's right to *consent*, *Re R* and *Re W*, by contrast, were concerned with her right to *refuse*, and that this enables them to be distinguished. Yet this is hardly logical. If the competent child's right to consent prevails over a parent's right to object, the converse should be true. This is especially so since a doctor's decision to examine or treat a child against that child's wishes is a potential assault, whereas a doctor's refusal to do so cannot be. The case is, if anything, stronger for giving precedence to the child's views in this situation. Lord Donaldson's distinction between determination and consent cannot overcome the essential reality that, where a doctor is aware of a disagreement between parent and child, he must, of necessity, choose between the two opposing views. If he elects to comply with what the parent wants, then he effectively gives to that parent a veto over the child's wishes, and this would appear to conflict directly with the decision in *Gillick*.

Yet if it is accepted that the competent child ought to have the decisive say in the event of a conflict, this does not necessarily mean that parents should be completely excluded from the process. Can it be said that, although deprived of decision-making capacity, parents yet have a right to be *notified* of dealings between their children and the medical profession? This immediately runs into the problem of medical confidentiality[1]. Of all the matters a young person might want to keep from her parents, those arising from sexual activity are the most likely and, of these, abortion is the one which has generated the greatest amount of litigation in the USA[2]. There, it has been held that States may not constitutionally give to parents an absolute and abitrary right of veto over abortion[3]. But, in some circumstances, it can be constitutional for a State to require notification of an abortion to parents[4]. States may also act constitutionally in requiring either parental notification or, alternatively, the consent of a judge[5]. The effect of *Gillick* on this would seem to be to preserve the right of the competent child to confidentiality where the doctor is unable to persuade her to inform her parents. The position is less certain in relation to a child who is adjudged incompetent[6].

---

responsibility for the girl, which was at issue. But the principles would appear to be the same whether parental responsibility is held by a parent or by someone else.

1   See fn 4 at p 254 above.

2   The leading US Supreme Court decisions on the constitutional framework for abortions on minors are *Planned Parenthood of Central Missouri v Danforth* 428 US 52 (1976); *Bellotti v Baird* 428 US 662 (1979); *Bellotti II* 443 US 662 (1979); *HL v Matheson* 450 US 398 (1981); *Ohio v Akron Center for Reproductive Health* 110 S Ct 2972 (1990); and *Hodgson v Minnesota* 110 S Ct 2926 (1990). For a recent exploration of the issues surrounding abortions on minors, see J Herring 'Children's Abortion Rights' (1997) 5 *Medical Law Review* 257.

3   *Danforth* and *Bellotti* (above).

4   *HL v Matheson* (above).

5   *Ohio* and *Minnesota* cases (above).

6   See the discussion above and also J Montgomery 'Confidentiality and the Immature Minor' [1987] Fam Law 101.

The question did not arise in *Re R* and *Re W*, and in *Gillick* it was conflated with the consent issue. It may be that this will be an area in which attempts may be made to find a middle course between giving absolute control to either parent or child over a decision which may affect the functioning of the whole family. On balance, the argument for preserving medical confidentiality is probably the stronger[1].

The role of the court

Should the courts have power to override the wishes of a competent child? Staughton LJ warned, in *Re R*, that 'good reason must be shown before the State exercises any power to control the decisions of a competent person whether adult or minor, which only concern his own well-being'. It has, moreover, been argued that, whatever may be the letter of the law, the *spirit* of Gillick requires that the courts should not arrogate to themselves a right to intervene in the lives of children which is denied to natural parents[2]. It should also be said that there must be a danger that a parent might invoke the court's jurisdiction in an attempt, for example, to force an abortion against the wishes of a competent child. This has the potential for driving a coach and horses through the *Gillick* decision. The view which is ultimately taken of these interventions must depend on a judgment as to the appropriate level of paternalism in promoting children's rights. Is this only justified to enable children to become rationally autonomous adults or should the courts continue to exercise a protective jurisdiction in the face of evidence that this rationality has, in fact, been achieved before majority[3]?

The Children Act 1989 gives conflicting messages in this respect. While many of its provisions reject the notion that children's views ought to be decisive[4], it supports the right of a child (in the context of certain proceedings) who 'has sufficient understanding to make an informed decision' to refuse to submit to medical or psychiatric examination or treatment, even where a court is otherwise minded to direct it[5]. The decisions in *Re R* and *Re W* are difficult to reconcile with these provisions, since their underlying principle seems to be that the competent child should have a *conclusive* right of objection.

Yet it is possible to take a more positive view of the role of the courts in these decision-making processes. It can be argued that, since many of these medical decisions are irreversible and of long-term significance to the young people concerned, an objective view is, if not strictly necessary, nevertheless desirable. Given the uncertainty about who in law does have the right to take the final decision, the use of the court is a way of resolving this. In England, there is no mandatory judicial procedure except that judicial authority is considered a necessary precaution before a sterilisation is performed on a handicapped minor. In the USA, greater use is made of judicial procedures for these purposes. A

---

1   A convincing defence of confidentiality in all minor cases is to be found in the judgment of Marshall J in *Matheson* (above) at 438–440.
2   J Eekelaar 'The Eclipse of Parental Rights' (1986) 102 LQR 4 at pp 7–8.
3   Chapter 3 above discussed this question. See also A Bainham 'Children, Parents and the Law: Non-Intervention and Judicial Paternalism' in P Birks (ed) *The Frontiers of Liability* (Oxford University Press, 1993). The issue arises particularly in relation to the exercise of the inherent jurisdiction, as to which see Chapter 11 below.
4   See Chapter 2 above.
5   See ss 38(6), 43(8), 44(7) of, and Sch 3, para 4(4) to, the Children Act and the discussion in Chapters 11 and 12 below.

number of States have enacted 'judicial by-pass' procedures which attempt to accommodate the interests of both parents and adolescents. Typically, the legislation will require notification of an abortion decision to one or possibly both parents and will allow a short time, perhaps 48 hours, to elapse after notification and before the operation is performed. But the notice requirement may be waived, on application to the court, where the court is satisfied that a specified ground is established. The grounds usually include a finding that parents have been guilty of abuse or neglect, that the child is mature and competent to take her own decision, or that the court, for other reasons, finds it to be in her best interest that the abortion should go ahead without parental notification[1]. While parental consent statutes[2] and parental notification statutes without by-pass procedures[3] have been struck down as unconstitutional[4], appropriately drafted notification statutes incorporating adequate by-pass procedures have been held to be constitutional[5].

In England, as in the USA, the challenge is to find a middle course which allows for a degree of autonomy in decision-making for adolescents but which does not exclude the opportunity for potentially beneficial parental involvement[6]. Whether a judicial by-pass could provide the answer depends on the unanswerable question of whether judges are better qualified than others to take what may be seen ultimately as value judgments about the desirability of medical interventions[7].

---

1   A particularly good example is the Minnesota legislation reviewed in *Hodgson v Minnesota* 110 S Ct 2926 (1990).
2   As in *Planned Parenthood of Central Missouri v Danforth* 428 US 52 (1976).
3   As in *Bellotti v Baird* 428 US 662 (1979).
4   Except, as in *HL v Matheson* 450 US 398 (1981), where they relate to notification in the case of an immature and unemancipated minor.
5   As in *Ohio v Akron Center for Reproductive Health* 110 S Ct 2972 (1990) and *Minnesota* (above).
6   The arguments for regarding parental involvement as potentially beneficial, rather than negative, are rehearsed in the *Minnesota* decision (above).
7   There may also be seen to be a need for clear principles to govern the activities of the medical profession to avoid the necessity of seeking judicial authorisation in every case.

Chapter 9

CHILDREN, MONEY AND PROPERTY

INTRODUCTION

Historically, children's financial interests have not been well served by the law: there was, in theory, a common law duty on a father to maintain his legitimate children, but no procedure was available to enforce that right[1], while children were not entitled as of right to any share in a deceased parent's property[2]. This chapter first summarises the rules governing children's rights in relation to property and the evolution of the obligation to provide financial support for children is summarised. The text then outlines some of the most significant features of the welfare benefits system as it affects young people and seeks to summarise the child support legislation. Finally, it analyses the residual role of the courts in making financial orders for children.

CHILDREN AND PROPERTY[3]

Children's capacity to own property

Most of the distinctive rules relating to children's interests in property stem from the common law notion that a child has no legal capacity[4]. Although (as has already been seen[5]) the *Gillick* decision[6] means that this denial of legal capacity is no longer absolute, the rules governing children's ownership of property are in general[7] founded on express statutory provisions unaffected by the *Gillick* approach to legal capacity. For example, statute provides that an infant cannot

---

1 A father was not even obliged to reimburse a person who supplied his child with necessary goods or services: *Mortimer v Wright* (1840) 6 M&W 482. However, someone who supplied a wife with goods necessary for a child might be able to recover from the husband under the doctrine of agency of necessity: *Bazeley v Forder* (1868) LR 3 QB 559.
2 The feudal lord became entitled to the profits of land during an heir's minority. The right was abolished by the Tenures Abolition Act 1660.
3 For an extremely helpful article which looks at the various angles of children's interests in property and which incorporates discussion of the recent Trusts of Land and Appointment of Trustees Act 1996, see E Cooke 'Children and Real Property – Trusts, Interests and Considerations' [1998] Fam Law 349.
4 See generally Chapter 13.
5 See Chapters 3 and 8.
6 *Gillick v West Norfolk and Wisbech Area Health Authority* [1986] 1 AC 112.
7 But not always. See, for example, the rule that a child cannot give a valid receipt for a legacy paid to him: *Philip v Paget* (1740) 2 Atk 80; *Re Somech; Westminster Bank Ltd v Phillips* [1957] Ch 165. It appears that, as a result of provisions defining parental responsibility contained in the Children Act 1989, s 3(2), any person with parental responsibility may now give such a receipt on the child's behalf. For a discussion of the position before the enactment of the Children Act, see Law Com Working Paper No 91 *Guardianship* (1985) at paras 2.32–2.35.

hold a legal estate[1] in land[2]. Statute denies an infant the right to make a will[3] (unless he[4] is a soldier in actual military service or a mariner or seaman at sea[5]), and a child cannot be appointed a trustee[6], nor act as an administrator[7].

Management of children's property

The rules debarring a child from holding a legal estate are probably of little practical significance. This is because – as a result of legislation[8] and professional practice – most property to which a child is entitled is held by trustees on the child's behalf; and the Trustee Act 1925 contains provisions[9] which facilitate the making of maintenance payments from property which is held in trust for a child[10].

It should also be noted that – in addition to the court's general jurisdiction in respect of the administration of a child's property in wardship[11] – statute[12] specifically empowers the court to approve trust variations on behalf of infants and others incapable of themselves consenting, provided the scheme is beneficial to the persons concerned.

Guardians have parental responsibility for the child, and consequently they have the power to administer a child's property. In certain specified circumstances[13], the Official Solicitor may be appointed to be guardian of a child's estate.

---

1 Nor can a child be registered as a registered proprietor of registered land: Land Registration Act 1925, s 2(1).

2 Law of Property Act 1925, s 1(6), and see now Sch 1, para 1 to the Trusts of Land and Appointment of Trustees Act 1996. However, this does not mean that a child may not hold an equitable interest in land. There is no prohibition on a child disposing of property, but any deed executed by a child is voidable and can be repudiated during minority or within a reasonable time after attainment of full age.

3 Wills Act 1837, s 7.

4 *In the estate of Stanley* [1916] P 192; *In the estate of Rowson* [1944] 2 All ER 36.

5 Wills Act 1837, s 11, as amended by the Wills (Soldiers and Sailors) Act 1918.

6 Supreme Court Act 1981, s 118.

7 *Re Manuel* (1849) 13 Jur 664.

8 See, for example, Sch 1, para 1(1) to the Trusts of Land and Appointment of Trustees Act 1996 (repealing the Law of Property Act 1925, s 19): conveyance of legal estate to a minor takes effect as a declaration of trust; legal estate conveyed to a child jointly with one or more other persons of full age vests in those of full age on trust for the minor.

9 Trustee Act 1925, s 31.

10 This provision will apply where a child is entitled under the statutory trusts arising on an intestacy: see p 285 below. For a consideration of the trustees' broad discretion under the Trustee Act 1925, see *J v J (C Intervening)* [1989] 1 FLR 453.

11 See Chapter 1.

12 Variation of Trusts Act 1958, s 1(1)(a).

13 See s 5(11) of the Children Act; RSC Ord 80, r 13 (as inserted by the Rules of the Supreme Court (Amendment No 4) 1991). Such appointments are made, for example, for the purpose of administering an award to the child under the Criminal Injuries Compensation Scheme where it would be unsuitable for the parents to be involved – for example if they had caused the injuries: see Law Com Working Paper No 91 *Guardianship* (1985) at p 51, note 95.

Inheritance rights

English law – in contrast to the law of Scotland and many other legal systems[1] – does not give members of the family any legal right to share in a deceased relative's estate, and, to that extent, English law still embodies the traditional common law principle of freedom of testation. It is true that children do have rights to succeed on the intestacy of a parent, but, in practice, those rights are often not of any real significance. This is because English law treats a surviving spouse generously and treats the deceased's children correspondingly ungenerously. In outline, the rule is that a spouse is entitled to a statutory legacy (currently amounting to £125,000[2]) and to a life interest in one half of any balance of the estate. Hence, it is only in cases where the deceased had significant means that the children's rights to succeed are likely to prove valuable. The extent of this preference for the surviving spouse may be questioned in an era of high divorce and remarriage. It might be argued that proportionately greater weight should be given to the claims of the deceased's biological children from a former marriage vis-à-vis the claims of the surviving spouse than is so under the existing law[3].

Subject to the interest of the surviving spouse, the deceased's estate is held 'on the statutory trusts' for the deceased's issue[4]. Under the statutory trusts[5], the intestate's children may receive maintenance out of income until they are 18, and any income not applied for their maintenance is accumulated for the children's benefit. On reaching 18 years of age, a child becomes entitled to the appropriate share of the capital. If any of the intestate's children predeceases the intestate (or dies subsequently, but before attaining the age of 18 years) leaving issue, the issue take the child's presumptive share.

Failure to provide for children

There are two situations in which a child may be left without adequate financial provision on the death of a relative. First, the child may be disinherited by a will which makes no provision for him or her and, secondly, the rules of intestacy may (in consequence of the preference they embody for a surviving spouse) leave a child without any provision. For example, in *Re Sivyer*[6], the intestate left a widow, and a 13-year-old daughter by a previous marriage. The widow was entitled, under the rules of intestacy, to the whole of his estate; the child was entitled to nothing.

Even more strikingly, in *Re Collins, dec'd*[7], Mrs Collins had obtained a decree nisi of divorce before her death, but the decree had not been made absolute. In the result, her husband was, at law, entitled on her intestacy to the whole of her estate,

---

1 For example, the law of Germany: see *MT v MT (Financial Provision: Lump Sum)* [1992] 1 FLR 362.
2 Family Provision (Intestate Succession) Order 1993, SI 1993/2906.
3 For a comparative discussion of the policy underlying the inheritance laws of England, the United States, France and Germany, see MA Glendon *The Transformation of Family Law* (University of Chicago Press, 1989) at pp 238–251. For a critique of the attempts to reform the English law of intestacy, see SM Cretney 'Reform of Intestacy: The Best we can do?' (1995) 111 LQR 99.
4 The term issue now extends equally to those born in wedlock and to the illegitimate: Family Law Reform Act 1987, s 18(1).
5 See *J v J (C Intervening)* [1989] 1 FLR 453.
6 [1967] 1 WLR 1482.
7 [1990] Fam 56.

and her children – a son of Mr and Mrs Collins and an illegitimate daughter – were not entitled, under the rules of intestacy, to anything.

Court's power to order that reasonable financial provision be made

The Inheritance (Provision for Family and Dependants) Act 1975 permits certain defined categories of 'dependant' to apply to the court for reasonable financial provision to be made for them out of the deceased's estate. If the court considers that the will or intestacy does not make such provision, it may make appropriate orders (for example, for periodical income payments, or for payment of a lump sum). The categories of dependant include a child of the deceased, and also:

> 'any person (not being a child of the deceased) who in the case of any marriage to which the deceased was at any time a party, was treated by the deceased as a child of the family in relation to that marriage.'

The term 'child' extends to illegitimate, adopted and posthumous children of the deceased, and there is no restriction of age or marital status so that an adult child is entitled to apply. This is an interesting illustration of the way in which, at least for some purposes, the relationship of parent and child and wider kinship links endure for life and do not end on the child attaining majority.

The category of 'children of the family' is similar to, but not identical with, that in the legislation governing financial provision on divorce[1]: under the divorce legislation, the child must have been treated as a child of the family by *both* parties to the marriage, but under the inheritance legislation, the criterion is treatment *by the deceased* in relation *to the deceased's marriage*. Thus, in *Re Leach*[2], the deceased was the applicant's step-mother who had married the applicant's father at a time when she was aged 32. The applicant had a good relationship with her step-mother and became particularly close to her after her father's death. The judge rejected an argument that the 'treatment' which was required was treatment at or about the time of the marriage; and he did not regard it as directly relevant that most of the treatment in this case had occurred after the end of the marriage.

Exercise of the court's discretion

In deciding whether 'reasonable financial provision' has been made, and if not, what order it should make, the court is given certain guidance. In all cases of applications by children, the court is required to have regard to the following matters[3]:

> '(a) the financial resources and financial needs which the applicant has or is likely to have in the foreseeable future;
> (b) the financial resources and financial needs which any other applicant for an order made under the Act has or is likely to have in the foreseeable future;
> (c) the financial resources and financial needs which any beneficiary of the estate of the deceased has or is likely to have in the foreseeable future;
> (d) any obligations and responsibilities which the deceased had towards any applicant for an order or towards any beneficiary of the estate of the deceased;
> (e) the size and nature of the net estate of the deceased;

1　See pp 310–311 below, where the scope of the definition is discussed.
2　[1986] Ch 226.
3　Inheritance (Provision for Family and Dependants) Act 1975, s 3(1).

(f) any physical or mental disability of any applicant for an order under the Act or any beneficiary of the estate of the deceased;

(g) any other matter, including the conduct of the applicant or any other person, which in the circumstances of the case the court may consider relevant',

and the court is also to have regard to the manner in which the applicant was being or in which he might expect to be educated or trained[1].

Where the applicant is someone who makes a claim as a 'child of the family' in relation to the deceased, the court is also required to have regard to the following matters:

'(a) whether the deceased had assumed any responsibility for the applicant's maintenance and, if so, to the extent to which and the basis upon which the deceased assumed that responsibility and to the length of time for which the deceased discharged that responsibility;

(b) whether in assuming and discharging that responsibility the deceased did so knowing that the applicant was not his own child;

(c) the liability of any other person to maintain the applicant.'

These provisions obviously give the court a wide discretion. In respect of applications by illegitimate children, it has been held that the children are to be treated on the same basis as legitimate children[2]. In *Re C (Deceased)*[3], for example, the eight-year-old daughter of the deceased was granted permission to make an application for provision out of time through her mother as next friend. The deceased was wealthy whereas the applicant child and her mother lived in humble circumstances. The court held that the fault for delay in making the application lay with the mother and that this should not bar the child, the merits of whose claim were clear – the more so since the estate had not yet been distributed.

What is the position of the 'child' now grown up? On the one hand, it has been held that claims by adults are not exceptional, but it has to be remembered that the policy of the Inheritance (Provision for Family and Dependants) Act 1975, is not to decide how the deceased's assets should be fairly divided. Instead, it is concerned with making reasonable provision for *dependants* and, accordingly, it is not surprising that the courts have adopted the view that claims for maintenance by able-bodied and comparatively young men who are in employment and able to maintain themselves, will be rare and are to be approached with a degree of circumspection[4]. This does not mean that a claim by a son is viewed with disfavour; rather it means that, faced with a claim by a person who is physically able to earn his own living, the court will be inclined to ask 'why should anybody else make provision for you if you are capable of maintaining yourself?'[5]

The leading case is now *Re Jennings (Deceased)*[6]. The deceased and his wife had separated as long ago as 1945 when the applicant, their son, was aged two. The applicant had thereafter been raised by his mother and step-father. The deceased left the bulk of his estate to charities and remote relatives. The applicant was married with two children and successfully acquired two companies which provided his family with a comfortable standard of living. He applied for financial

---

1   Inheritance (Provision for Family and Dependants) Act 1975, s 3(3).
2   *In the estate of McC* (1978) Fam Law 26.
3   *Re C (Deceased) (Leave to Apply for Provision)* [1995] 2 FLR 24.
4   *Re Coventry, dec'd* [1980] Ch 461 at 495.
5   *Re Dennis, dec'd* [1981] 2 All ER 140 at 145.
6   [1994] 1 FLR 536.

provision out of the estate and succeeded at first instance largely on the basis that the deceased had failed to discharge his moral and financial obligations to the applicant during his minority. The Court of Appeal, however, held that the Act could not be construed to include obligations and responsibilities in the distant past but, as a general rule, should be confined to those which the deceased had immediately before his death. The relationship of father and son could not, as such, impose on the deceased a continuing financial obligation up to the time of death. Neither had it been demonstrated that financial provision was reasonably required for the applicant's maintenance since no further provision was necessary to enable the applicant to discharge the cost of his daily living at a standard appropriate to him. The case is an interesting illustration of the way in which the mere presence of a genetic link is not enough, at least under this legislation, to trigger moral and legal financial responsibilities[1]. The position should be contrasted with that under the child support legislation (discussed below), where entirely the opposite is true, albeit in relation to minor, not adult, children.

Another example, this time involving an adopted daughter, is provided by *Williams v Johns*[2], where the applicant (who was 43, unemployed, impecunious and divorced with no capital beyond the houseboat in which she lived) had had a stormy childhood after being adopted as a baby by the deceased. She was a delinquent, and this caused emotional distress and suffering to her adoptive parents who, nevertheless, continued to assist her financially and morally whenever possible. She had not done anything to help the deceased, and indeed it was suggested that the deceased was afraid of her. The deceased made no provision in her will for the adopted daughter, and left a written statement that she felt no obligation towards her. The court held that, in these circumstances, it was not unreasonable for the deceased to have made no financial provision for the applicant.

In contrast, in *Re Debenham (Deceased)*[3], the applicant was an unwanted child brought up by her grandparents abroad. When she discovered the facts about her parentage she tried to establish a link with her mother, but these attempts were unsuccessful and the deceased continued to remain aloof, distant and indeed cruel to her daughter. It was held that a legacy of £200 out of an estate of £172,000 was not, in all the circumstances, reasonable provision for the daughter. In particular, the daughter was an epileptic and any mother might have felt some obligation to help her in those circumstances. The court ordered payment of a small capital sum to meet the claimant's immediate needs, and a payment of £4,500 per annum by way of income payments.

Re Abram (Deceased)[4] is a recent example of a successful claim by an adult son against his mother's estate. Here, the mother had owned a prosperous warehouse business and substantial family home. The applicant was her only son who had, since the age of 17, worked long hours in the business for a minimal wage. He eventually married and broke clear of the home in the face of strong opposition by his mother. The deceased had made a will leaving the whole of her estate to her

---

1   Note, however, that the Court of Appeal has recently held in *Re Hancock (Deceased)* [1998] 2 FLR
    346 that the applicant does not necessarily have to show that the deceased owed him a moral
    obligation or that there were other special circumstances.
2   [1988] 2 FLR 475.
3   [1986] 1 FLR 404.
4   [1996] 2 FLR 379.

son but later revoked this, disinheriting him. She never changed this will although there was evidence that she had intended to do so. Matters were complicated following the death of the deceased in that her company had failed and the sole asset was the family home. The applicant had also hit on hard times. His own business had failed and he had entered into an individual voluntary arrangement with creditors under the Insolvency Act 1986.

The court held that these were special circumstances and that the deceased had been under a moral obligation to provide for her son. In view of the arrangement under the Insolvency Act (under which any capital paid to the applicant would have to go to his creditors), the court ordered a settlement under which, inter alia, the income from 50% of the estate would be paid to him for life.

EVOLUTION OF THE OBLIGATIONS TO PROVIDE FINANCIAL SUPPORT FOR CHILDREN

As has been seen, enforcement of the obligation to maintain is governed entirely by statute, and a brief account of the historical development of the law will help put the modern law in context.

The Matrimonial Causes Act 1857 first gave English courts power to dissolve marriages, and it provided that the court granting a decree could make such order as it deemed just and proper with respect to the 'custody, maintenance and education' of children, the marriage of whose parents was in issue[1]. The court's powers to make financial orders in divorce and other matrimonial causes were greatly extended[2] over the years, and courts were given power to make orders for the children in other proceedings.

In 1878, magistrates were given power[3] to make what were, in effect, separation orders where a wife had been the victim of assault by her husband, and they were empowered to give custody of any children under the age of 10 to the wife, and to make financial orders. Magistrates also had power to make financial orders against the father of an illegitimate child in affiliation proceedings[4]. In 1886, the Guardianship of Infants Act[5] empowered the court to make a custody or access order on the application of a child's mother, and legislation[6] subsequently provided that the court could order a father to pay the mother weekly or other periodical sums by way of maintenance.

The Children Act 1989 reformed and assimilated the private law provisions governing financial provision and property adjustment for children, extended the

---

1 Matrimonial Causes Act 1857, s 35.
2 Both in respect of the types of order which could be made and in respect of the class of children eligible to benefit: the Matrimonial Proceedings (Children) Act 1958 gave the divorce court power to make orders for a child of one spouse who had been 'accepted' by the other; and the Matrimonial Proceedings and Property Act 1970 gave the court its present wide powers to make both capital and income payments to, or for the benefit of, any 'child of the family': see p 308 below.
3 Matrimonial Causes Act 1878, s 4.
4 This jurisdiction dates back to the Poor Law Amendment Act 1844: the history of the obligation to maintain is traced in the *Report of the Committee on One-Parent Families* ('the Finer Report') (1974) (Cmnd 5629).
5 Guardianship of Infants Act 1886, s 5.
6 Ibid, s 3.

court's powers, and achieved a substantial measure of simplification, rationalisation and harmonisation. The magistrates' court retained its power to make maintenance orders[1] in matrimonial proceedings and the divorce court retained its extensive powers to make orders over capital or income for the benefit of children of the family[2]. The Children Act itself[3] provided for a wide range of financial orders to be made in respect of children, on the application of a parent, a guardian, a person who had a child residing with him under a court order, and (in certain circumstances) a child of 18 years or over. The scheme of the legislation was that financial support for a child could be sought as an incident in matrimonal proceedings between the child's parents, and that in other cases – for example, where the mother of an illegitimate child wanted an order for financial support for the child – similar relief would be available under the Children Act.

The impact of the Child Support Act 1991 on the private law governing financial provision for children

Although the provisions of the matrimonial legislation and of the Children Act remain on the statute book and in force, their practical importance has been greatly reduced by reason of the coming into force on 5 April 1993 of the Child Support Act 1991 ('the 1991 Act')[4]. The general principle of the 1991 Act is that child support should be dealt with by the administrative procedure established by the Act, and that the court's powers should only be exercisable to fill gaps in the statutory child support scheme. The 1991 Act provides[5] that in any case where a child support officer would have jurisdiction to make a maintenance assessment, with respect to a qualifying child and an absent parent, on an application duly made by a person entitled to apply for such an assessment with respect to that child, no court shall exercise any power which it would otherwise have, to make, vary or revive any maintenance order (ie an order to make periodical payments – orders for lump sum payments are not within the definition), in relation to the child and absent parent concerned[6]. Hence, the first question to be asked, in any case in which an issue relating to the provision of financial support for a child arises, must be whether the provisions of the 1991 Act debar the court from proceeding because a child support officer would have jurisdiction to make a maintenance assessment if an application were made under the 1991 Act. Before seeking to explain the provisions of the child support legislation, however, it may be helpful to summarise the relevant provisions governing entitlement to welfare benefits.

---

1   And orders for the payment of small lump sums.
2   See pp 310 et seq below.
3   Schedule 1.
4   It should be noted at the outset of this discussion that the Labour Government is committed to a radical 'root and branch' reform of the current system of child support, see the Green Paper *Children First: A New Approach to Child Support* (HMSO, July 1998) and the final section to this chapter.
5   Section 8(1).
6   Ibid, s 8(3).

WELFARE BENEFITS AND THEIR IMPACT

The Finer Report [1]: welfare benefits as the third system of family law

As long ago as 1974, the Finer Committee on One-Parent Families produced the Finer Report which made a telling analysis of the inadequacy of the procedures then available to provide financial support for children. The Committee pointed out that there were, in effect, three systems of law governing financial support: the system administered by the divorce court; the system administered by the magistrates' courts in domestic proceedings; and what it described as the 'third system of family law' embodied in the system of welfare benefits, administered by an administrative agency. The Finer Report drew attention to the defects caused by this division of function, and to the hardship thereby caused to one-parent families, and made far-reaching proposals under which many issues relating to the quantification and enforcement of financial support obligations would be dealt with by an administrative agency by reference to clear guidelines rather than by the courts in the exercise of a loosely structured discretion. The Finer Report also proposed the creation of a so-called 'guaranteed maintenance allowance' which was intended to provide an income for single-parent families which was significantly higher than what was then available to them by way of welfare benefits.

Although the Finer Report had a profound impact on opinion, nothing was done to give effect to the Committee's proposals. The law continued to develop in separate compartments.

Changing approaches to the State's role

The State has, ever since the enactment of the Elizabethan Poor Law, assumed some obligation to provide for those persons who would otherwise be completely destitute, but a dramatic change in the philosophy underlying the principles on which provision for the poor should be made took place with the creation of the Welfare State in the period immediately following the end of the Second World War[2]. This change was first manifested in the context of the provision of support for the family in the system of family allowances introduced in 1945. That benefit was replaced in 1975 by child benefit, which is now payable to everyone who is responsible for a child under 16 years old (or under 19 years if certain prescribed conditions are met). This benefit is tax-free, does not depend on the making of contributions, and is not means-tested. The standard weekly rates of benefit with

---

1   *Report of the Committee on One-Parent Families* (1974) (Cmnd 5629).

2   These changes followed the publication in 1942 of the Beveridge Report (*the Report on Social Insurance and Allied Services* (1942) (Cmnd 6404)). For a concise account of the evolution of social security and social policy in Britain, see Ogus, Barendt and Wikeley *The Law of Social Security* (4th edn) (Butterworths, 1995) ch 1.

effect from 6 April 1998 are £11.45 for the first or only child; £17.10 for the first or only child of a lone parent[1] and £9.30 for every other child[2].

Means-tested benefits for the poor: supplementary benefit and family income supplement

The most important change in policy governing welfare benefits was achieved by the abolition of the Poor Law in 1948 and the creation of the supplementary benefit system under which every person in Great Britain of or over the age of 16 years, whose resources (as defined) were insufficient to meet his requirements (defined, at a modest level, in statute), became entitled to receive a supplementary allowance. At that time, it was the policy of the law to eradicate the stigma attached to the Poor Law, and to insist that supplementary benefits were 'the subject of rights and entitlement and that no shame attached to the receipt of them'[3].

Reducing the burden of welfare benefit provision

Over the years, the supplementary benefit system became increasingly burdensome to the taxpayer. Part of this increase was attributable to the costs apparently caused by family breakdown: the number of lone-parent families in Great Britain rose to over one million in 1986, and such families now constitute 19% of all families with dependent children[4]. It has always been an important principle that, although the State would provide financial support for a family in danger of destitution, the State should be entitled to recover the amounts disbursed from any person legally bound to support the claimant (that is to say the so-called 'liable relative'). It should be noted in passing that adult children are no longer legally liable to support their parents, but this is not so in every jurisdiction. Singapore has, for example, recently enacted the Maintenance of Parents Act 1995 which enables parents who are unable to support themselves adequately to apply to the court for maintenance from any or all of their children[5]. In England, such obligations (including obligations to support wider kin) existed under the Poor Law but were finally abolished with the advent of the post-war Welfare State[6]. But with changing attitudes it increasingly came to be said that the law failed, in

---

1   This higher figure, which incorporates the differential formerly attributable to one-parent benefit, has been controversially frozen by the Government while the other rates have been increased. We consider the policy underlying this in the conclusion to this chapter.
2   The detailed rules governing entitlement are complex: see Part IX of the Social Security Contributions and Benefits Act 1992, and the Child Benefit (General) Regulations 1976, SI 1976/965. The rates of benefit are governed by the Child Benefit and Social Security (Fixing and Adjustment of Rates) Regulations 1976, SI 1976/1267, as amended (most recently by the Social Security Benefits Up-rating Order 1998, SI 1998/470).
3   *Reiterbund v Reiterbund* [1974] 1 WLR 788 at 797, per Finer J.
4   The percentage has more than doubled since 1971: see *Social Trends 28* (1998) Table 2.10.
5   See P de Cruz 'Singapore: Maintenance, Marital Property and Legislative Innovation' in A Bainham (ed) *The International Survey of Family Law 1996* (Martinus Nijhoff, 1998) at p 401.
6   For a concise discussion, see M Maclean and J Eekelaar *The Parental Obligation* (Hart Publishing, 1997), especially at pp 41–44.

practice, to give effect to the 'clear moral duty' which all parents have to maintain their children until the children are old enough to look after themselves[1].

In response to these pressures, the supplementary benefit system was replaced by 'income support'[2], and legislation was introduced[3] to reinforce the obligations of parents and others. The 1991 Act is an ambitious system intended to ensure that absent parents meet their fair share of the cost of supporting their children[4]. Spouses remain liable in public law to maintain *each other* (as well as their children) while separated but this public liability ceases on divorce. Thus, in practice, the Child Support Agency takes responsibility for enforcing the public liability to support *children* while the Department of Social Security continues to enforce any public liability to maintain a *spouse* under the 'liable relative' procedure governed by the Social Security Administration Act 1992.

Benefits for school-leavers

A second change of emphasis related to the age at which a person becomes entitled to claim income support in his or her own right. Disquiet came to be expressed about the ease with which (so it was said) young people leaving school at the age of 16 could claim income support and thus be supported by the State rather than seeking work or training for work; and the 1987 Conservative Party election manifesto included a pledge that young persons who chose to be unemployed would be denied benefit[5]. The general rule until 7 October 1996 was that a person did not become entitled to income support in his own right[6] until the age of 18 years[7]. However, there were exceptional circumstances in which a person aged between 16 and 18 would be entitled to income support; and lone parents, persons who were temporarily unemployed but remained available to be re-employed, and a person registered for work who of necessity had to live away from his parents because he was estranged from them, in physical or moral danger, or because there was a serious risk to his physical or mental health[8] were allowed to claim in their own right. The Secretary of State could also direct that income support be paid to a person who would otherwise suffer severe hardship[9].

As from 7 October 1996 the minimum age for claiming income support has been reduced again to 16, but to qualify a person must fall within 'a prescribed category'. This change makes little difference in practice to those young people eligible for benefit since it is merely consequential on the replacement of income

---

1   Per Lord Mackay of Clashfern *Hansard*, Vol 526, col 775 (25 February 1991).
2   Social Security Act 1986.
3   Now the Social Security Administration Act 1992, s 106; Income Support (Liable Relative) Regulations 1990, SI 1990/1777.
4   See p 296 below.
5   See Ogus, Barendt and Wikeley *The Law of Social Security* (4th edn) (Butterworths, 1995) at pp 465–467. It should be noted that the income support regulations had always required that a claimant be 'available for work'; and in 1986 an additional requirement that a claimant be 'actively seeking' work was introduced: Social Security Contributions and Benefits Act 1992, s 124(1)(d).
6   The benefit entitlement of the parent or other person responsible for a young person in full-time (but not advanced – eg degree level) education was increased to take account of the needs of the young person concerned.
7   Social Security Contributions and Benefits Act 1992, s 124(1)(a).
8   Income Support (General) Regulations 1987, SI 1987/1967, Sch 1A, para 9A.
9   Social Security Contributions and Benefits Act 1992, s 125.

support by income-based jobseeker's allowance for those required to be available for work as a condition of receiving benefit. To be entitled to the jobseeker's allowance (under the Jobseekers Act 1995, s 3) a person must usually be aged 18, subject to similar (but not identical) exceptions to those which applied to income support[1].

Amount of benefit

The income support scheme attributes a so-called 'applicable amount' to each claimant and, in principle, the claimant is entitled to income support to bring the income up to that amount. The necessary calculations are complex: the 'applicable amount' is the aggregate of a prescribed personal allowance, premiums, and housing costs. The Income Support (General) Regulations 1987 prescribe 16 different 'personal allowances' depending on such factors as the claimant's age and whether or not he or she is a lone parent (that is to say 'a member of the family [who] has no partner'). For example, a single claimant or lone parent who is aged less than 18 years has a personal allowance of £30.30 weekly (although this is increased to £39.85 weekly if, for example, the claimant has to live away from his parents for the reasons set out in the previous paragraph)[2]. To this personal allowance there is added an amount – ranging from £17.30 for a person under 11 years to £30.30 for a person of 18 years or over – in respect of any child or young person who is a member of the claimant's family.

These different rates of personal allowance show considerable flexibility with respect to individual circumstances, but the Regulations, in further pursuance of the policy of targeting benefits without it being necessary to make detailed enquiries into personal needs, provide for the inclusion of weekly *premiums* in the applicable amounts of claimants who satisfy the prescribed conditions. For example, a 'family premium' is payable where at least one member of the family is a child or young person. Since April 1997 the family premium has been paid at two rates. The higher rate incorporates the former lone parent premium and is paid where the claimant is a lone parent and does not qualify for one of the pensioner or disability premiums. This rate from April 1998 is £15.75 (which has been frozen from the previous year) while the lower family premium for two-parent households has been uprated from £10.80 to £11.05. This is part of a deliberate policy begun by the former Conservative Government and continued by the Labour Government of reducing or eroding the additional benefits paid to lone parents.

The means test

Income support is a means-tested benefit. The general principle is that the whole of the earnings and other income of members of the family – including maintenance payments made under a court order or child support paid under the 1991 Act – is calculated on a weekly basis and goes to reduce the amount of benefit entitlement, while a claimant who has capital – other than disregarded capital,

---

1   See Jobseeker's Allowance Regulations 1996, SI 1996/207, regs 57–68.
2   Income Support (General) Regulations 1987, SI 1987/1967, Sch 2, Part I, as amended (most recently by the Social Security Benefits Up-Rating Order 1998, SI 1998/470). A single parent aged 18 years or over has a personal allowance of £50.35; as does a single claimant aged 25 years or over.

such as the house the claimant occupies – worth £8,000 or more, is normally debarred from benefit[1].

Maximising welfare benefits following family breakdown: welfare benefit planning

Lawyers soon began to appreciate that welfare benefits could be a significant resource for families after divorce, and (in particular) could be used to make practicable the 'clean break' philosophy embodied in the divorce legislation after the Matrimonial and Family Proceedings Act 1984. Three features of the welfare benefit legislation were particularly relevant. First, income support (as mentioned above) made allowance for a claimant's 'housing costs' and, subject to certain restrictions, income support payments would cover the interest paid on a mortgage taken out to buy the house or to buy out the interest of a divorced partner. Secondly, although the social security legislation[2] imposed an obligation to maintain the spouse and children, there was no such obligation to maintain a former spouse. Moreover, although the obligation to maintain children continued notwithstanding divorce and was not affected by the terms of any order made by the divorce court[3], it seemed that, in practice, the DSS did not attach a high priority to seeking to recover income support from parents and others[4]. Thirdly, the courts increasingly began to take account of the availability of State benefits in deciding how to exercise their powers to make financial orders on divorce. In particular, it began to be questioned whether a man should be made to go on paying maintenance out of his own small income when the payments would be of no benefit for the former wife but would merely reduce the amount of income support for which she was eligible. This point of view was put eloquently by Waite J[5]:

> 'no humane society could tolerate – even in the interest of saving its public purse – the prospect of a divorced couple of acutely limited means remaining manacled to each other indefinitely by the necessity to return at regular intervals to court for no other purpose than to thrash out at public expense the precise figure which the one should pay the other – not for any benefit to either of them, but solely for the relief of the tax-paying section of the community to which neither of them has sufficient means to belong.'

The welfare benefit 'clean break'

An appreciation of these factors increasingly led to financial orders being made under which the family home would be transferred to the wife outright. She would give up any claim to periodical maintenance and a small – perhaps even nominal – periodical payment order would be made for the children. In some cases, the wife would increase the mortgage on the house so that she could make a lump sum payment to the husband, sufficient to enable him to pay a deposit on a house for himself and his new family. The outcome would be as follows: the wife would remain eligible for income support, and the costs of meeting interest payments on

---

1 Income Support (General) Regulations 1987, reg 45, as amended.
2 The relevant provisions are now consolidated in the Social Security Administration Act 1992, ss 78(6) and 105(3).
3 *Hulley v Thompson* [1981] WLR 159.
4 National Audit Office Report *Support for Lone Parent Families* (1990) HC 328.
5 *Ashley v Blackman* [1988] 2 FLR 278.

the mortgage would be added to her basic entitlement. The DSS would have no right to pursue the former husband in respect of income support payments made to the wife; and, although the DSS would be entitled to recover income support paid in respect of the children, it may be that this right would not be vigorously exercised. The husband would have lost his interest in the former matrimonial home but he would have no on-going maintenance liability, and he would be in a position to buy another house on mortgage, and would be eligible for tax relief on the interest.

It seems probable that such planning became common. Certainly a large number of so-called clean-break orders were made[1] and, by 1989, less than one-quarter of families on income support were receiving periodical maintenance from the absent parent (whereas one half of such families had received maintenance 10 years earlier)[2].

The reaction to welfare benefit planning

These developments were not welcome to those responsible for the administration of the social security budget. Not only was the financial cost high, it was also thought that these developments played a part in eroding personal responsibility for the family. In this context, another matter of concern was the growing number of births outside marriage. In 1991, 31% of all live births were outside marriage[3], and it appeared that many children were born to young single mothers who became wholly dependent on welfare benefits, while no sustained effort was made to recover maintenance from the father.

FINANCIAL SUPPORT FOR CHILDREN UNDER THE CHILD SUPPORT ACT 1991

It has been seen[4] that some changes were made to the law to reduce the attractiveness of welfare benefits to young claimants, and attempts were made[5] to increase the effectiveness of the liable relative system. But much more radical change was to come: on 18 July 1990 the then Prime Minister[6] announced that the Government intended to set up a Child Support Agency which would have access to the information necessary to trace absent parents and to make them accept their financial obligations. Shortly afterwards, the Government published a White Paper[7] *Children Come First*, which gave the following diagnosis of the problem:

> 'The present system of maintenance is unnecessarily fragmented, uncertain in its results, slow and ineffective. It is based largely on discretion. The system is operated through the High and county courts, the Magistrates' Courts ... and the offices of the Department of Social Security. The cumulative effect is uncertainty and inconsistent decisions about how much maintenance should be paid. In a great many instances, the maintenance award is not paid or the payments fall into arrears and then take weeks to re-establish. Only 30% of lone mothers and 3% of lone fathers

---

1   See *Judicial Statistics Annual Report 1991* at Table 5.5.
2   *Children Come First* (1990) (Cmnd 1263) at para 1.5.
3   *Population Trends* No 68 (1992).
4   See p 293 above.
5   See the Maintenance Enforcement Act 1991; the Social Security Administration Act 1992, s 107; and the Income Support (Liable Relatives) Regulations 1990, SI 1990/1777.
6   Mrs Margaret Thatcher.
7   (1990) (Cmnd 1263).

receive regular maintenance for their children. More than 750,000 lone parents depend on income support. Many lone mothers want to go to work but do not feel able to do so.'

The White Paper set out further details about the role of the Child Support Agency which would trace absent parents and assess, collect and enforce maintenance payments. Responsibility for assessing claims for child maintenance was to be removed from the courts, and maintenance assessments would be calculated by reference to a non-discretionary formula intended to produce a level of maintenance reflecting both the day-to-day living costs of raising a child, and the essential living expenses of the person caring for a child and the absent parent.

The White Paper invited comments on its proposals, but the Child Support Act 1991 seems to have been intended to give effect to the proposals in *Children Come First* without any significant change. In particular, it is to be noted that the Act does not seem to reflect the then Prime Minister's statement that 'complicated cases' might still have to be referred to the courts and, in fact, the role of the courts under the English child support system is much less than that in comparable systems introduced elsewhere in the Commonwealth[1]. The Child Support Act 1995, which introduced the possibility of 'departure directions' in 'exceptional cases', was enacted in an attempt to meet some of the criticisms that the original scheme was too rigid and inflexible. We look more closely at this below.

The passage of the 1991 Act through Parliament was controversial[2] – although, perhaps surprisingly, the official opposition did not question the basic principles underlying the new law – but few amendments were made and the Act was brought fully into force on 5 April 1993[3]. All new cases – ie all cases in which there was no previous court order or maintenance agreement – were taken on by the Child Support Agency with effect from 5 April 1993. Between that date and April 1996, existing cases in which a claimant was on income support or family credit were taken over by the Agency, and by 1997 the Agency had assumed responsibility for all child support cases.

---

1 See, for example, M Harrison 'Child Maintenance in Australia: the New Era' in Weitzman and Maclean (eds) *The Economic Consequences of Divorce* (1991); 'Child Support in Australia: Children's Rights or Public Interest' (1991) 5 Int JL&F 24. On experience in the United States, see I Garfinkel *Assuring Child Support* (New York, 1992). On the scheme in New Zealand, see N Richardson 'The New Zealand Child Support Act' [1995] CFLQ 40. See also JT Oldham 'Lessons from the New English and Australian Child Support Systems' (1996) 29 *Vanderbilt J Transnat'l L* 691.

2 See R Bird *Child Maintenance: The New Law* (3rd edn) (Family Law, 1996) at ch 2. More generally on the child support legislation, see E Jacobs and G Douglas *Child Support: The Legislation* (Sweet & Maxwell, 1997) and for the practical application of the scheme, see R Bird *Child Support Calculation Pack 1998/99* (Family Law, 1998). For a penetrating analysis of the work of the Child Support Agency based on empirical research involving privileged access to the Agency's staff, see G Davis, N Wikeley and R Young, with J Barron and J Bedward *Child Support in Action* (Hart Publishing, 1998). Many important decisions on points of law relating to child support are taken by the Child Support Commissioners. Decisions of the Commissioners have been noted by E Knights in regular 'Child Support Updates' which appear in *Family Law*, the most recent of which is at [1998] Fam Law 474.

3 The effect of the transitional provisions was complex: see the Child Support Act 1991 (Commencement No 3 and Transitional Provisions) (Amendment) Order 1993, SI 1993/966.

General principles of the child support legislation

Support for parents, not payments to children

The law governing child support has traditionally been concerned with applications by parents and other adults for financial support in respect of a child's maintenance. Only in exceptional circumstances[1] could a child or young person seek financial support by way of court order and, as has been seen[2], the income support scheme also contains provisions intended to confine eligibility to adults in all save exceptional circumstances. The 1991 Act follows this traditional policy. It makes no provision for a child to seek support but is concerned to define the liability of each parent of a qualifying child to support that child, to assess the amount of periodical payments of maintenance which will be treated as sufficient to discharge the absent parent's responsibility for maintaining children, and to provide machinery for enforcing that responsibility. In this context, it is interesting to note that in Scotland a qualifying child who has attained the age of 12 years may apply for a maintenance assessment in his or her own right[3].

Child Support Act 1991 concerned only with parent/child obligations

As already noted, the legislation dealing with financial orders relating to children had gradually extended the basis upon which a person was to be treated as having an obligation to support a child, and liability could usually be imposed on anyone who had treated a child as a child of his or her family[4], with the result that a step-parent would, for example, be liable to maintain a step-child. The 1991 Act, however – in this respect following the 'public law' model, whereby welfare benefits paid in respect of a child's needs can be recovered from a liable relative[5] – is concerned only with the obligations of a parent and this word is defined to mean any person who is, in law, the mother or father of the child[6]. The 1991 Act is therefore not directly concerned with the liability of step-parents, or others who may have treated children as children of their family. Since around two-fifths of all marriages are now remarriages for at least one of the partners[7], it is inevitable that there are many cases in which the 1991 Act has an uneasy relationship with the private law.

Child Support Act 1991 concerned only with income payments

The 1991 Act is not concerned with capital: it contains no power to require a parent to make capital payments to a child, and it also largely ignores the fact that capital provision – for example, the transfer of a tenancy or other interest in the family home for the benefit of child – may have been made in satisfaction of the child's claims for support[8]. In this respect, the relationship between the new child support system and the older law has become a source of tension.

Two decisions illustrate this concentration on income and the failure of the 1991 Act to treat income and capital resources as interrelated.

---

1 See p 316 below.
2 See p 293 above.
3 Section 7(1) of the 1991 Act.
4 See p 312 below.
5 See p 292 above.
6 Section 54 of the 1991 Act.
7 *Social Trends 28* (1998) Chart 2.17.
8 See *K v K (Minors: Property Transfer)* [1992] 2 FLR 220, CA.

In *Crozier v Crozier*[1] the divorcing parties had agreed to an all too typical consent order under which the husband was to transfer his interest in the former matrimonial home to the wife in return for being released from any maintenance obligations towards the wife and paying only nominal maintenance for the five-year-old child. The wife had always been in receipt of income support and the Secretary of State for Social Security was content with a contribution of £4 per week in respect of the child from the husband. When the husband subsequently received the documentation from the Child Support Agency it was anticipated that his liability under the 1991 Act would amount to £29 per week for the child. In these worsened circumstances he applied to have the consent order set aside or varied. Both parties by this time had new partners and, indeed, both had a child of their new relationships.

Booth J refused leave to appeal out of time against the order. The 'clean break' approach which applied in the divorce jurisdiction had no application to *public* obligations to support children arising under the child support legislation. This public liability to maintain children remained on both parents irrespective of their intentions. Although the wife was prepared to assume sole legal liability to maintain the child she could not in fact do so without public assistance. The State was not bound by any agreement between the parties designed to trade off capital provision against liability for child support.

Crozier illustrated the inflexible nature of an income-based scheme which fails to take proper account of capital transfers which in reality might be viewed as a form of capitalised maintenance. This has only been partially ameliorated by the reforms introduced by the Child Support Act 1995 which we discuss below. *Crozier* was a case in which the father found himself the worse off for having parted with his capital. *Phillips v Peace*[2] illustrates the opposite problem – the way in which the child support scheme can be artificially generous to a man who has substantial capital but little or no income. Here, the father successfully owned and operated a company which dealt in shares. He lived in a house worth £2.6m but, applying the child support formula, it was found that he had no actual income. Hence, a child support assessment could not be made against him. Johnson J said it was absurd that the legislation resulted in the father's liability to support the child being assessed at zero. It was, however, open to the court to order a lump sum for the benefit of the child, exercising its jurisdiction under the Children Act, s 15 and Sch 1. It should not, however, do so in a way designed to circumvent the policy of the child support legislation. A lump sum ought only to be ordered to meet the need of the child in respect of a particular item of capital expenditure. A sum of £90,000 was ordered to enable the mother to buy a house plus £24,307.51 for furniture and birth and other expenses.

Child support and the welfare of the child

We noted in Chapter 2 that the 'welfare principle' applies in only a limited number of legal contexts and that the weight to be attached to children's welfare varies depending on the kind of proceedings in question. So far as the child

---

1 [1994] 1 FLR 26. For other cases exploring the relationship between the clean break and child support, see *Mawson v Mawson* [1994] 2 FLR 985 and *Smith v McInerney* [1994] 2 FLR 1077. Specifically on the relationship between lump sum orders and liability for child support, see *AMS v Child Support Officer* [1998] 1 FLR 955.
2 [1996] 2 FLR 230.

support scheme is concerned, there was a good deal of Government rhetoric about how this was intended to give priority to the interests of children but in fact the statutory commitment on a closer examination is really rather weak. It is provided[1]:

> 'Where, in any case which falls to be dealt with under this Act, the Secretary of State or any child support officer is considering the exercise of any discretionary power conferred by this Act, he shall have regard to the welfare of any child likely to be affected by his decision.'

Hence, welfare is not the 'first' consideration, let alone the 'paramount' consideration, and it is only in cases where there is any *discretion* that the welfare of the child will be relevant at all. As will be seen, there is little discretion in the child support system which rather involves the mandatory application of rigid rules, albeit somewhat tempered by the possibility of a 'departure direction'. Thus the welfare of the child is, in practice, unlikely to play much of a part in the calculation and enforcement of child support. Any redress on the basis that the Child Support Agency has failed to give any or proper weight to the welfare of the child will be restricted to the limited possibility of a challenge by way of judicial review[2].

Scheme of the Child Support Act 1991

The underlying principle of the 1991 Act was said to be that parents have a clear moral duty to maintain their children until they are old enough to look after themselves. Events may change the relationship between the parents but they cannot change their responsibilities towards their children[3]. The 1991 Act seeks to give effect to this philosophy in several ways: first by providing formulae whereby the liability of parents in respect of their children's maintenance is to be met; secondly by laying down rules for assessing the protected income – ie the minimum level below which a parent's income is not to be reduced by the application of the 1991 Act; thirdly by conferring wide powers to obtain information on the officials charged with the administration of the 1991 Act; and fourthly by giving wide powers of enforcement and collection in respect of maintenance assessments.

Administration of child support

The Government established a Child Support Agency with the responsibility of administering the provisions of the 1991 Act but the Act itself makes no mention of the Agency: it imposes responsibilities and confers powers on the Secretary of State and provides that he shall appoint persons to be known as 'child support officers' for the purposes of the legislation[4]. The responsibility for the administration of the Act therefore remains with a Minister responsible to Parliament but the actual administration of its provisions has been delegated to a Government Agency.

---

1   Section 2 of the 1991 Act.
2   See *R v Secretary of State for Social Security ex parte Lloyd* [1995] 1 FLR 856 and *R v Secretary of State for Social Security ex parte Biggin* [1995] 1 FLR 851.
3   *Children Come First* (1990) (Cmnd 1263).
4   Section 13(1) of the 1991 Act. The Act, under s 15, also empowered the Secretary of State to appoint persons to act as inspectors who have powers of entry, questioning, etc: see p 307 below. There is a Chief Child Support Officer who must make an annual report which must be published: 1991 Act, s 13(3)–(5).

Liability to maintain: absent parents

The underlying principle of the 1991 Act is that each parent of a 'qualifying child' is responsible for maintaining that child[1], but a child is only a 'qualifying child' if one or both of his parents is, in relation to him, an 'absent parent'[2]. This provision underscores the fact that the 1991 Act is concerned with the situation in which child and parent are living apart. The Act is not concerned to define the level of support appropriate to a child living under the same roof with the parents.

Who is a parent?

The fact that the 1991 Act is solely concerned to impose obligations on 'parents' has already been mentioned[3], and the Act states that the term 'parent', in relation to any child, means any person who is, in law, the mother or father of the child[4] (ie the natural parent, an adoptive parent, or a person treated as a child's parent under the Human Fertilisation and Embryology Act 1990[5]). The 1991 Act provides that no maintenance assessment is to be made against a person who denies parentage, unless a finding of parentage has been made in certain specified proceedings[6], and application may be made to the court for a declaration[7] of parentage for the purposes of the Act. It has been held that blood tests should be directed on such an application unless the court is satisfied that to do so would be against the child's best interests[8]. No statutory right of appeal was provided in relation to a declaration by magistrates that a person is a 'parent' for the purposes of the Act. It has, however, been held that the High Court has a discretion under

---

1 Child Support Act 1991, s 1(1).
2 Ibid, s 3(1). The parent of any child is an absent parent in relation to him if that parent is not living in the same household with the child and the child has his home with a person who is, in relation to him, a 'person with care'. A person with care is defined as a person with whom the child has his home and who usually provides day-to-day care for the child, whether exclusively or in conjunction with any other person, and who does not fall within a prescribed category of person: ibid, s 3(3).
3 See p 298 above.
4 Section 54 of the 1991 Act.
5 See *Re M (Child Support: Parentage)* [1997] 2 FLR 90. In this case, children who were conceived by AID were born in 1981 and 1986 respectively. The Secretary of State sought a declaration of parentage under s 27 of the 1991 Act in relation to the mother's husband on the basis that he had consented to the procedure. The husband denied that he had consented and argued that he was not therefore the 'parent' of the child. Bracewell J found the issue of consent to be immaterial since the status provisions of the 1990 Act did not have retrospective operation and it was clear that the husband was not the genetic father. If these facts were to recur today the matter *would* turn on whether or not the husband consented to the procedure.
6 Section 26(1) of the 1991 Act. It is to be noted that a finding that a child is a 'child of the family' for the purposes of the Matrimonial Causes Act 1973 (see Chapter 4) is not sufficient.
7 Which will be effective only for the purposes of s 27(3) of the 1991 Act. Note, however, that the Lord Chancellor's Department is consulting on whether it is possible and desirable to introduce a single procedure for obtaining a declaration of paternity from a court which would be valid for *all* purposes. See Consultation Paper on *Court Procedures for the Determination of Paternity* (March 1998).
8 *Re E (A Minor) (Child Support: Blood Test)* [1994] 2 FLR 548, applying in this context the test laid down by the House of Lords in *S v S; W v Official Solicitor* [1972] AC 24.

RSC Ord 15, r 16 to make a contrary declaration where it is subsequently shown that the person concerned is not the parent[1].

The obligation

The 1991 Act provides that an absent parent is, for the purposes of the Act, to be taken to have met his responsibility to maintain any qualifying child of his by making periodical payments of maintenance with respect to the child, in accordance with the provisions of the Act[2], and it imposes a duty to make such payments on an absent parent in respect of whom a maintenance assessment has been made[3].

The formulae

The details of the formulae whereby maintenance is assessed under the 1991 Act are complex and do not lend themselves to easy exposition[4], but the basic principles are comparatively straightforward.

The maintenance requirement

The 1991 Act first provides formulae whereby the basic maintenance requirement[5] for the children concerned can be calculated. This is done by taking the amount which would be paid, by way of income support, to a parent in respect of each child[6]. To this amount there is added (if there is at least one child under 16) the amount of the 'personal allowance' which the parent who has care would receive (currently £50.35 where there is at least one child under the age of 11), and the amount of the income support 'family premium' (currently £15.75 if a lone parent and £11.05 if not a lone parent). There is then deducted the amount of child benefit payable in respect of the family, and the result is the weekly basic maintenance requirement for the children. In the case of a family consisting of a lone parent, with one child aged 10 years and one aged 13 years, the weekly basic maintenance requirement in respect of the two children would be £88.00[7].

The liability: the maintenance assessment

Having calculated the maintenance requirement in this way, the amount which the absent parent has to pay – the maintenance assessment – is arrived at by

---

1   *T v Child Support Agency and Another* [1997] 2 FLR 875, in which magistrates had made a declaration that T was the father of a child in his absence. Subsequent DNA testing proved that this was not the case.
2   1991 Act, s 1(2).
3   Ibid, s 1(3).
4   Copious worked examples can be found in the Child Support Agency's *Notes for Advisers*; and see also R Bird *Child Maintenance: The New Law* (3rd edn) (Family Law, 1996) at ch 5. See also R Bird *Child Support Calculation Pack 1998/99* (Family Law, 1998).
5   Schedule 1, para 1 to the 1991 Act; the Child Support (Maintenance Assessment and Special Cases) Regulations 1992, SI 1992/1815, reg 3.
6   Ie £17.30 for a person under 11 years, £25.35 for a person aged 11 or over but under 16 years, and £30.30 for a person aged over 16 years: see p 294 above.
7   The 1991 Act provides for an 'additional element' which will be relevant where the absent parent has means in excess of those required to discharge his liability in respect of the basic maintenance requirement. The principle underlying the calculation of this amount is that a parent should contribute one quarter of his or her excess assessable income until the amount paid in respect of the children is three times the weekly, basic, maintenance requirement.

working out the 'assessable income' of the absent parent (less any *exempt* income, which relates to certain personal expenses of the absent parent), adding to it any income of the parent with care[1] and dividing the aggregate by two. The assessable income is calculated after making allowance for personal expenditure (calculated at the social security rate of £50.35 in respect of the individual's personal allowance) and adding to that sum income support rates for any children living with the absent parent and also adding allowable housing costs. These allowable housing costs include rent[2], and mortgage interest. However, there is a ceiling on the amount of housing costs which are allowable[3], and if an absent parent has a partner – for example, the father has remarried or is cohabiting – the absent parent's allowable housing costs are reduced on the basis that the partner will be responsible for a quarter of the housing cost[4]. It should also be noted that the earnings taken into account are earnings after tax, but no allowance is made for travel expenses in the case of employed people. Some allowance for travel costs may be made, however, if a departure direction is given.

The additional element

The 1991 Act provides that, where the total assessable income exceeds the maintenance requirement, an additional amount of maintenance is to be calculated[5]. In essence, between 15% and 25% (depending on the number of qualifying children) of the assessable income remaining after the maintenance requirement has been met is to be added, until the maximum amount defined by the 1991 Act is reached. This maximum for the additional element is the basic element (calculated as above) plus three times each child's income support allowance and family premium.

Protected income

The method of calculating the obligation of an absent parent set out above takes no account of the possibility that the absent parent may have inescapable financial commitments, for example in respect of step-children who are receiving little or no maintenance from their biological parents. The 1991 Act[6] therefore contains provisions defining an absent parent's 'protected income', and giving effect to the principle that the amount of any maintenance assessment should be adjusted to secure that payment of the amounts assessed should not reduce the absent parent's disposable income below the protected income level. The protected income level is calculated by a formula designed to ensure that the absent parent should be no worse off than he would be if he were on income support, and, following amendments introduced by the Child Support Act 1995, that the absent parent is left with not less than 70% of his net income.

---

1 Including maintenance payments.
2 Less any housing benefit received.
3 Basically £80 weekly or half the relevant person's income whichever is the greater: the Child Support (Maintenance) Assessments and Special Cases) Regulations 1992, SI 1992/1815, reg 18.
4 There are further adjustments for children living with the absent parent.
5 Schedule 1, para 4 to the 1991 Act; the Child Support (Maintenance Assessment and Special Cases) Regulations 1992, SI 1992/1815, reg 6.
6 Schedule 1, para 6 to the 1991 Act.

The legislation also takes account of the possibility that the person with care has an income and of the situation in which the absent parent is cohabiting with someone else who can be expected to contribute to the outgoings of the new family unit.

In the same way that there is a maximum amount of maintenance requirement, there is also a minimum amount of child support maintenance. This is currently £5.10.

The Child Support Act 1995: departure directions

Following widespread public hostility concerning the rigidity and inefficient administration of the child support scheme, Parliament enacted the Child Support Act 1995 in an attempt to meet some of the more serious criticisms[1]. The 1995 Act principally sought to achieve this by amending the 1991 Act to allow for so-called 'departure directions'[2]. It also provides for a 'child maintenance bonus'[3] payable in circumstances prescribed by regulations to persons who have been in receipt of child maintenance and in respect of whom income support or a jobseeker's allowance is or has been paid.

Where a maintenance assessment is in force, the person with care or the absent parent may apply in writing to the Secretary of State for a departure direction. The application must indicate whether it is based on the effect of the current assessment or on a material change of circumstances[4]. The Secretary of State must then give the application preliminary consideration and may reject it where it appears that there are no grounds for the application or that the difference between the amount of the assessment and the revised amount is less than an amount prescribed by regulations[5]. The applicant for a departure direction may be required to make regular payments while the application is under consideration[6].

Part I of Sch 4B to the 1991 Act prescribes 'the cases' in relation to which a departure direction may be made. It is important to appreciate that there is no automatic entitlement to a departure from the formula in these cases. The success of the application depends on the exercise of the Secretary of State's discretion but, where the application has not 'failed', there is a right of appeal to the Child Support Appeal Tribunal[7]. The stipulated cases are as follows.

Special expenses[8]
These include:

(a) costs incurred in travelling to work;
(b) costs incurred by an absent parent in maintaining contact with any children for whom he is liable to pay child support maintenance;

---

1 For a commentary specifically on the changes made by the 1995 Act, see M Horton 'Improving child support – a missed opportunity' [1995] CFLQ 26.
2 Now ss 28A–28I of and Schs 4A and 4B to the Child Support Act 1991.
3 1995 Act, s 10.
4 1991 Act, s 28A.
5 Ibid, s 28B.
6 Ibid, s 28C.
7 Ibid, s 28D.
8 Ibid, Sch 4B, para 2.

(c) costs attributable to a long-term illness or disability of the applicant or a dependant of his;

(d) pre-existing debts incurred before the separation of the parents for their joint benefit or for the benefit of prescribed children;

(e) pre-1993 financial commitments from which it is impossible or unreasonable for the parent concerned to withdraw;

(f) costs incurred by a parent in supporting a child who is not his child but who is part of his family (most obviously, but not exclusively, step-children).

Property or capital transfers[1]

Where a transfer of property took place by court order or agreement before 5 April 1993 and its effect was to reduce the amount of periodical payments which would otherwise have been payable in relation to a child, the child support maintenance assessment may be reduced by a departure direction. The amount of the reduction is calculated in accordance with a formula designed to attribute an 'equivalent weekly value' to the transfer concerned. The intention here is to meet the kind of inequity which can arise where capital and income were treated as integrated in a divorce settlement[2].

Additional cases[3]

The categories of additional cases are not necessarily closed since the Secretary of State has a continuing power to prescribe other cases in which a departure direction may be given. But the Act itself gives examples of additional cases including the following:

(a) assets which do not currently produce income but which are capable of producing it;

(b) a person's lifestyle is inconsistent with his level of income;

(c) housing costs are unreasonably high;

(d) housing costs are in part attributable to housing persons (such as a partner) whose circumstances are such as to justify disregarding a part of those costs;

(e) travel costs are unreasonably high; and

(f) travel costs should be disregarded.

The Act stipulates certain 'general principles' which are to be taken into account by the Secretary of State in exercising his discretion. This is perhaps another recent example of the legislature attempting to articulate its view of appropriate 'family values' and should be compared with the general principles enunciated in the Family Law Act 1996[4]. The most significant of these general principles are that:

(a) 'parents should be responsible for maintaining their children whenever they can afford to do so'; and

(b) 'where a parent has more than one child, his obligation to maintain any one of them should be no less of an obligation than his obligation to maintain any other of them'.

---

1 Child Support Act 1991, Sch 4B, para 3.
2 See *Crozier v Crozier* [1994] 1 FLR 26 (discussed above) for the kinds of problems which can arise.
3 Child Support Act 1991, Sch 4B, para 5.
4 See Chapter 4 above.

Having taken the prescribed matters into account, the Secretary of State may then give a departure direction if:

(a) he is satisfied that the case falls within one of the prescribed cases;

(b) that it is his opinion that, in all the circumstances of the case, it would be just and equitable to give a departure direction. In so deciding he must have regard in particular to:

    (i) the financial circumstances of the absent parent;

    (ii) the financial circumstances of the person with care; and

    (iii) the welfare of any child likely to be affected by the direction.

It is clear that the provision for departure directions is very far from the root and branch reform of the child support system which its critics would like to see. Many will identify with Stephen Cretney's assessment of the 1995 Act:

> 'Only time will tell whether these rules will be effective in reducing the widespread sense of grievance to which the Child Support Agency's activities seem to have given rise, or whether their effect will be to increase the already great complexity of the scheme to such an extent that it becomes unworkable.'[1]

Reviews

The legislation contains provisions to enable assessments, once made, to be reviewed periodically and also to be reviewed if there is a change of circumstances[2].

Assessment will be made only on application

If (but only if) a maintenance assessment has been made, the absent parent is required to make payments. It is important to understand that there is no general obligation on a person who has care of children to apply for the making of a maintenance assessment against an absent parent[3]: the 1991 Act does not prevent parents from settling their financial affairs by agreement[4] and, indeed, substantial fees are payable to the Child Support Agency on the making of an assessment[5].

The position is different where the person with care of the child is in receipt of income support or family credit[6]: the 1991 Act provides[7] that, in those circumstances, the person with care must (if required to do so) authorise the taking of action to recover child support maintenance from the absent parent and failure to comply with the requirement to give the authorisation or provide the information required may result in the giving of a 'reduced benefit direction'.

---

1 SM Cretney *Family Law* (3rd edn) (Sweet & Maxwell, 1997) at p 145.

2 Section 17 of the 1991 Act.

3 The obligation to make payments is found in the provisions of the 1991 Act which state that where a maintenance assessment made under the Act requires the making of periodical payments it is the duty of the absent parent to make those payments (s 1(3)), and payments of child support maintenance under the assessment are to be made in accordance with regulations made by the Secretary of State (s 29(2)).

4 Section 9(2) of the 1991 Act provides that nothing in the Act should be taken to prevent any person from entering into a maintenance agreement.

5 The Child Support Fees Regulations 1992, SI 1992/3094, prescribe an assessment fee of £44, and a collection fee of £34. These fees are payable annually by both parents.

6 It should be noted that the Labour Government has announced the abolition of family credit, and its replacement from 1999 by a working families tax credit. See p 321 below.

7 By s 6.

The effect of such a direction is that the claimant's benefit support will be reduced by 40% of the income support personal allowance for three years[1].

The Secretary of State must not require someone to authorise action, however, if:

'there are reasonable grounds for believing that –
(a) if the parent were required to give that authorisation; or
(b) if she were to give it,
there would be a risk of her, or any child living with her, suffering harm or undue distress as a result.'[2]

Agreements cannot oust Agency's jurisdiction

Although there is no reason why a couple should not agree on the financial arrangements to be made for their children, it is expressly provided that the existence of a maintenance agreement[3] shall not prevent any party to the agreement (or any other person) from applying for a maintenance assessment with respect to any child to whom or for whose benefit periodical payments are to be made or secured under the agreement. Any provision in an agreement which purports to exclude the right to apply for a maintenance assessment is void[4]. In practice, therefore, every parent must assume that he or she may be made to support the children by way of periodical income payments up to the amount of any maintenance assessment which could be made under the 1991 Act.

Information

The Regulations[5] give the Secretary of State extensive powers to require an absent parent and a person with care to give information on a wide range of matters to enable the absent parent to be identified, and the maintenance assessment computed. There are also powers to require employers, local authorities and others to give information. Inspectors may be appointed[6] who have power to enter at all reasonable times any specified premises (other than premises used solely as a dwelling house) and any other premises used by a specified person for the purpose of carrying on any trade, profession, vocation or business, and to make such examination and enquiry there as the inspector considers appropriate. Any person who is, or has been, an occupier of the premises in question, or an employee, is required to furnish the inspector with all such information and documents as the inspector may reasonably require, and it is a criminal offence intentionally to delay or obstruct any inspector exercising those powers, or (without reasonable excuse) to refuse or neglect to answer any question or furnish any information or produce any document which is required under the provisions of the 1991 Act. The 1991 Act broke a long tradition by providing (in effect) that

---

1 Child Support (Maintenance Assessment Procedure) Regulations 1992, SI 1992/1813, reg 36, as amended. This represents a substantial increase as from 7 October 1996. The previous penalty was 20% of the allowance for 26 weeks and a 10% reduction thereafter.
2 Section 6(2) of the 1991 Act.
3 Defined as any agreement for making or for securing the making of periodical payments by way of maintenance to or for the benefit of any child: s 9(1) of the 1991 Act.
4 Ibid, s 9(4).
5 Child Support (Information, Evidence and Disclosure) Regulations 1992, SI 1992/1812.
6 Section 15(1) of the 1991 Act.

the child support authorities might obtain information from the Inland Revenue in order to trace the current address of an absent parent or the current employer of an absent parent[1]. It is intended that these powers will enable the Child Support Agency to trace absent parents, investigate their means, and exercise the powers[2] of collection and enforcement given to the authorities by the 1991 Act.

Information held by the Child Support Agency is confidential and not to be disclosed without lawful authority[3]. It has been held that the courts have no power under the Act to give leave to, or direct, the Secretary of State to disclose information to a child as to his father's whereabouts. A court may, however, *request* the Secretary of State to disclose it in the context of an application for a s 8 order[4].

Collection and enforcement

The 1991 Act contains exceptionally wide powers of collection and enforcement[5]. Among the methods of enforcement, there is power to require a person, from whom payments are due under a maintenance assessment, to make them by way of direct debit or standing order[6], and the Secretary of State may – without having to obtain any court order – require an employer to make deductions from earnings in order to satisfy a maintenance assessment[7]. However, there is a protected earnings rate, below which the employer must not reduce the payments made to the employee.

If there is a failure by a liable person to make a payment of child support and it appears to be 'inappropriate' to make a deduction of earnings order – for example because the person concerned is not in employment, or because such an order has proved ineffective[8] – the Secretary of State may apply to the magistrates for a liability order. The magistrates' court is required to make such an order if the court is satisfied that the payments in question have become payable and have not been paid. Apparently, following the precedent of the community charge legislation, the making of a liability order confers on the authorities a wide range of enforcement powers. In particular, distress may be levied[9], and it appears to be the intention to use distress in preference to other procedures[10]. If distress (or other enforcement procedure) fails, the Secretary of State may apply to the magistrates' court for an order committing the liable person to prison, and the

---

1 1991 Act, Sch 2, para 1.
2 See below.
3 Section 50 of the 1991 Act.
4 *Re C (A Minor) (Child Support Agency: Disclosure)* [1995] 1 FLR 201.
5 Sections 29–40 of the 1991 Act; and the Child Support (Collection and Enforcement) Regulations 1992, SI 1992/1989.
6 Child Support (Collection and Enforcement) Regulations 1992, SI 1992/1989, Part II.
7 Sections 31–32 of the 1991 Act. It has been held that disputes relating to quantification or validity of a maintenance assessment, in which it is alleged that a deduction of earnings order was defective, are to be dealt with through the review and appeal structure under the child support legislation and are outside the jurisdiction of the magistrates' court. See *Secretary of State for Social Security v Shotton and Others* [1996] 2 FLR 241.
8 1991 Act, s 33.
9 Ibid, s 35; Child Support (Collection and Enforcement) Regulations 1992, SI 1992/1989, regs 30–32.
10 A garnishee or charging order may be sought in the county court: 1991 Act, s 36.

court may commit the defaulter to prison if, but only if, it is of the opinion that he has been guilty of wilful refusal or culpable neglect[1].

The residual role of the court in relation to financial provision for children

The general rule is that where a child support officer would have jurisdiction to make a maintenance assessment, the court is debarred from exercising any power which it would otherwise have[2] to make, vary or revive any maintenance order, ie an order for *periodical* payments[3] in relation to the child and absent parent concerned[4]. The court may, however, revoke a maintenance order[5], and there are certain circumstances in which the court may still have a role. First, the court has power to make an order if the maximum child maintenance assessment is in force[6], provided that the court is satisfied that the circumstances of the case make it appropriate for the absent parent to make, or secure the making of, periodical payments in addition to those under the assessment. Secondly, the court may exercise its powers to make an order in cases where the child is, will be or (if the order were to be made) would be receiving instruction or training requiring provision of some or all of the expenses incurred in connection with the provision of the instruction or training[7]. Thirdly, in cases where a child is disabled, orders may be made to meet some or all of the expenses attributable to the child's disability[8]. Fourthly, the court may exercise its powers to make orders in the case of

---

1   Ibid, s 40(3). The maximum period of imprisonment is six weeks: ibid, s 40(7).
2   In *Department of Social Security v Butler* [1996] 1 FLR 65, the Court of Appeal said that the Child Support Act provided a complete code for assessing and enforcing the financial responsibility of absent parents. This was a comprehensive legislative scheme which left no lacuna to be filled by the High Court's jurisdiction, in this case to grant a *Mareva* injunction.
3   Orders for lump sum payments or other capital transfers are not within this definition.
4   Section 8(3) of the 1991 Act. 'Maintenance order' is defined in s 8(11) of the 1991 Act to mean an order which requires the making or securing of periodical payments under: Part II of the Matrimonial Causes Act 1973; the Domestic Proceedings and Magistrates' Courts Act 1978; Part III of the Matrimonial and Family Proceedings Act 1984; or Sch 1 to the Children Act.
5   1991 Act, s 8(4).
6   Ibid, s 8(6).
7   Ibid, s 8(7).
8   Ibid, s 8(8), (9). See *C v F (Disabled Child: Maintenance Orders)* [1998] 1 FLR 151 in which Sir Stephen Brown P upheld a magistrates' order that the father pay £190 per month to the mother for the benefit of the seriously disabled child. This represented the difference between the mother's total monthly expenditure attributable to the child's disability (£820) and what she actually received by way of disability benefit (£630). He held that the magistrates had been right to conclude that jurisdiction to make the order derived from the Child Support Act 1991, although the application itself was made under Sch 1 to the Children Act. Accordingly, he held that the order could not extend beyond the child's nineteenth birthday by virtue of s 55 of the 1991 Act. However, the Court of Appeal, at [1998] 2 FLR 1, allowed the mother's appeal both as to the duration of the order and as to the calculation of the appropriate amount. It held that s 8(8) did not restrict the court to making a 'top-up' order but allowed it to make a freestanding order under the Children Act. The age restriction of 19 which applied under the Child Support Act 1991 did not apply to such Children Act maintenance orders and therefore the order could extend beyond the child's nineteenth birthday. In calculating the appropriate maintenance, the magistrates had taken too narrow a view. They should have taken the broadest view of expenses, including costs associated with, for example, additional help, feeding those providing such additional help, a larger house, heating, clothing, running a car and respite care. The case was remitted to the family proceedings court for reconsideration on this basis.

17- and 18-year-olds who are not in full-time education[1]; and the bar on making periodical payments orders does not apply if, for any reason, the child support officer has no jurisdiction to make a maintenance assessment – perhaps, for example, because the absent parent is not habitually resident in this country. The court may also make periodical payment orders against the parent with care; and the court also has power[2] to make an order giving effect to a written agreement between the parties. It is, therefore, still open to a couple to make an overall financial settlement to be embodied in a consent order, but no such order or agreement can prevent a parent with care subsequently applying for a child support maintenance assessment[3].

The court's powers in respect of lump sums and property adjustment

The 1991 Act does not affect the court's power to make orders for lump sums, or transfers or settlements of property.

THE COURTS' POWERS TO MAKE FINANCIAL ORDERS FOR THE BENEFIT OF CHILDREN

Although the scope for the exercise of the courts' powers to make financial orders in respect of children is now greatly restricted[4], the powers themselves still exist and may, on occasion, be exercised. A brief account must therefore be given here.

The Children Act 1989 introduced a considerable measure of simplification and rationalisation into the law governing the circumstances in which the court may, in the exercise of its discretion, make financial orders intended to benefit children, but the situation is still somewhat complex. It is most easily understood on the basis that the law draws a distinction between divorce and other matrimonial proceedings, on the one hand, and applications by one partner against the other under the provisions of the Children Act, on the other.

Powers exercisable in matrimonial proceedings

Most orders about children were[5], as the Law Commission pointed out[6], made in the course of divorce or other matrimonial proceedings. Since the provisions relating to children could not readily be separated from those relating to adults, the statutory provisions enabling the court to make financial orders for children in divorce and other matrimonial proceedings are still contained in the relevant statutes dealing with the matrimonial proceedings.

Divorce is far and away the most important of these proceedings[7], but it should also be mentioned that either party to a marriage may apply to the court for an order, on the ground that the other spouse has failed to provide or make a proper

---

1 Such persons are not within the 1991 Act definition of 'child': see s 5(1).
2 Section 8(5) of the 1991 Act; the Child Maintenance (Written Agreements) Order 1993, SI 1993/620.
3 See p 306 above.
4 See p 290 above.
5 Ie prior to the coming into force of the 1991 Act.
6 Law Com No 172, *Guardianship and Custody* (1988) at para 1.8.
7 See p 311 below.

contribution towards reasonable maintenance for any child of the family[1]. If that ground is made out, the court has power to order either periodical payments (secured or unsecured) or payment of a lump sum. Furthermore, either party to a marriage may apply to the family proceedings court for an order – for periodical payments or a lump sum (not exceeding £1,000) – under the Domestic Proceedings and Magistrates' Courts Act 1978. The sole ground (following amendments introduced by the Family Law Act 1996) is that the respondent: (a) has failed to provide reasonable maintenance for the applicant; or (b) has failed to provide, or make a proper contribution towards, reasonable maintenance for any child of the family. These provisions are rarely relevant after the coming into force of the 1991 Act[2].

Powers of the divorce court: provision for parents and children

Provision for children may be either direct or indirect. The court has extensive powers to make orders in favour of the parties, and for the benefit of the children. The Matrimonial Causes Act 1973 (which, following amendments made by the Family Law Act 1996, now distinguishes between proceedings relating to divorce and separation and those relating to nullity) provides that, in the exercise of these financial powers[3], it is the duty of the court, in deciding to exercise its powers and, if so, in what manner, 'to have regard to all the circumstances of the case ... first consideration being given to the welfare while a minor of any child of the family who has not attained the age of 18'[4]. This statutory directive recognises that the financial position of children and their parents is interrelated. It has been said, for example, that it is not in the children's interest that their mother be in straitened circumstances[5] and it may, accordingly, be thought appropriate to make an order for periodical payments in favour of a wife so as to enable her the better to care for the children[6]. Again, the court may consider that this provision requires it to ensure that the children's housing needs are protected[7], and this may often best be done by making an order for the transfer of the house to the parent with whom the child is to live, or for settlement of the house on terms that it is not sold during the children's dependency[8].

The fact that orders in favour of parents may indirectly benefit their children assumes a new significance following the coming into force of the 1991 Act. The divorce court is still required, in exercising its financial powers, to give first consideration to the welfare of children of the family who have not attained the

---

1 Matrimonial Causes Act 1973, s 27.
2 For fuller consideration, see SM Cretney and JM Masson *Principles of Family Law* (6th edn) (Sweet & Maxwell, 1997) at pp 88 et seq.
3 Ie the power to make financial provision orders (divorce and separation): s 22A and s 22B; financial provision orders (nullity): s 23; property adjustment orders (divorce and separation): s 23A and s 23B; and property adjustment orders (nullity): s 24; and the power to order sale of the property: s 24A.
4 Matrimonial Causes Act 1973, s 25, as substituted by the Matrimonial and Family Proceedings Act 1984, s 3.
5 See *E v E (Financial Provision)* [1990] 2 FLR 233 at 249.
6 See *Waterman v Waterman* [1989] 1 FLR 380, CA.
7 See, generally, SM Cretney and JM Masson *Principles of Family Law* (6th edn) (Sweet & Maxwell, 1997) at pp 429 et seq.
8 The so-called *Mesher* and *Martin* orders.

age of 18 years, and the 1991 Act imposes no restriction on the exercise of powers
to make orders against parents.

Meaning of 'child of the family'

The court's powers and duties in divorce proceedings[1] arise in respect of any child
of the family, and this term is defined, in relation to the parties to a marriage, to
mean a child of both those parties, and any other child (not being a child who has
been placed with those parties as foster-parents by a local authority or voluntary
organisation) who has been treated by both of those parties as a child of their
family.

   This definition therefore brings within the category of children of the family all
children who have been 'treated' as a child of the family – apart from those placed
as foster-children[2] – and makes the existence of a biological[3] (or even a formal
legal relationship such as adoption) between the child and the parties irrelevant.
A step-child living with a married couple is the classic example of a child of the
family who is not the child of both spouses. Of course, such a step-child also
remains a 'child of the family' in respect of his birth parents, and the broad
definition thus accurately reflects the erosion of traditional kinship patterns
incidental to increasing divorce and remarriage: a child may have biological
and/or factual links with several different marriages and may move in and out of
several households[4].

   The one limitation which has been placed on the scope of the definition is that
it has been held to be impossible to treat an unborn child as a child of the family: if
a man marries a woman who is pregnant by someone else, the baby will be a child
of their family if the husband treats it as such after birth – even if only for a very
short time and even if the wife has deceived him into thinking that he is the father
– but if the relationship breaks down before the birth, the child will be outside the
definition, whatever the husband may have said about his intentions to treat the
baby as his own[5].

Orders the court may make

The court is given wide (but not limitless) powers[6]. It can, subject to the
restrictions imposed by the 1991 Act, make periodical payment orders. Those
orders may be either in favour of the other party to the marriage[7] or they may
direct payments to the child or to someone else on his behalf for the benefit of a
child of the family[8] – and they may be either secured or unsecured[9]. The court may

---

1   And in most of the other proceedings mentioned in this chapter.
2   The implication is that the local authority or voluntary organisation will be responsible for the
    provision of financial support for the child.
3   Or a relationship created by law by operation of the provisions of the Human Fertilisation and
    Embryology Act 1990.
4   For an illuminating study of the nature of the parental obligation as children move between
    households during the course of their minority, see M Maclean and J Eekelaar *The Parental
    Obligation* (Hart Publishing, 1997).
5   *A v A (Family: Unborn Child)* [1974] Fam 6.
6   For a detailed consideration see SM Cretney and JM Masson *Principles of Family Law* (6th edn)
    (Sweet & Maxwell, 1997) at pp 411–423.
7   Matrimonial Causes Act 1973, s 21(1)(a), (3)(a) and s 22A(1)(a).
8   Ibid, s 21(1)(a), (3)(b) and s 22A(1)(b).
9   Ibid, s 21(1)(b).

also order the payment of a lump sum or sums by one spouse to the other[1] or a payment for the benefit of a child of the family to the child or to someone else on his behalf[2].

The court may also order the transfer of specified property to the other party, or to a child, or to a third party on a child's behalf[3]. It may order the settlement of such property for the benefit of the other party and/or of the children of the family[4] and it may make an order varying any 'ante-nuptial or post-nuptial' settlement made on the parties to the marriage for the benefit of the parties to the marriage and/or of the children of the family[5].

If the court makes a secured periodical payments order, a lump sum, or a property adjustment order, it may also order the sale of any property in which one or both of the parties has a beneficial interest[6].

Factors influencing the exercise of the court's discretion

As has already been seen, the court is required, in the exercise of all these powers, to give first consideration to the welfare, while a minor, of any child of the family who has not attained the age of 18 years. However, notwithstanding this requirement, there was some evidence that, in the past, the courts have underestimated the cost of maintaining children. It seems that orders for conventional sums (rarely exceeding £20 weekly in respect of each child) were often made. In an attempt to remedy this situation, the courts were given details of the income support scale rates for children's requirements, produced by the National Foster Care Association (which were designed to show the actual cost of bringing up a child) and the rates actually paid by local authorities to foster-parents[7]. In practice, however, there will now be little need to refer to such scales since the maintenance requirement, calculated in accordance with the 1991 Act, will provide the baseline for any consideration of a child's needs[8].

Limitations on welfare directive

There were limitations on the application of the direction to give first consideration to the welfare of the children and, in particular (as the courts have emphasised), the legislation does not make the welfare of the children the

1 Matrimonial Causes Act 1973, s 21(1)(c), (3)(a) and s 22A(1)(a).
2 Ibid, s 21(1)(c), (3)(b) and s 22A(1)(b). It is specifically provided that an order for payment of a lump sum to the other spouse may be made for the purpose of enabling that other party to meet any liabilities or expenses reasonably incurred in maintaining any child of the family before making an application for an order, or for meeting any liabilities or expenses reasonably incurred by or for the benefit of the child of the family: ibid, s 23(4).
3 Ibid, s 21(2)(a), (3) and s 23A.
4 Ibid, s 21(2)(b) and s 23A.
5 Ibid, s 21(2)(c) and s 23A. The court may also make an order extinguishing or reducing the interest of either of the parties to the marriage under any such settlement, s 21(2)(d).
6 Ibid, s 24A.
7 Information about these scales should have been of real value to the court because, as Simon Brown J put it in *Cresswell v Eaton* [1991] 1 All ER 484 at 489, 'although not insubstantial, [the payments] are paid entirely by way of reimbursement of the expense incurred in maintaining children: food, clothing, heating, travel and so forth. The underlying philosophy of the fostering scheme is that it should not be undertaken for gain. There is thus no profit to be made from such payments, no reward for a personal care involved in fostering children'.
8 See the amendments to the Family Proceedings Rules 1991, SI 1991/1247, made by the Family Proceedings (Amendment) Rules 1993, SI 1993/295.

'paramount' consideration. It has been said that the court must simply consider all the circumstances, always bearing the children's welfare in mind, and then try to make a financial settlement which is *just* as between husband and wife.

For example, in *Suter v Suter and Jones*[1], an order had been made on the basis that the husband should pay the whole of the wife's mortgage outgoings. This was done because preservation of the home was considered necessary to ensure the welfare of the children. The Court of Appeal held that the court should have taken account of the fact that the wife had a cohabitant who could have been expected to make a contribution, and that the court had been wrong to attach overriding importance to the child's welfare.

Circumstances to be considered

It is now provided that, as regards the exercise of its powers to make periodical payment orders, transfer of property orders or orders for the sale of property in relation to a child of the family, the court should have regard to all the circumstances of the case and, in particular, to a list of specific matters which (it has been said) cover almost every conceivable factor[2]. These specified matters are as follows:

'(a) the financial needs of the child;
 (b) the income, earning capacity (if any), property and other financial resources of the child;
 (c) any physical or mental disability of the child;
 (d) the manner in which he was being and in which the parties to the marriage expected him to be educated or trained;
 (e) the considerations mentioned in relation to the parties to the marriage in paragraphs (a), (b), (c) and (e) of section 25(2) of the Matrimonial Causes Act 1973 [ie their financial resources, financial needs, the standard of living enjoyed by the family before the breakdown and any disability of either party to the marriage].'[3]

Orders against step-parents and others

As pointed out above[4], financial orders may be made against a spouse in respect of any child of the family, and this term is very broadly defined. The legislation seeks to structure the court's discretion by providing that, with regard to the exercise of its financial powers against the party to a marriage in favour of a child of the family who is not the child of that party, the court is also to have regard to the following specified matters:

'(a) to whether that party assumed any responsibility for the child's maintenance, and, if so, to the extent to which, and the basis upon which, that party assumed such responsibility and to the length of time for which that party discharged such responsibility;
 (b) to whether in assuming and discharging such responsibility that party did so knowing that the child was not his or her own;
 (c) to the liability of any other person to maintain the child.'[5]

---

1 [1987] 2 FLR 232.
2 *Mortimer v Mortimer-Griffin* [1986] 2 FLR 315 at 318 per Sir J Donaldson MR.
3 Matrimonial Causes Act 1973, s 25(3).
4 See p 312.
5 Matrimonial Causes Act 1973, s 25(4).

Applications by a child in parents' divorce proceedings

The divorce legislation is primarily concerned with applications by one spouse for an order against the other, but it has been held[1] that a child of the family who has attained the age of 18 years may make an application for financial relief by intervening in the parents' matrimonial proceedings – notwithstanding the fact that the decree may perhaps have been granted many years ago. Such a child may also intervene to seek a variation of an existing order[2].

Duration of orders and age limits

The divorce legislation now provides as follows:

(1) Financial provision orders and transfer of property orders cannot be made in respect of a child who has attained the age of 18[3].

(2) Periodical financial provision (whether secured or unsecured, and whether in nullity, divorce, judicial separation or failure to maintain proceedings) will not, in the first instance, be ordered beyond the child's attaining the upper limit of compulsory school age[4]. However, the court may extend the obligation to make the payments to a later date (but not beyond the age of 18 years) if it considers that, in the circumstances of the case, the welfare of the child so requires[5].

(3) Periodical orders must terminate when the child attains the age of 18[6].

However, these three restrictions do not apply if: (a) the 'child is, or will be or [if provision extending beyond 18 years of age were made] would be, receiving instruction at an educational establishment, or undergoing training for a trade, profession or vocation, whether or not he is also or will also be in gainful employment'; or (b) there are 'special circumstances which justify' the making of a different order[7].

These restrictions do not apply to the court's powers to order a settlement of property or to vary a nuptial settlement. However, it has been held[8] that a court should not normally exercise the power to order a settlement of property so as to order life-long provision for a child who is under no disability and whose education is secured.

The basic principle of the legislation is thus that special justification must be shown if an order is to be made or continued in respect of an adult child. This

---

1 *Downing v Downing (Downing Intervening)* [1976] Fam 288. However, the court can only make orders continuing after a child's eighteenth birthday if the child is receiving education or training or there are special circumstances: see below.

2 Matrimonial Causes Act 1973, s 31.

3 Ibid, s 29. A child attains a particular age at the commencement of the relevant anniversary of his birth: Family Law Reform Act 1969, s 9.

4 Ibid, s 29(2).

5 Ibid, s 29(2)(a).

6 Matrimonial Causes Act 1973, s 29(1), (2)(b).

7 Ibid, s 29(3). See *B v B (Adult Student: Liability to Support)* [1998] 1 FLR 373 in which a father unsuccessfully argued that his daughter's full maintenance grant while at university and any supplementary income she might make during those substantial parts of the year when she was not required to be in residence should absolve him of any continuing financial liability for her. For a useful round-up of the circumstances under which parents may be liable to provide support for their adult children, see the comment on this decision by S Cretney at [1998] Fam Law 131.

8 *Lilford (Lord) v Glynn* [1979] 1 WLR 78; *Chamberlain v Chamberlain* [1973] 1 WLR 1557.

justification will often relate to the child's education (which is specifically referred to) but there may be other 'special circumstances', such as disability or ill-health, or the fact that a parent had given a child to understand that support would continue until the child had completed a course of professional training.

Finally, it should be noted that periodical payments orders[1] in favour of a child terminate on the death of the payer, whether or not the order so provides[2].

Financial orders for children under the Children Act 1989

Before the coming into force of the Children Act there were a number of ill-related procedures for getting financial provision orders for children outside matrimonial proceedings. Of these, the most commonly invoked was the procedure whereby an affiliation order could be sought against the putative father of an illegitimate child. There were also powers to make orders in guardianship proceedings and in proceedings in which parents simply sought orders about the upbringing of their children and did not seek any order about their own marriage. The Children Act reformed and assimilated the various private law provisions relating to the courts' powers to order financial provisions in proceedings which are not connected with the marriage of a child's parents. The Act adopted the divorce legislation as a model and, to a large extent, generalises for all children the benefit of principles which have already been established in the context of particular proceedings[3].

Qualified applicants

The following persons may apply for a financial order in respect of a child[4].

(1) *A parent*: this expression extends to adoptive parents and to both parents of an illegitimate child. The ordinary meaning of the word is extended so as to 'include any party to a marriage (whether or not subsisting) in relation to whom the child … is a child of the family'. Hence, it will be possible for a child's biological parent to initiate proceedings claiming support for the child against the child's step-parent[5] or for the step-parent to seek an order against the biological parent.

(2) *A guardian.*

(3) *Any person in whose favour a residence order is in force with respect to a child*: a residence order settles the arrangements to be made about where a child is to live; and accordingly anyone who has been given the right to care for a child by court order can now seek a financial order for the child's support.

(4) *An adult student or trainee or person who can show special circumstances*: anyone from this category may make an application for an order. However, in this case, there are two restrictions on the court's powers. First, no order may be made if the parents are living together in the same household[6], so that it is still

---

1 But not a *secured* periodical payments order.
2 Matrimonial Causes Act 1973, s 29(4).
3 Law Com No 172 *Guardianship and Custody* (1988) at para 4.63, and Children Act, s 15 and Sch 1.
4 Children Act, Sch 1, paras 1 and 2.
5 But a parent's cohabitant is not within this definition, irrespective of the length of time for which he has been in loco parentis to the child: *J v J (Property Transfer Application)* [1993] 2 FLR 56.
6 Children Act, Sch 1, para 2(4).

impossible for a child to compel parents who are living in a conventional relationship to provide support. Secondly, the court's powers on such an application are limited to making periodical payment or lump sum orders and the power to make periodical payment orders is now severely restricted by the 1991 Act[1].

In addition, there are certain circumstances in which the court may make a financial order even though no application for such an order has been made. It is provided that the court may make a financial order whenever it makes, varies or discharges a residence order[2] – and a residence order may be made in any family proceedings, whether or not applied for, if the court considers that the order should be made. The court can also make financial orders if the child is a ward of court, whether or not any application has been made for such an order[3].

Orders which may be made

The range of orders available is now very wide, on the pattern of the range of orders available for children in divorce proceedings. On an application under the Children Act, the court may order the child's parent or parents[4]:

(1) to make periodical payments, secured or unsecured;
(2) to pay a lump sum (and it is expressly provided[5] that such an order may be made to enable expenses in connection with the birth or maintenance of the child which were reasonably incurred before the making of the order to be met);
(3) to make a transfer or settlement of specified property to which the parent is entitled either in possession or reversion. This power gives the court greater flexibility in dealing with the home in which an unmarried couple have lived. It has been held that there is power to order the transfer of a secure tenancy to the other parent for the child's benefit[6], and it is possible for the court to order a settlement of such property on trust for the child – perhaps until the child ceases full-time education[7].

Interim orders and variation of orders

The court has wide powers[8] to make interim orders, and to vary periodical payment orders.

---

1   Children Act, Sch 1, para 2(2).
2   Ibid, Sch 1, para 1(6).
3   Ibid, Sch 1, para 1(7).
4   Defined to include step-parents, etc: see above.
5   Children Act, Sch 1, para 5(1).
6   *K v K (Minors: Property Transfer)* [1992] 2 FLR 220; but it seems that a cautious approach will be taken to the exercise of this power: *J v J (Property Transfer Application)* [1993] 2 FLR 56. It should be noted, however, that much wider powers to transfer certain tenancies are now given to the courts under Part IV of the Family Law Act 1996 where an unmarried cohabitation breaks down. These powers may well be exercised in future to provide a continuing home for the children. See Family Law Act 1996, s 53 and Sch 7, and S Bridge 'Transferring Tenancies of the Family Home' [1998] Fam Law 26.
7   Children Act, Sch 1, para 1(1)(d). For examples of the settlement of capital sums to provide homes for children, see *H v P (Illegitimate Child: Capital Provision)* [1993] Fam Law 515 and *Phillips v Peace* [1996] 2 FLR 230.
8   The powers of a (magistrates') family proceedings court in relation to financial orders are limited: such a court cannot make orders for transfer or settlement of property, or for secured

The exercise of the discretion

The Children Act[1] lays down guidelines for the exercise of the court's powers which largely follow the precedent of matrimonial law[2]. It is provided[3] that, in deciding whether to exercise its powers and if so in what manner, the court shall have regard to all the circumstances including:

(a) the income, earning capacity, property and other financial resources which the applicant, parents[4] and the person in whose favour the order would be made has or is likely to have in the foreseeable future;

(b) the financial needs, obligations and responsibilities which each of those persons has or is likely to have in the foreseeable future;

(c) the financial needs of the child;

(d) the income, earning capacity (if any), property and other financial resources of the child;

(e) any physical or mental disability of the child;

(f) the manner in which the child was being, or was expected to be, educated or trained[5].

The legislation also contains a provision similar to that in the matrimonial legislation dealing with the factors to be taken into account where the 'parent' against whom the order is sought is not the child's mother or father[6].

The provisions of the 1991 Act have made these provisions somewhat academic, in the vast majority of cases, in relation to the power to order periodical payments. It is only when the question of a payment in excess of the level provided for by the 1991 Act is a possibility – for example to pay school fees for independent education – that the court will be likely to be asked to exercise its powers to make periodical payments – and, indeed, it is only in such unusual circumstances that it will have jurisdiction to do so[7].

The 1991 Act does not, however, affect the exercise of the courts' powers to make lump sum or property adjustment orders, and it may be that there will be more applications for such orders than in the past – not least because, where a couple are not married, the court has only limited powers to make orders as between the adults concerned in respect of their family home. Accordingly, any such order must usually be sought in proceedings under the Children Act.

---

periodical payments, and its power to order a lump sum is restricted to a maximum payment of £1,000: Children Act, Sch 1, paras 6 and 7 (variation) and 9 (interim orders).

1   Ibid, Sch 1, para 4(1).

2   Law Com No 172 *Guardianship and Custody* (1988) at para 4.64.

3   Children Act, Sch 1, para 4(1).

4   This states the general effect of Sch 1, para 4(1)(b) to the Children Act; but not the distinction drawn in the Act between applications for orders for persons over 18 and others.

5   There are minor differences between the guidelines for the exercise of the discretion in proceedings instituted under the Children Act and those laid down in relation to divorce and other matrimonial proceedings. The divorce legislation does not require the court (in relation to orders sought for children) to have regard to the contributions which each of the parties has made or is likely, in the foreseeable future, to make to the welfare of the family. In proceedings under the Children Act there is no reference to the standard of living enjoyed by the family before the breakdown of the marriage, and there is no reference to the age of each party to the marriage and the duration of the marriage.

6   Schedule 1, para 4(2) to the Children Act.

7   See p 309 above.

However, in the past, the courts have been reluctant to make capital provision orders in respect of children[1].

For example, in *Kiely v Kiely*[2], the Court of Appeal pointed out that lump sum orders in favour of chidren and, in particular, of children whose parents were of limited means, were rare[3] and stated that the statutory scheme of the divorce legislation was to enable the court to make proper financial provision for children as children or dependants[4].

Conversely, in *J v J (C Intervening)*[5], the court again drew a distinction between the provision of maintenance (which was the proper function of the divorce court) and the preservation of capital which a child could be expected to inherit. Custody of two children was given to the mother in divorce proceedings and the father was ordered to pay maintenance. The mother subsequently died, leaving a will under which her two children were the sole beneficiaries. The only asset which she had was the former matrimonial home. On her death, the children were cared for by their grandmother and an application was made for the increase of the maintenance payments which had originally been ordered for the children – £15 weekly for the 16-year-old boy, and £12 weekly for the 11-year-old girl. The first instance court refused to increase the amounts notwithstanding the fact that the children's needs had never been fully quantified. A factor influencing the court's decision was that the income from the children's inheritance was such that it should be taken into account. The Court of Appeal held that this was the wrong approach. It was the father's duty to maintain his children in accordance with his means; and it was wrong to treat the trust fund which had only come into existence as a result of the mother's death as representing something of a windfall for the father and absolving him to a great extent from the burden he would otherwise have to bear in maintaining the children. Although the existence of the fund could properly be taken into account, the first instance court had misdirected itself in simply assuming that the whole income from the capital should be available for the children: a balancing exercise was called for to ensure that the children's needs were met without requiring the father to pay more than he could possibly afford, whilst at the same time not placing improper pressure on the trustees with regard to the exercise of the discretion which they had[6]. In the event, the maintenance orders were increased from £15 to £21, and from £12 to £19 weekly[7].

---

1 In *A v A (A Minor: Financial Provision)* [1994] 1 FLR 657, Ward J held that property adjustment orders should not ordinarily be used to make an outright transfer to a child. They should normally only be made to provide for the child's maintenance during minority or until the child completes education. In this case, the property was settled on trust for the ten-year-old child for a term expiring six months after she attained 18 or completed full-time education (including tertiary education).
2 [1988] 1 FLR 248, CA. See also *Lilford (Lord) v Glynn* [1979] 1 WLR 78.
3 Ibid at 251 per Booth J.
4 Ibid at 252.
5 [1989] 1 FLR 453.
6 Under the Trustee Act 1925, s 31.
7 It will be noted that these figures are still significantly below the children's maintenance requirements calculated according to the 1991 Act formula.

FINANCIAL RESPONSIBILITY FOR CHILDREN: SOME CONCLUDING POLICY CONSIDERATIONS

Ultimately, the question of financial support for children is about the appropriate apportionment of responsibility between the two parents concerned (or, perhaps more accurately, the two households concerned) and the wider community. The child support legislation shifted the emphasis decisively towards the notion that the *primary* responsibility rests with parents and any obligation on the part of the State is *secondary*. Yet, even if this is accepted, the respective *levels* of responsibility remain a contentious issue as does the view that these obligations of parenthood should fall very largely on biological parents[1] to the exclusion of the legal and moral obligations of social parenthood[2]. The fact that almost everyone would agree with the principle that parents have *some* continuing financial responsibility for their children even where they no longer live with them does not mean that there is anything like a consensus about precisely what this responsibility should be. As one policy publication of the Child Poverty Action Group put it: 'the superficial simplicity of support for this principle hides a complex and shifting array of attitudes about family obligations. Public agreement with the general principle does not necessarily mean that people think it should be unconditional or overriding'[3].

Another angle to this issue is the inconsistency in the legal treatment of the financial obligations of parents in ongoing, intact households as compared with those in separate households. The child support regime applies only where a parent is 'absent' and has left the household in which the children are present. The law does not concern itself directly with the management of family finances while the family remains intact[4]. This can lead to the ironic situation in which an 'absent' father is legally required to pay more, perhaps much more, for children than he would ever have done had the family remained a going concern. The irony is heightened in those cases in which the man concerned was never in the household at all and whose only link with the child is genetic. As Harry Krause has put it: 'it does not seem at all obvious that the same (or a greater) level of parental responsibility that makes sense in the ongoing family should be grafted (1) onto consanguinity based on what is understood as permissible recreational sex or (2) onto the essentially terminated post-divorce relationship between the typical

---

1   But not entirely, since non-genetic parents may be regarded in law as parents in the case of adoption and some instances of assisted reproduction under the status provisions of the Human Fertilisation and Embryology Act 1990. See Chapter 3 above.
2   Social parents may have legal, as well as moral, obligations towards children who are treated as 'children of the family'. See p 312 above. It should also be remembered that the presence of a working social father in a household would, under the aggregation rules which apply to social security entitlements, often preclude a mother from making an independent claim for herself and her children for means-tested income support and other benefits. In this sense, there is an assumed indirect legal responsibility on the man concerned to support his 'second' family. For discussion of the aggregation rule, see Ogus, Barendt and Wikeley *Law of Social Security* (4th edn) (Butterworths, 1995) at pp 470 et seq.
3   F Bennett *Child Support: Issues for the Future* (CPAG Ltd, 1997) at p 23.
4   For a concise and useful discussion, see M Maclean and J Eekelaar *The Parental Obligation* (Hart Publishing, 1997) at pp 37–44.

father and his child' and he urges a search 'for a level of responsibility that is commensurate with the social reality of the situation'[1].

In searching for the appropriate level of financial responsibility to place on the so-called 'absent father' (and the great majority of 'absent parents' are of course fathers) another issue needs to be confronted. Is parenthood and its obligations really a matter of genetics or a matter of assumed social responsibility[2]? Whichever it is, there is currently an inconsistency at the heart of English law. This is that, while genetics is apparently all important for *financial responsibility*, it is not so regarded for the wider aspects of *parental responsibility*, at least outside marriage[3]. It is difficult to resist the conclusion that the law would command more respect if it made this connection between the financial and non-financial elements of parental responsibility. There are two ways essentially in which this might be achieved. The first would be to emphasise the responsibility of the social parent and to remove the financial responsibility of the 'absent' genetic parent along with the wider aspects of parental responsibility. The second (and, it is submitted, much the preferred course) would be to recognise, along with financial responsibility, the wider parental responsibility of the absent genetic parent. There are signs that the new Labour Government is sympathetic to the latter proposal since the Lord Chancellor's Department has recently reopened the question of automatic parental responsibility for the unmarried father[4]. The Consultation Paper recognises that it is 'a particular source of grievance for some unmarried fathers that they may be forced to support their children financially, whether or not they have acquired parental responsibility under the Children Act'[5].

A final question is the extent of the State's obligations concerning the cost of raising children. This is a question which of course relates not just to children whose parents have separated but also to intact families with children. As we have seen, it has long been accepted, and certainly in the post-war period, that the cost of raising children is something to be met by parents and the State acting in partnership. In recent decades, the State's contribution has largely manifested itself in the provision of benefits through the social security system but, as we have seen, it was this burden which foreshadowed the introduction of the child support legislation. The Labour Government has signalled, particularly in its 1998 budget[6], a change of direction and a new 'welfare to work' philosophy. The details are beyond the scope of the present discussion but the central proposals may be briefly sketched.

The principal objective is for the State to support families by a package of measures designed to assist people in moving away from welfare dependency and into work. There will be a new 'working families tax credit' which will replace the social security means-tested benefit family credit. Under the new tax credit, every family with someone working full-time will have a guaranteed income of £180 per

---

1 HD Krause 'Child Support Reassessed: Limits of Private Responsibility and the Public Interest' in Kay and Sugarman (eds) *Divorce Reform at the Crossroads* (Yale University Press, 1990) at p 181.
2 We discuss this general question in Chapter 3 above.
3 See Chapter 5.
4 Consultation Paper, *Court Procedures for the Determination of Paternity: The Law on Parental Responsibility for Unmarried Fathers* (Lord Chancellor's Department, March 1998).
5 Ibid, para 54.
6 For the details see *The Times* and *The Financial Times* for Wednesday, 18 March 1998.

week and no income tax will be paid on earnings below £220 per week. This will be accompanied by a significant increase in child benefit of £2.50 per week over and above the rate of inflation[1]. The strategy for lone parents is essentially to assist them into work by the provision of tax credits for child care and a massive increase in nursery provision. There will be a new tax credit which will cover 70% of child care costs up to £100 per week for the first child and up to £150 per week for two or more children. Nursery provision will be provided for all four-year-olds under a partnership between the public and private sectors, although there is some anxiety that the supply of nursery provision and after-school clubs will be found to be lagging behind demand when the child care tax credits take effect in October 1999[2]. The Government has also announced a major reform of the welfare system in a Green Paper[3] which will include a 'root and branch' review of the Child Support Agency. A subsequent Green Paper has now been published dealing specifically with the Government's proposals for the child support system[4]. In essence, the intention is to move to a much simplified system and formula based on flat-rate payments. As the former Secretary of State for Social Secretary, Ms Harriet Harman, put it:

> 'It relies only on identifying the number of children the father has, where the children live and how much income he has after deduction of tax and national insurance.'

It is envisaged that the liable parent will pay 15% of his net income for one child, 20% for two children and 25% for three or more. There will be no return to the discretionary jurisdiction of the courts but there will instead be a right of appeal to a tribunal which will have power to vary the amounts payable as where, for example, a father incurs expenses in visiting a child or has already met some of the first family's housing costs.

As expected, there has been a mixed reception to the proposals from various interested parties, and the usual speculation about winners and losers.

Whether these ambitious plans result in greater public satisfaction with the division of responsibility for the cost of raising children remains to be seen. The only certainty is that this will remain a controversial matter.

---

1   It should be noted that this must be seen alongside the Government's controversial policy of phasing out the preferential treatment of lone parents through the erosion of 'one-parent benefit'. The Government has also hinted that child benefit may be taxed in the case of higher earners.

2   See (1998) *The Times*, 18 March at p 14.

3   Green Paper, *New Ambitions for Our Country: A New Contract for Welfare* (March 1998). See (1998) *The Times*, 27 March.

4   Green Paper, *Children First: A New Approach to Child Support* (July 1998). A summary of the principal points in the Green Paper appears in (1998) *The Times*, 7 July.

PART III
CHILDREN AND LOCAL AUTHORITIES

Part III, 'Children and Local Authorities', is deliberately not called 'Children and the State'. The concept of the State, broadly defined, impinges on children and families in many different ways – through social security and fiscal policy, education and employment, the criminal law, and in a host of other ways. Yet the relationship between local authorities and families is crucial since it is local authorities which have the primary statutory responsibility for supporting families and for protecting children who are thought to be at risk of abuse or neglect. The historical development of these responsibilities was discussed in Part I.

Chapter 10 analyses the *supportive* and *preventive* functions of local authorities. It also deals briefly with the regulation of substitute care arrangements, in relation to which local authorities have a central role. The focus in Chapters 11 and 12 is on *protection* rather than support. Chapter 11 discusses the statutory regime for compulsory action whether through care or supervision. Chapter 12 considers the critical question of short-term protection for children. Here, the emphasis is on immediate legal remedies for dealing with emergencies.

In theory, a sharp distinction can be drawn between *voluntary* assistance governed by Part III of the Children Act 1989 (see Chapter 10) and the *compulsory* measures under Parts IV and V of the Act (see Chapters 11 and 12). Yet, for various reasons, it is not a true reflection of what goes on in practice to postulate so rigid a demarcation. It is important to get some sense of the relationship between voluntary services and more coercive action and this should be constantly kept in mind when reading this Part of the book.

Chapter 10

LOCAL AUTHORITY SUPPORT FOR CHILDREN AND FAMILIES

INTRODUCTION

Part III of the Children Act 1989, which regulates support services for families and the powers and duties of local authorities towards children looked after by them, has received less exposure than the new regime for compulsory action in Parts IV and V of the Act[1]. In this chapter, we sketch the legal framework of Part III. Perhaps it is inevitable that the legal boundaries for *compulsory* State intervention in the family should be the subject of close critical evaluation. But to see these powers as relatively more important, and voluntary services as relatively less important, would be an unbalanced and distorted way of looking at things. In a nutshell, one of the primary purposes of the support services under Part III is to prevent, wherever possible, the circumstances under which it becomes necessary for compulsory action to be taken. Court orders for care and supervision are, in this sense, very much the ambulance at the bottom of the cliff while the support services are the (however inadequate) fence at the top.

This emphasis on voluntary assistance to families in difficulty, or those who would be in difficulty but for that assistance, is consistent with the general thinking behind the Children Act which was identified in earlier chapters[2]. Essentially, it is that first responsibility for children rests with the family. Public support should be viewed as positive, designed to underscore the primary role of parents and not to emphasise their failure. Thus, the local authority's powers should be exercised in *partnership* with parents, implying full participation in decisions, even where the child is looked after by the local authority. Court orders should only be made where they are strictly necessary[3]. Reunification with the family[4] and promotion of contact with relatives and friends[5] should be an important objective. The local authority should be accountable for its actions through an adequate system of internal reviews and procedures for accommodating representations and complaints.

---

1 The genesis of the reforms in Part III is the DHSS *Review of Child Care Law* (1985), Part II and the White Paper *The Law on Child Care and Family Services* (1987) (Cmnd 62), ch 2. The most detailed academic treatment of the subject is MDA Freeman *Children, Their Families and the Law* (Macmillan, 1992) at ch 4. Also useful is the account in SM Cretney and JM Masson *Principles of Family Law* (6th edn) (Sweet & Maxwell, 1997) at pp 767–785, which cites many helpful sources from social work. See also J Thoburn 'The Children Act 1989; Balancing Child Welfare with the Concept of Partnership with Parents' [1991] JSWFL 331. For a longer perspective taking in the post-war period, see N Parton *Governing the Family* (Macmillan, 1991) at ch 2. For the official guidance on this part of the legislation, see *The Children Act 1989 Guidance and Regulations Vol 2 Family Support, Day Care and Educational Provision for Young Children* (HMSO, 1991).
2 See particularly Chapter 2 above.
3 Ibid.
4 See, particularly, s 17(1)(b).
5 Schedule 2, para 15.

Removal of connotation of failure from legislation?

The legislation differentiates between children 'in care' and children 'looked after' or 'accommodated' by local authorities[1]. It aims to clarify the difference between seeking voluntary help from social services and the circumstances in which compulsion can be justified. It removes from the seeking of voluntary help any pejorative connotation of failure or inadequacy. Any features of the former law which could be interpreted as inconsistent with this ideal were removed[2]. Yet it has been questioned how far this is really a true reflection of what occurs in practice. Judith Masson has argued that the provision of services for children in need can be characterised, not so much as voluntary assistance, as a form of 'diversion' from the more coercive forms of intervention[3]. She argues that the Childen Act 'contains separate but interlinked frameworks for managing risk with and without court orders'. On this analysis, the primary preoccupation of social services will be with those children who are thought to be at risk. As she puts it:

> 'The fact that there is no order should not be taken as indicating that the relationship between the family and the local authority is entirely voluntary. The local authority has duties to provide services and to protect children; the family accepts services against the coercive backdrop of the authority's powers to take proceedings.'[4]

The Children Act Advisory Committee in its final report[5] has commented adversely on the inappropriate use of voluntary accommodation of children under Part III as an alternative to an application for a care or supervision order. Yet, local authority sources are finite and there is evidence that the decisive factor influencing authorities in some cases is the cost involved in taking a child into care[6]. It may well be that the alleged philosophy of 'non-intervention' which is said to permeate the legislation and the 'no-order' principle in s 1(5) of the Act have also had some influence in persuading social services to go down the voluntary route where there is doubt that the basis for a care order would be established[7]. In these ways, the apparently clear distinction between *voluntary* 'services' and *compulsory* 'care' may be less sharp in practice than in theory.

---

1   In fact this is not entirely accurate since the expression 'looked after' is a generic term for both children 'in care' and those in local authority accommodation under voluntary arrangements. Where it is necessary to distinguish the two groups it may therefore be preferable to describe the 'voluntary' children as 'accommodated'.
2   See Chapter 2 above and the discussion below.
3   JM Masson 'Managing Risk Under the Children Act 1989: Diversion in Child Care?' (1992) 1 *Child Abuse Review* 103. The concept of 'diversion' is familiar in the context of juvenile justice.
4   Ibid at p 119.
5   *The Children Act Advisory Committee Final Report June 1997* (Lord Chancellor's Department, 1997) at pp 29–30. See below.
6   See, for example, *Nottinghamshire County Council v P* [1994] Fam 18. See also the discussion, in Chapter 11, of the House of Lords decision in *Re C (Interim Care Order: Residential Assessment)* [1997] 1 FLR 1, where financial considerations loomed large at the interim stage of care proceedings.
7   It is not easy to find hard evidence for this. The raw figures for care and supervision orders reveal that they have remained reasonably level at around 5,000 plus per annum. It is, however, interesting to note that the number of applications for care and supervision orders which have

Children in need: eligibility for services

The concept of 'children in need' is central to the operation of Part III of the Children Act[1]. It constitutes an all-important threshold, since it creates an eligibility for a wide range of statutory services. The local authority *must* provide these services to children once it has been determined that a child is in need. The claims of such children are described as an 'eligibility' rather than a 'right' or 'entitlement'. This is because local authorities have very wide discretions in determining how precisely to discharge their many statutory duties. While, therefore, a blanket refusal to provide *any* services to such children could render an authority's decision susceptible to judicial review[2], it will frequently be difficult, perhaps impossible, to argue that the children have a legal right to any *particular* service. The legislation does not give children in need unlimited rights of recipience, and the enforcement of the local authority's duties is highly problematic[3].

This leads us to the 'universality versus selectivity' debate which has so dominated policy-making in the field of social security provision[4]. In the present context, the question is whether publicly provided benefits for children ought to be regarded as available to *all* children on a universal basis or only to *some* children by applying selective criteria. Children are major beneficiaries of State provision of health, education, social security, housing and other welfare needs of the public[5]. In broad terms, it might be said that all children are in need of adequate provision in these areas and that, accordingly, they might have a *right* to claim, and society a *duty* to make available, the best possible provision. Universalist claims like these litter international commitments to children, most obviously in the United Nations Convention on the Rights of the Child[6]. The concept of 'children in need' in the Children Act is not used in this sense. It has a much narrower and technical definition, the purpose of which is to mark out those families who need the help of specialist services offered by local authorities. Thus, during the parliamentary debates on the Children Bill, the Government rejected the argument that, since nursery education is generally acknowledged to be beneficial to young children, *all* children in the relevant age-group could be said to be 'in need' of it, since they could all profit from it[7]. Such an interpretation would have necessitated

---

been *withdrawn* has more than doubled since 1992. See *Children Act Advisory Committee Final Report* (above), Appendix 2, Tables 2A and 2B.

1 Defined in s 17(10) and discussed below.
2 For a good discussion of judicial review in this context, see PM Bromley and NV Lowe *Bromley's Family Law* (8th edn) (Butterworths, 1992) at pp 548–550.
3 The possibilities are discussed at pp 354 et seq below.
4 As to which, see Ogus, Barendt and Wikeley *Law of Social Security* (4th edn) (Butterworths, 1995) at p 17.
5 Indeed, many of these benefits are specifically geared to children or, at least, to families with children. Obvious examples are child benefit and the 'priority need' which arises where a homeless person has dependent children.
6 Take, for example, Article 27(1) which requires States to 'recognize the right of every child to a standard of living adequate for the child's physical, mental, spiritual, moral and social development'.
7 The debate on this provision took an entire session at the Committee Stage of the Children Bill. See *Hansard*, 16 May 1989 (afternoon). The current Labour Government has, however, announced that nursery provision will be made for all four-year-olds under its general reform of the Welfare State. See p 335 below.

comprehensive nursery provision which the Conservative Government wanted to resist. The debate highlights the chief dilemma in this area. This is that, however well-intentioned the legislation, and however laudable the efforts of local authorities to implement it, its effectiveness is largely determined by the level of resources committed to it[1]. This has promoted one commentator to conclude thus:

> 'Government policies to improve services but to control local authority spending are in direct conflict. Despite a common legal framework, there are huge differences in provision of children's services nationally which relate to many things including variations in resources. Implementation of legislation relating to children's services involves changes in attitude, reformulation of local policies, and the development of new services ... Without new services, provision will continue to be resource rather than needs-led. ... There is now a wide recognition amongst local authorities that without an adequate level of resources there will be no development of services for children in need.'[2]

Central and local government: division of functions

Finally by way of introduction, something should be said about the division of functions between central and local government and the important principle of inter-agency co-operation at the local level. This was very much a theme of the reforms and finds expression in several places in the Children Act[3]. Central government responsibility for child care now resides in the Department of Health, which took over from the former Department of Health and Social Security in 1989. Its brief includes the formulation of policy, preparation of legislation and the issuing of guidance[4]. There is a Social Services Inspectorate which has responsibility for inspecting social services departments[5]. The responsibility for day-care, family support and protection of children is delegated by the Department of Health to local authorities. The legislation defines a local authority as a county council, metropolitan district or London Borough[6]. These councils are obliged to establish social services departments under the overall control of a Director of Social Services[7]. They replaced the former children departments and have a much wider remit including responsibility for other potentially vulnerable groups such as the mentally ill and the elderly.

The lack of coordination in local services, especially between different departments within individual authorities, was a frequently voiced criticism prior to the Children Act[8]. The Act attempted to address these deficiencies, in part, by creating new duties of inter-departmental co-operation. Hence, the local

---

1 On resources for the Children Act generally, see the informative article by JM Masson 'Implementing Change for Children: Action at the Centre and Local Reaction' (1992) 19 *Journal of Law and Society* 320.
2 Ibid at pp 335–336.
3 Particularly in s 27.
4 The point has been forcefully made that there is no single government department responsible for policies affecting children and that this is one reason why an office of Children's Ombudsman is required. See M Rosenbaum and P Newell *Taking Children Seriously* (Gulbenkian Foundation, 1991) and critique by A Bainham (1992) JSWFL 552.
5 For further discussion of the relationship between central and local government in this field, see JM Masson (above).
6 Section 105(1).
7 Local Authority Social Services Act 1970.
8 Not least in public inquiries into the deaths of children in care – as to which see Chapter 11 below. The importance of inter-agency co-operation was promoted in *Working Together Under the*

authority's statutory responsibilities are imposed not simply on its social services department (although clearly this will bear primary responsibility) but also on related departments and authorities, especially those responsible for housing, education and health. These authorities are, subject to limited qualifications, required to co-operate with social services, and social services departments in different authorities are similarly required to co-operate with each other[1]. Local authorities must also coordinate the provision of services by themselves and other agencies, particularly voluntary organisations[2]. This is intended to ensure, as far as possible, consistency in the standard of provision and good practice across different regions.

SERVICES FOR CHILDREN AND FAMILIES

Before the Children Act, local authorities owed a duty to *all* children 'to make available such advice, guidance and assistance' as might promote their welfare 'by diminishing the need to receive children into or keep them in care ... or to bring children before a juvenile court'[3]. More specific powers and duties arose under other statutes relating to particular groups of children, including the mentally handicapped and the disabled[4]. There was a good deal of regional variation in the quality and extent of services provided to these different groups. The *Review* and the White Paper[5] accepted that it would be in the interests of all the children concerned to unify the relevant parts of child care law and health and welfare legislation, in particular to extend the protection of child care law to handicapped and disabled children. Part III, accordingly, constitutes a single code governing the voluntary services offered by local authorities to children and families, regardless of the particular reason why these services are needed.

Children Act 1989 (HMSO, 1991). The Government has now issued a consultation paper, in anticipation of a new edition, entitled *Working Together to Safeguard Children: New Government Proposal for Inter-Agency Co-operation.* See further 'Working Together – a Consultation Paper too Far?' [1998] Fam Law 532.

1 Authorities must only comply with a request for help 'if it is compatible with their own statutory or other duties and obligations and does not unduly prejudice the discharge of any of their functions' (s 27(2)). On the respective duties of social services and housing authorities for housing children in need, see the House of Lords decision in *R v Northavon DC, ex parte Smith* [1994] 2 AC 402. This decision illustrates the limitations of the legal duty on authorities to co-operate with one another. The housing authority refused to rehouse an 'intentionally homeless' family despite being requested to do so by the social services department. The House of Lords held that it was entitled to refuse given the legal framework of the housing legislation and that the burden fell instead on social services to offer the family assistance, financial or otherwise, under Part III. See G Holgate 'Intentional Homelessness, Dependent Children and their Statutory Rights of Accommodation' [1994] Fam Law 264 which comments on the Court of Appeal decision. See also D Cowan and J Fionda 'Housing Homeless Families – An Update' [1995] CFLQ 66 for comment on the House of Lords decision. Detailed consideration of the housing responsibilities of local authorities is beyond the scope of the present discussion. For an account of these and their relationship with the local authorities' responsibilities under the Children Act, see D Bedingfield *The Child in Need* (Family Law, 1998) at ch 4.

2 Section 17(5). This is another example of the 'partnership' theme in the legislation.

3 Child Care Act 1980, s 1.

4 The main statutes were the National Health Service Act 1977, the National Assistance Act 1948 and the Chronically Sick and Disabled Persons Act 1970.

5 DHSS *Review of Child Care Law* (1985) ('the *Review*') and *The Law on Child Care and Family Services* (1987) (Cmnd 62) ('the White Paper').

Reformulation of the general duty

The general duty of local authorities to provide services is now contained in s 17(1) of the Children Act which states:

> 'It shall be the general duty of every local authority (in addition to the other duties imposed on them by this Part) –
>
> (a) to safeguard and promote the welfare of children within their area who are in need; and
> (b) so far as is consistent with that duty, to promote the upbringing of such children by their families, by providing a range and level of services appropriate to those children's needs.'

It is crucial to appreciate that this general duty to provide welfare is not the same as being bound by the 'welfare principle' articulated in s 1 of the Act[1]. The Court of Appeal has made this clear in *Re M (Secure Accommodation Order)*[2]. Here, the question was whether the use of secure accommodation under s 25 of the Act was a matter to be governed by the welfare principle. The court held that, although the child's welfare was a relevant factor, the Act prescribed the circumstances under which secure accommodation might be used, including where the child was likely to cause injury to others, and accordingly there might be circumstances in which the exercise of the power would not be consistent with the idea that the child's welfare was paramount. But the court did not stop there. It went on to say that the welfare principle in s 1 did not apply to *any* of the powers and duties arising under Part III of the Act. Thus while the individual child's welfare is a factor, indeed an important factor, in the exercise of the authority's obligations under Part III it may be outweighed by other factors and policy considerations which the authority needs to take into account.

The duty in s 17 is a substantial recasting of the local authority's preventive role. Before the Children Act, the duty was to endeavour to avert not only compulsory care proceedings but also the need to receive children into voluntary care. The concept of voluntary care was abolished by the Children Act and replaced with the notion of children 'accommodated' or 'looked after' by local authorities. This voluntary provision of accommodation is now viewed as just one kind of service offered to children and families in difficulty and it was considered important that this should be seen as *positive* assistance and not as a negative or stigmatising procedure. Accordingly, local authorities are no longer required to diminish the need to accommodate children but it remains the case that they must attempt to prevent more coercive measures being required. This other aspect of the local authority's duty has to be ferreted out of Sch 2 to the Children Act, which lists a range of more specific duties. Here, there is a duty to take reasonable steps to reduce the need to bring proceedings for care or supervision orders, criminal proceedings against children, family proceedings which could result in them being placed in a local authority's care, or proceedings under the inherent jurisdiction of the High Court; to encourage children not to commit criminal offences; and to avoid the need to use secure accommodation[3]. The common characteristic of all these actions is that they are compulsory in nature and stand in contrast to voluntary family support. It is generally agreed that voluntary assistance, where possible, is preferable.

---

1   For the welfare principle generally, see Chapter 2.
2   [1995] 1 FLR 418.
3   Schedule 2, para 7.

The other respect in which the duty was refashioned was by the addition of the word 'general'. The view of most commentators was that the effect of this was to reverse a decision under the old law that the former preventive duty applied to individual children[1] and this interpretation has been confirmed by the courts[2].

Children in need

The statutory definition of 'children in need' is crucial. While it is true that some of the local authority's more specific duties and powers do extend to *all* children, even these are directed at a more restricted group since they exist 'for the purpose principally of facilitating the discharge of their general duty'[3]. Thus, specific duties like the duty to take reasonable steps to prevent the ill-treatment or neglect of children[4], or the duty to provide 'family centres'[5], are intended to prevent children from *becoming* children in need.

The importance of the classification of 'child in need' is that it operates as a threshold condition or 'passport' to the services offered by the local authority, and these are not simply those services offered by the social services department. The general duty binds all departments within the local authority and it has already been mentioned that they are under an obligation to co-operate with each other. An assessment that a child is, or is not, in need, may therefore have important repercussions, not simply for family support by social services, but in the determination of housing, health and educational priorities. In short, the legislation appears to authorise positive discrimination in favour of childen in need. The negative side of this is that the label 'child in need' could acquire a stigma akin to that which has often been thought to attach to means-tested social security benefits – some of which also have the 'passport' effect of securing entitlement to a range of other benefits. This might become a real danger if local authorities too readily equate 'child in need' with 'child at risk'. The official guidance to this part of the legislation makes it plain that to do so would be unlawful[6], but scarce resources and competing claims on those resources make it inevitable that local authorities will resort to some form of rationing device.

The Children Act defines a child as being in need if:

'(a) he is unlikely to achieve or maintain, or to have the opportunity of achieving or maintaining, a reasonable standard of health or development without the provision for him of services by a local authority under this part;

(b) his health or development is likely to be significantly impaired, or further impaired, without the provision for him of such services; or

(c) he is disabled.'[7]

This definition is pregnant with indeterminancy, except insofar as it is clear that we are dealing with a restricted category of children. The Childen Act does,

---

1   *A-G (ex rel Tilley) v London Borough of Wandsworth* [1981] 1 All ER 1162.
2   *R v London Borough of Barnet ex parte B* [1994] 1 FLR 592.
3   Section 17(2).
4   Schedule 2, para 4(1).
5   Schedule 2, para 9.
6   *The Children Act 1989 Guidance and Regulations Vol 2 Family Support, Day Care and Educational Provision for Young Children* (HMSO, 1991) at para 2.4, which states that such a restriction 'would not be acceptable'.
7   Section 17(10).

however, go on to define various components in the definition with greater particularity, if not precision. It is evident from the definition itself, that the local authority must concern itself not only with those children who are already in need (in the sense that they already have a low standard of health or development) but also with those who are likely to find themselves in that position unless services are provided. The inclusion of the prospective element emphasises prevention rather than cure and mirrors the reformulated ground for compulsory action[1]. 'Development' for these purposes is expressed to include 'physical, intellectual, emotional, social or behavioural development' and 'health' includes 'physical or mental health'. 'Disabled' means a child who is 'blind, deaf or dumb or suffers from mental disorder of any kind or is substantially and permanently handicapped by illness, injury or congenital deformity or such other disability as may be prescribed'[2]. The use of terminology like this was criticised as unduly stigmatic during the parliamentary debates and it has been said that it is inappropriate to the approaching twenty-first century[3]. The reasoning appears to be that Parliament wanted to ensure the specific inclusion of all those categories of children for whom it was intended that the local authority's duty should apply.

It has been held that the local authority's determination that a child is, or is not, in need is not susceptible to challenge except through the judicial review procedure. In *Re J (Specific Issue Order: Leave to Apply)*[4], a 17-year-old boy was refused leave to seek a specific issue order deeming him to be a child 'in need' and requiring the local authority to make appropriate provision for him. Wall J held that Parliament could not have envisaged that the exercise of the duties imposed on local authorities under Part III of the Act should be exposed to judicial intervention except where the statute expressly provided for this, for example in relation to secure accommodation. The courts had not been given any power under the legislation to regulate the selection of children in need or to enforce the statutory duty to accommodate such children.

Available services

If the definition of children in need is full of indeterminate concepts, so also is the statutory basis upon which a number of particular services are offered by local authorities. There are duties to 'take reasonable steps' or to make such provision 'as is appropriate'. The combined effect of such provisions (including the definition of 'children in need') is to give local authorities an almost unassailable controlling discretion and to make legal challenges very difficult.

Services may not only be made directly available to children but also to members of their family. A major aim of the legislation is to promote the upbringing of children within their own families and it is the duty of the local authority to try to give effect to this aim[5]. One aspect of this is that services may be offered to any member of the family of a child in need, provided that this is with a view to safeguarding the welfare of that child[6]. Suppose, for example, that the

---

1   Section 31(2) and see Chapter 11 below.
2   Section 17(11).
3   MDA Freeman *Children, Their Families and the Law* (Macmillan, 1992) at p 57.
4   [1995] 1 FLR 669.
5   Section 17(1)(b).
6   Section 17(3).

presence of a severely disabled child within a family is affecting the health or development of other children of the family and putting everyone under strain. The statutory provision would enable extra support to be provided for that child with a view to alleviating the overall family situation. 'Family' for these purposes has an extended meaning and includes 'any person who has parental responsibility for the child and any other person with whom he has been living'[1]. The local authority is therefore able to concentrate on those who have the actual care of a child, without having to concern itself with technical questions about who has parental responsibility.

As under the old law, services may include giving assistance in kind or, in exceptional circumstances, in cash[2]. Prima facie, it might appear more attractive for local authorities to spend a relatively small amount of money on improving the home conditions of a family in which there are children who might otherwise need to be accommodated by it. There is no question that the cost of accommodating the child would far exceed any cash assistance given under this provision. But the issue is politically sensitive, since to make widespread use of these payments could be seen as usurping the role of the social security system which, however inadequately, caters for the material needs of families. This is the true basis of the restriction that such payments may be made in only exceptional circumstances. Moreover, in keeping with the social security reforms of the 1980s, the local authority may, in some circumstances, require repayment of its assistance or its value[3]. It must, however, have regard to the means of parents and there is an automatic exemption from liability for those in receipt of the principal means-tested benefits[4].

The principle of inter-agency co-operation has been noted. Another facet of this is that local authorities are required to facilitate the provision by others of services which they themselves lack the power to provide, and to make arrangements for others to act on their behalf in the provision of any service[5]. This underlines the need for co-operation between the public, private and voluntary sectors. The specific services which local authorities are required or empowered to provide are largely contained in Sch 2 to the Children Act.

Specific powers and duties

It is not appropriate in a work of this nature to analyse every detail of Sch 2 to the Children Act. But it is necessary to gain a general sense of what local authorities are required to provide beyond their broad umbrella power, and to highlight some of the more significant services. Freeman has helpfully identified the general character of the services in question.

---

1 Section 17(10).
2 Section 17(6). This used to be referred to under the old law as 'section 1 money'.
3 Section 17(7). The obvious analogy is with the abolition of 'single payments' in 1988 and their replacement with loans under the newly constituted 'Social Fund'. For a discussion of these reforms under the Social Security Act 1986 (implemented in April 1988), see Ogus, Barendt and Wikeley *Law of Social Security* (4th edn) (Butterworths, 1995), ch 15.
4 Section 17(8) and (9). The principal means-tested benefits are now income support (formerly supplementary benefit), family credit (formerly family income supplement), disability working allowance and income-based jobseeker's allowance. Family credit is to be abolished and replaced with a working families tax credit from 1999. See Chapter 9.
5 Section 17(5)(a) and (b).

'Local authorities cannot be expected to meet every individual need, but they are to take "reasonable steps" to identify the extent of need in their area and then to use their discretion reasonably and sensibly to make decisions about service provision in the light of the information they receive and their statutory obligations. They must ensure that a range of services is available to meet the need they identify. What is required will vary from area to area but is likely to include day care, foster care, some provision of residential care. They will need to offer a range of placements to reflect the racial, cultural, religious and linguistic needs of the children of their area (s 22(5)(c)). They will also have to have a range of short-term and longer term accommodation as well as permanent placements.'[1]

We noted above some of the local authority's specific duties. Further duties are listed below, followed by a closer examination of those duties relating to day-care and other services offered to children who are living with their families.

Among the local authority's duties are:

(1) a duty to publicise the services provided by it and by others and to take such steps as are reasonably practicable to ensure that the information is received by those who might benefit from the services[2];

(2) a duty to review its provision of services and, having regard to the review, prepare and publish a plan for the provision of services under Part III[3];

(3) a duty to open and maintain a register of disabled children[4];

(4) a duty to minimise the effects of disability suffered by disabled children[5];

(5) a duty to take reasonable steps to prevent the ill-treatment or neglect of children by the provision of services[6];

(6) a power to assist someone (possibly through cash) with removal expenses and the costs of obtaining alternative accommodation where that person is living with a child and the child is suffering, or is likely to suffer, ill-treatment at the hands of the person in question[7];

(7) a duty to provide family centres at which a child, his parents and others may receive advice, guidance and counselling or take part in various activities of an occupational, social, cultural or recreational nature[8];

(8) a duty, where a child in need is living apart from his family, to take reasonable steps to enable him to live with them or to promote contact with them if, in the authority's opinion, it is necessary to do so to safeguard or promote his welfare[9].

---

1 MDA Freeman *Children, Their Families and the Law* (Macmillan, 1992) at p 53.
2 Schedule 2, para 1(2).
3 Schedule 2, para 1A, inserted by the Children Act 1989 (Amendment) (Children's Services Planning) Order 1996, SI 1996/785.
4 Schedule 2, para 2(1).
5 Schedule 2, para 6. The best discussion of the application of the Children Act to disabled children is Freeman (above) especially at ch 11.
6 Schedule 2, para 4.
7 Schedule 2, para 5. This provision should now be taken alongside the new provision enabling local authorities to ask for 'exclusion requirements' to be inserted into emergency protection orders and interim care orders under Part IV of the Family Law Act 1996. This followed the recommendations of the Law Commission in (1992) Law Com Report No 207 *Domestic Violence and Occupation of the Family Home*. We discuss the new regime in Chapter 12.
8 Schedule 2, para 9.
9 Schedule 2, para 10.

Day-care and pre-school provision

Section 18 sets out the duties and powers of authorities regarding day-care for pre-school children and supervision of school-age children outside school[1]. The matter proved controversial in Parliament and was unusual in being one issue during the progress of the Children Bill which divided the political parties. Contrary to the position elsewhere in Europe, there has been no national plan for day-care and nursery provision in the UK. It has been largely left to the individual discretion of local authorities and its amount and quality varies considerably. The former Conservative Government resisted pressure to impose stronger duties but did eventually accede to a late amendment which placed local authorities under a new duty to review periodically the whole range of day-care facilities provided across the public, private and voluntary sectors within their area[2].

Day-care for children in need

Local authorities *must* provide such day-care for children in need 'as is appropriate'[3]. They have power to provide day-care for children in their area who are *not* in need[4]. This reserves a wide discretion to individual local authorities. They are also empowered to provide back-up support for those people who are directly involved in providing day-care facilities[5]. In addition, they have corresponding duties to older children in need, who are attending school, to provide for such care or supervised activities as is appropriate outside school hours or during school holidays. Again, this provision extends to children who are not in need[6]. This is intended to assist working parents, after school hours but before the end of the working day, and during school holidays. It is for individual local authorities to decide how precisely to discharge these responsibilities, but the most obvious examples are day nurseries, playgroups, child-minding, out-of-school clubs, holiday schemes and parent and toddler groups[7]. Despite these provisions there remains, in many parts of the country, an unmet need. The Labour Government has now indicated its intentions to make a nursery place available for all four-year-olds, through a partnership between the public and private sectors, as part of its overall strategy for reform of the Welfare State[8].

Assistance for children living with their families

Schedule 2, para 8 to the Children Act requires local authorities to make 'such provision as they consider appropriate' for specified services to be made available

---

1 For a more detailed discussion, see Freeman (above) at pp 85–88.
2 Section 19. For discussion of the statutory obligations of local authorities in this area, see C Cameron and P Moss 'The Children Act 1989 and Early Childhood' (1995) JSWFL 417. For an excellent comparative critique of the policies relating to child care provision in the context of employment prospects for women and parental employment policies more generally, see S Fredman *Women and the Law* (Clarendon, 1997) at pp 208–224.
3 Section 18(1). Section 18(4) provides that 'day care' means 'any form of care or supervised activity provided for children during the day (whether or not it is provided on a regular basis)'.
4 Section 18(2).
5 Section 18(3).
6 Section 18(5) and (6).
7 Other examples are given in *The Children Act 1989 Guidance and Regulations Vol 2* (above) at paras 3.8–3.17.
8 See Green Paper *New Ambitions for Our Country: A New Contract for Welfare* (March 1998), and Chapter 9 above. Under the School Standards and Framework Act 1998, s 118, LEAs will

for children in need while they are living with their families. The services in question are:

(1)　advice, guidance and counselling;
(2)　occupational, social, cultural or recreational activities;
(3)　home help (including laundry facilities);
(4)　travel facilities or assistance with travelling to and from home for the purpose of taking advantage of services;
(5)　assistance to enable the child and the family to have a holiday.

This, then, is another duty which encapsulates the ethos of family support. As far as possible, every effort should be made to keep functioning families together. In some cases, for whatever reason, this may not be possible, and it may prove necessary for the local authority to look after a child itself. We now turn to the important duty to provide accommodation.

THE PROVISION OF ACCOMMODATION

Prior to the Children Act, children who were accommodated by local authorities with the consent of parents were 'in care' albeit 'voluntary care'. Yet, although the initial arrangement was voluntary, this could slip into compulsion with the passage of time. 'Voluntary care' began to acquire a negative, even 'threatening'[1], image as local authorities were empowered to pass administrative resolutions assuming parental rights[2]. Parents were required to give 28 days' notice before resuming the care of a child who had been in voluntary care for at least six months. Moreover, it was held that the local authority was not obliged to return the child immediately on demand, even where that child had been in care for less than six months and that the child remained in care despite the notice having been given[3]. This, it was said, gave the local authority a 'breathing space' to take further action to protect the welfare of the child, usually by passing a resolution to assume parental rights.

All of this was inconsistent with the objectives of the new legislation, in particular the voluntary partnership which is supposed to exist between parents and the local authority. Eekelaar and Dingwall have identified the problem confronted in the *Review* as the 'increasingly sharp distinction between being in and out of care'[4]. If this was the most significant distinction under the old law, the crucial legal distinction following the Children Act is between the children who are formally 'in care' under a court order and those who are not, either because

---

henceforth be under a general duty to 'secure that the provision (whether or not by them) of nursery education for children who: (a) have not attained compulsory school age, but (b) have attained such age as may be prescribed, is sufficient for their area'. Under s 119, every LEA will be required to establish an 'early years development partnership' and, in conjunction with that body, under s 120, prepare 'an early years development plan' for their area. There is extensive provision for the inspection of nursery provision under s 122 and Sch 26 which supersede the Nursery Education and Grant Maintained Schools Act 1996, which previously regulated the matter.

1　The description of J Eekelaar and R Dingwall *The Reform of Child Care Law* (Routledge, 1990) at p 74.
2　Under the Child Care Act 1980, s 3.
3　*London Borough of Lewisham v Lewisham Juvenile Court Justices* [1980] AC 273.
4　J Eekelaar and R Dingwall (above) at pp 74–75. See DHSS *Review of Child Care Law* (1985).
5　J Eekelaar and R Dingwall (above) at pp 74–75.

they are at home or because they are voluntarily accommodated. Yet, as Eekelaar and Dingwall go on to point out, it was not the intention of the *Review* to create such an obvious demarcation[5]. The *Review* sought to establish 'finer gradations' of voluntary accommodation which would have embraced 'respite care' and 'shared care'. *Respite care* (a concept previously utilised in connection with handicapped children) would have been a short-term arrangement of up to one month. Parents would not have been required to give any notice of removal, the local authority would have been wholly dependent on parental delegation, and parental responsibility would not have passed to the local authority[1]. *Shared care* would, in contrast, have involved a transfer of parental responsibility to the authority by agreement[2]. The 28 days' notice would have been preserved and, since it envisaged 'shared' control, the local authority would have been obliged to allow parents to participate in decision-making and plans for the child.

In the event, the Government rejected the distinction between respite care and shared care as unworkable[3]. Hence, *all* children who are not 'in care' under a court order are now not in care at all. Parental responsibility for them does not pass to the local authority, and parents may remove them without notice. There is no longer any power to assume parental rights without a court order. These issues are now governed by formal agreements between authorities and parents, and the law is in retreat from these voluntary arrangements. We now turn to the legal framework under which these agreements operate.

The duty to accommodate

Section 20(1) of the Children Act sets out the circumstances under which local authorities must accommodate children in need. It states:

> 'Every local authority shall provide accommodation for any child in need within their area who appears to them to require accommodation as a result of:
> (a) there being no person who has parental responsibility for him;
> (b) his being lost or having been abandoned; or
> (c) the person who has been caring for him being prevented (whether or not permanently, and for whatever reason) from providing him with suitable accommodation or care.'

In simple terms, the duty arises in relation to orphaned or abandoned children[4] and children whose parents or carers are prevented by temporary or long-term illness, disability or other reason from properly looking after them. The Children Act Advisory Committee in its *Final Report* commented on what were appropriate and inappropriate uses of the power to accommodate children[5]. The Committee said that accommodation was properly used by the local authorities to work in partnership with parents in a variety of circumstances of need, such as hospital admission of a parent, bereavement, housing difficulties and respite care. But it

---

1   See DHSS *Review of Child Care Law* (1985) at chs 6 and 7.
2   Ibid, at ch 7.
3   *The Law on Child Care and Family Services* (1987) (Cmnd 62) ('the White Paper') at para 26.
4   It should be noted that, since the accommodation of children under s 20 does not confer parental responsibility on the local authority, it may be desirable in the case of an orphan for the authority to seek a care order to enable it to plan for the child's long-term welfare. See *Re SH (Care Order: Orphan)* [1995] 1 FLR 746, and Chapter 11 below.
5   *Children Act Advisory Committee Final Report June 1997* (Lord Chancellor's Department, 1997) at pp 29–30.

went on to say that it was crucial that accommodation should not be regarded as an alternative to an application for a care order or supervision order since, if used inappropriately, drift and damaging delay could occur to the detriment of the child. There was evidence in some cases that parents were agreeing to accommodation, as an alternative to court proceedings, in return for generous contact with the child. This could lead to delay in decision-making and planning, a failure to address fundamental problems and failure to plan properly for the future. There was also evidence that some parents used accommodation too frequently as a means of crisis resolution, especially in the context of changes of school, resulting in harm to the child from instability.

The relevance of objections

It is the very essence of these arrangements that they are voluntary. This means that they cannot be effected in the face of opposition by parents, although this blanket statement requires some qualification in the case of divorced or unmarried parents. There is no requirement of positive consent since it is obvious that this will be unobtainable in the case of orphaned or abandoned children. Instead, what is required is an absence of *relevant* opposition. Where the arrangement is opposed by someone with the right to oppose it, the local authority will have to resort to compulsory measures if it wishes to take over the care of the child.

Right of objection if suitable alternative accommodation offered

The primary rule is that no child may be accommodated where a person with parental responsibility (most obviously a parent) objects[1]. This right of objection is qualified in that it must be shown that the objector is himself willing and able to provide accommodation for the child. It appears that this was inspired by concern that an estranged or 'absent' parent might seek to frustrate an arrangement between the caring parent and the local authority, with no intention of proposing a more suitable alternative. The second, and complementary, rule is that anyone with parental responsibility 'may at any time remove the child from accommodation provided by or on behalf of the local authority'[2]. Both rules are displaced where a residence order is in force and where the person or persons in whose favour it is made has agreed to the arrangement. The same applies where, instead of a residence order, there is an order under the inherent jurisdiction of the High Court[3]. In either case, where more than one person holds a residence order each of them must agree to the child being accommodated[4].

Operation of provisions in different family situations

How do these provisions operate in the case of the married family, the unmarried family and the divorced family? Where the parents are married and living together, an objection by *either* parent will preclude the arrangement and either parent may remove a child accommodated originally with the agreement of the

---

1   Section 20(7).
2   Section 20(8). It is of course implicit in this that the person with parental responsibility can object to the continuation of an arrangement previously made with his approval.
3   Section 20(9).
4   Section 20(10).

other. In practice, it is unlikely that parents will disagree over so fundamental an issue, but, it is not impossible, especially where their relationship is breaking down. The normal rule which allows parental responsibility to be independently exercised, even were parents disagree with each other, is clearly superseded by the statutory right of objection.

Where the parents are unmarried, the mother alone has parental responsibility. She may thus enter in an arrangement with the local authority, and the father has no right of objection or removal unless he has previously acquired parental responsibility. It has been pointed out that this puts the minority of unmarried fathers who have actual care of their children in a peculiarly vulnerable position vis-à-vis social services[1]. It would, of course, be open to an unmarried father to seek a parental responsibility order and/or a residence order, the effect of which would be to authorise removal of the child from the local authority. But where the child is by this time settled, perhaps in a foster-home, the court may be reluctant to upset the status quo.

Where parents are divorced, the primary rule will continue to apply, since a divorced parent, although physically absent, retains equal parental responsibility. This will be the situation in the majority of cases because of the 'no order' principle. In the minority of cases in which a residence order is made, its effect is to displace the primary rule and to 'trump' the non-residential parent's right of objection[2]. How far this is consistent with the notion of continuing parental responsibility has been questioned[3].

Abolition of statutory notice requirement

The abolition of the statutory notice requirement has caused concern. The fear is, as Freeman has put it, that local authorities may become 'dumping grounds'. Children might come in and out of local authority accommodation 'at a parent's whim, with no opportunity for planning, and little attention to the needs of the child for security and stability'[4]. The hope is that this sort of capricious behaviour on the part of parents will be avoided by carefully negotiated agreements which deal specifically with the issue of the child returning home. The possibility of an attempt by parents to remove their child suddenly from local authority care, cannot, however, be discounted, and this had led to widespread speculation about what action the local authority could legally take to forestall such an occurrence[5]. Most commentators agree that the local authority's general duty to safeguard the child's welfare, and the allied power which de facto carers have to do what is reasonable in the circumstances, would be sufficient to resist a summary removal and to fill what might otherwise be a legal vacuum[6]. But if the authority wished to

---

1   A Bainham *Children: The New Law* (Family Law, 1990) at para 4.25, citing the case of *Re L (A Minor)* (1984) *The Times,* June 21.

2   This is not of course a situation confined to divorce, but divorce is easily the most significant context numerically.

3   A Bainham (above) at para 4.26.

4   MDA Freeman *Children, Their Families and the Law* (Macmillan, 1992) at p 65.

5   The options are extensively canvassed by Freeman (above) at pp 66–69 and by J Eekelaar and R Dingwall *The Reform of Child Care Law* (Routledge, 1990) at p 77.

6   See ss 17(1) and 3(5). Cretney and Masson take the view that the legal position under the Children Act is uncertain, while it was not in doubt under the old law (see *Krishnan v Sutton London Borough Council* [1970] Ch 181) that local authorities were not under an *absolute* duty to

continue to hold the child, it would need to seek a care order, probably preceded by an emergency protection order[1]. Police protection could be invoked, or a foster-parent might conceivably seek a residence order or care and control in wardship proceedings[2]. Probably the most unsatisfactory aspect of not requiring at least a short period of notice, is that this may hinder the legitimate plans of local authorities in trying to ensure a smooth transition back to the family, possibly by means of a phased return. In some cases, the reluctance of social services to hand a child over on demand may simply reflect its wish to be satisfied that the home circumstances have improved sufficiently for the child to return. It would be extremely unfortunate if this wholly reasonable concern were to force the local authority into coercive action. An amendment in the House of Lords which would have required a mere 24 hours' notice was rejected as inconsistent with the voluntary partnership principle[3]. While it is likely that in most cases parents will stick to the agreements they make with social services, and will not try to remove children in inappropriate circumstances, it is still arguable that a statutory requirement would have been desirable.

The child's point of view

How far should children themselves be able to decide whether or not they wish to be admitted to local authority accommodation or, once there, to remain there or leave? The legislation distinguishes between those over 16 years of age and those under that age.

Provision for children over 16 years of age
The position of those over 16 years is clear. The Children Act provides that neither the parental right of objection nor of removal applies where a child of 16 years of age agrees to being provided with accommodation[4]. The authority *must* accommodate any child of 16 years 'in need', whose welfare it considers 'is likely to be seriously prejudiced if they do not provide him with accommodation'[5], and it *may* provide accommodation for any child in its area if it considers that to do so 'would safeguard or promote the child's welfare'[6]. The purpose of these provisions is to cater for teenagers who have a seriously dysfunctional relationship with their parents[7]. The local authority's duty is a very restricted one, although it retains a wider *discretion*. The reason why the local authority's duty is so restricted is not entirely clear, but it may serve as a controlling mechanism for those local authorities which might otherwise be swamped by demands for accommodation from homeless young people in this age group. Again, the relationship between

---

return the child. See SM Cretney and JM Masson *Principles of Family Law* (6th edn) (Sweet & Maxwell, 1997) at p 785.
1 As to which, see Chapters 11 and 12 below.
2 The status of foster-parents is discussed in Chapter 6 above.
3 House of Lords, Official Report, 20 December 1988, col 1335.
4 Section 20(11).
5 Section 20(3).
6 Section 20(4). This applies even though a person with parental responsibility for the child is able to provide him with accommodation.
7 A matter which hit the headlines in October/November 1992 with a string of cases in which children were seeking orders to live elsewhere from their parents. This phenomenon is discussed in Chapter 13 below. See also M Freeman 'Can Children Divorce Their Parents?' in *The Moral Status of Children* (Martinus Nijhoff, 1997) at ch 11.

this provision, social security provision and the statutory responsibilities of housing authorities is a politically sensitive one[1]. The legislation does not deal expressly with the issue of a child leaving accommodation but, since the local authority will have no statutory basis on which to retain a 16- or 17-year-old child against his wishes[2], the implication is that the child can discharge himself. The local authority will then have statutory duties to advise and assist that child.

These provisions fell for interpretation in *Re T (Accommodation by Local Authority)*[3]. Here, a 17-year-old girl had been accommodated informally by friends, Mr and Mrs B. She wished to be formally accommodated under s 20 since Mr and Mrs B would, in that event, be eligible for fostering allowances and she herself would be entitled to receive ongoing support from the local authority under s 24 of the Children Act which might otherwise terminate at the age of 18. The director of social services refused to accommodate T, despite a successful complaint by her to the authority's complaints review panel, taking the view that her welfare was not likely to be seriously prejudiced if she was not accommodated. Johnson J quashed this decision in judicial review proceedings. Although it was for the authority and not the court to judge the facts, the director of social services had erred in taking insufficient account of T's *future* needs and in attaching too much weight to its discretionary powers to offer assistance under s 17 of the Act. At the time of taking the decision, the director of social services could not have been sure that the local authority would continue to exercise its supportive discretionary powers.

Provision for children under 16 years of age

The position is less clear where the child is under 16 years of age, since, here, difficult questions arise surrounding the relationship between the wishes of 'competent' minors, parental responsibility and dealings with third parties (in this case social services) which have caused such consternation in other areas[4]. It could be argued that a '*Gillick*-competent' child should have the decisive say. Eekelaar and Dingwall have speculated that parents might lose the legal power to direct where the competent child is to live[5]. This argument probably takes insufficient account of the effect of relevant statutory provisions. It should be remembered that the '*Gillick* principle' must always be subject to express statutory provisions. The most relevant one here states that the local authority, before providing accommodation, shall:

'so far as is reasonably practicable and consistent with the child's welfare –
(a) ascertain the child's wishes regarding the provision of accommodation; and
(b) give due consideration (having regard to his age and understanding) to such wishes of the child as they have been able to ascertain.'[6]

This would appear to fall short of giving the competent child the exclusive right to decide, and it also has to be set against the more concrete parental right of objection. The result seems to be that, where a parent is objecting to the proposed arrangement, the child's wishes cannot prevail, and the local authority would

---

1 But note that housing authorities are required to co-operate with social services under s 27.
2 Neither may the authority make the young person a ward of court for this purpose, s 100(2) effectively reversing the decision in *Re SW (Wardship: Jurisdiction)* [1986] 1 FLR 24.
3 [1995] 1 FLR 159.
4 Most particularly in relation to medical issues. See Chapter 8 above.
5 J Eekelaar and R Dingwall *The Reform of Child Care Law* (Routledge, 1990) at p 78.
6 Section 20(6).

need a court order to accommodate the child. Most obviously, this could be sought where the child is alleging physical or sexual abuse. The converse position is more doubtful, ie where the parents want the child to be accommodated and the child is objecting. Here, the local authority will have to balance the views of parents and child and form its own judgment on whether its duty to accommodate has arisen. The Children Act does not, itself, attach greater weight to either view. The remaining issue is whether a competent child under 16 years of age could discharge himself from accommodation or insist on remaining there. There is a precedent, under the old law, which suggests that the local authority might not be obliged to return an objecting teenager[1]. Freeman discusses whether this might be a case in which the local authority could apply for leave to invoke the inherent jurisdiction of the High Court[2] or, alternatively, to seek a care order on the basis that the child is beyond parental control[3]. The parent's statutory right of removal would seem to prevail, short of compulsory action like this, but the argument for giving greater weight to the child's view is perhaps stronger where the child is already out of the family home than where he is still there. The teenager in local authority accommodation already has a kind of semi-independence.

POWERS AND DUTIES OF LOCAL AUTHORITIES TO CHILDREN LOOKED AFTER BY THEM

The powers and duties which local authorities exercise over children 'looked after' by them are derived in part from the legislation and in part from the agreements made with parents and others with parental responsibility. The expression 'looked after' includes children who are 'in care' and also those 'accommodated' under voluntary arrangements[4], provided that the accommodation is for more than 24 hours[5]. Yet there is a crucial legal distinction between these two groups. Whereas the local authority acquires parental responsibility (albeit shared with parents) over children in care[6], it does not acquire it where the children are merely 'accommodated'. Here, it depends for its powers, substantially, on the agreements reached with parents, although some powers are necessarily implied from the existence of its statutory duties. Where the child is in care, the local authority is *not* dependent on parental delegation of responsibility since it has this under the care order. Yet the statutory duties owed to each category of children are broadly similar, as they were under previous legislation[7].

1　*Krishnan v Sutton London Borough Council* [1969] 3 All ER 1367 where the court refused to order the return of a 17-year-old girl, against her wishes, to her father. There would seem to be no reason in principle why, with the current state of the law, this principle could not be applied to significantly younger children.
2　Under s 100(3).
3　Under s 31(2). See MDA Freeman *Children, Their Families and the Law* (Macmillan, 1992) at pp 68–69.
4　Section 22(1) is in fact somewhat wider than this since it embraces all children 'provided with accommodation by the authority in the exercise of any functions ... which stand referred to their social services committee under the Local Authority Social Services Act 1970'.
5　Section 22(2).
6　Section 33(3)(a), discussed in Chapter 11 below.
7　Child Care Act 1980.

Agreements

The powers which local authorities have by implication from their statutory duties and as a de facto carer are limited and do not, of themselves, provide them with adequate latitude in making their plans. Accordingly, it is vitally important that provision be made for such matters as placement, medical care and schooling. It is now a statutory requirement that local authorities should draw up a written plan for the child and should reach agreement on this with the parents, other persons with parental responsibility, or where there is no one with parental responsibility, the person caring for the child[1]. These agreements are not binding contracts and are not therefore enforceable. To have given them the force of law would, it was thought, have been to detract unacceptably from the voluntary principle.

The regulations and guidance made under the legislation go into considerable detail about what should be incorporated in these agreements[2]. Although each agreement is peculiar to the particular arrangement, most local authorities adopt standard form agreements. Indeed, to do otherwise might lead to unacceptable confusion about the extent of the local authority's powers in relation to different children and equally unacceptable variations in their treatment. The matters over which agreement should be reached include the type of accommodation; the respective responsibilities of the local authority, the parents, the child and others; the services to be provided; contact; the projected length of stay, and the procedure for terminating the arrangements and rehabilitating the child with his family[3]. The local authority must produce written copies of the agreement and must provide a copy to everyone with whom the agreement is made, and to the child, in understandable form[4]. The essence of these agreements is that the local authority and the parents should work together for the benefit of the child and this is further underscored by the statutory duties owed to all children looked after by the local authority.

Statutory duties

The general duty

The general duty which local authorities owed to children in their care used to be contained in s 18(1) of the Child Care Act 1980[5]. This was substantially recast in the Children Act which provides:

'It shall be the duty of a local authority looking after any child –
(a)   to safeguard and promote his welfare; and
(b)   to make such use of services available for children cared for by their own parents as appears to the authority reasonable in his case.'[6]

The former duty under the Child Care Act 1980 expressed the child's welfare to

---

1   Arrangements for Placement of Children (General) Regulations 1991, SI 1991/890, reg 3.
2   *The Children Act 1989 Guidance and Regulations Vol 3 Family Placements* (HMSO, 1991) at paras 2.13 et seq.
3   Arrangements for Placement of Children (General) Regulations 1991, reg 4 and Sch 4.
4   Ibid, reg 5(3).
5   This provided that: 'In reaching any decision relating to a child in their care, a local authority shall give first consideration to the need to safeguard and promote the welfare of the child throughout his childhood ...'.
6   Section 22(3).

be the 'first consideration' for the local authority[1]. The effect of this formula was thought to be that, although the interests of the child were not the local authority's sole or paramount consideration, they were to receive priority over other competing interests. Under the old law, this was relied on successfully in a number of judicial challenges to the closure of children's homes where the relevant local authorities had failed to give first consideration to the welfare of the individual children affected[2]. While the point is not free from doubt, it would seem that the former duty has been diluted and that similar challenges might fail under the new law[3].

It is not clear how far the local authority's general duty to safeguard and promote the child's welfare is qualified by other considerations, particularly those of administrative convenience. The local authority may have to balance the interests of particular children against those of other children or other potential clients, especially given the pressure of finite resources. One way in which the general duty is certainly limited is that the local authority is permitted to act inconsistently with it where it thinks it is necessary 'for the purposes of protecting members of the public from serious injury'[4]. The Secretary of State may also direct the local authority to act inconsistently and the local authority must comply[5]. It might be necessary, in such a case, to contemplate the use of secure accommodation[6]. Along with the issue of contact with children in care, the use of secure accommodation is unusual in being one type of decision by local authorities which is subject to judicial scrutiny on its merits[7].

Specific duties

Specific duties are many and various. Some are contained in the body of the Children Act while others are set out in Part II of Sch 2. We can do no more than point out some of the more important specific duties.

The duty to consult

The Children Act made much wider provision for consultation than was the case before it. It states:

> 'Before making any decision with respect to a child whom they are looking after, or proposing to look after, a local authority shall, so far as is reasonably practicable, ascertain the wishes and feelings of –
> (a)   the child;
> (b)   his parents;
> (c)   any person who is not a parent of his but who has parental responsibility for him; and

---

1   On the gradations of relevance of children's welfare in different legal contexts, see Chapter 2 above.
2   See, for example, *Liddle v Sunderland Borough Council* (1983) Fam Law 250; *R v Solihull Metropolitan Borough Council ex parte C* [1984] FLR 363; and *R v Avon County Council ex parte K* [1986] 1 FLR 443.
3   Freeman takes the view that the argument, once accepted in *AG v Hammersmith and Fulham London Borough Council* (1979) *The Times*, December 18, that the authority is entitled to consider a child's welfare *after* it has taken a decision to close a home, may again be tenable.
4   Section 22(6).
5   Section 22(7) and (8).
6   This is governed by s 25, the Children (Secure Accommodation) Regulations 1991, SI 1991/1505, and the Children (Secure Accommodation) (No 2) Regulations 1991, SI 1991/2034. For a general discussion, see A Bainham *Children: The New Law* (Family Law, 1990) at paras 4.57–4.61 and MDA Freeman *Children, Their Families and the Law* (Macmillan, 1992) at pp 155–160.
7   This kind of ordinary access to the courts should be contrasted with the more restricted mechanism of judicial review.

(d) any other person whose wishes and feelings the authority consider to be relevant, regarding the matter to be decided.'[1]

The local authority must then go on to give 'due consideration' to such views, in the case of a child commensurate with his age and understanding[2]. It must also, in making its decision, give due consideration to the child's 'religious persuasion, racial origin and cultural and linguistic background'[3], a recurrent theme in the legislation[4]. These considerations are probably of greatest relevance to the question of placement. They suggest that, all other things being equal, efforts should be directed to placing children in families of similar race, culture and linguistic background. But clearly this is only a guideline and there will be some instances in which this would be undesirable or impossible having regard to the overriding consideration of the child's welfare. If the only available foster-parents of similar cultural background are considered inappropriate, it may be necessary to place the child elsewhere.

There is no indication in the legislation of the relative weight to be attached to individual views where these conflict, and this must be a matter for the local authority's discretion.

The duty to provide accommodation

The options open to the local authority for accommodating a child who is looked after by the authority are set out in the legislation[5]. They are, to place him with a family, relative or other person (foster-parents), community home, voluntary home, registered children's home, home with special facilities or by making such other arrangements as seem appropriate to the authority. The legal regulation of these various placements is considered below.

An important option is to allow the child to remain at home, possibly subject to supervision. The local authority's general rehabilitative objective militates towards this solution but there is always the counter pressure of adequately protecting the child's welfare[6]. Several provisions in the Children Act reflect these considerations. On the one hand, there is a prima facie duty to make arrangements for the child to live with his family, unless to do so would not be reasonably practicable or consistent with his welfare[7]. There is a similar duty that accommodation which is not with the family should be near the child's home, and that siblings, who are looked after by the local authority, should be accommodated together[8]. On the other hand, there are regulations[9] which ensure that

---

1 Section 22(4). It was established in *R v North Yorkshire County Council ex parte M* [1989] 1 All ER 143 that where the child has a guardian ad litem he should be consulted.
2 Section 22(5)(a) and (b).
3 Section 22(5)(c).
4 There is a particularly useful discussion of these considerations in MDA Freeman (above) at pp 73–77 and, more generally, on cultural considerations in the context of children's rights, see M Freeman 'Children's Rights and Cultural Pluralism' in *The Moral Status of Children* (Martinus Nijhoff, 1997) at ch 7.
5 Section 23(2).
6 Chapter 11 below discusses these counter-pressures.
7 Section 23(6).
8 Section 23(7).
9 Section 23(5) and Sch 2, para 14, and the Placement of Children with Parents etc Regulations 1991, SI 1991/893. Under s 23(5A) (inserted by the Court and Legal Services Act 1990) the regulations apply only where the child lives with the relevant person for a continuous period of more than 24 hours.

there are sufficient safeguards where a child is allowed 'home on trial'[1]. The
regulations govern such matters as notification, consultation, medical and other
supervision.

The duty to maintain

The local authority is required to maintain a child looked after by it[2] but may, in
certain circumstances, recoup some of the cost by requiring a financial
contribution to the child's maintenance or services provided for him from certain
other persons[3]. The local authority must charge only what is reasonable, given the
financial means of the recipients of the service, but those on the principal
means-tested social security benefits are exempt[4]. Contributions towards maintenance are governed by a separate code[5]. These charges have always been
controversial and the Children Act brought about a change of emphasis whereby
local authorities are required to charge only where they consider it reasonable to
do so[6].

The duty to promote contact

Consistent with the rehabilitative thrust of the legislation, local authorities are
required to endeavour to promote contact, so far as is reasonably practicable and
consistent with his welfare, between the child, his family, relatives, friends and
others connected with him[7]. To this end, the local authority and persons with
parental responsibility are obliged to stay in touch with each other. The local
authority must take steps to keep them informed of the child's whereabouts and
they must keep the local authority informed of their respective addresses[8]. Local
authorities must also co-operate among themselves where a child moves into a
different area[9].

Other powers and duties

Other powers and duties are set out in Part II of Sch 2 to the Children Act. They
include assistance with travelling expenses where visits are made to children in
care, the appointment of independent visitors where visits by the family have
become very infrequent, assistance in arrangements for the child to live outside
England and Wales (subject to significant safeguards), and arrangements for the
funeral of a child who dies while being looked after by the local authority.

---

1   These provisions are the successors of the Children and Young Persons (Amendment) Act 1986,
    which legislation was inspired by public anxiety over the deaths of certain children at the hands
    of parents and others, most notably that of Jasmine Beckford. See *A Child in Trust: Report of the
    Panel of Inquiry Investigating the Circumstances Surrounding the Death of Jasmine Beckford* (London
    Borough of Brent, 1985).
2   Section 23(1)(b).
3   Section 29. Those who may be liable are the child's parents, a child over 16 years of age himself,
    and, where the service is provided for a member of the child's family, that person (s 29(4)). For
    the correct approach in assessing a parent's contribution, see *Re C (A Minor) (Contribution Notice)*
    [1994] 1 FLR 111.
4   Section 29(3). This will be likely to be a high proportion, given the close association between
    poverty and care.
5   Section 29(6) and Sch 2, Part III.
6   Schedule 2, para 21(2).
7   Schedule 2, para 15, which should be read with ss 17(1) and 23(6). Taken together they add up
    to a duty to endeavour to reunite the child with the family.
8   Schedule 2, para 15(2).
9   Section 20(2) and Sch 2, para 15(3) and (4).

Duties to children leaving accommodation

The Children Act substantially increased the duties of local authorities towards children ceasing to be looked after by them up to the age of 21 years[1]. The purpose was to assist these often vulnerable young people in making the difficult transition to independent living in the community. It was recognised that many of them would have no family on which to rely for support. The initial duty of local authorities is to the child while he is being looked after by them and is to 'advise, assist and befriend him with a view to promoting his welfare when he ceases to be looked after by them'[2]. Local authorities must then provide 'after-care' to certain young people by way of advice and assistance after they have ceased to be 'looked after'.

Those qualifying are young people in the area of the local authority who are under 21 years of age and who were, while 16 or 17 years of age, looked after by a local authority, accommodated by a voluntary organisation, a registered children's home, a health authority, a Special Health Authority or local education authority, a residential care home, a nursing home, a mental nursing home or in any accommodation provided by a National Health Service trust, or privately fostered, but who are no longer so looked after, accommodated or fostered[3].

The local authority may provide assistance in kind or, in exceptional circumstances, in cash[4] but, again, not as a substitute for income support under the social security system. A contribution may be made to expenses occasioned by a person needing to live near a place of employment, seeking employment, or receiving education or training[5]. There are the usual exemptions from liability to repay for those people who are on the major means-tested social security benefits[6], and there are provisions requiring co-operation between different local authorities[7]. Changes introduced by the Courts and Legal Services Act 1990 require local authorities to establish procedures for representations and complaints from relevant young people[8].

LEGAL REGULATION OF SUBSTITUTE CARE ARRANGEMENTS

The Children Act contains a mass of detail on regulating the different kinds of substitute care for children and a range of statutory instruments have also been

---

1 Following the recommendations in the DHSS *Review of Child Care Law* (1985) at ch 10; and see generally L Jordan 'Accommodation and Aftercare: Provision for Young People' (1992) 4 JCL 162.
2 Section 24(1).
3 Section 24(2). Where the young person concerned moves to another local authority area after attaining majority, it is the responsibility of *that* authority to provide the after-care required by the legislation. See *R v London Borough of Lambeth ex parte Caddell* [1998] 1 FLR 253.
4 Section 24(6) and (7).
5 Section 24(8).
6 Section 24(1) and s 17(9).
7 Section 24(11) and (12).
8 Section 24(14) and (15), and the Representations Procedure (Children) Regulations 1991, SI 1991/894, as amended.

made under its enabling powers[1]. Parts VI to XI and some of Part XII provide the framework. Much of this is a consolidation of previous law and is of limited academic interest[2]. But it is important to have at least some understanding of the general principles which govern the protection of children living away from home, and of the central role of local authorities in monitoring and supervising these arrangements. An attempt will be made to bring out the salient features of the statutory scheme as it applies to residential care, fostering arrangements, child-minding and day-care.

Residential care

The expression 'residential care' is used to refer to the accommodation of children outside families in various kinds of communal homes[3]. Broadly, the alternatives are community homes[4], voluntary homes[5], and registered children's homes[6]. The principal regulatory mechanism is *registration*. Voluntary homes are registered with the Secretary of State[7], and registered children's homes are registered with the local authority[8]. Voluntary homes are houses established and managed by voluntary organisations, and the legislation, in addition to regulating their conduct and management, spells out the general duties of voluntary organisations to children looked after by them[9]. Registered children's homes are essentially private homes and were largely unregulated prior to the Children Act[10]. The legislation contains corresponding provisions regarding the conduct and management of registered homes and the duties of those persons carrying on or in charge of registered homes[11]. The overall policy is to try to ensure that children receive similar standards of treatment and that their welfare is equally protected whether they are accommodated in the public, voluntary or private sector[12].

---

1 For a detailed discussion, see MDA Freeman *Children, Their Families and the Law* (Macmillan, 1992) at ch 9.
2 The law before the Children Act was extensively reviewed in M Freeman and C Lyon *The Law of Residential Homes and Day Care Establishments* (Sweet & Maxwell, 1984). On the new law, see A Bainham *Children: The New Law* (Family Law, 1990) at ch 7 and *The Children Act 1989 Guidance and Regulations Vol 4* (HMSO, 1991).
3 This chapter does not deal with children accommodated in health and educational establishments or in independent schools since it is more convenient to deal with this matter in Chapter 16 below.
4 Part VI and Sch 4 to the Children Act. Community homes are divided into two categories – 'controlled community homes' and 'assisted community homes'. The local authority has the management of the former whereas a voluntary organisation has the management of the latter (s 53(3)–(5)). What distinguishes them from 'voluntary homes' is the direct involvement of the local authority which is party to the instrument of management.
5 Part VII and Sch 5.
6 Part VIII and Sch 6.
7 Section 60(1).
8 Section 63(1).
9 Section 61. These correspond with the duties owed by local authorities to children looked after by them.
10 The Children's Homes Act 1982 did regulate these homes but the legislation was never implemented. The definition of 'registered children's home' is complex (CA 1989, s 63(3)). See A Bainham *Children: The New Law* (Family Law, 1990) at para 7.25 and MDA Freeman *Children, Their Families and the Law* (Macmillan, 1992) at pp 208–209.
11 Schedule 6, Part II.
12 See DHSS *Review of Child Care Law* (1985) at ch 11.

How is this achieved? In each case, the Children's Homes Regulations 1991[1] govern the conduct of these homes and provide for such matters as adequate staffing levels, suitable and proper equipment and furniture, proper sanitation, heating and lighting, important prohibitions on inappropriate disciplinary or control devices[2], dietary standards, religion, etc. For each child, a written case record must be maintained[3].

The main sanction for non-compliance with the statutory standards is, in the case of community homes, revocation of their designation by the Secretary of State. He may give written notice to the responsible body for the home that from a specified date the premises may no longer be used as a community home. This may be because the premises are considered unsuitable, or where the conduct of the home is in breach of the regulations, or where it is otherwise unsatisfactory[4]. No voluntary home may be carried on unless it is registered with the Secretary of State[5] and a registration may subsequently be cancelled where there is a breach of the regulations[6]. There is a procedure for representations and appeals in each case[7]. Although registration is with the Secretary of State, local authorities have important functions in relation to voluntary homes. Local authorities must satisfy themselves that voluntary organisations in their area are satisfactorily safe-guarding and promoting the welfare of the children looked after by them[8] and, where they are not satisfied, local authorities must, in effect, take over responsi-bility for protecting the welfare of those children[9]. They are obliged to visit the children[10] and they have powers of entry and inspection[11]. Largely corresponding provisions apply to registered children's homes[12]. A criminal offence is committed by anyone who carries on an unregistered home[13] and there are statutory disqualifications (based on those which apply to private foster-parents[14]) designed to prevent children coming into contact with undesirable adults.

Important new regulations designed to prevent children coming into contact with persons who have been convicted of or cautioned in relation to serious offences against children came into effect on 24 October 1997. The Children (Protection from Offenders) (Miscellaneous Amendments) Regulations 1997[15] apply widely to children who might be adopted, fostered or looked after in a children's home and amend the respective regulations governing disqualification

---

1 SI 1991/1506.
2 Such as, for example, corporal punishment, the deprivation of food and drink or a requirement that a child wear distinctive or inappropriate clothes (reg 8).
3 Arrangements for Placement of Children (General) Regulations 1991, SI 1991/890, reg 8.
4 Section 54.
5 Section 60(1).
6 Schedule 5, para 1(4).
7 Schedule 5, paras 3 and 5.
8 Section 62(1).
9 Section 62(5).
10 Section 62(3).
11 Section 62(6).
12 Sections 63 and 64.
13 Section 63(10).
14 Section 65.
15 SI 1997/2308.

in relation to those forms of caring for children.[1] The effect of the regulations is Draconian. There is a non-discretionary, absolute disqualification applying to anyone who has been either convicted of or cautioned in relation to a serious sexual offence or any offence of violence above the level of common assault or battery against a child. The disqualification applies to both prospective and existing foster-parents and anyone aged over 18 living in the same household. In *Lincolnshire County Council v RJ, X Intervening*[2] a foster-father, who had acted successfully as such for some years, received a caution on the basis of his admission of having caused actual bodily harm to a child in his care. The deputy High Court judge was obliged to hold that he was disqualified from fostering another child when this arose as a preliminary issue in care proceedings.

Fostering arrangements

The regulatory mechanisms are different as between local authority foster-parents and private foster-parents, yet the local authority has the key role in each case. The difference is that, in the case of local authority foster-parents, the local authority is, by definition, involved from the start, since it makes the arrangements, whereas it is not so involved where private arrangements are effected.

Local authority foster-placements

The definition of local authority foster-parent was noted earlier and the essential status involved was discussed[3]. This chapter is concerned with the legal controls on the standard and quality of these placements[4]. These are governed by the Foster Placement (Children) Regulations 1991[5]. There are essentially two controlling mechanisms: the approval of the prospective foster-parent, and the *written placement agreement*. Approval may not be given unless the authority has obtained references and detailed information concerning such matters as the age, health, personality and marital status of the applicant, particulars of the proposed accommodation, other members of the applicant's family, his religious persuasion, racial origin and cultural background, employment record, previous experience with children and so on[6]. Having approved someone as a foster-parent, the local authority must enter into a written agreement with him, governing the detailed aspects of the relationship between local authority, foster-parent and child[7]. The agreement must regulate such matters as: the information to be provided by the local authority to foster-parents about the child's history to enable them to carry out their task; financial support; dental and medical treatment; living and visiting arrangements; contact with parents and others; and the foster-parent's undertaking to co-operate with the local authority.

---

1   The Adoption Agencies Regulations 1983, SI 1983/1964; the Foster Placement (Children) Regulations 1991, SI 1991/910; and the Disqualification for Caring for Children Regulations 1991, SI 1991/2094.
2   [1998] 2 FLR 82.
3   See Chapter 6 above.
4   For a good general discussion, see MDA Freeman *Children, Their Families and the Law* (Macmillan, 1992), pp 79–85.
5   And see *The Children Act 1989 Guidance and Regulations Vol 3 Family Placements* (HMSO, 1991).
6   Regulation 3 and Sch 1.
7   Schedule 3.

Fostering allowances are paid to all local authority foster-parents by the authority in accordance with the regulations[1]. Although the amount paid varies between authorities, the National Foster Care Association annually recommends a minimum fostering allowance which depends on the age of the child and whether the child lives in London or elsewhere. The weekly rates from April 1997 (for children outside London) were: for children aged under 5, £58.35; for those aged between 5 and 10, £72.37; for those aged between 11 and 15, £90.08; and for those aged 16 and over, £116.70. The regulations go on to provide that the approving authority should review at intervals of not more than one year whether the foster-carer and his household continue to be suitable. Where the authority is not so satisfied, the approval is terminated[2].

The regulations impose minimum visiting requirements and also govern such matters as revocation of a placement where it ceases to be suitable, immediate placements in emergencies, registration of children in local authority foster-care and the maintenance of case records[3].

Private foster-parents

Again, the definition of private foster-parent has already been discussed[4]. The local authority would not, in the ordinary course of events, have any knowledge of privately arranged placements and this could be a cause for concern. Hence, the chief regulatory mechanism is *notification* rather than registration. The statutory scheme is contained in Part IX of, and Schs 7 and 8 to, the Children Act together with the Children (Private Arrangements for Fostering) Regulations 1991[5].

A prominent feature of the scheme is the requirement that the local authority should satisfy itself as to the welfare of privately fostered children in its area[6] and, where it is not so satisfied, take further specified action[7]. The notification requirements were tightened significantly by the Children Act. They now extend to parents, persons with parental responsibility and those involved directly or indirectly in making arrangements, as well as the foster-parents themselves. Notification is now required both of the proposal to make the arrangement and of its subsequent cessation[8]. The other key element in the statutory scheme is the

---

1 Schedule 3, para 2.
2 For an unsuccessful attempt by a foster-carer to challenge the authority's decision to terminate his approval as a foster-parent, see *R v Avon County Council ex parte Crabtree* [1996] 1 FLR 502.
3 See MDA Freeman (above) at pp 82 et seq.
4 See Chapter 6 above.
5 Which replace the Foster Children Act 1980.
6 Section 67(1). Under the Children (Private Arrangements for Fostering) Regulations 1991, SI 1991/2050, reg 2(2), the authority must satisfy itself in particular as to such matters as the intended purpose and duration of the arrangement, the child's development, financial arrangements, suitability of the accommodation, health, education, etc: in short, *all* matters relevant to the child's healthy development.
7 Section 67(5). They must essentially secure that the child's accommodation is taken over by a parent, person with parental responsibility, relative or, where that is not reasonably practicable, they must consider whether to exercise their functions under the legislation.
8 Children (Private Arrangements for Fostering) Regulations (above), regs 4–7.

disqualification of unsuitable persons from private fostering[1]. Those persons who are disqualified include parents whose children have been in care and those convicted of criminal offences against children. The local authority may also prohibit the use of unsuitable premises for private fostering[2]. There is an appeals system, and the disqualification provisions are backed up by criminal offences[3].

Child-minding and day-care for young children

Child-minding and day-care are regulated by Part X of, and Sch 9 to, the Children Act and regulations made under the Act[4]. These provisions replace the previous system of registration under the Nurseries and Child-Minders Regulation Act 1948, which was widely thought to be ineffective. *Registration* with the local authority remains the essential regulatory mechanism[5]. A major change in the system of registration introduced by the Children Act was to unify, in one register, all child-minders and day-carers, where previously separate registers had been maintained for child-minders and nurseries. The maximum age of children covered by the registration requirements has also been unified at eight years. Thus, the system protects mainly pre-school children but also younger children who take part in out-of-school and holiday activities. The aims of the scheme are to ensure compliance with adequate standards and to empower the local authority to take action where those standards are not achieved.

Who must register?

All local authorities are required to keep a register of child-minders and day-care providers[6]. The distinction is between those who look after children on 'domestic premises' (child-minders) and those who look after them on 'non-domestic premises' (day-carers)[7]. The key trigger condition for registration is that the child should be looked after by someone who is not a parent, or a person with parental responsibility or a foster-parent, for reward, for more than two hours in any day[8]. 'Nannies' are not child-minders and are not required to register unless they work for more than two employers[9]. There is also an 'occasional facilities' exemption where day-care is provided on any premises for less than six days per year, provided appropriate notice of their use is given to the local authority[10]. Occasional unregistered carers such as baby-sitters, although technically in breach of the regulations, are unlikely to receive enforcement notices[11].

---

1 Disqualification for Caring for Children Regulations 1991, SI 1991/2094.
2 Section 69(2)(b).
3 Section 70 and Sch 8, para 8.
4 Child Minding and Day Care (Applications for Registration) Regulations 1991, SI 1991/1689; Child Minding and Day Care (Registration and Inspection Fees) Regulations 1991, SI 1991/2076.
5 Sections 71–78.
6 Section 71(1).
7 Section 71(1).
8 Section 71(2).
9 Section 71(5) and (6). The children must be looked after wholly or mainly in the home of either of the employers.
10 Schedule 9, para 5(1).
11 Contravention of the registration requirement no longer automatically constitutes an offence. An enforcement notice is required (s 78).

Refusal or cancellation of registrations

The age-limit of eight years for children covered by the registration requirements was a compromise, designed to protect some younger school children but not to be set so high as to prevent any reasonable chance of enforcement. The local authority may refuse registration on the grounds that the applicant or the premises in question are unfit[1]. There are disqualifications similar to those which apply to private foster-parents[2].

In *London Borough of Sutton v Davis*[3], Anne Davis had been a child-minder under the previous legislation and she now sought to be registered under the Children Act. The local authority had formally adopted a 'no smacking policy' which entailed an automatic determination of unfitness in relation to any applicant who refused to undertake not to smack a minded child. Anne Davis's position on corporal punishment was that she wished to have the authority to 'smack gently' in accordance with parental wishes. She refused to give the required undertaking whereupon the authority, although satisfied that she met its child-minding criteria in every other respect, refused her registration.

The magistrates allowed her appeal against this refusal and their decision was upheld by the High Court. Wilson J held that there was nothing in the legislation which required the authority to adopt so inflexible a policy that Anne Davis was, by reason of her views on corporal punishment, per se unfit to be a child-minder. The magistrates had been entitled to look at the applicant's fitness more generally and to reach the conclusion that they did.

The local authority may also subsequently cancel a registration on specified grounds, the most significant of which is that 'the care provided by that person is ... in the opinion of the authority, seriously inadequate having regard to the needs of that child'[4]. Concern has been expressed that the inclusion of the word 'seriously' may imply that local authorities should accept people with whom they are less than happy[5]. There is provision for emergency cancellation of registrations where a child might otherwise be exposed to significant harm[6], and the local authority has powers of entry and inspection to enable it to carry out its

---

1 Section 71(7)–(10). It is a prerequisite to registration that suitable premises are available. In *Woodward v North Somerset District Council* [1998] 1 FLR 950, Mrs Woodward failed to be registered as a provider of nursery and other day-care services whereupon she forfeited the lease on the premises in which she had intended to run her business. Her appeal to the magistrates against refusal of registration failed on the preliminary ground that she had no premises in which such services could be provided and, thus, her personal fitness could not be assessed. Bracewell J held that this was the correct interpretation of the legislation since s 71 contemplated the registration of a person in respect of a particular set of premises.
2 Schedule 9, para 2.
3 [1994] 1 FLR 737.
4 Section 74(1) and (2). The other grounds for disqualification are where it appears to the authority that there are circumstances which would justify refusing to register the individual concerned or where the person concerned has contravened or failed to comply with any requirement of registration or has failed to pay the annual inspection fee.
5 This appeared to have been the case before the Children Act – a point made by Ms H Armstrong MP. See *Hansard*, 6 June 1989, col 402.
6 Section 75. An apparent lacuna is that there is no express provision for an inter partes hearing in such cases. However, it has been reported that a child-minder who had her registration cancelled under s 75 without the opportunity of putting her side of the case, succeeded in obtaining judicial review of the magistrates' decision and in obtaining an order of mandamus, requiring them to hold an inter partes hearing. See [1993] Fam Law 258.

duties[1]. The Children Act also instituted a *minimum* requirement that inspections of relevant premises be carried out at least annually[2]. Provision exists for appeals against refusals to register and cancellations of registrations[3], and it is a criminal offence to engage in unregistered activities, to obstruct inspections, to contravene the disqualification requirements or to fail to comply with any registration requirements imposed by the local authority[4].

Conditions for registration

Finally, the Children Act introduced important changes affecting the conditions of registration. First, the Act brought in fees for registration[5]. This was a controversial development. The argument in favour was that it would generate much-needed income for local authorities whose responsibilities for scrutiny of arrangements would increase under the legislation. Against this, it was said that the introduction of fees could operate as a disincentive to registration where existing day-care arrangements were already operating on a shoe-string budget. Secondly, authorities were, for the first time, given a *duty* to impose reasonable registration requirements, some of which, such as those relating to the maximum number of children who may be looked after, maintenance of premises, equipment and safety standards, and the duty to keep records of children and day-care assistants, are mandatory. Other conditions may be imposed at the discretion of individual local authorities[6].

QUESTIONING LOCAL AUTHORITIES' DECISIONS

What redress is available to someone who is aggrieved by a decision of the local authority affecting a child looked after by it? The potential remedies, in theory at least, apply equally to children in care and to accommodated children but, in practice, disputes are most likely to be about children in care, for several reasons. Since the local authority does not have parental responsibility over accommodated children it has less control. Allied to this is the fact that the agreement with the parents may well pre-empt potential areas of disagreement. More fundamentally, if a serious disagreement should arise, it would be open to the parents to demand the return of the child. This is not an option where the child is in care. However, since common principles apply to all children looked after by the local authority, they will be considered here. The general policy of the legislation is to vest managerial control in the local authority, and it was not thought appropriate to expose most areas of decision-making to judicial scrutiny. By way of exception, the decision to commit a child to care[7] or discharge a child from care[8] is left in the

---

1 Section 76.
2 Section 76(4).
3 Section 77.
4 Section 78.
5 Governed by the Child Minding and Day Care (Registration and Inspection Fees) Regulations 1991, SI 1991/2076.
6 Section 73.
7 Section 31(1).
8 Section 39.

hands of the courts, as is the emotive question of contact between children in care and their families[1].

We will now look at the possible avenues of redress[2], but it should be said at the outset that, apart from the statutory procedures for periodic reviews, representations and complaints, most of the other avenues are distinctly 'long-shots', although they do occasionally succeed. The courts have traditionally exhibited a reluctance to interfere with the plans of local authorities, except where they have plainly acted improperly[3].

It should be noted, however, that the local authority must produce a care plan to the court covering such matters as placement and contact with parents *before* the court will be willing to make a care order in the first place[4]. At present, there is no concrete statutory obligation to produce a care plan but the draft Adoption Bill 1996, if enacted, would amend the Children Act to provide for this[5]. The court also remains in control at the interim stage of care proceedings[6].

Reviews and representations

The local authority is obliged to keep under periodic review the case of each child looked after by it and it has a complementary duty to establish procedures to deal with representations and complaints[7]. Both are designed to subject local authorities to a measure of accountability and to encourage proper planning for every child. The *Review* was anxious to allow the authority to 'take a grip' on the case and did not want the courts to intrude into what was seen as the primary responsibility of the local authority. Instead, it recommended a strengthening and improvement of the existing system of reviews and the mandatory introduction of internal complaints procedures with an independent element[8]. The Children Act gives effect to these recommendations.

Reviews

Prior to the Children Act, there were no regulations dealing with the manner or conduct of reviews relating to children in care, although the power existed to make such regulations. The Review of Children's Cases Regulations 1991 now provide that the local authority must review the case of each child being looked after by it. The first review must be within four weeks of the child being accommodated, then within three months after that, and thereafter, at not more

---

1 Section 34. The use of secure accommodation is also subject to judicial control under s 25. See, for example, *Re W (A Minor) (Secure Accommodation Order)* [1993] 1 FLR 692; *Re M (Secure Accommodation Order)* [1995] 1 FLR 418; and *Re D (Secure Accommodation Order) (No 1)* [1997] 1 FLR 197. For discussion of the statutory regime, see C Smith 'Secure Accommodation' [1995] Fam Law 369; P Bates 'Secure Accommodation Orders – In Whose Interests?' [1995] CFLQ 70; and J Butler and S Hardy 'Secure Accommodation and Welfare' [1997] Fam Law 425.
2 An informative and detailed discussion of the possibilities is contained in PM Bromley and NV Lowe *Bromley's Family Law* (8th edn) (Butterworths, 1992) at pp 541–552. See also M Hayes 'Challenging Local Authority Decisions' (1993) 5 JCL 107.
3 The *locus classicus* being *A v Liverpool City Council* [1982] AC 363.
4 See *Re J (Minors) (Care: Care Plan)* [1994] 1 FLR 253.
5 See cl 87.
6 See *Re C (Interim Care Order: Residential Assessment)* [1997] 1 FLR 1.
7 Section 26, the Review of Children's Cases Regulations 1991, SI 1991/895, and the Representations Procedure (Children) Regulations 1991, SI 1991/894.
8 *Review*, at para 2.24.

than six-monthly intervals[1]. These requirements also apply to voluntary organisations and registered children's homes[2]. The regulations govern, inter alia, the
manner in which reviews are to be conducted, and the considerations to which the
local authority is to have regard[3]. Most significantly, for present purposes, the local
authority must, before conducting the review, seek and take into account the views
of the child, his parents, persons with parental responsibility and any other person
whose views it considers relevant[4]. It must also, as far as is reasonably practicable,
involve all the persons in the review, where appropriate, by attendance at
meetings, and must notify them of the result of the review[5]. Clearly, good practice
in the conduct of reviews can go a long way in meeting anxieties and heading off
complaints.

Representations and complaints

Local authorities are required to establish procedures for considering representations including complaints[6]. Those entitled to make representations are
children being looked after by the local authority, parents, persons with parental
responsibility, and local authority foster-parents. Others may be allowed to do so
where the local authority considers that they have a sufficient interest in the child
to warrant it. The representations may relate to the discharge of any of the local
authority's functions under Part III of the Children Act. They could relate to
serious issues such as a change of placement or a medical operation, or to
relatively trivial matters. The official guidance mentions complaints relating to
day-care, support services where the child is at home, accommodation, after-care
and decisions relating to the placement of a child or the handling of a child's
case[7]. The local authority must ensure that at least one person who is not a
member or officer of the local authority takes part in the procedure[8], but doubts
remain about how truly independent any internal procedure can be. The
procedure must be publicised by the local authority[9]. Beyond this, the Children
Act does not dictate the precise form of procedure to be followed but there are
prescribed minimum procedural requirements[10].

Once it has considered a representation, the local authority must have due
regard to the findings of those who considered it. It must then take such steps as
are reasonably practicable to give written notice of its decision, with reasons, and
any action taken or proposed in consequence, to the person making the
representation, the child (if the local authority thinks he has sufficient under-

---

1 Review of Children's Cases Regulations 1991, regs 2 and 3.
2 Ibid, reg 1.
3 Ibid, regs 4 and 5 and Schs 1, 2 and 3.
4 Ibid, reg 7(1).
5 Ibid, reg 7(2).
6 Section 26(3), and Representations Procedure (Children) Regulations 1991, SI 1991/894.
7 *The Children Act 1989 Guidance and Regulations Vol 3 Family Placements* (HMSO, 1991) at
   para 10.8.
8 Section 26(4).
9 Section 26(8). But one research study of the publicity of local authority complaints procedures
   found them to be insufficiently effective in bringing them to the attention of potential users.
   See C Williams and H Jordan 'Factors relating to publicity surrounding the complaints
   procedure under the Children Act 1989' [1996] CFLQ 337.
10 A detailed description of the procedure is to be found in PM Bromley and NV Lowe *Bromley's
   Family Law* (8th edn) (Butterworths, 1992) at p 544.

standing), and such other persons as appear to the local authority to be likely to be affected[1].

It will be some time before an evaluation can be given of the effectiveness of these procedures and whether they are an adequate substitute for judicial scrutiny. Moreover, as Freeman has said, they are no substitute for good practice, but they may be an integral part of good practice, contributing to a cultural change which encourages clients to express views about services and for these comments to be used as opportunities to improve services, relationships and, ultimately, the image of social services departments[2].

Other potential remedies

The first three possibilities discussed below are what might be called 'public law remedies' in that they are mechanisms for enforcing the proper discharge of public duties. Since local authorities have a vast amount of discretion under the children legislation, it does not follow that, because some third party might disagree with the line a local authority has taken, that that authority has acted beyond its powers or otherwise improperly. These remedies should not, therefore, be viewed as offering a great deal of hope to aggrieved individuals, except in the more obvious cases of abuse of power or failure to discharge public duties. For completeness, we also glance at the possibility of an application to the European Court of Human Rights, or an application for a private order.

Judicial review

Despite the restrictive nature of the remedy of judicial review, there has been a steady growth in applications for judicial review in recent years, no doubt reflecting the refusal of the courts to entertain wardship applications which were designed to challenge local authorities' decisions[3]. In order to succeed, the applicant must show that the local authority has acted in a way in which no reasonable authority would have acted[4], that it has acted *ultra vires*, ie exeeded its statutory powers[5], or that there has been a breach of the rules of natural justice[6]. Leave is required before an application may be brought. Apart from the narrowness of the grounds, the powers of the Divisional Court[7] are limited. It may

---

1   Section 26(7). It is arguable that this lacks teeth in that the complainant has no obvious redress where a complaint is upheld.
2   MDA Freeman *Children, Their Families and the Law* (Macmillan, 1992) at p 145.
3   In several cases it was held specifically that judicial review, rather than wardship, was the appropriate remedy. See particularly *Re RM and LM (Minors)* [1986] 2 FLR 205; and *Re DM (A Minor) (Wardship: Jurisdiction)* [1986] 2 FLR 122. For a general discussion see M Sunkin 'Judicial Review and Part III of the Children Act 1989' (1992) 4 JCL 109. But it has been held that the applicant must exhaust other remedies, particularly the statutory complaints procedure, before resorting to judicial review. See *R v Kingston upon Thames RBC ex parte T* [1994] 1 FLR 798 and *R v Birmingham City Council ex parte A* [1997] 2 FLR 841.
4   See, for example, *R v Lancashire County Council ex parte M* [1992] 1 FLR 109.
5   Good examples of ultra vires action under the old law arose where there was a failure to follow the correct procedure for passing a parental rights resolution, as in *Re L (AC)* [1973] 3 All ER 743. This was a successful challenge in wardship but would now be a matter for judicial review.
6   There have been several notable successes under this head. See, for example, *R v Bedfordshire County Council ex parte C* [1987] 1 FLR 239 and *R v Norfolk County Council ex parte M* [1989] QB 619.
7   The Divisional Court of the Queen's Bench Division. Judges from the Family Division may, however, sit in children cases.

order the local authority to discharge its statutory duty properly through the positive order of mandamus but, more likely, it will simply quash the local authority's decision through the negative order of certiorari. The court cannot go on to make orders which it considers to be in the best interests of the child as it can in wardship. The procedure contrasts sharply with the extremely flexible powers which the courts have under the Children Act, and its suitability in individual children cases must be doubted. Where it can prove useful is as a means of challenging *policy* decisions of local authorities. A formal decision, for example, to restrict services for children in need to those considered 'at risk' would clearly be susceptible to challenge.

The Secretary of State's default powers

The Secretary of State has a number of functions in the child care sphere[1], one of which is the so-called 'default power'. This enables him to intervene in limited circumstances where he is satisfied that a local authority has failed, without reasonable excuse, to comply with any of its duties under the legislation. He may then make an order, giving reasons and declaring the local authority to be in default with respect to the relevant duty[2]. The order may include directions to comply with that duty within a specified period[3], which may be enforced through judicial review and specifically by mandamus[4].

It is extremely unlikely that this kind of intervention by central government would be of assistance in individual cases. Again, where it does occur, it is likely to be directed against a policy decision of the local authority with regard to a *class* of children.

The local government ombudsman

It is possible to make a complaint to the Commissioner for Local Administration. This requires proof of 'maladministration' and the main disadvantage of the procedure is that it takes too long to be of immediate benefit to individual children, parents, or anyone else directly affected by an authority's decision[5]. Again, it may, if successful, be instrumental in securing the reversal of an ill-conceived policy.

The European Convention on Human Rights

It may be possible to allege before the European Commission and European Court of Human Rights a breach by the local authority of the European Convention on Human Rights. Although this has been a slow and cumbersome procedure, there have been some significant successes, notably in relation to contact with children in care[6] and access to their case

---

1 For a general discussion, see A Bainham *Children: The New Law* (Family Law, 1990) at paras 7.71–7.78.
2 Section 84(1) and (2). A similar power exists under the Education Acts, as to which see Chapter 16 below.
3 Section 84(3).
4 Section 84(4).
5 A case in which a complaint was successful was *Re BA (Wardship and Adoption)* [1985] FLR 1008 where the local ombudsman found procedural irregularities in the passing of a parental rights resolution. As a result the local authority agreed to the continuation of wardship proceedings and a sub-committee of the authority recommended that the resolution be rescinded.
6 *R v UK* [1988] 2 FLR 445.

case records[1]. The potential value of the European Convention and other international instruments in safeguarding children's rights is looked at in a later chapter[2]. It should be noted at this stage that the potential value of the European Convention as a basis of redress may be significantly enhanced by its incorporation into English law under the Human Rights Bill which is expected to reach the statute book before the end of 1998.

Civil actions

In recent years there have been attempts by adults to obtain damages from local authorities in tort for injuries caused to them when children, allegedly resulting from the acts or omission of the authorities concerned. The complaints have ranged from failure to act on reports of abuse made by doctors, teachers, neighbours and others[3]; the separation of a girl from her mother arising from the incorrect identification of an alleged abuser[4]; failure to prevent abuse by a foster-father through inadequate monitoring and supervision of the placement[5]; and failure to act as a reasonable parent would towards a child in care, allegedly resulting in a series of personal catastrophies in adulthood[6]. In all these cases, the claims failed whether they were based on common law negligence or breach of statutory duty. Although, in principle, the House of Lords has not ruled out the possibility of civil liability in other cases, it is clear that potential plaintiffs will be expected to have recourse to alternative remedies such as judicial review or the local government ombudsman[7]. It is also clear that the courts wish to discourage civil actions which they fear might impede local authorities in the performance of their statutory duties and that local authorities should be no more liable for mistakes made when essentially acting as parents than natural parents would be for their mistakes.

In *W v Essex County Council*[8], however, the Court of Appeal has held, by majority, that a local authority may in principle be liable in negligence and negligent misstatement in relation to specific assurances given by it and its social worker to foster-parents. The foster-parents alleged that a teenager was placed with them contrary to specific assurances that no adolescent known or suspected to be a sexual abuser would be fostered with them. The teenager concerned had been cautioned for indecent assault (a fact known to the authority) and went on to abuse sexually the foster-parents' four children who suffered psychiatric illnesses. The majority held that the case was distinguishable from *X (Minors) v Bedfordshire*

---

1   *The Gaskin Case* [1990] 1 FLR 167, and see R Pickford 'The Gaskin Case and Confidential Personal Information – whose secret?' (1992) 4 JCL 33. See also *McMichael v United Kingdom* [1995] Fam Law 478, in which the European Court found Scottish child care procedures under the Social Work (Scotland) Act 1968 to be in breach of parents' rights under Article 8(1) in denying them access to reports concerning adoption.
2   Chapter 17 below.
3   *X (Minors) v Bedfordshire County Council* [1995] 2 AC 633.
4   *M (A Minor) and Another v Newham London Borough Council v Others* [1995] 2 AC 663.
5   *H v Norfolk County Council* [1997] 1 FLR 384.
6   *Barrett v Enfield London Borough Council* [1997] 2 FLR 167. It should be noted that an appeal is pending before the House of Lords at the time of writing.
7   For a helpful commentary on all this case-law, see K Standley 'No duty of care to children in care' [1997] CFLQ 409.
8   [1998] 2 FLR 278.

County Council[1], in that *W v Essex* involved harm caused *by* a child in care to the family in which he was placed. There was, in particular, no evidence that liability in this sort of case would increase the burden on local authorities or lead to excessive caution, but there was a genuine fear that knowledge of any local authority immunity might decrease the number of potential foster-parents. The House of Lords will shortly have an opportunity to consider further the extent of local authorities' immunities in this area in the appeal in *Barrett v Enfield London Borough Council.*

Private orders

The final possibility is for the aggrieved individual to apply for a s 8 order. Where the child is 'accommodated' by the local authority, all s 8 orders are, in principle, available, subject to the leave requirement[2]. These orders are likely to be sought, if at all, by someone without parental responsibility, since those who have parental responsibility are able to terminate an accommodation arrangement.

Where the child is in care, the jurisdiction of the courts to make private orders is severely curtailed[3], but it is possible to apply for a residence order. This would only be an appropriate course for those persons who are willing and able to offer a home to the child. This course would not be appropriate if the person's grievance related only to some aspect of the local authority's plan for the child. Where the dispute is about contact (as it often is), there is now a statutory regime[4]. It was the case prior to the Children Act[5], and it is the case after it[6], that wardship may not be used as an extra-statutory device for challenging local authority decision-making. Although, technically, an application might be made under the inherent jurisdiction of the High Court, it has been argued that this '*Liverpool* principle' would be likely to preclude the court from exercising jurisdiction[7].

Conclusion

The general conclusion which must be drawn from this brief review is that, for most people, the internal procedures of the local authority, including informal negotiation with social workers, the review process and, as a last resort, the complaints procedure, represent the best and, perhaps, the only means of questioning the local authority's actions in relation to a particular child. The orthodox principles and remedies of administrative law are ill-adapted to the family context and are of limited use, except on the broader plane of policy-making in local government.

---

1   [1995] 2 AC 633.
2   Reversing, in effect, the House of Lords decision in *M v H* [1988] 3 All ER 5.
3   See Chapter 11 below.
4   Section 34, also discussed in Chapter 11 below.
5   *A v Liverpool City Council* [1982] AC 363 ('the *Liverpool* principle').
6   Section 100(2)(c).
7   PM Bromley and NV Lowe *Bromley's Family Law* (8th edn) (Butterworths, 1992) at p 547.

Chapter 11
CARE AND SUPERVISION

INTRODUCTION

It would be difficult to visualise a more striking failure of protection under the law than that which occurs when a defenceless young child is killed or seriously injured by an adult in the same household. However, it would be equally difficult to envisage a more serious invasion of civil liberties than that which arises where a child is unjustifiably removed from his family because of unwarranted suspicions of abuse. Here, then, is the dilemma for the law and for those, especially social workers, who have to apply it. The stakes could hardly be higher and, sadly, there have been plenty of examples (often attracting much media attention) of both kinds of failure. There has been a succession of public inquiries into apparent 'agency failure' to prevent the death or abuse of children who have been allowed to remain at, or return to, the family home[1]. In contrast, there have been a number of apparently over-zealous interventions in cases of suspected sexual abuse, most notably in Cleveland in 1987[2] and then in relation to alleged ritualistic abuse in Rochdale[3] and Orkney[4].

Errors on either side of the line usually provoke public outrage, and the difficulty of formulating grounds and procedures which achieve the right balance for compulsory interventions in the family must be apparent to everyone. It is also an issue which has generated substantial academic disagreement. During the 1980s, a number of influential works were published which conveyed the central message that there had been an unacceptable escalation in State intervention which called for the imposition of greater legal controls on social services departments[5]. This view of child protection practice was seriously challenged by a

---

1   See Chapter 2 above.

2   See the *Report of the Inquiry into Child Abuse in Cleveland 1987* ('the *Cleveland Report*') (1988) (Cmnd 412).

3   *Rochdale Borough Council v A* [1991] 2 FLR 192; and see the guidelines established for the investigation of such cases in *Re A (Minors) (Wardship) (Child Abuse: Guidelines)* [1992] 1 All ER 153.

4   As to which see R Brett 'Orkney – aberration or symptom?' (1991) 3 JCL 143; EE Sutherland 'The Orkney Case' (1992) *Juridical Review* 93; and A Bissett-Johnson 'Child Protection in Scotland – the Background to the Clyde Report' (1993) 5 JCL 28. The Orkney case was the subject of a major public enquiry: see *Report of the Inquiry into the Removal of Children from Orkney in February 1991* ('the *Clyde Report*') (HMSO, 1992). Wide-ranging reforms have since been made to the child protection and children's hearings system in Scotland by Part II of the Children (Scotland) Act 1995. These include reforms which are similar, but not identical, to the reforms introduced in England by the Children Act 1989. The 1995 legislation, inter alia, abolishes parental rights resolutions and place of safety orders and introduces child assessment orders, child protection orders and exclusion orders as alternative options for dealing with the short-term protection of children. For further discussion of the Scottish reforms, see EE Sutherland 'Scotland: Child Law Reform – At Last!' in A Bainham (ed) *The International Survey of Family Law 1995* (Martinus Nijhoff, 1997), p 435, at pp 444–452.

5   See, for example, H Geach and E Szwed (eds) *Providing Civil Justice for Children* (1983) and L Taylor, R Lacey and D Bracken *In Whose Best Interests?* (Cobden Trust, 1980).

study in three local authority areas which concluded that these charges were unsupported by hard empirical evidence[1]. The thrust of this research was that child protection agencies operated within a framework of cultural limitations which the authors called the 'rule of optimism'. They argued that the modus operandi of these agencies was to prefer the least coercive form of intervention in family life which was possible in the circumstances. On this analysis, parents would often be given the benefit of any doubt and only the worst cases of abuse or neglect would be the subject of compulsory action.

The task for the reformers of child care law was to come up with a framework for compulsory action which offered sufficient protection to vulnerable children but which also respected the rights of family members, most obviously those of parents but, increasingly, those of children themselves[2]. The Children Act 1989 attempts to achieve this primarily by rationalising and unifying the statutory ground for care or supervision, by creating more opportunity for participation in care proceedings, and by overhauling procedures for emergency protection. More recently, the Children Act has been amended by Part IV of the Family Law Act 1996 to allow for the possibility of 'exclusion requirements' to be inserted into emergency protection orders and interim care orders which, where made, will have the effect of removing the alleged abuser rather than the child from the family home[3]. This chapter concentrates on the first two aspects, and emergency and short-term protection is discussed in the next chapter. First it is necessary to discuss the attempts in the legislation to ensure that the various agencies involved in child protection 'work together' in their common endeavour to produce the right solution for a child who is thought to be at risk[4].

Emphasis on co-operation

The statutory emphasis for social security departments and other authorities to co-operate with each other has been noted, and 'partnership' has been identified as a central theme. The notion of partnership resurfaces here, with the expectation that lawyers, social workers, the police, the NSPCC, education and health personnel, health visitors, probation officers, representatives of voluntary organisations and anyone else professionally involved with a child, will pool their information and resources in the child's best interests.

Procedure before commencement of any action

The starting point for this discussion must be the realisation that compulsory action will not usually be commenced unless the option of voluntary assistance has first been explored. It is very much the philosophy of the legislation that the family should be supported in times of difficulty, that voluntary co-operation with

---

1   R Dingwall, J Eekelaar and T Murray *The Protection of Children: State Intervention and Family Life* (Basil Blackwell, 1983).

2   The *Cleveland Report* drew public attention to violations of children's rights by child protection agencies, especially in the sphere of repeated medical examination.

3   We discuss these reforms in Chapter 12. It should be noted that Scotland was ahead of England in this respect by making provision in the Children (Scotland) Act 1995 for 'exclusion orders'. See EE Sutherland 'Scotland: Child Law Reform – At Last!' (above).

4   See, generally, *Working Together – Under the Children Act 1989* (HMSO, 1991) ('*Working Together*'), revising the previous 1988 edition.

parents is the preferred option, and that compulsory orders should be a last resort. The Department of Health's *Guidance* makes this plain when it advises that 'a care or supervision order will be sought only where there appears to be no better way of safeguarding and promoting the welfare of the child suffering, or likely to suffer, significant harm'[1]. Accordingly, before proceeding with an application, social services should always take legal advice about alternative options and about those matters which would inform it as to whether a care or supervision order is really appropriate in the circumstances[2]. This advice should be sought within the context of a multi-disciplinary, multi-agency case conference. It is this case conference which performs the vital function of preparing the ground work for any application to the court. Still more importantly, the conference is the bridge between voluntary and compulsory action, conceptualised as distinct in the legislation, but, in practice often blurred as points on a spectrum of possible options to deal with a difficult family situation.

The child protection conference

Inter-agency co-operation is effected through the mechanisms of the child protection conference and the child protection register[3]. Overall planning and the formulation of policy in the different local authority regions is the responsibility of the area child protection committee. Both the committee and the conference are made up of members of the various professions mentioned above. Where, following a preliminary investigation[4], there is suspicion of abuse or neglect, a child protection conference will be called. Its purpose is not to decide the case (which will ultimately be left to the court); it rather 'brings together the family, and the professionals concerned with child protection and provides them with the opportunity to exchange information and plan together'[5]. At the initial conference, a decision will be taken about whether to place the child's name on the child protection register; a register, not of abused children, but of 'children for whom there are currently unresolved child protection issues and for whom there is an inter-agency plan'[6]. The conference must then decide on a plan for the child and appoint a 'key worker' whose functions will be to implement that plan to ensure protection for the child, inter-agency co-operation and the participation of parents or other carers in the plan[7]. After the initial conference there will be child protection reviews to monitor the implementation of the plan, the effectiveness of agency co-operation, and to decide whether the child's name should remain on the child protection register[8].

---

1   *The Children Act 1989 Guidance and Regulations Vol 1 Court Orders* (HMSO, 1991) at para 3.2.
2   Ibid, at para 3.12. The relevant matters include such things as whether the criteria for compulsory action would be likely to be satisfied, the implications of opposition to an order, whether the case might need to be transferred to a higher court, what the authority might be required to disclose in advance of the hearing and whether a s 8 order might be appropriate.
3   For a discussion of the role of each, see MDA Freeman *Children, Their Families and the Law* (Macmillan, 1992) at pp 95–97.
4   The local authority's investigatory duties are spelled out in s 47 of the Children Act – as to which see Chapter 12 below.
5   *Working Together* (above) at para 6.1.
6   Ibid at para 6.26.
7   Ibid at paras 6.4 et seq.
8   Ibid at para 6.9.

Attendance of parents at case conferences

An issue which has caused some controversy is the attendance of parents at case conferences. It has been held that it is not a breach of natural justice for parents not to be invited to attend a case conference[1], but the revised version of *Working Together*[2], and the spirit of the Children Act, require a justification for excluding them[3]. While parental involvement and the involvement of older children is a key feature of the legislation, so is the need to ensure that child protection agencies are not unduly inhibited in discharging their statutory functions. The shift brought about by the Children Act is that the onus now appears to be on those who would seek to deny participation since, as June Thoburn has put it:

> 'Practice, wisdom and research lead to the conclusion that the maximum involvement of parents and older children in the work, and honesty at the investigation and case conference stage, can lead to the sort of working together between professionals and family members which is most conducive to the long-term welfare of the children.'[4]

The importance of the case conference cannot be overstated. It has, in the recent past, been precisely the absence of this kind of coordinated approach and, in particular, the failure of agencies to pool vital information, which has led to some of the worst tragedies. Now, it has been said, 'with properly coordinated services there is a better chance of spotting warning signs of abuse or neglect and of constructive action being taken before crisis points have been reached'[5].

THE LEGAL BASIS FOR COMPULSORY ORDERS

Before the Children Act, there were many different routes by which a child might compulsorily enter the care of a local authority[6]. Broadly, these fell into three categories: cases in which children who were initially in voluntary care later became the subject of parental rights resolutions[7]; cases in which the local authority applied to the juvenile court for a care order under the Children and Young Persons Act 1969[8]; and cases where children were committed to care in

---

1   *R v Harrow London Borough Council, ex parte D* [1990] Fam 133; and see also *R v East Sussex County Council ex parte R* [1991] 2 FLR 358, and *R v Devon County Council ex parte L* [1991] 2 FLR 541.
2   *Working Together* (above) at para 6.15, which says that exclusion of a parent will be 'exceptional'. Where the parents do not attend it is emphasised that some other way should be found of communicating their views to the conference. Ibid at para 6.17.
3   For discussions of the issues involved in parents' attendance at conferences, see J Thoburn ' "Working Together" and parental attendance at case conferences' (1992) 4 JCL 11, P Thomson 'Parents at Case Conferences – a Legal Advisor's Viewpoint' (1992) 4 JCL 15, and D Savas 'Parental Participation in Case Conferences' [1996] CFLQ 57.
4   J Thoburn (above) at p 14.
5   PM Bromley and NV Lowe *Bromley's Family Law* (8th edn) (Butterworths, 1992) at p 510.
6   For an excellent discussion of the old law, see S Maidment 'The Fragmentation of Parental Rights and Children in Care' [1981] JSWL 21.
7   The grounds for passing resolutions were largely 'parent-centred' in that they concentrated on parental failings, such as unfitness arising from the parent's 'habits or modes of life' or consistent failure 'without reasonable cause to discharge the obligations of a parent'. See the Child Care Act 1980, s 3. For a critique of the former resolution procedure, see M Adcock, R White and O Rowlands *The Administrative Parent* (BAAF, 1983).
8   These grounds were 'child-centred' in that they focused on the child's condition as where the child was found to be 'exposed to moral danger', or his proper development was 'being unavoidably prevented or neglected' or he was 'beyond the control of his parent and guardian'.

family proceedings, most notably wardship, but also, for example, divorce, adoption or guardianship[1]. This system gave rise to a number of difficulties. The grounds for making a care order differed according to the proceedings in which it was sought[2], the effects of each type of order were far from clear[3], and there was growing concern that local authorities were beginning to rely too heavily on wardship. They were, in effect, invoking an extra-statutory basis for gaining compulsory control of a child where it was doubtful that the statutory grounds could be established[4].

The Children Act met these difficulties head-on by enacting a single ground for all care or supervision orders, by making these orders available in all 'family proceedings' and by closing-off wardship as an extra-statutory option[5]. The abolition of the resolution procedure means that the new ground is also the sole basis for compulsorily *retaining* a child who is currently voluntarily accommodated, and this also necessitates a court order. It should also be observed that there is no longer any legal means whereby parents may reach a voluntary arrangement that the child should enter the *care* of the local authority as opposed to merely being *looked after* by it. Since care proceedings are also 'family proceedings', the court is bound by the principles in Part I of the Children Act, although the manner of their operation in this child protection context is inevitably somewhat different from their undiluted application in private disputes. The principle that delay is prejudicial also applies and, again, the court must draw up a timetable with a view to expediting matters[6].

Who may apply for an order?

It is the policy of the legislation to locate primary responsibility for child care in local authorities' social services departments. It is they who are under a statutory duty to investigate the circumstances of any child in their area, where they have reasonable cause to suspect that he is suffering, or is likely to suffer, significant harm[7] and it is also they who may be directed by the court, in family proceedings,

---

In each case there was a further test that the child was in need of care and control which he was unlikely to receive unless the order was made. See the Children and Young Persons Act 1969, s 1.

1   Here, the test was whether there were 'exceptional circumstances making it impracticable or undesirable' for the child to be under the care of a parent or other individual. See, for example, the Matrimonial Causes Act 1973, s 43(1) and the Guardianship Act 1973, s 2(2)(b).
2   See, generally, the DHSS *Review of Child Care Law* (1985) at ch 15.
3   See the White Paper *The Law on Child Care and Family Services* (1987) (Cmnd 62) at para 7, which identified the lack of clarity in the mutual rights and responsibilities of parents and local authorities as the most striking defect of the law.
4   On the other hand, a more positive view of this use of the wardship jurisdiction was that it was a necessary 'safety-net' underpinning the statutory regime. See, for example, N Lowe 'Caring for Children' (1989) 139 NLJ 87.
5   But not entirely the use of the inherent jurisdiction of the High Court. See s 100(3)–(5) of the Children Act and the discussion at p 405 below.
6   Sections 1(2) and 32. We discuss the problem of delay in the context of care plans at p 372 below.
7   Section 47. For fuller discussions of local authorities' investigative duties under the Children Act see A Bainham *Children: The New Law* (Family Law, 1990) at paras 6.51–6.56 and D Bedingfield *The Child in Need* (Family Law, 1998) at ch 6.

to conduct an investigation into a child's circumstances[1]. The former power of the courts to make care orders of their own motion has been removed, except with respect to interim orders[2] in deference to this general principle of local authority responsibility. While the court may be concerned enough about a child to trigger an investigation, it is not for the court to usurp the functions of social services by dictating to the local authority, as it sometimes used to in wardship proceedings[3]. Similarly, while other agencies and individuals have their part to play in child protection work, they do not have legal responsibility for initiating action. There is no statutory duty in England which would require individuals to report suspected cases of abuse or neglect[4].

In keeping with this policy, only the local authority or an 'authorised person' may apply for a care or supervision order[5] and, for these purposes, only the NSPCC and its officers, with their historic and substantial contribution to child protection, have been authorised[6]. The police were formerly permitted to bring proceedings based on the so-called 'offence condition', but with the abolition of this ground and the redefinition of local authorities' responsibilities, it was no longer thought appropriate for them to retain the power[7]. Similarly, local education authorities, which used to be able to initiate proceedings based on truancy, are no longer empowered to do so following the abolition of this ground and its replacement with a new education supervision order[8]. Finally, there is no equivalent under the new law, to the former procedure whereby parents might require the local authority to bring proceedings in relation to a child who is beyond their control[9]. Proceedings must be brought by the 'designated authority', being the local authority in whose area the child is ordinarily resident or, where

---

1 Section 37, and A Bainham (above) at paras 5.57–5.61. In *Re H (A Minor) (Section 37 Direction)* [1993] 2 FLR 541, Scott-Baker J (in the first reported decision on the scope of the court's duty under s 37) adopted a liberal construction of the section. In his view, the statutory phrase 'the child's circumstances' should be widely construed to include any situation which might have a bearing on the child being likely to suffer significant harm in the future. In this case (which involved a lesbian couple in an arrangement analogous to surrogacy) the court was entitled to have regard in particular to the long-term, as well as the short-term, future of the baby concerned. See also *Re CE (Section 37 Direction)* [1995] 1 FLR 26. But a s 37 direction should not be used as a device for appointing a guardian ad litem where there is no real prospect of a care or supervision order being made, and a local authority may not be made a party to a private law application if it decides, following its investigations, not to seek a public law order (see *F v Cambridgeshire County Council* [1995] 1 FLR 516).
2 Section 38 discussed at p 400 below.
3 Particularly good examples of this are *Re E (SA) (A Minor) (Wardship)* [1984] 1 All ER 289, where the court directed a solution not sought by any of the parties; and *Re G-U (A Minor) (Wardship)* [1984] FLR 811, where the authority was reprimanded by the court for not referring back to it an abortion decision concerning a ward of court in its care. It has now been held that where the court is considering making an order not sought by the parties it must give them an opportunity to make submissions on the appropriateness of the order it is proposed to make. See *Devon County Council v S* [1992] 3 WLR 273 and *Croydon London Borough Council v A* [1992] 3 WLR 267.
4 There is such a mandatory reporting law in other jurisdictions, for example in the USA.
5 Section 31(1).
6 Section 31(9)(a).
7 See, generally, the DHSS *Review of Child Care Law* (1985) at paras 12.9–12.26.
8 Section 36.
9 Children and Young Persons Act 1963, s 3. But being beyond parental control remains an element in one of the alternatives under the new statutory ground in s 31(2). See p 386 below.

the child does not reside in any authority's area, the authority in whose area any circumstances arose in consequence of which the order is sought[1].

Which children?

Care or supervision orders may not be made in relation to a child who has reached the age of 17 years, or a married child who has attained 16 years of age[2]. While this corresponds with the old law, its effect is more dramatic, since there is no longer an option of warding children in this age group and securing care that way[3]. Opinion is divided on whether the removal of the power to take compulsory action, in relation to those older teenagers, was desirable. One view is that it leaves a potentially vulnerable group of adolescents unprotected[4]. An opposing view is that coercive orders grounded in non-criminal misbehaviour are open to civil libertarian objections and, in any event, would sit very uneasily with the philosophy of the legislation which finds expression in a number of other provisions[5]. This latter view is partly reinforced by the new provisions allowing troubled teenagers to seek a voluntary 'self-referral' into care[6], unless, of course, it can be argued that some will lack the resourcefulness to engage in self-help. In any event, the Children Act is clear and the embargo on 'public' orders is in line with the corresponding embargo on 'private' orders in relation to this age group[7].

Which proceedings and which orders?

It was observed above that care and supervision orders may be made in any family proceedings[8] and not only in what have traditionally been called 'care proceedings'. These latter proceedings, the sole purpose of which is to obtain a care or supervision order, are also now family proceedings for the purposes of the Children Act. Consequently, an application for these orders may be made on its own or during the course of family proceedings which are brought for some other purpose[9]. This, to some extent, corresponds with the old law, except that there is now only one ground for an order, whatever the nature of the proceedings. The statutory test, or threshold criteria, must be crossed, whether an order is requested in care proceedings, divorce proceedings or any other kind of proceedings.

---

1 Section 31(8). These provisions can give rise to legal wrangles between local authorities about which of them should be 'designated' and hence have the statutory responsibilities for a child who has moved between areas. See particularly *Re BC (A Minor) (Care Order: Appropriate Local Authority)* [1995] 3 FCR 598, *Gateshead Metropolitan Borough Council v L and Another* [1996] 2 FLR 179, *Re C (Care Order: Appropriate Local Authority)* [1997] 1 FLR 544 and *Re P (Care Proceedings: Designated Authority)* [1998] 1 FLR 80 (in which there were complications arising from the child spending a period of time in interim care).
2 Section 31(3).
3 As occurred in *Re SW (A Minor) (Wardship Jurisdiction)* [1986] 1 FLR 24 where the girl in question was 17 years of age.
4 See, for example, N Lowe 'Caring for Children' (1989) 139 NLJ 87.
5 See, for example, J Eekelaar 'Parents' Rights to Punish – Further limits after Gillick' (1986) 28 *Childright* 9. See also the discussion of controversial uses of the inherent jurisdiction in relation to older teenagers below.
6 See Chapter 10 above.
7 Section 8 orders may not usually be made in respect of children who have attained 16 years of age (s 9(6) and (7) and s 91(10)).
8 Section 8(3) and (4). We discuss the definition in Chapter 2.
9 Section 31(4).

A complementary feature of the new law is that, just as 'public' orders may be sought in private family proceedings, so 'private' orders may be sought in public family proceedings. Thus, the court considering an application for a care or supervision order must also consider the alternative of a s 8 order, especially a residence order. The court will also have at its disposal its general powers to attach conditions or give directions[1]. Unlike a care or supervision order, the court may also make s 8 orders, whether or not they have been requested and, of course, it is not necessary for the statutory threshold criteria for care or supervision to be reached. It has been suggested that this power may be useful where there is doubt that the threshold criteria will be satisfied[2] or, perhaps, to effect a 'phased rehabilitation' of the child with his family – a power which is not directly incorporated in the legislation[3]. In fact, it seems likely that the 'lesser' order (ie lesser in terms of its intrusion into family life) may prove valuable in cases at the margins of the statutory grounds[4]. A cautionary note should, however, be sounded. Too great a readiness in the courts to use s 8 orders in these circumstances could be interpreted as arrogating to themselves a wider power than Parliament intended. It could reopen all the old debates about wardship and its relationship to the statutory code – albeit in a rather different guise[5].

It is one thing for a private individual to seek private orders, or for a court to make them of its own volition in public family proceedings, and quite another for

1   Section 11(7). It has, however, been held in *Croydon London Borough Council v A (No 1)* [1992] 2 FLR 341 that the court does not have power to make a prohibited steps order prohibiting a father from having contact with a mother in care proceedings, since contact between spouses is not 'a step which could be taken by a parent in meeting his parental responsibility for a child'. In principle, of course, in appropriate cases, prohibited steps orders are available in public proceedings. But see also *Nottinghamshire County Council v P* [1993] 2 FLR 134, in which the Court of Appeal held that a local authority had erred in seeking a prohibited steps order instead of a care order in relation to two sisters at risk of sexual abuse by their father. The authority was in reality seeking to exclude the father. The effect of the order would be like that of a residence order which the authority was precluded from seeking under s 9(2).
2   PM Bromley and NV Lowe *Bromley's Family Law* (8th edn) (Butterworths, 1992) at p 522.
3   This was the issue in the House of Lords decision in *Re E (SA) (A Minor) (Wardship)* [1984] 1 All ER 289.
4   A further example, suggested by PM Bromley and NV Lowe (above), is that of an alcoholic or drug-addicted parent. Where there is a relative who could look after the child they suggest that a residence order may be appropriate. But it should be noted that the courts will not, other than in exceptional circumstances, make a residence order in favour of someone who does not want it. In *Re K (Care Order or Residence Order)* [1995] 1 FLR 675, the local authority, having originally applied for a care order, wanted a residence order to be made in favour of the grandparents. The grandparents, however, were getting on in years and did not wish to be exposed to the risk of private law proceedings being brought by the schizophrenic mother. Under a care order they would also be entitled to boarding-out allowances paid to local authority foster-parents. Stuart-White J held that a care order was appropriate in these circumstances to provide the children with the required protection and security.
5   The opposing arguments are extensively probed in Law Com Working Paper No 101 *Wards of Court* (1987) and see the discussion on the inherent jurisdiction below. And see now *Re RJ (Foster Placement)* [1998] 2 FLR 110 where Sir Stephen Brown P refused to entertain an application for a residence order by foster-parents, supported by the guardian ad litem, to preserve the status quo. The foster-father was disqualified from acting as a foster-parent by the newly implemented regulations (the Children (Protection from Offenders) (Miscellaneous Amendments) Regulations 1997) protecting children from individuals convicted of or cautioned in relation to serious offences against children. He held that to have allowed the application would have been contrary to public policy.

the State in the guise of the local authority to be allowed to seek private orders. Here, the policy of the legislation is that the local authority should normally be obliged to go down the *public* route, satisfying the threshold criteria and seeking *public* orders. Where the authority has already obtained a care order, the scheme of the Act is that the authority is 'in the driving seat' with parental responsibility for the child and should not normally be allowed to pass this responsibility to the courts by seeking orders in relation to the child's upbringing. In limited circumstances, where the authority's statutory powers are inadequate and the child's welfare requires it, the authority may with leave seek the assistance of the High Court under its inherent jurisdiction. We discuss the inherent jurisdiction below. For the moment we are concerned with the restrictions which the legislation places on the making of private s 8 orders in favour of local authorities and these are to be found in a cluster of provisions in s 9 of the Act.

First, where the child is already *in care* it is provided that no s 8 order may be made other than a residence order[1]. If a residence order were made in favour of an individual its effect would be to discharge the care order[2]. Such an application challenges the *source* of the authority's parental responsibility rather than its *exercise* and is not therefore inconsistent with the notion that the authority has parental responsibility under a care order. Secondly, no residence or contact order may be made in favour of a local authority[3]. Here, the policy is that if a local authority wishes to look after a child or have involvement with a child it must do so, unless it can secure the voluntary co-operation of the family, by means of the *public* care or supervision orders. As we have seen, a residence order may, of course, be made in favour of an *individual* in care proceedings. So far as contact is concerned, individuals must use the code in s 34 and not seek s 8 contact orders in relation to a child in care. We discuss the statutory contact regime below. Thirdly, no specific issue or prohibited steps order may be made with a view to achieving a result which could be achieved by making a residence or contact order or in any way which is denied to the High Court (by s 100(2)) in the exercise of its inherent jurisdiction with respect to children[4]. These provisions are complex and are not a good advertisement for parliamentary draftsmanship. They have given rise to major difficulties of interpretation, particularly in the case of *Nottinghamshire County Council v P*[5].

Perhaps the restrictions are best understood by concentrating on the limited circumstances in which local authorities *may* seek s 8 orders rather than when they may not seek them. The fact of the matter is that when all the restrictions of s 9 are added together there is very little scope left for the granting of private orders at the

---

1 Section 9(1).
2 Section 91(1).
3 Section 9(2).
4 Section 100(2) precludes the court from exercising its inherent jurisdiction:
  '(a) so as to require the child to be placed in the care, or put under the supervision, of a local authority;
  (b) so as to require a child to be accommodated by or on behalf of a local authority;
  (c) so as to make a child who is the subject of a care order a ward of court; or
  (d) for the purpose of conferring on any local authority power to determine any question which has arisen, or which may arise, in connection with any aspect of parental responsibility for a child.'
5 [1993] 2 FLR 134. Cf *Re H (Prohibited Steps Order)* [1995] 1 FLR 638. We consider these cases in the context of the discussion of excluding abusers from the family home in Chapter 12.

behest of the local authority. It is clear that residence and contact orders may *never* be made in favour of the local authority and that specific issue and prohibited steps orders may not be made where the child is *in care*. The net result is that the latter two orders may be made in favour of a local authority but not if their effect is to breach the embargo on making the former two orders. They are thus likely only to be used to resolve 'single issues' and, even here, the authority may instead seek leave to invoke the inherent jurisdiction. So, to an appreciable extent, private s 8 orders are beyond the reach of the State.

All applications for care or supervision orders will be made, in the first instance, at the magistrates' level to the family proceedings court, although both the county court and the High Court now have concurrent jurisdiction[1]. There is provision for proceedings to be transferred, vertically or horizontally, to another court in appropriate cases[2].

On what ground?

The statutory ground for care and supervision orders is crucial, as is its interpretation by the courts, since it is now the only basis for compulsory intervention. It is a complex provision with many constituent elements and prompted one commentator to warn:

> 'Each of these elements will require considerable judicial exegesis. Almost every word will require interpretation and analysis. Argument on the meaning of the language contained here (as filled out by later subsections) is likely to rage for as long as this legislation remains in force.'[3]

The all-important provision is s 31(2), but this must be read with *both* the later subsections of s 31 (which define certain elements in the ground), and with the central principles in s 1 of the Children Act.

Section 31(2) provides:

> 'A court may only make a care order or supervision order if it is satisfied –
> (a)   that the child concerned is suffering, or is likely to suffer, significant harm; and
> (b)   that the harm, or likelihood of harm, is attributable to:
>   (i)   the care given to the child, or likely to be given to him if the order were not made, not being what it would be reasonable to expect a parent to give to him; or
>   (ii)   the child's being beyond parental control.'

Essentially, this is a single composite ground comprising two elements. The first is the presence or risk of significant harm to the child. The second is the attribution of this harm or risk to parental upbringing or to loss of parental control. Close analysis will be needed of these two independent elements, both of which must be proved, but first it is necessary to explore the relationship between the statutory ground and the principles in Part I of the Children Act.

---

1   See Chapter 2 above.
2   Children (Allocation of Proceedings) Order 1991, SI 1991/1677. Detailed discussion of the procedural rules is beyond the scope of the present work but a useful account is to be found in PM Bromley and NV Lowe *Bromley's Family Law* (8th edn) (Butterworths, 1992) at p 518. See also D Bedingfield *The Child in Need* (Family Law, 1998) at pp 355–359.
3   MDA Freeman 'Care After 1991' in D Freestone (ed) *Children and the Law* (Hull University Press, 1990) at p 135.

The threshold criteria and s 1 principles

Care and custody proceedings under the old law

One of the principal distinctions between care proceedings and custody or related proceedings under the old law was that the welfare principle applied in the latter but not in the former. It was not unknown for judges, especially in wardship, to draw attention to this[1]. The point which they were making was that the application of a broad welfare criterion, like the 'best interests' of the child, could allow the court to take almost any action it considered appropriate to safeguard the child's welfare. This was not possible in care proceedings which were hedged about with technical, and arguably restrictive, grounds which could prevent the court from taking the desired action. This, of course, accounts for the popularity of wardship with local authorities in the years leading up to the reforms[2]. Under the Children Act, local authorities may now resort to the inherent jurisdiction only with leave of the High Court.

Rejection of the welfare principle

The *Review*[3] specifically rejected the idea that the welfare principle could be adopted as the basis for compulsory action. The thinking was that this could give rise to widely differing interpretations of welfare and thus expose the family to unrestricted intervention. In short, it would give the State too open-ended a power, and might lead to children being removed from their families simply because someone else could do better in raising them. Instead, it was accepted that, subject to certain minimal acceptable standards, parents should be allowed to continue raising their children in their own way. Hence, the statutory criteria are met only where there has been a failure to measure up to these minimum standards. This is sometimes known as the 'threshold stage'. The ultimate decision on whether to make a care order, supervision order or any other order will then turn on the best interests of the child. Thus, the welfare principle will apply, but only at this second 'welfare stage', as discussed below.

Safeguarding 'the best interests' of the child

The *Review* had proposed the inclusion of a third element in the new ground: that the order would be 'the most effective means available to [the court] of safeguarding the child's welfare'[4]. In essence, this third element has been grafted on to the statutory ground through the application of the welfare principle in s 1 of the Children Act. Both this and the no order principle in s 1(5) apply, and their cumulative effect is to prevent the making of a care or supervision order where this is not shown to be in the best interests of the child, or where it is not shown to be a better way of safeguarding the child's welfare than any other available option. But these broader considerations of welfare only come into play after the threshold criteria have been satisfied. If the conditions of s 31(2) cannot be proved, that is the end of the matter. If they can be proved, the court must then go on to consider

---

1 See, for example, the remarks of Dunn J in *Re D (A Minor) (Justices' Decision Review)* [1977] Fam 158.
2 Local authorities would sometimes 'waive the jurisdictional point' to enable the court to exercise its wardship jurisdiction for this purpose. Good examples of this phenomenon are *A v B and Hereford and Worcester Council* [1986] 1 FLR 289; and *Re JT (A Minor) (Wardship: Committal to Care)* [1986] 2 FLR 107.
3 DHSS *Review of Child Care Law* (1985) at para 15.10.
4 Ibid at para 15.24.

whether care or supervision is the best course of action, which it may not be, given the new emphasis on voluntary co-operation. If parents are willing to agree to the local authority's plan for the child, perhaps by allowing the child to be accommodated by the local authority, compulsion may be both unnecessary and undesirable. On the other hand, where there have been serious incidents of violence or sexual abuse, the court may conclude that the local authority requires the additional control which it can get from a care order.

Care plans

In order to enable the court to make an informed choice as between care, supervision, a s 8 order or no order at all, it is necessary for the local authority to have a care plan to put before the court[1]. The 1987 White Paper[2] acknowledged the importance of care plans. In *Manchester City Council v F*[3] Eastham J said that the care plan delivered by local authorities should accord, as far as is reasonably possible, with the *Guidance* issued under the legislation[4]. This advises that whereas there is no set format for a care plan it should be in writing and should set out the child's and the family's social history. It goes on to identify other key elements which should be included in the plan such as identifying the child's needs and how these should be met, the nature of the proposed placement, arrangements for contact and reunification, the duration of the placement and what is to happen if it breaks down, and arrangements for health care and education.

The Children Act Advisory Committee in its Final Report[5] has drawn attention to the serious difficulties experienced by some local authorities in drafting care plans where the satisfaction of the threshold criteria depends on proof of specific facts, such as 'was a child sexually abused or non-accidentally injured and, if so, by whom?'. There may have been no previous history of inadequate parenting or social services involvement. Thus, until those questions are answered, a care plan cannot sensibly be made and this can lead to unacceptable delays in the proceedings. The suggested solution, approved by Bracewell J in *Re S (Care Proceedings: Split Hearing)*[6], is that there ought to be a split hearing. The first

---

1   Although not yet on a statutory footing, in practice care plans are regarded as mandatory since without them the court is simply unable to make a judgment of what action is required as between the various alternatives. See *Re J (Minors) (Care: Care Plan)* [1994] 1 FLR 253. The care plan should be properly supported by the evidence. For the problems which can arise where it is not, see *Re H (Care: Change in Care Plan)* [1998] 1 FLR 193. See also *Re CH (Care or Interim Care Order)* [1998] 1 FLR 402, where the Court of Appeal quashed a final care order which had been made despite the fact that there was outstanding expert evidence to bring before the court. This evidence would have enabled the court to scrutinise properly the care plan and the differences of view between the local authority and the guardian ad litem. Cf *Re R (Care Proceedings: Adjournment)* [1998] Fam Law 454 where, on the evidence, the Court of Appeal held that there had been no realistic alternative to the making of an immediate full care order and that the judge had erred in adjourning the hearing for 3 months to enable the local authority to reconsider its care plan.

2   *The Law on Child Care and Family Services* (Cm 62) at para 10, where it was said that the 'amount of detail in the plan will vary from case to case depending on how far it is possible for the local authority to foresee what will be best for the child at that time'.

3   [1993] 1 FLR 419.

4   *The Children Act 1989 Guidance and Regulations Vol 3 Family Placements* (HMSO, 1991) at ch 2, para 2.62.

5   *The Children Act Advisory Committee Final Report June 1997* (Lord Chancellor's Department, 1997).

6   [1996] 2 FLR 773.

hearing will be to determine the relevant facts and whether the threshold criteria are met and then there will be, if necessary, a second hearing with a care plan to decide what order, if any, should be made. The Committee advises that in order to avoid delay it is essential that a decision to have a split trial should be made as early as possible in the proceedings and that, thereafter, the case should be timetabled as tightly and quickly as possible[1].

The significance of the care plan in the overall scheme of things cannot be over-estimated since, once a care order has been made, the general principle is that the court may not intrude into the authority's plans for the child by, for example, dictating to it about the appropriate placement of the child. Tensions between the courts and local authorities have, however, surfaced concerning the relationship between the care plan and the vital issue of contact with the family which has been subjected to judicial scrutiny under the legislation. We discuss this issue below.

How far can the no order principle be taken?
A final and vitally important preliminary question is how far the courts are likely to take the no order principle in practice. In the private sphere, particularly on divorce, the objection to court orders was that they were often unnecessary, merely upholding the status quo after, at best, a perfunctory investigation of welfare[2]. Care and supervision orders, however, have not been granted routinely but only after a full and often contested hearing before the court. If, therefore, there were to be a similar sharp decline in the number of care orders as there has been in the number of orders on divorce, this would be a matter of major public concern. This is especially so since the wardship procedure, which used to protect a number of children, is now no longer available.

The first element – significant harm

When must significant harm occur and how it is proved?
An early answer to the question whether the statutory threshold criteria should be interpreted restrictively or liberally was given by the Court of Appeal in *Newham London Borough Council v AG*[3]. The court was concerned with the interpretation of the new prospective element in the statutory threshold – that the child is 'likely to suffer' significant harm. Sir Stephen Brown P held that this was not to be equated with 'on the balance of probabilities' and expressed the hope that the courts would not be asked to perform in every case a strict legalistic analysis of the statutory meaning of s 31. Although the words of the statute had to be considered, Parliament could not have intended them to be unduly restrictive when the evidence clearly indicated that a certain course of action should be followed to protect a child.

The *Newham* case was concerned with what has become a recurrent problem and theme in the reported cases. This is the choice which often has to be made between care in the child's extended family (in this case with grandparents) and substitute care outside the birth family, perhaps leading to the child's ultimate adoption. The broad issue is how far the resources of the birth family must be

---

1 For a case in which the local authority was criticised for delay in seeking a care order and for not applying for a split hearing, see *Re CD and MD (Care Proceedings: Practice)* [1998] 1 FLR 825.
2 See Chapter 4 above.
3 [1993] 1 FLR 281.

exhausted before the State is entitled to pursue its preferred choice of substitute care under the force of a care order. In *Newham,* the Court of Appeal accepted the judge's assessment that the grandparents would be unable to offer the child adequate protection from the serious danger which the mother represented (she was seriously ill with a form of schizophrenia which manifested itself in neglect of the child).

The issue was to resurface again in dramatic fashion in *Re M (A Minor) (Care Order: Threshold Conditions)*[1], which is now the leading authority on the interpretation of the statutory threshold. Here, the father had murdered the mother in front of the children in particularly gruesome circumstances. The police took the children into emergency protection[2]. The father was convicted of the mother's murder and was serving a life sentence with a recommendation for deportation (he was Nigerian) on his eventual release. Three of the four children were placed with Mrs W, the mother's cousin, but initially she did not feel able to cope with the youngest child, M. So M, not yet four months old, was placed with a temporary foster-mother. In due course, Mrs W wanted to offer M a home with his half-siblings. It should be noted in passing that there were several different fathers of the children but that the father of M was the mother's husband. Since he was married to her, he continued to retain parental responsibility and, indeed, sought to influence the decision from prison on what was to happen to M[3]. The local authority, the guardian ad litem for M and the father all wanted a care order to be made and for M to be placed for adoption outside the extended birth family.

At first instance, Bracewell J made the care order but the Court of Appeal allowed Mrs W's appeal and substituted a residence order in her favour[4]. The House of Lords restored the care order, although by the time of the hearing it was accepted on all sides that M had settled well with Mrs W and her family and should stay with her. The point of law was this. In considering whether a child 'is suffering significant harm' is it permissible to look backwards to the time when the initial protective measures were instigated (in this case police protection) or does this test have to be satisfied at the time of the hearing at which the application is being considered? The significance of the issue was, of course, that by the date of the hearing M was no longer suffering significant harm, nor was he 'likely' to suffer it because he was by this time properly looked after and the danger had passed.

The House of Lords held that there was jurisdiction to make a care order in these circumstances. Lord Mackay LC said that on a correct interpretation of s 31(2)(a) the court was entitled to have regard to the whole period from the instigation of the protective measures until the final disposal of the case. Thus, Bracewell J had been right to look back to the situation as it was when emergency protection was taken. She had been entitled to conclude that *at that time* M was suffering significant harm by being permanently deprived of the love and care of

---

1   [1994] 3 WLR 55. For commentaries, see J Masson 'Social Engineering in the House of Lords: *Re M*' (1994) 6 JCL 170, J Whybrow '*Re M* – Past, Present and Future Significant Harm' (1994) 6 JCL 88 and A Bainham 'The Temporal Dimension of Care' (1994) CLJ 458.

2   For the powers of the police to protect children in emergencies, see Chapter 12.

3   There is no statutory power to revoke the parental responsibility of a *married* father short of the ultimate step of adoption. It is questionable whether a father in these circumstances should be able to retain it at all.

4   A particularly good example of the *private* s 8 order being made in *public* family proceedings. See, generally, Chapter 2 for the scheme of the Children Act in this respect.

his mother and that this was attributable to the fact that the 'care' given by the parent (the father) was not what it would have been reasonable to expect a parent to give to him[1]. The only limitation on this retrospective process of looking backwards was that the initial protective arrangements had remained continuously in place. The local authority could not, for example, terminate a temporary foster-placement, allow the child home and then, as it were, have a 'second bite at the cherry'. Lords Templeman and Nolan pointed out that to restrict evidence to that which was available at the hearing could mean that *any* temporary measures which removed the risk could preclude the court from making a final care order and that this could not have been Parliament's intention.

The decision raises a number of important questions of policy. First, the reader may wonder why, if the child M had settled happily with Mrs W, the local authority bothered to pursue the chance of obtaining a care order all the way to the House of Lords. Part of the answer to this was of course the need to obtain clarification of the important point of law about when precisely the threshold conditions must be proved to be satisfied. But there was more to it than this. The practical point of a care order in *Re M* itself was that it would enable social services to keep a 'watching brief' on M's situation and intervene quickly to remove him from Mrs W should the need arise. If the residence order in favour of Mrs W had stood, the authority would have had no such right, since parental responsibility would have vested in her and not in the authority. Secondly, there is the broader policy question, alluded to above, about whether the State should have the option of obtaining a compulsory order where the risk *in fact* has passed and there is no obvious future risk to the child. Surely the public law requirement of the Children Act is not intended to allow the State to remove children who are no longer at risk merely because it would have greater confidence in carers outside the family than those within it. The legislation is, after all, supposed to have a commitment to supporting the natural family, and reuniting the child with relatives, wherever possible[2]. In short, State intervention is not about finding the best available home for a child, and children are not to be taken into care merely because someone could make a better job of raising them than their own family. The decision in *Re M* has been subjected to scathing criticism along these lines by Judith Masson[3] and it is impossible here to do justice to the full force of her arguments.

Nevertheless, it is submitted, that on balance the positive aspects of the House of Lords ruling in *Re M* outweigh these objections for the following reasons. First, following the Court of Appeal's decision in the *Newham* case, it was important that the House of Lords should adopt a liberal and non-legalistic interpretation of the statutory threshold conditions which allows for some flexibility on the temporal question which had so bedevilled the previous legislation[4]. Secondly, it should be remembered that to cross the threshold is not per se sufficient to found a care order. The court will still need to be convinced, at the welfare stage, that a care order is in the best interests of the particular child and the authority will have to convince the court in its care plan that this is so. The court is not obliged to make a

---

1 A possible criticism of this logic, but not, it is submitted, a convincing objection, is that the father's behaviour, appalling though it was, had been directed towards the *mother* and not towards the child.

2 See Chapter 10.

3 See fn 1 at p 374 (above).

4 See p 377 below.

care order, supervision order or any other order if it sees no need for it at the date of the final hearing. Finally, while it is true that the potential contribution of the extended family should be properly explored, the authority will have to balance this with genuine anxieties it may have about whether the wider family, in which a parent has been shown to be unable to cope with a child, is actually the best environment in which that child should be raised. There is no better illustration of this than the facts of the *Newham* case.

Re M has been applied in several subsequent cases. In *Re K (Care Order or Residence Order)*[1], it was held that the court had jurisdiction to make a care order even though, at the relevant time, the children were well looked after by their grandparents. Although the local authority no longer sought a care order, it had originally applied for one and there was no principle that a care order should only be made in the family context in exceptional circumstances. There would be cases (and this was one) in which a care order would be the only way of protecting children placed with the extended family from significant harm.

What if the initial 'protective measures' envisaged in *Re M* are taken under Part III of the Children Act, ie they are 'voluntary' measures in the sense that they are not opposed by anyone with parental responsibility? Two decisions make it plain that the provision of such services to children, particularly accommodation, may be sufficient to found a care order if in due course the authority feels that it needs the additional security of a care order. In *Re SH (Care Order: Orphan)*[2], the child had had spells of voluntary accommodation with the local authority while his mother was in hospital. There had been allegations of sexual abuse of his half-brother in which the mother was implicated. The mother then died and within months the father also died. At that point, the local authority sought a care order which was opposed by the child's guardian ad litem on the basis that the threshold criteria were not satisfied and that, applying the 'no order' principle, the local authority had ample powers to continue to look after the child under Part III and particularly under its powers to accommodate under s 20. It was held that the words 'is suffering' in s 31(2) meant 'was suffering' significant harm at the time when the 'rescue operation' was instigated, provided that these measures were continuing at the time of the final hearing. The decision confirms that protective measures which start as voluntary accommodation qualify as the necessary rescue operation. Moreover, a care order offered more than the continuation of voluntary accommodation since it gave the local authority parental responsibility and the legal standing to find an early adoption placement, to authorise medical procedures, to resist applications by relatives, etc. Its voluntary powers were inadequate for these purposes and neither was guardianship (which was the appropriate procedure where an individual wished to take over the care of an orphan) apposite in the case of a local authority.

A similar conclusion was reached in *Re M (Care Order: Parental Responsibility)*[3] which confirms that the threshold conditions may be satisfied in relation to an abandoned baby. Here, a baby of Afro-Caribbean origin was found abandoned on the steps of a health centre when a few days old. It proved impossible to trace the child's family and he was placed with foster-parents. The baby was found to have

---

1   [1995] 1 FLR 675.
2   [1995] 1 FLR 746.
3   [1996] 2 FLR 84.

developmental and other abnormalities and it was likely that medical intervention in the future would be necessary. The local authority was concerned that without a care order its powers were limited in relation, for example, to medical testing. It sought a care order with a view to placing the child for adoption and argued that there was a need for *someone* to have parental responsibility. Cazalet J held that the fact of abandonment, with all the risks it entailed, meant that the baby was suffering from significant harm immediately before he was found. Given his special needs, he was 'likely' to suffer significant harm in the future as a result of being abandoned. It was therefore necessary that someone should have parental responsibility and that the local authority should acquire this through a care order.

A rather different temporal problem from the one which occurred in *Re M* had caused very considerable difficulty under the old law. A major problem with the former conditions for care orders was that they generally required proof of *existing* harm. The local authority could not usually take a pre-emptive strike to protect a child from apprehended harm[1]. It is true that, in every case, the court had to make an evaluation of future risk when deciding whether to make a care order, but it could not make one *solely* on the strength of this[2]. This restriction caused problems in certain kinds of cases, as where a local authority wished to forestall the removal of a child from a stable foster-home to an uncertain future with parents[3], or where it wished to prevent a new-born baby leaving hospital with parents known to have a propensity for abuse or neglect[4]. The problem, in each case, was that it was very difficult to pin down existing harm, let alone attribute this to parental failings. These difficulties were occasionally circumvented by warding the child or by straining the statutory language as occurred in the well-known *Berkshire* case[5]. It ought now to be possible for cases like this to be resolved, if necessary, exclusively on the strength of the risk to the child's welfare as disclosed by all the surrounding circumstances, although there has been a forceful dissent from this view[6]. It seems clear that purely past conduct will not meet the statutory criteria unless it also points to present or future harm[7] or unless, as discussed above, protective measures have been continuously in place since the conduct in question.

The Children Act 1989 Guidance and Regulations Vol 1 Court Orders[8] suggests that most cases of anticipated harm will arise where the child has suffered significant harm at some time in the past and 'is likely to do so again because of some recurring circumstance'. The examples given are:

---

1   By way of exception to this, the old grounds did allow a care order to be made largely on the strength of the risk to one child in the family arising from previous abuse or neglect of *another* child in the household, or risk to the child occasioned by the presence in the household of a child offender. See the Children and Young Persons Act 1969, s 1(2)(b) and (bb).
2   *Essex County Council v TLR and KBR (Minors)* (1978) Fam Law 15.
3   As in the *Essex* case (above).
4   Place of safety orders had, however, been granted, controversially, for this purpose for some considerable time before the Children Act. See MDA Freeman 'Removing Babies at Birth: A Questionable Practice' (1980) Fam Law 131.
5   *D (A Minor) v Berkshire County Council* [1987] AC 317.
6   MDA Freeman 'Care after 1991' in D Freestone (ed) *Children and the Law* (Hull University Press, 1990). Cf A Bainham 'Care After 1991 – A Reply' (1991) 3 JCL 99.
7   Issues raised by the pre-Children Act decision in *M v Westminster City Council* [1985] FLR 325.
8   (HMSO, 1991) at para 3.22.

'where physical abuse of a child is associated with bouts of parental depression; or where a newly-born baby, because of the family history, would be at risk if taken home; or where the welfare of a child who was being looked after by the local authority under voluntary accommodation arrangements . . . would be at risk if the parents went ahead with plans to return him to an unsuitable home environment.'

But the *Guidance* goes on to warn that 'the conditions are intended to place a sufficiently difficult burden of proof upon the applicant as to prevent unwarranted intervention in cases where the child is not genuinely at risk'.

How then is this difficult burden of proof to be discharged by the local authority? The issue fell to be determined by the House of Lords which found it sufficiently difficult that it was obliged to hand down a 3–2 majority decision. In *Re H and R (Child Sexual Abuse: Standard of Proof)*[1] a 15-year-old girl alleged sexual abuse over a long period by her mother's cohabitant who was subsequently tried for rape but acquitted. The local authority nonetheless wanted to secure care orders in relation to the three younger girls in the household. They invited the judge to find that on the balance of probabilities (viz the lower civil, as opposed to criminal, standard of proof) the man concerned had indeed abused the eldest girl or that there was a substantial risk that he had done so and that, accordingly, the younger girls were 'likely to suffer significant harm' if a care order was not made. The judge was suspicious of abuse and recognised the real possibility that the eldest girl had given true evidence. But he dismissed the application for the care order holding that he could not be sure to the 'requisite high standard of proof' that this was so and that the threshold criteria were not therefore satisfied. The Court of Appeal by majority dismissed the authority's appeal, as did the House of Lords.

The principal majority speech was given by Lord Nicholls (with whom Lord Goff and Lord Mustill agreed) but there were strong dissents by Lord Browne-Wilkinson and Lord Lloyd. The first point was unanimously accepted. Following the Court of Appeal's decision in the *Newham* case, the House confirmed that in order to establish the prospective element in the statutory threshold it was *not* necessary to show that it was *probable* that the child would suffer significant harm in the sense of there being more than a fifty–fifty chance of it occurring. A child might need protection just as much where there was a *real possibility* of harm that could not be ignored having regard to the nature of the harm feared. Where the majority and minority views differed was in what was required in order to establish this real possibility of harm to the court's satisfaction.

The majority held that the standard of proof was the ordinary civil standard of the balance of probabilities, but also took the view that, generally, the truth of specific allegations on which the authority was relying would have to be proved to this standard. More controversially, it was the view of the majority that, in applying this standard, the court should bear in mind that the more serious the allegations the less likely it was that the events had occurred and the stronger the evidence that would be required. The standard of proof itself was not higher in these cases but, since it was inherently unlikely that what was alleged had actually occurred, proportionately more cogent evidence would be required to overcome this improbability. It was further held that in assessing likelihood of harm the court had to determine disputed issues of fact. Suspicion was not enough since the

---

1   [1996] 1 FLR 80. For commentary, see H Keating 'Shifting Standards in the House of Lords' [1996] CFLQ 157, and A Bainham 'Sexual Abuse in the Lords' (1996) CLJ 209.

foundation of care orders was 'the language of proof not suspicion'. In this respect, the evidence required to found a care order was greater than that required for short-term orders such as child assessment orders, emergency protection orders or interim care orders where, respectively, 'reasonable cause to suspect', 'reasonable cause to believe' or 'reasonable grounds for believing' that the child is likely to suffer significant harm will suffice[1]. The majority did, however, concede that there would be cases where, although the alleged maltreatment was not proved, the totality of the evidence established a combination of 'profoundly worrying features' which affected the care of the child within the family. It was possible that 'likelihood' of harm could be established in these circumstances even though it could not be said that the child was presently suffering it. In *Re H and R* itself, the difficulty was that the *only* relevant fact was the alleged abuse of the eldest girl and it could not therefore be said that the younger girls were at risk unless this allegation could be proved. Parents, it was said, should not have their children taken away fom them solely on the basis of suspicion.

The essential difference between the majority and the minority was that the latter, but not the former, were prepared to accept that the eldest girl's evidence remained *evidence* which could be taken into account in making the prognosis of risk. It was not essential to discount it if the truth of the allegations could not be substantiated. Thus, the judge's conclusion that there was a real possibility that her version of events was true was *not* a finding based on suspicion alone but on the *evidence*. Lord Lloyd also commented adversely on the notion that because a risk is serious, it is less likely. As he put it, it 'would be a bizarre result if the more serious the anticipated injury, whether physical or sexual, the more difficult it became for the authority to ... secure protection for the child'.

The majority decision of course represents the law, and it has subsequently been applied by the Court of Appeal which had to consider the appropriate standard of proof at the welfare stage of care proceedings[2]. Having crossed the threshold and found either existing significant harm, or the risk of significant harm to the child, could it be argued that a lesser standard of proof should apply at the welfare stage, viz when the court is deciding whether or not it should make the care order? In *Re M and R*, the Court of Appeal emphatically rejected this argument, again holding that the court can only act on the basis of proven facts rather than suspicion. Here, the judge had made interim care orders on the basis of emotional abuse and neglect of the children but he found that serious allegations of sexual abuse of the children by the mother and two men had not been proved to the requisite standard. He thus refused to make a final care order but adjourned the case for three months. The Court of Appeal was not prepared to accede to the local authority's argument that, because the welfare of the child was paramount at the welfare stage, the standard of proof for establishing likely harm should be less than the preponderance of possibilities. So again, the judge's finding of the real possibility of sexual abuse was not sufficient to found a full care order.

The problem of the unborn child

One situation which has caused difficulty is that of the unborn child. Where the pregnant mother is already known to social services, perhaps because of drug or

---

1   See, respectively, s 43(1), s 44(1) and s 38(2). See also the discussion of the inherent jurisdiction below.
2   *Re M and R (Child Abuse: Evidence)* [1996] 2 FLR 195.

alcohol abuse, or previous difficulties with her other children, the local authority may be genuinely concerned about the welfare of the expected child. If the mother has a medical or psychiatric condition, the local authority may want to ensure that the mother co-operates in the provision of proper ante-natal care and that the birth itself should be under normal medical supervision. Whatever these anxieties, the legal position is that the foetus is not within the definition of 'child' which means 'a person under the age of eighteen'[1]. Moreover, the foetus may not be made a ward of court[2]. All the authority can normally do is 'offer' voluntary assistance and 'keep its fingers crossed' that the birth will be trouble-free[3]. These limitations reflect, in part, the strong libertarian objections to the coercion of pregnant women who, it is often asserted, have complete autonomy over their own bodies. The legal and philosophical difficulty is how to balance any rights the foetus may have against such rights of the mother – an issue which has been hotly debated in the context of abortion[4]. As reflected in abortion law itself, it may well be that different considerations ought to apply to the later stages of pregnancy than in the first or second trimesters[5]. The case for ruling out all judicial intervention where a foetus is close to term is not, it is submitted, a strong one.

The position may, however, be different if the High Court is prepared to exercise its inherent jurisdiction in relation to *the mother* herself, as it has done in a number of cases in order to authorise a Caesarean section in the face of opposition by a woman in labour[6]. The courts have been careful to avoid saying explicitly that these interventions are designed to protect the health or life of the foetus, and the decisions are at least formally justified on the basis of the best interests of the patient herself. But the effect will nevertheless usually be to ensure the safe delivery of the child. *A Metropolitan Borough Council v DB*[7] provides perhaps the best illustration of the court's willingness to intervene paternalistically to protect a young mother and her child in the period immediately before and after the birth. It also illustrates the use of the inherent jurisdiction in conjunction with statutory powers under the Children Act. Here, the mother was a 17-year-old crack-cocaine addict. She had a fear of doctors but her medical condition gave cause for concern since she had suffered eclamptic fits resulting from high blood pressure. A Caesarean section was performed under judicial authorisation and an emergency protection order was then obtained in relation to the baby once born.

---

1   Section 105(1), and see Chapter 3 above.
2   *Re F (In Utero)* [1988] Fam 122.
3   The word 'offer' is used since it may well be that social services will attempt to exert pressure to co-operate.
4   As to which, contrast J Jarvis Thomson 'A Defence of Abortion' and J Finnis 'The Rights and Wrongs of Abortion' both in RM Dworkin (ed) *The Philosophy of Law* (Oxford University Press, 1977).
5   For a discussion of English abortion law, see G Douglas *Law, Fertility and Reproduction* (Sweet & Maxwell, 1991) at ch 5. For a useful collection of materials on legal intervention, see J Bridgeman and S Millns *Feminist Perspectives in Law: Law's Engagement with the Female Body* (Sweet & Maxwell, 1998) especially at pp 352–379. See also for a recent thorough examination of the issues involved in balancing maternal rights and foetal welfare, M Brazier 'Parental responsibilities, foetal welfare and children's health' in C Bridge (ed) *Family Law Towards the Millennium: Essays for PM Bromley* (Butterworths, 1997) at ch 8.
6   See, for example, *Re S (Adult: Surgical Treatment)* [1993] 1 FLR 26, *Norfolk and Norwich Health Care (NHS) Trust v W* [1996] 2 FLR 613, and Chapter 8 (above).
7   [1997] 1 FLR 767.

The authority then successfully invoked the inherent jurisdiction to keep the mother in the hospital maternity ward, which for these purposes constituted 'secure accommodation', since she had threatened to discharge herself from the ward in life-threatening circumstances.

What is harm?: the 'Russian doll' provision

The concept of 'harm' is very wide and is the cornerstone of the new ground. It has been said that 'the categories of abuse are never closed'[2]. The legislation defines harm[3] as 'ill-treatment or the impairment of health or development' and then provides a definition of each of these components. 'Development' includes 'physical, intellectual, emotional, social or behavioural development'. 'Health' includes 'physical or mental health'. 'Ill-treatment' embraces 'sexual abuse and forms of ill-treatment which are not physical'. In short, the kinds of harm contemplated are neglect, physical injury, sexual abuse and emotional abuse[4].

Neglect

Neglect is not, as such, mentioned in the Children Act but is subsumed within the idea of 'ill-treatment or the impairment of health or development'. Examples of neglect may be failure to summon essential medical attention[5], failure to provide the child with sustenance or failure to prevent the child coming into contact with foreseeable hazards[6].

Physical injury and the problem of corporal punishment

Physical injury is understandable enough to the layman, but difficult questions can be asked about the line between corporal punishment and abuse. Some people would outlaw all corporal punishment (as in the Scandinavian countries, Austria and Cyprus) largely because of the danger that punishment can degenerate into abuse[7]. There is also an argument that to allow parental punishment of children violates Article 19 of the United Nations Convention on the Rights of the Child which, inter alia, protects the child from 'all forms of physical or mental violence'. Freeman's view is that 'nothing is a clearer statement of the position that children occupy in society, a clearer badge of childhood than the fact that children alone of all people in society can be hit with impunity'[8].

The whole question of corporal punishment underwent close scrutiny by the Scottish Law Commission[9]. Although the Commission was not addressing the question of when it is or is not abuse, for the purposes of care proceedings, its conclusions were nonetheless an interesting barometer of Scottish public

---

1   MDA Freeman *Children, Their Families and the Law* (Macmillan, 1992), at p 93.
2   Section 31(9).
3   Identified and expanded upon in *Working Together Under the Children Act 1989* (HMSO, 1991) (*'Working Together'*) at para 6.40. On the problems of defining child abuse, see C Wattam 'The social construction of child abuse for practical policy purposes – a review of *Child Protection: Messages from Research*' [1996] CFLQ 189, reviewing the Department of Health's overview of research findings (HMSO, 1995).
4   See Chapter 8.
5   See Chapter 15.
6   This is MDA Freeman's view in *Children, Their Families and the Law* (Macmillan, 1992) at p 105. See also *The Moral Status of Children* (Martinus Nijhoff, 1997) especially at pp 116–117 and pp 131–132.
7   Ibid at p 117.
8   Scot Law Com Report No 135 *Family Law* (1992) at paras 2.67–2.105.

opinion¹. This seemed to be that, while the spontaneous slap or smack by a loving parent was considered a legitimate exercise of parental control, the striking of a child of any age with an implement was not². The Commission was not prepared to recommend the total abolition of the parental right to administer 'moderate and reasonable chastisement'³. It seems clear that parents who operate within these limits⁴ (vague though they are) will not have 'ill-treated' the child for the purposes of the legislation, whereas those who exceed them may well have done⁵.

Sexual abuse
Sexual abuse is included within the expression 'ill-treatment' but is not otherwise defined in the legislation. It would be fair to say that this has been the area of greatest difficulty in recent years. Perhaps this is not so surprising since, as Freeman points out⁶, the phenomenon was only recognised to exist at all comparatively recently. *Working Together* defines it as 'actual or likely sexual exploitation of a child or adolescent'⁷. While the grosser forms of abuse (rape, incest, buggery, etc) are easily recognisable as physical abuse, and serious criminal offences, there is much difficult line-drawing to be done over matters such as 'horseplay' between parents and children⁸ or, as Freeman has speculated, the exposure of children to pornographic literature⁹. Proof of sexual abuse is often difficult as well have seen. Moreover, the courts may be willing to continue contact arrangements even where sexual abuse is established¹⁰. These features are perhaps evidence of continuing ambivalence in social and judicial attitudes to the problem¹¹.

Emotional abuse
Emotional abuse undoubtedly comes within the expression 'forms of ill-treatment which are not physical' and it was a recognised form of ill-treatment under the old law¹². Again, it is not defined in the legislation, but it would seem that it is unlikely to be established without psychiatric evidence pointing to abnormal behaviour on the part of the child¹³. An example of emotional abuse may be the refusal to recognise a child's gender by making the child dress in the clothes of the opposite sex¹⁴.

---

1 The Commission conducted a survey through System Three Scotland in September 1991. The results of this are recorded at Scot Law Com Report No 135 (above), at paras 2.100–2.102.
2 While, for example, 83% thought that it ought to be lawful for a parent to smack a three-year-old, only 3% thought that the use of a belt, stick or other object should be within the law.
3 A test established in *R v Hopley* (1860) 2 F&F 202.
4 The Children and Young Persons Act 1933, s 1(7), inter alia, excludes from the offence of cruelty the parental right to administer punishment to a child.
5 For a discussion of the issue of corporal punishment in the context of child-minding, see Chapter 10, and in educational institutions, see Chapter 16.
6 MDA Freeman *Children, Their Families and the Law* (Macmillan, 1992) at p 93 referring to the DHSS circular in 1980 on registers which made no reference to it.
7 *Working Together* (above) at para 6.40.
8 In *C v C (Child Abuse: Access)* [1988] 1 FLR 462 the judge found the father to have indulged in 'vulgar and inappropriate horseplay' with his daughter.
9 MDA Freeman (above) at p 104.
10 See Chapter 4 above.
11 Graphically revealed in the Cleveland crisis and the media attention it received.
12 *F v Suffolk County Council* (1981) FLR 208. For a post-Children Act case of emotional abuse, see the facts of *Re M and R (Child Abuse: Evidence)* [1996] 2 FLR 195.
13 Discussed further by MDA Freeman (above) at p 104.
14 MDA Freeman (above).

It goes without saying that the above categorisations should not necessarily be regarded as exhaustive since, sadly, the discovery of new forms of abuse[1], or the rediscovery of old ones, cannot be discounted.

What is significant?

The immense variation in the forms which abuse or neglect can take means that the crucial issue is usually a question of *degree* rather than kind. How much does a child have to suffer, and how much society tolerate, before the 'private realm' of family life can be invaded? The answer given by the legislation is that the harm must be 'significant'. Here, again, we confront one of the many essentially indeterminate concepts which litter the Children Act[2]. The Act, nonetheless, does attempt to provide some guidance on when the requisite level will be reached. Section 31(10) states:

> 'Where the question of whether harm suffered by a child is significant turns on the child's health or development, his health or development shall be compared with that which could reasonably be expected of a similar child.'

While there can be no precise way of measuring the extent of harm, it is agreed that not every minor deficiency in a child's health or development will constitute 'significant harm'. Indeed, it is clear that we are looking for some 'substantial deficit' in the standard of upbringing which could be expected for the child[3]. This can only be ascertained by making a comparison with the hypothetical 'similar child'. But what is a 'similar child' for these purposes? It is generally agreed that the expression was designed to incorporate any subjective or unusual character-istics of the child in question. Thus, disabled children require special care which children who are not disabled do not require. Yet even this may become problematic, and comparisons may need to be more sophisticated. It has been pointed out[4], for example, that a deaf child of deaf parents may not be directly comparable to a deaf child of hearing parents.

---

1   Eg satanic or ritualistic abuse which, if it does exist, has only in recent years been acted upon by child protection agencies.
2   A problem discussed in Chapter 10 above. The question of significant harm must also be related to the likelihood of it occurring. The greater the potential *gravity* of the harm, the stronger will be the case for a care order, as opposed, for example, to a supervision order. The point is well illustrated by *Re D (A Minor) (Care or Supervision Order)* [1993] 2 FLR 423. Here, Ewbank J made a care order, rather than the supervision order which the local authority had itself sought. The circumstances were that the children of the father's previous marriage had suffered non-accidental injuries and a baby in his care had been killed. The need for protection of the children of his present relationship was considered to be the decisive factor as between care and supervision.
3   See the *Review* (above) at para 15(15).
4   MDA Freeman *Children, Their Families and the Law* (Macmillan, 1992) at p 107.

Whether it is legitimate to go beyond the inherent characteristics of the child and explore his cultural or social background is more debatable and gave rise to an apparent difference of opinion between the Lord Chancellor and the Department of Health[1], and some academic debate[2]. One view is that cultural pluralism ought to be relevant, especially since the legislation has an ideological commitment to this[3]. According to this view 'Muslim children, Rastafarian children, the children of Hasidic Jews may be different and have different needs from children brought up in the indigenous, white, nominally Christian culture'[4]. The opposing view is that allowances for cultural background ought not to be made, except at the welfare stage of the court process[5], since, by definition, the threshold criteria set minimally acceptable limits of behaviour towards children. As such, society has a right to expect everyone from whatever cultural background to comply[6] and, in any event, allowances for ethnic background take insufficient account of the widely divergent attitudes to child-rearing held among the indigenous population[7]. The matter remains unresolved[8].

The second element: the standard of care
The second element has been described as 'causative'[9]. It has been argued, however, that a condition may be 'attributable' to some factor but not 'caused' by it[10]. Yet, the concept of causation in other areas of law is wide enough to embrace indirect influences which contribute to a situation[11]. What is agreed is that parental behaviour does not have to be the sole or direct cause of the child's predicament, as long as it indirectly contributes to it[12].

1 In the debates on the Children Bill, Lord Mackay LC suggested that background as opposed to attributes, should be left out of account (House of Lords, Official Report, col 354). *The Children Act 1989 Guidance and Regulations Vol 1 Court Orders* (HMSO, 1991) at para 3.20, however, states that account may need to be taken of 'environmental, social and cultural characteristics of the child'.

2 Freeman (above). Cf A Bainham 'Care after 1991 – A Reply' (1993) 3 JCL 99. For an extremely helpful discussion of the cultural question in the context of the competing philosophies of relativism, monism and pluralism, see M Freeman 'Children's Rights and Cultural Pluralism' in *The Moral Status of Children* (Martinus Nijhoff, 1997) at ch 7.

3 This is Freeman's view, although he would discount social inequality arising from poor socio-economic status.

4 Freeman (above) at p 153.

5 A Bainham (above) at p 103. In other words, culture should be relevant when the court decides what order is appropriate.

6 Freeman himself would accept that practices such as female circumcision, excessive corporal punishment, refusal of essential medical aid on religious grounds, and so on, ought properly to be regarded as 'significant harm'.

7 For example, on corporal punishment, the Scottish Law Commission survey also revealed that 10% of those questioned thought it *should* be lawful to strike a 15-year-old with a belt, stick or other object, and over two-thirds (68%) thought that smacking a young person of this age should be lawful. See Scot Law Com Report No 135 *Family Law* (1992) at para 2.101.

8 On what is a 'similar child' in the context of truancy, see *Re O (A Minor) (Care Order: Education: Procedure)* [1992] 2 FLR 7, discussed in Chapter 16 below.

9 A Bainham 'Care After 1991 – A Reply' (1993) 3 JCL 99 at p 101.

10 MDA Freeman *Children, Their Families and the Law* (Macmillan, 1992) at p 150.

11 A Bainham (above).

12 This is certainly the view expressed in SM Cretney and JM Masson *Principles of Family Law* (6th edn) (Sweet & Maxwell, 1997) at pp 805–806.

Parental upbringing

Here, it must be shown that the harm the child is suffering, or is likely to suffer, is attributable to 'the care given to the child or likely to be given to him ... not being what it would be reasonable to expect a parent to give to him'[1].

It was said by Lord Mackay LC, during the debates on the Children Bill[2], that the underlying objective of this requirement is to strike a balance between the conflicting pressures of ensuring that intervention in the family occurs only in carefully defined circumstances, and allowing it where harm, or risk of harm, can be traced to a perceptible deficiency in parental care.

It must be shown first, that the harm or risk is indeed attributable, at least in part, to the standard or projected standard of parental care. The view has been offered that harm which is *solely* attributable to moving a child from foster-care would not meet the test[3]. This view is questionable. Anxieties about such a move must postulate concern about the standard of care the child is likely to receive at home, if moved. Otherwise, every move of a child from foster-care would be seen as harmful. The reality is that the anxiety fixes not on the move itself but on the risk to the child's welfare on his return home, and this is squarely caught by the reference in the statutory ground to the care *likely to be given* to the child. The *Guidance*[4] states that 'harm caused solely by a third party is ... excluded (unless the parent has failed to prevent it)'. This might occur, for example, where a parent has a relationship with an undesirable adult, such as a child offender, which exposes the child to contact with that person.

It seems that the test of the adequacy of care is an *objective* one, although all the arguments about social or cultural background resurface again here[5]. The *Guidance* advises that the court will need professional assistance on what it would be reasonable to expect the parents to achieve in the circumstances[6]. But clearly, reasonableness must be assessed in relation to the particular child who is before the court, bearing in mind the needs of that child. The test is, therefore, what would a reasonable parent do for *this* child? Cultural considerations may well be relevant when the court has to apply the ultimate welfare test and decide on what order, if any, it should make. This is because the statutory checklist of factors applies and this includes a reference to the child's background[7].

Parental control

The alternative, on the second element, requires that the harm or risk to the child be attributable to 'the child's being beyond parental control'[8]. Under the old law,

---

1 Section 31(2)(b)(i).
2 House of Lords, Official Report, 19 January 1989, col 355.
3 PM Bromley and NV Lowe *Bromley's Family Law* (8th edn) (Butterworths, 1992) at p 515.
4 *The Children Act 1989 Guidance and Regulations Vol 1 Court Orders* (HMSO, 1991) at para 3.23.
5 Freeman is in no doubt (above) at p 108, that social deprivation must be discounted:
   'The care given to the child is not what it would be reasonable for *this* parent to give (in her high-rise flat, living on income support, with three children under five and a partner in prison), but what it would be reasonable to expect *a* parent to give.'
6 *The Children Act 1989 Guidance and Regulations Vol 1* (above) at para 3.23.
7 Section 1(3)(d).
8 Section 31(2)(b)(ii).

this was a freestanding ground for a care order and the former power of parents to initiate proceedings indirectly has already been noted[1]. This was, in essence, a 'status offence' and was open to the objection that compulsory action could be taken against a child for non-criminal misbehaviour. Under the new law, a care or supervision order may only be made where the child, being beyond parental control, is suffering significant harm or is exposed to the risk of doing so[2]. Whether the test is objective or subjective is not entirely clear[3] but the *Guidance* advises that it is not necessary to prove fault on the part of the parents[4]. It has been argued that the reference to 'parental' control is wide enough to include non-parents caring for a child, at least where they have parental responsibility[5].

It is possible, but not necessary, for both alternatives to be satisfied at the same time. Indeed, in one reported case[6] the judge indicated that the circumstances established *either* a lack of reasonable parental care *or* the child being beyond parental control.

The welfare stage

If the court finds that the statutory threshold is crossed it must then go on to consider what kind of order, if any, is in the best interests of the child. We discussed the welfare stage of care proceedings above.

CARE ORDERS

In some respects, there is considerable similarity between the respective legal positions of those children who are voluntarily accommodated by local authorities and those in care. They are all 'looked after' by the local authority whose general and specific duties apply to both groups[7]. Yet there are also important distinctions. This section looks at the distinctive legal effects of a care order and at the special regime which applies to contact with children in care.

The legal effects of a care order

Section 33 of the Children Act spells out the legal effects of a care order. There is now only one set of criteria for care orders and uniform legal effects whatever the proceedings in which the order was made. One important change is that the court, having made the care order, retains no residual control over the

---

1   See fn 9 at p 366 above.
2   This would seem to meet the above objections, especially since the order can only be sought in relation to younger teenagers, ie those under 16 years of age.
3   See MDA Freeman *Children, Their Families and the Law* (Macmillan, 1992) at p 100.
4   *The Children Act 1989 Guidance and Regulations Vol 1* (above) at para 3.25.
5   Freeman (above) at p 100. This certainly seems to be confirmed by the decision in *M v Birmingham City Council* [1994] 2 FLR 141 where the teenager concerned was in local authority accommodation but held to be beyond the parental control of her mother and partner. Stuart White J took the view that the statutory conditions could include a state of affairs which might be in the past, present or future.
6   *Re O (A Minor) (Care Order: Education: Procedure)* [1992] 2 FLR 7.
7   See Chapter 10 above.

management of the child's case[1]. The *Review* recommended that the local authority should be able to take a grip on the case by taking firm and early decisions, and should resist the temptation of passing responsibility to another body[2]. Accordingly, the former power of certain courts to give directions to the local authority about strategic plans for the child has been removed[3]. The court has the more limited power of directing an investigation in family proceedings, but it may not act of its own volition in making a care order or dictate to the local authority once an order is made.

Local authorities must receive and keep a child in their care

The first effect of a care order is to require local authorities 'to receive the child into their care and to keep him in their care while the order remains in force'[4]. Although parents do not lose their parental responsibility when a care order is made, they must not exercise this in a way which is incompatible with any order of the court[5]. Thus, they may not remove a child who is subject to a care order, since this would contravene the effect of that order.

Local authorities must assume/share parental responsibility

The second consequence of a care order is prescribed in s 33(3) and is more controversial. It provides:

'While a care order is in force with respect to a child, the local authority designated by the order shall –
(a)   have parental responsibility for the child; and
(b)   have the power (subject to the following provisions of this section) to determine the extent to which a parent or guardian of the child may meet his parental responsibility for him.'

The local authority, therefore, has parental responsibility by virtue of the care order and is not dependent, as where a child is voluntarily accommodated, for its legal powers on parental delegation. However, parents do not lose their parental responsibility merely because the local authority also acquires it[6]. Most other people who hold parental responsibility when a care order is made will lose it, since the effect of the order is to revoke a residence order[7]. Guardians and adoptive parents, however, retain parental responsibility, since they do not derive it from a residence order but from their status. The effect of s 33(3) is, therefore,

---

1   See p 405 et seq below.
2   DHSS *Review of Child Care Law* (1985) at para 2.24.
3   Powers used most frequently, but not exclusively, in wardship.
4   Section 33(1).
5   Section 2(8).
6   Section 2(5) and (6). In *Kent County Council v C* [1992] 3 WLR 808, Ewbank J held that once a care order was made the family proceedings court did not retain the power to direct that the guardian ad litem should continue his involvement with the child. Responsibility passed to the authority under the order. See also *Re B (A Minor) (Care Order: Review)* [1993] 1 FLR 421 in which Thorpe J held that a care order which incorporated provision for a review in six months of the operation of the order, progress in the care plan and contact, was manifestly ultra vires. What both of these cases establish is that the court may not make a *conditional* care order. The central effect of a care order is to give the local authority the power to regulate the management of the child's life in care except in so far as the statutory regime makes express contrary provision – for example in relation to contact or the use of secure accommodation. See the discussion of care plans and contact with children in care at p 389 below.
7   Section 91(2). A care order will also automatically revoke a supervision order (s 91(3)), wardship (s 91(4)), or a school attendance order under the Education Act 1996, s 437(2) (s 91(5)).

that the local authority must *share* parental responsibility with the parents. This was not the intention in the *Review* or the White Paper which, as Eekelaar has observed, clearly contemplated that a care order would involve a transfer of parental responsibility from the parents to the local authority[1]. It was, for Eekelaar, the Law Commission, which in 1988 'struck out in a new direction'. This sharing of parental responsibility, where the child is in care, has been the subject of trenchant criticism[2] on the ground that it dilutes the local authority's control over the child. In contrast to this, there has also been criticism that parents' participatory rights have been threatened by a late amendment to s 33(3), discussed below.

Sharing parental responsibility

What then does sharing entail? The theory is clear enough. Parents maintain an *equal* say in matters of upbringing and may exercise all aspects of parental responsibility, including, of course, the right of independent action, when the child is with them. But since the child will usually *not* be with them, all of this theory probably adds up, in practice, to little more than a right of consultation[3].

While the Children Bill was progressing through Parliament, concern began to be expressed that parents might use the opportunity, where a child was allowed home, to act in ways contrary to the wishes of the local authority[4]. In consequence, an amendment was introduced which is now s 33(3)(b). The intention was to try to ensure that, despite the notional equality of parents and the local authority and the idea of partnership, the local authority would remain in effective control of the situation. Thus, the Children Act gives the local authority power to control the *exercise* of parental responsibility by parents if this would undermine its plan for the child. The *Guidance* euphemistically advises that this power 'allows the local authority to deal with any conflict that may arise between the local authority and the parents in exercising their respective parental responsibilities'[5]. In fact, it allows the local authority to impose its will. As Freeman has put it, 'the local authority has the whip hand'[6]. He is scathing about what he sees as a largely illusory retention of parental responsibility by parents:

> 'There is concern that we are saying parents have responsibility but giving them no way of challenging the exercise by a local authority of its discretion to take that responsibility away.'[7]

It was envisaged that the power would only be exercised sparingly and it *can* only be exercised where it is necessary to safeguard or promote the child's welfare[8]. Also, it cannot prevent a parent or guardian with physical care of a child from doing what is reasonable in all the circumstances, for the purpose of safeguarding or promoting that child's welfare[9].

---

1   J Eekelaar 'Parental Responsibility: State of Nature or Nature of the State?' (1991) JSWFL 37 at p 43.
2   Ibid, especially at pp 41–42.
3   Section 22(4) and (5), and see Chapter 10 below. It would not appear that parents are under a concomitant duty to consult the authority and that this is one reason why s 33(3)(b) is required.
4   There could, for example, be arguments about whether what parents proposed to do was incompatible with the care order.
5   *The Children Act 1989 Guidance and Regulations Vol 1 Court Orders* (HMSO, 1991) at para 3.67.
6   See MDA Freeman *Children, The Family and the Law* (Macmillan, 1992) at p 121.
7   Ibid.
8   Section 33(4).
9   Section 33(5), which mirrors s 3(5) in relation to de facto carers.

It can be argued that the very idea of sharing parental responsibility, where a child has been compulsorily removed because of parental failings, is an unacceptable intrusion into the managerial control of the local authority. On this view, the concept of a partnership between social services and, for example, parents who are responsible for serious abuse, may be ill-conceived[1]. It is difficult to resist the conclusion that the provision was an unhappy compromise, cobbled together at the eleventh hour, which satisfies neither social services nor the advocates of parents' rights.

How much parental responsibility does the local authority acquire?

The parental responsibility which the local authority acquires is not quite as extensive as that of parents since there are some express statutory limitations. The general principle, which also applies to non-parents with parental responsibility[2], is that those legal incidents which are fundamental to the relationship of parent and child ought not to pass to others by any means short of adoption. The powers in question are the right to consent to or refuse an application to free the child for adoption, or a final adoption order, and the right to appoint a guardian[3]. None of these powers pass under a care order. There are also restrictions on changing the child's name and removing him from the country which correspond broadly with those restrictions which apply where a residence order is made[4]. In addition, the local authority must not 'cause the child to be brought up in any religious persuasion other than that in which he would have been brought up if the order had not been made'[5]. The effect of this is to prevent the local authority itself from unilaterally changing the child's religion. It does not preclude the child from taking his own decision as he grows older.

Contact with children in care

The background

There is no question that the issue of contact between a child in care and parents or relatives has generated more complaints and litigation than any other issue in this area of the law[6]. No doubt this was, in part, a reflection of the largely unrestrained power which local authorities used to wield over contact arrangements. The absence of effective mechanisms of redress led to a clamour in the early 1980s which culminated in successful challenges under the European Convention on Human Rights[7] and domestic legislation[8]. This legislation provided for judicial control over decisions to 'refuse' or 'terminate' access (as it then was). The current legislation builds on these foundations but goes much

---

1 This certainly seems to be the thrust of Eekelaar's position in 'Parental Responsibility: State of Nature or Nature of the State?' (1991) JSWFL 37.
2 See Chapter 6 above.
3 Section 33(6)(b).
4 Section 33(7) and (8). But the child may be allowed to leave the jurisdiction in accordance with arrangements made under Sch 2, para 19.
5 Section 33(6)(a).
6 See *The Children Act 1989 Guidance and Regulations Vol 1 Court Orders* (HMSO, 1991) at paras 3.75–3.86.
7 *R v The United Kingdom* [1988] 2 FLR 445.
8 The Health and Social Services and Social Security Adjudications Act 1983, s 6 and Sch 1, adding ss 12A–12G to the Child Care Act 1980.

further. In particular, it shifts the onus from aggrieved parents to local authorities where local authorities wish to refuse contact to a prescribed category of individuals.

Before turning to the new regime it is as well to put the contact question into perspective. It should be seen alongside the principles of parental responsibility for children, partnership, and the statutory responsibilities of local authorities to endeavour to effect a reunification of the child with his family and, to this end, to promote contact[1]. The contact code in s 34 must be seen in this wider context. The hope is that it will not have to come into play at all, since questions of the nature or extent of contact arrangements will be resolved at the time the care order is made. Indeed, the court is specifically empowered to make a contact order when it makes a care order[2]. More importantly, it must, before making a care order:

> '(a) consider the arrangements which the authority have made, or propose to make, for affording any person contact with a child ... and
> (b) invite the parties to the proceedings to comment on those arrangements.'[3]

Proposals for contact should, therefore, be an important element in the authority's care plan for the child which it puts before the court. The function of the contact code, constituted by s 34 and the Contact with Children Regulations 1991[4], is therefore, to resolve disputes and to make the local authority accountable for the discharge of its statutory duties.

The presumption of reasonable contact

The Children Act broke new ground by creating, for the first time, a presumption of reasonable contact with a child in care[5]. This is in favour of a parent, guardian, person who held a residence order or person who had the care of a child under an exercise of the inherent jurisdiction, immediately before the care order was made[6]. The local authority may refuse contact to these individuals only in very limited circumstances, ie where:

> '(a) they are satisfied that it is necessary to do so in order to safeguard or promote the child's welfare; and
> (b) the refusal –
>   (i)   is decided upon as a matter of urgency; and
>   (ii) does not last for more than seven days.'[7]

---

1 Particularly Sch 2, para 15.
2 Section 34(10).
3 Section 34(11).
4 SI 1991/891. It must be emphasised that the code does not govern contact with 'accommodated' children. Such children could, however, be the subject of a s 8 contact order.
5 It is interesting to note that there is no corresponding statutory presumption in favour of parents in the private law although the courts have, through their practice, effectively created one. See Chapter 4 above.
6 Section 34(1).
7 Section 34(6). Under reg 2 of the Contact with Children Regulations 1991 (above), the authority is then required to give written notice with reasons to the child (if he has sufficient understanding) and to any person entitled to the presumption of reasonable contact.

If the local authority then wishes to continue to disallow contact, it must get the court's authorisation, and the onus is on the local authority to bring the application[1]. The court has power to authorise or refuse contact[2]. This is a major shift of emphasis from the pre-Children Act position. Under the old law, the local authority's initial obligations were limited to giving notice of an intended refusal or termination of access. Now there are automatic restraints on the local authority's power to refuse contact and it is incumbent on the local authority, subject to emergencies, to justify this to the court.

There is undoubtedly a tension between the two principles, (1) that the courts are *not* allowed under the statutory regime to interfere with the implementation of the local authority's care plan, and (2) that they *are* authorised to regulate the question of contact with a child in care. The short point is that the question of contact with the family is itself a very important integral part of the care plan. The reported cases have given guidance on the proper relationship between these two principles. First, it should be recalled that the court must have regard to the authority's care plan before making a care order[3]. If, therefore, the court is not happy with what is proposed concerning contact, one obvious solution will be for it to refuse to make the care order in the first place[4]. Secondly, once the child is actually subject to a care order, the courts have made it plain that Parliament has given them the right and duty to determine the question of contact in the event of a dispute. Where, therefore, there are any prospects of the link between the child and the family being meaningfully maintained, it falls to the court to decide the reasonableness of continuing contact and either to authorise it or refuse it[5].

Applications for contact

The category of those who benefit from the presumption of contact is limited. Others, such as grandparents or other relatives, may apply, with leave of the court, for a contact order[6]. In *Re M (Care: Contact: Grandmother's Application)*[7], the Court of

---

1 Section 34(4). On such an application, the parent must be permitted to call such evidence as he or she sees fit, provided that this is presented in a professional and responsible manner. See *H v West Sussex County Council* [1998] 1 FLR 862.

2 Section 34(2) and (4). For a recent decision illustrating the complex relationship between contact and the overall care plan, see *L v London Borough of Bromley* [1998] 1 FLR 709. For some research findings about efforts to promote contact between children looked after by local authorities and their families, see J Masson 'Restoring Contact and Rebuilding Partnerships' [1998] Fam Law 142.

3 *Re J (Minors) (Care: Care Plan)* [1994] 1 FLR 253.

4 *Re T (A Minor) (Care Orders: Conditions)* [1994] 2 FLR 223.

5 See, particularly, the judgment of Hale J in *Berkshire County Council v B* [1997] 1 FLR 171. See also *Re B (Minors) (Termination of Contact: Paramount Consideration)* [1993] Fam 301, *Re T (Termination of Contact: Discharge of Order)* [1997] 1 FLR 517, and *Re D and H (Care: Termination of Contact)* [1997] 1 FLR 841. The court must not, however, attempt to control contact in a way which strikes at the heart of the local authority's care plan. For a case in which the court trespassed unjustifiably on the 'forbidden territory' of the care plan itself, see *Re S (A Minor) (Care: Contact Order)* [1994] 2 FLR 222. For commentary, see Smith 'Parental powers and local authority discretion – the contested frontier' [1997] CFLQ 243.

6 Under s 34(3)(b) 'any person' may apply with leave.

7 [1995] 2 FLR 86.

Appeal set out in some detail the principles to be applied where the applicant for leave to apply for contact with a child in care is not in the category of those who benefit from the presumption (in this case a grandparent). The court said that, as in private law, grandparents are not entitled to reasonable contact as of right. At the same time, the special place of relatives was acknowledged in the legislation, and grandparents should have a special place in any child's affections. Contact between the child and the birth family should be assumed to be beneficial and the local authority should file evidence to justify why it would not be consistent with the child's welfare to promote contact with relatives. The court went on to hold that, by analogy with private law applications for contact, the criteria in s 10(9)[1] governing applications for leave in that context, were apposite on applications for leave to seek contact under the public regime. The local authority's general duty to promote contact with the child also extends to 'any relative, friend, or other person connected with him'[2]. It should not, therefore, be difficult for relatives to surmount the leave hurdle, where the application is genuine[3]. It may prove more difficult for those with a less obvious connection with the child. The main difference between this group and those entitled to the presumption of contact is that the onus here is on the applicant and not on the local authority.

Where the issue is not the complete refusal of contact, but rather the level or nature of contact being allowed, the onus will always be on the person affected by the decision to bring the matter to court. The court may then specify the time, place and frequency of contact[4]. Those entitled to the presumption of reasonable contact, together with the local authority and the child, are entitled to apply without leave for defined contact[5]. Others require leave. This power to define contact is again wider than that which existed before the Children Act. Under the old law, the local authority had power to curtail access drastically, perhaps with a view to phasing it out completely, and this was not susceptible to challenge[6]. This is

---

1 See Chapter 4.
2 Schedule 2, para 15(1)(c).
3 The leave requirement was considered necessary to prevent a 'free for all' which could inhibit the authority in executing its plans for children in care. However, in *F v Kent County Council* [1993] 1 FLR 432, Sir Stephen Brown P said that the court should be slow to exercise its discretion under s 91(14) of the Children Act which enables it, on disposing of an application, to order that no application for an order of a specified kind be made without leave of the court. In this case the justices had made an order restricting applications by the parents for contact or discharge of the care order. This had been an improper exercise of their discretion since there was no evidence suggesting that the parents had behaved unreasonably or that their previous applications were vexatious or frivolous. Cf *Cheshire County Council v M* [1993] 1 FLR 463 for a case in which the circumstances justified a refusal to allow a father to seek a contact order where the children were in care. For the operation of s 91(14) in the context of applications for leave to seek private orders, see *Re N (Section 91(14) Order)* [1996] 1 FLR 356 where a father was granted contact but prevented from continuing to make applications about a range of aspects of upbringing without the leave of the court. Such leave will be granted where there is an arguable case. See *Re G (Child Cases: Parental Involvement)* [1996] 1 FLR 857.
4 Section 33(3) allows the court to 'make such order as it considers appropriate'.
5 Section 34(2) and (3)(a).
6 Under the Child Care Act 1980, s 12B(4) it was expressly provided that the authority was not to be taken to have terminated access where it proposed to substitute new arrangements for existing ones.

precisely what had happened in the leading wardship case *A v Liverpool City Council*[1] in which a mother's access had been cut to one hour's supervised visit per month at a day nursey. Decisions on the amount of contact are now opened up to judicial scrutiny.

The local authority might itself find it advantageous to apply to the court to define contact where it is anticipating a dispute which could inhibit its ability to make positive plans for the child. The child's standing to make an application may be important, not merely to establish or increase contact but, perhaps more significantly, where the child wishes to have it terminated[2]. When making its orders, the court, as usual, has flexible powers to impose such conditions as it thinks fit[3].

Changes to contact arrangements

The court may vary or discharge a contact order on an application by the local authority, child, or person named in the order[4]. But the regulations[5] also provide for circumstances under which the parties may, by agreement, depart from the terms of a court order or vary or suspend voluntary contact arrangements. Such variations require the child's consent, where he has sufficient understanding, and there are notification requirements relating to those affected. Again, the principle is that it is better to arrive at voluntary arrangements wherever possible. Judicial intervention should be a last resort.

Application of the welfare principle

Since contact proceedings are proceedings under Part IV, the principles in s 1 apply. Thus, the court must apply the welfare principle and the statutory checklist, together with the no order principle.

SUPERVISION

Supervision orders were traditionally used for two distinct purposes. One was to provide a measure of local authority control over a family situation, where there was concern that a child might be at risk, but a care order was not thought necessary. The other was to provide short-term assistance to parents, following separation or divorce. The Law Commission wanted to make this distinction clear. Thus, the second type of order has now been replaced by the family assistance order, discussed earlier[6]. The first type of order remains as an alternative to a care order and is regulated by s 35 and Parts I and II of Sch 3 to the Children Act. We

---

1   [1982] AC 363.
2   This is an especially pertinent point in the light of the sudden glut of cases in Autumn 1992 in which several children took to the courts in an attempt to secure the right to live apart from their parents. See Chapter 13 below.
3   Section 34(7).
4   Section 34(9).
5   Section 34(8)(b), and reg 3 of the Contact with Children Regulations 1991, SI 1991/891.
6   See Chapter 4 above.

also discussed earlier the fact that truancy used to be a ground for a care order[1]. The *Review* and the White Paper did not think it an appropriate use of care proceedings where absence from school was the *sole* reason for bringing them[2], although a care order could remain appropriate where absenteeism represented part of a wider family problem[3]. The 'education supervision order' has now been introduced to deal with truancy as such. Educational supervision will be looked at in the context of education generally[4]. The concern, for the moment, is with the more traditional use of supervision in care proceedings, itself the subject of significant reform[5].

When may a supervision order be made?

A supervision order may be used as an alternative to a care order[6] or may be made on discharging a care order[7]. The threshold criteria of s 31(2) must be satisfied in the ordinary way. Although supervision might be viewed as a less Draconian intervention in the family, the *Review* took the position that nothing less than the minimum conditions for a care order could justify compulsion, even at this lower level[8].

Although the threshold conditions for care and supervision orders are identical, the distinction between the legal effects of the two orders becomes crucial at the welfare stage when the court has to consider which order (if any) to make. We discuss the effects of supervision orders in more detail below. As between a care order or supervision order, the central question for the court will be whether the level of protection which can be offered to the child under a supervision order will be adequate or whether it is necessary to go further and make a full care order. The reported cases provide illustrations of instances in which the courts have felt it necessary to impose a care order and others in which they have decided a supervision order would suffice.

Re V (Care or Supervision Order)[9] is perhaps the best illustration of the first type of case. It reveals that one reason why a care order may be necessary is that it gives to the local authority parental responsibility which it will not acquire under a supervision order. The case concerned an adolescent boy approaching his seventeenth birthday (the age beyond which it becomes impossible to obtain a care order). He suffered from cerebral palsy, had spastic quadriplegia and learning disabilities. His father and mother quarrelled over the specialist school which he attended. The local authority was concerned at his absences and, fearing that his condition was regressing, sought a care order. The judge found that the

---

1 Children and Young Persons Act 1969, s 1(2)(e).
2 Chapter 16 discusses the position under the Children Act.
3 DHSS *Review of Child Care Law* (1985) at para 15.26, and the White Paper *The Law on Child Care and Family Services* (1987) (Cmnd 62) at para 59.
4 See Chapter 16 below.
5 See, generally, the *Review* (above) at paras 3.87–3.97.
6 Section 31(1)(b). On the circumstances in which a supervision order can be replaced by a care order, see *Croydon London Borough Council v A (No 3)* [1992] 2 FLR 350.
7 Section 39(4).
8 *Review* at para 18.18.
9 [1996] 1 FLR 776. See also *Re S (Care or Supervision Order)* [1996] 1 FLR 753 in which the Court of Appeal held that the judge, in making a supervision order, had not properly adverted to the difference between this and a care order. In this case the risk of the possibility of sexual abuse of the child justified the making of a care order.

threshold criteria were satisfied but refused to make the care order on the basis of the strain which this might place on the parents' marriage. Instead, he made a supervision order and attached conditions to it which, inter alia, required the boy to continue to attend the school as a weekly boarder.

The Court of Appeal allowed the guardian ad litem's appeal and substituted a care order. It was held that supervision orders with conditions do not fit into the framework of the Children Act. Requirements and directions in supervision orders could not be enforced other than by returning to court. Supervision orders depended rather on consent and co-operation, failing which the ultimate sanction was a care order. In this case, the risk to the parents' marriage was outweighed by the risk of harm to the boy if he was deprived of the specialist facilities at the school.

An example of the second type of case is *Re O (Care or Supervision Order)*[1]. Here, the proceedings concerned six children aged between 9 and 2. Health professionals and social workers had long been concerned about the children's development and about the neglect of certain specific health needs. On the other hand, it was accepted that their educational needs were largely being met, that their parents loved them and that present standards in the home were satisfactory. The local authority went to the family proceedings court for a supervision order to enable it to monitor the children's progress and continue to work with the family but the guardian ad litem wanted a care order so that the local authority, while leaving the children at home, could share parental responsibility with the parents. The justices made the care order but Hale J allowed the parents' appeal and substituted supervision orders in relation to all the children. Hale J held, inter alia, that the justices had given insufficient weight to the improvements which had taken place in relation to the children's condition, the co-operation of the parents, the intensification of the local authority's efforts and how best to develop that co-operation further. They ought to have looked more carefully at the effect of supervision orders before going on to the most Draconian order (the care order) permitted under the legislation.

What is its effect?

A supervision order will automatically terminate any existing supervision or care order[2]. It lasts, in the first instance, for one year but may be extended for up to three years from the date on which it was made[3] and will, in any event, terminate when the child attains 18 years of age[4]. The initial time-limit is designed to enable the court to control the effectiveness of the order.

---

1   [1996] 2 FLR 755. See also, in similar vein, *Re B (Care or Supervision Order)* [1996] 2 FLR 693 and *Oxfordshire County Council v L (Care Order or Supervision Order)* [1998] 1 FLR 70, in which Hale J sets out in some detail the reasons why a care order might be preferred over a supervision order and emphasises that although the court is empowered to make an order other than that sought by the local authority it should not make a more Draconian order unless there are cogent and strong reasons for doing so. In this case the local authority wanted supervision orders while the guardian ad litem pressed for care orders. On the facts, supervision orders were considered sufficient and were substituted for the care orders made by the justices.
2   Schedule 3, para 10.
3   Schedule 3, para 6.
4   Section 91(13).

The chief effect of a supervision order is to place the child under the supervision of a designated local authority or probation officer[1]. Parental responsibility does not pass to the local authority, as under a care order, but remains exclusively vested in the parents or in those who currently have it. The order places certain duties on the supervisor, the child and, for the first time under the Childen Act, the 'responsible person'[2].

Role of the supervisor

The supervisor has three duties:

'(a)   to advise, assist and befriend the supervised child;
(b)   to take such steps as are reasonably necessary to give effect to the order; and
(c)   where –
   (i)   the order is not wholly complied with; or
   (ii)   the supervisor considers that the order may no longer be necessary,
to consider whether or not to apply to the court for its variation or discharge.'[3]

The purpose of the second two duties is to try to prevent the situation of 'drifting' which arose under the old law and tended to discredit supervision orders for their ineffectiveness. Under the new law, the supervisor's duties are more specific, and he is obliged to take positive action where the order is proving ineffective. The hope is that local authorities will come to see supervision as a real alternative to care.

Making supervision work

The legislation provides that the order may empower the supervisor to give a range of directions to the child which may include where he is to live for specified periods, requiring him to present himself to a specified person or to take part in specified activities at particular places or times[4]. One of the main difficulties in making supervision work has been that parents or other carers could not be made to comply with the order. The position now is that the court may impose obligations on them but only with their consent. This sounds contradictory, but it should be remembered that supervision depends on co-operation, and, as Freeman has pertinently observed, it is likely that consent 'will be readily obtained where it becomes apparent that the alternative is a care order'[5]. Supervision is only one possible solution, the alternatives being care or, at the other end of the spectrum, voluntary assistance. The order may require the responsible person to take reasonable steps to ensure that the child complies with any requirement in the order or the various directions of the supervisor[6]. It may also require the responsible person to keep the supervisor informed of his own address where it differs from that of the child, and allow the supervisor to visit the child at the address where the child lives[7]. The supervisor has no power to direct the child to

---

1   Section 31(1)(b). The selection of supervisor is governed by Sch 3, para 9. In essence, the probation service will not be selected unless it has already been exercising its statutory duties in relation to another member of the child's household.
2   'Responsible person' is defined in Sch 3, para 1 as '(a) any person who has parental responsibility for the child; and (b) any other person with whom the child is living'.
3   Section 35(1).
4   Schedule 3, para 2.
5   MDA Freeman *Children, Their Families and the Law* (Macmillan, 1992) at p 130.
6   Schedule 3, para 3(1).
7   Schedule 3, para 3(3).

undergo medical or psychiatric examination or treatment[1]. The court may do so, subject to the general principle that where a child is capable of giving an informed consent, this must be obtained[2]. Other than in relation to this one matter, the child's consent is not required under the regime of supervision.

'Enforcement'

The 'enforcement' of supervision has always been problematic and, in some ways, it is a contradiction even to talk of enforcement of what is an essentially co-operative programme. However, failure to allow a supervisor access to the child could be a serious matter and, where this happens, the supervisor may apply to the court for a warrant or possibly take other emergency action, which is discussed in the next chapter[3].

PROCEDURAL FEATURES AND OTHER ORDERS

The minutiae of the procedural rules governing care and related proceedings are beyond the scope of this work[4]. The procedural peculiarities of care proceedings were the source of much discontent and certainly contributed to the impetus for reform. These peculiarities derived from the Children and Young Persons Act 1969 – a piece of legislation which governed both care proceedings and criminal proceedings arising from juvenile delinquency. Most of the defects of care proceedings were the result of the adoption of a quasi-criminal procedure, arguably suited to delinquency cases but certainly not appropriate in cases of alleged abuse or neglect. Under the procedure, only the child and the local authority had party status. Parents were not parties but, initially, might represent the child[5]. This was wholly inappropriate since, by definition, it was their upbringing of the child which was usually in issue[6]. The local authority had no right to appeal against the refusal to make a care order and would sometimes seek to circumvent this restriction by using wardship as an extra-statutory avenue of

---

1   See Chapters 8 and 12 for further discussion of the issues.

2   Schedule 3, paras 4 and 5.

3   *The Children Act 1989 Guidance and Regulations Vol 1 Court Orders* (HMSO, 1991) at para 3.95 emphasises that every effort should be made to secure co-operation before taking any such action.

4   The leading practitioner works are *Clarke Hall and Morrison on Children* (Butterworths) now in looseleaf format, and D Hershman and A McFarlane *Children Law and Practice* (Family Law) also in looseleaf format. A useful account of the procedure in care proceedings may also be found in D Bedingfield *The Child in Need* (Family Law, 1998) at pp 355–359.

5   Provision for separate representation for children in care proceedings was first recognised in the Children Act 1975 but those provisions were not brought fully into force until some years after that.

6   Parents themselves had only limited rights of participation in the proceedings, falling short of party status, and this initially meant that they were unable to obtain legal aid (*R v Worthing Justices, ex parte Stevenson* [1976] 2 All ER 194). Under the Children and Young Persons

appeal[1]. Neither did parents have any right of appeal against the making of a care order, at least in their own right[2].

The changes made by the Children Act sought to emphasise the *civil* nature of care and supervision proceedings by procedural changes and also by abolishing the use of care orders in criminal proceedings[3] and the 'offence condition' in care proceedings[4]. We will now look briefly at these changes and at the central features of the new law as it applies to interim orders and the discharge and variation of existing orders for care and supervision.

Procedural changes

Parties

As well as the child and the local authority, parents and others with parental responsibility now automatically have party status in care proceedings[5]. *Anyone* else may apply to the court to be joined as a party[6]. The White Paper had recognised the potential contribution which others might have to make in care proceedings[7]. The most likely candidates are grandparents, foster-parents or members of the extended family, but there is no restriction on those who may be joined. The child has a right to attend court by virtue of his party status, and the court has power to order attendance, where necessary, by authorising the police to bring the child to court[8]. In many cases, however, particularly those involving young children, the child will not attend but will be represented[9].

Representation of the child

Since the Children Act 1975, provision has been made for the separate representation of children in public proceedings[10]. The Children Act extended and reinforced the system of representation by a guardian ad litem ('GAL'). The court is now required in care and supervision proceedings[11] to appoint a GAL for the child 'unless satisfied that it is not necessary to do so in order to safeguard his interests.'[12]. In contrast to private proceedings, independent representation of children is therefore the norm in public proceedings. Later we look at the more general question of the legal representation of children[13].

(Amendment) Act 1986 parents did become entitled to party status but only where there had been an order for separate representation of the child.

1 See, for example, *Hertfordshire County Council v Dolling* (1982) FLR 423 and *Re R (A Minor) (Care: Wardship)* [1987] 2 FLR 400.
2 But they could exercise the child's right of appeal on his behalf (*B v Gloucestershire County Council* [1980] 2 All 746) but not where a formal order for separate representation of the child had been made (*A-R v Avon County Council* [1985] Fam 150).
3 Section 90(2).
4 Section 90(1).
5 Family Proceedings Courts (Children Act 1989) Rules 1991, SI 1991/1395.
6 Ibid.
7 The White Paper *The Law on Child Care and Family Services* (1987) (Cmnd 62) at paras 55–56.
8 Section 95, but this may often be inappropriate. See *Re G* (1992) *The Times*, November 19.
9 See further Chapter 13 below.
10 Ie care and related proceedings.
11 And in a range of other 'specified proceedings'. See s 41(6).
12 Section 41(1).
13 See Chapter 13 below.

Disclosure of evidence and discovery of documents

The *Review* recommended that there should be more advance disclosure and discovery of documents in care proceedings[1]. Care proceedings formerly always took place at the level of magistrates' courts (in the juvenile court), and evidence was oral rather than written. This could take parties by surprise, and it was felt that families should know in advance the essential nature of the case for a care order. The legislation now requires that written statements of the substance of the oral evidence which a party intends to adduce at the hearing be submitted in advance[2]. The same applies to copies of any documents upon which a party intends to rely, including experts' reports[3].

We consider later the question of evidence in children's cases and, more particularly, the evidence of children themselves[4].

Appeals

It was a logical consequence of the peculiar rules which governed party status in care proceedings that appeal rights were very restricted. Only the child had a right of appeal as such, although, initially, parents could (very inappropriately) exercise this on the child's behalf[5]. This right was later removed where there had been an order for the separate representation of the child at first instance[6], but one effect of this was to deny parents any right of appeal *at all* since they had no right independent of the child's.

The Children Act removed these restrictions at a stroke, by ushering in a new rule that *any* party to care proceedings should have an automatic right of appeal[7]. In keeping with the new civil character of care proceedings, the appeal now lies from the family proceedings court (ie the magistrates' court) to the High Court[8] and not as before to the Crown Court, with its almost exclusively criminal jurisdiction. Parents, local authorities and all other parties thus now have *independent* rights of appeal[9].

The legislation makes provision for preserving the status quo, pending an appeal against the court's refusal to make (or decision to discharge) a care or supervision order. The objective is to avoid the risk of unnecessary disruption to the child's current living arrangements. Where the child is already the subject of an interim order (a necessary pre-condition), the court may order that he remain in care or supervision for the 'appeal period'[10].

---

1 DHSS *Review of Child Care Law* (1985), ch 16, especially at paras 16.2–16.29.
2 Rule 17(1)(a) of the Family Proceedings Courts (Children Act 1989) Rules 1991, SI 1991/1395, and r 4.17(1)(a) of the Family Proceedings Rules 1991, SI 1991/1247.
3 Ibid, r 17(1)(b) and r 4.17(1)(b) respectively.
4 See Chapter 13 below.
5 See fn 2 at p 398 above.
6 Ibid.
7 Section 94(1), which provides for an appeal against the making or refusing of any order under the Children Act by magistrates.
8 Ibid.
9 For further discussion of the procedure on appeal, see PM Bromley and NV Lowe *Bromley's Family Law* (8th edn) (Butterworths, 1992) at p 527.
10 Section 40. The 'appeal period' is either the period between the making of the decision and the determination of the appeal or the period during which an appeal might be made against the decision (s 40(6)).

Interim orders

The old law governing interim orders was criticised in the *Review* for several reasons[1]. First, the orders were apparently routinely granted as part of the package of care proceedings and, in some cases, there could be many such orders before the final care hearing took place. This could result in the child being kept away from home for an indefinite and potentially unlimited time without proof of one of the grounds for a care order. Secondly, the test for granting interim orders was imprecise and inconsistently applied and amounted to no more than showing a prima facie case for a care order. Thirdly, the orders·were often made by single justices without an adequate opportunity for parents, or others affected, to be heard.

The Children Act now prescribes the circumstances under which the order may be made[2], restricts their maximum duration[3] and requires them to be sought before a properly constituted court[4]. In keeping with the new image of supervision, it is now possible for the court under the Children Act, for the first time, to make an *interim* supervision order. It *must* do so when making a residence order in care or supervision proceedings, unless it is satisfied that the child's welfare will be satisfactorily safeguarded without the order[5]. The objective is to balance the need to provide the child with necessary protection while proceedings are pending, but not to allow the child to remain in a state of limbo for longer than
> is necessary[6]. The court has an important power when making an interim order, to direct medical or psychiatric examination or other assessments of the child or to prohibit them[7]. This power is, again, subject to the mature child's right of objection.

Difficult questions have arisen concerning the extent to which the courts may direct local authorities to do certain things at the interim stage. The proper division of responsibility between the courts and local authorities under the Children Act is the general context in which this issue has been debated and there has been speculation about whether the court's function in public cases is meant

1   See the DHSS *Review of Child Care Law* (1985) at ch 17.
2   Under s 38(1) this is where proceedings for a care or supervision order are adjourned or where the court directs an investigation of the child's circumstances under s 37(1). The court must be satisfied under s 38(2) that there are reasonable grounds for believing that the threshold criteria in s 31(2) are satisfied in relation to the child. For an application of the test and its relationship to the principles in s 1, see *Humberside County Council v B* [1993] 1 FLR 257. Guidelines on the handling of applications for interim orders were given by Cazalet J in *Hampshire County Council v S* [1993] 1 FLR 559. See also *Re B (A Minor) (Interim Care Order: Criteria)* [1993] 1 FLR 815 especially on the attribution of harm or likely harm at the interim stage.
3   Under s 38(4) this is eight weeks in the first instance and there are complex rules governing the maximum duration of subsequent orders. On the duration of subsequent interim care orders, see *Gateshead Metropolitan Borough Council v N* [1993] 1 FLR 811. See also *Re C (A Minor) (Interim Care Order)* (1993) *The Times*, July 23 for some of the difficulties which have arisen.
4   This is implicit in s 38(1). It was held in *W v Hertfordshire County Council* [1993] 1 FLR 118 that the justices must give reasons when making or refusing interim orders. In *S v Oxfordshire County Council* [1993] 1 FLR 452 it was similarly held that reasons must be given when making a supervision order rather than a care order, especially where this conflicts with the recommendations of the child's guardian ad litem.
5   Section 38(3).
6   See *The Children Act 1989 Guidance and Regulations Vol 1 Court Orders* (HMSO, 1991) at para 3.35.
7   Section 38(6) and (7).

to be 'adjudicative' or 'participative'[1]. Sometimes the focus of tension between the courts and social services has been the use of limited resources. The authority may be resisting a particular course of action because it does not believe the cost is justifiable in the light of its competing priorities. Is it then open to the court to order it to conduct an expensive investigation against its better judgment? If a full care order has already been made the management of the child's care is a matter for the local authority and not for the court. But does this logic hold good for the interim stage? The legal effect of an interim care order is to place the child in care with the legal effects of a care order – most notably that the authority acquires parental responsibility[2]. On the other hand, the court still has to be satisfied about whether the conditions are made out for a full care order.

The question of the court's powers at the interim stage fell to be determined by the House of Lords in *Re C (Interim Care Order: Residential Assessment)*[3]. The narrow issue in this case was a matter of the correct technical interpretation of two subsections of the Children Act, but the broader issue was nothing less than the appropriate balance of power between the courts and local authorities at the interim stage.

The provisions in question (so far as they are relevant) were as follows. Section 38(6) of the Children Act provides:

> 'Where the court makes an interim care order, or interim supervision order, it may give such directions (if any) as it considers appropriate with regard to the medical or psychiatric examination or other assessment of the child ...'

Section 38(7) provides:

> 'A direction under subsection (6) may be to the effect that there is to be –
> (a) no such examination or assessment; or
> (b) no such examination or assessment unless the court directs otherwise.'

The facts were that the local authority had obtained an emergency protection order and interim care order in relation to a baby taken to hospital with serious non-accidental injuries. The parents were very young (father 16, mother 17). Social workers, a clinical psychologist and the child's guardian ad litem all favoured an in-depth assessment of parents and child together at a residential unit. The local authority disagreed. The initial objection appeared to be on the basis of cost which was projected at between £18,000–24,000. Later, the Assistant

---

1   See J Dewar 'The Courts and Local Authority Autonomy' [1995] CFLQ 15.
2   Section 31(11).
3   [1996] 3 WLR 1098. For commentary, see A Bainham 'Authority Over the Authority' [1997] CLJ 267. The issue had come before the courts on a number of previous occasions. See, for example, *Re C (Minors) (Care: Procedure)* (1993) Fam Law 288 which held that a local authority might be directed by the court to arrange for a child to be assessed by a suitably qualified social worker. Without this direction, there might have been substantial delay because of pressure on the authority's resources. The court's power to direct assessment by a *named* social worker has also been recently confirmed by the Court of Appeal in *Re W (Assessment of Child)* [1998] 2 FLR 130. The court held, however, that this should not be encouraged since the court had no means of forcing an unwilling individual to act. The court should take into account the resources of the local authority employing the social worker and any difficulties there might be regarding its responsibility for and duty to supervise that individual. The better direction would be that an assessment be carried out by a 'suitably qualified social worker'. See also *Re O (Minors) (Medical Examination)* [1993] 1 FLR 860 in which Rattee J held that the court had power on making an interim care order to direct the local authority to have the children medically tested for HIV.

Director of Social Services put it differently to the court, arguing that the assessment would expose the child to an unacceptable level of risk. The authority instead pressed for a final care order with a view to adoption.

The judge directed the residential assessment but the Court of Appeal reluctantly allowed the authority's appeal following its own earlier decision in *Re M (Interim Care Order: Assessment)*[1]. The House of Lords allowed the parents' appeal and ordered the assessment.

On the proper construction of s 38(6), the Court of Appeal had adopted a narrow interpretation of the court's power to direct an assessment. It had held that the words 'other assessment of the child' had to be construed *ejusdem generis* with 'medical or psychiatric examination'. It also attached importance to the fact that the statute made no reference to the assessment of anyone other than the child (specifically not the parents) and it thought that to direct the child's residence would be to usurp the local authority's powers to regulate where the child was to reside.

The House of Lords preferred a broader, more purposive interpretation to give effect to the underlying intentions of Parliament. The House accepted that a child in interim care was subject to control by the local authority and that the court had no power to interfere except where specified in the legislation. But the subsections in question created exceptions to this principle. Their purpose was to enable the court to obtain the information necessary for its final decision as to whether the threshold was crossed and a care order was required. The court therefore had power to override the authority to the extent that it was necessary to enable it to reach this decision. It was not for the authority to decide what evidence was to go before the court, and the court should not allow the authority by administrative decision to pre-empt its own judicial decision. Moreover, the prohibition of assessments under subs (7) must have been intended to extend to the prohibition of assessment of *parents* as well as children so that, by analogy, subs (6) ought also to cover assessments of parents.

The decision does not provide the answer to the broader policy question of where precisely the balance should be struck between the powers of the courts and local authorities in child protection cases. The following observations may, however, be offered. First, this case is one of a number[2] in which the courts have exhibited frustration at their inability to direct local authorities to take action in certain circumstances, where the authorities are reluctant to do so, but where the court feels that action is warranted in the best interests of the child. Secondly, the House of Lords has made it plain that, at least at the interim stage, the court remains in control. Thirdly, there is the question of the allocation of scarce resources and whether the court or the authority is best placed to determine these priorities. It is certainly arguable that local authorities should be reasonably free from judicial interference in making these difficult choices. The money spent on the expensive assessment in this one case could conceivably have been better deployed in providing voluntary assistance under Part III of the Act. The House of Lords acknowledged the force of this policy argument but did not feel that it could affect the proper construction of the Act. The courts in directing assessments should, however, take into account the cost and limitations on local authority

---

1   [1996] 2 FLR 464.
2   See also particularly *Nottinghamshire County Council v P* [1993] 2 FLR 134.

budgets. The correct balance of power between the courts and local authorities remains a matter of legitimate debate.

Discharge of care orders and discharge or variation of supervision orders

The defects in the old law which applied to interim orders also applied to care and supervision orders. Only the child or the local authority could apply for a discharge order. The parents had no right to do so except on behalf of the child[1] and this despite a clear conflict of interest between them. After all, what was usually at stake was the question of parental fitness to resume care of the child and the adequacy of the home environment. Recognising these conflicts of interest and providing for separate representation of the child did not offer a complete solution either, since this raised difficult issues about the parents' relationship with the child's GAL. It was not clear how far parents might pursue a discharge application where the GAL opposed it[2], and it was held that parents had no right to exercise the child's appeal against refusal to discharge a care order where the GAL refused to do so[3]. The grounds for discharge were vague. The court simply had to be satisfied that it was 'appropriate' and there was a distinct feeling that the courts were more concerned with issues of parental fitness than with the broader question of the child's welfare[4].

The Children Act increased the category of those persons who are eligible to apply for discharge and makes children rather than parents the focus of attention through the application of the welfare principle.

Discharge of care orders

The child himself, the local authority, and anyone with parental responsibility may now apply for discharge of a care order[5]. Variation of care orders (except, indirectly, by substituting supervision orders) is not permitted since this would conflict with the principle that management of the child's case is under the control of the local authority. Parents, unmarried fathers with parental responsibility[6] and guardians thus now have independent rights to apply for discharge[7]. Those who do not have parental responsibility may not apply but may instead

---

1 Section 21(2) of the Children and Young Persons Act 1969.
2 *R v Wandsworth West Juvenile Court* [1984] FLR 713.
3 *A-R v Avon County Council* [1985] Fam 150.
4 See DHSS *Review of Child Care Law* (1985) at paras 20.11 et seq.
5 Section 39(1). It has been established that a child (in this case a 14-year-old boy) has a statutory right to seek discharge of a care order and does not require leave as is the case with private law applications for a s 8 order. See *Re A (Care: Discharge Application by Child)* [1995] 1 FLR 599.
6 Unmarried fathers *without* parental responsibility should, under the Family Proceedings Rules 1991, be joined as parties to applications to discharge care orders but the court also has a discretion to discharge any party from the proceedings. In *Re W (Discharge of Party to Proceedings)* [1997] 1 FLR 128, the father was serving a life sentence for the murder of his step-daughter. The mother, who was seeking to discharge a care order in relation to their two children, successfully applied to have the father discharged from the proceedings to prevent him from having any involvement.
7 Non-parents by definition are ineligible since they cannot hold parental responsibility while a care order is in operation. They could only derive it from a residence order and a care order revokes a residence order (s 91(2)).

apply for a residence order, the effect of which would be to discharge the care order[1].

Discharge applications are now governed by the welfare principle and by the other principles in Part I of the Children Act[2]. It should be emphasised that, in contrast to the position where a care order is *sought*, this is an undiluted application of the welfare principle, and the threshold criteria have no part to play. Indeed, it is expressly provided that the statutory criteria do not have to be proved again where the court wishes to substitute a supervision order for the existing care order[3]. Conversely, the substitution of a supervision order with a care order *does* necessitate proof of the threshold criteria, since this involves a higher level of intervention.

The new provisions do not expressly allow a 'phased return' of the child. This was an issue which led, as already seen, to litigation before the Children Act[4]. There has been speculation that, where a phased rehabilitation is considered desirable, the court may be able to sanction this indirectly through its power to control contact decisions[5], or to attach conditions or give directions when making s 8 orders[6]. It would have been preferable if the legislation had confronted the issue directly, both because it is an important matter and because failure to do so may push applicants into inappropriate discharge applications[7].

A final matter is that, where an application (the 'previous application') for discharge of a care or supervision order, or for the substitution of a supervision for a care order, has been disposed of, no further application can be made until six months have elapsed[8]. Again, the thinking is that the local authority should be given a reasonable chance of implementing its plans for the child without the constant interference of court applications.

Variation or discharge of supervision orders

A supervision order may be varied or discharged on the application of the child himself, any person with parental responsibility, or the supervisor[9]. It is also provided that a person who is not entitled to apply for discharge may apply for variation where the child is living with him and where the supervision order imposes a requirement which affects that person[10]. This reflects the obligations

---

1 Where someone qualifies to apply for either discharge *or* a residence order, the only advantage of the latter would appear to be where there is disunity between two or more eligible applicants such as estranged parents. The residence order would not simply discharge the care order but would also determine the child's residence.
2 This is because Part I applies to proceedings under Part IV of the Children Act.
3 Section 39(4). In *Manchester City Council v Stanley* [1992] Fam Law 16 this was done where the local authority had mismanaged the care of two girls committed to its care in wardship proceedings.
4 See, particularly, *Re J (A Minor) (Wardship: Jurisdiction)* [1984] 1 WLR 81. Cf *Re M (A Minor)* [1985] Fam 60.
5 Under s 34.
6 Under s 11(7). See PM Bromley and NV Lowe *Bromley's Family Law* (8th edn) (Butterworths, 1992) at p 529.
7 This might occur where, for example, parents are unhappy with the pace of a rehabilitative programme.
8 Section 91(15).
9 Section 39(2).
10 Section 39(3).

which the legislation imposes on 'responsible persons'[1]. Applications in relation to the discharge or variation of supervision orders are also governed by the welfare principle.

WARDSHIP AND THE INHERENT JURISDICTION

One of the aims of the Children Act was to render wardship less necessary by incorporating its more valuable features into the statutory code. The flexible powers given to the court in family proceedings, especially those relating to specific issues and prohibited steps, are designed to have this effect. The possible future use of wardship in private cases has been commented on[2].

We now turn our attention to the relationship between wardship or the inherent jurisdiction of the High Court and the public law embodied in the Children Act. The effect of the legislation is greatly to reduce the possibilities for recourse to these jurisdictions but, whereas wardship and local authority care are now totally incompatible, local authorities may still, in limited circumstances, be able to invoke the inherent jurisdiction. What then is the difference between these two jurisdictions? It should be said immediately that wardship is itself one manifestation of the inherent jurisdiction. In essence, the distinction is this: where the court is exercising its wardship jurisdiction, but not where it is otherwise exercising its more general inherent jurisdiction, the court has 'custody' of the child (in the old terminology) or 'parental responsibility' for the child (in the new terminology)[3]. As such, the court has all-embracing, automatic and ongoing control of major issues in the child's life which have to be referred back to the court. This is not the case where the court exercises its inherent jurisdiction in relation to children who are *not* wards of court.

Wardship and local authorities

Wardship proceedings are 'family proceedings' (as are all proceedings under the inherent jurisdiction) for the purposes of the Children Act[4]. It therefore follows that there is no reason, in principle, why the court in wardship proceedings should not make a care or supervision order. But it may *not* do so otherwise than in accordance with the statutory criteria in s 31(2)[5]. It is the wider basis for committing wards to care, based on broad welfare considerations, which had proved so popular with social services, which was abolished by the legislation.

This result was achieved in a number of ways. Where a ward is committed to care, properly applying the statutory criteria, the care order will terminate the wardship[6]. The former power under s 7(2) of the Family Law Reform Act 1969, to

---

1 See p 396 above.
2 Chapter 6 above. There is an extremely informative and detailed discussion of wardship in PM Bromley and NV Lowe (above) at ch 14.
3 Of necessity, the physical 'care and control' of the child has to be delegated to an individual by the court.
4 Section 8(3).
5 See, generally, *The Children Act 1989 Guidance and Regulations Vol 1 Court Orders* (HMSO, 1991) at paras 3.98–3.103.
6 Section 91(4).

place a ward of court in care or under supervision, was repealed[1], as was the court's inherent power to do so[2]. Conversely, no child who is already in care may be made a ward of court[3]. Neither may the inherent jurisdiction be used to require a local authority to accommodate a child[4], nor to confer on it any power to decide questions concerned with any aspect of parental responsibility for the child[5]. These restrictions apply equally to wardship and other exercises of the inherent jurisdiction. The common reasoning behind the restrictions is that local authorities, the courts and everyone else must operate within, rather than outside, the carefully crafted statutory parameters for compulsory intervention.

It must be emphasised that these restrictions apply only where the child is *in care*. They do not apply where the child is merely 'accommodated'. In principle, wardship is not incompatible with voluntary accommodation arrangements, but it cannot be used initially to bring about such an arrangement[6]. Whether the courts will be prepared to entertain applications to ward accommodated children is highly questionable. There are perhaps two reasons for this. The first reason is that the *Liverpool* principle had been extended by the courts to voluntary cases[7], and it is likely that the courts will follow a similar policy under the new law. The second reason is that the courts are very unlikely to allow wardship to be used where they think the purpose can be achieved under the statutory code itself. The important consideration here is that s 8 orders, especially specific issue and prohibited steps orders, are available[8]. It is therefore unlikely that the courts will allow wardship to be used by or against local authorities in voluntary accommodation cases. The conclusion must be that wardship as such is redundant in public law cases[9].

The inherent jurisdiction and local authorities

The realisation that the High Court has a more general inherent jurisdiction to protect children outside wardship appears to be a comparatively recent phenom-

---

1 Section 100(1).
2 Section 100(2)(a).
3 Section 100(2)(c).
4 Section 100(2)(b).
5 Section 100(2)(d).
6 Section 100(2)(b). Once a child is accommodated, accommodation and wardship, unlike care and wardship, are not incompatible.
7 *W v Nottinghamshire County Council* [1986] 1 FLR 565.
8 The restrictions in s 9(1) apply only where the child is in care.
9 See Chapter 10 for possible alternatives to wardship. For a good example of the flexibility which can now be achieved in public cases under the Children Act, see *C v Solihull Metropolitan Borough Council* [1993] 1 FLR 290 in which Ward J indicated that a conditional residence order could be made alongside the interim supervision order. This could avoid the two extremes of a final supervision order or a care order. The court could, in effect, continue to preserve a degree of control over the child's situation where it thought this necessary, by an imaginative use of its statutory powers. But it should be noted that there are *some* limits to the flexibility of the statutory scheme. Thus, it was made plain by Booth J in *Hounslow London Borough Council v A* [1993] 1 FLR 702 that care orders and residence orders are incompatible. Where, therefore, the justices had made a care order they were deemed to have dismissed the father's application for a residence order. The proper course, where there remained some uncertainty about the father's role, would have been for the justices to have made an interim care order and adjourned both applications until the authority had had a chance to assess the father as carer.

enon[1]. The effect of invoking the inherent jurisdiction is not to trigger the extremely wide-ranging effects of wardship but rather to invite the High Court to determine certain specific issues of difficulty. It is in effect a 'single issues' jurisdiction. Local authorities, but not others, require leave for this purpose. It is, prima facie, a derogation from their responsibilities that local authorities should wish to hand over a decision affecting a child in their care. A limited exception to this principle has been allowed because it was appreciated that there can be some particularly sensitive or complex questions where it may be appropriate for local authorities to seek the assistance of the courts[2].

The Children Act allows the inherent jurisdiction to be invoked by local authorities with leave[3]. This will be granted where the court is satisfied that:

(a) the result which the authority wishes to achieve could not be achieved through the making of any other order available to the authority under the legislation; and

(b) there is reasonable cause to believe that, if the inherent jurisdiction is not exercised, the child is likely to suffer significant harm[4].

There are, thus, two key elements in obtaining leave. The first ought not to be difficult to satisfy since, where the child is in care, the legislation prevents the courts from making specific issue or prohibited steps orders[5]. The inherent jurisdiction will probably be the only mechanism where the local authority wishes to obtain the court's ruling on a 'single issue'. The second requirement is the familiar 'significant harm' test which applies elsewhere in the legislation[6]. Its suitability here as a pre-condition for leave has been thought by some commentators to be unnecessarily restrictive[7]. On the other hand, it might be argued that it is unduly liberal since it effectively lowers the statutory threshold for State intervention. We discuss this further below.

What kind of circumstances then might justify leave[8]? It seems to be agreed that the most likely issues will revolve around serious medical procedures[9], restricting harmful publicity[10] or restraining other harmful interferences with the child[11]. There is some doubt as to the precise extent of the court's powers but the view has

---

1 This, at least, is the view of PM Bromley and NV Lowe *Bromley's Family Law* (8th edn) (Butterworths, 1992) at p 479.

2 But the Court of Appeal has held that county courts do *not* have an inherent jurisdiction to grant injunctions to supplement public law orders in favour of local authorities. See *Devon County Council v B* [1997] 1 FLR 591.

3 Section 100(3), and see JM Masson 'Leave, Local Authorities and Welfare' [1992] Fam Law 443.

4 Section 100(4).

5 Section 9(1).

6 Ie in Parts IV and V. But note that whereas under s 31(2) the court must be satisfied that *the child is suffering, or likely to suffer, significant harm*, under s 100(3) it need only be satisfied that *there is reasonable cause to believe* that if the inherent jurisdiction is not exercised with respect to the child, the child is likely to suffer significant harm.

7 See, for example, A Bainham *Children: The New Law* (Family Law, 1990) at para 8.55, and J Eekelaar and R Dingwall 'The Role of the Courts under the Children Bill' (1989) 139 NLJ 217.

8 PM Bromley and NV Lowe *Bromley's Family Law* (8th edn) (Butterworths, 1992) at p 483; MDA Freeman *Children, Their Families and the Law* (Macmillan, 1992) at pp 161–162.

9 See Chapter 8 for examples.

10 As in *Re L (A Minor) (Wardship: Freedom of Publication)* [1988] 1 All ER 418. See also *Re Z (A Minor) (Freedom of Publication)* [1996] 1 FLR 191.

11 As in *Re JT (A Minor) (Wardship: Committal to Care)* [1986] 2 FLR 107.

been expressed judicially that they are co-extensive with the court's powers in wardship[1]. Clearly, these powers extend beyond the court's statutory powers under the Children Act and also exceed the power of a natural parent[2].

It is fair to say that in recent years there have been some controversial uses of the inherent jurisdiction by local authorities which have led to suggestions that it is being used in a way which subverts the intentions of Parliament. We will return to some of this case-law in Chapter 12. For the moment it is sufficient to note that one area of difficulty has concerned the refusal to consent to treatment or medical procedures by young people who have attained the age of 16 but are below the age of majority. We discussed the leading case of *Re W (A Minor) (Medical Treatment: Court's Jurisdiction)*[3] in Chapter 8. This case was followed by the decision of Wall J in *Re C (Detention: Medical Treatment)*[4], another case involving a 16-year-old suffering from anorexia nervosa who was refusing all treatment. Here, it was held that the inherent jurisdiction might be exercised at the behest of the local authority not merely to authorise treatment but also to restrain the young patient in a secure unit[5].

Cases like this raise serious questions about the autonomy aspect of children's rights[6] but they also provoke consideration of the limits of State paternalism under the legislation. Superficially it might appear that intervention via the inherent jurisdiction is, because of the requirement of leave, just as constrained by the threshold test of 'significant harm' to the child as is intervention by means of a care or supervision order. Yet this is not really the case and the decision of the House of Lords in *Re H and R (Child Sexual Abuse: Standard of Proof)*[7] makes this clear. In that case, the House was at pains to emphasise the difference between proof of the statutory threshold conditions and the kind of reasonable suspicions of harm which would be sufficient to found emergency protection orders or interim care orders. When we turn to s 100(4), which governs the criteria for granting leave to invoke the inherent jurisdiction, we find that it is *not* satisfaction of the threshold criteria which is required but *reasonable cause to believe* that the child would otherwise be likely to suffer significant harm. It might be replied that where we are concerned only with a 'single issue' and not with removal of the child from the family, a less stringent test for intervention is justified. But it is also legitimate to reflect on whether the State, through the High Court, is effectively arrogating to itself a wider power of compulsory intervention than that envisaged when the public law affecting children was reformed.

---

1   *Re W (A Minor) (Medical Treatment: Court's Jurisdiction)* [1993] Fam 64.
2   A point made plain in relation to wardship in *Re R (A Minor) (Wardship: Consent to Treatment)* [1992] Fam 11, discussed in Chapter 8 above.
3   [1993] Fam 64. See also *A Metropolitan Borough Council v DB* [1997] 1 FLR 67.
4   [1997] 2 FLR 180.
5   He also held that the secure unit in this case did not amount to 'secure accommodation' under s 25 of the Children Act so as to require an application for a 'secure accommodation order' under that section.
6   See Chapters 3 and 8 above.
7   [1996] 3 WLR 1098 (discussed above).

Chapter 12

INVESTIGATION AND SHORT-TERM PROTECTION

INTRODUCTION

This chapter looks at the investigative duties of local authorities where children are suspected to be at risk, and the legal framework within which short-term or emergency protection is undertaken. The connection between investigation and protection is a necessary one since it has been emphasised that no court is likely to grant either a child assessment order or an emergency protection order unless there has been a prior investigation of the circumstances[1]. The focus of attention here is on short-term remedies for the purposes of assessment and dealing with emergencies, as distinct from the medium and long-term solutions of care and supervision.

Historical background to the reforms

Emergency procedures were arguably criticised even more than other areas of child care law – understandably, since they regulate the initial stages of compulsory intervention in the family. They have, in the past, been associated with Draconian and unceremonious removals of children from their homes, of which the so-called 'dawn raids' in Orkney and Rochdale were glaring examples[2]. Place of safety orders were the chief mechanism for emergency action, but there was much evidence of their misuse. In many instances, orders appeared to be used, not in genuine emergencies, but as a means of gaining control of children for diagnostic or investigatory purposes. The orders were apparently routinely granted, often ex parte, by single magistrates from home[3]. They came to be seen by some social services departments as stage one of a three-stage process leading to a care order[4]. The process lacked elementary procedural fairness, bearing in mind the seriousness of the intrusion. The grounds were based on the applicant's belief that one of the conditions for a care order might be satisfied[5]; the removal of children was authorised for as long as 28 days; and the effects of the order were vague, especially regarding the powers and obligations of the local authority.

The most damning criticism of emergency procedures was the way in which they could be used to ride roughshod over the rights of parents and children. Parents had little input into the process. They had no rights of prior notification, consultation or appeal, and only a limited right to an explanation of the reasons

---

1   *The Children Act 1989 Guidance and Regulations Vol 1 Court Orders* (HMSO, 1991) at para 4.78. On orders under Part V of the Children Act generally, see ch 4 of the *Guidance*.

2   See, particularly, *Re A (Minors) (Child Abuse) (Guidelines)* [1992] 1 All ER 153.

3   'A Magistrate sitting at home in his pyjamas', in the graphic phrase of Stuart Bell MP (*Hansard*, 23 Oct 1989, col 594).

4   The process would begin with a place of safety order which would be followed up by one or more (usually more) interim care orders and finally the full care order.

5   The test was part objective in the sense that it focused on the *reasonableness* of the applicant's belief, but partly subjective in that it was the *applicant's* belief not the court's which was crucial.

for the order once made. The absence of proper avenues of redress led to applications by parents for interim care orders, as a back-door mechanism for challenging place of safety orders[1]. Even this option was, in due course, removed[2]. It was the large-scale use of place of safety orders in dubious circumstances in Cleveland which was the 'last straw' and led to a clamour for immediate reform[3]. At the same time, there remained widespread anxiety about undetected child abuse in general, and sexual abuse in particular[4].

The emergency protection order

The aim of Part V of the Children Act 1989 is therefore, as the *Guidance* puts it, 'to ensure that effective protective action can be taken when this is necessary within a framework of proper safeguards and reasonable opportunities for parents and others connected with the child to challenge such actions before a court'[5]. The legislation tried to achieve this by revamping the investigative duties of local authorities, requiring other authorities to co-operate, and by replacing the discredited place of safety order with a new emergency protection order ('EPO') with more stringent grounds, more clearly defined legal effects, and shorter time-limits for detaining children in emergencies.

The need for a 'half-way house': the child assessment order

While the Children Bill was progressing through Parliament, a major issue arose as to whether another type of order for assessment of children was required as an alternative to an EPO. The idea had its origins in the *Carlile Report*[6]. There was concern that there could be many cases in which there was suspicion of abuse, but insufficient evidence to justify emergency action. In such cases, the aim of social services is to make an assessment of the child's situation and, where suspicion of abuse persists, to obtain an accurate diagnosis. This, of course, may require medical and/or psychiatric examination of the child. But what if parents are refusing to co-operate either to let social services see the child at all or to allow the child to be examined? The dilemma for the social worker caught in this situation has been whether to take highly interventionist emergency action to remove the child, or to do nothing.

It was asserted in Parliament that a 'half-way house' was needed which would require a child to be produced and authorise an assessment but which would not necessarily lead to the removal of the child. There was considerable disagreement

---

1   *R v Lincoln (Kesteven) County Justices, ex parte M* [1976] QB 957.
2   *Nottinghamshire County Council v Q* [1982] Fam 94.
3   The evidence in Cleveland was that between 1 January 1987 and 31 July 1987 there were 276 applications for place of safety orders. Of these, 174 were granted by a single justice from home. See *Report of the Inquiry into Child Abuse in Cleveland 1987* (HMSO, 1988) (Cmnd 412) at para 10.9.
4   Considerable media attention was devoted to this, most notably in the BBC television programme 'That's Life' which led to the establishment of 'Childline'.
5   *The Children Act 1989 Guidance and Regulations Vol 1 Court Orders* (HMSO, 1991) at para 4.1. For further discussion of the basis of the reforms in Part V of the Children Act, see the *Review of Child Care Law* (1985) at chs 12 and 13, and the White Paper *The Law on Child Care and Family Services* (1987) at ch 4.
6   *A Child in Mind: Protection of Children in a Responsible Society, Report of the Commission of Inquiry into the Circumstances surrounding the death of Kimberley Carlile* (1987).

about whether the additional order was really required, not least between professional bodies such as the NSPCC and the Association of Directors of Social Services. The opponents of the order were worried about the possible confusion which might arise about when to seek each order and also the potential of the assessment order, as they saw it, for undermining attempts at voluntary co-operation with parents[1]. The proponents of the order stressed that this would not be so, especially since parental responsibility would not pass to the local authority. They argued that the 'lesser' order would allow action to be taken where there was serious, but not urgent, concern for the child's well-being.

It was this view which ultimately prevailed with the introduction of the innovative child assessment order ('CAO'). The features of the CAO, as it eventually emerged, when compared with those of the EPO are evidence of the compromise which had to be struck[2]. The extremely short time-limit (seven days), for example, reflects the perceived need to make this shorter than the limit for EPOs (eight days). Both orders can be utilised in 'non-access' cases, and both make provision for medical and psychiatric examination. This is, at least in part, the result of grafting on to the statutory scheme, at the eleventh hour, an alternative mechanism for dealing with some of the difficulties which had already been addressed when formulating the EPO[3]. Nevertheless, conceptually at least, the two orders are quite distinct and, as the *Guidance* says, the CAO 'is emphatically not for emergencies'[4].

Other reforms under the Children Act

The legislation also redefined police powers to protect children and powers of entry and search. These powers should not be underestimated since, in the worst cases of severe violence against children, the police will need to be involved. Finally, the legislation reformed the law governing abduction of children from care, and addressed, for the first time, the legal position of those organisations which provide assistance to young 'runaways'.

INVESTIGATION

Local authorities, it will be recalled, are required to use the voluntary services offered to families under Part III of the Children Act to 'take reasonable steps ... to prevent children within their area suffering ill-treatment or neglect'[5]. It is not necessary to mention again here the connection between voluntary and

---

1   Baroness Faithfull, for example, said in the House of Lords that a court-ordered medical examination would be likely to 'upset an enormous number of good parents who have a finger pointed at them' (House of Lords Official Report, 19 January 1989, col 429).
2   For a further informative discussion of the parliamentary background, see, generally, N Parton *Governing the Family* (Macmillan, 1991) at ch 6. For critical commentary on child assessment orders and their operation in practice, see R Lavery 'The Child Assessment Order – a reassessment' [1996] CFLQ 41, and Dickens 'Assessment and Control of Social Work – analysis or reasons for the non-use of the child assessment order' (1993) JSWFL 88.
3   A point made very well by MDA Freeman in *Children, Their Families and the Law* (Macmillan, 1992) at pp 173–175.
4   *The Children Act 1989 Guidance and Regulations Vol 1 Court Orders* (HMSO, 1991) at para 4.4.
5   Schedule 2, para 4(1).

compulsory action or the primary focus on the former[1], but what this means is that where social services, because of the information available to them, believe a child may be at risk, they will first have to consider whether this risk can adequately be met through voluntary assistance to the family. A good example of this working is where an alleged abuser can be induced to move out of the home, perhaps with assistance from the local authority[2].

Sources of initial information

How do local authorities get their initial information? There is no single source. Neighbours may hear suspicious noises, or fail to see a child for some time; social services may have had previous dealings with the family and be aware of the problems; the child himself may be sufficiently resourceful to contact social services direct or, more likely, confide in a trusted adult; the family doctor or health visitor may become aware of what looks like a non-accidental injury. Perhaps the most likely source of information in the case of older children is the school. Children spend almost as much time at school as they do at home, and teachers and welfare assistants are in direct contact with them for substantial periods of the day. As such, they are uniquely placed to observe behavioural aberrations (which could point to sexual abuse) or to notice signs of physical injury. Physical education classes and swimming activities provide opportunities for discreet observation, and it is not unknown for a school to hold an impromptu class where a child is suspected to have been abused. It must be stressed again, that there is no mandatory reporting law in England[3], but various authorities, including local education authorities ('LEAs'), are required to assist social services with their investigations, unless it would be unreasonable to expect them to do so in all the circumstances[4].

Local authority's investigations

The local authority's investigative duties may arise by direction of the court in family proceedings[5], and also in certain other circumstances specified in s 47 of the Children Act. These circumstances are where the local authority is informed that a child living or found in its area:

(1) is the subject of an EPO;
(2) is in police protection; and
(3) where the local authority has reasonable cause to suspect that the child is suffering, or is likely to suffer, significant harm.

In each case, the local authority must make, or cause to be made, 'such enquiries as it considers necessary to enable it to decide whether it should take any action to safeguard or promote the child's welfare'. It is a broader and more positive obligation to conduct enquiries than the pre-Children Act duty. This was limited to making enquiries on receipt of any information which suggested that

---

1   See Chapters 10 and 11 above.
2   Under Sch 2, para 5. The issue of removing adults rather than childen is discussed below.
3   This was not favoured in the DHSS *Review of Child Care Law* (1985) at para 12.4.
4   See p 413 below.
5   Under s 37(1).

there were grounds for care proceedings, unless the local authority was satisfied that this was unnecessary[1]. The new duty is more directly focused on the child's welfare. Where the child is already subject to an EPO or in police protection, by definition that child is considered to be at risk and this is an automatic trigger for social services to investigate.

Possible courses of action following enquiries

The legislation requires the local authority to decide, following its enquiries, whether to seek a CAO, an EPO, or a care or supervision order or to offer voluntary assistance under Part III[2]. Where a child who is subject to an EPO is not currently in local authority accommodation, the local authority must consider whether the child should be placed there for the duration of the EPO. Where the child is in police protection, the local authority must determine whether it would be in the child's best interests to apply for an EPO. The strongest duty arises where, in the course of the local authority's enquiries, an officer of the authority is refused access to the child or denied information as to his whereabouts. Here, the local authority *must* apply for an EPO, care order or supervision order unless satisfied that the child's welfare can otherwise be satisfactorily safeguarded[3].

Following its investigations, the local authority may conclude that an order is not required. Where it takes the view that no order is necessary, it must still consider whether there should be a later review of the child's circumstances and, if so, it must fix a date for the review to begin[4]. Where it decides that it *should* act to safeguard or promote the child's welfare, it is obliged to take that action, insofar as it is within its power and reasonably practicable for it to do so[5]. Eekelaar has drawn attention to the local authority's 'peculiar position of being allowed to decide whether or not to put itself under additional duties' and has been critical of the absence of a 'clear and unambiguous duty to take action on the basis of the results of the inquiries where the child is likely to be harmed if no such action is taken'[6]. He speculates on whether it could be lawful for the local authority to decide to do no more, for example, because of pressure of resources. And he contrasts the position with the local authority's duty where there has been a s 37 direction to justify to the court a decision to take no action[7]. It is arguable that the local authority is not accountable enough for the proper discharge of these duties.

The value of co-operation

The importance of inter-agency co-operation is stressed again at this preliminary investigative stage. Local authorities must co-operate with each other in the

---

1   Children and Young Persons Act 1969, s 2(1).
2   Section 47(3).
3   Section 47(6).
4   Section 47(7). It should be remembered that the authority may not have decided to do 'nothing' since it may well be offering voluntary assistance under Part III of the Children Act.
5   Section 47(8).
6   J Eekelaar 'Investigation Under the Children Act 1989' [1990] Fam Law 486 at p 487.
7   The relevant provision is s 37(3) which requires the authority to inform the court of the reasons for its decision, any service or assistance which it has provided, or intends to provide, for the child and his family and any other action which it has taken, or proposes to take, with respect to the child.

investigation of child abuse[1]. Where, as a result of its enquiries, an authority decides that there is an educational issue which requires investigation it must consult the relevant LEA[2]. Housing authorities, health authorities and others specified by the Secretary of State must assist the local authority with its enquiries, if called upon to do so, by providing information and advice[3], unless this would be unreasonable in all the circumstances of the case[4]. Freeman has questioned whether the police should have been left off this list, arguing that some police forces have been obstructive in the past[5]. The spirit of the Act certainly requires police co-operation and, in most cases, no doubt this will be forthcoming.

CHILD ASSESSMENT ORDERS

The *Guidance*[6] describes the CAO as 'a lesser, heavily court-controlled order dealing with the narrow issue of examination or assessment of the child in specific circumstances of non-co-operation by the parents and lack of evidence of the need for a different type of order or other action'. The hope is that the assessment ordered by the court will provide this evidence and enable the local authority to decide what action (if any) is required.

It cannot be emphasised strongly enough that the CAO is not suitable for emergencies, which must be the subject of applications for EPOs. Indeed, the court is precluded from making a CAO where it is satisfied that there are grounds for making an EPO and that it ought to make this order rather than the CAO[7]. It may then treat the application for the CAO as an application for an EPO[8]. The local authority must, in every case, decide whether the case is a genuine emergency or whether there is sufficient doubt about this to push it instead in the direction of a CAO.

Who may apply and on what grounds?

In contrast to the EPO (which may be sought by anyone), the CAO may only be requested by a local authority or 'authorised person' (the NSPCC). The rationale for this distinction is that in *emergencies* anyone should be able to act decisively to protect a child but that, in non-urgent cases, the policy should be to leave action to the primary child protection agencies. The court is empowered to make a CAO where:

'(a)   the applicant has reasonable cause to suspect that the child is suffering, or is likely to suffer, significant harm;

---

1   Section 47(12) provides that, where a local authority is making enquiries with respect to a child who appears to it to be ordinarily resident within the area of another authority, it must consult the other authority, which may undertake the necessary enquiries in its place.
2   Section 47(5).
3   Section 47(9) and (11).
4   Section 47(10).
5   MDA Freeman *Children, Their Families and the Law* (Macmillan, 1992) at p 178.
6   *The Children Act 1989 Guidance and Regulations Vol 1 Court Orders* (HMSO, 1991) at para 4.4.
7   Section 43(4).
8   Section 43(3).

(b) an assessment of the state of the child's health or development, or of the way in which he has been treated, is required to enable the applicant to determine whether or not the child is suffering, or is likely to suffer, significant harm; and

(c) it is unlikely that such an assessment will be made, or be satisfactory, in the absence of an order under this section.'[1]

The order is thus designed to enable social services to satisfy themselves about the welfare of children where they have suspicions of abuse or neglect but lack hard evidence. As the *Guidance* at para 4.8 advises:

'The order is for cases where there are suspicions, but no firm evidence, of actual or likely significant harm in circumstances which do not constitute an emergency: the applicant considers that a decisive step to obtain an assessment is needed to show whether the concern is well founded or further action is not required, and that informal arrangements to have such an assessment carried out have failed.'

Rather like the grounds for care and supervision orders, those for CAOs (and for EPOs) involve the satisfaction of minimum threshold criteria, followed by the application of the general principles in Part I of the Children Act. Taking the threshold criteria first, the first element requires the court to be satisfied about the reasonableness of the *applicant's* belief regarding the risk of significant harm to the child. 'Significant harm' for these purposes bears the same meaning as it does in s 31. A more stringent test is required for EPOs where the *court itself* must be satisfied about the risk. This reflects the more intrusive nature of the order. The other two elements in the CAO criteria require the court to satisfy itself that an assessment is really needed and that it cannot be arranged voluntarily. No doubt the court will want to hear evidence of the attempts to persuade parents to co-operate.

As with care and supervision orders, the s 1 principles only come into play once the threshold has been crossed. Ultimately, the court must consider whether a CAO is the right course of action, applying the welfare principle and s 1(5). However, in this context there are two points of distinction. The first is that proceedings under Part V of the Children Act are outside the definition of 'family proceedings' so that the court may not make s 8 orders in lieu of a CAO. The second is that the statutory checklist of factors in s 1(3) does not apply[2]. The reasoning is that Part V is an essentially separate code governing short-term remedies. It would be inappropriate for the court to be inhibited in its ability to act expeditiously, by having to plough through a range of factors in relation to which there may well, as yet, be insufficient information.

An important difference between the CAO and the EPO is that the application for a CAO must be brought before a full court on notice and involves an inter partes hearing[3]. By definition, this is not an emergency and, therefore, parents, those with parental responsibility, anyone with a contact order and the child himself must be given a proper opportunity to participate in the proceedings.

The *Guidance* suggests that the CAO 'will usually be most appropriate where the harm to the child is long-term and cumulative rather than sudden and severe'[4]. Examples given are of nagging concerns about a child apparently failing to thrive;

---

1 Section 43(1).
2 Part V proceedings are not within those proceedings specified in s 1(4) as attracting the application of the checklist.
3 Section 43(11).
4 *The Children Act 1989 Guidance and Regulations Vol 1 Court Orders* (HMSO, 1991) at para 4.9.

parents ignorant of, or unwilling to face up to the child's condition; and sexual abuse. In all these cases the child must not appear to be at immediate risk.

What are the effects of the CAO?

Compulsory production of the child/authorisation of assessment

A CAO has two automatic effects. The first is to require production of the child by anyone able to do so to the person named in the order and thereafter to comply with any directions the court makes regarding assessment[1]. The second effect is to authorise the assessment itself[2]. Parental responsibility does not vest in the applicant. It is expected that the court will spell out with some particularity what the assessment is to involve and, in doing so, it should take advice from those presenting the case and from other professionals. The most obvious directions are likely to relate to medical and/or psychiatric examination, but the assessment may range wider than this to cover other aspects of the child's health and development[3]. Again, a child of sufficient understanding to make an informed decision may refuse to submit to any examinations or form of assessment[4]. The *Guidance* suggests that the child's GAL, with the assistance of professionals from other disciplines, may advise the court of the child's level of understanding, after talking the matter through with the child, but it emphasises that this process must not result in coercion of the child[5].

The effect of this provision, together with similar provisions which apply to directions made where a court makes an EPO or interim care order[6], is diluted by the power of the High Court to override the child's objections under its inherent jurisdiction[7]. This exercise of the inherent jurisdiction is controversial since it appears to run contrary to the spirit, if not the letter, of the legislation. This appears to give to 'mature minors' a clear right to refuse to submit to such examinations and assessments. The issue is at the heart of the debate about the nature of children's rights[8]. Suppose, for example, there is suspicion that a teenage girl is being sexually abused by her father, and social services succeed in obtaining either an EPO, a CAO or an interim care order. They need to have the girl medically examined in order to determine whether or not there is sufficient evidence of sexual abuse. The court orders the examination but the girl objects to it. Is it her right to do so or is it her right to be protected from the risk of sexual abuse on the assumption that it may have occurred? The answer to this question must ultimately turn on the view which is taken of children's rights and the balance which is struck between autonomy and protection.

1　Section 43(6).
2　Section 43(7) authorises any person carrying out the assessment, or any part of the assessment, to do so in accordance with the terms of the order.
3　*The Children Act 1989 Guidance and Regulations Vol 1 Court Orders* (HMSO, 1991) at para 4.14.
4　Section 43(8).
5　See *The Children Act 1989 Guidance and Regulations Vol 1* (above) at para 4.13, and see further Chapter 13.
6　Sections 44(7) and 38(6) respectively.
7　*South Glamorgan County Council v W and B* [1993] 1 FLR 574. See also (in a rather different context but again involving the court's power to override mature minors) *Re K, W and H (Minors) (Medical Treatment)* [1993] 1 FLR 854.
8　As to which, see Chapter 3.

Keeping the child away from home

The CAO, unlike the EPO, is not designed to remove the child from home. As a general proposition, therefore, the child should only be kept away from home where this is strictly necessary for the purposes of the assessment. Overnight stays can be authorised, but this requires a specific direction from the court, and the child may be kept away only for the period or periods specified in the order[1]. The *Guidance* emphasises that this is a 'reserve provision' and that the number of overnight stays should be kept as low as possible[2]. Assessment should be carried out with as little trauma to children and parents as possible, and the CAO should not be regarded as a variant of the EPO. Examples of when an overnight stay might be justifiable are where the child has eating difficulties, seriously disturbed sleeping patterns or other symptoms which might appear to require 24-hour observation and monitoring.

Where the child is kept away from home, the court must give directions about contact between the child and the parents or others[3]. Restrictions on contact can only be justified where contact would unduly interfere with the assessment process. The *Guidance* suggests that consideration should be given to providing facilities for parents to remain overnight with the child[4].

How long does the order last?

Somewhat controversially, the maximum duration of a CAO is seven days from the date specified in the order[5]. But, significantly, there is no power to extend this. A CAO is therefore strictly a 'one-off' order. No further application for a CAO may be made within six months of the disposal of the last, without the leave of the court[6]. Seven days is not a long time and it is imperative that the local authority should make the necessary arrangements for the assessment in advance of the commencement date. The official view is that, if this is done, it should give enough time for an 'initial multi-disciplinary assessment of the child's medical, intellectual, emotional, social and behavioural needs'. It is said that this 'should be sufficient to establish whether the child is suffering, or likely to suffer, significant harm and, if so, what further action is required'[7]. Some scepticism has been expressed about this and about the adequacy of the eight-day limit for EPOs[8]. The argument is that a proper diagnosis of a child's condition may take several weeks and that the rigid time-limit for the CAO might force the local authority to seek an interim care order. This could be seen by everyone as 'a significant escalation in the interventive process'.

Finally, to put CAOs in perspective, it should be remembered that a formal order will often not be required, since even the suggestion of an application for this (a fortiori one for an EPO) may bring about voluntary co-operation by the parents.

---

1 Section 43(9).
2 *The Children Act 1989 Guidance and Regulations Vol 1 Court Orders* (HMSO, 1991) at para 4.15.
3 Section 43(10).
4 See *The Children Act 1989 Guidance and Regulations Vol 1* (above) at para 4.16.
5 Section 43(5).
6 Section 91(15).
7 See *The Children Act 1989 Guidance and Regulations Vol 1* (above) at para 4.12.
8 J Eekelaar 'Investigation Under the Children Act 1989' [1990] Fam Law 486 at p 488.

EMERGENCY PROTECTION ORDERS

The *Guidance* states that the purpose of the EPO is 'to enable the child in a genuine emergency to be removed from where he is, or be kept where he is, if and only if this is what is necessary to provide immediate short-term protection'[1]. It stresses that every aspect of the law governing EPOs whether relating to grounds, duration, effect or opportunities for challenge is different from that which applied to place of safety orders. The EPO, it advises, is an 'extremely serious step' which should not be undertaken lightly or regarded as a routine first step to initiating care proceedings[2]. The order authorises the immediate removal of a child from a dangerous or potentially dangerous environment, or the detention of the child in a safe place, in emergencies.

Who may apply and on what grounds?

Applications

Unlike CAOs, care orders or supervision orders, EPOs may be sought by *anyone* and not only by the local authority or NSPCC, except where 'non-access' is the basis of the application[3]. This may also be contrasted with the rules governing standing to apply for private orders. Whilst there is much more flexibility under the Children Act, the applications are, nevertheless, still restricted, either by the class of applicant, or by the requirement of leave. EPOs are the one example in the legislation of wholly unrestricted access to the courts. The reasoning is obvious. Where a child is thought to be in immediate danger, the policy is not to stand on ceremony but to allow any concerned individual to act post haste to protect the child. It is anticipated that this will, in the vast majority of cases be the local authority or NSPCC but the *Guidance* speculates that in 'dire circumstances' a concerned relative or neighbour (to which we could perhaps add a teacher, doctor or other professional) may find it necessary to seek the order[4]. The police might also wish to apply but are more likely to rely on their independent emergency powers in the legislation[5]. However, regulations now provide that, where the applicant is not the local authority, the local authority may take over the order, and the power and responsibilities which go with it, where it considers that this would be in the child's best interests[6]. In deciding whether to do so, the local authority must consult the applicant and must have regard to a range of factors

---

1   *The Children Act 1989 Guidance and Regulations Vol 1 Court Orders* (HMSO, 1991) at para 4.28 et seq.
2   Ibid at para 4.30.
3   Section 44(1) provides that 'any person' may be the applicant. This was the position regarding place of safety orders and the DHSS *Review of Child Care Law* (1985) found no evidence of abuse (see para 13.7). If someone other than the local authority succeeds in obtaining an EPO, this will trigger the authority's investigative duties under s 47(1). There were 2,565 EPOs and EPO extensions made in 1996 – a fall of 16% from 1995. See *The Children Act Advisory Committee Final Report June 1997* (Lord Chancellor's Department, 1997) at Appendix 2.
4   See *The Children Act 1989 Guidance and Regulations Vol 1* (above) at para 4.32.
5   Under s 46 which is discussed at p 434 below.
6   Section 52(3), and the Emergency Protection Order (Transfer of Responsibilities) Regulations 1991, SI 1991/1414.

reminiscent of those in the statutory checklist in s 1(3) [1]. It is not thought that these transfer powers will be exercised in relation to the NSPCC, since it is expected that there will be local dialogue and consultation between the NSPCC and the local authority.

Ex parte applications

An important procedural distinction between the EPO and the CAO is that the EPO may, and usually will, be made ex parte[2]. While the court has power to direct an inter partes hearing, 'the very fact that the situation is considered to be an emergency requiring immediate action will make this inappropriate or impracticable in most cases'[3]. The application must be made in the magistrates' family proceedings court and there is no provision for transfer to a higher court[4]. As was the case with place of safety orders, the application may be made to a single justice[5] and in most cases this will be necessary – not least because emergencies arise when courts are not sitting[6]. Time will usually be of the essence. The rules provide that, wherever possible, the application should be made to the court. This reflects concern that place of safety orders were too often requested of single justices where an application to a full court would have been possible. On the other hand, the *Guidance* warns that, in certain instances, to give parents notice of the application might be to place the child in great danger[7].

Where the application is heard ex parte the rules require the applicant to serve a copy of the application and the order within 48 hours on the parties to the proceedings, anyone with the care of the child and the local authority where it is not the applicant[8]. They emphasise the crucial need to inform parents of their rights and responsibilities under the order – something severely neglected in the past.

Identification of the child in the order

Any child may be the subject of an EPO and, wherever practicable, the order should name the child. Where it does not do so, it should identify him as clearly as possible[9]. In some situations, the name of the child who is thought to be in danger will not be known to the applicant.

Grounds

There are three alternative grounds for obtaining an EPO set out in s 44(1), the first of which is open to any applicant. This may be relied on where the court is satisfied that:

---

1   Emergency Protection Order (Transfer of Responsibilities) Regulations 1991 (above), reg 3 provides that the authority must have regard to the wishes and feelings of the child; his physical, emotional and educational needs; the likely effect of any change of circumstances on him; his age, sex and family background; the circumstances which gave rise to the application for the EPO; any court order or directions; the relationship of the applicant to the child and any plans which the applicant may have for the child.

2   Family Proceedings Courts (Children Act 1989) Rules 1991, SI 1991/1395, r 4(4).

3   *The Children Act 1989 Guidance and Regulations Vol 1 Court Orders* (HMSO, 1991) at para 4.46.

4   Children (Allocation of Proceedings) Order 1991, SI 1991/1677, arts 3(1)(g) and 7(2).

5   Family Proceedings Courts (Children Act 1989) Rules 1991 (above), r 4(4).

6   Most obviously in the middle of the night or at weekends.

7   See *The Children Act 1989 Guidance and Regulations Vol 1* (above) at para 4.46.

8   Family Proceedings Courts (Children Act 1989) Rules 1991 (above), r 21(8).

9   Section 44(14).

'there is reasonable cause to believe that the child is likely to suffer significant harm if –
(i)   he is not removed to accommodation provided by or on behalf of the applicant or
(ii)   he does not remain in the place in which he is then being accommodated.'

Satisfying the court of significant future harm

The first point is that it is the *court* rather than the applicant which must be satisfied that the statutory criteria are met[1]. 'Significant harm' bears the same interpretation as elsewhere in the legislation[2]. Where the application of the statutory test differs in this context is that the grounds for an EPO are *entirely* prospective in nature. Past or present harm will not be sufficient to found an EPO and are relevant only to the extent that they indicate future risk. The court or magistrate must be satisfied of the likelihood of significant harm occurring or recurring.

How likely does 'likely' have to be?

It seems that, in applying this test, the court will need to relate the chance of harm occurring to the gravity of harm if it should occur. Where there is even an outside chance that the child could be exposed to someone convicted of offences against children, this may be seen as an unacceptable risk to run. Equally, where the nature of the possible harm is less grave, it may be that the court should look for a higher risk of its occurrence[3].

Removing or detaining the child

This ground covers two alternative situations. The first is where the intention is to *remove* a child from where he is currently living – most obviously where abuse or neglect is alleged against the parents. Here, it is not necessary for the applicant to prove that the need for the child's removal is *immediate*[4]. The EPO is intended to be flexible enough to cover the situation where, on investigation, the applicant concludes that it is not necessary to remove the child immediately. An example would be where a suspected adult is prepared 'voluntarily' to leave the home and to undertake not to return to it[5]. The EPO allows the local authority to adopt a 'wait and see' policy, albeit over a short period. The power to remove the child remains for the duration of the order. Thus, in the above example, if the alleged abuser agrees to leave immediately, but 24 hours later is still in the home, steps could then be taken to remove the child without having to go back to court.

The second alternative relates to the situation where the child is currently in a safe environment but there is a threat that he may shortly be removed to a potentially unsafe one. Chapter 11 looked at the two most obvious examples, namely the child in hospital or settled in a foster-home. In each case, the concern may be that a sudden removal by inadequate parents may expose the child to risk of harm.

---

1   Cf the 'non-access' grounds, discussed below, in relation to which it is the *applicant's* belief which is crucial.
2   Ie in relation to care, supervision and child assessment orders.
3   This is rather contrary to what was suggested by the majority of the House of Lords in *Re H and R (Child Sexual Abuse: Standard of Proof)* [1996] 1 FLR 80, where it was suggested by Lord Nicholls that the more serious the allegation the less likely it was that the conduct alleged had occurred. It was suggested in Chapter 11 that this reasoning is less than convincing in the context of applications for full care orders. It is further suggested, a fortiori, that it has no place in relation to EPOs.
4   See Lord Mackay LC, House of Lords, Official Report, 19 January 1989, col 426.
5   See p 425 below.

No other requirements
It must be appreciated that there is no second element to the test for an EPO corresponding with that which forms part of the test for care and supervision orders. It does *not* have to be shown that the risk of harm is attributable to a likely lack of parental care or the child being beyond parental control. The thinking is that at the emergency stage it is not possible to conduct the kind of forensic inquiry which could determine this issue. Valuable time could be lost and the child might be exposed to unnecessary danger.

Frustrated access: alternative grounds for an EPO
Section 44(1) goes on to prescribe two further alternative grounds for an EPO. They apply to local authorities[1] and authorised persons (the NSPCC)[2] respectively and are designed to cater for emergencies arising from 'frustrated access'. In each case it is provided that an order may be made where:

(1) the applicant is making enquiries into the child's welfare; and
(2) those enquiries are being frustrated by access to the child being unreasonably refused to a person authorised to seek access and the applicant has reasonable cause to believe that access to the child is required as a matter of urgency.

In the case of the NSPCC, but not local authorities, there is a third requirement that the applicant has reasonable cause to suspect that the child is suffering, or is likely to suffer, significant harm.

EPO or CAO?: degree of urgency
The obvious question is: when should an EPO be requested in non-access cases, given the existence of similar grounds for a CAO and given that the CAO was largely introduced to deal with these situations? The answer lies in the degree of urgency which is felt about the child's situation. Where the circumstances suggest that the child is in imminent danger, the EPO is appropriate. Where this is not the case, but an investigation and assessment of the child's circumstances is required, the CAO will be appropriate. It all depends on the circumstances surrounding the refusal and whether they add up to an emergency[3]. In this context, the test is whether the *applicant*, and not the court, has reasonable cause to suspect that access is required urgently.

Whichever ground is relied on, the principles of s 1 again apply, although the statutory checklist does not. What this means is that the court must ultimately exercise a discretion as to whether the order is really necessary and in the best interests of the child. It is not obliged to make the order. Having said that, unless there is voluntary co-operation to avert the emergency, it is difficult to visualise circumstances in which the court would not feel bound to act to protect a child exposed to imminent danger.

---

1   Section 44(1)(b).
2   Section 44(1)(c).
3   As to which see *The Children Act 1989 Guidance and Regulations Vol 1 Court Orders* (HMSO, 1991) at para 4.39.

What are the effects of the EPO?

An EPO has three automatic legal effects under s 44(4) while it remains in force. It:

> '(a)   operates as a direction to any person who is in a position to do so to comply with any request to produce the child to the applicant;
>
> (b)   authorises –
>
>   (i)   the removal of the child at any time to accommodation provided by or on behalf of the applicant and his being kept there; or
>
>   (ii) the prevention of the child's removal from any hospital, or other place, in which he was being accommodated immediately before the making of the order; and
>
> (c)   gives the applicant parental responsibility for the child.'

Acquisition of parental responsibility by the applicant

This partly reflects the fact that, unlike the position under a CAO, the child will not be at home and will have to be looked after by arrangements made by the applicant[1]. But there are restrictions on the *exercise* of parental responsibility, which reflect the transient nature of the applicant's position. Hence, this may only be exercised 'as is reasonably required to safeguard or promote the welfare of the child (having regard in particular to the duration of the order)'[2]. The applicant must, therefore, ensure that the child is properly looked after while away from home, but should not take major or irreversible decisions which affect the longer-term interests of the child. In keeping with this, the child must not be kept away from home for longer than is strictly necessary. The legislation provides that the child must, accordingly, be allowed to return home or be removed (as the case may be) where it appears to the applicant safe to do so, even though the EPO remains in force[3]. Where this duty arises (which does not involve a return to court) the child must be returned to the care of the person from whom he was removed. Where this is not reasonably practicable, the child must be returned to his parent, a person with parental responsibility or someone else whom the applicant (with the approval of the court) thinks appropriate[4]. Importantly, however, the applicant retains the power, while the order remains in force, to remove the child again if this should prove necessary[5].

Reasonable contact

An EPO gives rise to a presumption of reasonable contact in favour of prescribed individuals, rather like the situation which applies where the child is in care[6]. Subject to any directions by the court, the applicant must allow the child reasonable contact with his parents, persons with parental responsibility, persons with whom he was living before the EPO, those who have contact orders, and any

---

1   Under s 21(1) the local authority is obliged to make provision for the reception and accommodation of children who are removed or kept away from home under Part V of the Children Act.

2   Section 44(5)(b).

3   Section 44(10).

4   Section 44(11).

5   Section 44(12).

6   Under s 34(1), discussed in Chapter 11 above.

person acting on their behalf[1]. The court may give specific directions about contact[2] when the order is made or while it remains in force[3], and it may impose conditions[4]. What is 'reasonable' will depend on the circumstances, and in many cases it may be necessary to have supervised contact, in view of the nature of the allegations[5]. At the same time there are dangers, well-illustrated in Cleveland, of depriving parents of contact, only to find that the allegations against them are unsubstantiated. The *Guidance* sees the contact question as largely a matter for the local authority's discretion and for negotiation[6]. In view of the short time-scale, it is unlikely that the courts will seek to interfere unduly with this process. The drastic reduction in the allowable period of emergency detention, in itself, goes some way in removing grievances about contact[7].

Other directions which the court can make

These include the power to direct that medical and/or psychiatric examinations or assessments should, or should not, take place[8]. Again, the competent child has a right to refuse to co-operate[9]. It has been pointed out that the applicant, by virtue of having parental responsibility, could, in any event, probably provide a valid consent, and this may not be wholly dependent on the court's direction[10]. But it would be unwise not to seek this in so sensitive a matter – especially bearing in mind the uncertainties involved in establishing the child's level of understanding[11]. It is possible that the EPO may be used *primarily* with a view to securing an examination of some sort where parents are unwilling to co-operate. This can, of course, be achieved under a CAO where the matter is not urgent. The EPO has the advantage that, if the parents should fail to comply with the court's directions, the local authority will have an automatic right to remove the child.

The court may give other ancillary directions to assist with the enforcement of the EPO[12]. First, where it appears to the court that adequate information about the child's whereabouts is not available to the applicant, but is available to someone else, the court may order that person to disclose the information[13]. Secondly, the court may authorise the applicant to enter specified premises and search for the child[14]. This may extend to other childen, where the court is reasonably satisfied that there may be another child on the premises with respect to whom an EPO

---

1 Section 44(13).
2 Section 44(6)(a).
3 Section 44(9)(a).
4 Section 44(8).
5 See the DHSS *Review of Child Law* (1985) at para 13.17.
6 *The Children Act 1989 Guidance and Regulations Vol 1 Court Orders* (HMSO, 1991) at para 4.62.
7 From 28 days to eight days.
8 Section 44(6)(b) and (8).
9 Section 44(7), and see the discussion in Chapter 8 above. But again, the competent child's refusal may be overridden by the High Court exercising its inherent jurisdiction. See above.
10 PM Bromley and NV Lowe *Bromley's Family Law* (8th edn) (Butterworths, 1992) at p 540. This is not the case where a CAO is made since parental responsibility does not pass to the applicant under this.
11 And also the uncertain relationship between adolescent capacities and the exercise of parental responsibility explored in Chapter 8 above.
12 Section 48.
13 Section 48(1).
14 Section 48(3).

ought to be made[1]. Where a second child is then found on the premises, the court's order may operate as an EPO and authorise removal of *that* child[2], subject to a duty to notify the court[3]. Thirdly, where it appears that the use of force may be necessary, the court may grant a warrant authorising a police constable to assist in the exercise of powers under an EPO, using reasonable force if necessary[4]. When executing the warrant, the constable must allow the applicant to accompany him, unless the court directs otherwise[5], and the court may also direct that the applicant be accompanied by a 'registered medical practitioner, registered nurse or registered health visitor if he so chooses'[6]. None of these directions are automatically part and parcel of an EPO. They must be specifically sought where the applicant, on the strength of information received or his knowledge of the family situation, thinks they may prove necessary.

How long does the EPO last?

One of the most important reforms was the major reduction in the length of time for which emergency orders can last, or remain unchallenged, and in the number of 'extensions' which can be made. As was seen, this is also a feature of interim care orders[7].

The legislation prescribes eight days, rather than 28 days, as the initial maximum duration of an EPO[8]. A limited extension for a further seven days may be granted where the applicant is the local authority or NSPCC, but not where it is an individual[9]. Only one extension is allowed and the maximum period of emergency protection is therefore 15 days[10]. The expectation is that extensions will be uncommon since the initial eight-day period is thought to give the applicant sufficient time in which to decide what further action (if any) to take, and particularly to decide whether to seek an interim care order[11].

There is no appeal, as such, from the making of an EPO, but there is an opportunity for judicial challenge by an application to discharge the order. This may be brought by the child, the parents, persons with parental responsibility and any person with whom the child was living immediately before the order[12], but not

1 Section 48(4).
2 Section 48(5).
3 Section 48(6).
4 Section 48(9). The court may grant a warrant where it appears to it that a person attempting to exercise power under an EPO has been prevented from doing so by being refused entry to premises or access to the child or that he is likely to be so prevented. These powers are complementary to the general power of the police to act in 'dire emergencies' under the Police and Criminal Evidence Act 1984, ss 17(1)(e) and 25(3)(e) – as to which see *The Children Act 1989 Guidance and Regulations Vol 1 Court Orders* (HMSO, 1991) at para 4.57.
5 Section 48(10).
6 Section 48(11).
7 See Chapter 11 above.
8 Section 45(1). Special provision is made for holidays (s 45(2)). Where the EPO follows police protection, the eight-day period runs from the first day on which the child was taken into police protection (s 45(3)).
9 Section 45(4).
10 Section 45(6).
11 *The Children Act 1989 Guidance and Regulations Vol 1* (above) at para 4.66. See also the DHSS *Review of Child Care Law* (1985) at para 13.23.
12 Section 45(8), (10). For a case in which practical difficulties occurred in applying these provisions, see *Essex County Council v F* [1993] 1 FLR 847.

before 72 hours has elapsed since the order was made[1]. No discharge application may be made where the potential applicant was given notice of the original hearing and was present at it[2]. In the majority of cases, this will not be the case, since the order will have been made ex parte. But, where it was made following an inter partes hearing, an opportunity for challenge has already arisen. To allow a 'second bite at the cherry' would be unacceptably disruptive of protection procedures.

The local authority has no right of appeal against the refusal of justices to extend an EPO. *Re P (Emergency Protection Order)*[3] was a disturbing case which illustrates the problems which can arise where there is a refusal to extend the order. Here, a young baby nearly died from what was suspected to be an attempt by his mother to suffocate him. There was clear medical evidence by a paediatrician, later confirmed by a brain scan, that there was no medical cause for what had happened. The local authority did eventually obtain a care order but only after prolonged investigations by experienced paediatricians. Johnson J criticised the justices for their failure to extend the EPO in the face of firm medical evidence pointing to the risk of life-threatening abuse. He considered that there was a lacuna in the legislation and a need for some mechanism of review. Meanwhile, the only options open to a local authority in this situation are to apply immediately for a care order and seek an interim care order or to seek to have the matter transferred to the county court.

Can the alleged abuser be removed instead?

The background: before the Family Law Act 1996

Few people would argue with the general proposition that children are better off left in the family wherever possible. This is, of course, central to the philosophy of the legislation. Removal from home should be confined to those cases in which it is really necessary. One possible solution, and perhaps a better one for the child, may be to remove the alleged abuser from the home. This will be a more viable option where that person's partner or spouse is in agreement with the proposal. It will be much more difficult where this co-operation is not forthcoming and, a fortiori, where there is collusion in the abuse.

As the law stood there was no public law remedy which was available to evict an alleged abuser. The options were to try to persuade the abuser to leave voluntarily or to persuade his partner to pursue private law remedies which could at least authorise temporary exclusion. The *Guidance* advised that these options be explored[4]. It stated that the local authority would always want to canvass the possibility of providing voluntary services to the person concerned, perhaps also providing alternative housing or even cash assistance[5]. The same result might be achieved if the non-abusing parent was prepared to apply for an ouster order under the domestic violence legislation[6]. The *Guidance* suggested that this might

---

1   Section 45(9).
2   Section 45(11).
3   [1996] 1 FLR 482.
4   *The Children Act 1989 Guidance and Regulations Vol 1 Court Orders* (HMSO, 1991) at para 4.31.
5   Under Sch 2, para 5 to the Children Act.
6   Ie under the Domestic Violence and Matrimonial Proceedings Act 1976, s 1 (county court) or the Domestic Proceedings and Magistrates' Courts Act 1978, s 16 (magistrates' courts).

be particularly appropriate where sexual abuse was alleged. In this instance, the non-abusing parent might have no wish to protect or shield the alleged abuser but immediate removal of the child might well not be in the child's best interests.

Family law commentators, at least for the purposes of exposition, have been much inclined to put child abuse and domestic violence into different compartments. Yet in reality this distinction has always been somewhat artificial. If a man is being violent towards children, or threatening them with violence, this can be viewed both as child abuse which might give rise to *public* care proceedings or domestic violence which could trigger the *private* remedies relating to non-molestation or ouster from the family home. In the years between the implementation of the Children Act 1989 and of Part IV of the Family Law Act 1996[1], local authorities, not wishing to take the ultimate step of seeking a care order, began to explore whether they might exclude an alleged abuser by resorting to the private law orders under s 8 of the Children Act.

The matter came to a head in *Nottinghamshire County Council v P*[2] where the Court of Appeal found, for partly technical reasons arising under the provisions of s 9 of the Children Act and partly on broader policy grounds, that in general local authorities were precluded from invoking *private* s 8 orders, and, in fulfilling their statutory child protection role, ought instead to pursue the *public* remedies which Parliament had provided in the Children Act. Indeed, the court was very critical of Nottinghamshire's failure to do so. What had happened in this case was that there were allegations of sexual abuse against the father of three girls by the eldest girl who claimed that he had been abusing the three of them. The local authority successfully obtained leave to seek a prohibited steps order preventing the father from living in the household and from having contact with the girls. Ward J at first instance held that he was prevented by s 9(5) of the Children Act from making the orders and his decision was upheld by the Court of Appeal.

Sir Stephen Brown P held that in reality the effect of the prohibited steps order (if made) would be for the father to be ordered to have 'no contact' with the children and that a 'no contact' order was equivalent to a contact order. The authority was directly precluded from seeking such a contact order by the provisions of s 9(2) and indirectly by the provisions of s 9(5). From a broader policy perspective, the President said that 'the route chosen by the local authority in this case was wholly inappropriate'. He went on to criticise the authority for not taking steps under Part IV of the Children Act specifically to seek a supervision order to protect the children, and expressed deep concern at 'the absence of any power to direct this authority to take steps to protect the children'.

This decision did not prevent a prohibited steps order being subsequently made by the Court of Appeal (in a case in which the local authority had already obtained a care order in relation to one child and supervision orders in relation to the other children in the household) to restrain a man who was *not* living with the mother and the children from having or seeking to have, contact with the children[3]. The distinction drawn by Butler-Sloss LJ was essentially that this was to prevent an *external* threat to the children and that a 'no contact' order against the man could not be made since he did not live with the children. Local authorities also

---

1   Part IV of the 1996 Act was brought into force on 1 October 1997.
2   [1993] 2 FLR 134.
3   *Re H (Prohibited Steps Order)* [1995] 1 FLR 638.

succeeded in a couple of reported decisions[1] in obtaining ouster orders by invoking the inherent jurisdiction, although the extent of this jurisdiction to protect children was not clear[2]. The distinctions drawn in these cases were often subtle and technical and it was a matter of some doubt whether they could be regarded as at all consistent from a policy perspective.

In 1992 the Law Commission considered the issue[3]. Having rejected the idea that undertakings could provide an adequate solution[4], the Law Commission went on to recommend a new power for the court to make a short-term emergency ouster order when making an EPO or interim care order[5]. The order would be dependent on proof of the criteria for these orders but there would also be additional criteria. First, it would have to be shown that there was reasonable cause to believe that the likelihood of harm to the child would not arise if the named person were to be removed from the household. Secondly, there would have to be another parent or other person in the household who was willing and able to provide reasonable care for the child and that that person consented to the order being made[6]. Importantly, the Law Commission also recommended that the court would have power to attach a power of arrest to the order to offer immediate protection to the child in the event of a breach[7].

The new law: Part IV of the Family Law Act 1996

These recommendations have been substantially implemented by Part IV of the Family Law Act 1996[8]. Similar, but somewhat less restrictive, reforms were introduced into Scots law by the Children (Scotland) Act 1995[9]. In a text about children it is inappropriate to go into the intricacies of the new scheme governing domestic violence and occupation of the family home. It is, however, possible here to sketch the principal features of the scheme and to draw attention to the way in which the new law is likely to impact on the protection of children and to interact with the emergency and short-term protective remedies which are the focus of this chapter.

---

1   *Re S (Minors) (Inherent Jurisdiction: Ouster)* [1994] 1 FLR 623 and *Devon County Council v S* [1994] Fam 169.

2   See particularly *Pearson v Franklin* [1994] 2 All ER 137.

3   Law Com Report No 207 *Domestic Violence and Occupation of the Family Home* (1992).

4   Ibid at para 6.15. The Law Commission was particularly bothered by the fact that, since proceedings for EPOs were usually ex parte, there would have to be an adjournment during which time the child might be exposed to risk. It also thought that a power of arrest could not very appropriately be attached to undertakings as opposed to orders.

5   Ibid at para 6.18.

6   Ibid at para 6.20.

7   Ibid at para 6.22.

8   On Part IV of the Act generally, see R Bird *Domestic Violence and Protection from Harassment: The New Law* (2nd edn) (Family Law, 1997). For a concise account of what Part IV is trying to achieve, which takes account of its interrelationship with the subsequent Protection from Harassment Act 1997, see SM Cretney *Family Law* (3rd edn) (Sweet & Maxwell, 1997) at ch 6. For detailed commentary on the individual provisions of Part IV, many of which are technical and complex, see M Freeman *The Family Law Act 1996* (Sweet & Maxwell, 1996).

9   For a concise summary of the new 'exclusion order' available to local authorities in Scotland, see E Sutherland 'Scotland: Child Law Reform – At Last!' in A Bainham (ed) *The International Survey of Family Law 1995* (Martinus Nijhoff, 1997) at pp 449–450.

Essential features of the new scheme

Part IV of the Family Law Act 1996 repeals the various statutes which governed domestic violence and occupation of the family home[1] and gathers together in one place a consistent set of remedies obtainable on common criteria, under a concurrent jurisdiction exercised by the magistrates' (family proceedings) court, the county court and the High Court[2]. These courts may, at their discretion, make 'non-molestation orders' and 'occupation orders'. The former protects from 'molestation' which, of course, includes violence but is a concept wide enough to cover a range of conduct which can broadly be described as 'pestering' or 'harassment'[3].

Standing to seek a non-molestation order depends on the applicant being 'associated' with the respondent, and the Act contains a definition of 'associated persons'[4], the effect of which is to extend essentially familial or domestic remedies to a very wide range of individuals not hitherto treated as family members for other purposes by English law[5]. For present purposes it is sufficient to note that the definition of 'relevant child' in the legislation is drawn extremely widely and extends to many children who would not, for example, have been regarded as a 'child of the family' as required by some of the earlier legislation[6]. It is hard to visualise any children whose status would preclude the court from making a non-molestation order if it feels inclined to do so. Also of note is that the definition of 'associated persons' includes in relation to a child the two parents of that child, persons with parental responsibility and adoptive (or prospective adoptive) parents[7]. And the term 'relative', which also has the effect of rendering two people 'associated', can surely never have been so widely defined in legislation here or anywhere else[8]. So the scope for protective non-molestation orders being made in relation to children is very considerable. It should be remembered, however, that these orders can only be made on the application of a private individual, usually but not necessarily by the mother, and not by the local authority.

---

1   The Domestic Violence and Matrimonial Proceedings Act 1976, the Domestic Proceedings and Magistrates' Courts Act 1978 (to the extent that it governed these remedies) and the Matrimonial Homes Act 1983.
2   In this respect it follows the pattern set by the Children Act 1989.
3   It should be noted that the Protection from Harassment Act 1997 has created criminal offences of 'harassment' and putting people in fear of violence. Where these offences are committed or threatened, the victim may have a civil remedy (damages and/or injunction) and a 'restraining order' may be made to prevent a recurrence of the behaviour. The remedies under this Act will be particularly useful where individuals fall outside the definition of 'associated persons' in Part IV of the Family Law Act 1996. The details of the 1997 legislation are beyond the scope of the present discussion, especially since they are more likely to be relevant to the protection of adults than the protection of children.
4   Section 62(3).
5   For commentary on the significance of this definition in the wider context of conceptual change in family law, see A Bainham 'Changing families and changing concepts: reforming the language of family law' [1998] CFLQ 1.
6   'Relevant child' is defined in s 62(2) as:
    '(a) any child who is living with or might reasonably be expected to live with either party to the proceedings;
    (b) any child in relation to whom an order under the Adoption Act 1976 or the Children Act 1989 is in question in the proceedings; and
    (c) any other child whose interests the court considers relevant.'
7   Section 62(4) and (5).
8   See s 63(1).

Standing to seek an occupation order is exceedingly complex as are the criteria which the court must apply. Pressures from the ultra-conservative wing of the Conservative party (then in government) and the tabloid press culminated in a piece of legislation which seeks to draw distinctions between those who have a property interest of some sort in the family home and those who do not; and between spouses and cohabitants. It is a moot point, as Gillian Douglas has observed, whether the purpose 'is as much to stress Parliament's concern for the importance of property rights as it is to emphasise the importance of marriage'[1].

Either way, the Act draws distinctions between so-called 'entitled applicants' and 'non-entitled applicants', the latter category being further sub-divided into 'former spouses' on the one hand and 'cohabitants' and 'former cohabitants' on the other. In essence, 'entitled applicants' are those with 'matrimonial home rights' (which with very limited exceptions will include all spouses who do not otherwise have a proprietary interest in the home) and those 'entitled to occupy a dwelling house by virtue of a beneficial estate or interest or contract or by notice of any enactment giving them the right to remain in occupation'[2]. Entitled applicants may seek an occupation order where the home in question has been the home of the applicant and an associated person or was intended to be their home. Former spouses, cohabitants, and former cohabitants must therefore apply as 'non-entitled' applicants unless they have an interest in the property and the overall effect in practice will be that the overwhelming majority of spouses will be 'entitled' while very many of those who live together outside marriage will be 'non-entitled'. The practical effect of falling into one or other category will not become totally clear until the legislation has been in force for some time and judges have had the opportunity to interpret and apply it[3]. What can be said at the time of writing is that the criteria for making occupation orders differ depending on the category of the applicant as does the potential duration of any order made[4]. The differential criteria may conceivably be important to the question of the relative weight to be attached to children's interests and we discuss this below in assessing the impact of Part IV on children.

If made, an occupation order, as its name suggests, may regulate the occupation of a home in various ways. In particular (and perhaps most relevant to the current context of child protection), it may oust an alleged abuser from the home, or may go further and exclude him from 'a defined area in which the dwelling-house is included'[5]. An important change brought about by the Act relates to powers of arrest. While it was the case that such powers could be attached to orders under the previous legislation, judges were reluctant to do so unless a pattern of flouting the court's orders had developed. Under the new law, the court must attach a

---

1 'England and Wales: "Family Values" to the Fore?' in A Bainham (ed) *The International Survey of Family Law 1996* (Martinus Nijhoff, 1998) at p 176.

2 FLA 1996, s 33(1).

3 The point being that, given the width of discretion under the Act, it is not at all clear with what enthusiasm judges will attempt to draw distinctions between the married and the unmarried by, for example, limiting the duration of orders in relation to the latter.

4 As to duration, the essential difference is that an order of unlimited duration may conceivably be made in relation to 'entitled applicants' whereas for 'non-entitled former spouses' there may be successive six-monthly orders and for 'non-entitled cohabitants and former cohabitants' the six-month order may be extended only once and is thus bound to be seen as a temporary and not a permanent order.

5 Section 33(3)(g).

power of arrest to the order 'if it appears to the court that the respondent has used
or threatened violence against the applicant or a relevant child ... unless satisfied
that in all the circumstances of the case the applicant or child will be adequately
protected without such a power of arrest'[1].

As in the case of 'non-molestation' orders, it should be carefully noted that
occupation orders may be sought only by individuals, usually the mother of the
children, and that the local authority has no standing under the legislation to
make a 'free-standing' application.

The impact of Part IV on children

Undoubtedly the most innovative and potentially significant reform introduced
by Part IV as it applies to children is the amendment of the Children Act to allow
local authorities to seek 'exclusion requirements' as adjuncts to emergency
protection orders and interim care orders. But before we consider the new
provisions it may be helpful to highlight certain other ways in which the Act is
arguably attaching greater weight to the interests of children to be protected.
These are, respectively, the reformulation of the statutory criteria for occupation
orders, provision for applications by children themselves and the possible
extension of separate legal representation to children in proceedings under the
1996 Act.

(i) Reformulation of criteria for occupation orders

One of the matters which caused the greatest amount of difficulty under the
former jurisdiction to grant 'ouster orders' was the weight which the court should
attach to the welfare of children vis-à-vis other factors, particularly the conduct of
the respondent, in deciding whether to make the order. The Court of Appeal had
been inconsistent in the guidance which it had given to the lower courts, and the
issue eventually came before the House of Lords in *Richards v Richards*[2]. Here, it
was held that the matter was governed by the criteria in the Matrimonial Homes
Act 1983, which made reference to 'the conduct of the spouses in relation to each
other and otherwise to their respective needs and financial resources, to the needs
of any children and to all the circumstances of the case'[3]. Hence, it was not
permissible for the court to treat the welfare of the children as the 'paramount', or
even the 'first', consideration but rather it had to be taken into account alongside
the other specified factors with no preconceived weighting as between them.

These criteria have been substantially re-enacted in the Family Law Act 1996[4],
but, grafted onto them is a so-called 'balance of harm' test which the court must
apply and which may appear to some to be tilting the balance in the direction of
children's welfare vis-à-vis the respondent's conduct. It is provided, in the case of

---

1   Section 47(2).
2   [1984] AC 171.
3   MHA 1983, s 1(3).
4   The provision which applies to 'entitled applicants' and which, with some controversial
    additions, applies to the various categories of 'non-entitled' applicants prescribes that the court
    must have regard to all the circumstances including:
    '(a) the housing needs and housing resources of each of the parties and of any relevant child;
    (b)   the financial resources of each of the parties;
    (c)   the likely effect of any order, or of any decision by the court not to exercise its powers, on the
          health, safety or well being of the parties and of any relevant child; and
    (d)   the conduct of the parties in relation to each other and otherwise.'

applications by 'entitled' applicants and by 'non-entitled former spouses', that where the applicant or any relevant child is likely to suffer significant harm attributable to the conduct of the respondent, the court *must* make the occupation order unless it appears to it that the respondent or any relevant child is likely to suffer significant harm if the order is made and that this harm is as great or greater than the harm attributable to the respondent's conduct if the order is not made[1]. This 'balance of harm' must also be considered on applications by 'non-entitled cohabitants and former cohabitants' but, in this case, there is no statutory presumption that the order will be made where the balance weighs on the side of the applicant or children[2].

Not everyone agrees that the provisions of the Act as drafted will be effective if the intention was to emphasise welfare considerations at the expense of conduct in these cases of actual or threatened 'significant harm'. Stephen Cretney[3] argues that since it is only harm 'attributable to the respondent's conduct' which is taken into account under the test 'the effect seems to be to preserve the decision of the House of Lords in *Richards v Richards*'. In other words, 'rubbishy' or 'flimsy' allegations of adverse conduct by the respondent (as occurred in that case) will not be enough to trigger effectively the balance of harm test, if the real problem is just relationship breakdown and/or poor housing conditions.

What does seem clear (and this does offer greater potential protection to children) is that where there is significant harm, or the threat of it, which does arise from the respondent's conduct, there is now clear statutory guidance that the welfare of the applicant and children is to be the primary consideration for the court. Only time will tell how much difference this will really make in practice.

(ii) Applications by children and legal representation

The 1996 Act provides for the first time that children themselves may bring applications for non-molestation orders and occupation orders. Hitherto they have in reality been dependent on applications being brought on their behalf – usually by their mothers. In many, perhaps most, cases of domestic violence, the mother will be seeking orders to protect herself and the children and their interests will coincide. But there may be instances in which they diverge. An extreme case might be where the mother is herself abusing the child or colluding in abuse by the father. Perhaps social services are unwilling or feel unable to intervene. In circumstances like this, the new standing to bring proceedings may be very beneficial to a minority of children.

Where the child has attained the age of 16, he or she will be able to seek a non-molestation order as an 'associated person'[4]. Where the child is under the age of 16, the 1996 Act follows the pattern of the Children Act 1989 and provides that such a child may not apply for a non-molestation or occupation order 'except with the leave of the court'[5]. Leave may only be granted for these purposes if the court is satisfied that 'the child has sufficient understanding to make the proposed

---

1   Sections 33(7) and 35(8).
2   Section 36(7) and (8).
3   SM Cretney *Family Law* (3rd edn) (Sweet & Maxwell, 1997) at p 101.
4   We looked at the definition of 'relevant child' in fn 6 on p 428 above.
5   Section 43(1).

application'[1]. We consider what is involved in this in the context of children's applications for private s 8 orders in Chapter 13.

The 1996 Act also provides that the Lord Chancellor may by regulations provide for the separate representation of children in proceedings which relate to any matter in respect of which a question has arisen, or may arise, under certain specified Acts[2], including Part IV of the 1996 Act itself[3]. Generally speaking, the separate legal representation of children has been confined to specified 'public' proceedings and has not been extended to the essentially 'private' field of remedies for domestic violence – we discuss this general issue further in Chapter 13.

(iii) Action by the local authority: the new exclusion requirements

We have seen that the local authority is precluded from applying for non-molestation or occupation orders under Part IV and to a large extent from resorting to the private s 8 orders of the Children Act. But, following the recommendations of the Law Commission, Part IV of 1996 Act has amended the Children Act to allow the court, in prescribed circumstances, to add 'exclusion requirements' to emergency protection orders and interim care orders[4]. While these requirements are likely to be specifically requested by the local authority concerned, there would appear to be no reason why the court should not insert such a requirement of its own volition. It is important to appreciate that these requirements may only be inserted in the two orders in question and may not, for example, be included in child assessment orders.

The circumstances in which an exclusion requirement may be included in the above orders are:

'(a) that there is reasonable cause to believe that, if a person ("the relevant person") is excluded from a dwelling-house in which the child lives, the child will cease to suffer, or cease to be likely to suffer, significant harm; and
(b) that another person living in the dwelling-house (whether a parent of the child or some other person) –
  (i) is able and willing to give to the child the care which it would be reasonable to expect a parent to give him, and
  (ii) consents to the inclusion of the exclusion requirement.'[5]

The exclusion requirement may be one or more of the following:

(a) a provision requesting the relevant person to leave a dwelling-house in which he is living with a child;
(b) a provision prohibiting the relevant person from entering a dwelling-house in which the child lives; and

---

1 Section 43(2).
2 Section 64(1). At the time of writing no such regulations had been made.
3 We discuss the other legislation to which this provision may apply and the policy underlying it in Chapter 13.
4 See ss 38A and 44A of the Children Act 1989.
5 CA 1989, s 38A(2). Section 44A(2) is in broadly similar terms.

(c) a provision excluding the relevant person from a defined area in which a dwelling-house in which the child lives is situated[1].

A power of arrest may be attached to the exclusion requirement[2]. The court may provide for this to have effect for a period shorter than the exclusion requirement itself[3].

The likely impact of these provisions is hard to assess since much will depend on how far social services are prepared to use them. Two limitations on the use of the exclusion requirements should be noted. The first is that since they may only accompany emergency protection orders or interim care orders they are dependent on the authority being able to establish the grounds for those orders[4] and they must cease to have effect when the principal orders themselves expire. They are thus by definition only temporary in nature and this may give rise to anxiety that an alleged abuser may return to the home once the temporary exclusion requirement has expired. The second is that the requirements may not be included unless 'another person' in the home is able and willing to care for the child and consents to the inclusion of the requirement. Although this category is not confined to the child's parent, in the overwhelming majority of cases we are likely to be talking about the child's mother. There will be concern that the mother in some cases will not be willing to consent in view of the impact this might have on her marriage or relationship with the 'relevant person'.

These are genuine concerns but, it is submitted, they are capable of being exaggerated. Where an interim care order is made, although ultimately limited in time, the relevant person may be excluded for at least some months and in many cases this will help to resolve the problem. As to the mother's consent to the exclusion requirement, it needs to be appreciated that failure to consent may lead to the local authority pursuing a full care order with a view to removing the child from the home. Put crudely, the mother may in some cases have to decide whether she would prefer her husband or partner to be excluded or for her child to be removed. In these circumstances it seems likely that some mothers will be persuaded (albeit reluctantly) to consent.

In this area, as in others, the division between voluntary co-operation and compulsion may be more apparent than real. So far as local authorities themselves are concerned, one attraction in seeking the new exclusion requirements will surely be that there will be a considerable saving of hard-pressed resources if the abuser can be removed rather than if a care order, and the extensive ongoing responsibility that goes with it, has to be pursued.

---

1 CA 1989, ss 38A(3) and 44A(3).
2 Ibid, ss 38A(5) and 44A(5). For the procedural requirements, see *President's Direction: Children Act 1989: Exclusion Requirement* [1998] 1 FLR 495.
3 Ibid, ss 38A(4) and 44A(4).
4 Although the amount of evidence required to establish the grounds for an EPO or interim care order is significantly less than is required for a full care order, as to which see particularly *Re B (A Minor) (Care Order: Criteria)* [1993] 1 FLR 815.

POLICE PROTECTION

The police have important powers to protect children in cases of real urgency[1]. The raison d'être of these powers is that the police are able to act *immediately* without a court order where they find a child in need of protection. Thereafter, they must act expeditiously to pass responsibility for the child to the local authority which has the primary statutory responsibility for the child's welfare.

Direct action

Where a police constable has reasonable cause to believe that a child would otherwise be likely to suffer significant harm, he may remove the child to 'suitable accommodation' and keep him there. Alternatively, the constable may take reasonable steps to ensure that the child's removal from a hospital or other place in which he is accommodated is prevented[2]. These powers mirror those conferred by an EPO but, here, the police may take direct action on the basis of their own belief. The powers do not include any rights of entry or search, so that if the police require these rights, they will have to apply to the court for an EPO along with a warrant where appropriate[3]. These powers can, therefore, only relate to children who are found by the police. Typically, they have been used to pick up and hold runaways[4], glue-sniffers, abandoned children and those found living in unhygienic conditions[5]. Such children are said to be in 'police protection' and may be kept there without legal challenge for up to 72 hours[6]. This is the same period of allowable detention as under an EPO before a discharge application can be made. It is a considerable reduction from the eight days allowed under the old law[7], and is in keeping with the general policy to restrict the length of operation of emergency powers. At the end of this period, the child must either be released or detained further under the authorisation of an EPO[8].

Obligations which police must fulfil

As soon as practicable after a child is taken into police protection, the constable concerned must ensure that the case is inquired into by a senior officer appointed by the chief officer of the police area[9]. This officer is then known as the 'designated officer' and has independent statutory duties to those of the constable. The constable must, inter alia: inform the local authority of the situation; inform the child (where the child is capable of understanding) of the steps being taken, with reasons, and ascertain the child's wishes and feelings; ensure that where the child is not already in local authority accommodation or a

---

1 *The Children Act 1989 Guidance and Regulations Vol 1 Court Orders* (HMSO, 1991) at paras 4.71 et seq. For a particularly good example of the exercise of this power, see the facts of *Re M (A Minor) (Care Order: Threshold Conditions)* [1994] 2 AC 424, where the initial protective measures were taken by the police following the murder of the mother by the father.
2 Section 46(1).
3 Section 44(1).
4 See the discussion of refuges at p 437 below.
5 See *The Children Act 1989 Guidance and Regulations Vol 1* (above) at para 4.71.
6 Section 46(6).
7 Children and Young Persons Act 1969, s 28(4).
8 CA 1989, s 46(5).
9 Ibid, s 46(3)(e).

refuge, that he is moved to such accommodation; and inform the parents, persons with parental responsibility or others with whom the child was living, of the steps that are being taken, with reasons[1]. The designated officer must inquire into the case. He may, where appropriate, apply for an EPO, whether or not the local authority agree to it or are aware of it[2]. The *Guidance* states, however, that good effective channels of communication ought to mean that the police never find themselves in this position. No extension of an EPO obtained by the police is possible. The maximum period of police-instigated protection is, therefore, eight days. Thereafter the local authority must be involved if further protection is necessary. The *Guidance* emphasises the importance of inter-agency communication and co-operation between the police and the local authority. This ought to be reviewed and monitored at regular intervals. The aim is to ensure that no child taken into police protection need be accommodated in a police station and that his reception into local authority accommodation is achieved with the minimum of trauma[3].

No parental responsibility

The police do not acquire parental responsibility where a child is in police protection. The designated officer is, however, required to do what is reasonable in all the circumstances for the purpose of safeguarding or promoting the child's welfare (having regard, in particular, to the length of time during which the child will remain under police protection)[4]. Beyond the power of removal and detention, the powers of the police are, therefore, in essence, limited to those held by anyone with the de facto care of a child[5]. The designated officer must also allow prescribed individuals to have such contact with the child as is, in his opinion, reasonable and in the child's best interests[6]. Those concerned are the parents, others with parental responsibility, contact orders or with whom the child was living before he was taken into police protection[7]. Again, contact under supervision may be the only realistic option during the first 72 hours of an emergency.

ABDUCTION OF CHILDREN AND REFUGES FOR CHILDREN AT RISK

Runaways

We noted above the practice of the police to pick up 'runaways'. The problem of teenage runaways is not a new one but, in recent years, the incidence of

---

1 Section 46(3).
2 Section 46(7) and (8).
3 *The Children Act 1989 Guidance and Regulations Vol 1 Court Orders* (HMSO, 1991) at para 4.77.
4 Section 46(9)(b).
5 Cf s 3(5) and the discussion in Chapter 2 above.
6 Section 46(10). Under s 46(11) this is the obligation of the local authority where a child taken into police protection is in local authority accommodation.
7 Ibid.

homelessness among young people has increased[1]. The legal position of adolescents who run away has never been entirely clear, not least because the law has not set a definite age at which a young person may live independently[2]. Organisations such as the Children's Society, which have habitually given assistance to young runaways, particularly by providing them with temporary accommodation, until the Children Act had a dubious legal basis for doing so. The Children's Society especially, was concerned to put its activities on a firmer legal footing and to counter any possible charge that they might constitute a criminal offence.

Criminal offence of abduction

The Children Act reaffirmed the criminal offence of abduction relating to children in care, but at the same time exempted from prosecution bona fide organisations, through a process of certification. The starting point is s 49(1), which provides:

> 'A person shall be guilty of an offence if, knowingly and without lawful authority or reasonable excuse, he –
> (a) takes a child to whom this section applies away from the responsible person;
> (b) keeps such a child away from the responsible person; or
> (c) induces, assists or incites such a child to run away or stay away from the responsible person.'

'Responsible person' for these purposes means any person who, for the time being, has care of the child by virtue of a care order, an emergency protection order, or as a result of the child being taken into police protection[3]. The offence is therefore concerned with children absconding from public care as opposed to fleeing the parental home[4]. The court may make a 'recovery order' where it appears that a child has been taken or kept away from the responsible person unlawfully, where the child has run away, is staying away or missing[5]. Recovery orders may not be made in respect of children who are voluntarily 'looked after' by local authorities but the *Guidance* counsels that authorities should also report to the police immediately where these children abscond[6]. The recovery order requires production of the child by any person able to produce him and disclosure

---

1   The Children's Society has estimated that 98,000 young people go missing each year in Britain. For an informative discussion of the work of the Society in relation to runaways, see C Newman *Young Runaways – Findings from Britain's First Safe House* (The Children's Society, 1990). See also C Abrahams 'Understanding "running away" – findings from recent NCH research' (1993) 5 JCL 84.

2   For a discussion of the point, see A Bainham *Children, Parents and the State* (Sweet & Maxwell, 1988) at pp 63–64.

3   Sections 49(2) and 50(2).

4   Chapter 17 below discusses abduction from parents in the context of international child abduction.

5   Section 51(1). For the first reported decision on the use of recovery orders, see *Re R (Recovery Orders)* [1998] 2 FLR 401, in which Wall J provides detailed guidance on the provisions of s 50. In this case, a recovery order was made where a boy aged 13 was the subject of a care order on the basis that he was beyond his mother's control. He refused to return to the boarding-school which he was required to attend as part of the care plan. The order was made and upheld after the local authority had revised the care plan nominating foster-parents, rather than the boy's mother, to care for him during the holidays – thus making them 'responsible persons' for the purposes of a recovery order.

6   *The Children Act 1989 Guidance and Regulations Vol 1 Court Orders* (HMSO, 1991) at para 4.90.

of his whereabouts by any person with such information. It also authorises his removal, and authorises a police constable to enter specified premises and search for the child, using force if necessary[1]. The order may be sought by any person with parental responsibility for the child, under a care order or EPO, or by the designated officer where the child is in police protection[2].

Exemption of children's refuges

The legislation exempts from all offences relating to the abduction or harbouring of children, voluntary or registered children's homes which provide a refuge for children who appear to be at risk of harm and which have a certificate from the Secretary of State[3]. Local authority or voluntary organisation foster-parents may also fall within the terms of the certificate where they also provide a refuge[4]. The issue and withdrawal of certificates is governed by the Refuges (Children's Homes and Foster Placements) Regulations 1991[5]. It is not anticipated that such certificates will be readily granted to just *anyone* claiming to assist children, and it was said in Parliament that it would be necessary to separate the 'sheep' from the 'goats'. Without proper scrutiny, there would be a risk of exploitation of vulnerable adolescents by unscrupulous individuals. A key requirement is that, where any child is admitted to, or leaves, a refuge, the police must be notified[6]. Where a refuge fails to measure up to the required standards its certificate may be withdrawn and there is no right of appeal against this[7].

---

1 Section 50(3).
2 Section 50(4).
3 Section 51(1).
4 Section 51(2).
5 SI 1991/1507.
6 Ibid, reg 3.
7 Ibid, reg 4.

PART IV
CHILDREN AND SOCIETY

Part IV of this book is concerned primarily with issues which arise in relation to the child's activities outside the family. This is not an easy distinction to make since the family is often (if not always) affected by these activities. But such a distinction can be made for the purposes of exposition and analysis. It is certainly the case that, whereas Parts II and III have been principally concerned with what might be described as 'mainstream family law', the subjects under discussion in Part IV take the family lawyer into largely uncharted waters. And whereas Parts II and III have been predominantly concerned with the statutory code constituted by the Children Act 1989, Part IV involves an examination of many other pieces of legislation, common law rules and international instruments.

Chapter 13 highlights an issue crucial to the position of children in the legal system – their standing before the courts. This chapter concentrates on the two issues of representation and evidence in children cases including the evidence of children themselves. Chapter 14 discusses the position of children, or more accurately children and young persons, under the criminal law. Chapter 15 does the same in relation to the civil law concentrating, particularly, on the two great areas of the common law, contract and tort, but also pausing to look at the thorny issues surrounding children's employment. Both of these chapters identify, as central features of the law applying to children, the twin concepts of protection and responsibility. Chapter 16 examines education law, so crucial to the rights of children and parents, and undoubtedly a 'boom' area of children law. Finally, Chapter 17 concludes by taking a wider perspective of children's rights within the international community. We considered the International Convention on the Rights of the Child as a basic source of children law in Chapter 2. Chapter 17 is concerned with other international Conventions and concentrates particularly on those Conventions dealing with the major problem of international child abduction and the European Convention on Human Rights about to be incorporated into English law.

Chapter 13

CHILDREN IN COURT

INTRODUCTION

Rights of children historically

The greater awareness of the independent interests and capacities of children, noted elsewhere in this work, has also manifested itself in recent changes to the legal standing of children in the courts. Indeed, without these changes it might have been difficult to speak with any conviction about children's rights. Rights are arguably of little value, and certainly of less value, where the machinery does not exist for their enforcement[1]. In the case of children, there is an initial difficulty in that the protection of their rights or interests is usually dependent on the intervention of interested adults, most obviously their parents. Children generally suffer from a natural disability, reflected in a legal disability, which prevents them from commencing and concluding legal proceedings on their own account. In the case of young children, this factual dependency on adults is self-evident. It is less so in the case of older children, especially adolescents. But whatever the age of the child there is an ever-present danger that there may be a conflict of interest between the child and the adult on whom he or she is dependent for taking action. As has been seen[2], this became apparent in public law cases in the 1970s when the Children Act 1975 first provided for the separate representation of children in care proceedings.

This dependency on adults is illustrated by many features of the legal procedures which govern children cases. In ordinary civil litigation, children are usually required to commence and conduct proceedings through an adult known for these purposes as 'next friend'. In private family proceedings, children are rarely parties and their independent interests are usually represented, if at all, through welfare reports by welfare officers or, sometimes in wardship proceedings, by the Official Solicitor[3]. No public official is charged generally with the responsibility of bringing proceedings on behalf of children[4]. Moreover, rules of evidence relating to child witnesses have traditionally incorporated warnings about placing too much reliance on children's evidence and have, on the whole, been unsympathetic to the special difficulties which they face when confronting the intimidating environment of the courts[5].

---

1 This is not to deny the value of international normative standards as reflected in Conventions like the United Nations Convention on the Rights of the Child, as to which see Chapter 2 above.
2 In Chapter 11 above.
3 On the functions of the Official Solicitor in wardship generally, see NV Lowe and R White *Wards of Court* (2nd edn) (Barry Rose/Kluwer, 1986) at ch 9.
4 It is not, for example, the function of the Official Solicitor to *initiate* wardship proceedings but only to act in existing proceedings. See Heilbron J's remarks in *Re D (A Minor) (Wardship: Sterilisation)* [1976] Fam 185 at 197.
5 Again wardship, with its inquisitorial approach, has been something of an exception.

A new philosophy: the importance of children's views

The new philosophy of the Children Act 1989, with its emphasis on the importance of children's views[1] and the primacy of their interests, necessitated change on several fronts. The Act allows children to commence and conduct certain types of family proceedings in their own right in specified circumstances; they are given party status in a wider range of proceedings and there is much greater provision for their separate representation. Changes to the law of evidence (some in the Children Act and some outside it) were designed to give greater credence to the evidence of children and to make the process of giving evidence a less stressful one for them.

These changes are best seen as incremental moves in the right direction. In particular, the greater representation of children in the public sphere has not been extended to private law cases, although the Family Law Act 1996 does empower the Lord Chancellor to provide by regulations for the separate representation of children in certain specified proceedings[2]. There are some who think that the evidential changes which have been made fall well short of tackling the fundamental problem as they see it – that children should not appear as witnesses in court at all[3].

This chapter highlights these changes. It begins by looking briefly at the rules governing the way in which legal proceedings involving children are commenced and conducted. It then turns to the crucial question of representation and concludes with a section on the rules applying to child witnesses in legal proceedings both civil and criminal. Further reforms may well be required in future to comply with the European Convention on the Exercise of Children's Rights which seeks to extend procedural and participatory rights to children in proceedings affecting them. We consider the provisions of the Convention in Chapter 17.

COMMENCING AN ACTION

Traditional procedure

The basic rule of civil litigation is that a child is a person under a 'disability'. As such he:

> 'may not bring, or make a claim, in any proceedings except by his next friend and may not acknowledge service, defend, make a counterclaim or intervene in any proceedings, or appear in any proceedings under a judgment or order notice of which has been served on him, except by his guardian ad litem.'[4]

It is one of the incidents of parenthood that a parent has the prima facie right to act as the child's next friend and the duty to act as his guardian ad litem ('GAL') in

---

1   See Chapter 2 above. But for a case evincing a more cautious attitude to the significance of children's views in care proceedings, see *Re C (A Minor) (Care: Child's Wishes)* [1993] 1 FLR 832. See also the cases granting leave to children to commence proceedings at pp 444 et seq.

2   Section 64, discussed at p 455 below.

3   See, for example, JR Spencer 'Child Witnesses, Video-Technology and the Law of Evidence' [1987] Crim LR 76.

4   RSC Ord 80, r 2(1).

legal proceedings[1]. An obvious example might be where the child has allegedly been injured by the negligence of some third party. The court does, however, have power to remove a parent and substitute another adult as next friend or GAL where a parent is acting improperly or against the child's best interests[2].

Exceptions under the Children Act 1989

This normal rule of civil proceedings applies also in 'family proceedings' but is now subject to significant exceptions introduced by the Children Act 1989 and the rules of court made under it[3]. The starting point is r 9.2 of the Family Proceedings Rules 1991 which essentially reproduces the general rule that a person under a disability (a child for present purposes) may only begin and prosecute any family proceedings by next friend and may only defend such proceedings by GAL[4]. But this rule is subject to exceptions in r 9.2A providing that minors who are entitled to begin, prosecute or defend proceedings under the Children Act 1989 or the inherent jurisdiction of the High Court[5] may do so *without* a next friend or GAL in two alternative sets of circumstances. These are either:

(1) that the leave of the court is obtained[6]; *or*
(2) where a solicitor:
  (a) considers that the minor is able, having regard to his understanding, to give instructions in relation to the proceedings; *and*
  (b) has accepted instructions from the minor to act for him in the proceedings and, where the proceedings have begun, is so acting[7].

The rules go on to provide that a minor may apply for leave to remove an existing next friend or GAL where he wishes to prosecute or defend the remaining stages of the proceedings himself[8].

This ability of the child to commence proceedings without a next friend is most likely to become relevant where the child obtains the leave of the court to seek a s 8 order. The Act allows a child to seek leave to apply for *any* s 8 order[9]. This may be granted by the court where 'it is satisfied that he has sufficient understanding to make the proposed application'[10]. The same test of 'sufficient understanding' also governs the court's decision whether to allow the child to appear without a next friend or GAL[11] and is generally thought to be a statutory application of the *Gillick*

---

1 *Woolf v Pemberton* (1877) 6 Ch D 19.
2 *Re Birchall, Wilson v Birchall* (1880) 16 ChD 41; *Re Taylor's Application* [1972] 2 QB 369.
3 Family Proceedings Rules 1991, SI 1991/1247, r 9.2A.
4 It is not necessary for the court to appoint the GAL under this rule.
5 Family Proceedings Rules 1991, SI 1991/1247, r 9.1(3).
6 The child does not need to have a next friend or GAL in order to apply for leave which may be sought by filing a written request or by making an oral request at the hearing (ibid, r 9.2A(2)).
7 On how solicitors go about the task of assessing a child's competence, see C Sawyer 'The competence of children to participate in family proceedings' [1995] CFLQ 180.
8 Family Proceedings Rules 1991, SI 1991/1247, r 9.2A(4). For the principles to be applied on such an application by a child, see *Re S (A Minor) (Independent Representation)* [1993] 2 FLR 437 discussed at p 446 below.
9 Section 10(2)(b).
10 Section 10(8).
11 Family Proceedings Rules 1991, SI 1991/1247, r 9.2A(6) requiring that the court grant leave 'if it considers that the minor concerned has sufficient understanding to participate as a party in the proceedings concerned or proposed without a next friend or guardian ad litem'.

test[1]. Where leave is refused, the child may be able to persuade an interested adult to apply for the order. Where leave is given, the child may wish to seek: a residence order preserving his existing home or authorising him to live somewhere else[2]; a contact order or an order prohibiting contact with a relative he does not wish to see; or, perhaps, a prohibited steps or specific issue order to regulate areas of disagreement with his parents or other carers. In this connection, it should be recalled that *Gillick*, subject to its controversial interpretation by the Court of Appeal[3], appears to support the right of the competent child to decide matters within his capacity, thus overriding parental views.

When can a child invoke these procedures?

There has been much speculation about the circumstances in which children might be allowed to invoke these procedures. There was concern that there might be an abuse of the procedures by young people who, following some temporary tiff with their parents, seek a 'divorce' from them[4]. On the other hand, it is not difficult to visualise circumstances in which children who are the alleged victims of physical or sexual abuse or other offensive behaviour could find these procedures an invaluable self-help mechanism. The same might be said of the new right of children to seek orders in cases of domestic violence under Part IV of the Family Law Act 1996 which was discussed in the previous chapter.

On the whole, it is the first view which seems to have characterised the reported decisions of the courts[5]. The case-law has made it plain that even where the court finds that the child has the requisite understanding that is not the end of the matter. The court still retains a discretion in deciding whether or not to grant leave and the key question has been whether this residual discretion should be exercised restrictively or liberally. Unlike in the case of adults where the Act[6] specifies the criteria the court is to apply, the Act is silent on the considerations which should govern children's applications for leave.

In *Re C (A Minor) (Leave to Seek Section 8 Orders)*[7], a 14-year-old child who did not get on with her parents went to stay with a friend's family and did not want to return. With the consent of the friend's father she sought leave to apply for a residence order to enable her to continue living with the family and a specific issue

1 *Gillick v West Norfolk and Wisbech Area Health Authority* [1986] 1 AC 112. See, particularly, Chapter 8 above and the cases discussed below for what is involved.
2 On this question, it should also be remembered that minors who have reached 16 years of age may effectively seek a 'self-referral' into local authority accommodation (s 20(3) and (11)), and see Chapter 10 above.
3 In *Re R* and *Re W*, as to which see Chapter 8 above.
4 In fact, the idea is not such a revolutionary one. Legal procedures have long existed in certain jurisdictions, particularly in the United States, for the legal emancipation of certain children, but usually only those who had already achieved de facto independence from their parents. On the doctrine of emancipation, see A Bainham *Children, Parents and the State* (Sweet & Maxwell, 1988) at pp 67–69 and the sources cited there. For a more recent analysis of the phenomenon of 'divorcing parents', see M Freeman 'Can Children Divorce Their Parents?' in *The Moral Status of Children* (Martinus Nijhoff, 1997) at ch 11 which also cites many useful sources dealing with the position in North America.
5 For a general commentary, see A Bainham ' "See you in Court, Mum": Children as Litigants' (1994) 6 JCL 127.
6 Section 10(9).
7 [1994] 1 FLR 26.

order to allow her to take a holiday with them in Bulgaria. Johnson J refused leave on the specific issue application and adjourned the application relating to residence. In his view, there was no advantage in an order being made at that time in relation to a matter which should be resolved internally within the family. He also took the view that Parliament had intended the jurisdiction only to be exercised in relation to matters of importance and that the issues here were not serious enough to warrant judicial orders. Controversially, he also held that the question of leave was governed by the central principles of the Children Act including the welfare principle. The effect of applying a welfare test to the issue of leave would be, as here, to reserve to the court a wide discretion to refuse leave and to filter out applications by children thought by the courts to be against their best interests. In contrast, two subsequent decisions of the Family Division have held that, on children applications, as on adult applications, for leave to seek s 8 orders, the welfare principle does *not* govern the issue.

In *Re SC (A Minor) (Leave to Seek Residence Order)*[1], another adolescent girl wanted to live with a friend's family but her circumstances were very different. She had been in care for many years and had suffered a number of breakdowns in foster-placements. Her mother was opposed to her obtaining a residence order and wanted her to remain in care, even though she was herself unable to provide a home. Booth J granted the child leave to seek a residence order. In her view, assuming the child passed the test of understanding (which she did here) the court in exercising its discretion should then simply have regard to the likelihood of success of the substantive application. It should be satisfied that this was not a 'non-starter' doomed to failure. She further held that the child's welfare was *not* paramount on the leave question since the issue of the child's upbringing did not arise at that stage. This case also confirmed that a child was capable of seeking a residence order in favour of an adult since it was Parliament's intention that all s 8 orders should, in principle, be available to children even though the residence order, because of its form, could not be framed in favour of the child herself.

This decision was followed in *Re C (Residence: Child's Application for Leave)*[2]. Here, there had been a long history of proceedings between the two parents since they had separated. The child, another 14-year-old girl, felt that her views had never been properly represented by the court welfare officer. She had a fervent wish to live with her mother but felt under pressure from her father. Stuart-White J held that the welfare principle did not govern the leave question but that applications for leave by children should be treated cautiously. Making a child party in proceedings between warring parents might, for example, expose the child to the evidence of the parents and to matters which it might be better for the child not to hear. However, in this case, he held that the girl had the necessary understanding and leave should be granted. Her application concerned an important matter and it had a reasonable prospect of success.

These latter two decisions perhaps illustrate a more relaxed judicial attitude to children applications, certainly where the issues raised are undeniably serious. It remains the case, of course, that the child concerned must pass the preliminary test of understanding. The leading authority on what is required in this respect is

---

1   [1995] 1 FLR 96.
2   [1995] 1 FLR 927.

Re S (A Minor) (Independent Representation)[1], a case in which a boy aged 11 sought to 'sack' the Official Solicitor who was acting as his GAL in acrimonious proceedings concerned with whether he should live with his father or his mother. Sir Thomas Bingham MR said that the Children Act required a judicious balance to be struck between two considerations. The first was that children were human beings with individual minds, wills, views and emotions which should command serious attention. They should not be discarded merely because they were children. The second was that a child is, after all, a child. The law should be sensitive to the need to protect children who were likely to be vulnerable and impressionable, lacking the maturity to weigh the longer term against the short term amongst other things. In this case, the court concluded that the judge's ruling to the effect that the child lacked sufficient understanding to participate as a party without representation by a GAL, in what were emotionally complex and highly fraught proceedings, was impregnable. It is to the matter of representation that we now turn.

REPRESENTATION

Background

English law has never given minors a generalised right to representation in legal proceedings or any automatic party status. The process of conferring statutory rights in this area has been an evolutionary one and the changes in the Children Act were another stage in this process. Traditionally, it has been more usual for courts to call for welfare reports on children's 'best interests' rather than for the children themselves or their views to be represented as such. This duty to provide reports has fallen on different people depending on the nature of the proceedings. The welfare test is, as has been seen[2], an indeterminate one, and it has been said that 'the approach taken in each child's case could be as different as the people called upon to discharge the task of representing them to the court'[3]. The notion of more comprehensive reform requiring *every* court in *all* kinds of proceedings to consider whether children should be separately represented or joined as parties has been mooted for a considerable period of time. It was the subject of an abortive private member's Bill introduced by Dr David Owen in the

---

1   [1993] 3 All ER 36.
2   See Chapter 2 above.
3   CM Lyon 'Safeguarding Children's Interests? – Some Problematic Issues Surrounding Separate Representation in Care and Associated Proceedings' in MDA Freeman (ed) *Essays in Family Law* (University College, London, 1985) at p 1. Lyon's essay is an excellent introduction to the law on representation of children's interests before the reforms of the Children Act. See also I Robertson 'Acting in Children's Cases – The Future of Specialisation' [1993] Fam Law 103, indicating that the admission of solicitors to The Law Society's Children Panel is carefully controlled to ensure suitability. See also PM Harris 'Procedural problems in representing children' (1995) JCL 49. For more recent academic commentaries, see J Masson 'Representations of Children' (1996) *Current Legal Problems* 245, and J Fortin *Children's Rights and the Developing Law* (Butterworths, 1998) at ch 7. Much useful information on the practical concerns involved in representing children may be found in the quarterly journal *Representing Children* (formerly *Panel News*) published by the National Youth Advocacy Service.

mid-1970s. The idea was closely associated with the establishment of a family court and an independent court welfare service[1].

Current trends

This has not materialised, largely, it appears, because of its resource implications, and there remains a patchwork of different kinds of representation. The trend, however, is undoubtedly towards *more* representation. The effect of the reforms first begun in the Children Act 1975 and built upon in the 1989 Act is to increase, very substantially, the provision for representation of children in *public* law cases. The essential feature of child representation in the modern law is that in *public* law cases it will be the rule rather than the exception while in *private* law cases it will be the exception rather than the rule[2], although in future there is likely to be at least some increased representation of children in private cases following the Family Law Act 1996[3]. It should be said that, since private law cases vastly exceed public law cases numerically, in most 'family proceedings' the child will be neither a party, nor separately represented[4]. The effect of this divergent policy is to preserve, at least on this issue, a distinct dichotomy of public and private children cases. This might be thought rather contrary to the general thrust of the legislation which has been to harmonise the two through common procedures and common principles[5]. It is thus necessary to take public and private law separately for the purposes of this discussion.

Public family proceedings

An earlier chapter considered[6] the background to the provision of separate representation for children in care proceedings. The Children Act significantly increased this in two ways. First, it created a presumption of appointment of a GAL in 'specified proceedings' and, secondly, it enlarged the range of proceedings in which the presumption of appointment applies. The child will also automatically be a party in such proceedings.

Appointment of a separate representative
Where the child is separately represented, this will be by a GAL and/or a solicitor. The relationship between these two kinds of representative is discussed below. The concern for the moment is with the circumstances of appointment.

Appointment of a GAL
Section 41(6) of the Children Act 1989 and the accompanying rules of court[7] specify a long list of proceedings in which the court *must* appoint a GAL for the child 'unless satisfied that it is not necessary to do so in order to safeguard his

---

1 CM Lyon (above) at p 2.
2 The term 'representation' is used here to refer to representation of the *child* as such rather than investigations into the child's *interests*.
3 See p 454 below.
4 This is, of course, principally accounted for by the very high incidence of divorce.
5 See Chapter 2 above.
6 At Chapter 11 above.
7 Family Proceedings Rules 1991, SI 1991/1247 ('FPR 1991') and the Family Proceedings Courts (Children Act 1989) Rules 1991, SI 1991/1395 ('FPC(CA 1989)R 1991').

interests'[1]. It was envisaged by the Lord Chancellor, during the passage of the Children Bill, that an appointment would need to be made in the vast majority of cases falling within the specified proceedings[2]. The wording of the legislation is a reformulation of the former statutory language and was designed to remove the wide discretion which the courts previously had in deciding whether to appoint a GAL[3]. The small minority of cases in which a GAL is not appointed are likely to be mainly those in which the child wishes to instruct his own solicitor and is found to be competent to do so. In 'specified proceedings' the child is automatically entitled to be a party[4] and may instruct a solicitor where he has sufficient understanding and wishes to do so[5]. In 'non-specified proceedings', which expression includes mainly private law cases under the Children Act[6], the child is not usually a party but the court has a discretion to join him at his request and also to appoint a GAL or solicitor[7].

What are 'specified proceedings'?

Essentially, specified proceedings are all proceedings which involve public intervention in the family[8]. They include, most obviously, applications for care or supervision orders and, significantly since the Children Act, applications for the short-term remedies of EPO and CAO. Other proceedings included are: those in which a s 37 direction has been made or the court is considering whether to make an interim care order; applications for discharge or variation of care or supervision orders; and applications for residence or contact orders where a child is in care and appeals against the making or refusal of these orders. Also now included are: secure accommodation applications; applications by a local authority to change the child's name or remove him from the UK; and applications to extend supervision orders and appeals in any of these proceedings.

---

1   Section 41(1). On the appointment and functions of GALs generally, see *The Children Act 1989 Guidance and Regulations Vol 7 Guardians ad Litem and other Court Related Issues* (HMSO, 1991).

2   House of Lords Official Report Vol 503, col 408 (19 January 1989). But for a case in which the court held that the appointment of a GAL in specified proceedings was unnecessary on the facts, see *Re J (A Minor) (Change of Name)* [1993] 1 FLR 699. Here, a 12-year-old girl in care and living with long-term foster-parents wished to use their name. This was not opposed by the Official Solicitor and there was no longer any contact between the girl and her natural parents following a history of severe abuse. Booth J said that a GAL could not have said any more than counsel for the local authority and there was no conflict of interest. Neither was it appropriate here to serve either the parents or the girl or for her to be present in court.

3   In some courts, appointments were evidently made in only a small proportion of cases. See *R v Plymouth Juvenile Court ex parte F and F* [1987] 1 FLR 169 at 178.

4   FPR 1991, r 4.7(1) and App 3, col (iii); FPC(CA 1989)R 1991, r 7(1) and Sch 2, col (iii).

5   Section 41(3), (4)(b).

6   'Relevant proceedings' for these purposes are any proceedings under the Children Act, under any statutory instrument made under it or any amendment made by the Children Act in any other enactment (s 93(1)–(3)).

7   See, for example, *Re CE (Section 37 Direction)* [1995] 1 FLR 26 where a GAL appointed following a s 37 direction by a district judge continued to represent a 14-year-old child (who had left her parents to live with her boyfriend's family) even though the local authority decided not to seek a public law order following its investigations. Section 37 should not, however, be used purely as a device to secure the appointment of a GAL since the normal course is for the child's views to be presented by the court welfare officer in private proceedings. Neither should wardship be used for the purpose of foisting a GAL on a child. See *Re CT (A Minor) (Wardship: Representation)* [1993] 2 FLR 278.

8   See fn 7 at p 447 above.

In addition, GALs continue to be appointed in adoption proceedings under the Adoption Act 1976.

Although the appointment of a GAL can be made at any stage of the proceedings[1] the rules require the court to make the appointment as soon as possible after the commencement or transfer of the proceedings[2]. It is thus foreseen that GALs will be involved at an early stage and consequently should be able to advise the court about short-term orders, such as EPOs and interim orders, and directions the court may wish to make in the initial stages of protective intervention[3].

Appointment of the Official Solicitor
The Official Solicitor has traditionally represented certain children in wardship proceedings[4]. Wardship has effectively been abolished in public law cases[5] but the representative role of the Official Solicitor's Department has not been so abolished. Involvement of the Official Solicitor has decreased by virtue of the restrictions on wardship and the fact that a GAL may now be appointed for proceedings in both the county court and High Court as well as the magistrates' court. Further, where a case starts in a lower court and is then transferred to the High Court, an appointed GAL is able to continue[6].

The circumstances in which the Official Solicitor should be appointed to represent the child in public law cases was the subject of a direction by the Lord Chancellor[7]. Where, in specified proceedings, the child does not have a GAL and the court considers that there are 'exceptional circumstances which make it desirable in the interests of the welfare of the child' that the Official Solicitor be appointed rather than a panel guardian, he may be appointed to represent the child. Factors which the courts ought to take into account are spelt out in the direction and include cases with a foreign element, those involving a number of children or a child already represented by the Official Solicitor in the proceedings, and any other circumstances the court considers relevant. In any event, the Official Solicitor will only be appointed where a case reaches the High Court and the child is without a GAL. Where he is appointed as a GAL his duties will be the same as those imposed on other GALs. The Official Solicitor may also give advice and assistance as he considers appropriate to any appointed GAL in specified proceedings in the High Court. The Lord Chancellor's Direction has been reinforced by a Practice Note[8] issued by the Official Solicitor which governs more generally the appointment of the Official Solicitor in family proceedings whether public or private. We consider its application to private family proceedings below.

---

1 FPR 1991, r 4.10(4) and FPC(CA 1989)R 1991, r 10(4).
2 FPR 1991, r 4.10(1) and FPC(CA 1989)R 1991, r 10(1).
3 As to which see Chapter 12 above.
4 See NV Lowe and R White *Wards of Court* (2nd edn) (Barry Rose/Kluwer, 1986).
5 Section 100, discussed in Chapter 11 above.
6 See Lord Mackay LC, House of Lords Official Report Vol 503, 19 January 1989 at cols 421–422.
7 *Lord Chancellor's Direction: Duties and Functions of Official Solicitor under the Children Act 1989* [1991] 2 FLR 471, made under s 41(8).
8 *Practice Note: The Official Solicitor: Appointment in Family Proceedings* [1995] 2 FLR 479 superseding the previous Practice Note published at [1993] 2 FLR 641.

The *Guidance*[1] notes that the Official Solicitor's Department has 'great expertise in regard to High Court procedures and child care cases where wider issues of public policy and complexity are present'. It advises that managers of panels of GALs should establish good liaison links between their panel and the office of the Official Solicitor. It has, however, been observed that the methods of working and background training of panel GALs and the Official Solicitor's staff are quite distinct and that this may lead to some variation in the quality of representation[2].

Appointment of a solicitor

It is not the function of the GAL to represent the child at the hearing in court. This is undertaken, as one would expect, by a solicitor and, where appropriate, counsel[3]. Where a solicitor has not already been appointed, one of the functions of the GAL is to appoint one and thereafter give instructions to him. We consider below the thorny question of what happens where the instructions of the GAL do not accord with the wishes of the child. Where no solicitor has been appointed, the court may itself make an appointment where:

(1) no GAL has been appointed for the child;
(2) the child has sufficient understanding to instruct a solicitor and wishes to do so; and
(3) it appears to the court that it would be in the child's best interests for him to be repesented by a solicitor[4].

The appointed solicitor must then represent the child in accordance with rules of court[5].

Civil legal aid is available for *all* proceedings under the Children Act 1989[6] and this includes the representation of children. The normal 'means and merits' test will apply but this is not so in relation to certain 'special Children Act proceedings'[7]. In these cases, children have a right to non-means, non-merits-tested legal aid which has come to be known as 'free legal aid'. These special proceedings are again confined to *public* family proceedings but are a more restricted class than the 'specified proceedings' for the purposes of representation. Included are cases under s 31 (care and supervision orders), s 43 (CAOs), s 44 (EPOs), s 45 (duration and discharge of EPOs) and s 25 (secure accommodation applications). In these proceedings, time will often be of the essence and the special rules mean that a solicitor will be able to get on with the case immediately. In 'non-special' cases (ie all other children cases), civil legal aid may be applied for in the normal way and it is important to remember that this could

---

1   *The Children Act 1989 Guidance and Regulations Vol 7 Guardians ad Litem and Other Court Related Issues* (HMSO, 1991) at para 2.73.
2   See J Masson 'The Official Solicitor as the child's guardian ad litem under the Children Act 1989' (1992) 4 JCL 58. The article compares and contrasts the work of panel guardians with that of the Official Solicitor's staff.
3   There is much valuable information about the nature of the solicitor's role in representing children in P King and I Young *The Child as Client* (Family Law, 1992).
4   Section 41(3) and (4).
5   Section 41(5) and FPR 1991, r 4.12.
6   Legal Aid Act 1988, s 15, as amended, and the Civil Legal Aid (General) Regulations 1989, SI 1989/339, as amended. Section 99 of the Children Act extended civil legal aid to care proceedings but it is not available to the local authority or GAL.
7   Legal Aid Act 1988 (Children Act 1989) Order 1991, SI 1991/1924, and the Legal Aid Act 1988, s 15(3)(c).

include emergency legal aid over the telephone where necessary. The ability of the solicitor to act quickly is important, not least to avoid offending the general principle in the legislation that delay is prejudicial to children[1].

The specialised nature of the work involved in representing children is recognised by The Law Society which has established a Children Panel with regional branches, in an effort to ensure that solicitors chosen to represent children will have the necessary expertise.

The role of the GAL

General

GALs are individuals with qualifications in social work who are required to have a thorough knowledge of both social work theory and child care law. The principal function of the GAL system is to ensure that 'the court is fully informed of the relevant facts which relate to the child's welfare and that the wishes and feelings of the child are clearly established'[2]. They are described by the *Guidance*[3] as having a 'proactive role' in relation to the conduct of the proceedings, including timetabling and advising the court on the range of orders available. The general duty of the GAL, as expressed in the Children Act, is 'to safeguard the interests of the child' in the manner prescribed by rules of court[4]. It should be noted that these rules only govern GALs appointed in 'specified' Children Act proceedings. There are no comparable rules governing the conduct of next friends or GALs appointed to represent children in other kinds of proceedings. The rules[5] spell out in some detail the more specific duties of GALs.

Specific duties

The GAL is required to attend all directions, appointments and hearings, unless excused by the court, and to advise the court on the following matters:

'(a) whether the child is of sufficient understanding for any purpose including the child's refusal to submit to a medical or psychiatric examination or other assessment that the court has power to require, direct or order;

(b) the wishes of the child in respect of any matter relevant to the proceedings, including his attendance at court;

(c) the appropriate forum for the proceedings;

(d) the appropriate timing of the proceedings or any part of them;

(e) the options available to it in respect of the child and the suitability of each such option including what order should be made in determining the application;

(f) any other matter concerning which the court seeks his advice or concerning which he considers that the court should be informed.'[6]

In addition to this advisory role the GAL must[7], inter alia:

(1) appoint a solicitor, advise the child as is appropriate having regard to his understanding, and instruct the solicitor;

---

1 See Chapter 2 above.
2 *Children Act Advisory Committee Annual Report 1992/3* (Lord Chancellor's Department, 1993) at p 14. See also D Dinan-Hayward 'The Changing Role of the Guardian ad Litem' [1992] Fam Law 555.
3 *The Children Act 1989 Guidance and Regulations Vol 7 Guardians ad Litem and Other Court Related Issues* (HMSO, 1991) at para 2.2.
4 Section 41(2).
5 FPR 1991, r 4.11 and FPC(CA 1989)R 1991, r 11.
6 FPR 1991, r 4.11(4) and FPC(CA 1989)R 1991, r 11(4).
7 Ibid.

(2) file a written report advising on the interests of the child, not less than seven days before the date fixed for the hearing; and

(3) make such investigations as may be necessary for him to carry out his duties, including, in particular, interviewing, inspection of records and obtaining professional assistance.

Regarding the inspection of records, the Children Act, as amended by the Courts and Legal Services Act 1990[1], gives the GAL access to the records of social services departments which may be inspected and copies taken. This right does not, however, extend to the records of health authorities, except where health records form part of the local authority's own records[2]. As regards the GAL's report, the Act provides that the court may take account of any statement made by the GAL in the report and any evidence given in respect of matters referred to in it where, in its opinion, these are relevant to the issue it is considering[3]. The broad effect of this provision was to disapply the hearsay rule, reflecting the inquisitorial nature of children proceedings[4]. Children cases are, however, no longer distinctive in relation to the hearsay rule since, under the Civil Evidence Act 1995, hearsay is now admissible in civil proceedings generally.

Relationship between the GAL and the child's solicitor

Clearly, the GAL and the child's solicitor are required to work closely together in the child's best interests[5]. It will usually be the GAL who appoints and instructs the solicitor. Although the solicitor presents the child's case in court, he must act on the GAL's instructions in determining the manner of presentation. Difficulties can arise where the views of the GAL diverge from those of the child, especially if it is an older teenager who disagrees strongly with the GAL's view of his or her welfare. A particular problem may be a difference of opinion between the GAL and the solicitor about the competence of the child. It has been suggested[6] that this can lead to acute problems, for example in sexual abuse cases. Here, the solicitor may wish to take instructions from the child direct if, having taken into account the GAL's views and any court directions, he considers that the child wishes to give instructions which conflict with those of the GAL and he has sufficient understanding to do so. The rules allow him to deal directly with the child in these circumstances[7]. In this eventuality, the GAL remains in office and will continue to discharge all his duties other than instructing the solicitor[8].

The child's ability to instruct a solicitor was considered in *Re H (A Minor) (Care Proceedings: Child's Views)*[9]. In that case, Thorpe J emphasised that a child must

---

1   Section 42(1), and the Courts and Legal Services Act 1990, Sch 16, para 18.

2   For further analysis of s 42, see MDA Freeman *Children, Their Families and the Law* (Macmillan, 1992) at p 169.

3   Section 41(11).

4   On the shift towards inquisitorial procedures in children cases under the Children Act, see Chapter 2 above.

5   See, generally, P King and I Young *The Child as Client* (Family Law, 1992) at ch 7 and MR Bell and R Daley 'Social Workers and Solicitors: Working Together?' [1992] Fam Law 257.

6   MDA Freeman *Children, Their Families and the Law* (Macmillan, 1992) at p 168.

7   FPR 1991, r 4. 12(1)(a) and FPC(CA 1989)R 1991, r 12(1)(a).

8   He is entitled to legal representation but not to legal aid. See *The Children Act Advisory Committee Annual Report 1992/3* (Lord Chancellor's Department, 1993) at p 29. It is for the court to decide how the child should be represented in these circumstances. See *Re M (Minors) (Care Proceedings: Child's Wishes)* [1994] 1 FLR 749.

9   [1993] 1 FLR 440.

have sufficient understanding and rationality and that this may not be so where the child is suffering from intense emotional disturbance. Where there is any issue as to the child's rationality, the question should be the subject of specific expert opinion from experts already involved in the case.

The GAL panel service

Local authorities are required to set up panels from which GALs are drawn[1]. They must ensure that there are sufficient numbers of GALs to meet, in full, the requirements imposed on them by the legislation[2]. Because of the earlier involvement of GALs in proceedings, many panels have set up 'duty systems' to provide a quick response to requests for appointments. While the responsibility for management of the panels rests with the local authority, certain tasks may be delegated to other agencies such as voluntary organisations. The authority must appoint a panel manager who is responsible, inter alia, for: arranging the training, remuneration and administrative support of panel members; managing the panel budget; dealing with complaints about the service; and preparing an annual report on the panel's activities. A panel committee also has to be established, whose task is to assist with liaison between the local authority and the courts, in relation to the operation of the panel[3].

There has been considerable debate about the independence of panel members from the local authority, and this continues to be an issue[4]. GALs are either self-employed social workers (full-time or part-time) or self-employed probation officers. The danger of a conflict of interest is obvious, and rules of court seek to meet this difficulty. The person selected in a particular case must not:

(1) be a member, officer or servant of a local authority or authorised person party to the proceedings, unless employed solely as a member of the panel[5];
(2) be, or have been, at any time in the past, a member, officer or servant of a local authority or voluntary organisation directly concerned in arrangements for the care, accommodation or welfare of the child during the last five years[6]; or
(3) be a serving probation officer[7].

Despite these safeguards, the issue remains sensitive, since there is concern that the independence of GALs may be compromised by the fact that they are paid employees of the local authority. While acknowledging the legitimacy of this concern, the Children Act Advisory Committee, in its first Annual Report, took the view that funding per se need not threaten independence[8]. The courts, too, have been alive to the issue. In *R v Cornwall County Council*[9], Sir Stephen Brown P

---

1 Guardians ad Litem and Reporting Officers (Panels) Regulations 1991, SI 1991/2051, and s 41(7) of the Children Act.
2 Guardians ad Litem and Reporting Officers (Panels) Regulations 1991, SI 1991/2051, reg 2(3).
3 There is a wealth of information on matters relating to the operation of the panels in *The Children Act 1989 Guidance and Regulations Vol 7 Guardians ad Litem and Other Court Related Issues* (HMSO, 1991) at ch 2.
4 It was, for example, one of three issues singled out by *The Children Act Advisory Committee Annual Report 1992/3* (Lord Chancellor's Department, 1993) at pp 28–29.
5 FPR 1991, r 4.10(7)(a) and FPC(CA 1989)R 1991, r 10(7)(a).
6 FPR 1991, r 4.10(7)(b) and FPC(CA 1989)R 1991, r 10(7)(b).
7 FPR 1991, r 4.10(7)(c) and FPC(CA 1989)R 1991, r 10(7)(c). For a case in which this rule was contravened, see *Devon County Council and Others v S and Others* [1993] 1 FLR 842.
8 *The Children Act Advisory Committee Annual Report 1992/3* (above) at p 29.
9 [1992] 1 WLR 427.

quashed a decision of the local authority limiting the maximum number of hours which a GAL should spend on each case. The President emphasised the importance of the court and the public having confidence in the service, and GALs themselves feeling confident of their independent status. This independence should not be compromised in any way by placing restrictions, directly or indirectly, on the discharge of their statutory duties.

Private family proceedings

The contrast between representation for children in public and private proceedings could hardly be more striking. The issue can be disposed of much more quickly in the private context, since representation of the child, as such, occurs in only a tiny minority of cases. Objective assessments of the child's best interests through welfare reports take place in a larger number of cases, but the proportion of the total is still very small, principally because of the large number of divorce cases in which there is no dispute over children and no need for a court order. Sometimes children's interests are very intimately involved and there is no better illustration of this than divorce. There can be few matters which have the potential for affecting children so deeply as the breakdown of their parents' marriage, yet they are rarely represented in divorce proceedings, and welfare reports are usually only ordered in the small minority of cases in which there is a real contest over the arrangements for the children[1]. In certain other jurisdictions, there is a more systematic investigation of children's interests in private proceedings[2], and there is no doubt that the lack of provision for representation in English law has been influenced, to some extent, perhaps heavily, by resource implications – a fact indirectly acknowledged by the Law Commission[3]. It is, perhaps, a fair question to pose whether there is any justification, other than pressure on resources, for the preservation of the current distinctions between public and private law on this issue.

In recent years there has been increasing pressure from children's rights organisations for the creation of greater opportunities for the representation of children in private family proceedings. This pressure lead to the insertion of an empowering provision in the Family Law Act 1996[4]. Under this provision the Lord Chancellor may by regulations provide for the separate representation of children in certain specified private proceedings. The proceedings specified are those under Part II of the Family Law Act 1996 (divorce and separation); Part IV of the 1996 Act (occupation of the family home and domestic violence); the Matrimonial Causes Act 1973 (principally now proceedings relating to property and financial matters on divorce or annulment) and proceedings under the Domestic Proceedings and Magistrates' Courts Act 1978 (effectively now proceedings relating to financial relief during marriage). It should be noted that private Children Act proceedings are not specified and it should also be appreciated that

---

1 The court is not, however, confined to contested cases. See Chapter 4 above.
2 See, for example, the role of the family advocate in South Africa in I Schäfer 'The Family Advocate in South Africa' in A Bainham, DS Pearl and R Pickford (eds) *Frontiers of Family Law* (2nd edn) (John Wiley & Sons, 1995) at p 30.
3 See Law Com Report No 172 (1988) at para 6.15 where the Law Commission recognised that welfare officers' time was limited and 'must be targeted on the cases in which it will be most valuable'.
4 Section 64.

the regulations (which have not been made at the time of writing) 'may provide for such representation only in specified circumstances'[1]. As Freeman has pointed out[2], it may be that the regulations will provide that separate representation is not necessary where a court welfare officer is involved. Such a restriction, should it be imposed, would severely curtail the use of separate representation in private proceedings.

There remains the broader policy question of exactly how far it is desirable for children to be independently represented in such proceedings. Freeman deplores the 'unfortunate omission'[3] to include private Children Act proceedings in the range of specified civil proceedings and it is not difficult to visualise circumstances under which children ought to be represented in private disputes. *L v L (Minors) (Separate Representation)*[4] is a good illustration. Here, the parents and three children aged respectively 14, 12 and 9 were Australian. The parents had separated, the mother having formed a new relationship, and the children remained with their father. There was some suggestion that they might be taken back to Australia. There was a dispute as to residence and the amount of contact with the mother. The children expressed their view to the court welfare officer that existing contact with their mother was inadequate. The welfare officer took the position that she could not adequately reflect the views of the children in court and the judge therefore ordered the children to be separately represented by a solicitor from the child care panel. The Court of Appeal upheld this decision and also directed that the children be joined as parties to the proceedings.

Other instances in which children might appropriately be parties and separately represented spring to mind. Clearly, this would be so where a child is the applicant for an order under Part IV of the Family Law Act 1996 where, as previously discussed, the division between what is 'public' and what is 'private' is in any event artificial. In acrimonious divorce proceedings in which there is a bitter ongoing battle over the children, it is equally clear that the case for separate representation which acknowledges the conflict of interest between the parents and the children is also very strong. But these cases are exceptional. The overwhelming majority of divorce cases are not like this. There is not usually a dispute over the children and in a very high proportion of cases an order in relation to the children is neither sought nor necessary[5]. It would therefore seem right that, unlike in public proceedings in which a conflict of interest between parents and children is rightly presumed, in private proceedings independent representation should continue to be regarded as exceptional but nevertheless important in the minority of cases in which there is a real dispute and real conflict.

Welfare reports in private proceedings

Some of the principles applying to welfare reports have already been noted[6] and they will not be repeated here. Instead, we will focus briefly on the essential differences between representation by a GAL in public proceedings and the

---

1   Section 64(2).
2   M Freeman *The Family Law Act 1996* (Sweet & Maxwell's Legislation Handbook, 1996) annotations to s 64.
3   Ibid at the Introduction.
4   [1994] 1 FLR 156.
5   See Chapter 4 above.
6   Section 7, and Chapter 4 above.

involvement of welfare officers in private cases. We also touch upon the role of the Official Solicitor in wardship proceedings, which is somewhat different from that of either GALs or welfare officers.

The first point to emphasise is that a welfare officer is *not* the child's representative and his role is not to represent the child's interest. Rather, it is to provide the court with an objective evaluation, through a report, of the child and his background. There is no reason, in principle, why the court should not appoint a GAL *and* seek a welfare report, but the Court of Appeal has warned against unnecessary duplication which might occur where two reports are obtained[1]. Such cases are therefore likely to be rare.

Welfare reports are obtained from either court welfare officers, who are qualified probation workers, often specialising in family work, or from officers of the local authority. However, it is unlikely that the latter would be asked to report, unless the authority is already involved with the child or the family[2].

The duty of the welfare officer is to conduct a thorough investigation of the child's circumstances and prepare a written report for the court. This investigation must extend beyond the child himself, to all other members of the child's family and adult figures in the child's life. This entails interviewing all relevant parties and, perhaps also, inquiries among relatives, the child's school or health authorities. Conciliation is not part of the welfare officer's function and should not be undertaken[3]. When his investigations are completed, the welfare officer produces a report which must be filed in the time prescribed by the court or, in any event, within 14 days of the hearing[4]. This will then be served on the parties, and on the GAL, where one is appointed. Only the parties, their legal representatives, the GAL, the legal aid authorities and a welfare officer are entitled to have access to the report, without the leave of the court[5]. In due course, the welfare officer must, unless excused by the court, attend the hearing, and may be questioned about the report by the court or the parties[6]. The influence of welfare reports on the ultimate decision of the court was considered previously[7].

What are the salient differences between the process of obtaining welfare reports and representation by a GAL? In essence, the welfare officer is an officer of the court with an investigative and reporting role. He is in no sense a representative or witness for the child or any other party. There are, of course, some similarities in what welfare officers and GALs do, but the functions of the latter are much wider than just investigation and report. It is the representative element of their duties which is the real point of distinction. Apart from the small

---

1   *Re S (A Minor) (Guardian ad Litem/Welfare Officer)* [1993] 1 FLR 110, a *public* case concerning the question of whether an additional report from a welfare officer should be obtained where an appointed GAL already had responsibility to provide a report. Cf *Re W (Welfare Reports)* [1995] 2 FLR 142, discussed in Chapter 4 above, which confirms that the court has an unfettered discretion to order more than one welfare report where it considers this appropriate. For a general comparison of the roles of the court welfare officer and the GAL, see C Jackson 'Reporting on Children: The Guardian ad Litem, the court welfare officer and the Children Act 1989' [1992] Fam Law 252.

2   See the discussion in *Bromley's Family Law* (8th edn) (Butterworths, 1992) at p 378.

3   *Scott v Scott* [1986] 2 FLR 320, and *Re H (Conciliation: Welfare Reports)* [1986] 1 FLR 476.

4   FPR 1991, r 4.13(1) and FPC(CA 1989)R 1991, r 13(1).

5   FPR 1991, r 4.23(1) and FPC(CA 1989)R 1991, r 23(1).

6   FPR 1991, r 4.13(3) and FPC(CA 1989)R 1991, r 13(3).

7   At Chapter 4 above.

proportion of private cases in which children are actually joined as parties, as the law stands, they will be unrepresented either by a GAL or a solicitor. A further point of distinction is that there is no *presumption* of welfare involvement in private cases which corresponds to the statutory presumption of representation by a GAL in public cases. It is certainly arguable that more still needs to be done to ensure an adequate voice for the child and representation of his independent interests and views in the private sphere, and it remains to be seen how far this will be taken under the empowering provisions of the Family Law Act 1996.

The appointment of the Official Solicitor in private proceedings

Wardship proceedings continue to take place in the private law context despite the reforms. Wardship has always been special and has many peculiarities which emphasise the inquisitorial, rather than adversarial, nature of the proceedings[1]. The nature of wardship involves a wide-ranging investigation into the circumstances of the child and this often results in the appointment of the Official Solicitor to represent the ward. Appointments are not, however, routinely made[2] but are made in complex or sensitive cases, perhaps involving serious medical issues or a foreign element. The Official Solicitor is often appointed to represent older children in dispute with their carers, usually, but not invariably, where they have formed what is considered to be an 'undesirable association'[3].

The appointment of the Official Solicitor in family proceedings is now the subject of a detailed Practice Note[4] which governs not only the specified public proceedings discussed earlier but also the appointment in 'non-specified' private law proceedings under the Children Act and proceedings under the inherent jurisdiction of the High Court (which include wardship). In brief, the principles are as follows.

In most private cases, the child's interests will be sufficiently safeguarded by a court welfare officer's report. Only where this is not so will the consideration of the appointment of the Official Solicitor arise and, even then, involvement should be seen as exceptional rather than automatic. He will accept appointment where, in these exceptional circumstances, it is desirable that the child be separately represented. Such exceptional cases include those with a foreign element, exceptional or difficult points of law, unusual or complicating features, or conflicting or controversial medical evidence; those where a child is ignorant of the truth of his parentage or is refusing contact with a parent and where there may be a need for a psychiatric assessment; and those where the Official Solicitor is acting for the child in other proceedings. In certain types of case the Official Solicitor will almost invariably accept appointment. These include cases where there is doubt as to the child's competence to instruct a solicitor[5]; where the child is represented but the court needs the Official Solicitor's assistance as amicus curiae[6]; where difficult issues of medical confidentiality arise[7]; and in 'special

---

1   See, generally, NV Lowe and R White *Wards of Court* (2nd edn) (Barry Rose/Kluwer, 1986) and *Bromley's Family Law* (above) at pp 468–469.
2   See *Practice Direction* [1982] 1 All ER 319.
3   The so-called 'teenage wardships'.
4   [1995] 2 FLR 479.
5   See *Re CT (A Minor) (Wardship Representation)* [1993] 2 FLR 278 and *Re S (A Minor) (Independent Representation)* [1993] Fam 263.
6   *Re H (A Minor) (Role of Official Solicitor)* [1993] 2 FLR 552.
7   *Note: HIV Tests* [1994] 2 FLR 116.

category' cases, such as those involving sterilisation and abortion, where application should be made under the inherent jurisdiction[1]. The Official Solicitor may also act as next friend to a child seeking leave to make an application or in respect of a mother who is herself a minor and whose child is the subject of the proceedings. The Official Solicitor should also be consulted in all cases where it is sought to restrain publicity about a child[2].

Where an appointment is made, the child will be joined as a party in the proceedings and the Official Solicitor will act as the GAL. The Official Solicitor has something of a hybrid role, combining the functions of GALs and welfare officers and those of a lawyer. Thus, as well as representing the ward, he is his own solicitor and may represent the child in the conduct of the proceedings[3]. Yet he is also, like welfare officers, an officer of the court, responsible for conducting the investigation into the child's circumstances, reporting to the court and making recommendations to it about how best to protect the ward's welfare. The Official Solicitor's staff, unlike panel GALs and court welfare officers, are not trained in social work but have acquired specialist skills in the particular kinds of cases in which the Official Solicitor's Department has traditionally been involved[4]. Sometimes the Official Solicitor will 'sub-contract' his work in private proceedings to GALs who may be members of the panel but not acting in their capacity as panel members[5].

EVIDENCE

How is evidence obtained in children cases? Are children themselves competent to give evidence and, if so, ought their evidence to be given the same credence as that of adults, or ought allowances to be made for the age of the child witness? Should the legal system make special arrangements for accommodating child witnesses to counteract the ordeal of a court appearance, often arising in connection with alleged abuse of the child concerned? Ought children to attend court at all[6]? These are some of the questions which law reform agencies have had to face in recent years. In considering the answers which the legal system currently gives to these questions, it is necessary to distinguish between *civil* and *criminal* proceedings.

Family proceedings are civil proceedings, and the dominant principle is that the importance of the child's welfare requires the court to have regard to *all*

1　*Re HG (Specific Issue Order: Sterilisation)* [1993] 1 FLR 587.
2　*Re H (Minors) (Injunction: Public Interest)* [1994] 1 FLR 519.
3　FPR 1991, r 9.2.
4　For a comparison of the work of the role of panel GALs and the Official Solicitor's staff, see J Masson 'The Official Solicitor as the child's guardian ad litem under the Children Act 1989' (1992) 4 JCL 58.
5　See *The Children Act Advisory Committee Annual Report 1992/3* (Lord Chancellor's Department, 1993) at p 29 for discussion of some of the difficulties which have arisen.
6　The most comprehensive treatment of these issues and of children's evidence generally is JR Spencer and R Flin *The Evidence of Children* (2nd edn) (Blackstone Press, 1993). See also H Dent and R Flin (eds) *Children as Witnesses* (1992), especially JR Spencer 'Reforming the Law on Children's Evidence in England: The Pigot Committee and After' at ch 7. See JR Spencer, G Nicholson, R Flin and R Bull (eds) *Children's Evidence in Legal Proceedings* (1990), distributed

available evidence[1]. This gave rise to a substantial relaxation in the ordinary rules of evidence, most particularly the hearsay rule. While this had long been a feature of some children proceedings, especially wardship, the effect of the Children Act was to extend the principle more generally to civil cases involving children.

In contrast, in criminal proceedings, the primary focus is not on the welfare of the child victim or witness but on the issue of the guilt or innocence of the accused. That being the case, a balance has to be struck between the needs of children in court as witnesses, whether victims or not, and the traditional safeguards afforded the accused by English criminal procedure. This involves weighing the potential benefits to children of being spared certain aspects of the ordeal of appearing in court against possible prejudice to the accused which might thereby be occasioned. There has been a perceptible shift in thinking in recent years. This reflects a growing appreciation that justice is not served if children are so intimidated by the legal process that their evidence is rendered less reliable or, more seriously, that they feel unable to give evidence at all.

Civil proceedings

There are perhaps three major issues concerning civil proceedings. The first is the question whether a child is *entitled* to attend court or can be *compelled* to attend as a witness. The second is the question of the *competence* of child witnesses and the weight to be attached to their *own* evidence. The third is how *other* evidence is obtained.

Attendance at court and compellability
There are really two sides to this question. The first is whether children are *entitled* to attend family proceedings affecting them when they wish to do so. The second is whether they can be *compelled* to attend as witnesses where they do *not* wish to do so. These issues have been addressed mainly in the context of care proceedings.

It used to be the case that children over the age of five were required to attend care proceedings if an interim care order was to be made[2]. However, now, under the Children Act[3] the court has a discretion which can mean that they may be required to attend where they do *not* wish to do so or may not be allowed to attend where they *do*. The higher courts have generally discouraged the attendance of children and prefer to rely on obtaining evidence about the child's situation from adults[4], although children often attend hearings in the magistrates' family

---

by the Faculty of Law, University of Cambridge. See also the report by the Royal College of Psychiatrists *The Evidence of Children* (1996) Council Report CR 44.

1 For a recent illustration of this principle, see *Re S (Contact: Evidence)* [1998] 1 FLR 798, where the Court of Appeal granted leave to issue a subpoena duces tecum to compel production of video evidence held by the police. The father wished to challenge allegations of sexual abuse of his five-year-old daughter with whom he had hitherto enjoyed extensive contact but which was now under threat. The court held that it had a duty to decide whether the allegations were true and could not allow the local authority or the police to decide the case. The court needed to have access to the best available evidence, and the parents had to have the opportunity of considering it.

2 Children and Young Persons Act 1969, s 22.

3 Children Act 1989, s 95(1).

4 See, for example, *Re C (A Minor) (Care: Child's Wishes)* [1993] 1 FLR 832 and *Re W (Secure Accommodation Order: Attendance at Court)* [1994] 2 FLR 1092.

proceedings court[1]. Exclusion of children from civil proceedings has been criticised by Masson[2] who contrasts the position with the shift in social work practices towards the participation of children in meetings and case conferences and with the requirement that the child must attend criminal proceedings. She finds it 'paradoxical that children should be excluded when the "benign jurisdiction" is being exercised but required to attend in the punitive atmosphere of the criminal courts'.

So far as compelling children to attend as witnesses is concerned, the courts have made it plain that a party may not demand as of right that a child attend if this would have an adverse effect on the child and there is an alternative means of introducing the child's evidence into the proceedings. The leading case is *R v B County Council, ex parte P*[3] in which the Court of Appeal upheld the decision of the magistrates not to issue a witness summons against a 17-year-old girl who had accused her step-father of sexually abusing her. In the care proceedings the step-father sought to have her called (the local authority having decided not to do so itself) principally as a way of having her cross-examined. The Court of Appeal held that it was for the local authority to determine what evidence was required to support its case in the care proceedings and that the decision not to call the girl was not amenable to judicial review. A summons should not be issued where its effect would be oppressive or so inimical to the child's welfare as to outweigh the legitimate interest of the person seeking to call her. As Butler-Sloss LJ put it:

> 'Research has shown the adverse effects upon some children of the requirement to give evidence in cases of sexual abuse. In cases of young children, such harm may well be inferred. ... The introduction of the Order of 1990 [now the Children (Admissibility of Hearsay Evidence) Order 1993, SI 1993/621] clearly envisages an alternative to oral evidence and cross-examination and to make it possible for children making allegations of, inter alia, sexual abuse to do so without the additional stress of a court hearing. The philosophy behind the Children Act 1989 would be thwarted by the abuser himself being able to require the attendance of the child at court. A court should be very cautious in requiring the attendance of a child in these cases, reinforced as it must be by considerations as to how to deal with refusal to give evidence after the issue of the summons.'

At the same time, the court did acknowledge one possible disadvantage in the failure of the child to give evidence, namely that this may weaken the case against the alleged abuser because issues will arise about the *weight* which ought to be attached to hearsay evidence. The court warned that magistrates should take great care in assessing how much weight is to be attached to the hearsay evidence of statements from children of mature years making serious allegations against a parent, where there has been no opportunity for cross-examination. It was accepted that different considerations would apply in the case of young children.

The Court of Appeal has recently given further guidance on the principles applicable to the issue of a witness summons against a child in care proceedings. In *Re P (Witness Summons)*[4] the court made it clear that in taking into account the great relevance of the child's welfare, the matter was not, however, governed by the 'welfare principle' as such since the issue was not one which related to the

---

1   For a more detailed discussion, see J Fortin *Children's Rights and the Developing Law* (Butterworths, 1998) at pp 179–182.
2   J Masson 'Representations of Children' (1996) *Current Legal Problems* 245 at pp 259–262.
3   [1991] 1 WLR 221.
4   [1997] 2 FLR 447.

child's upbringing[1]. The court went to say that, in principle, the older the child the more likely it was that the application to call the child would succeed. It was, however, to be expected that in most cases involving a child aged 12 or younger (here, the girl was 12) the court would favour the absence of oral evidence even though that might mean weakening, perhaps even fatally, the evidence against the adult.

Children as witnesses: competence

The difficulty with child witnesses before the Children Act was that the civil law required them to understand the nature of an oath before being allowed to give evidence. While this is usually assumed in the case of an adult, this is not so with a child. The court will inquire into the *competence* of a child under the age of 14 years who is to be sworn in. The leading case is *R v Hayes*, in which Bridge LJ identified the important consideration as being:

'whether the child has a sufficient appreciation of the solemnity of the occasion and the added responsibility to tell the truth, which is involved in taking an oath, over and above the duty to tell the truth which is an ordinary duty of normal social conduct.'[2]

The problem with this test is that, while some children may make competent and credible witnesses[3], they will not necessarily understand abstract concepts like an oath or 'the truth' or the technicalities of the legal system. Rhona Flin has given some colourful illustrations, from a study of child witnesses, of some of the misconceptions which children have about 'law'[4]. Thus, a six-year-old child offered the view that judges 'teach people dancing'; a 10-year-old child said of a jury, 'They ask the criminal questions, then he gives up and they sit down'; an eight-year-old child thought that a lawyer 'gives money to the poor'; and some children in a similar US study thought that a lawyer 'loans money', 'sits around', 'plays golf' or 'lies'[5].

The Children Act 1989 sought to overcome these difficulties, by abolishing the competency requirement and admitting the *unsworn* evidence of children, subject to a different test. This test, which formerly governed the admission of unsworn evidence of children of 'tender years' in *criminal* proceedings[6], is based on more general powers of understanding. It allows children with the requisite level of understanding to give unsworn evidence which is not dependent on appreciation of an oath. It provides that a child's evidence may be heard, notwithstanding the child's inability to understand the nature of an oath, where the court is of the opinion that:

'(a) he understands that it is his duty to speak the truth; and
(b) he has sufficient understanding to justify his evidence being heard.'[7]

This provision applies only where a child is, in fact, incapable of understanding an oath under the *Hayes* test. Thus, children may now conceivably give sworn *or* unsworn evidence in civil proceedings depending on their level of understanding.

---

1 On the application of the welfare principle generally, see Chapter 2.
2 [1977] 1 WLR 234 at p 237.
3 As to which see JR Spencer and R Flin *The Evidence of Children* (2nd edn) (Blackstone Press, 1993) at ch 11, and R Flin 'Child Witnesses: The Psychological Evidence' (1988) 138 NLJ 608.
4 R Flin 'Child Witnesses: The Psychological Evidence' (above).
5 Ibid at p 610.
6 Children and Young Persons Act 1933, s 38.
7 Section 96(1) and (2).

It is younger children who are more likely to give evidence unsworn. There remains the question of the credibility or weight which ought to be attached to the evidence of particular child witnesses, but this is also an issue in relation to adults.

Other evidence in family proceedings

Hearsay

The key feature of civil proceedings involving children is now the disapplication of the hearsay rule, although under the Civil Evidence Act 1995 it has now been disapplied more generally in civil cases. This general rule of evidence, where it applies, renders inadmissible as proof of facts evidence given by someone as to what someone else said or did. If applied in children cases it could prevent the court from relying on evidence in welfare reports and the reports of GALs about what children said to the writer of the report, perhaps concerning incidents of abuse.

The rule was abolished in all *civil* proceedings affecting children[1] before its more general abolition in civil proceedings, the result being that the court can admit a wide range of documentary evidence[2] and simultaneously avert the need for the child to attend court and give oral evidence[3]. While the grounds for challenging the *admissibility* of hearsay have thus been removed, the *weight* to be given to hearsay evidence is a matter within the discretion of the judge, and it is even open to him to disregard it completely[4]. Such weight may well diminish in the case of second or even more remote hearsay. Where it is the child's hearsay evidence, the court will need to take into account factors such as the child's age, the context and circumstances in which the statement was made, the child's previous behaviour, etc. It may also take account of the child's opportunities to have acquired the information elsewhere, and any predilection he may have for fantasising or telling untruths. The courts have also taken the view that, in cases of alleged sexual abuse, the court should rarely be satisfied of the abuse on the balance of probabilities purely on the strength of an unsupported allegation by the child[5].

The rules admitting hearsay are very important in care and other public law proceedings. Prior to the Children Act 1989, care proceedings took place exclusively in the juvenile court – a specialised magistrates' court[6]. Magistrates, subject to limited exceptions, had to apply the hearsay rule and refuse to admit hearsay statements and documentary evidence, such as reports, as evidence of the facts to which they related. The *Review of Child Care Law* recommended an extension of the rules of civil evidence to care proceedings[7]. The broad effect of

---

1 Children (Admissibility of Hearsay Evidence) Order 1993, SI 1993/621, made under the Children Act, s 96(3).
2 Formerly this was largely proved by means of affidavits but these have now been displaced by written statements.
3 On the attendance of children in care proceedings, see pp 459–461 et seq above.
4 See *Re W (Minors) (Wardship: Evidence)* [1990] 1 FLR 203 and *R v B County Council ex parte P* [1991] 1 FLR 470.
5 Ibid.
6 Now replaced by the youth court. The civil side of the former juvenile court's work has now been taken over by the family proceedings court. On the implications of the change from the juvenile court to the youth court, see the research of C Ball 'Youth justice and the youth court – the end of a separate system?' [1995] CFLQ 196.
7 DHSS *Review of Child Care Law* (1985) at paras 16.30–16.38.

s 96 of the Children Act was to apply the new rules in *all* civil proceedings affecting children[1], including care proceedings, which should always start in the magistrates' family proceedings court.

The relaxation of the rules of evidence in children cases has other implications. In recent years the courts have made it clear that normal rules of evidence applicable in an adversarial legal system do not necessarily apply in children cases[2]. This is especially so regarding the disclosure of documents[3]. Thus, parents are required to disclose to the court all the documents in their possession, including expert reports commissioned by them, even if they are not favourable to their case[4]. Likewise, the local authority must disclose to the parents all relevant documents in its possession[5].

Examination and assessment of the child

The court carefully controls the medical examination or other assessment of children[6]. No person may, without the leave of the court, medically or psychiatrically examine or otherwise assess a child, for the purpose of preparing evidence for use in any proceedings[7]. Without such leave, any evidence resulting from the examination or assessment is inadmissible. This rule is complementary to the right of a competent child to refuse to undergo such examinations or assessments[8].

The privilege against self-incrimination

In a further attempt to ensure that the court in public law cases hears *all* evidence relevant to the welfare of children, the Children Act[9] removed the privilege against self-incrimination in relation to proceedings under Part IV (care and supervision) and Part V (EPOs and CAOs). In these proceedings, a person is not to be excused from giving evidence on any matter, or answering any question put to him in the course of giving evidence, on the ground that doing so might incriminate him or his spouse of an offence. The provision is something of a 'trade-off' since, in return for the loss of this privilege, any such statement or admission will not be admissible in evidence against the person making it, or his spouse, for any offence other than perjury[10]. It should be remembered that many

---

1 The rule is thus also disapplied in civil proceedings which fall outside the definition of family proceedings in the Children Act.
2 For a general discussion of these developments, see C Tapper 'Evidential privilege in cases involving children' [1997] CFLQ 1, L Mendoza 'Confidentiality in Child Proceedings' [1998] Fam Law 30, and J McEwan 'The privilege of parents and the protection of the child – where do priorities lie?' in C Bridge (ed) *Family Law Towards the Millennium: Essays for PM Bromley* (Butterworths, 1997) at ch 5.
3 The issue of disclosure has involved the courts in a delicate balancing exercise involving conflicting considerations of public policy. For particularly good illustrations of the difficult balance which must be struck and how the courts go about it, see *A County Council v W and Others (Disclosure)* [1997] 1 FLR 574 and *Re R (Disclosure)* [1998] 1 FLR 433.
4 See *Oxfordshire County Council v M* [1994] 2 All ER 269 and *Re L (Minors) (Police Investigation: Privilege)* [1996] 1 FLR 731.
5 *R v Hampshire County Council, ex parte K* [1990] 2 All ER 129.
6 FPR 1991, r 4.18 and FPC(CA 1989)R 1991, r 18.
7 FPR 1991, r 18(1) and FPC(CA 1989)R 1991, r 18(1).
8 See Chapter 8 above.
9 Section 98(1).
10 Section 98(2).

instances of child abuse or neglect are also criminal offences[1] and could lead to prosecution. The rule is thus of considerable importance where the allegation of significant harm to the child is founded on accusations of parental abuse.

The courts have, however, drawn a distinction between investigation by the police and prosecution. Thus, while court documents and transcripts in family proceedings may not be admitted as evidence in any subsequent criminal proceedings, they may well be disclosed to the police to assist them with their investigations – especially bearing in mind the need to protect *other* children not involved in the family proceedings[2]. It has also been held by the House of Lords that medical reports prepared by a medical expert engaged by a parent in care proceedings are not protected by legal professional privilege and may be disclosed to the police[3].

Criminal proceedings

The three major issues relating to child witnesses in criminal proceedings have been identified as *competence, credibility* and *stress*[4]. Before considering these issues, the preliminary question arises, as it does in relation to civil proceedings, whether a child is a compellable witness in criminal proceedings. The general rule is that a child *can* be compelled to attend and give evidence in any criminal trial[5]. A child's failure to give evidence would, at least in theory, amount to contempt of court unless the child was aged under 10 and thus below the age of criminal responsibility. But, again, in deciding whether to issue a witness summons against the child, the court must balance the interests of justice and fairness to the accused against the possible detriment to the child in having to appear.

In *R v Highbury Corner Magistrates' Court ex parte D*[6] the defendant to an assault charge relating to this former cohabitant sought to have a witness summons issued against their nine-year-old son who saw the incident. The materiality of the witness was accepted but the metropolitan magistrate refused to issue the summons taking the view that the detriment to the boy's welfare if he were obliged to give evidence outweighed the interests of the defendant. His judgment was set aside in judicial review proceedings on the basis that it was premature. The balancing act,

---

1 See Chapter 14 below.
2 See *Re EC (Disclosure of Material)* [1996] 2 FLR 725 and *Re G (A Minor) (Social Worker: Disclosure)* [1996] 1 WLR 1407.
3 *Re L (Police Investigation: Privilege)* [1996] 1 FLR 731. In this case the report cast doubt on the mother's account of accidental ingestion of methadone by her child. See also *Re M (Disclosure)* [1998] 1 FLR 734 in which the Court of Appeal ordered disclosure of litigation materials in care proceedings not just to the police (as the judge had determined) but also to the health authority. The court emphasised that the child protection conference relied upon the contribution made by the relevant medical and health professionals and that the judge's attempt to exclude them from the conference at which disclosure would be made to the police was absurd. Another recent decision of the Court of Appeal which also emphasises the importance of the inter-agency partnership in child protection which may require disclosure is *Re W (Disclosure to Police)* [1998] 2 FLR 135. Here, the court said that this partnership required the sharing and exchange of relevant information between social workers and the police when the withholding of information will prejudice the welfare of children and that a judge should hesitate before refusing to provide significant information to the police.
4 R Flin 'Child Witnesses: The Psychological Evidence' (1988) 138 NLJ 608.
5 Criminal Procedure (Attendance of Witnesses) Act 1965, s 2(2); Magistrates' Courts Act 1980, s 97.
6 [1997] 1 FLR 683.

it was held, should be performed at the court of trial when the moment arose and a decision had to be taken on whether to call the child. Schiemann LJ pointed out that, by that stage, the picture may have become clearer since something might, or might not, be admitted. It is also evident from the tenor of the judgment that the court in criminal cases should take into account not merely the welfare of children but also their *duties* as citizens to society to an extent appropriate to their age and understanding[1]. This might suggest that a witness summons is perhaps more likely to be issued against a child in criminal than in civil proceedings.

Competence

There was, until recently, only one way in which a child under 14 years of age could give evidence in civil proceedings (ie sworn). Now, as discussed earlier, there are two ways (ie sworn and unsworn). Confusingly, the converse is true of criminal proceedings. For, whereas before the recent reforms the child under 14 years of age could give evidence in two ways (sworn and unsworn)[2], now there is only one way (unsworn)[3]. The situation is a classic illustration of the problems of piecemeal reform.

Under the amended provision introduced by the Criminal Justice Act 1991[4] it was feared that the statutory test might operate harshly to exclude the evidence of young children who were incapable of understanding the abstract concepts involved in the duty to tell the truth[5]. These concerns have now been met by a further amendment to the Criminal Justice Act 1988 made by the Criminal Justice and Public Order Act 1994[6]. Under the new provision, an intelligibility test governs the issue of competence as follows:

> 'A child's evidence shall be received unless it appears to the court that the child is incapable of giving intelligible testimony.'

The Court of Appeal in *R v Hampshire*[7] has agreed with the view of John Spencer[8] that this 'appears to be a less rigorous test of competence than that derived from s 38 of the 1933 Act' in that 'it appears to remove the need to determine on a question of competence, whether a child knows the difference between truth and a lie and the importance of speaking the truth'.

The new requirement prescribes no minimum age for competence so that, in principle, a child of any age might pass the test. In *DPP v M*[9] the Divisional Court allowed the prosecution's appeal by way of case stated where, on appeal to the Crown Court, that court had refused to view the video-taped evidence of a four-year-old girl (the victim of an alleged indecent assault by a 12-year-old boy). The Crown Court had taken the view that by reason of her age alone she was not a

---

1 On the concept of children's duties, see Chapter 3. See also *Re F (Specific Issue: Child Interview)* [1995] 1 FLR 819 and the remarks of Lord Donaldson in *Re A (A Minor) (Wardship: Witness in Criminal Proceedings)* [1991] 2 FLR 95 on which the court relied.
2 Children and Young Persons Act 1933, s 38.
3 Criminal Justice Act 1991, s 52, inserting s 33A into the Criminal Justice Act 1988.
4 Ibid.
5 See, particularly, J Spencer 'Children's Evidence and the Criminal Justice Bill' (1990) 140 NLJ 1750.
6 Section 33A(2A) of the 1988 Act, inserted by Sch 9, para 33 to the 1994 Act.
7 [1995] 2 All ER 1019.
8 *Archbold News* (1994) issue 6. See also M Childs 'Children's Evidence in Criminal Cases' [1996] CFLQ 81.
9 [1997] 2 All ER 749.

witness on whom they should rely. The Divisional Court held that the statutory test of intelligibility was mandatory and that the child's evidence *must* be received whatever her age, unless it appeared to the court that she was incapable of giving intelligible testimony. There was no wider discretion to refuse to receive it. In order to make this assessment, the judge should watch any video-taped interviews or ask various general questions of the child, or both, to determine whether she was able to understand questions and to answer them in a coherent and comprehensible manner. In this case, the extreme youth of the complainant properly raised concern as to her competence but it was not of itself conclusive.

It has also been held by the Divisional Court in *G v DPP*[1] that whether or not a child is capable of giving intelligible evidence is a simple test well within the capacity of a judge or magistrate and that it does not require any input from an expert.

Credibility

The next question is, having admitted the evidence of a child, how credible is it? At common law, the judge was required to warn the jury about convicting on the strength of a child's uncorroborated evidence. Similar warnings were, until recently, given in sexual cases whether the alleged victim was a child or an adult.

The Pigot Committee, reporting in 1989[2], was highly critical of the corroboration rules in sex cases and recommended their abolition. It disapproved of the underlying assumption that women or children were more likely to be untruthful than the ordinary experience and knowledge of jurors might suggest. The corroboration rule as it applied to children was grounded in the notion that children have a propensity for imagining things, lack moral responsibility, have weaker powers of observation and recollection, and are more likely to be open to suggestion. On the last point, similar claims were made for many years in family proceedings and have been used as a reason for discounting, or treating with suspicion, the views of children on residence or contact questions[3]. These claims did not appear to be substantiated by the psychological evidence. Thus, it was asserted by some psychologists[4] that moral understanding is not proved to be a reliable predictor of honesty in *adults* (and hence should not be seen as such for children either), and that moral knowledge should not be equated with intelligence. Moreover, it was said that comparisons between children and adults were often founded on an exaggerated view of adult competence.

The Criminal Justice Act 1988[5] went some way towards meeting these objections, by abolishing the corroboration rule in relation to children. It is provided that:

> 'Any requirement whereby at a trial on indictment it is obligatory for the court to give the jury a warning about convicting the accused on the uncorroborated evidence of a child is abrogated in relation to cases where such a warning is required by reason only that the evidence is the evidence of a child.'[6]

---

1 [1997] 2 All ER 755.
2 *The Report of the Advisory Group on Video Evidence* (Home Office, 1989), as to which see, generally, J McEwan 'In the Box or on the Box? The Pigot Report and Child Witnesses' [1990] Crim LR 363.
3 See Chapter 4 above.
4 See, for example, R Flin 'Child Witnesses: The Psychological Evidence' (1988) 138 NLJ 608.
5 Section 34(2).
6 The provision applies only to 'trials on indictment'. *Quaere* whether magistrates have to apply it by implication.

The effect of this reform is that it is now at least possible for a conviction to be sustained solely on the basis of the unsworn evidence of a single child, and it also allows the unsworn evidence of one child to be corroborated by the evidence of another child. The 1988 Act did not, however, strike at the rule requiring an official warning regarding the uncorroborated evidence of a *sexual* complainant. In many cases the child might well be the victim of a sexual offence. However, the former mandatory requirement of a warning in sexual cases has now also been abolished by s 32 of the Criminal Justice and Public Order Act 1994.

The effect of these reforms is to remove the obligatory judicial warnings and to leave the question of what warning (if any) is appropriate to the judge's discretion. The Court of Appeal (Criminal Division)[1] has said that whether the judge chooses to give a warning and in what terms will depend on the circumstances of the case, the issues raised, the context and quality of the witness's evidence and whether there is any evidential basis for suggesting that the evidence of the witnesses may be unreliable. Moreover, where such a warning is given the judge shoud give it as part of his general review of the evidence and his comments to the jury on how they should evaluate it. Any warning should not be delivered in the traditional manner used when corroboration warnings were mandatory.

Stress

Anyone who has been a witness in court will know that it can be a stressful and worrying experience. These natural anxieties can be magnified in the case of children to such an extent that they may break down in the witness box or become unable to continue at all. Most of the cases will involve highly distasteful sexual allegations. The prospect of the child having to relive the experience in the presence of the alleged offender will be harrowing. It is one reason why many prosecutions for sexual offences against children either failed to get off the ground at all, collapsed, or resulted in acquittals.

Use of screens and other assistance

The courts have tried to mitigate the problem through a number of ad hoc devices. As long ago as 1919, in *Smellie*'s case[2], the defendant was required by the judge to sit on the stairs leading out of the dock, out of sight of his 11-year-old daughter whom he was alleged to have beaten for stealing[3]. The Court of Appeal dismissed Smellie's appeal, rejecting arguments by defence counsel that the girl might be inclined to say untrue things which she would not have said in her father's presence, and that the jury might be adversely influenced by his removal. Lord Coleridge LCJ laconically responded that there was nothing to prevent the judge from securing the ends of justice by removing the accused from a witness he might intimidate.

More recently, in *R v X*[4], the Court of Appeal approved the use of wooden screens to conceal the victims from the defendants during the victims' evidence. In this case, the children in question were alleged to have been abused 'in almost every permutation of sexual perversion'. Counsel could plainly see the children, and the judge expressly warned the jury not to allow the mere presence of the

---

1   *R v Makanjuola; R v Easton* [1995] 3 All ER 730.
2   (1919) 14 Cr App R 128.
3   The actual conviction was for 'assaulting, ill-treating and neglecting' his daughter.
4   *R v X; R v Y; R v Z* [1990] Crim LR 515.

screen to prejudice them in any way against the defendants. In refusing leave to appeal, the court emphasised that the trial judge had to see that justice was done. This meant that he had to ensure that the system operated fairly, not only to the defendants, but also to the prosecution and the witnesses. It was a matter of the balance of fairness, and the judge had been right to conclude that the necessity of trying to ensure that the children were able to give evidence outweighed any possible prejudice to the defendants. To some extent, the usefulness of screens has now been overtaken by video technology, but they remain an alternative in those courts, particularly magistrates' courts, where the new technology is not available[1].

In *R v Smith*[2], the Court of Appeal considered the balance which has to be struck between the need to protect a child witness and the interests of justice and possible prejudice to the defendant. The accused here was convicted of rape and gross indecency with a 12-year-old girl. He appealed against his conviction on the basis of alleged procedural irregularities at the trial. During her evidence, a social worker had sat beside the girl. When the girl broke into tears the social worker had comforted her and talked quietly to her. After lunch, and while the jury were present but before the judge returned, the complainant had left court through the judge's door accompanied by, among others, the judge's clerk and the social worker. It transpired that she had been taken to a lavatory to avoid possible confrontation with the defendant's relatives who were outside court.

Dismissing the appeal, the Court of Appeal held that it was the judge's duty to order a procedure which reduces the strain on child witnesses without prejudicing the interests of the defendant. In this case it was clear that there had been no contact between the child witness and the judge and any allegations of procedural irregularity should have been made by counsel at the trial. The court went on to say that in future it was important that anyone providing comfort or support to a child witness should not talk to the child while she is giving evidence and that this should be made clear publicly. To do otherwise would arouse suspicions that something was being said about the evidence. It was therefore desirable that anyone performing that role should say as little as possible to the witness and preferably nothing.

---

1   Crown Court centres equipped with live television facilities and suitable for transfer of cases involving video evidence by children are listed in a Practice Note issued by Lord Taylor of Gosforth LCJ [1992] 3 All ER 922.
2   [1994] Crim LR 458.
3   *The Report of the Advisory Group on Video Evidence* (Home Office, 1989). See also Department of Health *Memorandum of Good Practice in Video Recorded Interviews with Child Witnesses for Criminal Proceedings* (1992). See also: JR Spencer 'Child Witnesses, Video-Technology and the Law of Evidence' [1987] Crim LR 76; G Smith 'Good practice or yet another hurdle: video recording children's statements' (1993) 5 JCL 21; J Aldridge and K Freshwater 'The preparation of child witnesses' (1993) 5 JCL 25; and J McEwan 'Where the prosecution witness is a child: the memorandum of good practice' (1993) 5 JCL 16. For a discussion of the implications of video technology for *civil* cases, see PM Smith, 'Child Witnesses: Implications for Civil Proceedings' [1993] Fam Law 110. For more recent evaluations of the video-link facilities, see G Davis, C Wilson, R Mitchell and J Milson *Videotaping Children's Evidence: An Evaluation* (Home Office, 1995), *The Child, the Court and the Video* (Social Services Inspectorate, 1994), and H Wescott and J Jones *Perspectives on the Memorandum* (Arena, 1997).

Video technology

The advent of video technology has increased the options open to the courts and was the subject of a report by the Pigot Committee in 1989[1]. Before that, the Criminal Justice Act 1988[2] allowed children under 14 years of age to give evidence from outside the courtroom via closed-circuit television, in sex, cruelty and assault cases. This age-limit was raised to accommodate those under 15 years for offences of violence, and those under 18 years in sex cases, by the Criminal Justice Act 1991[1]. The argument is that the live television link ameliorates the child's ordeal without an unacceptable risk of prejudice to the defendant. Although the system is recognised to have drawbacks for children[3], there is some evidence that children are less likely to break down under cross-examination and less likely to refuse to give evidence in the first place[4]. The system is reinforced by another provision in the Criminal Justice Act 1991 which prohibits cross-examination by an unrepresented defendant of a child under 14 years, where the offence is one of violence, or a child under 17 years, where it is a sexual offence[5]. The child may be either the victim or simply a witness to the commission of the alleged offence.

Should children have to appear at all?

Should the law go further and obviate the necessity for child victims to appear as witnesses in criminal proceedings at all? Some advocate this approach through a greater use of video technology, which would enable the courts to rely, instead, on pre-recorded interviews with children. The difficulty with this is caused by the retention of the hearsay rule in criminal proceedings. The Pigot Committee recommended radical reform along these lines, but the Criminal Justice Act 1991, which followed it, opted for a much more selective response which incurred the wrath of some commentators[6]. The new rule is that, subject to the judge's discretion, and rules of court, videos of pre-trial interviews of a child who is an accused are permitted in trials in the Crown Court and youth courts, in cases involving sexual offences or offences for violence or cruelty.

In *R v Lee*[7] the Court of Appeal (Criminal Division) dismissed an appeal from a conviction for arson being reckless as to whether life was endangered. The appellant had gone to his former cohabitant's home and set fire to her clothing in front of the children. At his trial a video from his six-year-old son was played and the boy was cross-examined on a live television link. The appellant argued that the video should not have been admitted because s 32A(2)(a) which refers to an 'offence which involves an assault on or injury or threat of injury to a person' did not apply to an offence of arson. He further argued that the provisions of s 32A had been intended to protect children for whom the trauma of evidence could be severe but they were not needed where, as here, it was not suggested that he

---

1 Section 32.
2 Section 54(7). Where a child aged over 14 years gives oral evidence via a live television link, the child should take the oath or make an affirmation before giving it. Failure to do so may render the evidence inadmissible. See *R v Sharman* [1998] 1 FLR 785.
3 By increasing their feeling of isolation, by being intimidated or distracted by the camera or by having difficulty concentrating on a face or voice speaking over a television monitor.
4 G Davies and E Noon *An evaluation of the live-link for child witnesses* (Home Office, 1991), which is the subject of an editorial comment at (1992) 4 JCL 145.
5 Criminal Justice Act 1991, s 55.
6 Section 54 of the Criminal Justice Act 1991, inserting new s 32A into the Criminal Justice Act 1988, and see, for example, J Spencer 'Children's Evidence and the Criminal Justice Bill' (1990) 140 NLJ 1750 commenting on the provision in the Bill.
7 [1996] Crim LR 412.

intended to threaten or injure the boy. It was held that the statutory requirements related to the circumstances of the offence and not to the state of mind of the offender. They did not necessarily require threat of injury to any particular person and the 'person' envisaged did not have to be the child giving video evidence. When viewed objectively the consequences of reckless arson did involve a threat of injury to a person. DJ Birch commented on this decision[1] that as a matter of policy it might be preferable if s 32 were further amended to allow video and live-link facilities to be made available 'wherever the child is likely to be traumatised by confrontation with the accused'. In the meantime, the courts may achieve the same result by a broad interpretation of the statute as occurred in this case.

The Home Office and Department of Health have issued a Memorandum of Good Practice relating the use of video-recorded interviews with children[2]. It has been held in *G v DPP*[3] that where the guidelines set out in the memorandum are not followed the evidence of young children may be dangerously suspect. This might result in the evidence not being admitted at all or, depending on the circumstances, the breaches of good practice might merely go to weight rather than to admissibility. A video-recording may be admitted in whole or in part. Where part of it is excluded, it must be edited by the person seeking to introduce it into the proceedings[4].

The catch, and it is a major catch, is that the device may only be used for evidence-in-chief and the child must be made available for cross-examination at the trial, if necessary, by live television link. This is a very considerable dilution of what Pigot proposed, since the ordeal of cross-examination is, depending on how extensive the cross-examination is, much worse than examination-in-chief by a supportive and well-disposed lawyer. Having said that, the child is at least spared the experience of having to relive the incidents twice. It remains to be seen whether yet more radical advances can be made in the years to come.

---

1   [1996] Crim LR 412 at 414.
2   *Memorandum of Good Practice on Video Recorded Interviews with Child Witnesses for Criminal Proceedings* (HMSO, 1992). The Court of Appeal has recently made it clear in *Re D (Child Abuse: Interviews)* [1998] 2 FLR 10 that, although the guidelines for interviewing children in the *Memorandum of Good Practice* were primarily designed for criminal trials, the underlying principles were applicable in both care and private law family proceedings.
3   [1997] 3 All ER 755.
4   *Practice Note: Video Recordings of Children's Evidence* [1992] 3 All ER 909.

Chapter 14

CHILDREN AND THE CRIMINAL LAW

INTRODUCTION

This chapter explores the relevance of the criminal law to children or, more accurately, 'children and young persons'. The civil law does not distinguish between children of various ages as a matter of status. Anyone below the age of majority is a 'child' or a 'minor'[1]. This is not the case with the criminal law where an important distinction is made between minors under the age of 14 years who are known as 'children' and those over 14 but under 18 years who are known as 'young persons'[2]. Collectively, they are referred to as 'juveniles' although the former 'juvenile court' was re-named the 'youth court' by the Criminal Justice Act 1991[3]. That Act also introduced a very significant reform by bringing within the jurisdiction of the youth court young persons aged 17 years who had previously, although still minors, been treated as *adults* by the criminal law. One of the principal distinctions between 'children' and 'young persons' was that it had been intended, under the Children and Young Persons Act 1969, to abolish criminal prosecutions of 'children' and, instead, to deal with young offenders below the age of 14 years, through the more welfare-orientated care procedures. In fact, this never happened[4] for a variety of reasons, some of them political[5]. The distinction is thus not as important as it might have been, but it remains of significance in a number of respects, not least until 1998 in determining criminal responsibility.

It is impossible, in a general introductory work of this nature, to do justice to the multifarious aspects of the criminal justice system as it applies to children and young persons[6]. The aim here is rather to provide an understanding of the various ways in which the criminal law treats children *differently* from adults. It should always be remembered that children are *people* or citizens and, as such, like everyone else, enjoy the protection of the ordinary criminal law. Conversely, and

---

1   There are, of course, many age-related rules which distinguish between children of different ages for specific purposes.
2   The principal legislation is the Children and Young Persons Acts of 1933, 1963 and 1969, the Criminal Justice Act 1991, the Criminal Justice and Public Order Act 1994 and the Crime and Disorder Act 1998.
3   Criminal Justice Act 1991, s 70, and see below.
4   Children and Young Persons Act 1969, s 4, now repealed by s 72 of the Criminal Justice Act 1991.
5   For a succinct discussion of the vacillations of policy in juvenile justice, see C Ball 'Young Offenders and the Youth Court' [1992] Crim LR 277, especially at pp 278–283.
6   See, generally, *Clarke Hall and Morrison on Children* (Butterworths), Vol 3, Section B; and HK Bevan *Child Law* (Butterworths, 1989) at chs 9, 10, 12 and 13. For a theoretical rights perspective, see MDA Freeman *The Rights and Wrongs of Children* (Frances Pinter, 1983) at ch 4. For an international perspective, see G van Bueren 'Child-Oriented Justice – An International Challenge for Europe' (1992) 6 IJLF 381. More recent commentaries may be found in: S Uglow *Criminal Justice* (Sweet & Maxwell, 1995) at ch 9; J Fortin *Children's Rights and the Developing Law* (Butterworths, 1998) at chs 18 and 19; and D Bedingfield *The Child in Need* (Family Law, 1998) at ch 9. For a concise account of the procedure relating to the trial of juveniles, see J Sprack *Emmins on Criminal Procedure* (7th edn) (Blackstone Press Ltd, 1997) at ch 10.

subject to major qualifications, they are also responsible for their own actions under the criminal law. These dual ideas of *protection* and *responsibility* are the theme of this chapter and they are also very much a feature of the *civil* law, which is examined in the next chapter.

The differential treatment of children and adults is a pervasive feature of English criminal law and procedure. Thus, to take *protection* first, there are numerous special offences which relate only to children. Further, those offences which apply more generally to children *and* adults, particularly sexual offences, often have special features in their application to children, which reflect their greater vulnerability. The law and procedure governing the *responsibility* of juveniles is riddled with rules which distinguish them from adults at every stage of the criminal process. The criminal responsibility of 'children' has been determined differently: different factors influence the decision whether to prosecute; there are special protections for children where the police are carrying out their investigations; there is segregation of children and adults while in court or in custody; and, if convicted, the disposal options open to the courts are markedly different in the case of juvenile offenders.

This chapter will endeavour to highlight some of these more important features of the criminal justice system. The chapter begins by looking at the *protection* side of the system. It then looks at the other side, describing first the process of determining *responsibility* or liability for criminal acts, and then examining the criminal process for dealing with juvenile offenders. The chapter concludes with a brief description of the provisions of the Crime and Disorder Act 1998 insofar as they relate to youth justice.

PROTECTION

This section is concerned with crimes *against* children which, for the purposes of exposition, can conveniently be put into three categories: those which relate to violence and physical harm; sexual offences; and special offences designed to eradicate or control activities which are thought to be harmful to children. There is a good deal of overlap between these categories. Sexual offences, for example, frequently involve violence and physical harm. Many of the special offences in the third category also involve physical harm but are distinctive in that they are ad hoc legislative responses to particular dangers for children which arise from time to time.

An issue which needs to be confronted immediately is the fact that a high proportion of crimes against children are committed by members of the same family or household. Most instances of child abuse or neglect also involve criminal offences so that, to some extent, child protection agencies face a choice about whether to prosecute or to invoke the civil remedies[1]. In some cases, it may be necessary to take action on both fronts. Until recently, the prospects of bringing a successful prosecution, especially in cases of sexual abuse, were substantially hindered by the restrictive rules regarding children's evidence. The reforms in this area[2] should now render prosecution a more realistic alternative and it has

---

1   See Chapters 11 and 12 above. See Chapter 13 on the question of disclosure to the police of documents in family proceedings.
2   See Chapter 13 above.

been argued that in some cases prosecution may serve to remove an abuser (rather than the child) from the family home – and is, in that sense, consistent with the thinking in the Children Act 1989[1].

On the other hand, the Childen Act supports the primary responsibility of parents to raise children, and the principle that the relationship between children and parents should be fostered, except where this is outweighed by considerations of harm to the child. In many cases, child abuse will be the result of stress on parents who themselves have inadequate family backgrounds and who lack sufficient understanding of child development or basic child care techniques. In cases like these, social work support and education may be a more appropriate response than either prosecution or care proceedings[2]. It may also be in the child's best interests for the family unit to be preserved, despite the instances of abuse, and for residential or foster-care to be avoided. In other cases, the abuse may be so serious or abhorrent as to necessitate a prosecution in the public interest. In such cases, it may, in any event, be difficult to conceive of any possible benefit to the child in preserving his 'relationship' with the adult concerned. The broad question, in any given case, must be whether the beneficial consequences of criminal proceedings are likely to outweigh the potential harm to the child and the family[3].

Violent crimes and physical harm

Homicide
The law governing murder and manslaughter applies just as much to child victims as it does to adult victims[4]. However, there are two features in relation to children which deserve special attention. These are deaths of infants within a short time of birth and deaths of children, of whatever age, as a result of neglect or omission.

Childbirth and the law of homicide
A charge of murder or manslaughter may only be brought in relation to 'any reasonable creature in rerum natura'[5] or, in other words, a human being. There can be some difficult line-drawing for these purposes. The essential test is that the child should have 'an existence independent of its mother'. This involves

---

1 C Cobley 'Child Abuse, Child Protection and the Criminal Law' (1992) 4 JCL 78. It is increasingly likely, however, that removal of the abuser will be possible under the new powers to add 'exclusion requirements' to EPOs and interim care orders under Part IV of the Family Law Act 1996 and this may well represent a better alternative than prosecution in some cases. See Chapter 12.
2 See, eg, JG Hall and DF Martin 'Crimes Against Children' (1992), 142 NLJ 902. See also A Wilcznski and A Morris 'Parents who kill their children' [1993] 1 Crim LR 31 and R Mackay 'The consequences of killing very young children' [1993] 1 Crim LR 21.
3 See, for example, C Cobley's argument in 'Child Abuse, Child Protection and the Criminal Law' (1992) 4 JCL 78 at p 80, that prosecutions in cases of intra-familial sexual abuse may not always be justified in either the public interest or in the interests of the child victim.
4 For a general analysis of the law of homicide, see JC Smith and B Hogan *Criminal Law* (8th edn) (Butterworths, 1996) at ch 12, and MJ Allen *Textbook on Criminal Law* (4th edn) (Blackstone Press Ltd, 1997) at ch 9. For an incisive academic critique of the underlying principles, see A Ashworth *Principles of Criminal Law* (2nd edn) (Clarendon, Oxford, 1995) at ch 7. For its more specific application to child victims, see HK Bevan *Child Law* (Butterworths, 1989) at ch 9, paras 9.06–9.33.
5 Coke, 3 Inst 47.

expulsion from the mother's body, an independent circulation and breathing after birth[1]. Any killing of a foetus before this constitutes (if anything) the offence of child destruction or falls within the abortion laws. Detailed discussion of the status of the 'unborn child' and the criminal law is beyond the scope of the present work[2].

On the other hand, there may be liability for the homicide of a child where the injury is inflicted on the foetus before birth, the child is born alive and then subsequently dies as a result, at least in part, of the injury. The Court of Appeal so held in *Attorney-General's Reference (No 3 of 1994)*[3] through an ingenious use of the doctrine of transferred malice[4]. In this case, the accused had stabbed his girlfriend, who was 26 weeks' pregnant, cutting the abdomen of the foetus. The child was born prematurely, survived 120 days and then died as a result of stress from operations and immaturity. The accused was acquitted on a charge of murder by direction of the trial judge. The Court of Appeal held that this direction was wrong since the foetus could be regarded as part of the mother's body. The 'malice' towards the mother could thus be transferred to the child at the point where the child was born and became an independent person. An intention to cause serious harm to the mother was an intention to cause serious harm to part of the mother. This could be transferred and there was no requirement that the person to whom it was transferred had to be in being at the time of infliction of the injury. The House of Lords[5] subsequently rejected the application of the doctrine of transferred malice in the circumstances of this case, but held that liability could instead lie in constructive manslaughter. The mother and foetus were to be regarded as 'two distinct organisms living symbiotically, not a single organism with two aspects'. On the other hand, the child, once born, could be regarded as falling within the defendant's mens rea when he stabbed the mother. The decision appears somewhat strained in terms of principle in order to arrive at what was thought to be the right conclusion on policy grounds[6]. In particular, the House declined to hold that murder, rather than manslaughter, could be an appropriate charge.

Where a child was killed by his mother within a short time of birth, there was a traditional reluctance on the part of juries to convict her of murder, and public and professional disapproval of treating these cases as ordinary murders. Many such cases arose, historically, through the fear of unmarried mothers of the stigma of giving birth to an illegitimate child. The special offence of infanticide exists, in essence, to reduce what would otherwise be murder to the equivalent of manslaughter. The offence is committed in the following circumstances:

> 'Where a woman by any wilful act or omission causes the death of her child being a child under the age of twelve months, but at the time of the act or omission the balance of her mind was

---

1　For further discussion of the point, see JC Smith and B Hogan (above) at pp 338 et seq. See also the discussion of the offence of concealment of birth under s 60 of the Offences Against the Person Act 1861, which essentially makes it an offence to conceal the dead body of a child after birth: ibid at pp 389–391.

2　Ibid at pp 396–408.

3　[1996] 2 FLR 1. For commentary, see J Keown 'Homicide, Fetuses and Appendages' (1996) CLJ 207.

4　On the doctrine of transferred malice, see JC Smith and B Hogan (above) at pp 77–78, and for commentary on this case, see ibid at p 339.

5　[1997] 3 WLR 421.

6　See J Keown 'Homicide by Prenatal Assault Revisited' (1998) CLJ 240.

disturbed by reason of her not having fully recovered from the effect of giving birth to the child or by reason of the effect of lactation consequent upon the birth of the child[1]'.

There are difficulties in justifying the retention of the offence in the modern law[2]. The causal link between the mother's mental imbalance and the killing may not be easy to establish, the defence of diminished responsibility is now generally available as a defence to murder and the offence may be criticised for being gender-specific[3]. On the other hand, the option of prosecuting for infanticide avoids the need to charge the mother with murder.

Death by neglect or omission
As a general proposition, admittedly subject to significant exceptions, the criminal law does not punish for omission or inactivity[4]. The point was graphically made by Stephen[5] who said that no offence was committed by a person who could save someone from drowning merely by holding out his hand. Morally reprehensible though it would undoubtedly be, it seems that failure to rescue a drowning child from a shallow pool is not homicide on the part of the bystander. It is different for parents and others who have a duty to protect the child. Where a *duty* to act can be established, the criminal law applies[6]. In the case of parents, this duty of protection is an incident of parental responsibility but others who have 'responsibility' for children, in the less technical sense of assuming their physical care, are also bound by this duty[7]. Thus, as long ago as 1918[8], a conviction for murder was upheld where a female cohabitant withheld food from her male cohabitant's child resulting in the child's death. She was held to have assumed responsibility for the child by living with the man and accepting from him money for food. In most cases, manslaughter is more likely to be the charge, but where an *intention* to kill or cause grievous bodily harm can be established, it is murder, in the absence of an exculpatory defence[9].

Non-fatal offences

Assaults under the Offences Against the Person Act 1861
The Offences Against the Person Act 1861 still governs the various criminal offences arising from assault. The main offences are assault occasioning actual bodily harm[10], and wounding or grievous bodily harm with[11] or without intent[12].

---

1 Infanticide Act 1938, s 1(1).
2 See JC Smith and B Hogan (above) at pp 394–396. See also D Maier-Katkin and R Ogle 'A rationale for infanticide laws' [1993] Crim LR 903 and R Mackay 'The consequences of killing very young children' [1993] Crim LR 19.
3 See A Ashworth *Principles of Criminal Law* (2nd edn) (Clarendon, Oxford, 1995) at pp 281–283.
4 Discussed, generally, in JC Smith and B Hogan (above) at pp 45–52.
5 *Digest of Criminal Law* (4th edn) (1887) at Art 212.
6 The imposition of liability for inactivity more generally in the criminal law has been the subject of more than one theory, but the duty theory is probably the most convincing and was the basis of the decision in *R v Miller* [1983] 2 AC 161.
7 See below for those who have potential liability for neglect under the Children and Young Persons Act 1933, s 1.
8 *R v Gibbins and Proctor* (1918) 13 Cr App Rep 134.
9 The leading cases are now *R v Hancock* [1986] AC 455; *R v Moloney* [1985] AC 905; and *R v Nedrick* [1986] 3 All ER 1.
10 Offences Against the Person Act 1861, s 47.
11 Ibid, s 18.
12 Ibid, s 20.

Where an injury is intentionally or recklessly inflicted on a child by an outsider who does not have responsibility for him, one of these charges will be appropriate, depending on the extent of the injury and the mental state of the assailant. Again, as with homicide, these are general offences which are not confined to child victims.

Cruelty to childen under 16 years of age

Where, as is more likely, the injury to the child has been caused by one of his 'carers', the offence in s 1(1) of the Children and Young Persons Act 1933 will apply. However, the offence is a good deal wider in its coverage than simply assaults. It extends to various forms of neglect, ill-treatment, abandonment and exposure, as well as to physical assaults[1]. The offence is committed by 'any person who has attained the age of sixteen years' who 'has responsibility for any child or young person under that age'. The concept of 'responsibility' reflects the change of terminology in the Children Act and replaces the former expressions 'custody, charge or care'[2]. The general idea is of someone who either has parental responsibility formally, most obviously a parent or someone with a residence order, but also anyone else who is de facto looking after the child at the relevant time, for example a relative, babysitter or foster-parent.

This potential liability for failure to care adequately for the child is really the obverse of s 3(5) of the Children Act which, as we saw[3], gives to such de facto carers the power to take necessary action to promote the child's welfare. It is also plain that someone who does, formally, have parental responsibility cannot 'contract out' of liability under this offence by delegating responsibility to someone else[4] but, where proper care has been taken to ensure the adequacy of a substitute caring arrangement, it would be unlikely that the parent would have the requisite mens rea. Problems can arise where it is not clear which of more than one person with parental responsibility has caused the injury, but there is authority that the court may be able to infer that they are jointly responsible[5].

What is wilful neglect?

The Children and Young Persons Act 1933 goes on to create certain presumptions of neglect which can be applied to parents, guardians and persons who are legally liable to maintain the child. Such persons will be deemed to have neglected the child 'in a manner likely to cause injury to his health' where they have failed 'to provide adequate food, clothing, medical aid or lodging' or have failed to procure

---

1   For discussion of the offence in the context of failure to summon medical aid for the child, see Chapter 8 above.
2   On the interpretation of these expressions, see HK Bevan *Child Law* (Butterworths, 1989) at paras 9.48–9.55.
3   At Chapter 6 above.
4   Children Act, s 2(11).
5   *R v Gibson and Gibson* [1984] Crim LR 615. Cf *R v Aston and Mason* [1991] Crim LR 701. In *R v Young* (1993) 97 Cr App R 280, the Court of Appeal held that as long as the jury were unanimous that cruelty in the sense alleged by the prosecution had been established, it was not necessary for them to agree on the specific evidence which led to a finding of guilt. They might legitimately differ on the emphasis to place on different incidents. Lloyd LJ said that it might, however, be wrong for the jury to be given the impression that they could convict if some of them were satisfied that *neglect* was established while others were satisfied of *assault* or *ill-treatment*. But there was no evidence in this case that the jury had been given that impression.

these things for the child[1]. All forms of conduct or omission envisaged by the offence must be committed 'wilfully'. It has been held by a majority of the House of Lords that this requires subjective recklessness[2]. The unintelligent or inadequate parent who does not appreciate, as would an average person, the health and other needs of the child, will not be liable[3].

How far can parental discipline go?
An issue which arises both in relation to this offence and in relation to ordinary assaults is how far a parent might be able to rely on the defence that the conduct in question was a proper exercise of parental discipline. The matter turns on whether the purported chastisement was 'moderate and reasonable'. The issue has already been discussed in the context of 'significant harm' in care proceedings[4] and is discussed in the context of intentional torts in Chapter 15 below.

Prosecutions
Before 1988, prosecutions for wilful neglect were uncommon[5]. This doubtless reflected, in part, the low maximum punishment which, in 1988, was two years' imprisonment. The Criminal Justice Act 1988[6] raised this to 10 years, and there were immediate signs that prosecutions were increasing. This is the maximum and, of course, within it, actual sentences will vary depending on such factors as the extent of the child's injuries and the circumstances surrounding the conduct in question. Where poverty and social deprivation have played a part, this may be expected to have an influence, but not necessarily so in the most atrocious cases of abuse. It has been observed that where a mother and step-father are jointly charged, the tendency has been to impose a more severe sentence on the step-father[7].

---

1 Section 1(2)(a) of the Children and Young Persons Act 1933. Section 1(2)(b) also deals with the death of an infant under three years of age by suffocation. Where the suffocation was not caused by disease or a foreign body in the throat or air passages of the infant, and the infant was at the time in bed with someone over 16 years of age, that person is, if he was under the influence of drink when he went to bed, 'deemed to have neglected the infant in a manner likely to cause injury to its health'.
2 *R v Sheppard* [1981] AC 394 and see Chapter 8 above.
3 For a criticism of the case, see HK Bevan *Child Law* (Butterworths, 1989) at para 9.37. Note also that the offence will be committed where there is a failure to summon medical aid even if in fact there was no help which a doctor could have given (*R v S and M* [1995] Crim LR 486). See Chapter 8 above.
4 At Chapter 11 above.
5 In 1987, only 145 persons were sentenced for the offence while, by 1989, 189 women and 192 men were prosecuted and 105 women and 107 men were convicted. See JG Hall and DF Martin 'Crimes Against Children' (1992) 142 NLJ 902.
6 Section 45.
7 A point made by HK Bevan (above) at para 9.57, citing as an example the *Jasmine Beckford* case where the step-father received a 10-year sentence for manslaughter, to run concurrently with an eight-year sentence for cruelty, while the mother was sentenced to only 18 months' imprisonment for wilful neglect.

Sexual offences

General considerations

There are a great many sexual offences on the statute book[1]. Many relate to children and adults alike, while others have specific application to children or, more accurately, young girls. It is this policy of protecting under-age girls which is the most striking feature of this part of the criminal law as it applies to children. The greater vulnerability of girls, in the matter of pregnancy and abortion, and the much greater propensity for sexual interferences by men against women goes a long way in explaining this differentiation between the sexes. It is, nonetheless, surprising that there is not a single offence specifically enacted to protect boys[2].

The other salient feature of these offences is that, in almost all instances, rape being the exception, it does not matter whether the sexual activity was consensual or non-consensual[3]. The consent of a child will generally be no defence since the offences are paternalistic in nature. It is deemed to be in children's interests, and in the public interest, that they are protected from what is thought to be premature sexual activity. These considerations of public policy came to the fore in the *Gillick* litigation when it was argued, but rejected by a majority in the House of Lords, that medical personnel would be secondary parties to a criminal offence in providing contraceptives to under-age girls[4].

Specific sexual offences

Rape and buggery

Recent changes to the law of rape and buggery have removed some of the previous gender-specific aspects of these offences[5]. It is important to consider the two offences alongside one another in their application to children since the definition of rape was extended in 1994[6] to incude anal, as well as vaginal, intercourse. Therefore, the newly defined offence of rape now incorporates what was previously non-consensual buggery[7]. Buggery thus now exists to catch cases of consensual anal intercourse but, by virtue of further amendments introduced in 1994[8], the offence is not committed where the act takes place in private and both parties have attained the age of 18 years. Where either party is under the age of 18,

---

1 About 40 in all. See JC Smith and B Hogan *Criminal Law* (8th edn) (Butterworths, 1996) at ch 14, MJ Allen *Textbook on Criminal Law* (4th edn) (Blackstone Press Ltd, 1997) at paras 10.2 et seq, and A Ashworth *Principles of Criminal Law* (2nd edn) (Clarendon, Oxford, 1995) at sections 8.4 et seq.
2 But see below for the potential liability for indecent assault on boys.
3 Even in the case of rape it may be difficult to show that a child *in fact* gave a real consent to intercourse. See below.
4 *Gillick v West Norfolk and Wisbech Area Health Authority* [1985] 3 WLR 830. But note the vigorous dissent of Lord Brandon, based squarely on considerations of public policy. For him, the distribution of contraceptives to an under-age girl whether by a parent, doctor or social worker necessarily involved 'promoting, encouraging or facilitating the having of sexual intercourse, contrary to public policy, by that girl with a man'. See ibid at p 865. The girl herself is *not* a secondary party to the offence, again based on the notion that the policy behind the offence is to protect her. See *R v Tyrell* [1894] 1 QB 710.
5 For rape, see JC Smith and B Hogan (above) at pp 467–474; for buggery, ibid at pp 492–494.
6 By the Criminal Justice and Public Order Act 1994, s 142.
7 The definition of buggery under the Sexual Offences Act 1956, s 12 embraced anal intercourse with a person or an animal. We do not discuss here buggery involving animals.
8 By the Criminal Justice and Public Order Act 1994, s 143.

both commit the offence. Homosexual and heterosexual buggery fall within the offence so, unlike rape, a woman may commit an act of buggery where, for example, the male 'partner' or 'agent' is under the age of 18[1]. The age of consent for anal intercourse, whether given by a man or a woman, is therefore 18 which, although in the case of a man was reduced in 1994 from 21, is still a matter of controversy since the age of consent for vaginal intercourse in the case of girls is 16[2].

The broad effect of these reforms as they apply to children is that a boy or girl may be the victim of rape where there is non-consensual vaginal or anal intercourse, or buggery where there is consensual anal intercourse. As we shall see, there is a separate offence of unlawful sexual intercourse with *girls* (but not with boys) under the age of 16 and either a girl or a boy under that age may be the victim of an indecent assault. In the case of these last two offences, the consent of the girl or boy is irrelevant.

Rape is committed where a man has unlawful sexual intercourse (whether vaginal or anal) with a person who, at the time, does not consent to it and he either knows of that person's lack of consent or is reckless about this[3]. Unusually, a mental element, namely the victim's lack of consent, is an essential ingredient in the actus reus. So far as children are concerned, it is possible for a child to give a real consent which can be defence to rape[4]. If it were not so, every instance of consensual intercourse between precocious school-girls and their male partners would be rape. But the younger the child, the less likely it will be that she has, in fact, given a real consent or that the accused could genuinely have believed it[5]. It has been suggested that the defence would rarely be established where the victim is a child (ie under 14 years of age)[6]. While this may be overstating the situation in 1998, it is undoubtedly the case that most instances of genuinely consensual activity will be in the 14- or 15-year age range. In *R v Larter and Castleton*[7] a conviction for rape of a 14-year-old girl was upheld where it appeared that she slept throughout the incident.

Unlawful sexual intercourse

There are two offences here which overlap. They are unlawful sexual intercourse with a girl under 13 years of age[8], and unlawful sexual intercourse with a girl under

---

1 In relation to buggery, the person effecting the intercourse is known as the 'agent' and the other party as the 'patient'.
2 See the discussion of the offence of unlawful sexual intercourse with girls below. An amendment to the Crime and Disorder Bill 1998 which would have reduced the age of consent for homosexual activity to 16 had to be dropped, at least temporarily, in July 1998, when it was defeated in the House of Lords. The Government dropped the clause to prevent the loss of the entire Bill, the clause having been defeated in the Lords on 22 July. See (1998) *The Times*, July 23.
3 Sexual Offences Act 1956, s 1(1), as amended, and the Sexual Offences (Amendment) Act 1976, s 1(1).
4 Although the same act of intercourse could constitute the offence of unlawful sexual intercourse with a girl despite her consent.
5 On the question of what is consent for the purposes of rape, see *R v Olugboja* (1981) 73 Cr App Rep 344, *R v Elbekkay* [1995] Crim LR 163, *R v Linekar* [1995] 2 Cr App Rep 49, and JC Smith and B Hogan *Criminal Law* (8th edn) (Butterworths, 1996) at pp 469–472.
6 HK Bevan *Child Law* (Butterworths, 1989) at para 10.16.
7 [1995] Crim LR 75.
8 Sexual Offences Act 1956, s 5.

16 years of age[1]. Unlike rape, these offences remain gender-specific and protect girls exclusively. There is no distinctive offence of unlawful sexual intercourse with boys. The first offence is now really an aggravated form of the second, given the very low age of the girls to whom it applies. It has a maximum punishment of life imprisonment. The second offence covers the case of girls at the margins of lawful sexual intercourse and, therefore, has some defences built into it to cater for certain (but by no means all) bona fide mistakes about the girl's age. The consent of the girl is irrelevant to both offences.

The man who invalidly 'marries' and has sexual intercourse with a girl under 16 years of age has a defence where he can prove that he believed her to be his wife and had reasonable grounds for that belief[2]. A man under 24 years of age also has a defence where he has not previously been charged with a like offence and he also reasonably believed the girl to be over 16 years of age. This is designed to make allowances for the relatively young man who has not previously had formally brought to his attention the serious consequence of under-age sexual activity[3], but this is the limit of the exceptions. In other cases, a belief, even where reasonable, that the girl is over 16 years is no defence[4].

Procuration of a girl under 21 years of age

It is no offence to have sexual intercourse with a girl *over* 16, but it is 'to procure a girl under the age of 21 to have unlawful sexual intercourse in any part of the world with a third person'[5]. Again, a reasonable belief that the girl is over-age is not a defence, nor is her consent, but it must be established that intercourse did actually take place.

Incest

Incest involves heterosexual intercourse between two people within a prohibited range of relationships[6]. Consent is, again, no defence whatever the age of the parties. The relevant relationships are grand-daughter, daughter, sister or mother, where a man is charged, and the male equivalents, where a woman is charged. In each case, relationships of the half-blood and 'illegitimate' relationships are included[7]. The basis of the offence appears to be largely eugenic, although the opportunities for undue influence within the family are probably a more convincing justification today[8]. It might be argued on this basis, for example, that brother–sister incest is less culpable than incest involving the parental or grandparental relationship and that the former, but not the latter, should be

---

1   Sexual Offences Act 1956, s 6(1).
2   Ibid, s 6(2).
3   Ibid, s 6(3). Under this provision it is not necessary to show that a conviction was sustained on the previous charge since merely being charged with the offence would have brought it to the accused's attention.
4   *R v Prince* (1875) LR 2 CCR 154.
5   Sexual Offences Act 1956, s 23(1).
6   The range is narrower than the prohibited degrees for the purposes of marriage under Sch 1 to the Marriage Act 1949.
7   Sexual Offences Act 1956, ss 10 and 11. Note also the Criminal Law Act 1977, s 54 which makes it an offence for a man or boy to incite a girl under 16 years of age, whom he knows to be his grand-daughter, daughter, sister or half-sister, to have intercourse with him.
8   Especially in the context of father and daughter.

taken out of the ambit of the special offence of incest and be dealt with under the general law of sexual offences[1].

Offences of indecency

This is the area in which some technical legal difficulties surrounding sexual activity with children have arisen. We consider first, the main offence of indecent assault and then, briefly, the special offences under the Indecency with Children Act 1960 and the Protection of Children Act 1978.

It was noted above that the consent of a child may be a defence to rape. Nevertheless, the same facts may produce a conviction for indecent assault, since a child under 16 years of age may not, in law, give a valid consent to prevent this offence[2]. The charge of indecent assault may be constituted by an assault or battery[3], coupled with circumstances of indecency. What is 'indecent' is an objective test of what would be regarded as such by a 'right-minded person'. The result of *R v Court*[4], the leading case, appears to be that where the external circumstances of the assault are not unambiguously indecent, the purpose of the defendant (indecent or otherwise) becomes a relevant element in the mens rea.

Indecent assaults may be perpetrated on boys as well as girls and, again, the consent of the boy is no defence[5]. While there is no offence of unlawful sexual intercourse with boys, a woman who persuaded a 12-year-old boy to have intercourse, and thereby infected him with venereal disease, was found guilty of indecent assault[6]. For these purposes, it seems that purely passive submission by a woman to sexual intercourse with a boy would not be sufficient. But if, as is more likely, she indulges in foreplay which involves touching the boy, the actus reus is established and it does not matter that the activity culminates in sexual intercourse[7].

Problems arose in relation to the applicability of indecent assault to children where there was evidently no assault but merely an invitation to touch the penis of the accused[8]. These were the circumstances in *Fairclough v Whipp*[9] where it was held that such an invitation could not, per se, amount to an assault. For some years

---

1 See J Temkin 'Do We Need the Crime of Incest?' (1991) 44 *Current Legal Problems* 185.
2 Sexual Offences Act 1956, ss 14 and 15.
3 Battery involves a 'touching' of the victim whereas assault includes a 'psychic assault' where the victim apprehends a touching which does not in fact occur. The victim does not, however, have to apprehend an *indecent* touching. In *R v Sargeant* [1997] Crim LR 50 the appellant had grabbed a boy aged 16 on his way home from school (and hence had assaulted him) and forced him to masturbate into a condom. The Court of Appeal rejected his argument that for indecent assault there must be a threat of indecent touching. It was sufficient for a physical assault (here the threat of violence) to have occurred in circumstances of indecency.
4 [1988] 2 All ER 221.
5 Sexual Offences Act 1956, s 15. In *Attorney-General's Reference No 34 of 1997* [1998] 1 FLR 515, the Court of Appeal held that such offences call for an immediate custodial sentence to mark the public condemnation of such conduct, to punish the offender and to deter others. In this case, the defendant had pleaded guilty to six counts of indecently assaulting three different boys aged between six and 11 who were friends of the family. The original *suspended* sentence of 18 months' imprisonment was substituted by a sentence of 15 months' immediate imprisonment.
6 *R v Hare* [1934] 1 KB 354.
7 *Faulkner v Talbot* (1981) 74 Cr App Rep 1.
8 It was also anomalous that the maximum penalty for indecent assault on a female was two years' imprisonment while for indecent assault on a male it was 10 years. The law has now been amended to make the maximum penalty for both 10 years.
9 [1951] 2 All ER 834.

it was also thought that an assault required 'hostility' which might often be lacking, although it is now established that this is not a requirement[1]. The problem of no act other than incitement to touch was remedied by the 1960 legislation which created a special offence of indecency with children, of which incitement is the principal ingredient[2]. The offence is committed by someone who *either* 'commits an act of gross indecency with or towards a child under the age of 14, or who incites a child under that age to such an act with him or another'. Invitations to touch are therefore caught, even where, as may often be the case, the child refuses to respond in the manner suggested, although children aged 14 and 15, while still below the age of consent, are unprotected by this offence.

Another special offence was created in 1978[3] to deal with the perceived problem of pornographic photography of children. The legislation followed the decision in *R v Sutton*[4] in which the touching of naked boys under 16 years of age, solely to indicate a pose, was held to lack the element of indecency. It is now an offence to take, permit to be taken, possess or publish indecent photographs of persons under 16 years[5]. The Court of Appeal has recently held in *R v Land*[6] that the offence is one of strict liability. There is no necessity to prove that the defendant knew or was reckless as to the age of children depicted in indecent photographs. Neither was it necessary for the prosecution to call expert evidence of the onset of puberty. The jury, it was held, was as well placed as an expert to assess whether or not the person depicted was under 16.

Special offences relating to children

Restrictions and prohibitions on sale of harmful goods

There are numerous statutory offences regulating various activities which may cause harm to children. Some of these are in the Children and Young Persons Act 1933, while others, like those above involving indecency, are scattered about the statute book. Little purpose would be served by reproducing a catalogue of these offences[7] but it is important to get a sense of the breadth of coverage of the criminal law. The offences include, most obviously, restrictions on the sale of alcohol[8] and tobacco[9] and road safety regulations[10]. These are widely known to the general public. Also well known are those offences relating to firearms[11], crossbows[12] and explosives, incuding fireworks[13]. The rationale of these offences is

1 *R v McCormack* [1969] 3 All ER 371.
2 Indecency with Children Act 1960.
3 Protection of Children Act 1978, as amended by the Criminal Justice Act 1988, s 160.
4 [1977] 3 All ER 476.
5 See *R v Owen* [1988] 1 WLR 134.
6 [1998] 1 FLR 438.
7 They are examined extensively in HK Bevan *Child Law* (Butterworths, 1989) at chs 9 and 10, and more recently in D Bedingfield *The Child in Need* (Family Law, 1998) especially at paras 5.198–5.216.
8 Licensing Act 1964, s 169.
9 Protection of Children (Tobacco) Act 1986 and the Children and Young Persons (Protection from Tobacco) Act 1991 which increased the penalties for sale of tobacco to persons under 16 years of age.
10 Thus, persons under 17 years of age are not allowed to drive motor vehicles on public roads.
11 Firearms Acts 1968 and 1982.
12 Crossbows Act 1987.
13 Explosives Act 1875, as amended by the Explosives (Age of Purchase etc) Act 1976.

partly to protect the children themselves and partly to protect society from the anti-social conduct which might result from allowing children and traders complete freedom of action.

Offences centred on protection
Other offences are more overtly centred on protection of children. The prohibition on tattooing of minors[1], the restrictions on the employment of children[2] and the offence relating to the exposure of children under 12 years to the risk of burning[3] would all seem to fall into this category.

Restriction of children's liberty
A feature of many of these special statutory offences is that they restrict not only the activities of adult society towards children but also the liberty of children themselves. This raises the general issue of how far the State has a legitimate interest in imposing these restraints. One of the freedoms which adults enjoy is the right to make mistakes. Many adults are not, for example, conspicuously competent drivers or noted for their restraint with alcohol, tobacco or in sexual matters. Yet the law generally does not step in to prevent them from behaving contrary to their own interests, objectively judged. What then is the case for denying children the right to make mistakes? The justification would seem to reside in the overriding obligation of the State to uphold the public interest in the well-being of children. But ultimately the view which is taken of the proper limits of State paternalism depends on the individual's own stance on the general question of children's rights[4].

Compensation for criminal injuries

This section concludes with a few words about compensation for criminal injuries sustained by child victims[5]. The Criminal Injuries Compensation Board formerly made ex gratia payments to the victims of crimes of violence who had sustained personal injury which, for these purposes, also included certain sexual offences. Generally, claims had to be made within a three-year time-limit from the date of the injury in question. The Board, however, indicated that it would treat sympathetically late claims made on behalf of children if made within a reasonable time of their attaining majority[6]. Normally, the application would be made on behalf of a child by his parent or other person with parental responsibility[7]. Where the child suffered injury within the family, the compensation question could be

---

1 Tattooing of Minors Act 1969.
2 Mainly in the Children and Young Persons Act 1933. See Chapter 15 below.
3 Children and Young Persons Act 1933, s 11 as amended. A more recent example of such legislation is the Horses (Protective Headgear for Young Riders) Act 1990. A very recent example is the Confiscation of Alcohol (Young Persons) Act 1997 which enables a police constable to confiscate intoxicating liquor from young persons under the age of 18 in prescribed circumstances.
4 See Chapter 3 above.
5 See, generally, RL Denyer QC 'The Criminal Injuries Compensation Board: Applications by or on Behalf of Children' [1993] Fam Law 34 and, more generally on the Criminal Injuries Compensation Scheme, P Duff 'The Measure of Criminal Injuries Compensation: Political Pragmatism or Dog's Dinner?' (1998) 18 *Oxford Journal of Legal Studies* 105.
6 RL Denyer QC (above).
7 Where the child is in care, the application would be made by the local authority.

delicate and the Board had to consider whether it was in the child's best interests for an award to be made[1]. In some cases, it was possible to secure an award on the basis of findings of abuse in family proceedings where a prosecution was considered inappropriate[2]. The Criminal Injuries Compensation Scheme has now been placed on a statutory footing by the Criminal Injuries Compensation Act 1995. The legislation governs, inter alia, the basis upon which compensation is to be calculated, the making of claims and awards, and reviews of decisions and appeals.

It may also be possible for the child to bring a _civil_ action for damages for trespass to the person (arising from physical or sexual abuse) but such actions must be brought within the appropriate limitation period which is six years from the date of the child attaining majority. The House of Lords so held in _Stubbings v Webb_[3]. A subsequent complaint that the limitation period infringed the applicant's rights under the European Convention on Human Rights, in particular rights of access to courts, was rejected by the European Court of Human Rights in 1996[4].

RESPONSIBILITY

Criminal responsibility of children and young persons

The criminal law until the implementation of the Crime and Disorder Act 1998 divides juveniles into three distinct age groups for the purposes of criminal liability[5]. As we discuss below, the 1998 Act abolishes the doli incapax presumption as it applies to children aged over 10 but under 14 years, so that in future it will only be necessary to distinguish between two groups of children, viz those over and those under 10 years. We begin by describing the traditional threefold categorisation commenting on the reasoning behind the 1998 reform.

Children under 10 years of age

Children under the age of 10 years are conclusively presumed to be doli incapax ('incapable of evil') or incapable of committing any offence[6]. They are thus

---

1   In particular, it needed to consider whether an award might exacerbate family tensions. See RL Denyer (above) at p 36.
2   Ibid. Indeed, it was established in _Re G (A Minor) (A Ward: Criminal Injuries Compensation)_ [1993] 1 FLR 103 that it was not even necessary that a finding of abuse should have been made. In this case the father had been exonerated in wardship proceedings of sexual abuse, but the Court of Appeal, nonetheless, upheld the judge's decision giving leave for the Official Solicitor (acting as the GAL) to make an application to the Criminal Injuries Compensation Board. The essential point was that the Board was not bound by the ordinary rules of evidence and did not require any finding against an alleged perpetrator. It merely had to be satisfied, on the balance of probabilities, that the applicant had been the subject of a crime of violence.
3   [1993] 1 FLR 714.
4   See _Stubbings and Others v The United Kingdom_ [1997] 1 FLR 105.
5   The Act received Royal Assent on 31 July 1998 and will be implemented on days appointed by the Secretary of State (see s 121). See, generally, HK Bevan _Child Law_ (Butterworths, 1989) at paras 12.05–12.09, JC Smith and B Hogan _Criminal Law_ (8th edn) (Butterworths, 1996) at pp 194–197, and MJ Allen _Textbook on Criminal Law_ (4th edn) (Blackstone Press Ltd, 1997) at pp 107–110.
6   Children and Young Persons Act 1933, s 50, as amended by Children and Young Persons Act 1963, s 16.

completely immune from prosecution. Historically, at common law, the principle evolved that young children should be exempt from criminal liability and, when an age was first fixed by law, seven years was chosen[1]. This was raised to eight years in 1933 and to 10 years in 1963, where it remains today. Article 40(3) of the United Nations Convention on the Rights of the Child requires 'the establishment of a minimum age below which children shall be presumed not to have the capacity to infringe the penal law' but does not go on to specify what this should be. The age of criminal responsibility in England is set lower than in most other European countries and has been the subject of extensive criticism[2].

Two consequences flow immediately from the rule. The first is that, since the child is, in law, incapable of committing a crime, anyone over the age of criminal responsibility, who incites a child to commit a criminal act, will be liable as principal offender and not as a secondary party. The child is an 'innocent agent' and this can have some unexpected consequences. In *Walters v Lunt*[3], the parents of a boy aged seven years were accused of receiving from him a stolen tricycle. Since the boy himself was incapable of theft, the tricycle was not 'stolen' and the parents had to be acquitted. The second consequence is that, where young children commit acts which but for the age rule would be criminal, they can only be dealt with, if at all, through the public law procedures of the Children Act. In many cases, this will involve social services providing the family with voluntary assistance. As has been seen[4], the abolition of the 'offence condition' means that proceedings for compulsory care or supervision may no longer be instigated simply on the strength of delinquency. It has to be shown that the child is also at risk of 'significant harm', applying the statutory criteria and, ultimately, the welfare principle.

Children aged 10 years but under 14 years

Before its abolition by the Crime and Disorder Act 1998[5] the presumption of incapacity applied to this age group but here it was a *rebuttable* presumption. The prosecution was required to prove that the child had what was termed a 'mischievous discretion'. This was in addition to the normal burden of proof on the prosecution to establish the actus reus and appropriate mens rea which has to be proved for the offence whether committed by a child or an adult. In 1994 there was an attempt by the Divisional Court in *C v DPP*[6] to abolish the common law presumption on the basis that it was outdated, but the House of Lords[7] subsequently held that, although reform was desirable, this was a matter for Parliament and not for the courts. It therefore reasserted the existence of the

---

1   The historical development of the rule is discussed by HK Bevan (above) at para 12.05.
2   For a particularly helpful discussion, see J Fortin *Children's Rights and the Developing Law* (Butterworths, 1998) at pp 439–449 and the sources cited there.
3   [1951] 2 All ER 645.
4   Section 90(1) of the Children Act.
5   Section 34 provides that 'the rebuttable presumption of criminal law that a child aged 10 or over is incapable of committing an offence is hereby abolished'.
6   [1994] 3 WLR 888, and for commentary on the Divisional Court's decision, see ATH Smith 'Doli Incapax Under Threat' (1994) CLJ 426.
7   [1995] 2 WLR 383. For commentary, see ATH Smith 'Reshaping the Criminal Law in the House of Lords' (1995) CLJ 486. For a wider critique of the doli incapax presumption, see G Douglas 'The Child's Right to Make Mistakes: Criminal Responsibility and the Immature Minor' in G Douglas and L Sebba *Children's Rights and Traditional Values* (Ashgate, 1998) at ch 15.

presumption only for the Labour Government to incorporate its abolition as part of a wider package of measures to tackle youth crime in the 1998 legislation.

What then is meant by a 'mischievous discretion' where the presumption applied? The broad effect of the case-law was that it entailed on the part of the child an appreciation of 'serious wrongdoing' which went beyond mere 'naughtiness'[1]. It was, in short, necessary to adduce some evidence of capacity which went beyond the performance of the act in question. Merely running away from the scene was, for example, equivocal. Thus in *C v DPP*, C, aged 12, together with another boy, was seen using a crowbar to tamper with a motor cycle in a driveway. He ran away but was caught and arrested. He was subsequently convicted by the youth court of interfering with a motor vehicle with intent to commit theft under s 9(1) of the Criminal Attempts Act 1981. Allowing C's appeal, the House of Lords held that there was no evidence beyond the commission of the act which was capable of rebutting the presumption. As Laws J had accepted in the Divisional Court, running away was equivocal in this case, since flight from the scene could just as easily follow a naughty action as it could a wicked one.

Where the act is one that any normal child of the relevant age would know to be seriously wrong, it was necessary to establish that the child was of normal mental capacity for his age and not simply that an average child of that age would have appreciated the gravity of the wrongdoing. The leading case was *JM (A Minor) v Runeckles*[2], in which a 13-year-old girl hit another girl with a bottle and then stabbed her with the broken part of it. Her conviction for assault occasioning actual bodily harm was upheld by the Divisional Court. The following factors enabled the presumption of incapacity to be rebutted in her case:

(1) her coherent statement, made shortly after her arrest, was very similar to the victim's account;
(2) her handwriting was commensurate with the average ability of a 13-year-old;
(3) her actions before the stabbing were provocative; and
(4) she ran away from the police and admitted that she thought they were looking for her.

The younger the child was, within the 10- to 14-year spectrum, the more difficult it was to rebut the presumption[3]. It was accepted that police officers engaged in interviewing child suspects should be trained and encouraged to ask direct questions as to the child's perception of what he had done but they should not suggest the answer to the child[4]. Where the prosecution was relying on the normality of the child it was necessary to prove this specifically and not merely to rely on a presumption of normality[5].

Views were inevitably divided on the merits of the presumption. The Labour Government saw its abolition as an integral part of its more general policy for reinforcing personal and parental responsibility for youth crime[6]. It believed that

1   *R v Gorrie* (1919) 83 JP 136. But this was not so for offences involving 'dishonesty' since if the child appreciated what was involved in the concept of dishonesty he had, by definition, a 'mischievous discretion'. See *T v DPP* [1989] Crim LR 498.
2   (1984) 79 Cr App Rep 255.
3   *X v X* [1958] Crim LR 805. Cf *R v Sheldon* [1996] 2 Cr App R 50.
4   *L (A Minor) v DPP* [1996] 2 Cr App R 500.
5   *CC (A Minor) v DPP* [1996] 1 Cr App R 375.
6   See White Paper *No More Excuses – A New Approach to Tackling Youth Crime in England and Wales*, Cm 3809 (1997), ch 4.

'in assuming that children of this age generally do not know the difference between naughtiness and serious wrongdoing, the notion of doli incapax is contrary to common sense[1]. It also took the view that 'the practical difficulties which the presumption presents for the prosecution can stop children who should be prosecuted and punished for their offences from being convicted or from even coming to court'[2]. Others have pointed out that the existence of the presumption should have been seen alongside the very low age of criminal responsibility in England and that it was perhaps more justifiable in the light of this[3]. It is also questionable how far the abolition of the presumption is consistent with the notion of gradual or gathering independence for children. As was argued in Chapter 3, the notion of children's responsibilities or duties ought to go hand in hand with the extent of their autonomy. The Government appeared to accept this in its White Paper on Youth Crime which states:

> 'As they develop, children must bear an increasing responsibility for their actions, just as the responsibility of parents gradually declines – but does not disappear – as their children approach adulthood.'[4]

Yet this is precisely what the abolition of the doli incapax presumption will not achieve, for instead of a gradual recognition of increasing responsibility of children for crime what we will have is the sudden acquisition of responsibility at the age of 10. As Tony Smith has graphically put it, referring to the earlier decision of the Divisional Court in *C v DPP*, 'we now have a law which holds that a person is completely irresponsible on the day before his tenth birthday, and fully responsible as soon as the jelly and ice-cream have been cleared away the following day'[5].

There used to be a special rule applying to sexual offences and boys under 14 years of age. There was a *conclusive* presumption that a boy of that age was incapable of sexual intercourse and therefore could not commit rape, offences involving sexual intercourse or buggery[6]. Acts which might, but for that presumption, have constituted the above offences might instead have founded a prosecution for indecent assault. It became increasingly appreciated that the presumption did not accord with reality and it was eventually abolished by s 1 of the Sexual Offences Act 1993.

Young persons over 14 years of age
Young persons over 14 years of age, but below the age of majority, are assumed to have the normal capacity for forming the mens rea required for particular offences[7]. They are treated for these purposes as adults. There are, however, major distinctions in their *treatment* both under criminal procedure and in the sentences which may be imposed on conviction. Essentially there is a more welfare-

---

1   White Paper (above) at para 4.14.
2   Ibid.
3   For a detailed discussion, see J Fortin *Children's Rights and the Developing Law* (Butterworths, 1998) at pp 439–449.
4   White Paper (above) at para 4.1.
5   ATH Smith 'Doli Incapax Under Threat' (1994) CLJ 426, at 427.
6   *R v Groombridge* (1836) 7 C&P 582; *R v Waite* [1892] 2 QB 600; *R v Tatam* (1921) 15 Cr App R 132, respectively.
7   It is interesting to compare this age rule with the civil law which, for many purposes, tends to draw the line for civil capacity at 16 years of age. See Chapter 15 below.

orientated approach than in the case of adults. As we discuss below, there has been a palpable shift in the 1990s towards a more punitive, authoritarian approach.

Responsibility of parents

Should parents be responsible for the criminal acts of their children? The former Conservative administration thought so and, to the surprise of many, the incoming Labour Government has introduced legislation firmly grounded in the same philosophy. But many commentators on juvenile justice evidently doubt the validity of this[1].

Before 1990, the law was that parents might be made liable for fines imposed on their children. It was the duty of the court to order that a fine, compensation, or costs be paid by a parent or guardian unless it was satisfied that the parent or guardian could not be found, or that the order would be unreasonable in the circumstances. It is understood, however, that the power was rarely used[2].

Enforcing parental responsibility
In a White Paper published in February 1990[3], the Conservative Government expressed its intention to go further in the direction of enforcing parental responsibility in this area. Originally it wanted to make it a criminal offence for parents to 'fail to prevent their children from committing offences'. The proposal was heavily criticised by, among others, the Magistrates' Association and was subsequently dropped. The main criticisms were that most delinquents came from families which were inadequate in some way – often lacking an appropriate father-figure. It was argued that resources could better be diverted to helping the families, through education and social work support and, it was further argued, that the proposal was likely to be counter-productive in that it might lead to the complete disintegration of already fragile family units. The connection between excessive corporal punishment and child abuse was also noted[4].

Measures to make parents more accountable
Despite these criticisms, the Conservative Government pressed ahead with a package of measures designed to make parents more accountable. These were incorporated in the Criminal Justice Act 1991[5]. This followed a White Paper in which the Government had expressed its view of the importance of parents attending court and taking responsibility for financial penalties. Accordingly, where a child or young person under 16 years of age *is* charged with a criminal offence, the court must now require a parent to be present in court unless, in all the circumstances, this would be unreasonable[6]. It has a discretion to require a

---

1   For two succinct criticisms of the idea, see JG Hall and DF Martin 'Child Delinquency and Parental Responsibility' (1990) JPN 604; and D Boyd 'Blaming the Parents' (1990) 2 JCL 65.
2   Children and Young Persons Act 1933, s 55. This was the experience at least of JG Hall (a retired circuit judge) and DF Martin (a former principal in the Lord Chancellor's Office) (above).
3   *Crime, Justice and Protecting the Public* (1990) (Cmnd 965).
4   See JG Hall and DF Martin (above) for a neat summary of these objections.
5   Criminal Justice Act 1991, ss 56–58.
6   Ibid, s 56, creating a new s 34A of the Children and Young Persons Act 1933.

parent's presence where the young person is over 16 years[1]. The court's duty to require parents to pay fines, compensation and costs continues where a child is under 16 years of age but this is now only a *power* in relation to young persons over 16 years[2]. The thinking, similar to that which has inspired reforms in the civil law[3], is that many in this age group will have de facto independence from their parents and, therefore, should be made directly responsible for their own financial penalties. Local authorities were, for the first time, made directly responsible for financial penalties incurred by offenders, under the age of 18 years, who are looked after by them[4]. Where the child is merely accommodated, as opposed to being in the care of the local authority, a parent may not be liable for offences committed by the child if the parent has no control of the child at the relevant time[5].

More controversially, the criminal courts have a duty to bind over the parents of a child or young person under 16 years if satisfied, in the circumstances, that the exercise of this power 'would be desirable in the interests of preventing the commission by him of further offences'[6]. Where the court is not so satisfied, it must give reasons in open court[7], the effect of which is to create a presumption of binding over[8]. There had been a proposal that the power be extended to the parents of children over 16 years in full-time education and living at home, but this was withdrawn. The court may also order a parent or guardian to enter into a recognisance in a sum not exceeding £1,000 to take proper care of the offender and exercise proper control over him[9]. This requires the consent of the parent or guardian, but this is more illusory than real, since the court may fine him where it considers his refusal unreasonable[10]. The recognisance may then be forfeited if further criminal offences are committed[11]. The controversial bind-over provisions of the Criminal Justice Act 1991 were taken a stage further by the Criminal Justice and Public Order Act 1994. This amended the 1991 Act[12] to empower the courts to bind over parents not merely where their children re-offend but also where they fail to comply with the requirements of a community sentence.

---

1 Children and Young Persons Act 1933, s 34A(1).
2 Criminal Justice Act 1991, s 57, inserting a new s 55(1B) into the Children and Young Persons Act 1933.
3 See the discussion of the Age of Legal Capacity (Scotland) Act 1991 in Chapter 15 below.
4 Criminal Justice Act 1991, s 57, inserting a new s 55(5) into the Children and Young Persons Act 1933 and effectively reversing the decision in *Leeds City Council v West Yorkshire Metropolitan Police* [1983] 1 AC 29. The liability of the local authority will turn in individual cases on whether it has behaved reasonably and properly in its efforts to control the child. See *D (A Minor) v DPP* [1995] 2 FLR 502 and *Bedfordshire County Council v DPP* [1995] Crim LR 962.
5 *TA v Director of Public Prosecutions* [1997] 2 FLR 887.
6 Criminal Justice Act 1991, s 58(1)(a).
7 Ibid, s 58(1)(b).
8 The Government's intention was clearly to persuade the courts to exercise these powers much more frequently than they had done before the Criminal Justice Act 1991. For an analysis of that Act as it applies to parental responsibility, see M Wasik and RD Taylor *Blackstone's Guide to the Criminal Justice Act 1991* (Blackstone Press, 1991) at paras 4.5–4.8.
9 Criminal Justice Act 1991, s 58(2) and (3).
10 Ibid, s 58(2)(b).
11 But interesting questions may arise as to what precisely constitutes a failure 'to take proper care of [the child] and exercise proper control over him'. Can this simply be assumed because the child or young person has committed further offences?
12 1991 Act, s 58(2).

Objections to these powers

These powers come the closest to the Conservative Government's original, more radical, proposal to fix parents themselves with criminal responsibility. There are some formidable civil libertarian objections to these powers and serious questions about imposing liability for the criminal actions of others. It is not at all clear how well the idea accords with the civil concept of parental responsibility under the Children Act or how far it acknowledges the conflict of interest which may arise between the child and the parent who has done everything in his or her power to control the child but has failed. The trend in the civil law since *Gillick* has been very much away from the notion of parental control and towards independence for adolescents. The binding-over power seems to jar with this.

The new parenting order

Far from reversing the authoritarian trend towards punishing parents for the sins of their children instigated by the former Conservative Government, the new Labour administration takes us yet further in the same direction by the introduction in the Crime and Disorder Act 1998 of the new 'parenting order'[1]. The Government's thinking is set out in a White Paper which preceded the legislation[2]. Essentially, this is that research has established an association between inadequate parental supervision and juvenile offending. While, therefore, parents of young offenders might not be directly to blame for the crimes of their children, they do have to be responsible for providing their children with proper care and control. The courts, it is thought, need powers to help and support parents more effectively to keep their children out of trouble.

The parenting order will generally be available to parents of convicted young offenders, parents of children who have been the subject of the new anti-social behaviour order, sex offender order or child safety order[3], and parents who have been convicted in truancy cases[4]. The order will require parents to attend counselling or guidance sessions for no more than once per week and for no longer than three months[5]. Where the court thinks it necessary the order may impose additional requirements which may apply for up to one year, for example to ensure that the child attends school every day or that he or she is home by a certain time each night[6]. Parents may be fined for failing without reasonable excuse to comply with any requirement included in the order[7]. Where a person under 16 years of age is convicted of an offence, the court *must* make a parenting order (if the other conditions for the order exist) or, if no order is made, it must state the reason why it is not in open court[8].

In its White Paper, the Government gave the following example of how the parenting order could work. A 13-year-old boy has committed a number of crimes at night and does not attend school regularly. Here, a parenting order might be

---

1 Sections 8–10.
2 See White Paper *No More Excuses – A New Approach to Tackling Youth Crime in England and Wales* (1997) (Cm 3809) ch 4, especially at paras 4.6–4.12.
3 See pp 505 et seq below.
4 For the duty of parents to ensure school attendance and the related offences, see Chapter 16 below.
5 Section 8.
6 Ibid.
7 Section 9.
8 Ibid.

imposed which requires his parents to attend training and which might include additional requirements to ensure his attendance at school and that one parent or another responsible adult be at home at night to supervise him.

The new parenting order will exist alongside the bind-over powers discussed above but the Government has signalled its intention to reconsider the latter in the light of the experience of piloting the parenting order. The new order might be viewed by some as an attempt to provide support and encouragement to the parents of young offenders, while others will see it as fundamentally authoritarian, an attack on civil liberties and an extraordinary invasion by the State into family autonomy – so richly prized elsewhere in the law[1].

YOUNG OFFENDERS AND THE CRIMINAL PROCESS

Prevention and diversion

The emphasis on inter-agency co-operation in the civil context has already been noted[2]. This is also very much a feature of the criminal processes which may or may not be invoked against young offenders. Local authorities' social services departments have statutory obligations to provide support services to children and families[3]. These include a duty to take reasonable steps designed to reduce the need to bring criminal proceedings against children, to encourage children within their areas not to commit crime, and to avoid the need for children to be placed in secure accommodation[4]. Early local authority involvement is also secured by requiring the prosecuting authorities[5] to give notice of any decision to prosecute a juvenile to the relevant local authority. While this ought to, and often will, involve co-operation and consultation *before* the decision to prosecute is taken, there is no statutory requirement to this effect. In practice, there is usually close liaison between the police, social services, education authorities and the probation service[6].

The use of cautions

The above consultations will be directed in particular to the question whether the offender should be cautioned rather than prosecuted. There has been a considerable expansion in the system of cautioning in recent years as part of a wider strategy of 'diversion' of juveniles from the criminal justice system. This was very much the philosophy behind the unimplemented provisions in the Children and Young Persons Act 1969[7]. If these had been brought into effect, criminal proceedings against children, ie children under 14 years of age, would have been abolished altogether[8] and would only have been brought against those over 14 years as a last resort[9]. The increased preference for cautioning was part of the same

---

1 White Paper (above) at para 4.12.
2 See particularly Chapters 10 and 11 above.
3 See Chapter 10 above.
4 Schedule 2, para 7 to the Children Act.
5 The Police, and the Crown Prosecution Service ('CPS').
6 The probation service must be notified where the juvenile is over 13 years old before a prosecution can be brought: the Children and Young Persons Act 1969, s 34(2).
7 Now repealed by the Criminal Justice Act 1991, s 72.
8 Children and Young Persons Act 1969, s 6.
9 Ibid, s 5.

thinking, but the practice itself is not on a statutory footing[1]. The Home Office has issued guidance on the criteria which must be followed[2]. It must be appreciated that the caution is a *formal* alternative to prosecution, as contrasted with an informal warning[3]. A caution may, thus, only be administered where guilt is admitted or there is sufficient evidence to give a realistic prospect of conviction, and, importantly, the parent or guardian must understand the nature of a formal caution and give an informed consent to it.

The Labour Government took the view that the current system of cautioning was not effective in the prevention of re-offending especially where there have been repeated cautions. Accordingly, the Crime and Disorder Act 1998 abolishes cautioning for young offenders and replaces it with a statutory police reprimand and final warning scheme. We discuss this in the context of the Act's other provisions below.

Overruling decisions on prosecution

An issue which has come before the courts is whether the decision of the prosecuting authorities is final or susceptible to judicial review. Several cases have established that judicial review could lie in respect of decisions *not* to prosecute[4]. More recently, in *R v Chief Constable of Kent*[5] the question was whether a decision to continue a prosecution, against the advice of the local Juvenile Offender Liaison Team, could be impugned. The Home Office criteria for cautioning were satisfied, but the police, nevertheless, decided to go ahead with the prosecution. This decision received the endorsement of the Crown Prosecution Service ('CPS'). The decision was reached on the basis that the injuries sustained exceeded the usual incidents of juvenile violence and that it was therefore in the public interest to prosecute[6]. The Divisional Court held that a decision of the CPS to continue or discontinue criminal proceedings was, in principle, susceptible to judicial review but only in very restricted circumstances[7]. It would have to be shown that the decision contravened a settled policy of the DPP, evolved in the public interest. Such instances of a complete disregard of public policy would be rare. The decision, in this case, has been criticised on the basis that it largely ignored the welfare considerations involved in prosecution versus cautioning,

---

1 The matter is governed by Home Office Circular No 18/1994 *The Cautioning of Offenders*.
2 Ibid at Annex B.
3 Informal warnings or cautions may be given by the police but they do not have the implications of formal cautioning discussed below.
4 See *R v Metropolitan Police, ex parte Blackburn* [1968] 2 QB 118; and *R v Bar Council ex parte Percival* [1990] 3 WLR 323. In *R v DPP, ex parte C* [1995] 1 Cr App R 136 the decision of the DPP not to prosecute in a case of alleged non-consensual buggery by a husband on his wife was set aside by the Divisional Court and remitted to the DPP for further consideration. The court said that the power to review the decision not to prosecute was to be exercised sparingly, but in this case there had been a failure to follow the Code for Crown Prosecutors issued by the DPP under s 10 of the Prosecution of Offences Act 1985.
5 *R v Chief Constable of Kent and Another ex parte L* [1991] Crim LR 841. See the commentaries on the case in C Eades 'The Decision to Prosecute Juveniles – No Review of the Actions of the Police and Crown Prosecution Service' (1991) JPN 358, and S Uglow, A Dart, A Bottomley and C Hale 'Cautioning Juveniles – Multi-Agency Impotence' [1992] Crim LR 632.
6 The victim had sustained a fracture to the maxillary spine of his nose and had been knocked to the ground. As he lay there it was alleged that the accused had kicked him in the head.
7 It was held that the initial decision of the police was not susceptible to judicial review since their power to prosecute had been severely limited by the setting up of the CPS.

making these secondary to legalistic questions of due process, and undermining the role of the non-statutory liaison body[1].

The investigative process

In general, the powers of arrest and detention which the police have are governed by the Police and Criminal Evidence Act 1984 ('PACE 1984'). Under s 66 there is a Code of Practice regulating the detention, treatment and questioning of persons by police officers. This Code makes special provision for the treatment of young suspects.

The juvenile in police custody

Where a juvenile is arrested, the arresting officer must, where practicable, ascertain the identity of the person responsible for that juvenile's welfare and must notify that person of the arrest[2]. This will normally be the juvenile's parent or guardian or, perhaps, social services, where he is being looked after by the local authority[3]. If the juvenile is then held in custody he must be told of his rights to have someone informed of his whereabouts and he has the right to a solicitor[4]. The 'appropriate adult' must then generally be present at any interview with the juvenile[5]. Any caution must be administered in the presence of the appropriate adult or repeated in his presence later. The juvenile must not be detained in a police cell without good reason and must not be allowed to come into contact with adult suspects[6]. As soon as practicable after the arrest, the 'custody officer'[7] must determine whether or not there is sufficient evidence to charge the juvenile. If not, he must be released, with or without bail, unless his further detention is necessary: (1) to secure or preserve evidence relating to an offence for which he is under arrest; or (2) to obtain such evidence by questioning him[8]. The maximum period of detention without charge is 24 hours, but this may be extended on the authority of a superintendent or the court[9].

Further detention of a juvenile

Where the juvenile is charged and further detention is necessary, PACE 1984[10], as amended by the Criminal Justice Act 1991[11], imposes important duties on the custody officer. The central principle is that juveniles who are charged and

---

1 Uglow et al (above) at p 640.
2 Children and Young Persons Act 1933, s 34(2) and (3).
3 Ibid, s 34(5)(b) refers to 'any other person who has for the time being assumed responsibility for his welfare'. And see 'At the Police Station. The Role of the "Appropriate Adult"' (1991) 74 *Childright* 9.
4 PACE 1984, ss 56 and 58.
5 See the *Code of Practice for the Detention, Treatment and Questioning of Persons by Police Officers (Code C)* at para 11.
6 Children and Young Persons Act 1933, s 31, which also prescribes that a girl should be under the care of a woman.
7 The 'custody officer' is a designated police officer who is charged with the responsibility of ensuring that the statutory requirements and Code of Practice under PACE 1984 are observed. See PACE 1984, s 36(3) which provides that the officer appointed must be of at least the rank of sergeant.
8 PACE 1984, s 37(2).
9 Ibid, ss 41, 42 and 43.
10 Ibid, s 38(6).
11 Ibid, s 59.

detained ought, in all but exceptional circumstances, to be looked after by social services in local authority accommodation and not held in police custody. This was the original intention reflected in PACE 1984 itself but there was evidence that the practice of police forces throughout the country differed significantly. The purpose of the amendments in the Criminal Justice Act 1991 was to reinforce the policy of passing responsibility for the juvenile's accommodation to the local authority[1].

Where the custody officer authorises an arrested juvenile to be kept in police detention, he must now secure that the juvenile is moved to local authority accommodation, unless he certifies:

(1) that, by reason of specified circumstances, it is impracticable for him to do so; or

(2) in the case of an arrested juvenile who has attained the age of 12 years, that no secure accommodation is available and that keeping him in other local authority accommodation would not be adequate to protect the public from serious harm from him[2].

Where an arrested juvenile is charged with a 'violent offence' or a 'sexual offence' there is a statutory definition of 'protecting the public from serious harm'. This means 'protecting members of the public from death or serious personal injury, whether physical or psychological, occasioned by further such offences committed by him'[3].

Remands and committals of juveniles

The Criminal Justice Act 1991[4] also amended the law relating to remands and committals of juveniles and applies essentially the same policy regarding their accommodation while in custody. Thus, where a court remands a child or young person charged with or convicted of one or more offences, or commits him for trial or sentence, and he is not released on bail, the remand must be to local authority accommodation[5]. The court is required to designate the relevant authority which will be where the child is being 'looked after' by an authority, that authority, or the authority in whose area the child resides, or where one of the offences was committed[6]. The court may require the juvenile to comply with any condition which can be imposed under the Bail Act 1976[7], and the relevant authority may be given the responsibility of securing compliance with the conditions imposed[8].

On a remand or committal, the court may, after consultation with the local authority, require it to comply with a 'security requirement' by placing or keeping

---

1 For further discussion, see C Bell 'New Criminal Justice Act amends PACE on detention of juveniles' (1991) 79 *Childright* 7.
2 PACE 1984, s 38(6), as amended by the Criminal Justice Act 1991, s 59.
3 Ibid, s 38(6A).
4 Criminal Justice Act 1991, s 60.
5 Children and Young Persons Act 1969, s 23(1).
6 Ibid, s 23(2).
7 Such conditions typically relate to place of residence, reporting to the police, curfew requirements, etc.
8 Children and Young Persons Act 1969, s 23(9) and (10).

the juvenile in 'secure accommodation'[1]. This is defined as 'accommodation which is provided in a community home, a voluntary home or a registered children's home for the purpose of restricting liberty, and is approved for that purpose by the Secretary of State'[2]. The Criminal Justice Act 1991[3] requires local authorities to ensure that they have sufficient secure accommodation for these purposes and others. The power to impose a security requirement is, however, carefully restricted. It may be stipulated only where the young person is at least 15 years of age[4] and either:

(1) he is charged with, or has been convicted of, a violent or sexual offence or an offence punishable, in the case of an adult, with at least 14 years' imprisonment; or

(2) he has a recent history of absconding while remanded to local authority accommodation and is charged with, or has been convicted of, an imprisonable offence alleged, or found to have been committed, while he was so remanded.

In either case, the court must be of the opinion that the protection of the public from serious harm justifies the security requirement[5]. Where the court does impose a requirement, it must explain the reasons for its decision in open court and in ordinary language which the young person can understand[6].

Consistency of practice
The overall objective of the provisions is to produce consistency of practice between the different police forces and as between detentions while under arrest, on remand or on committal[7].

The criminal courts

Provision for the child's welfare
Since the early part of the twentieth century, the principle has been accepted that there should be a separate system of criminal courts for dealing with juvenile offenders[8]. The objective is to prevent children and young persons coming into contact or associating with adult suspects, while awaiting trial, during the trial

---

1 Children and Young Persons Act 1969, s 23(4). The provisions relating to 'secure accommodation' are dependent on s 60 of the Criminal Justice Act 1991 being brought into force. In the meantime, under transitional provisions, a young person aged under 17 may be remanded to a remand centre and, if aged at least 15, to prison.

2 Ibid, s 23(12).

3 Criminal Justice Act 1991, s 61(1).

4 Section 97 of the Crime and Disorder Act 1998 amends s 23 of the Children and Young Persons Act 1969 to allow courts to remand young persons aged 12 or over direct to local authority secure accommodation and to enable the Secretary of State to implement the provisions in stages. Section 98 amends s 23 to provide for 15- and 16-year-old boys who meet specific criteria to be remanded to prison or a remand centre and for vulnerable 15- and 16-year-old boys to be remanded to local authority secure accommodation if a place is available.

5 Children and Young Persons Act 1969, s 23(5).

6 Ibid, s 23(6).

7 For criticisms, see C Bell 'New Criminal Justice Act amends PACE on detention of juveniles' (1991) 79 *Childright* 7.

8 The historical background is traced by HK Bevan *Child Law* (Butterworths, 1989) at paras 12.01 et seq.

itself, and while in custody[1]. The general rule is, therefore, that a juvenile should be tried in the youth court and not in the adult magistrates' court or the Crown Court. Where, exceptionally, it is necessary for the trial of the juvenile to take place in one of the adult criminal courts[2], the principle (again subject to limited exceptions) is that, if convicted, the juvenile should be remitted to the youth court to be dealt with by it[3]. Whichever court is dealing with a child or young person, either as an offender or otherwise, it must have regard to his welfare and must, in a proper case, 'take steps for removing him from undesirable surroundings, and for securing that proper provision is made for his education and training'[4]. This welfare provision in the criminal context is, however, quite different from the 'welfare principle' which applies in family proceedings[5]. Welfare is not 'paramount' in criminal proceedings but is one important factor in the court's decision-making process. Clearly, there are wider considerations of the public interest at stake here, especially the need to protect the public.

The youth court

The youth court is a specialised magistrates' court comprised of justices of the peace who are members of the youth court panel for their area. The court will usually be constituted by three members, at least one of whom must normally be a woman[6]. The court abides by the ordinary rules and procedures of magistrates' courts, except where these are expressly modified[7].

Before the Criminal Justice Act 1991, the youth court was known as the juvenile court and the youth court panel as the juvenile court panel. The change of nomenclature reflected a shift in the demographic make-up of those appearing before the court[8]. In 1988, approximately 90% of those appearing were in the 14- to 16-year age group but it is now predicted that, in future, three-quarters will be 16 or 17 years of age. This shift came about as a result of a number of other changes. First, before the Criminal Justice Act 1991, 17-year-olds were dealt with in the adult court system while 16-year-olds were brought before the juvenile court. The Government did not think that this differential treatment of 16- and 17-year-olds could continue to be justified and thought that *both* should be dealt with in the youth court as 'near adults'. The Criminal Justice Act 1991 brought 17-year-olds within the youth court's jurisdiction for most purposes except

---

1   See the Children and Young Persons Act 1933, s 31.
2   The main exceptions relate to homicide and cases in which the juvenile is jointly charged with an adult or in relation to which an adult is charged as a secondary party or vice-versa. See the Children and Young Persons Act 1933, s 46, the Children and Young Persons Act 1963, s 18 and *Clarke Hall & Morrison on Children* (Butterworths) at paras B55 and B56 which sets out the position in helpful tabular form. A useful and concise account of the circumstances in which the trial of juveniles may take place on indictment, in an adult magistrates' court and a youth court, is to be found in J Sprack *Emmins on Criminal Procedure* (7th edn) (Blackstone Press Ltd, 1997) at pp 159–165.
3   Children and Young Persons Act 1933, s 56(1) which provides for remission to the youth court unless the adult court is 'satisfied that it would be undesirable to do so'.
4   Ibid, s 44.
5   See Chapter 2 above.
6   See, generally, *Clarke Hall & Morrison on Children* (above) at paras B34 et seq.
7   Magistrates' Courts Act 1980, s 152.
8   See M Wasik and RD Taylor *Blackstone's Guide to the Criminal Justice Act 1991* (Blackstone Press, 1991) at para 4.14.

remand[1]. Alongside this change, the court lost its former substantial *civil* jurisdiction over children in need of care and protection, which was transferred to the 'family proceedings court'[2]. The practical effect of this, was to remove from the court's jurisdiction many younger children.

Special procedural rules

Special procedural rules protect the anonymity of children appearing before the youth court[3]. The court must not sit in a room which is used for normal criminal proceedings within one hour either side of such proceedings[4]. There are restrictions on publicity and the categories of those entitled to be present are severely restricted[5]. The words 'conviction' and 'sentence' must not be used in relation to juveniles dealt with summarily, and are replaced by the more neutral 'finding of guilt' and 'order made on a finding of guilt'[6].

Disposals: dealing with young offenders

Policies of dealing with young offenders have been the subject of considerable vacillation by governments of different complexion over a great many years. In particular, there has not been a consistent view about how to strike the balance between issues of the welfare of the young offender and considerations of justice or punishment. During the 1960s it seemed that the welfare model was in ascendancy and, although it can be argued that an increasingly punitive approach has been taken for several decades, there was still, until comparatively recently, an emphasis on diversion from the criminal courts and a preference for community-based rather than custodial sentences[7]. In the 1990s, however, there has been a distinctly authoritarian shift, and the sentencing of juveniles has taken on an increasingly punitive ethos. Once again, juvenile crime is being seen predominantly as a matter of personal responsibility, rather than principally the product of adverse social conditions or a disadvantaged family background. This appears to be the philosophical basis of the Crime and Disorder Act 1998 which is described briefly at the end of this chapter. Before coming to this, we will summarise the current range of sentencing options in relation to young offenders. The full range of disposals in the youth court is extensive[8]. Yet this requires qualification, since the alternatives in any individual cases are cut down by various criteria which determine when each can be used. Thus, for example, custodial sentences may only be imposed where the offence is 'so serious' that only a custodial sentence can be justified[9] and, where a community sentence is proposed, it must be shown

---

1   Criminal Justice Act 1991, s 68.
2   See Chapter 2 above.
3   Children and Young Persons Act 1933, s 47.
4   Ibid, s 47(2).
5   Those allowed are members and officers of the court, the parties, their lawyers and others directly concerned with the case, witnesses, bona fide representatives of newspapers or newsagencies and others specially authorised by the court.
6   Children and Young Persons Act 1933, s 59(1).
7   On the 'justice' versus 'welfare' debate, see C Ball 'Young Offenders and the Youth Court' [1992] Crim LR 277.
8   These are comprehensively set out in *Clarke Hall & Morrison on Children* (Butterworths) at paras B161 et seq.
9   Criminal Justice Act 1991, s 1(2).

that the offence is 'serious enough' to warrant such a sentence[1]. Other sentences are restricted by the age of the offender and by whether the offence would be punishable by imprisonment in the case of an adult.

Sentencing in the criminal courts is largely governed by the Criminal Justice Act 1991. A key principle in that Act is 'proportionality' – that the sentence or order imposed should be broadly commensurate with the seriousness of the offence[2]. The various disposals can be conveniently categorised into discharges, financial penalties and orders, community sentences, custodial sentences and orders for dealing with mentally disordered offenders[3].

Discharges

In cases which are perceived by the courts to be at the least serious end of the spectrum, they may either discharge the offender absolutely, or discharge him subject to a condition that he commits no further offences during a specified period not exceeding three years[4]. If he then re-offends, he will be in breach of the order, and may be brought back before the court and dealt with as the court had power to do originally. Discharges have the advantage that they do not count as convictions against the child or young person, except for limited purposes[5].

Financial penalties and orders

It has already been noted here that it is the duty of the court to order that a parent or guardian be responsible for payment of a juvenile's financial penalties. These penalties broadly divide into fines, compensation and deprivation of property orders.

Fines

Magistrates' courts and youth courts may impose fines subject to maximum levels prescribed by the statutes which create the various offences. The particular fine within the appropriate scale is then fixed in accordance with the 'unit fine system'. This involves applying a formula which takes into account the gravity of the offence, the means of the person responsible for payment and any mitigating circumstances[6].

Compensation orders

Instead of, or in addition to, dealing with the offender in any other way, the court may order the offender to pay compensation to the victim for any personal injury, loss, or damage resulting from the offence, or any other offence taken into account[7].

---

1 Criminal Justice Act 1991, s 6(1).
2 For a general account of the aims of the Act, see M Wasik and RD Taylor *Blackstone's Guide to the Criminal Justice Act 1991* (Blackstone Press, 1991) at pp 1–9.
3 For a detailed description of each sentence or order, see *Clarke Hall & Morrison on Children* (Butterworths) at paras B161 et seq.
4 Under the Powers of Criminal Courts Act 1973, s 1A the court may grant a discharge where it is of the opinion 'having regard to the circumstances including the nature of the offence and the character of the offender, that it is inexpedient to inflict punishment'.
5 Ibid, s 1C(1).
6 Criminal Justice Act 1991, s 18.
7 Powers of Criminal Courts Act 1973, s 35(1).

Deprivation of property order

Deprivation of property orders are designed to ensure that the offender does not profit from his wrongdoing in relation to offences involving property such as theft and related offences. The court may, instead of, or in addition to, dealing with the offender in any other way, make a forfeiture order depriving the offender of any rights in the property to which the offence relates[1].

Community sentences

Community sentences, while falling short of custodial sentences, do involve a significant interference with liberty. As such, the criteria for imposing them are more restrictive than for financial penalties but less restrictive than for custodial sentences. Three conditions must be satisfied which are:

(1) that the offence, or the combination of the offence and one or more offences associated with it, was *serious enough* to warrant such a sentence[2];
(2) the particular order or orders comprising or forming part of the sentence is or are the *most suitable* for the offender[3]; and
(3) the restrictions on liberty imposed are such as are *commensurate* with the seriousness of the offence, or the combination of the offence and other offences associated with it[4].

In considering the suitability of the various community orders, the court must obtain and consider a pre-sentence report on the offender[5]. Community orders include a probation order, a community service order, a combination order, a curfew order, a supervision order or an attendance centre order[6].

Probation order

A probation order places the offender under the supervision of a probation officer for not less than six months or more than three years. The court may make the order where it is of the opinion that it is desirable in the interests of securing rehabilitation of the offender, protecting the public from him, or preventing the commission by him of further offences[7]. The primary obligation of the offender is to stay in touch with the probation officer. Conditions may also be attached to the order which may, for example, require him to attend from time to time at approved places to take part in various activities[8].

Community service order

This order may be imposed where the offender is over 16 years of age and the offence would be punishable by imprisonment in the case of an adult[9]. The consent of the offender is again required. The order entails undertaking specified unpaid work in the community. The court must be satisfied that provision for such work can be made and must specify the number of hours to be served[10].

---

1 Powers of Criminal Courts Act 1973, s 43.
2 Criminal Justice Act 1991, s 6(1).
3 Ibid, s 6(2).
4 Ibid.
5 Ibid, s 7(3).
6 Ibid, s 6(4).
7 Powers of Criminal Courts Act 1973, s 2(1).
8 Ibid, s 3(1) and Sch 1A.
9 Ibid, s 14(1).
10 Ibid, s 14(2A), (4).

Combination order

The court may, instead of imposing one kind of order, combine more than one order to constitute, together, a community sentence. The court must, before doing so, have regard to the suitability of the order, to the offender's circumstances and to the seriousness of the offence or offences. Orders of probation and community service may not, however, be combined other than to form a combination order[1]. They may not be used together to constitute a community sentence.

Curfew order

A curfew order requires an offender to remain for specified periods at a place specified in the order[2]. When originally introduced, the order applied only to offenders over the age of 16 years but, following amendments made by the Crime (Sentences) Act 1997[3], the order has been extended to cover those aged under 16. In the case of the former, the order may not last more than six months, and in the case of the latter, for more than three months. The order must include provision for a 'responsible person' to monitor the curfew. Compliance with the order may also be monitored by electronic tagging[4]. The practice is controversial and it has been questioned whether it is in compliance with Art 40(1) of the United Nations Convention on the Rights of the Child which requires States parties to recognise 'the right of every child alleged as, accused of, or recognised as having infringed the penal law to be treated in a manner consistent with the promotion of the child's sense of dignity and worth'[5].

Supervision order

This places the offender under the supervision of a designated local authority or probation officer for a period of not more than three years[6]. There are no restrictions on the kind of offences for which the order may be made and the consent of the offender is not a condition[7]. The local authority will usually be appointed supervisor, except where the probation service has already been involved with the household, the juvenile is 13 years old or over, and the local authority requests it[8]. The statutory duty of the supervisor is to 'advise, assist and befriend' the offender[9]. The order may impose a range of conditions relating to such matters as residence, education, participation or non-participation in various activities[10].

Attendance centre order

An attendance centre is 'a place at which offenders under 21 years of age may be required to attend, and be given under supervision, appropriate occupation or instruction'[11]. The court may make the order where the offence would usually be

---

1 Criminal Justice Act 1991, ss 6(3) and 11.
2 Ibid, s 12.
3 Section 43.
4 Criminal Justice Act 1991, s 13.
5 J Fortin *Children's Rights and the Developing Law* (Butterworths, 1998) at p 463.
6 Children and Young Persons Act 1969, s 70(1) and s 11.
7 By virtue of amendments made by the Crime (Sentences) Act 1997, parental consent to the imposition of certain requirements is no longer necessary.
8 Children and Young Persons Act 1969, s 13(2).
9 Ibid, s 14.
10 Ibid, s 18(2)(b).
11 Criminal Justice Act 1982, s 16(2).

punishable with imprisonment or where there has been a failure to comply with previous orders of the court, such as conditions of probation or refusal to pay a fine[1]. The centre must be reasonably accessible to the offender and the court must specify the number of hours of attendance[2].

Custodial sentences

In the most serious cases of violent or sexual offences there may be no alternative but to pass a custodial sentence, if only to protect the public. As noted above, in recent years there has been an increased use of custodial sentences particularly in the case of persistent young offenders.

Detention in a young offender institution

The principal custodial sentence is now detention in a 'young offender institution'. The maximum period which may be imposed by either the youth court or the Crown Court is 24 months[3]. The restrictions on custodial sentences are substantial under the Criminal Justice Acts of 1982 and 1991[4].

Before a sentence of detention may be imposed, the offender must be at least 15 years of age and the offence must be punishable with imprisonment if committed by someone over 21 years of age[5]. In addition, the court must be satisfied:

(1) that the offence, or the combination of the offence and one or more offences associated with it, was *so serious* that only such a sentence can be justified for the offence; and

(2) where the offence is a violent or sexual offence, that only such a sentence would be adequate to protect the public from serious harm from him[6].

These conditions do not prevent the court from passing a custodial sentence where the offender refuses to give his consent (where required) to a community sentence proposed by the court[7]. This is clearly intended to force the 'consent' of reluctant offenders to community-based orders.

Detention in a secure training centre

As noted above, the maximum period of detention in a young offender institution was increased from 12 to 24 months by the Criminal Justice and Public Order Act 1994. The same legislation[8] introduced the new 'secure training order' with a view to dealing with a small number of persistent offenders at the younger end of the

---

1   Criminal Justice Act 1982, s 17(1).
2   Ibid, s 17(7) and s 17(4) and (5) which prescribe the minimum and maximum aggregate number of hours which may be imposed.
3   The maximum term was doubled by the Criminal Justice and Public Order Act 1994, s 17, amending the Criminal Justice Act 1982, s 1B. The normal maximum term which the youth court can impose for a single offence is six months (Magistrates' Courts Act 1980, s 133).
4   See *Clarke Hall & Morrison on Children* (Butterworths) at paras B308 et seq.
5   For guidance on the interrelationship between the maximum sentence of detention in a young offender institution and detention under the Children and Young Persons Act 1933, s 53(2), see the recent Court of Appeal decision in *R v AM and Others* [1998] 1 FLR 900. See also *R v Secretary of State for the Home Department, ex parte Furber* [1997] Crim LR 841 and *R v Zinga* [1997] Crim LR 904. More recently, see the Court of Appeal (Criminal Division) decision in *R v Brown* [1998] Crim LR 588 and the helpful commentary on the changes to custodial sentences for young offenders which will be made by the Crime and Disorder Act 1998.
6   Criminal Justice Act 1991, s 1(2).
7   Ibid, s 1(3).
8   Section 1.

spectrum who were believed to be responsible for a disproportionate amount of crime. The secure training order empowers the courts to order children aged from 12 to 14 years to be detained for a minimum of six months and a maximum of two years. The order may be made where the juvenile is convicted of an imprisonable offence when at least 12 years old; has been convicted of at least three imprisonable offences; and has, either on the present occasion or on an earlier occasion, been found to be in breach of a supervision order or convicted of an imprisonable offence while subject to such an order[1]. The order consists of two parts. The first part involves detention in a secure training centre while the second entails supervision in the community.

Detention during Her Majesty's pleasure
Children and young persons who are convicted of murder must by law be detained at Her Majesty's pleasure[2]. The trial for murder must be on indictment in the Crown Court. A child or young person may also be committed for trial in the Crown Court for certain other serious offences, ie manslaughter or offences in relation to which the maximum adult punishment is at least 14 years' imprisonment. If there is a conviction, and the Crown Court is satisfied that none of the other methods in which the case may legally be dealt with is suitable, the court may order detention for a period not exceeding the maximum period which could be imposed on an adult offender for the offence[3]. Detention under either of the above provisions will be 'in such place and on such conditions as the Secretary of State may direct' which will not be an ordinary young offender institution.

In recent years the law relating to s 53 offenders has been the subject of extensive domestic and international criticism largely revolving around the indeterminate nature of the sentences. In February 1996 the European Court of Human Rights in *Hussain v The United Kingdom*[4] found that English law was in breach of Art 5(4) of the Convention which provides:

> 'Everyone who is deprived of his liberty by arrest or detention should be entitled to take proceedings by which the lawfulness of his detention shall be decided speedily by a court and his release ordered if his detention is not lawful.'

Mr Hussain complained that he had not been able at reasonable intervals to have judicial, rather than executive, assessment of his continued detention during Her Majesty's pleasure and the European Court agreed with him. As a result, the UK found it necessary to amend s 53[5] to transfer responsibility for the decision on eventual release of a s 53 offender from the Home Secretary to the Parole Board.

Hussain concerned the so-called 'post-tariff' period of detention but further widely publicised issues have arisen in relation to the initial period of detention or the 'tariff' itself. A two-year-old toddler, James Bulger, was abducted from a shopping centre in Merseyside and killed under horrific circumstances by two boys, Thompson and Venables, both of whom were just 10 years old at the time. They were subsequently convicted of his murder and sentenced, as they had to be,

---

1 Criminal Justice and Public Order Act 1994, s 1(5).
2 Children and Young Persons Act 1933, s 53(1), and see 'Detained at Her Majesty's Pleasure' (1991) 76 *Childright* 15.
3 Children and Young Persons Act 1933, s 53(2). For a recent illustration of the use of this provision, see *R v Sheffield Youth Justices ex parte M* [1998] 1 FLR 929.
4 (1996) 22 EHRR 1.
5 By the Crime (Sentences) Act 1997, s 28.

to be detained under s 53. Questions then arose as to the appropriate 'tariff'. The trial judge recommended that it should be eight years but this was increased by the then Lord Chief Justice, Lord Taylor LCJ, to 10 years. In an atmosphere of 'moral panic' and near public hysteria the then Home Secretary, Michael Howard, taking into account the public clamour, increased the tariff again to 15 years.

In *R v Secretary of State for the Home Department ex parte Thompson and Venables*[1] the legality of the Home Secretary's decision fell for consideration by the House of Lords. Meanwhile, Thompson and Venables had also taken their case to the European Commission on Human Rights. The House of Lords was deeply divided but held by majority that the Home Secretary had erred in law when he stated that the mandatory sentence for life imprisonment for murder, including the tariff principle, imposed in the case of an adult offender was equivalent to a sentence of detention imposed on a child murderer under s 53. There was a difference in philosophy between the two sentences which could be traced back to the Children Act 1908 and was also reflected in s 44 of the Children and Young Persons Act 1933 which required courts dealing with young offenders to have regard to their welfare. The tariff policy adopted by the Home Secretary in this case was therefore unlawful. Any tariff policy in relation to young offenders would have to be sufficiently flexible that it could take into account by continuing review any progress or development of the child in addition to the considerations of retribution, deterrence and risk. The House went on to hold that the Home Secretary had misdirected himself and been procedurally unreasonable in taking into account petitions and other correspondence submitted by the victim's family. This consisted of a petition signed by 278,000 members of the public calling for a full-life sentence and another signed by 5,900 members of the public calling for a minimum of 25 years' detention. There were also 4,400 letters submitted by the family. It was held that, while the Home Secretary was entitled to have regard to broader considerations of a public character, in fixing the penal element he was exercising a function closely analogous to a sentencing function. He had erred in failing to distinguish between legitimate public concern of a general nature and public clamour over a particular case.

The result of the Thompson and Venables case is that while an initial tariff may continue to be set in s 53 cases there will need to be provision for regular review of the progress of s 53 offenders and the appropriateness of early release.

Special orders relating to mentally disordered offenders

Under the Mental Health Act 1983[2] the court may, if the offence would normally be punishable by imprisonment, and certain medical conditions are satisfied, make an order authorising the offender's admission to a hospital (a hospital order) or placing him under the guardianship of social services (a guardianship order). Detailed discussion of the mental health legislation is beyond the scope of this work[3].

---

1   [1997] 2 FLR 471.
2   Mental Health Act 1983, s 37.
3   For detailed treatment, see B Hoggett *Mental Health Law* (4th edn) (Sweet & Maxwell, 1996).

The effect of the Children Act 1989

The Children Act[1] abolished care orders in criminal proceedings. The main objection to such orders was that they were ineffective as preventive measures and indeterminate. Instead, the court is now empowered, in appropriate cases, and in accordance with specified criteria, to add a requirement to an existing supervision order that an offender reside in local authority accommodation for a period of up to six months[2].

THE CRIME AND DISORDER ACT 1998

The Crime and Disorder Act 1998, inter alia, provides the basis for a root and branch reform of the youth justice system[3]. We have already discussed some of the reforms, particularly the abolition of the doli incapax presumption and the new parenting orders, earlier in the chapter. We set out below the salient features of the new legislation as it affects youth crime and conclude with a brief comment on its underlying philosophy and how this may relate to the thinking behind other legislation relating to children. The reader should bear in mind that a number of new orders, including child safety orders, parenting orders, reprimands and warnings, action plan orders and reparation orders, will be piloted before their full implementation.

The Act essentially reforms the law of juvenile justice in three ways. First, there are what might be called *institutional changes* to the criminal justice system (Part III). Secondly, there are measures for the *prevention* of crime and disorder many of which relate specifically to youth crime (Part I). Finally, there are reforms relating to the options for *dealing with young offenders* (Part IV).

Institutional changes

Part III of the Act sets out the aims of the youth justice system, contains provisions relating to youth justice services, provides for the creation of a new Youth Justice Board and the establishment of local youth offending teams.

The principal aim of the youth justice system is to prevent offending by children and young persons and it is to be the duty of all persons and bodies carrying out functions in relation to the youth justice system to have regard to that aim[4]. Local authorities must ensure the availability of appropriate youth justice services, and police authorities, probation committees and health authorities are required to co-operate in securing that such services are available[5]. The Act goes on to specify and define the meaning of 'youth justice services'[6]. In particular, each local authority must establish one or more youth offending teams[7]. Local authorities, in

---

1   Section 90.
2   Schedule 12 to the Children Act, and the Children and Young Persons Act 1969, s 12AA.
3   The Labour Party's proposals for reform of the youth justice system were set out in the consultation paper *Tackling Youth Crime: Reforming Youth Justice* (May 1996). This was followed by other consultation papers culminating in the White Paper *No More Excuses – A New Approach to Tackling Youth Crime in England and Wales* (November 1997) (Cm 3809).
4   Section 37.
5   Section 38.
6   Sections 38–41.
7   Section 39.

consultation with the above authorities, must formulate and implement an annual youth justice plan which sets out how youth justice services in their area are to be provided and funded and the composition, funding and functions of the youth offending teams[1]. There is to be a Youth Justice Board whose function will be to monitor the operation of the youth justice system, promote good practice and advise the Home Secretary on the operation of the youth justice system and the setting of national standards[2]. The Board will be located in the Home Office and will 'have a wide ranging membership drawn from different backgrounds with expertise in tackling youth offending'[3].

Prevention of youth crime

Part I of the Act contains a number of radical measures designed to prevent crime and anti-social behaviour by adults and young offenders. Our concern here is only with the latter and we have already discussed the new parenting orders. In addition to these measures to reinforce parental responsibility, the Act provides for a new 'child safety order' which is designed to enable the courts to protect children under the age of 10 (viz below the age of criminal responsibility) who are at risk of becoming involved in crime or have already begun to behave in an anti-social or criminal manner[4]. The order, if made, will place the child under the supervision of a specified, responsible officer and require the child to comply with arrangements aimed at ensuring that he receives appropriate care, protection and support and is subject to proper control. It might, for example, require the child to be home by a certain time or to avoid a certain area. The court, before making such an order, will be required to take into account information about the family circumstances and must explain to the parent in ordinary language the effect and consequences of the order[5].

Allied to above order will be a new power given to local authorities to make a 'local child curfew scheme' under which a curfew notice may be given banning children of specified ages (below the age of 10) from being in a public place during specified hours unless they are under the control of a responsible adult[6]. The police will be required to inform the local authority where they believe the child is contravening a curfew notice and a police constable will be empowered in these circumstances to return the child to his home[7].

Dealing with young offenders

Part IV of the Act contains a number of new measures for dealing with young offenders.

As noted earlier, the existing system of cautioning young offenders is to be abolished and replaced with a new system of reprimands and warnings[8]. Where a police constable warns a child or young person, that person will be referred to a youth offending team for assessment and, where appropriate, provision must be

---

1 Section 40.
2 Section 41 and Sch 2.
3 Consultation Paper *Tackling Youth Crime: Reforming Youth Justice* (May 1996).
4 Section 11.
5 Section 12.
6 Section 14.
7 Section 15.
8 Sections 65 and 66.

made for him to participate in a programme to prevent re-offending and to secure his rehabilitation[1]. A child who receives a final warning will be given guidance and support to cut down the risks of re-offending but any further re-offending is then likely to result in a significant punishment from the courts. It is expressly provided that the courts should not, other than in exceptional circumstances, conditionally discharge young offenders convicted of an offence within two years of a warning[2].

Part IV also provides for several completely new sentencing options for young offenders. There will be a 'reparation order' which requires a young offender to make a reparation to the victim of an offence, a person otherwise affected by it or to the community at large[3]. Before making the order, the court will be required to consider a written report about the type of reparation and the views of the victim and to explain the order to the young offender[4]. The Act also amends the Children and Young Persons Act 1969 to enable reparation conditions to be attached to supervision orders[5]. There will be an 'action plan order' which is a new community penalty requiring a young offender to comply with an action plan intended to address his offending[6]. It is expected that the order will combine reparation, punishment and rehabilitation and will involve the offender's parents. The court will be required to consider the family circumstances, information about the proposed action plan and the attitude of the offender's parent or guardian. The court must then explain the effect of the order to the young offender and it is empowered to fix a hearing within 21 days of making the order to review its effectiveness and the extent to which it has been implemented[7]. Finally, the Act enables the court to sentence a young offender to a detention and training order ('DTO') which will require the offender to be subject to a period of detention and training, followed by a period of supervision[8]. The new order is intended to be a generic custodial sentence to replace the various custodial sentences currently available in relation to juveniles as discussed above. The Government has made it clear that the new DTO will be subject to the restrictions on the use of custody laid down in the Criminal Justice Act 1991[9].

The philosophy of the legislation

The hallmark of the 1998 Act as indicated by the title to the White Paper preceding it – 'No More Excuses' – is personal responsibility for crime which is shared between young people themselves and their parents. We have alluded above to the ongoing debates about the appropriate balance between 'justice' and 'welfare' and it must be doubted whether the increasingly punitive, authoritarian approach to juvenile crime, involving as it does Draconian restraints on liberty and

---

1 Section 66.
2 Ibid.
3 Section 67.
4 Section 68.
5 Section 71.
6 Section 69.
7 Section 70.
8 Sections 73–79.
9 For the thinking behind the new order, see the White Paper (above), ch 6.

family autonomy, is consistent with a commitment to the civil liberties of young people or with international obligations[1].

How far the legislation is consistent with the philosophy embodied in other legislation affecting children, most notably the Children Act 1989, is also open to doubt[2]. On the one hand, the increasing autonomy of adolescents, acknowledged in the Children Act, might be thought consistent with the emphasis on personal responsibility in the Crime and Disorder Act. Indeed, we commented in Chapter 3 on the failure of the law to articulate clearly enough the responsibilities or duties which should go with gathering independence. On the other hand, the Children Act supports the notion of *gradual*, not sudden, emancipation for children as they grow older, and the inflexible imposition of criminal responsibility on children at the age of 10 and the use of custodial sentences for those as young as 12 is hardly consistent with this. Perhaps most striking of all is the notion of *dual* responsibility of children and parents for crime. Elsewhere in the law, the idea is of dwindling parental control as the child gets older. Yet, in the criminal context, the notion persists that parents remain fully in control and responsible for their children. There is little recognition here of the potential for a conflict of interest between the parent and child and indeed it is not entirely clear who should be regarded as a 'parent' for these purposes[3]. The new 'parenting orders' may be made against a 'parent or guardian' but this may well be inadequate to cover the case of many children who are raised not by genetic parents but by social parents such as step-parents. More fundamentally, it is certainly questionable whether a parent, however defined, is actually able to be in control of a teenage child. Making parents legally liable in these circumstances may only serve to exacerbate the tensions between adolescents and parents with which the law has had to grapple in other contexts.

---

1 The UN Committee on the Rights of the Child was, for example, highly critical of the introduction of secure training orders for children as young as 12 and, more generally, of the weight being placed on imprisonment and punishment in the juvenile justice system. See *Concluding Observations of the Committee on the Rights of the Child: United Kingdom of Great Britain and Northern Ireland*, CRC/C/15/Add 34 (January 1995).

2 On the philosophy of the Children Act, see Chapter 2 above.

3 On the difficulties of defining parenthood, see Chapter 3 above.

Chapter 15
CHILDREN AND THE CIVIL LAW

INTRODUCTION

We now turn our attention from the criminal law to the civil law. Family law, with which most of this book is concerned, is itself a branch of the civil law but we are concerned in this chapter with those areas which are not directly related to the child's position in the family. We are dealing primarily with those legal issues which can arise from the child's activities outside the home. We have already seen[1] that young people do not acquire capacities and responsibilities all at once, on attaining majority, but at different ages, depending on the activity in question[2], and it has been noted that this can give rise to difficult questions about the relationship between the child's own capacities and the responsibilities of parents[3]. We now concentrate on three key and related areas of the civil law – the law of tort, contract and employment. Each is something of a 'Cinderella' area as it applies to children. Little is written on these subjects beyond what can be gleaned from the standard texts. Useful comparisons can, however, be made with Scots law where, following a wide-ranging report on the legal capacities and responsibilities of minors and pupils in 1987, there was legislation on the subject in 1991[4].

The central themes of the civil law, like those of the criminal law, are *protection* and *responsibility*. What special protections are afforded children where they are injured by the actions of third parties or where children purport to enter into contracts (whether of employment or otherwise) which are, objectively judged, not in their best interests? To what extent are children responsible for their own actions which lead to the injury of third parties or to commercial loss, as where a trader has dealt fairly with a minor who then defaults? The answers which the law gives reflect a compromise between the desire to protect children either from themselves or from the exploitation of others, and the need to avoid unnecessary hardship to those who deal with children in good faith.

CHILDREN AND THE LAW OF TORT

There are two broad aspects of the law of tort which affect children. The first is the question of civil liability for interferences with, or injuries to, children by third parties or by their carers. The second is the issue of the liability which children themselves have for their own tortious acts. In each case, difficult questions arise

---

1 At Chapter 3 above.
2 For a good review of the various age limits, see 'At What Age Can I?' (1991) 73 *Childright* 11.
3 See especially Chapter 8 above in relation to medical issues where most of the difficulties have arisen.
4 Scot Law Com No 110 *Report on the Legal Capacity and Responsibility of Minors and Pupils* (1987) implemented by the Age of Legal Capacity (Scotland) Act 1991. For commentary on the Act, see JM Thomson *Family Law in Scotland* (3rd edn) (Butterworths, 1996) at ch 9.

about the extent of the parental duty to *protect*[1]. Where a child is injured at home, this may be the result of negligence by the parent or other carer or it may be a pure accident. Essentially, this turns on what ought to have been expected of the reasonably prudent parent. Where a child is injured outside the home, this may again be attributable to the negligence of the carer, that of a third party or the negligence of both of them, but again, it may be an accident for which no one is to be held responsible. Conversely, where a child causes injury to someone, this may be solely the responsibility of the child, the result of negligence by the carer or, again, just accidental.

The extent of control, as an aspect of parental responsibility, is also a central feature of the so-called 'intentional torts' involving trespass to the person whether by assault, battery or false imprisonment. It is accepted that the right to control and discipline the child is an element of parental responsibility and, indeed, a failure to exercise that responsibility might conceivably give rise to an action in negligence against the parent. But how far does this go? As the child gets older, the *Gillick* case and the Children Act[2] both support the notion of a gradual relaxation of parental authority and control. Thus, certain purported exercises of parental discipline may themselves be tortious, if they exceed the bounds of reasonableness. A related issue here is the extent to which (if at all) a third party may be held liable for interfering with parents in the discharge of their responsibilities.

Protection of children

Torts based on negligence
The tort of negligence is committed where a duty of care is owed, there is a breach of that duty, and someone (a child for present purposes) is injured as a result[3]. In order to establish this, it needs to be proved, on the balance of probabilities, that the defendant failed to avoid acts or omissions which were foreseeably likely to injure the child. The child will then have a claim for damages.

As a general proposition, the standard of care required *towards* children is higher than that towards adults[4]. Conversely, children themselves (especially young children) are not expected to exercise the same degree of care as adults[5]. While these are general principles of the law of negligence, they have been applied more specifically by statute in the context of occupiers' liability. This

---

1   The duty which is recognised by implication in the Children and Young Persons Act 1933, s 1, as to which see Chapters 8 and 14 above.
2   See Chapter 3.
3   See, generally: *Winfield and Jolowicz on Tort* (14th edn) (Sweet & Maxwell, 1994) at ch 5; *Street on Torts* (9th edn) (Butterworths, 1993) at chs 11–14; and *Salmond and Heuston on the Law of Torts* (21st edn) (Sweet & Maxwell, 1996) at ch 9.
4   The general standard of care was summed up by Alderson B in *Blyth v Birmingham Waterworks Co* (1856) 11 Ex 781 at p 784 where he said:
    'Negligence is the omission to do something which a reasonable man, guided upon those considerations which ordinarily regulate the conduct of human affairs, would do, or doing something which a prudent and reasonable man would not do.'
    Clearly, a reasonable man would appreciate the need for greater caution where children are concerned. An obvious example would be child pedestrians.
5   See below. On children's duties generally, see Chapter 3 above.

legislation governs the liability of 'occupiers'[1] for injuries caused to those on land or structures under their control. The natural curiosity of children and their propensity for straying into hazardous environments has generated a mass of reported cases over a substantial period of years[2].

The chapter begins by looking at the principles which have emerged in this area of applied negligence. It then considers the tort of negligence itself, in its application to parental failings.

Occupiers' liability

The liability of occupiers is governed by the Occupiers' Liability Acts of 1957 and 1984. The extent of the duty owed depends on whether the injured person was a 'visitor' (the 1957 Act) or a 'non-visitor' (the 1984 Act). Essentially, the distinction is between those persons who were invited onto the property or were otherwise there with the express or implied permission of the occupier, and those who were not – usually, but not always, trespassers[3]. In the case of children, the distinction is not as marked as with adults and many of the cases have, for obvious reasons, involved at least technical trespasses by children[4].

Children as visitors – the Occupiers' Liability Act 1957

The 'common duty of care' owed to visitors is 'a duty to take such care as in all the circumstances of the case is reasonable, to see that the visitor will be reasonably safe in using the premises for the purposes for which he is invited or permitted by the occupier to be there'.

The duty is, therefore, not an unlimited one, but is only to take such precautions as are *reasonable*. In deciding whether there has been a breach of duty, account must be taken of the degree of care, or want of care, which would ordinarily be looked for in the visitor[5]. For these purposes, the Occupiers' Liability Act 1957 singles out children as a special case and provides that 'an occupier must be prepared for children to be less careful than adults'[6].

What then is the requisite standard of care? It is first established that allowances must be made for the greater vulnerability of children. Something which would not be a danger to an adult might be a danger to a child. This is illustrated by *Moloney v Lambeth Borough Council*[7] where a four-year-old child fell through a

---

1   Essentially, the concept of 'occupier' is related to control rather than ownership of property although the two will frequently coincide. The test is laid down in *Wheat v Lacon & Co Ltd* [1966] AC 552.

2   For an excellent review, see R Kidner 'The Duty of Occupiers Towards Children' (1988) 139 *Northern Ireland Legal Quarterly* 150.

3   The Occupiers' Liability Act 1957 abolished the former distinction between 'invitees' and 'licensees'. See *Winfield and Jolowicz on Tort* (14th edn) (Sweet & Maxwell, 1994) at pp 228 et seq, *Street on Torts* (9th edn) (Butterworths, 1993) at pp 287 et seq, and *Salmond and Heuston on the Law of Torts* (21st edn) (Sweet & Maxwell, 1996) at pp 269 et seq. In fact, the position is somewhat more complex than this since there is a category of those who enter by virtue of a legal right, such as the use of a public right of way, who are neither visitors nor trespassers. The effect of the House of Lords ruling in *McGeown v Northern Ireland Housing Executive* [1995] 1 AC 233 is that there is no liability for negligent non-feasance in these circumstances. Thus the occupier is under a duty not to add to the danger but not to take positive steps to avoid it. In this case there was no liability for failure to keep a footpath in good repair.

4   See, for example, *Glasgow Corp v Taylor* [1922] 1 AC 44.

5   Occupiers' Liability Act 1957, s 2(3).

6   Ibid, s 2(3)(a).

7   (1966) LGR 440.

balustrade protecting a staircase leading from a ground-floor to first-floor flat. The gaps in the railings were not wide enough for an adult to fall through but *were* wide enough for a child of the age and size of the plaintiff. The defendant council was held liable on the basis that it ought to have anticipated that young children would use the staircase when unaccompanied by adults. The design of the staircase did not conform with the council's common duty of care owed to a child of that age. A second, long-established, principle is that an occupier may be liable where he has created, or is aware of, an 'allurement' to children, but fails to guard against it. Seventy years ago, Glasgow Corporation fell foul of this principle[1]. It was held liable to the father of a deceased seven-year-old child who had eaten poisonous 'deadly nightshade' berries from a shrub in public gardens controlled by the Corporation. The berries were attractive and accessible to children and the Corporation was aware that the area was frequented by them. Yet it took no steps either to fence off the shrub or warn of the danger.

The courts have had to confront the difficulty in the case of young children that virtually anything can be a danger. Is there then an obligation on occupiers to make their premises as safe as a nursery? The courts have avoided this extreme conclusion, first by finding that children were trespassers in some circumstances where unaccompanied by adults[2], and secondly, more realistically, by limiting occupiers' duties to take into account parents' own responsibilities to young children. The essential point is that where a young child comes into contact with a man-made or natural hazard this may be at least as much the fault of the parent, for failing to supervise the child, as it is the fault of the occupier.

In *Phipps v Rochester Corporation*[3], a boy aged five years, out picking blackberries with his seven-year-old sister, broke his leg when he fell into a trench which his sister had safely negotiated. The trench was part of a building site adjoining the plaintiff's home. In exonerating the council, Devlin J held that the council would discharge its duty of care if it reduced the dangers present to those which would either be obvious to a parent or, if not obvious, it warned against them. He emphasised the *primary* duty of parents to ensure that young children did not wander about on their own or that, if they did, they were allowed to go only to safe places. If, on the other hand, an occupier ought to have anticipated the presence of young unaccompanied children, this could impose a duty to take appropriate precautionary measures. These principles were applied to natural hazards in *Simkiss v Rhondda Borough Council*[4]. Here, the seven-year-old plaintiff slid down a Welsh mountainside on a picnic blanket. The mountain had a bluff or steep slope which became very steep at the bottom. The plaintiff sustained a fractured skull when she fell 30 to 40 feet onto the road below. The Court of Appeal held that the council was not obliged either to fence the mountain or to warn of the sharp drop, despite the evidence that unaccompanied children were known to play in the vicinity. The prudent parent, it was said, would warn his children of such natural hazards. As Dunn LJ remarked, an occupier was not bound to fence every tree simply because a child might climb it and fall out of it. It should be remembered, however, that this principle applies only to those hazards, natural or unnatural,

---

1   *Glasgow Corp v Taylor* [1922] 1 AC 44. The concept of allurement could have the effect of
    preventing the child being regarded as a trespasser.
2   The so-called 'conditional licence'.
3   [1955] 1 QB 450.
4   (1983) 81 LGR 460.

which would be *obvious* to a prudent parent. Where the danger is latent or concealed, the duty is squarely on the occupier, if he knows of it, to take precautions.

Where the plaintiff is an older child, the occupier's duty will be discharged more easily and the standard of care owed to adolescents may not differ markedly (if at all) from that owed to adults[1].

Children as trespassers – the Occupiers' Liability Act 1984

At common law an occupier was not liable at all to trespassers, except where the injury was caused deliberately or maliciously. No distinction was made between adults and children, and the rule could operate very harshly, as it did in *Addie v Dumbreck*[2]. Here, a four-year-old boy was crushed in the wheel of a haulage system operated at a colliery. The wheel was in a field known to be frequented by children. It was attractive to them but inadequately protected. The House of Lords held that, since the child had no express or implied permission to be on the premises, he had to be classed as a trespasser and hence no duty of care was owed to him. The harshness of the rule was mitigated over the years by several devices, including the concepts of allurement and the implied licence, before a more generalised duty of 'common humanity' towards trespassers was fashioned by the House of Lords in *British Railways Board v Herrington*[3]. This extended beyond the duty merely to refrain from deliberately causing injury to a duty to take precautionary measures where there was knowledge of the circumstances of the danger and the actual or likely presence of trespassers. The duty to 'non-visitors', including trespassers, is now contained in the Occupiers' Liability Act 1984[4]. The test for liability now comprises three elements as follows:

(1) the occupier must be aware of the danger or have reasonable grounds to believe it exists;

(2) he must have known, or had reasonable grounds to believe, that the non-visitor was in, or might have come into, the vicinity of the danger; and

(3) the risk of injury must have been one against which, in all the circumstances, the occupier might have been expected to offer the non-visitor some protection.

The duty is then 'to take such care as is reasonable in all the circumstances of the case to see that [the non-visitor] does not suffer injury on the premises by reason of the danger concerned'[5]. The circumstances which give rise to a duty of care do, therefore, have elements of subjectivity and it is also provided that the duty may be discharged in appropriate cases by giving a warning[6]. However, it has been doubted whether, in its application to children, there is any appreciable difference from the common duty of care owed to child visitors. Clearly, the precautions which might be expected of occupiers towards child trespassers are greater than those one would expect for burglars. And it is unlikely that the duty could be discharged merely by giving a warning since this might well be incomprehensible to young children.

---

1 See, for example, *Titchener v British Railways Board* [1983] 3 All ER 770.
2 *Robert Addie and Sons (Collieries) Ltd v Dumbreck* [1929] AC 358.
3 [1972] AC 877.
4 Occupiers' Liability Act 1984, s 1(3).
5 Ibid, s 1(4).
6 Ibid, s 1(5).

Negligence of parents and other carers

As was seen above, the duties of the prudent parent to protect his child might absolve a third party from liability, but under what circumstances might a parent *himself* be liable for the child's injuries, arising from failure to take proper care of him? There is no reason, in principle, why a child should not sue his parent, although he would need, as in other ordinary civil actions, to act by a 'next friend'[1]. However, since the child and his parent will usually be part of a family which constitutes a single economic unit, there will seldom be any point in suing, unless the parent is insured. That exception will, of course, apply where a child is injured through the negligent driving of his parent[2].

Some case-law has been concerned with the liability of foster-parents but the principles can be extrapolated to parents and other carers. Accidents frequently occur at home and the question is: what standard of care is it reasonable to expect the ordinary parent to achieve in the domestic context? The matter arose in *Surtees v Kingston-upon-Thames Borough Council*[3], where the two-year-old plaintiff, while a foster-child, suffered serious foot injuries from immersion in hot water. The facts were disputed, but the court accepted the version of the foster-parents that, while the foster-mother was absent from the bathroom, the child contrived to stick her foot into the wash basin and to turn on the hot water tap. It was not disputed that the foster-mother sought immediate medical attention for the child. A majority of the Court of Appeal held that an injury of the kind suffered was not foreseeable, taking into account the foster-mother's domestic circumstances. The court was mindful of the need to avoid imposing too high a standard of care, given the stress and preoccupation with household tasks which usually characterise parents' domestic circumstances[4].

Clearly, the line must be drawn somewhere, but it ought to be remembered that parents and others with responsibility may be criminally liable for cruelty or neglect and that the circumstances which suffice for this would, almost by definition, also be enough for civil liability[5]. This would also be the case if parents failed to ensure the suitability or adequacy of substitute carers such as babysitters,

---

1 See Chapter 13 above. The child's parent will normally act as next friend although this will clearly be impossible where the parent is the defendant.

2 This is also the one exceptional situation in which a child may sue his mother in relation to congenital defects caused before birth. See the Congenital Disabilities (Civil Liability) Act 1976, s 2.

3 [1991] 2 FLR 559.

4 Sir Nicolas Browne-Wilkinson V-C said that the court should be wary to hold parents in breach of a duty of care owed to their children. The duty owed by a foster-parent to a child in care was the same as that owed by the ordinary parent to his or her own children. There were, he thought, very real public policy considerations to be taken into account if the conflicts inherent in legal proceedings were to be brought into family relationships. But see the dissent of Beldam LJ.

5 For a New Zealand decision in which negligence was established against a parent, see *McCallion v Dodd* [1966] NZLR 710 and the analysis of the case in *Bromley's Family Law* (8th edn) (Butterworths, 1992) at p 317. See also *S v Walsall Metropolitan Borough Council* [1986] 1 FLR 397 in which the Court of Appeal upheld the liability of a foster-mother for severe burns to the soles

and the child came to harm as a result[1]. Where the child is injured, partly as a result of the negligence of a third party, and partly as a result of the contributory negligence of a carer, it has been held that the child's damages should not be reduced[2]. Where, of course, the negligence of the carer is the *major* cause of the child's injury, the court may conclude that the third party is not negligent at all.

Intentional torts

Children, as persons, are protected from civil wrongs in the ordinary way, just as they are protected by the criminal law[3]. In the context of the intentional torts of assault, battery and false imprisonment, special considerations apply to parents and others who exercise lawful authority over children. In short, certain bodily interferences with children which would, without doubt, be tortious if carried out on adults *may* be justifiable if they can be regarded as proper acts of parental discipline. Yet, especially after *Gillick*, there are limits to this principle[4]. The responsibility of parents to control the actions of their children also raises the question of whether a third party may commit a tort against the *parent* by interfering.

The limits of parental discipline

Parents will have a defence to the torts of assault and battery where they can show that the physical 'touchings' were proper exercises of parental discipline being moderate and reasonable. Young children, especially, often have to be restrained physically by parents from placing themselves in danger, and some parents resort quite lawfully to low-level corporal punishment, such as smacking. If this does not become excessive, whatever the morality of the practice, it is not tortious[5]. Similarly, parents are known to confine children to the home, or perhaps a bedroom, for misbehaviour. Their special authority deriving from parental

---

of a child's feet caused by her negligence. The council was held not to be liable since the foster-parents could not be regarded as agents of the local authority. In *S v W and Another (Child Abuse: Damages)* [1995] 1 FLR 862 the 29-year-old plaintiff succeeded in an action for damages against her mother arising from her mother's breach of duty in failing to protect her, while a child, from repeated physical and sexual abuse by her father. Her claim against her father himself (which was based on trespass to the person) was statute-barred. She succeeded against her mother on the basis that she could take advantage of the longer limitation period applicable to negligence claims under the Limitation Act 1980, s 11.

1   See the Children Act 1989, s 2(11).
2   *Oliver v Birmingham and Midland Omnibus Co Ltd* [1933] 1 KB 35.
3   See, generally, *Winfield and Jolowicz on Tort* (14th edn) (Sweet & Maxwell, 1994) at ch 4, *Street on Torts* (9th edn) (Butterworths, 1993) at chs 2, 3 and 6, and *Salmond and Heuston on the Law of Torts* (21st edn) (Sweet & Maxwell, 1996) at ch 7.
4   *Gillick v West Norfolk and Wisbech Area Health Authority* [1986] 1 AC 112. On the specific issue of consent and potential tortious liability in medical matters, see Chapter 8.
5   Note, however, that the European Court of Human Rights is expected to rule on the compatibility of the English test of 'moderate and reasonable chastisement' with the European Convention in the autumn of 1998. This case is being brought by a teenage boy who was repeatedly caned by his step-father. The latter was acquitted of assault in a criminal trial at the Crown Court. The European Commission found unanimously that English law 'failed to provide the applicant with adequate and effective protection against corporal punishment which was in the circumstances of the case degrading within the meaning of Article 3 of the Convention'. The case will provide the European Court with the opportunity of ruling on the legality of the whole practice of corporal punishment within the home. For an account of the case, see M Gardner 'No, beating children is not "reasonable" ' (1998) *The Times*, June 23.

responsibility is, again, a defence to what might otherwise amount to false imprisonment.

It is equally well established that, in principle, a parent behaving *unreasonably* may be criminally liable and, by deduction, liable also in tort. In *R v D*[1], the House of Lords held that a parent might be guilty of the common law offence of kidnapping and, in *R v Rahman*[2], a father who tried to take his teenage daughter, by force, to Bangladesh, had his conviction for the common law offence of false imprisonment upheld. Lord Lane CJ said that a parent could act unlawfully where the detention of the child was 'for such a period or in such circumstances as to take it out of the realm of reasonable parental discipline'. The circumstances of the case are instructive and suggest that physical restraints and punishments of older children, especially teenagers, may at best be inappropriate and at worst positively unlawful.

Powers of control and discipline are also exercised by schools, for the purposes of maintaining good order, but these were severely curtailed as regards the use of corporal punishment by legislation in 1986. In *Campbell and Cosans v United Kingdom*[3], the UK was found to be in breach of the European Convention on Human Rights by failing to respect the philosophical convictions of certain Scottish parents who were opposed to the use of corporal punishment on their children. As a result, corporal punishment was prohibited in all State schools and in relation to State-funded pupils in independent schools[4] by s 47 of the Education (No 2) Act 1986. Although it remained lawful in independent schools, the *Guidance* under the Children Act[5] indicated that its continued use should be regarded as exceptional, and that it should not be used for trivial offences or applied indiscriminately to whole classes of children. It was advised that it should normally only be administered by the head teacher, and should be properly recorded in the school punishment book[6].

Then, in *Costello-Roberts v United Kingdom*[7], the European Court of Human Rights, by a narrow 5 : 4 majority, held that corporal punishment inflicted on a seven-year-old pupil in a private boarding school was not a violation of the European Convention on Human Rights. The boy had been struck three times on the buttocks with a rubber-soled gym shoe. The court held that this did not reach the required minimum threshold of severity as to constitute degrading punishment under Article 3 of the Convention. The narrowness of the result and the tone of the judgments, however, necessitated amending legislation which made it

---

1 [1984] AC 778.
2 (1985) 81 Cr App R 349. On the other hand, it was reported at (1993) *The Times*, April 20, that a mother's conviction for assault on her nine-year-old daughter had been quashed on appeal. She had admitted hitting the girl's bare bottom with a slipper but contended that it was a reasonable punishment for stealing sweets. Judge McLean preferred the view that 'if a parent cannot slipper a child the world is going potty'. But see the prohibition on the use of corporal punishment in schools discussed below.
3 (1982) 4 EHRR 293.
4 Education (No 2) Act 1986, s 47 applied to all maintained schools (including special schools), grant-maintained schools, non-maintained special schools, independent schools for 'assisted places' pupils and other pupils whose fees were partly or entirely paid out of public funds.
5 *The Children Act 1989 Guidance and Regulations Vol 5 Independent Schools* (HMSO, 1991) at paras 3.9.1 et seq.
6 Ibid at para 3.9.5.
7 [1994] ELR 1.

explicit that, insofar as corporal punishment was still used in the independent sector, it could not be administered in a way which was 'inhuman or degrading' since this would be in breach of the Convention[1]. The way was paved for the total abolition of corporal punishment in independent schools and this has now been achieved by an amendment to the Labour Government's School Standards and Framework Act 1998[2]. It remains to be seen whether the legality of corporal punishment by parents in the home will survive the ruling of the European Court of Human Rights[3].

The *Guidance* went on to deal with restriction of liberty of children in independent schools. It advised that to restrict the liberty of a child by, for example, locking him in his bedroom, should be regarded as a serious and potentially unlawful step, having regard to the restrictions on the use of secure accommodation imposed on local authorities under s 25 of the Children Act 1989[4]. Schools which resort to locking up children will now run the risk of an action for assault or false imprisonment.

Interference with parental responsibility

If parents have primary responsibility for the care and upbringing of their children (and, usually, are the only people formally vested with parental responsibility) can it be tortious for an outsider to intervene in their affairs? It might be thought that, since only the persons with parental responsibility have legal authority to take decisions in relation to the child[5], another person trying to frustrate this would be acting unlawfully as that person would have no legal basis for doing so. Yet, in *F v Wirral Metropolitan Borough Council*[6], the Court of Appeal denied that parents had *independent* rights which were capable of being infringed[7]. The former action which a parent could bring for loss of his child's services[8] had become anachronistic and was abolished by the Administration of Justice Act 1982. Any right a parent possessed, therefore, was subordinate to the welfare of the child. There was no tort of interference with parental rights known to the law.

It should be noted, however, that it may in certain circumstances be possible for what is in reality a financial loss to the parent to be recovered as an element in the child's damages. Thus, in *Donnelly v Joyce*[9], the child's injuries required regular re-bandaging which would normally have been undertaken by a nurse but which was in fact carried out by his mother, herself a nurse. The Court of Appeal allowed

---

1 The original provision in the Education Act 1993 was later consolidated in the Education Act 1996, s 584(2). It was also provided in s 549(3) that, in applying the test of whether the punishment was inhuman or degrading, regard was to be had to 'all the circumstances of the case, including the reason given for it, how soon after the event it is given, its nature, the manner and circumstances in which it is given, the persons involved and its mental and physical effects'.

2 Section 131.

3 See fn 5 at p 515 above.

4 *The Children Act 1989 Guidance and Regulations Vol 5* (above) at para 3.10.1.

5 Children Act 1989, ss 2 and 3, and see Chapter 2 above. It should be remembered of course that de facto carers have a limited amount of authority under s 3(5).

6 [1991] Fam 69.

7 For a critique of the decision see A Bainham 'Interfering with Parental Responsibility – A New Challenge for the Law of Torts?' (1990) 3 JCL 3.

8 The former action is discussed at length in *Bromley's Family Law* (6th edn) (Butterworths, 1981) at pp 329 et seq.

9 [1974] QB 454.

the child to recover in damages the cost of the wages which his mother lost by devoting an hour a day to her son's special care. The result could be achieved only by the rather artificial characterisation of the child's loss as the existence of the need for care, rather than the incurring of nursing expenses and this reasoning has been criticised as unconvincing by the House of Lords[1].

Any tortious action by a parent against a third party must, therefore, be grounded in a tort against the *child* and not against the parent. In the case of physical touchings, it may be possible to establish an infringement of the child's rights[2] but this will be very difficult where the complaint is merely that an outsider is acting contrary to parental wishes and encouraging the child to do likewise[3]. In this situation the only option would seem to be for the parent to seek a 'prohibited steps' order under the Children Act or an analogous order under the inherent jurisdiction. But each of these actions would depend on the exercise of the court's discretion in determining what is in the child's best interests; the court would not seek to enforce any independent parental claim. As the law stands, the onus would seem to be on the parent to commence legal action. Arguably, the third party interference should be prima facie unlawful, so that the onus of proof is shifted onto the outsider[4].

Fatal accidents constitute something of an exception. Where a third party has unlawfully brought about the death of a parent or a child, the survivor will have a claim for damages under the Fatal Accidents Act 1976[5].

Congenital Disabilities (Civil Liability) Act 1976

Children born disabled as a result of injuries before their birth caused to their parents may have a cause of action under the Congenital Disabilities (Civil Liability) Act 1976[6]. The action is 'derivative' in that the child must establish that the defendant would have been actually or potentially liable to the *parent* in respect of the injury[7], but it is not necessary to show that the parent did, in fact, sustain injury. Thus, if a pregnant mother takes a negligently manufactured drug which causes her child, when born, to be disabled, an action will lie against the manufacturer, even though the mother suffers no ill-effects[8]. The mother herself

---

1 See *Hunt v Severs* [1994] 2 AC 350. If the parent should also be the tortfeasor the effect of this decision is that the child would be unable to recover the cost of nursing by that parent.

2 See the discussion in the medical context in Chapter 8 above.

3 An example would be various advice agencies. There is nothing tortious about giving advice (unless it amounts to negligent misstatement), but a parent might wish to stop the child from visiting whatever agency it is. See the discussion in Chapter 16 below of the former Conservative Government's circular on sex education and advice given by teachers to individual pupils about sexual matters.

4 See fn 7 at p 517 above.

5 Section 1, as substituted by s 3(1) of the Administration of Estates Act 1982.

6 This Act followed the Law Com Report No 60 *Injuries to Unborn Children* (1974). See, generally, *Winfield and Jolowicz on Tort* (14th edn) (Sweet & Maxwell, 1994) at pp 708 et seq, and *Street on Torts* (9th edn) (Butterworths, 1993) at pp 195–196. The common law position was uncertain until 1992 when, in *Burton v Islington Health Authority* [1993] QB 204, the Court of Appeal held that an action lay at common law for injuries caused to an unborn child by negligence. The action crystallises on the birth of the child. In practice, the common law action will only need to be utilised in respect of births before 1976 since the 1976 legislation governs births after that time.

7 Congenital Disabilities (Civil Liability) Act 1976, s 1.

8 The example given in *Winfield and Jolowicz on Tort* (above) at p 709.

is not generally liable where, for example, she neglects her own body through alcohol or drug abuse while pregnant[1]. The exception is where she is driving a car[2], in which case the real defendant will be the insurers. The father does not have the same immunity, and may be liable if, for example, he assaults the mother while she is pregnant. However, it has been pointed out that the mother might be unenthusiastic or unwilling about acting as the child's next friend in an action against the father[3].

Since an action under the 1976 Act is derivative in nature, the child's claim may be defeated or reduced by defences available to the parent. Thus, there is no liability for an occurrence preceding the time of conception if, at that time, either or both of the parents knew the risk of the child being born disabled[4]. Similarly, where the responsibility for the child being born disabled is shared by the parent and the defendant, the damages may be reduced as the court thinks just and equitable having regard to the extent of the parent's responsibility[5]. Finally, any term of a contract excluding or restricting liability to the parent binds the child[6].

A major problem for many children who are born disabled is to establish causation and prove that the congenital defects were actually brought about by negligence. The Pearson Committee[7] thought that the Congenital Disabilities (Civil Liability) Act 1976 would benefit only a minute proportion of children born with these defects. In recent years, attention has been focused on group actions by children alleged to have suffered birth defects or developed childhood diseases as a result of local environmental factors[8].

Responsibility for children's acts

Two general principles govern liability for tortious acts committed by children. The first principle is that children themselves are prima facie liable and there is no defence of minority as such[9]. A minor is therefore as liable to be sued as an adult. The second principle is that parents (and others exercising parental responsibility) are not usually liable for torts committed by children. Both of these principles require qualification.

Liability of children

The standard of care required for the tort of negligence is that of the reasonable man. Some torts require proof of malice. In either case, the age of a child may be relevant to show that the child did not possess the requisite mental state. Most of the reported cases have been concerned with the issue of contributory negligence. In many such cases, children have been found not to be negligent where, in similar circumstances, adults would have been. The test appears to be the degree of care for his own safety which it would have been reasonable to expect a child of

---

1   But this might lead to local authority intervention. See *D (A Minor) v Berkshire County Council* [1987] 1 All ER 20, and Chapter 11 above.
2   See fn 2 at p 514 above.
3   HK Bevan *Child Law* (Butterworths, 1989) at para 9.83.
4   Congenital Disabilities (Civil Liability) Act 1976, s 1(4).
5   Ibid, s 1(7).
6   Ibid, s 1(6).
7   *Compensation for Personal Injuries* (1978) (Cmnd 7054).
8   For a good discussion of the issues, see E Palmer 'Children and Toxic Torts' (1992) 4 JCL 156.
9   See, for example, *Gorely v Codd* [1967] 1 WLR 19.

the particular age reasonably to take[1]. It is not clear whether this test is entirely objective or whether the child's subjective characteristics, such as maturity and understanding, may be taken into account[2].

The standard of care expected of children is illustrated by the Australian case of *McHale v Watson*[3] where a boy of 12 years of age threw a piece of steel welding rod, sharpened to a spike, at a post. The spike glanced off the post hitting a nine-year-old girl who was standing nearby, causing injuries to her eye. It was established that the boy had no intention of hitting the girl or frightening her. The High Court of Australia upheld the judge's decision that this did not amount to negligence, applying the standard of care reasonably to be expected of a child of the same age, intelligence and experience. As Kitto J put it:

> 'It is, I think, a matter for judicial notice that the ordinary boy of 12 suffers from a feeling that a piece of wood and a sharp instrument have a special affinity. To expect a boy of that age to consider before throwing the spike whether the timber was hard or soft, to weigh the chances of being able to make the spike stick in the post, and to foresee that it might glance off and hit the girl, would be, I think, to expect a degree of sense and circumspection which nature ordinarily withholds till life becomes less rosy.'

Until recently, there was no direct English authority on the standard of care required of children, but in *Mullin v Richards*[4] the Court of Appeal addressed the issue and substantially adopted the reasoning of the High Court of Australia in *McHale v Watson*.

Teresa and Heidi were 15-year-old Birmingham schoolgirls. At the end of a maths lesson they were engaged in a mock 'sword-fight' with plastic rulers when tragedy struck. One of the rulers snapped and a fragment of plastic entered Teresa's eye causing her to lose all useful sight in it. Teresa sued Heidi together with Birmingham City Council, alleging negligence on the part of Miss Osborne, the maths teacher. The judge found that the latter had not been negligent and dismissed the claim against the education authority. But he found that both the girls had been negligent and that Teresa's injury was the foreseeable result. Accordingly, he awarded damages subject to a 50% reduction for contributory negligence.

Allowing the appeal, the Court of Appeal held that where the defendant was a child the test was not that of the ordinary prudent and reasonable adult but that of the ordinary prudent and reasonable child of the same age as the defendant in the defendant's situation. The judge had indeed referred to the fact that the girls were aged 15 but there had been insufficient evidence to justify his conclusion that the accident was foreseeable. There was no evidence of the propensity of such rulers to break, that the practice of playing with rulers was frowned upon or barred by the school or that either of the girls had used excessive or inappropriate violence. All that had occurred was a schoolgirls' game and there was no justification for attributing to the girls foresight of any significant risk of likelihood of injury. Butler-Sloss LJ referred with approval to the judgment of Kitto J in *McHale v Watson* where it was said that 'children, like everyone else, must accept as they go

---

1   *Yachuk v Oliver Blais Co Ltd* [1949] AC 396.
2   Such authority as there is suggests that, although a child's age may be taken into account, the test is otherwise entirely objective. See *Watkins v Birmingham City Council* (1976) 126 NLJ 442.
3   [1966] ALR 513. On the standard of care expected of children, see *Salmond and Heuston on the Law of Torts* (21st edn) (Sweet & Maxwell, 1996) at pp 411–412 and, in the context of occupier's liability, at pp 273–274.
4   [1998] 1 All ER 920.

about in society the risks from which ordinary care on the part of others will not suffice to save them. One such risk is that boys of 12 may behave as boys of 12.' And she added that 'girls of 15 playing together may play as somewhat irresponsible girls of 15'.

One of the reasons why there is a shortage of English authority on the standard of care required of children, at least outside the context of contributory negligence, is that a child will generally not be worth suing[1]. One way around this problem, in an appropriate case, is to sue the child's parent or, perhaps, the education authority, where an accident was near the child's school.

Liability of parents and other carers

There are two recognised exceptions to the rule that parents are not liable for the torts of their children. The first exception is where they have specifically authorised the child's actions, or where the child is employed by them. Here, they will be vicariously liable. A similar principle applies to contracts authorised by parents[2].

The second, and more significant, exception arises where the parent *himself* is found to be negligent in failing to prevent the act or omission of the child which has injured a third party[3]. A number of the reported cases have concerned firearms. Thus, a father was held liable where he gave his 15-year-old son an air gun and allowed him to keep it after he had smashed a neighbour's window with it. The son then went on to injure the eye of another boy with the gun[4]. However, a father was held not liable where his 13-year-old son resiled on a promise never to use an air rifle outside the house and did so injuring the plaintiff. It was accepted that the father had taken all reasonable precautions and the son's disobedience was unforeseeable[5].

Similar principles apply to school authorities where the standard of care is that of the reasonably prudent parent[6]. The leading case is the decision of the House of Lords in *Carmarthenshire County Council v Lewis*[7]. Here, the local authority was held liable for the lack of supervision at a nursery school. This led to a young child, not yet four years of age, running out of school and into the road, which caused the death of a lorry driver in the accident which followed. School authorities may also be liable where the child is injured owing to their negligence[8].

It would seem fair to conclude that *anyone* who has assumed responsibility for a child, such as a child-minder taking a child to or from school, could be liable on

---

1   This is not, however, inevitably so since the child is capable of owning substantial personal property. See Chapter 9 above.

2   For the child's *own* contractual capacity and liability, see pp 522 et seq below.

3   As to liability to pay the child's fines and other responsibility for children's crimes, see Chapter 14 above.

4   *Bebee v Sales* (1916) 32 TLR 413. Liability was also established in *Newton v Edgerley* [1959] 1 WLR 1031.

5   *Donaldson v McNiven* [1952] 2 All ER 691.

6   *Ricketts v Erith Borough Council* [1943] 2 All ER 629. For an extensive review of the liability of schools in relation to health and safety, see N Harris *The Law Relating to Schools* (2nd edn) (Tolley Publishing Co Ltd, 1995) at ch 13. See also N Harris 'Legal Liability in Respect of School Premises' (1991) 3 *Education and the Law* 125.

7   [1955] AC 549.

8   As in *Barnes v Hampshire County Council* [1969] 1 WLR 1563. Here, school children were let out of school five minutes earlier than was the normal practice. A five-year-old child was injured when she wandered into the street, her mother having not yet arrived. The local education

similar principles if either a child or a third party is injured as a result of their lack of supervision.

CHILDREN AND THE LAW OF CONTRACT

Trietel has observed that the law governing minors' contracts is based on two principles[1]. The first principle is that 'the law must protect the minor against his inexperience, which may enable an adult to take unfair advantage of him, or to induce him to enter into a contract which, although in itself fair, is simply improvident'. The second principle is that 'the law should not cause unnecessary hardship to adults who deal fairly with minors'.

The result of attempting to follow a policy which embraces these two, somewhat conflicting, principles is that the law is complex and, in some respects, quite vague. Some contracts are valid, others are voidable, and yet others are completely unenforceable against the minor. The first principle underlies the general rule that a minor is not bound by his contracts. But this principle is only one of 'qualified unenforceability' since, under the second principle, the minor will be liable under certain types of contract from the outset, while others will bind him unless he takes steps to repudiate them. He may also incur some liability in tort, restitution, or under the Minors' Contracts Act 1987[2]. This section examines the current state of English law regarding the various kinds of contract which a minor may purport to make.

It should be appreciated that the practical significance of the issue diminished when the age of majority was lowered from 21 to 18 years of age, by the Family Law Reform Act 1969[3]. Many of the older cases related to young people in this age group such as, for example, undergraduates at the universities of Oxford and Cambridge[4]. Such people are now young adults with full contractual capacity[5].

---

authority was held responsible, since the injury was foreseeable. Cf *Wilson v Governors of Sacred Heart Roman Catholic School* [1998] 1 FLR 663. Here, a nine-year-old boy was injured at the end of the school day when he was hit in the eye by a coat which had been deliberately whirled around like a lasso by another pupil. The Court of Appeal allowed the school's appeal against a finding of negligence arising from alleged failure to supervise children leaving through the school gates. Supervision was in fact provided during the lunch break when large numbers of children were in the playground. But the lunch period was contrasted with the very short period in which, and very short distance over which, children were engaged in leaving the school. It was not standard procedure to supervise children leaving school and the need for such supervision was not demonstrated.

1   GH Treitel *The Law of Contract* (9th edn) (Sweet & Maxwell, 1995) at p 494. See also Cheshire, Fifoot and Furmston's *Law of Contract* (13th edn) (Butterworths, 1996) at pp 440 et seq.
2   Following Law Com Report No 134 *Minors' Contracts* (1984).
3   Following the *Report of the Committee on the Age of Majority* (the Latey Committee) (1967) (Cmnd 3342).
4   *Nash v Inman* [1908] 2 KB 1 concerned an action by a Savile Row tailor against a Cambridge undergraduate with respect to 11 fancy waistcoats. The action failed since he had not adduced sufficient evidence that the clothes were suitable to the condition in life of the minor or that he was not already adequately supplied with clothes. By contrast, Viscount Middleton, during the second reading of the Infants Contracts Bill 1874, referred to the decisions of juries at Oxford which had found, inter alia, that champagne and wild ducks and studs of emeralds set in diamonds were necessaries for Oxford undergraduates! See (1874) *Hansard*, Vol 219, Ser 3, col 1225.
5   And with full civil capacities for other legal purposes such as making a will or owning real property.

Having said that, we are witnessing in other areas of the law a gradual emancipation of older minors[1], and there are certain areas, such as entertainment and sport, in which minors regularly do enter into contracts. Children, sometimes quite young, also routinely engage in everyday transactions, such as purchasing sweets, which, although trivial, have contractual implications.

We conclude this section with a brief look at the position in Scotland where, following a wide-ranging report by the Scottish Law Commission[2], statutory reforms to Scots law have simplified the law on minors' contracts and other civil law capacities. We pose the question whether English law should not be similarly reformed, in pursuit of what the Scottish Commission identified as a third central principle which ought to inform the law: 'that the law should be clear and coherent and should accord with modern social and economic conditions'[3].

Valid contracts

Two kinds of minors' contracts have long been recognised as exceptions to the principle of unenforceability. They are contracts for 'necessaries' and contracts of service. In each case they are only binding on the minor if, on balance, they are *beneficial* to him. Beyond these two special kinds of contract there is no wider principle that a minor is bound by beneficial contracts. Thus, it is equally well established that trading contracts are not binding on a minor, however beneficial the terms might be for him[4].

Contracts for necessaries

A minor is liable to pay for necessaries, whether goods or services, which have been supplied to him under a contract. The concept of necessaries clearly includes the essentials of life such as food, clothing and lodging, but it is wider than this. It extends to what is appropriate to maintain the *particular* minor in his ordinary way of life and this can vary, depending on the lifestyle to which he is accustomed. Pure luxuries are not included, but some of the older cases recognised as necessaries luxurious articles which were also articles of utility[5]. In the case of goods, there is a statutory definition of necessaries, namely 'goods suitable to the condition in life of the minor ... and to his actual requirements at the time of sale and delivery'[6]. The latter part of the definition makes it plain that, as well as being capable of being regarded as necessaries in law, the minor must actually have had need of the items in question[7].

---

1 See Chapter 3 above.
2 Scot Law Com No 110 *Report on the Legal Capacity and Responsibility of Minors* (1987).
3 Ibid at para 2.12. The other two principles broadly corresponded with those identified by GH Treitel (above):
    '(a) that the law should protect young people from the consequences of their immaturity without restricting unnecessarily their freedom of action;
    (b) that the law should not cause unnecessary prejudice to adults who enter into transactions with young people.'
4 See, for example, *Cowern v Nield* [1912] 2 KB 419, although there may be some liability in restitution (see below).
5 See *Chapple v Cooper* (1844) 13 M&W 252.
6 Sale of Goods Act 1979, s 3(3).
7 Thus, in *Nash v Inman* (above) there was no evidence that the minor did not already possess sufficient waistcoats.

The contract will be enforceable against the minor only if it does not contain harsh or onerous terms so that it is, on balance, substantially for his benefit[1]. The concept of necessaries has now been abandoned in Scotland and replaced by a less technical and more wide-ranging notion of 'ordinary transactions' being everyday transactions commonly entered into by a child of the transacting child's age[2].

Contracts of service

It is established that a minor is bound by contracts of apprenticeship or service[3] on the basis that it is 'to his advantage that he should acquire the means of earning his livelihood'[4]. Again, as with necessaries, this will be so only where the contract, construed as a whole, is beneficial to the minor. Where it is not, he is free to repudiate it. The issue is again a question of balance, and the minor will not be able to escape liability merely because some of the terms of the contract are onerous. The standard texts[5] contrast two cases.

De Francesco v Barnum[6]

This case is an example of the oppressive sort of contract which is not binding on minors. Here, a 14-year-old girl entered into an apprenticeship deed to be taught stage dancing for seven years. The agreement prevented her from marrying during the apprenticeship, or from accepting professional engagements without the plaintiff's permission. However, the obligations were one-sided, since the plaintiff did not bind himself to provide the girl with professional engagements or to maintain her, if unemployed, and the stipulated remuneration was very poor. Fry J found the terms of the deed unreasonable and unenforceable since the girl was at the complete disposal of the plaintiff without commensurate obligations on his part.

Clements v London and North Western Railway Co[7]

This case illustrates the kind of contract of service which is regarded as broadly beneficial to minors and hence enforceable. The minor entered the service of the Railway Company as a porter, agreeing to join the company's insurance scheme and to relinquish his right to sue for personal injury under the Employers' Liability Act 1880. This occupational insurance scheme was more favourable to the minor than the statutory scheme, since it provided for compensation in a greater range of accidents but, on the other hand, it fixed a lower scale of compensation. Overall, it was held that the agreement was to the minor's advantage and thus binding on him.

Voidable contracts

Voidable contracts are those which are valid and binding on minors, unless they repudiate them during minority or within a short time of attaining majority. Four types of such contract have been recognised to exist, namely: contracts

---

1   See *Roberts v Gray* [1913] 1 KB 520.
2   Age of Legal Capacity (Scotland) Act 1991, s 2(1)(a).
3   GH Treitel *The Law of Contract* (9th edn) (Sweet & Maxwell, 1995) at pp 498 et seq, and Cheshire, Fifoot and Furmston *Law of Contract* (13th edn) (Butterworths, 1996) at pp 444 et seq.
4   Ibid.
5   GH Treitel (above) at pp 498–499, and Cheshire et al (above) at pp 445–446.
6   (1890) 45 Ch D 430.
7   [1894] 2 QB 482.

concerning land; the acquisition of shares in companies; partnership agreements; and marriage settlements[1]. The basis for placing these contracts in a separate category is not clear. The view of the commentators is that the common factor is the quality of relative permanence which attaches to them. They are all contracts under which the minor acquires an interest in some subject-matter, ie a subject-matter to which continuous or recurring obligations are incident[2]. As such, the obligations continue, unless and until the minor decides to put an end to them. It would then be unjust to allow him to retain his interest in the subject-matter without carrying out his own obligations. Where the minor repudiates the contract in time, he will be freed from future liabilities under it but cannot recover money paid over unless there has been a total failure of consideration[3].

The continued existence of this exceptional category of contracts has been questioned, for it has been said that special treatment has been based on 'social and economic factors which have long since passed away'[4].

Unenforceable contracts: liability under the Minors' Contracts Act 1987, in restitution or in tort

Where a contract does not fall within any of the categories mentioned above, it is unenforceable against the minor. This does not necessarily mean that it has no legal effect. First, the other party remains bound by it and then certain legal consequences for the minor may also flow from it.

Liability under the Minors' Contracts Act 1987

Where the contract is partially carried out, property may pass to the minor under the ordinary principles of contract of sale. It would be unjust to allow the minor to retain this property where he has resiled from his part of the bargain. The issue is now governed by s 3 of the Minors' Contracts Act 1987[5]. This provides:

'(1) Where –
(a) a person ("the plaintiff") has after the commencement of this Act entered into a contract with another ("the defendant") and
(b) the contract is unenforceable against the defendant (or he repudiates it) because he was a minor when the contract was made, the court may, if it is just and equitable to do so, require the defendant to transfer to the plaintiff any property acquired by the defendant under the contract, or any property representing it.
(2) Nothing in this section shall be taken to prejudice any other remedy available to the plaintiff.'

Most obviously, this provision can catch a minor who has obtained goods on credit and is now refusing to pay for them, but the remedy is discretionary and there is no guarantee that the court will order the transfer of the property. Moreover, the remedy is limited to the property itself transferred under the contract, or 'any property representing it'. In other words, the court does not have carte blanche to order the minor to pay the price of the goods or otherwise to pay out of his wider assets. There may be some difficult 'tracing' issues about whether property really does represent that which was originally transferred[6]. The

---

1 See GH Treitel (above) at pp 501–504, and Cheshire et al (above) at pp 446–451.
2 Cheshire et al (above) at p 434.
3 *Steinberg v Scala (Leeds) Ltd* [1923] 2 Ch 452.
4 GH Treitel *The Law of Contract* (9th edn) (Sweet & Maxwell, 1995) at p 504.
5 For a concise review of the Act, see J Holroyd 'The Minors' Contracts Act 1987' (1987) 84 LS Gaz 2266.
6 These are explored with examples by GH Treitel (above) at pp 507–509.

reasoning for the restriction is that, to allow the minor's wider assets to be touched, would be to enforce indirectly an unenforceable contract. It has been suggested that, in exercising its discretion, the court will probably wish to take into account the intrinsic fairness of the original contract, such as the price the minor was required to pay. Where this was unreasonable, the court might order the minor to return the property unless he pays a reasonable price for it, fixed by the court[1].

Liability in restitution

The Minors' Contracts Act 1987 preserves any other legal remedy available to the plaintiff. Under the equitable doctrine of restitution, a minor who has obtained goods by fraud may be obliged to disgorge them, if they are still in his possession, on the basis of unjust enrichment. This remedy is not available where the minor has already disposed of the goods and, in this respect, it is more limited than the statutory remedy which allows limited tracing[2]. Moreover, the statutory remedy, unlike the equitable one, is not dependent on proof of fraud.

Liability in tort

The issue here is whether a minor could incur tortious liability for acts directly connected with unenforceable contracts. The general principle is that an unenforceable contract may not be indirectly enforced against a minor by framing the cause of action in tort. Where, however, the wrongful event can be sufficiently divorced from the contract that it can be regarded as an independent wrong, the minor may not escape tortious liability. Two old cases, both involving horse-riding, resulted in different conclusions on this point.

In *Jennings v Rundall*[3], it was held that the minor was not liable in the tort of negligence where he hired a mare for riding and injured her through excessive and improper riding. However, in *Burnard v Haggis*[4], the opposite conclusion was reached where, contrary to the express instructions of the horse's owner, the minor injured the horse while jumping her, having hired her simply for riding. The point of distinction is elusive but is thought to turn on whether or not the wrongful act was contemplated by the contract. In the first case, riding clearly was contemplated (albeit not excessive riding) while, in the second case, jumping was positively excluded under the agreement.

A Scottish solution for England?

The English Law Commission, over a decade ago, considered the possibilities of simplifying the law by adopting a general rule that minors of 16 years or over should be fully liable on *all* contracts while those under that age would be immune from liability[5]. In the event, it opted for more limited reforms which found their way into the Minors' Contracts Act 1987[6].

---

1 Suggested by GH Treitel (above) at p 509.
2 The limitations of the doctrine of restitution are well illustrated by *Leslie Ltd v Sheill* [1914] 3 KB 607.
3 (1799) 8 Term Rep 335.
4 (1863) 14 CB(NS) 45.
5 Law Com Working Paper No 81 *Minors' Contracts* (1982) Part XII.
6 One of these was that minors' contracts should generally be capable of being ratified by the minor on attaining majority.

Meanwhile, in Scotland, the Scottish Law Commission had embarked on a major examination of the legal capacities and responsibilities of minors and pupils in Scots law[1]. Its review included, but was considerably wider than, the contractual capacity of young people. Its concern was with what, in Scots law, was termed 'active' capacity to perform civil acts having legal effect as opposed to 'passive' capacity simply to hold rights[2]. This active capacity included the capacity 'to enter contracts, make promises, grant conveyances or discharges, make a will, give consent, participate in court proceedings or perform any act of legal significance in the field of private law'[3]. After an extensive consultation, the Scottish Law Commission proposed a two-tier system of legal capacity. Children from the ages 0 to 16 years would, subject to limited but important exceptions, have no legal capacity[4], while those young people from 16 to 18 years would, subject to limited protections, enjoy full legal capacity for all those acts listed above[5]. Transactions purportedly entered into by those under 16 years of age would be void, unless ratified on attaining 16 years, but there would be an important exception, whereby they would have capacity to engage in 'ordinary transactions' – being reasonable transactions of a kind commonly entered into by a child of the same age and circumstances[6]. Transactions entered into by those over 16 years of age would be valid, but the court would have a discretion to set a transaction aside on a young person's application made before attaining 21 years of age, if satisfied that it had caused or was likely to cause him 'substantial prejudice' and was not of a kind 'which a reasonably prudent person acting in the same circumstances, would have entered into'[7]. These recommendations were implemented by the Age of Legal Capacity (Scotland) Act 1991[8].

Effects of the reformed Scots law

The broad effect of the new law was to draw a reasonably clear line for contractual (and other civil) capacity at 16 years of age. This is subject to the very significant exception for 'ordinary transactions'. The gist of this is that the legal capacity of children to do those things which children habitually do is legally recognised, and this varies, depending on the age of the child. The Scottish Law Commission gave the examples of the five-year-old child buying sweets and the 15-year-old child purchasing a cinema ticket. Neither of these examples comes within the traditional category of necessaries, but ought to be placed, the Commission thought, on a proper legal footing[9]. The advantage of the 'ordinary transactions' formula was thought to be that it would be flexible enough to cater for children at

1   Before the Age of Legal Capacity (Scotland) Act 1991, Scots law distinguished between 'minors' who were boys between the ages of 14 and 18 years and girls between 12 and 18 years and 'pupils' who were boys under 14 and girls under 12 years. For further discussion of the Scottish Law Commission's work and the 1991 legislation, see A Bainham 'Growing Up in Britain: Adolescence in the Post-Gillick Era' (1992) *Juridical Review* 155 at pp 169–172, and JM Thomson *Family Law in Scotland* (3rd edn) (Butterworths, 1996) at chs 9 and 10.
2   Scot Law Com No 110 *Report on the Legal Capacity and Responsibility of Minors* (1987) at para 3.22.
3   Ibid.
4   Ibid at paras 3.21 et seq.
5   Ibid at paras 3.97 et seq.
6   Ibid at paras 3.41–3.51.
7   Ibid at paras 3.102 et seq.
8   This Act received Royal Assent on 25 July 1991 and came into force on 25 September 1991.
9   Scot Law Com Report No 110 *Report on the Legal Capacity and Responsibility of Minors* (1987) at para 3.41.

the two extremes of the age group. Thus, a child of five years would have the capacity to engage in transactions appropriate to his age group, but not those appropriate to an older child. Accordingly, the rule would have built-in recognition of the different levels of understanding of children of different ages[1]. The Commission acknowledged that there might be an element of vagueness, but thought that this would be no worse than that which surrounded the concept of necessaries. It believed that the new formula could cover, inter alia: small shopping transactions; payment of bus or train fares; payment for skating lessons or a haircut; Saturday or holiday jobs; booking accommodation at a Youth Hostel; and the operation of bank deposit accounts[2].

The new scheme also made it possible to sweep away, at a stroke, the existing rules governing the exceptional cases of valid contracts. It thought that it was unnecessary to retain contracts for necessaries as an exception to the general rule of incapacity. It also thought that these items would usually be provided by the parent or guardian and that, where they were not, they would be covered by the ordinary transactions rule[3]. Similarly, the Commission thought that there should be no exemption relating to employment or trading contracts since, where appropriate, they too would fall within the general exception – the most obvious examples being contracts for Saturday or holiday jobs[4].

Reform for England?
Whether such a scheme would be suitable for England is legitimately the subject of debate, but there is no question that Scots law now has a more coherent and rational system. Reform along the lines of the Scottish legislation would also be consistent with the changes in the Children Act regarding young people over 16 years of age[5]. A comprehensive review of the legal capacities and responsibilities of children and young people is overdue, but at the time of writing there has been no indication from the English Law Commission that it intends to embark on this task.

THE EMPLOYMENT OF CHILDREN AND YOUNG PERSONS

It has been seen that a minor may enter into a valid contract of employment, or other contract whereby he makes a living professionally, if it is substantially for his benefit, but the contractual rules are subject to extensive and complex legislation which places restrictions on the employment of children. Some of these restrictions are general, while others relate to specific kinds of employment.

Historical background

Legislative intervention can be traced back to the early nineteenth century and was a response to the appalling working conditions and long hours which prevailed in factories, mines and shops during the industrial revolution. This

---

1   Scot Law Com Report No 110 (above) at para 3.42.
2   Ibid at para 3.48.
3   Ibid at paras 3.87–3.88.
4   Ibid at para 3.92.
5   See Chapter 2 above.

legislation began to impose controls over the hours which children and young people (and women) were permitted to work, at first in textile factories, and later underground or as shop assistants. Other, early legislation dealt with health and safety, dangerous and unhealthy industries, and the education of children.

A comprehensive review of this legislation is beyond the scope of the present work[1] but the following were some of the principal landmarks in the nineteenth century. The Factory Act 1833 prohibited the employment of children under nine years of age in textile factories and regulated the employment of older children. The Factory Act 1847 imposed a maximum daily limit of 10 hours' work for women and young persons employed in textile factories. The Factory and Workshop Act 1878, following the report of a Royal Commission, extended the protections to all factories, raised the minimum age of employment to 10 years of age, and limited the hours of children under 14 years of age to half the normal day. The Education Act 1880 introduced compulsory school attendance up to 10 years of age, and this was extended to 13 years of age for those with poor attendance records. The connection between compulsory education and the restrictions on employment is an obvious and significant one and remains a feature of the law today[2].

Further protective legislation continued to be introduced from time to time throughout the twentieth century[3]. The Employment of Women, Young Persons and Children Act 1920, for example, prohibited (with limited exceptions) the employment of women and young persons at night in industrial undertakings and established 14 years of age (the then school leaving age) as the minimum age for employment in such undertakings. The Children and Young Persons Act 1933 imposed the general restrictions on the employment of children under 13 years of age which continue to apply today although the age restriction has been recently raised to 14. The Mines and Quarries Act 1954 consolidated previous legislation regulating the employment of women and children underground in mines, or above ground in quarries, and the Shops Act 1950 was a similar consolidation of legislation, mainly controlling the hours of work of young people in shops. The Education Act 1944 raised the compulsory school leaving age to 15 and this was subsequently raised to 16 (or just under) in 1972, where it remains[4]. More recently, the Employment Act 1989 brought about a substantial 'deregulation' of the employment of young persons (as opposed to children) by sweeping away most of the protective employment legislation applying to this age group. However, in 1994, the Council of the European Union issued a Directive on the Protection of Young People at Work[5] which has already necessitated some reform of domestic employment legislation affecting children and young people and which will require yet further reform.

---

1   There is a detailed review of this legislation in the Department of Employment's Consultative Document *Restrictions on Employment of Young People and the Removal of Sex Discrimination in Legislation* (1987).
2   See also Chapter 16 below.
3   A selective approach is necessary here, but for a full review see the Consultative Document (above) at paras 2.6 et seq.
4   Raising of the School Leaving Age Order 1972, SI 1972/444.
5   Council Directive No 94/33/EC of 22 June 1994. For a critique of the Directive and of English legislation as it applies to the employment of children in 'family work', see A Bond 'Working for the family? Child employment legislation and the public/private debate' (1996) JSWFL 291. For a recent review of the issues surrounding children's work in the UK, see B Pettitt (ed) *Children and Work in the UK: Reassessing the Issues* (CPAG, 1998).

The current situation

The key distinction in current employment law is therefore between 'children' and 'young persons'. This is not, however, the same distinction which exists for the purposes of the criminal law where, as was seen[1], those under 14 years of age are children while those over 14 years of age are 'young persons'. In the employment sphere, the crucial divide is the compulsory school leaving age: those below it are 'children' while those above it are 'young persons'. It would be convenient, for the student's purposes, if a precise age were fixed in this respect, but the position is not quite as straightforward as this. Although 16 years of age is the benchmark, the school leaving age fluctuates slightly depending on the date of the individual pupil's birthday and its relationship to the statutory school leaving dates. In practical terms, this means that it may apply to someone as young as 15 years and eight months or as old as 16 years and seven months[2]. The distinction is, nonetheless, important since there are extensive restrictions on the employment of children but practically none on the employment of young persons.

The employment of children

Restrictions on the employment of children may be divided into two categories – general restrictions and specific restrictions.

General restrictions
The general restrictions are contained in the Children and Young Persons Act 1933, as recently amended[3]. This provides that children may not be employed:

(1) who are under the age of 14 years;
(2) to do any work other than light work;
(3) before the close of school hours on any school day (except where leave to be absent can be, and is, given);
(4) before 7 am or after 7 pm on any day;
(5) for more than two hours on any school day;
(6) for more than two hours on any Sunday;
(7) for more than eight hours or, if the child is under the age of 15 years, for more than five hours in any day:
    (i)   on which he is not required to attend school, and
    (ii) which is not a Sunday;
(8) for more than 35 hours or, if the child is under the age of 15 years, for more than 25 hours in any week in which he is not required to attend school; or
(9) for more than four hours in any day without a rest break of one hour; or

---

1 At Chapter 14 above.
2 Education Act 1996, s 8, and the Education (School Leaving Date) Order 1997, SI 1997/1970. On compulsory attendance at school, see Chapter 16 below.
3 Children and Young Persons Act 1933, ss 18–21, as amended by the Children (Protection at Work) Regulations 1998, SI 1998/276. The Regulations, which came into force on 4 August 1998, make various amendments to the 1933 Act and the Children and Young Persons Act 1963 to implement in relation to children the EC Directive on the Protection of Young People at Work. In particular, they raise from 13 to 14 years the age at which a child may be employed in any work other than as an employee of his parent or guardian in light agricultural or horticultural work on an occasional basis.

(10) at any time in a year unless at that time he has had, or could still have, during a period in the year in which he is not required to attend school, at least two consecutive weeks without employment.

These restrictions may be augmented by other restrictions imposed by local authority bye-laws. Conversely, such bye-laws may allow children under 14 years of age to be employed in limited circumstances[1]. Under the unimplemented Employment of Children Act 1973, the Secretary of State has wide powers to regulate the employment of children, the intention being to remove regional variations and impose uniform standards. It is a criminal offence for an employer to engage a child in breach of any of the above restrictions, but he will have a defence where it can be shown that the contravention was due to the act or default of some other person and that he himself used all due diligence to secure compliance with the statutory requirements[2].

Specific restrictions

Various pieces of legislation impose specific restrictions on children participating in particular kinds of employment. Thus, no child may be employed in an industrial undertaking[3], factory[4], mine or quarry[5], in a shop[6], or aboard a UK registered ship[7].

Children may not, generally, be employed in street-trading[8], but local authorities are empowered to make bye-laws which authorise children of 14 years or over (but not younger children) to be employed by *their parents* in street-trading to a specified extent. The bye-laws may provide for the granting of licences and specify conditions relating to their issue, suspension and revocation. In particular, the bye-laws may determine the days, hours and places during which the children concerned may take part in street-trading[9].

The employment of children in entertainment and performances is strictly regulated by the Children and Young Persons Acts of 1933 and 1963. Detailed discussion of the minutiae of these provisions is not appropriate here[10]. Suffice it to note that the 1933 Act prohibits the participation by children in dangerous public performances[11]. The training of children to take part in dangerous performances or to be employed outside the UK in singing, playing, performing or being exhibited for profit is controlled by local authority licences[12]. The 1963 Act extended the licensing system to performances more generally, including those on film, television or in broadcasting. Again, a local authority licence must be obtained. This will not be granted unless the authority is satisfied that the child

---

1 Children and Young Persons Act 1933, s 18(2).
2 Ibid, s 21(1).
3 Employment of Women, Young Persons and Children Act 1920, s 1(1).
4 Factories Act 1961, s 167.
5 Mines and Quarries Act 1954, s 124.
6 Shops Act 1950, s 74(1) and Part II.
7 The Merchant Shipping Act 1995, s 55.
8 Children and Young Persons Act 1933, s 20(1).
9 Ibid, s 20(2).
10 But such a discussion may be found in HK Bevan *Child Law* (Butterworths, 1989) at paras 11.71–11.76.
11 Children and Young Persons Act 1933, s 23, as amended, refers to any performance in which the child's 'life or limbs are endangered'.
12 Ibid, s 24.

is fit to take part in the performance, that proper provision has been made to secure his health and kind treatment, and that his education will not suffer[1].

Enforcement of restrictions

Local education authorities are empowered to institute proceedings in respect of offences under Part II of the Children and Young Persons Act 1933[2]. They may also prohibit or restrict the employment of children where it appears to them that a child is 'being employed in such a manner as to be prejudicial to his health or otherwise to render him unfit to obtain the full benefit of the education provided for him'[3]. The parent or employer may also be required to provide information necessary to ascertain whether the child is being employed in that manner[4]. Failure to comply with a local authority's request for information, or notice of prohibition, constitutes a criminal offence[5].

There is substantial evidence that enforcement of the statutory restrictions is ineffective and that there is widespread contravention of the law. A report by the Low Pay Unit, following a National Child Employment Study[6], found a vast amount of illegal employment of children in Birmingham and concluded that large numbers of children were at risk of economic exploitation, physical risk and educational disadvantage. Among the report's more significant findings were that 43 per cent of children between the ages of 10 and 16 years of age had some sort of job: 74 per cent of these were illegally employed, of which one-quarter were under 13 years of age, and many were employed in work prohibited for children or were working illegal hours; 35 per cent had had an accident including cuts, burns, broken bones and assault; and children were generally underpaid with one-quarter of them earning less than £1 per hour. The report called for immediate implementation of the Employment of Children Act 1973, a thorough review of all employment legislation affecting children, minimum wage protection for children and young persons and action, at a European level, to provide greater protection for children at work under the European Social Charter. It remains to be seen how effective the European Directive is in achieving these aims.

Family decisions and the employment of children

Children are, of course, members of families as well as individuals, and this raises issues about the application of family law principles in the context of the employment of children[7]. Two problematic and inter-related issues may be identified. The first issue is the impact of parental responsibility on employment decisions. The second issue is the relationship between child autonomy or '*Gillick*-competence' and the restrictions on employment.

---

1   Children and Young Persons Act 1963, s 37(4).
2   Children and Young Persons Act 1933, s 98.
3   Education Act 1996, s 559(1).
4   Ibid, s 559(2).
5   Ibid, s 559(3).
6   C Pond and A Searle *The Hidden Army: Children at Work in the 1990s* Low Pay Pamphlet No 55, and see the summary at (1991) 76 *Childright* 17.
7   For a damning critique of the law relating to the employment of children by their families, see A Bond 'Working for the Family? Child employment legislation and the public/private divide' (1996) JSWFL 291.

Employment and parental responsibility

Bevan has noted how, historically, the absolute nature of parental rights was used as a justification for child slavery, whereby a father sold his child to an employer. This influence of parental rights, according to Bevan, also contributed indirectly to the wretched conditions of apprenticeship in the nineteenth century. The father/child and master/servant relationships were considered so closely analogous that, just as the father could make unrestricted demands on the services of his child, so also could the master or employer – thus giving the barbaric conditions of apprenticeship 'an aura of respectability'[1].

Parental rights, now responsibilities, are no longer absolute, as has been shown, but an unresolved question is how far a parent might legally be able to interfere with the relationship of child and employer which does not contravene the statutory restrictions. What, for example, is the legal position if a 14-year-old agrees to take a Saturday job but his parents object? Can they prohibit the potential employer from engaging the child? The one point which is clear is that, if the employer should decide to flout the parents' wishes, no action would lie against him in tort[2]. From a practical point of view this may be all that we need to know, but the theoretical question remains. Does the parent, or the child acting in conjunction with the employer, have the right to decide? The answer would again appear to turn on the uncertain interpretation of *Gillick*. The later Court of Appeal decisions in *Re R* and *Re W* suggest that the employer, if satisfied that the child is '*Gillick*-competent', would be acting lawfully *either* in deciding to employ the child *or* in following the parents' wishes and deciding not to do so[3]. Any disputes could, at least theoretically, be resolved by application to the court, with leave, for a s 8 order.

Gillick competence and employment restrictions

A respectable argument can be mounted for saying that those children who have acquired *Gillick* competence should be liberated from the statutory restrictions on employment and the corresponding requirements of compulsory education. Why should such children not decide to work rather than stay on in school? This is an argument which undoubtedly appeals to some advocates of the liberationist school of children's rights[4]. The opposing argument, in favour of the employment restrictions and compulsory education, is that the child's 'developmental' and 'basic' interests require that he receive a certain level of education and be protected from premature exposure to work[5]. The essence of this argument is that it is only through proper education that a child can acquire the capacity for meaningful independence later in life, and this justifies imposing statutory restrictions before he matures into adulthood.

---

1   HK Bevan *Child Law* (Butterworths, 1989) at para 11.67.
2   *F v Wirral Metropolitan Borough Council* [1991] Fam 69.
3   *Gillick v West Norfolk and Wisbech Area Health Authority* [1986] 1 AC 112, *Re R (A Minor) (Wardship: Medical Treatment)* [1992] Fam 11, and *Re W (A Minor) (Medical Treatment: Court's Jurisdiction)* [1993] Fam 64. And see Chapter 8 above.
4   See also the discussion in MP Grenville 'Compulsory School Attendance and the Child's Wishes' [1988] JSWL 4.
5   See A Bainham *Children, Parents and the State* (Sweet & Maxwell, 1988) at pp 166–169.

The employment of young persons

Until comparatively recently, there were innumerable statutory provisions
regulating the employment of young persons[1]. Most of these related to night work
in industrial undertakings and the number of hours which young people were
permitted to work in specified occupations, mainly related to the delivery of goods
and the running of errands[2].

Abolition of most protective legislation
The Employment Act 1989[3] swept away practically all the protective legislation
applying to young people as distinct from children. Only a few restrictions which
were considered necessary, on health and safety grounds, remain. The legislation
involved denunciation of part of the European Social Charter, the main provision
being Article 7(8) governing night work, which requires contracting parties 'to
provide that persons under 18 years of age shall not be employed in night work
with the exception of certain occupations provided for by national laws and
regulations'. The power of local authorities to make bye-laws governing the
employment of young persons was removed, while the Secretary of State was given
wide powers to repeal or amend other relevant statutory provisions. The
Employment Act 1989 was part of a wider government policy for the 'deregulation' of the labour market by the removal of discriminatory and protective
legislation and the relaxation of certain employment protection rights[4]. The
position is, for the present, very straightforward. There is effectively no special
protective employment legislation and no general legal restrictions on the
employment of young persons.

The legislation was controversial and followed a Consultative Document issued
by the Department of Employment in 1987. This contended that there was 'no
evidence that long hours, shift work or night work have a different effect on young
people than on adults'[5]. Another argument in favour of deregulation was that the
existing regulations were piecemeal, complex and difficult to understand. As
such, they constituted an administrative and clerical burden for employers. It was
also said that the legislation was selective in its coverage, without any evidence of
greater exploitation in the protected spheres than in the unprotected ones[6]. It was
conceded that some form of regulation might need to be retained, on health and
safety grounds, or on 'moral' grounds as, for example, to protect young people
from exposure to drinking and gambling[7].

Deakin[8] has criticised the legislation for taking away the, admittedly selective,
protections for young workers, without making more general provision for
maximum hours of work, rest periods and working at weekends. While conceding

---

1   As to which see HK Bevan (above) at para 11.81.
2   The principal legislation was the Employment of Women, Young Persons and Children Act
    1920 and the Young Persons (Employment) Acts 1938 and 1964.
3   Employment Act 1989, s 10 and Sch 3.
4   For a critique of the Employment Act 1989, see S Deakin 'Equality Under a Market Order: The
    Employment Act 1989' (1990) 19 *Industrial Law Journal* 1.
5   Department of Employment's Consultative Document *Restrictions on Employment of Young People
    and the Removal of Sex Discrimination in Legislation* (1987) at para 1.8.
6   Ibid.
7   Ibid, at para 1.6.2.
8   S Deakin (above) at pp 18–19.

that there may be no evidence of an extra risk to the health and safety of young workers in the 16- to 18-year age group, Deakin put forward a more compelling reason for restricting their hours of work, namely 'to facilitate their integration into society'[1]. This, he argued, required that they have positive incentives to train and pursue their education in the transitional period between leaving school and entering fully waged work. The legislation, in his view, 'contributes further to the undervaluing of youth training and education which began with the linking of YTS to a policy of disguising unemployment and coercing the young unemployed into work through cuts in social security'[2]. He concluded that government employment policy in the UK was increasingly out of step with international and European domestic labour standards, which recognise 'that a high level of social protection is a pre-condition of a fair and efficient labour market'[3]. It should be noted that the European Directive applies to 'adolescents' as well as to children, although its requirements are understandably less exacting in relation to the latter. 'Adolescent', for these purposes, is defined by Article 3 as 'any young person of at least 15 years of age but less than 18 years of age who is no longer subject to compulsory full-time schooling under national law'. The Directive prescribes maximum daily working times for adolescents and a prohibition on night work which, despite a partial opt-out for the UK, should require a significant reform of English legislation.

The near abolition of protective legislation applying to young persons and the signal failure to enforce that which applies to children presents us with a curious paradox – that the area of law in which there has perhaps, historically, been the largest amount of legislative intervention is also the one in which the legal system has most emphatically failed to protect children and young people.

---

1 Citing the Council of Europe *Nightwork, Comparative Study of Legislation and Regulations, Problems and Social Repercussions* (1981) at p 48.
2 These wider aspects of employment policy are beyond the scope of this work.
3 S Deakin (above) at p 19.

Chapter 16
CHILDREN AND EDUCATION

INTRODUCTION

While the previous chapter was concerned with the 'Cinderella' aspects of children law, this chapter examines what is, undoubtedly, the growth area of law: education. The last decade or so has seen a burgeoning interest in educational issues and major legislative change. Education law has become an accepted academic discipline in its own right[1]. The fundamental right of children to be educated is recognised in a number of international Conventions. One of the most important is the United Nations Convention on the Rights of the Child. Article 28(1) provides:

> 'States parties recognize the right of the child to education, and with a view to achieving this right progressively and on the basis of equal opportunity, they shall, in particular:
> (a) make primary education compulsory and available free to all;
> (b) encourage the development of different forms of secondary education, including general and vocational education, make them available and accessible to every child, and take appropriate measures such as the introduction of free education and offering financial assistance in case of need;
> (c) make higher education accessible to all on the basis of capacity by every appropriate means;
> (d) make educational and vocational information and guidance available and accessible to all children;
> (e) take measures to encourage regular attendance at schools and the reduction of drop-out rates.'

Similarly broad statements about the right of the child to education may be found in the Universal Declaration of Human Rights[2] and the European Convention on Human Rights and Fundamental Freedoms[3]. Increasingly, also, the education of children has become relevant under European Community law[4].

The law relating to education was, until 1996, to be found in a host of Education Acts having as their foundation the Education Act 1944. Education law has, however, now been consolidated in the mammoth Education Act 1996 ('the 1996

---

1 The best introductory work is probably N Harris *The Law Relating to Schools* (2nd edn) (Tolley, 1995). For a more analytical analysis of education law and policy, see N Harris *Law and Education: Regulation, Consumerism and the Education System* (Sweet & Maxwell, 1993). The standard practitioner work is P Liell and JB Saunders *Law of Education* (Butterworths) (in looseleaf format). Many useful articles may be found in the specialist periodical *Education and the Law*. Many important decisions on all aspects of education law are now reported in the *Education Law Reports* (ELR).
2 Universal Declaration of Human Rights, Article 26(1) states:
  'Everyone has the right to education. Education shall be free, at least in the elementary and fundamental stages. Elementary education shall be compulsory.'
3 European Convention on Human Rights, Article 2, Protocol 1 provides, inter alia, that, 'No person shall be denied the right to education'.
4 See, particularly, M Gould 'Children's Education and the European Court of Justice' in D Freestone (ed) *Children and the Law* (Hull University Press, 1990) at ch 7; and N Bernard 'Education and EEC Law: Gravier and after' (1992) 4 JCL 43.

Act') and references in the text will usually be to the relevant section of the 1996 Act. But such is the propensity for governments of all complexion to legislate in the educational arena that the 1996 Act has already been amended by the Education Act 1997. The new Labour Government's School Standards and Framework Act 1998 also received Royal Assent on 24 July 1998. We describe briefly the principal objectives of this legislation at the end of this chapter.

Resources and parental choice

The above provisions are general statements of principle. The particular kind of education which individual children receive is influenced to a large extent by local educational provision and by parental choice. These factors are also acknowledged in international Conventions. Thus, the European Convention on Human Rights requires States parties to 'respect the right of parents to ensure such education and teaching in conformity with their own religious and philosophical convictions'[1]. The United Nations Convention explicitly recognises the discretion which States have in determining educational provision, provided that it accords with the fundamental principles of the European Convention and with the minimum standards of domestic law[2].

Minimum standards

The required minimum standards in English law are contained in s 10 of the 1996 Act which puts the Secretary of State under a general duty 'to promote the education of the people of England and Wales'. The more specific duty falls on local education authorities ('LEAs') and it is to secure that there are sufficient schools available for their area. The 1996 Act provides that they will not be deemed sufficient unless they are sufficient 'in number, character, and equipment to provide for all pupils the opportunity of appropriate education'[3]. 'Appropriate education' for these purposes means:

'education which offers such variety of instruction and training as may be desirable in view of –
(a)   the pupils of different ages, abilities and aptitudes, and
(b)   the different periods for which they may be expected to remain at school,
including practical instruction and training appropriate to their different needs.'

---

1   European Convention on Human Rights, Article 2, Protocol 1.
2   Ibid, Article 29(2). The fundamental principles themselves are set out in Article 29(1) which provides that the education of the child shall be directed to:
  '(a)   the development of the child's personality, talents and mental and physical abilities to their fullest potential;
  (b)   the development of respect for human rights and fundamental freedoms, and for the principles enshrined in the Charter of the United Nations;
  (c)   the development of respect for the child's parents, his or her own cultural identity, language and values, for the national values of the country in which the child is living, the country from which he or she may originate, and for civilizations different from his or her own;
  (d)   the preparation of the child for responsible life in a free society, in the spirit of understanding, peace, tolerance, equality of sexes, and friendship among all peoples, ethnic, national and religious groups and persons of indigenous origin;
  (e)   the development of respect for the natural environment.'
3   Education Act 1996, s 14(2).

The duty is deliberately broad, and legal attempts to challenge the general level of educational provision have usually failed[1]. In particular, the service provided by LEAs is severely constrained by the financial resources available. Indeed, many of the points made earlier about the general duties of social services departments towards children and families are pertinent here[2]. The establishment of a National Curriculum has, however, to some extent clarified the basic minimum education which LEAs and individual schools are required to provide[3].

Parental choice

Without question, the dominant ethos of education policy under the former Conservative Government was consumer choice, the dilution of the role of LEAs and the exposure of the education system to market forces. This was accompanied by greater centralisation in the provision and content of education[4]. The cornerstone of that Government's policy was parental choice, a principle encapsulated in the so-called 'parents' charter' issued by the then Department of Education and Science in 1991. The Conservative Government sought to give effect to this principle, directly and indirectly, in many different ways.

The Education Act 1980 tightened the procedures for allowing parents to express a preference as between schools and sought to entrench parental choice[5]. The Education (No 2) Act 1986, following the White Paper *Better Schools*[6], increased parents' representation on governing bodies and stipulated that articles of government require governors to prepare an annual report for parents[7] and to hold an annual parents' meeting[8]. The Education Reform Act 1988 took the process further and established the principle of 'open enrolment' (which required schools to admit pupils to the limit of their physical capacity) and 'local management of schools' ('LMS') (which delegated to governing bodies the financial management of the school's budgetary allocation)[9].

---

1 See, particularly, *Secretary of State for Education and Science v Tameside Metropolitan Borough Council* [1977] AC 1014; and the useful discussion in P Meredith 'Individual Challenge to Expenditure Cuts in the Provision of Schools' [1982] JSWL 344.
2 See Chapter 10 above.
3 See pp 553 et seq below.
4 Such as in the areas of religious and sex education and the ban on political indoctrination, discussed below.
5 For reasons of space we do not consider here the statutory regime governing school admissions. The principles are discussed in the first edition of this book, together with the question of parents' statutory rights to information about schools, at pp 555–563. See also N Harris *The Law Relating to Schools* (2nd edn) (Tolley, 1995) at ch 7. The leading case on appropriate admissions criteria for schools is the House of Lords decision in *Choudhury v Governors of Bishop Challoner Roman Catholic Comprehensive School* [1992] 3 All ER 277. Disputes between parents over choice of school may be resolved in family proceedings of which the best example is probably *Re P (A Minor) (Education)* [1992] 1 FLR 316. Here, the court held that the wishes of a 14-year-old boy to attend a day school rather than a boarding-school tipped the balance where the mother and father were in dispute. The law on school admissions is now consolidated in Part VI of the Education Act 1996, as amended by Part III of the Education Act 1997, and is further amended by Part III of the School Standards and Framework Act 1998.
6 (1985) (Cmnd 9469).
7 Education (No 2) Act 1986, s 30.
8 Ibid, s 31. This has now been put on a direct statutory footing by the School Standards and Framework Act 1998, s 43.
9 Education Reform Act 1988, ss 26 and 36 respectively.

Yet more radically, the Education Reform Act 1988 introduced a new category of school, the 'grant-maintained school'. Such schools were given the opportunity to 'opt out' of LEA control altogether and to receive a direct grant from central government[1]. The Education (Schools) Act 1992, intending to give effect to the provisions of the 'parents' charter', attempted to increase further the account-ability of schools to parents by providing for regular inspections of every State school and increasing the information available to parents about all local schools by requiring the publication of 'performance tables'[2].

The Education Act 1993 gave to parents a statutory right to withdraw their children from sex education classes analogous to their long-standing right to withdraw them from religious education and collective worship[3]. The Labour Government has also adopted as one of its central themes the concept of *partnership*, so familiar elsewhere in children law, in which parents will work with schools, LEAs and others in the commitment to raise educational standards. Key features of this partnership under the School Standards and Framework Act 1998 are 'home–school agreements', better information for parents and increased representation of parents on governing bodies and LEAs[4].

Rights versus responsibilities

No student of children law, looking at education, can fail to be struck by the contrast between the emphasis on parents' *rights* in education alongside the movement from rights to *responsibilities* elsewhere in the law. However, too much should not be read into this, for it is undoubtedly the case that parents do have *responsibilities* regarding their children's education[5] and many of the reforms in the Children Act, although couched in the terminology of parental responsibility, are founded on the philosophy that parents have primary control of their children. A more valid contrast is perhaps the lack of emphasis which the education legislation seems to place on *children's* rights, particularly (but not exclusively) in the matter of ascertaining and taking into account their views. While this is very much a feature of reforms elsewhere, it is certainly not a prominent feature of education law, much of which seems to be predicated on the assumption of an identity of interests between parent and child. Indeed, one can find examples in the education reforms of a reverse trend, as in the abolition of pupil governors[6]. One question which the student should, therefore, keep constantly in mind when looking at educational issues is the extent to which the *independent* interests or rights of children are being upheld.

It is, of course, true that the interests of children are bound to be affected, albeit indirectly, by every aspect of educational provision whether relating to the kinds of

---

1   Chapter IV of the Education Reform Act 1988. For further discussion, see P Meredith
    'Educational Reform' (1989) 52 MLR 215 at pp 224–228.
2   See J Robinson 'The Law of Education in 1992' (1992) 142 NLJ 24.
3   Section 241.
4   See White Paper *Excellence in Schools* (1997) (Cm 3681) at ch 7.
5   Especially in relation to their registration and attendance at school, discussed below. We also
    noted in Chapter 14 above the increased emphasis given to parental responsibility for the
    crimes of children.
6   Education (No 2) Act 1986, s 15(14), criticised in D Pannick 'School Student Governors – no
    legal obstacle' (1986) 25 *Childright* 15. Another example is the lack of independent
    representation and appeal rights against an exclusion. See further p 552 below.

schools provided, their financial and managerial arrangements, the adequacy of teachers and equipment, the role of the governors and so on. These wider issues cannot be explored here[1]. Instead, this chapter will concentrate on those legal questions which *directly* affect children. The following section considers the legal framework governing attendance and discipline. This is followed by a discussion of the *content* of education and the National Curriculum. Two special areas in education law are then examined – religious education and worship, and special educational needs. We then take a brief look at reforms introduced by the Children Act 1989 to protect the welfare of children who are being educated in independent schools or have long-term residential placements in various other establishments. The chapter concludes with a short summary of the principal changes to the education system to be expected under the Labour Government's School Standards and Framework Act 1998.

ATTENDANCE AND DISCIPLINE

Attendance

The legal obligation to secure a child's attendance at school is placed on parents and is not an express legal duty of the child himself. The principle of compulsory education is, thus, achieved through a combination of this duty and the statutory obligations of LEAs to provide schools[2].

Parents' obligations

The starting point is s 7 of the 1996 Act which provides:

'The parents of every child of compulsory school age shall cause him to receive efficient full-time education suitable –
(a)   to his age, ability and aptitude, and
(b)   to any special educational needs he may have, either by regular attendance at school or otherwise.'

The compulsory school age is from five to 16 years. The child begins to be of compulsory school age essentially when he attains the age of five[3]. He ceases to be of compulsory school age effectively at the school leaving date (the last Friday in June for 1998) closest to his sixteenth birthday[4].

Parental discretion over this aspect of upbringing is therefore curtailed to the extent that parents may not decide to withhold from their child an appropriate

---

1   But they should be borne in mind throughout this discussion. Clearly, inadequacy of resources can render much of this academic. For an academic treatment of the subject, see N Harris *Law and Education: Regulation, Consumerism and the Education System* (Sweet & Maxwell, 1993).

2   See p 538 above.

3   In fact, he will be of compulsory school age on a day prescribed by the Secretary of State which will either coincide with his fifth birthday or be the next prescribed day following his fifth birthday – Education Act 1996, s 8(2), as amended by the Education Act 1997, s 52.

4   Ibid, s 8(3) and the Education (School Leaving Date) Order 1997, SI 1997/1970. The Labour Government has signalled its intention to implement changes to the rules governing the school leaving date to prevent a child who has attained the age of 16 from leaving school at Easter and hence missing the GCSE examinations which take place just a couple of months later. It is concerned that as many as 17,000 young people leave school with no qualifications at all and that this damages their life-chances. See the White Paper *Excellence in Schools* (1997) (Cm 3681) at p 58.

education. In determining the *manner* of this education, however, they have a considerable say. They are not, strictly speaking, obliged to send the child to school at all if they can meet the statutory requirements by educating the child at home. But is is very unlikely that many attempts to do so would comply with these requirements, especially since the introduction of the more stringent requirements of the National Curriculum[1]. In any event, it is arguable that to deprive a child of the experience of a school life would, in itself, be a denial of children's rights and a failure to discharge parental responsibility.

Registration and attendance

There are two aspects to the parents' duty. The first is to secure the child's *registration*[2] at a school. The second is to ensure his regular *attendance* thereafter. Failure to comply with the first duty will lead to the invocation of school attendance procedures, and a possible prosecution under s 443 of the 1996 Act. These procedures begin with the LEA serving on the parent a notice which requires the parent to satisfy the education authority, within a specified time of not less than 15 days, that the child is being educated in accordance with s 7[3]. Where the parent does not satisfy the LEA, the LEA must serve a school attendance order ('SAO')[4]. If this is not complied with, the parent commits a criminal offence[5] which is punishable by a fine, but no longer by imprisonment[6]. It has been held[7] that, once there has been a prosecution in respect of an SAO, no further prosecution may be brought on that order. This has cast doubt on the effectiveness of criminal sanctions in the case of repeated offences, and it seems likely that LEAs will increasingly prefer the civil option of the education supervision order, introduced by the Children Act 1989[8]. The more common breach of duty relates to failure to secure the child's regular attendance which constitutes an offence under s 444 of the 1996 Act[9]. The question here, is usually whether parents can avail themselves of one of the prescribed statutory excuses for non-attendance[10]. These are:

(i)   absence with leave;
(ii) sickness or other unavoidable cause[11];
(iii) days of religious observance[12];

---

1 LEAs have a right to inspect the education provided at home. See *R v Surrey Quarter Sessions Appeal Committee ex parte Tweedie* (1963) 107 Sol Jo 555.
2 On the significance of the school register, see N Harris *The Law Relating to Schools* (2nd edn) (Tolley, 1995) at p 293.
3 Section 437 of the 1996 Act.
4 The procedure was amended by the Education Act 1980, ss 10 and 11 to accommodate the then new procedures regarding choice of school.
5 Section 443 of the 1996 Act.
6 Ibid.
7 *Enfield London Borough Council v F and F* [1987] 2 FLR 126.
8 Discussed at p 544 below.
9 It has been held that the offence is one of strict liability and that ignorance of the child's truancy is no defence. See *Crump v Gilmore* (1970) 68 LGR 56. The child's persistent late arrival at school may amount to non-attendance. See *Hinchley v Rankin* [1961] 1 WLR 421.
10 Section 444(3) and (4) of the 1996 Act.
11 This must, however, be an emergency and must relate to the child's position rather than the parents'. See *Jenkins v Howells* [1949] 2 KB 218; and, for a full discussion of the sickness provision, see MP Grenville 'Sickness and Compulsory School Attendance' (1989) 1 *Education and the Law* 113.
12 See, generally, the discussion below of religious issues in schools.

(iv) if the school is not within walking distance of the child's home and no suitable arrangements have been made by the LEA or the funding authority for the child's transport to and from the school or for boarding accommodation at or near the school, or for enabling him to become a registered pupil at a school nearer to his home[1].

The last issue has twice been to the House of Lords, not surprisingly, bearing in mind the financial implications of the duty to provide 'free transport'. In reality, the issue is not usually an absence of appropriate transport facilities but rather whether the cost should be borne by the parents or the LEA. In this respect, the LEA has a statutory duty under s 509 of the 1996 Act[2] to make provision for free transport with a view to 'facilitating' the attendance of pupils at school. In discharging this duty, the LEA must be guided by the considerations in s 509(4) of the 1996 Act which provides:

> 'In considering whether or not they are required ... to make arrangements in relation to a particular person, a local education authority shall have regard (amongst other things) –
> (a) to the age of the person and the nature of the route, or alternative routes, which he could reasonably be expected to take, and
> (b) to any wish of his parent for him to be provided with education at a school or institution in which the religious education provided is that of the religion or denomination to which his parent adheres.'

It was the interaction of the respective statutory duties of parents and LEAs which fell for determination by the House of Lords under the former provision in the 1944 Act[3]. 'Walking distance' is defined in the 1996 Act as two miles, or three miles where the child is aged eight years or over, measured by the nearest available route[4]. In *Rogers v Essex County Council*[5], it was held that a route did not cease to be *available* because it would be dangerous for an unaccompanied child. The nearest available route was the nearest along which the child could walk to school with reasonable safety when accompanied by an adult. The House of Lords thought that an interpretation which would render the route unavailable simply because of dangers which could confront an unaccompanied child was too vague. The decision was followed in *George v Devon County Council*[6] where the House held that an LEA exercising its discretion under s 55 of the 1944 Act (now s 444 of the 1996

---

1   Section 444(4).
2   For interpretation of this duty, see *R v Rochdale Metropolitan Borough ex parte Schemet* [1994] ELR 89 which inspired an amendment to the legislation to require LEAs in exercising their duty to make transport arrangements to take account of the religious preferences of parents. See also *R v Essex County Council ex parte C* [1994] ELR 273. Here, it was confirmed by the Court of Appeal that the statutory duty to provide transport only arises where the school (being more than three miles from the child's home) is the authority's choice. In this case, the LEA's choice of school for a child with special educational needs was not that of the parents. The parents chose a school some 14 miles away. While the LEA was willing to accede to the parents' choice of school, it was unwilling to bear the whole cost of the transport. It was held that the LEA was under no obligation to do so since the child's needs could have been met at a closer school.
3   Section 55 of the 1944 Act. See J Matthews 'Free Transport to School within Walking Distance' (1990) 134 Sol Jo 800; and S Luke 'Provision of free school transport (or keep fit by walking 60 miles a week)' (1989) 1 JCL 85.
4   Section 444(5) of the 1996 Act (formerly s 39(5) of the 1944 Act).
5   [1986] 3 All ER 321.
6   [1988] 3 All ER 1002. More recently, in *R v Kent County Council ex parte C* [1998] ELR 108, it was held by McCullough J that the LEA had not acted unlawfully when it refused to provide free transport for a pupil who had been selected for a grant-maintained grammar school on the

Act) was entitled to refuse free transport if it was reasonably practicable for the child in question to be accompanied to school. In this case, the child had an unemployed step-father who was in a position to do this. The principle underlying these cases is that where a child lives within the statutory limit, the *primary* responsibility for getting the child to school rests with the parent. Normally this will be discharged by the parent accompanying the child to school himself or by making alternative arrangements. The LEA has a discretion, over and above its statutory duty, to give assistance, but this is increasingly unlikely to be exercised given the constraints on public expenditure[1].

Does the child have a duty to attend school?

The child's obligation to go to school arises only by implication from the parent's duty, and the various enforcement procedures. Nowhere is this explicitly laid down in statute[2]. Given the increased autonomy of older children it could be argued that a '*Gillick*-competent' child ought to be able to decide whether or not to stay on in school. The issue is, essentially, the same as that which applies to the restrictions on child employment and the alleged right of the child to work, which was discussed in that context[3]. For the reasons given earlier, it is felt that the compulsory education system is not only compatible with, but positively mandated by, the concept of children's rights. Nevertheless, it has been argued that the independent powers and duties of parent and child are insufficiently defined and ought to be spelled out in legislation[4]. It has also been argued that parents might be able to raise, as a defence to prosecution, the unwillingness of a *Gillick*-competent child to attend school[5]. There are difficulties with this view, not least the short point that *Gillick* governs the common law and cannot be applied in the face of a conflicting statutory provision.

The enforcement of school attendance – education supervision orders

Where a child is not attending school regularly, the LEA has the option of taking criminal or civil action. It may decide to mount a prosecution for breach of s 444 of the 1996 Act, just as it can for breach of s 443[6], but this has often proved ineffective. Before the Children Act 1989, the LEA was obliged to consider whether it was appropriate, instead of, or as well as, prosecuting, to bring care proceedings based on the truancy condition in the Children and Young Persons Act 1969[7]. It had to be shown, in addition to the fact of failure to attend school, that the child was in need of 'care and control' which he was unlikely to receive unless the court made a care order. Yet this condition was interpreted in such a way that it was virtually redundant since proper 'care' was said to require proper education[8]. At the same time, there was a growing appreciation that taking

---

basis that it was not the nearest 'suitable' school. The fact that the grammar school was *more* suitable for her did not make the nearer wide-ability school unsuitable.

1   Section 509(3) of the 1996 Act.
2   It can of course be argued that the child *should* be placed under such a statutory duty. On the concept of children's duties, see Chapter 3.
3   At Chapter 15 above.
4   MP Grenville 'Compulsory School Attendance and the Child's Wishes' [1988] JSWL 4.
5   Ibid at p 18.
6   Above at fn 1, and see, generally, V Smith 'Non-School Attendance after the Children Act 1989' (1992) 156 JPN 387.
7   Children and Young Persons Act 1969, s 1(2)(e).
8   *Re S (A Minor)* [1978] QB 120.

children into care was not the way to combat the rise in truancy, and in Leeds a system of adjournments in care proceedings was pioneered with the objective of putting parents under pressure to carry out their responsibilities[1]. The legality of the so-called 'Leeds system' had been questioned but the Interdepartmental Committee reviewing child care law concluded that care orders were generally not the way to deal with truancy. The *Review*[2] reasoned that care proceedings were inappropriate where the *only* problem was the child's absenteeism. This was an educational issue and it was proposed that a new education supervision order ('ESO') should be introduced to deal with it. Where the child's absences were part of a wider family problem representing a risk to the child's welfare, the *Review* proposed that care proceedings should remain an available option. Here, the LEA would no longer be the applicant, since these wider problems were properly a matter for social services.

Education supervision orders
The Children Act 1989 gave effect to these recommendations. The LEA may now apply for an ESO simply on the grounds that the child is of compulsory school age and is not being properly educated[3]. The Act provides that this will be so 'only if he is receiving efficient full-time education suitable to his age, ability and aptitude and any special educational needs he may have'[4]. Unless proved to the contrary, it will be assumed that the child is not being properly educated where he is the subject of an SAO or where he is not attending regularly the school at which he is registered within the meaning of s 444 of the 1996 Act[5]. An ESO may not be made in relation to a child who is in the care of a local authority, the assumption being that the authority will properly discharge its obligations in relation to the education of children in its care[6]. The effect of an ESO is to place the child under the supervision of the 'designated authority'[7] which must, before applying for the order, consult with the relevant social services department[8]. Before instigating criminal proceedings against parents for offences relating to failure of their child to attend school, the LEA must consider whether it would be appropriate to apply for an ESO. The court, in criminal proceedings against the parents, may also direct the LEA to apply for an ESO. While the LEA is not obliged to follow the direction, it must give reasons to the court for not doing so within eight weeks of the direction being given[9].

Other possibilities
The court has a number of other options instead of making an ESO. Since these are 'family proceedings', the court may wish to consider making a s 8 order to resolve an educational issue. This could be apposite where, for example, parents

---

1 As to which, see R Hullin 'The Leeds Truancy Project' (1985) 149 JPN 488.
2 DHSS *Review of Child Care Law* (1985) at para 12.22.
3 Children Act 1989, s 36(3).
4 Ibid, s 36(4).
5 Ibid, s 36(5).
6 Ibid, s 36(6).
7 Ibid, s 36(7).
8 Ibid, s 36(8). This is one example of liaison and co-operation between LEAs and social services departments. Another is s 47(5) which provides for reciprocal consultation where it is the social services department which is initially involved with the child, and an educational issue arises.
9 Education Act 1996, s 447.

are at loggerheads over the child's education with the result that he is not attending school at all. Such a dispute might be resolved by a specific issue order or perhaps even by a residence order changing the child's residence to enable the more responsible parent to assume daily responsibility for the child[1]. Another possibility is that the very fact of court intervention might be enough to bring about a more responsible attitude in one or both parents. The general principles in the legislation apply, and the court will not therefore make an ESO, or any other order, unless satisfied that this would do more good than harm, applying the principles in Part I of the Children Act 1989[2]. A final possibility is that the court will take the view that matters are serious enough to satisfy the threshold provisions of s 31(2) of the Children Act 1989 and that it ought to make a care order. This is likely to be an uncommon situation, given the policy of the Act to abandon care orders as a response to purely educational problems. Yet in *Re O (A Minor) (Care Order: Education: Procedure)*[3], Ewbank J upheld the decision of magistrates to make a care order in relation to a 15-year-old girl who had been truanting from school for a three-year period and had only attended on 28 days during the last year. He held that it was open to the justices to conclude that her social, intellectual and educational development suffered consequential harm which was significant enough to warrant a care order[4].

Legal effects of an ESO

Part III of Sch 3 to the Children Act sets out in greater detail the legal effects of an ESO. The ESO will last for one year but the LEA may apply for it to be extended within three months of its expiration[5]. Where the ESO is in force, the duty of parents to secure regular school attendance is superseded by their duty to comply with directions under the ESO[6]. These directions are given by an educational welfare officer or education social worker whose duty under the ESO is to 'advise, assist and befriend' the child and his parents[7]. He should consult with the parents before giving directions and take note of their preferences, especially regarding the place of education[8]. Both parent and child must notify the supervisor of the child's address and must allow visits[9]. Failure to adhere to these directions is a criminal offence[10]. Where the child 'persistently fails to comply with any direction' under the ESO, the LEA must notify the social services department which then has a duty to investigate the child's circumstances. The ESO may be discharged on an application by the child, the parent or the LEA and will be automatically discharged by a care order or when the child ceases to be of compulsory school age[11].

---

1 Various options are discussed by V Smith 'Non-School Attendance after the Children Act 1989' (1992) 156 JPN 389.
2 Children Act 1989, s 1(1) and s 1(5) in particular. See Chapter 2 above.
3 [1992] 2 FLR 7.
4 On the 'parental failing' limb of s 31(2), see Chapter 11 above.
5 Part III, Sch 2, para 15.
6 Ibid, Part III, Sch 2, para 13.
7 Ibid, Part III, Sch 2, para 12.
8 Ibid, Part III, Sch 2, para 12(2) and (3).
9 Ibid, Part III, Sch 2, para 16.
10 Ibid, Part III, Sch 2, para 18.
11 Ibid, Part III, Sch 2, paras 15(6) and 17(1).

Discipline

Discipline in schools is considered important, partly to protect individual children from bullying, but more generally to create an environment in which education can operate effectively. It is recognised that standards of teaching and learning suffer where there is a breakdown of good order. The whole question of discipline in schools was the subject of a Report by the Elton Committee in 1989[1]. This made a number of significant recommendations which, inter alia, emphasised the importance of striking a balance between punishment and reward. Part II of the Education Act 1997 made a number of important changes to the law on school discipline concerning particularly the power of teachers to use reasonable force to restrain pupils, detention and the procedures relating to exclusions. That Act also gave statutory recognition to so-called 'home–school agreements'. The latter are now included in the School Standards and Framework Act 1998 which, as we have seen, also provides for the abolition of corporal punishment in the independent sector. This section examines the responsibility of schools for disciplinary matters and the legal limits on punishment. Since we discussed earlier the abolition of corporal punishment in schools[2], this chapter is confined to the other disciplinary measures open to schools.

Responsibility for discipline

As its broadest level, discipline falls within the overall conduct of schools, which in the case of State schools is under the direction of the governing body[3], but, in relation to discipline, the head teacher is given a central role to determine and make known the particular disciplinary regime for the school, and the standards of behaviour which are considered acceptable. The governing body is now under a specific statutory duty to 'ensure that policies designed to promote good behaviour and discipline on the part of its pupils are pursued at the school'[4]. The head teacher must now publicise the school's disciplinary regime in a written document and make this available within the school and to parents. At least once a year, he or she must take steps to make the school's disciplinary measures known to parents, pupils, teachers and other employees of the school[5]. The 1996 Act sets out in some detail the general objectives the head teacher should seek to fulfil. The head teacher should determine and enforce measures with a view to:

'(a)   promoting, among pupils, self-discipline and proper regard for authority;
(b)   encouraging good behaviour and respect for others on the part of pupils and, in particular, preventing all forms of bullying among pupils;
(c)   securing that the standard of behaviour of pupils is acceptable; and
(d)   otherwise regulating the conduct of pupils.'

In determining disciplinary measures, the head teacher must act in accordance with the current written statement of general principles prepared by the governing body and must have regard to any particular matters arising from the notification of guidance given to him by the governing body[6].

---

1   *Discipline in Schools: Report of the Committee of Inquiry chaired by Lord Elton* (1989).
2   At Chapter 15 above.
3   Education Act 1996, s 154, as amended by the Education Act 1997, s 2. See now School Standards and Framework Act 1998, s 61.
4   Section 154(1), now the School Standards and Framework Act 1998, s 61.
5   Section 154(7), now ibid, s 61(7).
6   Now the School Standards and Framework Act 1998, s 61(7).

Within these general guidelines, the governing body, and more especially the head teacher, have a good deal of discretion to determine the particular regime of discipline for the school and it is acknowledged that this may need to vary from school to school. The School Standards and Framework Act 1998 also contains a 'reserve power' which enables the LEA to intervene in the case of a complete breakdown in discipline at one of its schools. Thus, they are empowered to 'take such steps in relation to a maintained school as they consider are required to prevent the breakdown, or continuing breakdown, of discipline at the school'[1]. They may only do so where, in their opinion (if action is not taken), the 'education of any registered pupils at the school is (or is likely in the immediate future to become) severely prejudiced'[2]. It is not clear what the LEA might do in these circumstances, but it seems likely that it would at least seek to influence the action taken by the governing body to contain the situation.

Disciplinary measures: the legal limits

The limits of teachers' authority over children are largely determined at common law. There was considerable uncertainty both about the legal basis of this authority and its extent, so much so that the Elton Committee recommended that teachers' disciplinary authority be put on a firm statutory footing – a recommendation not immediately acted upon by the Government[3]. By way of exception, we have seen that corporal punishment has for some time been regulated by statute, and this is also the case regarding exclusion, the most serious disciplinary option.

The Education Act 1997 took this process further by clarifying teachers' powers of restraint, putting the practice of detention on a statutory footing and making amendments to the law and procedure governing exclusions. The School Standards and Framework Act 1998 requires all maintained schools to adopt home–school agreements, an important aspect of which will be the school's disciplinary regime[4].

The legal basis of a teacher's authority

The traditional view was that a teacher's authority derived from implied delegation of parental authority. The teacher was, as it were, in loco parentis during the school day and, as such, had the same power and authority as a parent. The modern view is that teachers possess this authority *independently,* by virtue of their status as teachers[5]. The Elton Committee proposed that this latter view be made explicit in statute and that there should be a statutory statement of the extent of teachers' disciplinary powers. The Committee thought that this should make clear, inter alia, the general authority of teachers to maintain discipline for educational reasons, to enforce school rules and to impose reasonable

---

1 School Standards and Framework Act 1998, s 62.
2 Ibid, s 62(2).
3 For further discussion, see N Harris 'Discipline in Schools: The Elton Report' (1990) JSWL 110.
4 Under ss 110–111, such agreements are now referred to as 'home–school agreements'. Under the Education Act 1997, s 13 they were previously known as 'home–school partnership documents'.
5 This appeared to some to have been given implied statutory recognition in the Children and Young Persons Act 1993, s 1(7). The subsection provided, in relation to the offence of cruelty to children, that 'nothing in this section shall be construed as affecting the right of any parent, teacher, or other person having the lawful control or charge of a child or young person to administer punishment to him'.

punishments (consistent with the school's disciplinary policy and the general law) and to exercise discipline over pupils out of school in certain circumstances[1].

Before turning to the legal framework governing particular disciplinary measures, it is appropriate to begin with a brief description of home–school agreements since these encapsulate the ethos of partnership between schools and parents (and to an extent the children themselves) in securing co-operation over, inter alia, the school's disciplinary regime.

Home–school agreements

The idea of the home–school agreement is that all schools should work in strong partnership with parents. The agreements are not to be legally binding but are intended to be 'powerful statements of intent'[2]. Although the detail will vary from school to school, 'all agreements are likely to include expectations about the standard of education, the ethos of the school, regular and punctual attendance, discipline, homework, and the information schools and parents will give to one another'[3]. The Government views them as 'important in helping engage parents in raising pupils' achievements and in action to combat truancy, bullying and unacceptable behaviour which undermines pupils' progress'[4].

Under the School Standards and Framework Act 1998[5], such agreements will be mandatory in maintained schools and the governing body will be required to take reasonable steps to secure a signed 'parental declaration' by every qualifying parent. The purpose of the declaration will be to record that parents 'take note of the school's aims and values and its responsibilities and that they acknowledge and accept the parental responsibilities and the school's expectations of its pupils'[6]. The Act also provides that the governing body may invite the pupil to sign the parental declaration as an indication that he acknowledges and accepts the school's expectations of its pupils but, essentially adopting the test of *Gillick* competence, only where they are satisfied that the pupil 'has a sufficient understanding of the home–school agreement as it relates to him'[7]. The hope is obviously that the creation of a partnership ethos and co-operation between schools, parents and children will pre-empt the need for the use of the different disciplinary measures discussed below.

General legal constraints on disciplinary action

The general, albeit rather vague and unhelpful, proposition which can be stated with some confidence is that teachers must, in resorting to any disciplinary measure, act within the law. As with other principles of the common law, this seems, in the end, to come down to proportionality and reasonableness[8]. Subject to this underlying principle, the law does authorise the use of classroom sanctions

---

1 *Discipline in Schools: Report of the Committee of Inquiry chaired by Lord Elton* (1989) at para 74, and see N Harris 'Discipline in Schools: The Elton Report' (1990) JSWL 110 at pp 115–116. See also 'Teachers must learn to play safe' (1993) *The Times*, February 15, in which it was suggested that, since the Children Act 1989, teachers had become statistically more likely to have complaints brought against them in relation to exercises of discipline.
2 White Paper *Excellence in Schools* (1997) (Cm 3681) at p 55.
3 Ibid.
4 Ibid.
5 Sections 110–111.
6 Section 110(2).
7 Section 110(5).
8 This is broadly in line with principles of the tort of negligence, discussed in Chapter 15 above.

such as the withdrawal of privileges, confiscation of property and detention. The common law principles are derived, in part, from cases on corporal punishment, decided before its abolition in schools, especially the nineteenth-century case of *R v Hopley*[1]. In this, Cockburn CJ laid down the test, now generally accepted in relation to both parents and schools, that punishment must be moderate and reasonable. This test originally applied specifically to the use of corporal punishment, but it has been argued that the test can be applied, by analogy, to *all* forms of punishment in schools[2]. There is a dearth of direct authority on disciplinary sanctions falling short of exclusion and it has been suggested that this may well reflect a consensus among parents that low-level disciplinary measures are really a matter for individual schools.

There was, however, until recently, uncertainty concerning the legality of teachers' use of physical restraint. Since 1987, corporal punishment has been outlawed in the State sector (and will be outlawed in the independent sector under the 1998 Act). The question has been how far teachers might be entitled to use physical force in restraining pupils without this degenerating into unlawful corporal punishment. The line was blurred and teachers overstepping it would run the risk of committing a battery on the child. In an effort to clarify the position, the Education Act 1997[3] conferred a new statutory power on members of staff to use 'such force as is reasonable in the circumstances' for the purpose of preventing a pupil from:

'(a) committing any offence;

(b) causing personal injury to, or damage to the property of, any person (including the pupil himself); or

(c) engaging in any behaviour prejudicial to the maintenance of good order and discipline at the school or among any of its pupils, whether that behaviour occurs during a teaching session or otherwise.'

It appears that this provision was designed to take away from teachers the fear of prosecution where they use moderate physical restraints, for example to break up fights between pupils. Ultimately, the limits of this power will turn again on the necessarily vague notion of what is reasonable in the particular context.

Detention

There is comparatively recent authority on the limits of parental control over the physical movements of children which can be applied, by analogy, to schools. In *R v Rahman*[4], Lord Lane CJ held that the detention of a child by a parent could be unlawful and amount to false imprisonment where it was 'for such a period or in such circumstances as to take it out of the realms of reasonable parental discipline'. In the context of schools, detention, when used, should be motivated by proper considerations[5] and should be for a reasonable time. What is reasonable will vary, depending on the circumstances and the ages of the pupils. Detention of whole classes is now of dubious legality and should be avoided since it is insufficiently related to the misdemeanours of individual pupils[6].

---

1   (1860) 2 F&F 202.
2   N Harris (above) at pp 314 et seq.
3   Inserting a new s 550A into the Education Act 1996.
4   (1985) 81 Cr App R 349.
5   Otherwise it may amount to false imprisonment, as to which see *Fitzgerald v Northcote* (1865) 4 F&F 656.
6   See N Harris (above) at p 124.

The Education Act 1997[1] amended the 1996 Act to give express statutory recognition to the authority of schools to detain badly behaved children after school without their parents' consent thus removing the risk of legal action for false imprisonment. The head teacher must have previously made it known within the school that detention is part of the school's disciplinary regime. Steps must have been taken to bring this to the notice of parents and the particular pupil's parents must have been given at least 24 hours' notice of the proposed detention[2].

The new provision also prescribes the factors which go to determining whether the detention complies with the general test of reasonableness[3]. These are:

'(a) whether the detention constitutes a proportionate punishment in the circumstances; and
(b) any special circumstances relevant to its imposition on the pupil which are known to the person imposing it (or of which he ought reasonably to be aware).' [These include the pupil's age, any special educational needs he may have, religious factors and transport arrangements.]

Confiscation of property

There is no real authority on the legality of this practice but on general principles it is regarded as lawful[4]. Indeed, in the case of a dangerous object, the teacher might expose the school authorities to a possible negligence action if the item were not confiscated and a child suffered injury as a result[5]. Teachers must operate within the criminal law and civil law, which generally impose liability for permanent taking or destruction of property belonging to others[6]. It has, therefore, been argued, that to avoid any possible legal liability, the confiscated item should be returned to the child or his parent at the earliest opportunity, preferably at the end of the school day[7].

Exclusion

Exclusion is a drastic measure to deal with serious breaches of discipline and is now closely regulated by statute[8]. The minutiae of the legal procedures are beyond the scope of this chapter, but the salient features of the law are as follows[9].

The decision whether to exclude a pupil from the school is for the head teacher in the first instance. Where the exclusion is for a fixed term, this must not exceed 45 school days in any one school year[10]. Where he decides to exclude a pupil, the head teacher must inform the child's parents of the decision, giving reasons and the period of the exclusion[11]. He must inform the parents again if he decides to

1 Education Act 1997, s 5, inserting a new s 550B into the Education Act 1996.
2 Education Act 1996, s 550B.
3 Ibid, s 550B(4).
4 See N Harris (above) at p 325.
5 Sharp instruments, for example. On the negligence of school authorities, see Chapter 15 above.
6 Particularly theft and related offences and the tort of conversion.
7 N Harris (above).
8 Education Act 1996, ss 156–160 and Schs 15 and 16, as amended by the Education Act 1997. The matter will be further governed by ss 64–68 of and Sch 18 to the School Standards and Framework Act 1998 when implemented.
9 For a more detailed discussion, see N Harris *The Law Relating to Schools* (2nd edn) (Tolley, 1995) at pp 314–322, and N Harris 'Discipline in Schools: The Elton Report' (1990) JSWL 110 at pp 120–122.
10 Education Act 1996, s 156, as amended. The limit prior to the Education Act 1997 was 15 school days per term. The amendment was designed to give greater flexibility to schools. See now School Standards and Framework Act 1998, s 64.
11 Education Act 1996, s 157(2) and School Standards and Framework Act 1998, s 65.

exclude the child permanently. The parents, and the child where he is over 18 years of age, must be informed of their right to make representations to the governing body or the LEA[1]. Whenever a child is excluded for more than five days in total in a single term, or the exclusion would result in the pupil losing the opportunity to take a public examination, the head teacher must inform the governors and LEA without delay[2]. The governing body will then normally determine the question of reinstatement but can be overridden by the LEA itself which has power to direct it[3]. Where the child has been expelled, or the exclusion was indefinite, the LEA *must* consult the governing body and *may* direct reinstatement[4]. Where the exclusion was for a fixed period, *both* the LEA and the governing body have power to order a reinstatement and the head teacher is bound to comply with this[5]. If their directions conflict, the head teacher must follow that direction which would lead to the earlier reinstatement[6].

There is a right of appeal to an appeal committee[7]. This may be exercised by the parents, or the child where he is over 18 years of age, against a permanent exclusion and a decision by the LEA against reinstatement[8]. The arrangements for hearing appeals against exclusions or decisions not to reinstate were modified by the Education Act 1997 to inject more procedural fairness into the areas of rights of appearance, representation and stipulation of the criteria to which the appeal committee should have regard. In particular, there is now a *duty* on the appeal committee to allow the parent or pupil to be represented or accompanied by a friend. The governing body also has a right of appeal where the LEA has directed the head teacher to reinstate a permanently excluded pupil. It should, however, be noted that the pupil himself, except in the tiny minority of cases in which he is over 18 years of age, has no appeal in his own right, or right of representation – something which is questionable both in terms of children's rights and on more general principles of natural justice. It contrasts starkly with the greater legal rights of children in other areas, especially in care proceedings[9]. Indeed, the extent to which the current law on discipline in schools is really 'child-centred' or gets to grips with the independent interests of children (as distinct from those of parents) can be called into question.

In its White Paper *Excellence in Schools*[10] the Labour Government recognised that schools need the ultimate sanction of exclusion, but also that the present number of exclusions is too high. It was also concerned about the unjustified variation in exclusion rates across schools and the disproportionate exclusion of pupils from certain ethnic groups and from children looked after by local authorities. It is

---

1 Education Act 1996, s 157(2).
2 Ibid, s 157(3).
3 Ibid, Sch 15, para 5.
4 Ibid, Sch 15, para 2.
5 Ibid, Sch 15, para 5(1).
6 Ibid, Sch 15, para 5(2).
7 Ibid, Sch 16, as amended by the Education Act 1997, s 7. On the nature and extent of the appeal committee's duty to give reasons, see *R v Northamptonshire County Council ex parte W* [1998] ELR 291.
8 Ibid.
9 See Chapters 11 and 13 above; and see *R v Fernhill Manor School ex parte A* [1993] 1 FLR 620, in which Brooke J held that an expelled pupil at an independent school had no public law right to challenge the expulsion. Her parents might, however, seek a declaration in private law.
10 Paragraphs 19–21.

expected that new guidance[1] will be issued concerning the appropriate circumstances for exclusion, appeals and arrangements for the subsequent education of excluded pupils.

THE CURRICULUM

Under the 1944 Act, control of the secular curriculum was vested entirely in LEAs. Whether parents had any right even to be consulted was a matter of some doubt[2]. Central control of the curriculum was limited to religious education which was compulsory[3]. The effect of the educational reforms of the 1980s was to wrest control of the curriculum from LEAs and to establish central direction of the curriculum, both secular and religious, while at the same time increasing the influence of governing bodies (and hence parents)[4]. The role of the LEA itself has been marginalised. The central pillar of this policy has been the establishment of a National Curriculum and, alongside this, there has been significant central intervention in specific matters, including religious worship in schools, sex education and political issues. The legal framework may be conveniently examined under three headings: general principles applying to the whole curriculum; the secular curriculum; and religious education. In the case of the latter, consideration must be given not only to the religious education and worship in schools but also to the principles applying to religious upbringing as an aspect of parental responsibility.

General principles

Under the 1996 Act we saw that the Secretary of State has a general duty to 'promote the education of the people of England and Wales'[5]. LEAs were given a similarly broad duty to 'contribute towards the spiritual, moral, mental and physical development of the community'. These general promotional duties and underlying aims were fleshed out by the Education Reform Act 1988 (now consolidated in the Education Act 1996). They apply to what is referred to as the 'whole curriculum' which includes the 'basic curriculum' but extends beyond it. The 'basic curriculum' refers to the secular and religious education which schools are bound to provide, while the concept of the 'whole curriculum' includes the essential aims of education which cut across all aspects of the curriculum and other activities of the school. As Harris has put it:

> 'There is an important cross-curricular aspect to the "whole curriculum", involving the inculcation of various skills and emphasising themes such as economic and industrial understanding, careers education and guidance, environmental education, health education and citizenship.'[6]

1 The current guidance is DFE Circular 10/94 *Exclusions from School.* For a further useful discussion of the legal issues surrounding exclusion, see J Fortin *Children's Rights and the Developing Law* (Butterworths, 1998) at pp 141–148.
2 Goff J in *Wood v Ealing London Borough Council* [1996] 3 WLR 1209 at 1221 seemed to imply that there was a right of consultation, as a matter of interpretation of s 76 of the 1944 Act.
3 And still is, as discussed below.
4 See P Meredith 'Educational Reform' (1989) 52 MLR 215 at pp 216–221.
5 Education Act 1996, s 10.
6 N Harris *The Law Relating to Schools* (2nd edn) (Tolley, 1995) at p 190.

The responsibility for the whole curriculum is shared between the Secretary of State, LEAs, governing bodies and head teachers who must all have regard to certain guiding principles expressed at a very broad level of generality. Under the Education Act 1996[1], they must exercise their respective functions with a view to securing that the curriculum of a school is 'balanced and broadly based' and that it promotes the 'spiritual, moral, cultural, mental and physical development of pupils at the school and of society' and that it prepares such pupils 'for the opportunities, responsibilities and experiences of adult life'.

In addition, certain other responsibilities regarding the curriculum were already in place, having been introduced by the Education (No 2) Act 1986. This Act required LEAs to keep under review their policy in relation to the secular curriculum and to publish and keep up to date a written statement of it[2]. Articles of government were to require governing bodies to consider the LEA's policy and, in the light of their opinion as to the aim of the secular curriculum at the school, consider whether, and if so how, it should be modified in its application to the school[3]. The head teacher was required to ensure that the organisation of the curriculum was compatible with the LEA's policy, as amended by the governors (where relevant) and with the general law. Governing bodies were to have regard to any representations made to them by 'any persons connected with the community served by the school' and particularly any made by the Chief Constable 'and which [were] connected with his responsibilities'[4].

The Education Act 1996[5] requires every maintained school[6] in England and Wales to establish a 'basic curriculum' which must include:

(1) provision for religious education for all registered pupils at the school;
(2) a curriculum for all registered pupils at the school of compulsory school age (to be known as 'the National Curriculum');
(3) in the case of a secondary school, provision for sex education for all registered pupils at the school; and
(4) in the case of a special school, provision for sex education for all registered pupils at the school who are provided with secondary education.

Since religious education needs to be discussed alongside collective worship and parental upbringing (matters falling outside the National Curriculum) it is convenient to begin by looking at the secular curriculum.

Secular education: the National Curriculum

The origins of the National Curriculum can be traced back at least as far as the White Paper *Better Schools* published in 1985, in which the Conservative Government signalled its intention to seek a broad consensus on the aims of the secular

---

1 Section 351.
2 Education (No 2) Act 1986, s 17.
3 Ibid, s 18.
4 Ibid, s 18(3).
5 Section 352.
6 There are many different categories of maintained schools as opposed to independent schools. The classification of schools is complex, but an excellent account is to be found in N Harris *The Law Relating to Schools* (2nd edn) (Tolley, 1995) at pp 29–45. It should be noted, however, that the categorisation of schools will be altered by the School Standards and Framework Act 1998. See p 571 below.

curriculum. One view of the National Curriculum is that by 1988 this had been achieved, and that the legal framework in the Education Reform Act 1988 '[was] a mere statutory endorsement of the consensus which [had] emerged over the past 10 years or so over the curriculum, and [was] thus a welcome, timely and uncontroversial tidying up measure bringing our practice more into conformity with our European partners where centralised prescription of what is taught in schools is much more advanced'. An alternative view is that it was more a reflection of the desire to by-pass LEAs in the way that has occurred in other aspects of the educational reforms. On this view, the National Curriculum was 'a notable exercise in centralisation and a serious undermining of the role of LEAs and the professional autonomy of teachers'[1]. In any event, LEAs, governing bodies, and head teachers are required to implement the National Curriculum in force at the relevant time[2].

Scheme of the National Curriculum

The scheme of the National Curriculum is that there are certain *core*[3] and other *foundation* subjects[4] and in relation to these there are *attainment targets, programmes of study*[5] and *assessment arrangements*[6] which are to be promulgated by order from time to time. For each of the core and foundation subjects, the Secretary of State is required to establish a 'complete' National Curriculum and to revise it whenever he considers it necessary or expedient[7]. The attainment targets, programmes of study and assessment arrangements are related to four *key stages* which broadly approximate to the age ranges 5 to 7, 8 to 11, 12 to 14 and 15 to 16 years of age[8]. Standard assessment tasks ('SATs') take place at the end of each key stage. Before promulgating orders specifying *attainment targets* and *programmes of study*, the Secretary of State must refer draft proposals to the Qualifications and Curriculum Authority[9] which has responsibility for keeping all aspects of the curriculum for maintained schools under review, advising the Secretary of State, and conducting programmes of research and development[10]. In practice, initial proposals for submission to the Council are first referred to subject

---

1 P Meredith 'Educational Reform' (1989) 52 MLR 215 at 217.
2 Education Act 1996, s 357.
3 Ibid, s 354(1)(a) which defines the core subjects as Mathematics, English and Science. Welsh is a core subject in Welsh-speaking schools (s 354(1)(b)).
4 Ibid, s 354(2) defines other foundation subjects to include technology, physical education, history, geography, art and music (in relation to key stages 1–3); and a modern foreign language (in relation to key stages 3 and 4).
5 Ibid, s 353(a) defines attainment targets as 'the knowledge, skills and understanding which pupils of different abilities and maturities are expected to have by the end of each key stage'. Ibid, s 353(b) defines programmes of study as 'the matters, skills and processes which are required to be taught to pupils of different abilities and maturities during each key stage'.
6 Assessment arrangements are defined by ibid, s 353(c) as 'the arrangements for assessing pupils at or near the end of each key stage for the purpose of ascertaining what they have achieved in relation to the attainment targets for that stage'.
7 Ibid, s 356(1).
8 Ibid, s 355.
9 Formerly the School Curriculum and Assessment Authority and before that the National Curriculum Council.
10 Education Act 1997, s 23.

working groups, although the Secretary of State has not always followed their recommendations[1]. The LEA, governing body and head teacher of a maintained school are required to publish detailed information about the curriculum and they must establish a complaints procedure relating, inter alia, to curricular matters[2].

Exceptions to these requirements

Limited exceptions to the requirements of the National Curriculum may be specified by the Secretary of State. Pupils with special educational needs and who are 'statemented' under the Education Act 1996 may be exempted from the whole or part of it[3].

Other specific aspects of the Curriculum are centrally prescribed as follows.

External qualifications and examination entry

Maintained schools are precluded from offering to pupils of compulsory school age courses which lead to qualifications authenticated by outside bodies unless the qualifications have been approved by the Secretary of State or a designated body[4]. Governing bodies must secure that all pupils are entered for *public* examinations for which they are being prepared by the school[5]. Exceptionally, a particular pupil may not be entered for educational reasons, if his parents request this in writing[6].

Charging for education

Under the Education Act 1944, maintained schools and LEAs were prevented from charging for the education they provided[7]. The principle of 'free education' was largely preserved but the Education Reform Act 1988 (now consolidated in the 1996 Act) does allow charging in certain specified instances involving such things as individual music tuition, the cost of residential trips, 'optional extras' in school, and education provided outside school hours[8].

Political issues

The Education Act 1996 as amended requires the head teachers and governing bodies of all maintained and grant-maintained schools to forbid 'the pursuit of partisan political activities' by junior pupils of the school (or such activities off the school if organised by a member of staff) and 'the promotion of partisan political views in the teaching of any subject in the school'[9]. Further, LEAs, head teachers, and governing bodies must 'take such steps as are reasonably practicable to secure that where political issues are brought to the attention of pupils' while at school or

---

1   See the examples given by P Meredith 'Educational Reform' (1989) 52 MLR 215 at 219.
2   Education Act 1996, ss 408 and 409.
3   Ibid, s 364.
4   Education Act 1997, s 37.
5   Education Act 1996, s 402(1).
6   Ibid, s 402(2).
7   Education Act 1944, s 61, as to which see *R v Hereford and Worcester Local Education Authority ex parte Jones* [1981] 1 WLR 768.
8   See, generally, Education Act 1996, ss 449 et seq.
9   Ibid, s 406.

involved in extra-curricular activities organised for registered pupils, 'they are offered a balanced presentation of opposing views'[1]. These provisions were largely a reaction to what the Conservative Government saw as political indoctrination by left-wing teachers. It had in mind, in particular, 'Peace Studies'. It has been said that the ban on partisan political activities extends beyond purely *party* political matters and that, for example, environmental issues such as nuclear power could fall within it[2]. It is, of course, a possible criticism of these provisions that they were themselves motivated by partisan political considerations appealing to the government of the day.

Sex education

Much the same point can be made in relation to the attempt to influence the content of sex education in schools in the Education (No 2) Act 1986. The purpose of the legislation is to impose a moral framework on the provision of sex education. It requires LEAs, governing bodies and head teachers to 'take such steps as are reasonably practicable to secure that where sex education is given . . . it is given in such a manner as to encourage . . . pupils to have due regard to moral considerations and the value of family life'[3].

Before 1993, it was left to the governing bodies in maintained schools to determine whether sex education should be included in the secular curriculum[4]. It was doubted by the commentators whether it was consistent with the general duty which schools had in preparing pupils for the 'opportunities, responsibilities, and experiences of adult life' and the National Curriculum Science Targets (which referred to human reproduction), for sex education not to be offered[5]. A government circular of the time recognised 'the widely accepted view that schools have a responsibility to their pupils to offer at least some education about sexual matters'. But, in a foretaste of what was to come, it also advised that governing bodies should take full account of the strong objections of some parents based on religious grounds[6].

It was, therefore, no great surprise that when the former Conservative Government decided to legislate on the matter in 1993 it did so in a way which ostensibly made sex education compulsory in maintained schools but which also attempted to skew the *content* of what formed part of the National Curriculum to allow objecting parents to remove their children from what might be termed 'value-free' instruction about sexual matters[7]. Under what is now s 352 of the Education Act 1996[8], sex education is a compulsory element in the *Basic Curriculum* of all maintained schools and this is explicitly defined to include education about:

---

1 Education Act 1996, s 407.
2 N Harris *The Law Relating to Schools* (2nd edn) (Tolley, 1995) at p 199.
3 Education Act 1996, s 403.
4 Education (No 2) Act 1986, s 18(2)(a).
5 See N Harris in his report for the National Consumer Council entitled *Complaints About Schooling* (1992) at p 29.
6 DES Circular 11/87 *Sex Education in Schools*.
7 For detailed treatment of the whole subject of sex education in schools, focusing particularly on the reforms introduced by the Education Act 1993, see N Harris (ed) *Children, Sex Education and the Law* (National Children's Bureau, 1996).
8 Formerly the Education Act 1993, s 241.

'(a)   Acquired Immune Deficiency Syndrome and Human Immunodeficiency Virus; and
(b)   any other sexually transmitted disease.'[1]

Crucially, however, these matters do not form part of the *National Curriculum*, and the 1996 Act goes on to give to parents an *absolute* right to withdraw their children, wholly or partly, from sex education except so far as it is comprised in the National Curriculum. The result is that while instruction about the biological aspects of human sexual development and reproduction is compulsory, the National Curriculum excludes knowledge of AIDS, HIV, other sexually trans- mitted diseases and other aspects of human sexual behaviour. It should be noted that parents are not required to give reasons for exercising their rights of withdrawal and that any such request must be complied with by the school authorities. Moreover, these rights extend to all registered pupils, which will include those aged over 16 – the age for consensual sexual activity and marriage, at least with parental consent.

Following the change to the law in 1993, the then Conservative Government issued a further circular on sex education[2]. This purports, inter alia, to advise on the question of counselling and advice given by teachers to individual pupils about sexual matters, especially pupils' own sexual behaviour[3]. Schools are warned that dealings between teachers and pupils 'should never trespass on the proper exercise of parental rights and responsibilities' and there is, in relation to contraceptive advice, a dark hint at illegality: 'teachers are not health pro- fessionals, and the legal position of a teacher giving advice in such circumstances has never been tested in the courts'. The clear implication is that a teacher giving such advice without parental knowledge or consent might be acting unlawfully and the Circular expressly states that it 'would be an inappropriate exercise of a teacher's professional responsibilities'. It is submitted that this advice is without foundation and, indeed, displays surprising ignorance of the state of the law. The short point is that it has been established that there is no tort of interference with parental 'rights'[4] and the advice jars badly with this and with the principles established by the House of Lords in the *Gillick* case[5]. It is difficult to see how merely talking to a child could be viewed as unlawful vis-à-vis the child and it is tempting to ask where it would all end. The better view is surely that advice agencies, teachers, professionals and other third parties must be presumed to be acting within the law in having dealings with children unless and until they have been specifically restrained by the courts from doing so[6].

---

1   Section 405.
2   DFE Circular 5/94 *Sex Education in Schools*.
3   Paragraphs 38–42.
4   *F v Wirral Metropolitan Borough Council* [1991] Fam 69.
5   See Chapters 3 and 8 above.
6   For further discussion, see A Bainham 'Sex Education: A Family Lawyer's Perspective' in N Harris (ed) *Children, Sex Education and the Law* (above) at pp 37–39.

Is there a right to sex education?

The current law on sex education in schools is not a conspicuous advertisement of the UK's commitment to children's rights and it does provoke the question whether there is indeed a right to such information[1]. What can be said with confidence is that it is not contrary to *parents'* rights under the European Convention on Human Rights for the State to introduce compulsory sex education which covers all aspects, provided that it is not delivered in a way which is intended to indoctrinate, but is objective. The European Court on Human Rights so held in *Kjeldsen, Busk Madsen and Pedersen v Denmark* over 20 years ago[2]. But this decision was not concerned directly with *children's* rights and it cannot be concluded that to allow the parental right of withdrawal is necessarily contrary to children's rights under the Convention. The United Nations Convention is, moreover, probably too broad and general in its references to education for it to be said that a universal right to sex education is recognised by that Convention[3].

From a theoretical and policy perspective, the current position is difficult to defend. The case for all children receiving appropriate sex education in an effort to prevent unwanted teenage pregnancy, abortion and sexually transmitted disease is a strong one and one which is justified by more than one theory or component of children's rights[4]. Along with the analogous parental right of withdrawal of children from religious education and collective worship[5], the case of sex education brings into sharp focus the problems which can arise where the interests/rights of children are too closely and uncritically identified with those of their parents. At the international level, this is one of a number of areas in which there is likely to be some difficulty in upholding contemporaneously what may be thought to be the fundamental (but perhaps conflicting) rights of parents and children[6].

Religious education, worship and parental upbringing

Religious education ('RE') forms part of the 'basic curriculum' and is compulsory in the State sector[7]. LEAs, governing bodies and head teachers have statutory responsibilities to ensure that it is provided to *all* pupils, including those over compulsory school-leaving age[8]. The matter is now governed by the 1996 Act. This requires county schools to teach RE in accordance with an agreed syllabus drawn up by a local conference. It must not be 'distinctive of a particular religious

---

1   The UN Committee on the Rights of the Child was distinctly unimpressed by the Government's record. See *Concluding Observations of the Committee on the Rights of the Child: United Kingdom of Great Britain and Northern Ireland* CRC/C/15/Add 34 (January 1995).
2   (1976) 1 EHRR 711.
3   See further, A Bainham (above) at pp 30–33.
4   Ibid at pp 25–28.
5   See below.
6   See Chapter 17 below.
7   See, generally, N Harris *The Law Relating to Schools* (2nd edn) (Tolley, 1995) at pp 205–214. See also C Hamilton *Family, Law and Religion* (Sweet & Maxwell, 1995) and C Hamilton and B Watt 'A discriminatory education – collective worship in schools' [1996] CFLQ 28. The matter is also the subject of DFE Circular 1/94 on *Religious Education and Collective Worship*.
8   Education Act 1996, s 384. It should be noted that the matter will be regulated by the School Standards and Framework Act 1998, s 69 and Sch 19, when implemented.

denomination'[1]. These requirements do not apply to *voluntary* schools which will often be of a religious character. In the case of voluntary schools, whether controlled, aided or special agreement schools, RE must be taught in accordance with either the agreed syllabus, the trust deed for the school, or the practice which operated before the school acquired voluntary status[2]. Special provisions also apply to grant-maintained schools[3].

The Education Reform Act 1988 also controversially required all agreed syllabuses for RE adopted on or after 29 September 1988 to 'reflect the fact that the religious traditions in Great Britain are in the main Christian whilst taking account of the teaching and practices of the other principal religions represented in Great Britain'[4]. A similar requirement applies to collective worship and we will consider the issues in that context along with the provision which gives parents a right to insist that their child be excused from RE or worship. Such rights are exercisable in all maintained schools. Maintained schools may also be obliged under the Education Act 1996 to make alternative arrangements for a child to receive particular denominational instruction during school hours. They must be satisfied that to do so would only interfere with his attendance at the beginning or end of the school day[5].

The 1996 Act[6] requires every LEA to constitute a standing advisory council on religious education (SACRE) which must advise the LEA on all matters relating to the agreed syllabus and collective worship in county schools. Importantly, it must also deal with applications to lift or modify the requirements relating to *Christian* collective worship[7] – a significant role in those areas in which there is a concentration of ethnic minorities. The council is constituted by representatives drawn from school governing bodies, the principal religious traditions in the area, teachers' associations, the LEA and co-opted members.

Collective worship

The provisions in the 1944 Act which required schools to hold a daily act of collective worship[8] were repealed by the Education Reform Act 1988, but only to put in their place more prescriptive requirements. The then Conservative Government previously made plain its view that religious education and worship had a 'special contribution' to make, in its White Paper *Better Schools*. It proposed that it should continue to receive 'the significance which it deserves within the curriculum', but that this should have a distinctively Christian flavour. Thus, 'within the statutory framework an introduction to the Christian tradition [it thought] remains central to the religious education provided in our schools'. It also indicated that it would look to LEAs and schools to ensure that these requirements were met[9].

The Education Act 1996 now requires (subject to the important parental right of withdrawal) all pupils at maintained schools to 'take part in an act of collective

---

1   Education Act 1996, s 376.
2   Ibid, ss 377–378.
3   Ibid, ss 379–383.
4   Education Reform Act 1988, s 8(3), now Education Act 1996, s 375(3).
5   Education Act 1996, s 389(3), (4).
6   Section 390.
7   Section 387.
8   Education Act 1944, s 25(1).
9   *Better Schools* at para 55.

worship' on each school day[1]. This may be a single act of worship for all pupils or different acts for different groups. It must be 'wholly or mainly of a broadly Christian character'[2]. It will be regarded as such 'if it reflects the broad traditions of Christian belief without being distinctive of any particular Christian denomination'[3]. It is not necessary for every act of collective worship to comply with this if, taking the school term as a whole, most of the acts which take place in the school do comply with the principle[4]. It has been held that the broadly Christian character of worship is not lost by the inclusion of elements common to Christianity and other religions which enable children of other faiths to participate[5].

These provisions were the result of a House of Lords' amendment to the Education Reform Bill and caused controversy from the outset. The concern seems to have been that schools were failing to get across the principal tenets of Christianity by, as some peers saw it, 'dabbling' in other religions[6]. Of course, this pre-supposes that schools *should* be trying to get across this message and that there is a proper place for religion in State schools. Other jurisdictions, with different traditions, have exercised great caution to ensure that State schools preserve neutrality as between different religions[7], and the principle of equality of religious belief is also a feature of the decisions of the family courts[8]. The English requirements which seek to elevate in importance one particular religion, Christianity (albeit maintaining neutrality between the many different Christian denominations), do not square with the position elsewhere, and can be a source of antagonism for the ethnic minorities. They are one manifestation of the existence of an established church, binding together church and State, itself something which has been called into question in recent years[9]. As one commentator has pertinently inquired, 'is it not incongruous in our multi-faith society for collective worship in schools to be "wholly or mainly" Christian?'[10].

Religious upbringing

There is no legal obligation on parents to raise their children in a particular religion or, indeed, in any religion. They have complete discretion to raise them as atheists, agnostics, or in any religion of their choice, but religion has often been a

---

1 Education Act 1996, s 385. The matter will be regulated by the School Standards and Framework Act 1998, s 70 and Sch 20, when implemented. See P Cumper 'School Worship and the Education Reform Act 1988' (1989) 139 NLJ 1203; S Poulter 'The Religious Education Provisions of the Education Reform Act' (1990) 2 *Education and the Law* 1; and C Hamilton and B Watt (above).

2 Education Act 1996, s 386(2).

3 Section 386(3).

4 Section 386(4).

5 *R v Secretary of State for Education ex parte R and D* [1994] ELR 495.

6 See P Cumper 'School Worship and the Education Reform Act 1988' (1989) 139 NLJ 1203.

7 The approach in the United States is to outlaw religion in State schools. For a review of some of the constitutional cases there, see A Bainham *Children, Parents and the State* (Sweet & Maxwell, 1988) at pp 179–180. For a discussion of the rather different approach to the problem in France, but one which still maintains the principle of equality, see J Bell 'Religious observance in secular schools: a French solution' (1990) 2 *Education and the Law* 121.

8 See below.

9 For an American perspective on the relationship between church and State, see ME Smith 'Relations Between Church and State in the United States: With Special Attention to the Schooling of Children' (1987) 35 Am J Comp Law 1.

10 P Cumper (above) at 1204.

fertile area of dispute between parents and other carers in proceedings relating, for example, to residence or adoption[1]. Several principles have emerged from the jurisprudence of the courts on religious issues. The first is that the courts should be reluctant to change the settled religion of a child. This has sometimes resulted in orders for custody (now residence) or adoption being made conditional on the carer or adoptive parent undertaking to secure the continuation of the child's religious upbringing[2]. The same principle underlies the statutory provisions which preclude local authorities and voluntary organisations from changing the religion of a child in their care[3]. The second principle is that the courts usually do not discriminate between the comparative worth of different religions. They take a neutral stance between them so that the adherence of one parent to a certain religion, or to no religion at all, should not, per se be decisive as to the child's welfare[4]. A third principle is that they will intervene where the social practices attaching to a particular sect or religion are considered positively harmful to the child. The best example is probably their willingness to intervene to protect the health of children whose parents, for religious reasons, are opposed to certain forms of medical aid[5]. More contentiously, they have occasionally intervened to prevent the chid being exposed to what has been seen as 'brainwashing' or social isolation[6].

The courts must be careful, however, not to discriminate between parents in residence and contact disputes purely on the basis of religion since this might violate parental rights under the European Convention on Human Rights. The European Court held by a narrow 5 : 4 margin in *Hoffmann v Austria*[7] that the Austrian Supreme Court's decision requiring the mother (who was a Jehovah's Witness) to hand over the children, who had been with her for the last two years, to the father infringed her rights under Article 8 taken in conjunction with Article 14. The majority accepted that there were adverse 'social factors' relating to Jehovah's Witnesses which might tip the balance in favour of the other parent. But crucially in this case the Austrian Supreme Court had attached decisive importance to Austrian federal legislation which prevented either parent from unilaterally changing the religion of the child or from the religion shared by both parents. The mother had done this when she had ceased to be a Roman Catholic and had become a Jehovah's Witness. The Supreme Court had essentially based its

---

1 Reviews of relevant case-law may be found in B Walsh 'Religious Considerations in Custody Disputes' [1988] Fam Law 198 and C Yates 'Religious education and upbringing – child right or parent prerogative?' (1989) 1 JCL 89. See also, more generally, C Hamilton *Family, Law and Religion* (Sweet & Maxwell, 1995) at chs 4 and 5.

2 For an example of an access dispute revolving around religious questions, see *Re S (Access: Religious Upbringing)* [1992] 2 FLR 313. For religious factors in medical cases, see Chapter 8 above.

3 See Chapters 10 and 11 above.

4 In *Re Carroll* [1931] 1 KB 317 at 336, Scrutton LJ said:
   'It is, I hope, unnecessary to say that the Court is perfectly impartial in matters of religion, for the reason that it has as a Court no evidence, no knowledge, no views as to the respective merits of the religious views of various denominations.'
   More recently, see *Re R (A Minor) (Residence: Religion)* [1993] 2 FLR 163 in similar vein.

5 Discussed in Chapter 8 above.

6 Perhaps the most striking example of this line of cases is the virtual condemnation of Scientology in *Re B and G (Minors) (Custody)* [1985] FLR 493.

7 Publ Eur Ct HR, Series A No 2552, 1993. For commentary, see A Bainham 'Religion, Human Rights and the Fitness of Parents' [1994] CLJ 39.

decision concerning residence (in the English sense) on religion alone and this violated the Convention.

Religious upbringing is, therefore, an area in which parents enjoy a great deal of discretion and this is reflected in the unusual deference which is attached to parental wishes in the education legislation. Whereas the so-called parental choice of school is, in reality, a qualified right to express a preference, the right to withdraw a child from religious education classes and collective worship is a strict legal right, since the educational authorities have an absolute duty to comply[1]. Quite where this leaves the independent rights of the child, especially the '*Gillick*-competent' child, over religious matters is highly questionable[2].

SPECIAL EDUCATIONAL NEEDS

Children with special educational needs ('SENs') are entitled to special educational provision under Part IV of the Education Act 1996[3]. Justice cannot be done here to the detail and complexity of the statutory regime but we will attempt to describe its principal features[4].

The purpose of the Education Act 1981 was to reverse the marginalisation of children with SENs, to remove any stigma and to integrate them, wherever possible, into ordinary schools. It sought to achieve this by the creation of legally defined and coherent procedures for assessment of need and special educational provision[5]. Thus, in a nutshell, although children with the most severe learning difficulties are usually expected to attend special schools, those with less severe difficulties (but still having special learning requirements) are expected to be catered for by special provision in mainstream schools[6]. Part IV of the Education Act 1996 must also be read with the Children Act 1989 which, as we saw[7], requires close co-operation between LEAs and social services departments and which places the latter under statutory duties to provide services for 'children in need'. Many children with SENs will also be children in need, and the legislation requires social services to assist any LEA with the provision of services for any child who has

---

1 First given to parents in the nineteenth century and now contained in the Education Act 1996, s 389(1).

2 There is an argument that it amounts to a denial of the child's rights under the European Convention on Human Rights. See A Nelson 'School Religion Law may break Convention' (1988) 44 *Childright* 7. The European Court of Human Rights in *Angeleni v Sweden* (1988) 10 EHRR 123 held that Article 9(1) of the Convention prohibits religious indoctrination at school but the court was here concerned with parents' rights against the State and not with the independent rights of children. Cf the discussion of sex education (above).

3 The Act consolidates the Education Act 1981, as amended by the Education Act 1993, which latter legislation made significant changes to the original scheme under the 1981 Act. See, generally, N Harris *The Law Relating to Schools* (2nd edn) (Tolley, 1995) at ch 9; S Oliver and L Austen *Special Educational Needs and the Law* (Jordans, 1996); and J Friel *Children with Special Needs: Assessment, Law and Practice* (Jessica Kingsley, 1995). For a study of the role of the special educational needs tribunal (SENT) which also contains a concise introduction to the legal principles, see N Harris *Special Educational Needs and Access to Justice* (Jordans, 1997).

4 See the illuminating two-part article, N Harris 'Special Education and the Law: further progress?' (1992) 3 JCL 104 and 147.

5 N Harris notes that, in 1989, LEAs held statements of SENs in respect of 138,679 pupils or 1.8% of the school population.

6 The policy referred to as 'integration' but more often now as 'inclusion'.

7 At Chapters 2 and 10 above.

SENs[1], and, equally, LEAs are required to assist social services[2]. The legal framework is especially complex because of interlinking and 'relativistic' definitions which broadly require a comparison to be made between the educational requirements of the individual child and ordinary educational requirements[3].

General duties towards children with SENs

The Education Act 1996 requires the LEA to ensure that there are sufficient schools in its area. An aspect of this is that it must have regard 'to the need for securing that special educational provision is made for pupils who have special educational needs'[4]. The Act defines this special educational provision as educational provision of any kind for a child under two years[5] and, for children over that age, 'educational provision which is additional to, or otherwise different from, the educational provision made generally for children of his age in schools maintained by the local education authority (other than special schools) or grant-maintained schools in their area'[6].

The governing body of a county, voluntary or grant-maintained school, and the LEA in relation to a maintained nursery school, have a statutory duty to *identify* children with SENs and use their best endeavours to ensure that special educational provision is made for them[7]. Where the head teacher or appropriate governor is informed by the LEA that a child has SENs, the head teacher or governor must make this known to anyone who is likely to teach the child[8].

The definition of special educational needs

The Education Act 1996 provides that a child has SENs where he has 'a learning difficulty which calls for special educational provision to be made for him'[9]. 'Learning difficulty' is further defined as either:

(a) 'a significantly greater difficulty in learning than the majority of children of his age'; or
(b) 'a disability which either prevents or hinders him from making use of educational facilities of a kind generally provided for children of his age in schools within the area of the local education authority'.

The Act also provides that a child under five years old has a learning difficulty if he is likely to fall within (a) or (b) (above) after attaining that age or would do so if special educational provision was not made for him[10].

---

1 Education Act 1996, s 324.
2 Children Act 1989, s 27(1) and (3).
3 N Harris 'Special Education and the Law: further progress?' (1992) 3 JCL 104 at p 105.
4 Section 14(6).
5 The legislation as it applies to children with special educational needs is not confined to children of school age. For a discussion of local authority obligations regarding day-care and nursery provision for pre-school children, see Chapter 10 above.
6 Section 312(4).
7 Education Act 1996, s 317(1)(a) and (c). See also the Code of Practice on the *Identification and Assessment of Special Educational Needs* (DFE, 1994). It is the duty of the governing bodies, LEAs and the SENT to have regard to the provisions of the Code as revised from time to time (Education Act 1996, s 313).
8 Ibid, s 317(1)(b).
9 Ibid, s 312(1).
10 Ibid, s 312(2).

The child's needs are therefore not to be considered in a detached way but must be related to what is considered ordinary and what special educational provision is available, and here there has been some litigation. In *R v Hampshire Education Authority ex parte J*[1], it was held by Taylor J that dyslexia suffered by a highly intelligent child could amount to a 'disability' for these purposes. The argument for the council was that provision for dyslexia could not be 'special educational provision' within the meaning of the legislation since *some* provision was made to deal with the problem in LEA schools through dyslexic units. Taylor J rejected this contention, taking the view that the statutory reference to educational provision 'made generally for children of his age' meant that which was made 'to the general run of normal children, to the normal majority'. Thus, even though each school might have a dyslexic unit or, for example, a deaf unit, this provision could still be special educational provision under the then Education Act 1981[2]. This decision was followed in *R v Lancashire County Council ex parte M*[3] in which the Court of Appeal, casting doubt on an earlier decision to the contrary[4], held that a need for speech therapy was almost always going to constitute SENs calling for special educational provision. It has, however, been held that the requirement of a lift in a school for a disabled pupil would not amount to educational provision[5].

The choice of school

It was noted above that the policy of the legislation is for *inclusion* wherever possible of children with SENs in the ordinary education system by attendance at mainstream schools. This philosophy is given statutory expression in s 316 of the Education Act 1996 which applies to 'statemented' children. These are children in respect of whom the LEA maintains a 'statement' of SENs and are those with the most severe learning difficulties[6]. Despite this, the 1996 Act requires the LEA (provided the following conditions are met) to secure that the child is educated in a mainstream (viz not special) school. The conditions are that educating the child in a mainstream school will be compatible with:

(a) his receiving the special educational provision which his learning difficulty calls for;
(b) the provision of efficient education for the children with whom he will be educated; and
(c) the efficient use of resources.

Education of the child at a mainstream school must not be 'incompatible with the wishes of his parent'[7].

In principle, also, the policy is that statemented children should follow the National Curriculum except insofar as this is modified to take into account their

---

1   (1985) 84 LGR 547.
2   For further analysis of the case, see N Harris 'Special Education and the Law: further progress?' (1992) 3 JCL 104 at p 105.
3   [1989] 2 FLR 279, and see T McKevitt 'Speech Therapy as "Special educational provision"' (1990) 2 JCL 45.
4   *R v Oxfordshire County Council ex parte W* [1987] 2 FLR 193.
5   *R v London Borough of Lambeth ex parte MBM* [1995] ELR 374.
6   For the statementing procedure, see pp 566 et seq below.
7   Education Act 1996, s 316(1).

SENs. All children with SENs, whether statemented or not, are expected to engage in the activities of the school together with those children who do not have SENs[1].

Where, however, the child's needs are especially severe, it may be necessary for him to attend a special school which, since the Children Act 1989, may with public assistance be situated abroad. A special provision was inserted into the legislation to allow local authorities to provide financial and other assistance to families who wished to take advantage in particular of the programme of 'conductive education' at the Peto Institute in Budapest for those suffering from cerebral palsy[2].

Quite protracted legal disputes can arise between parents and LEAs where parents themselves are requesting that a child be educated at a special school at the authority's expense[3] or, conversely, where the parents wish the child to attend a mainstream school and the LEA is pressing for the child to be educated at a special school[4]. The Education Act 1993 conferred on parents the right to express a preference in relation to the school to be named in a statement[5]. Where the LEA decides not to comply with the request it must inform the parents of their right to appeal to the SENT[6].

Identification and assessment of children with SENs

The statutory duties of LEAs and schools to identify children with SENs were noted above. These are most likely to become apparent during the teaching process, but might also first come to light through health problems, of which the health authorities and National Health Service Trusts are aware. There is, thus, a corresponding duty on health authorities in these circumstances to inform parents in the first instance and then, after giving them an opportunity to discuss the matter, to inform the LEA[7]. Much of the process of identifying and acting upon SENs may be informal and co-operative[8], but the legislation does provide a formal assessment procedure which is designed to safeguard the child's needs and parents' rights, and to make schools and LEAs accountable[9].

This procedure is now laid down in the Education Act 1996 and the regulations made under it[10]. We can do no more than set it out in skeletal form[11]. The procedure is intended to provide for parental involvement at all stages, and

---

1 Education Act 1996, s 317(4).
2 Ibid, s 320.
3 As in *R v Hampshire Education Authority ex parte J* (1985) 84 LGR 547. See also *L v Kent County Council and the Special Educational Needs Tribunal* [1998] ELR 140.
4 As in the wardship case *Re D* (1988) 86 LGR 442.
5 See now Education Act 1996, Sch 27, para 3.
6 Ibid, para 8. See further p 568 below.
7 Education Act 1996, s 332.
8 Informal assessment will be carried out at the school in up to three stages of assessment. See S Oliver and L Austen *Special Educational Needs and the Law* (Jordans, 1996) at ch 2 for the details.
9 For some robust criticisms of the way the procedure worked under the Education Act 1981, see J Robinson 'Reforming the Reforms' (1992) 142 NLJ 685.
10 Education Act 1996, ss 323, 328–331 and the Education (Special Educational Needs) Regulations 1994, SI 1994/1047.
11 For greater detail, see N Harris *The Law Relating to Schools* (2nd edn) (Tolley, 1995) and S Oliver and L Austen (above) at ch 3.

parents may themselves instigate an assessment[1]. Parents must be served with a notice in prescribed form that the authority proposes to assess the child. They must also be informed of the name of the officer within the LEA from whom further advice may be obtained and of their right to make representations and written submissions[2]. The child may be examined as part of the process and it is an offence for parents not to comply with this, although they have a right to attend the examination[3]. If the LEA decides, following the assessment, not to determine special educational provision, parents have a right of appeal to the SENT[4]. Where the LEA *does* decide to make such a determination it must maintain a *statement* of the child's SENs in prescribed form, which should include the professional advice on which the assessment was made[5]. Litigation has made two principles clear. The first principle is that LEAs have a wide discretion in the first instance in deciding whether or not a child should be statemented. The second principle is that once LEAs have decided that this is the appropriate course, they must thereafter adhere strictly to the formal requirements in the legislation. Harris, noting that the Code of Practice advises that educational provision should be specified only if adequate provision cannot be made from the school's own resources, says that the decision 'often comes down to the question whether the provision the child requires can, *in the opinion of the LEA*, be met from the resources normally allocated to mainstream schools in the area'[6].

As to the first principle above, in *R v Secretary of State for Education and Science ex parte Lashford*[7], a distinction was drawn between the finding of fact that a child had SENs and the determination of the LEA that it should itself make provision for those needs through the formal process of statementing. The Court of Appeal upheld the LEA's decision *not* to make a statement, the effect of which was that the girl in question remained in an ordinary school and was not sent to an independent special school as the parents had requested. As to the second principle, the Court of Appeal has held in *R v Secretary of State for Education and Science ex parte E*[8] that where a statement of special educational needs *is* made by the authority, the concomitant statement of special educational provision to be made for those needs must be spelt out precisely, and must deal with each and every educational need that the child has been found to have[9]. Parents have rights of appeal to the SENT relating to the various aspects of the statementing process and, from there, appeal to the High Court on a point of law[10]. Appeals may be

1 Education Act 1996, s 329. This is what happened in *R v Hampshire Education Authority, ex parte J* (1985) 84 LGR 547.
2 Within a time-limit, currently 29 days. See the Education Act 1996, s 323(1).
3 Education Act 1996, Sch 26, paras 4 and 5.
4 Ibid, s 325.
5 Ibid, s 324 and Sch 27.
6 N Harris *Special Educational Needs and Access to Justice* (Jordans, 1997) at p 10.
7 [1988] 1 FLR 72. See also *R v Isle of Wight County Council ex parte RS and ex parte AS* [1993] 1 FLR 634 in which the Court of Appeal held that serving a parent with a *proposed* statement of SEN following an assessment of a child did not give rise to a duty on the part of the LEA to go on to determine special educational provision. The authority was entitled to make a 'no' decision on this at any time up to the issue of the final statement.
8 [1992] 1 FLR 377. See also *L v Clarke and Somerset County Council* [1998] ELR 129.
9 But it is not required to spell out precisely any non-educational provision. See *R v Hereford and Worcester County Council ex parte P* [1992] 2 FLR 207.
10 Education Act 1996, ss 325 and 326, and the Tribunals and Inquiries Act 1992, as amended.

brought against the decision of the LEA not to make a statement[1], against the description of the statement of the authority's assessment of the child's SENs, against the special educational provision specified in the statement, or against the authority's decision not to name a school in the statement[2]. There is also a right of appeal in relation to a decision by the LEA to cease to maintain a statement[3].

We noted above that the Education Act 1993 gave to parents for the first time the opportunity to express a preference as to choice of school. Where it makes a statement, the LEA must include the name of that school in the statement unless:

(a) the school is unsuitable to the child's age, ability or aptitude or to his SENs; or
(b) the attendance of the child at the school would be incompatible with the provision of efficient education for the children with whom he would be educated or the efficient use of resources[4].

The question of the allocation of scarce resources can loom large in the determination of the choice of school and much of the growing litigation in this area boils down to arguments about whether the cost should be borne by the LEA or by the parents[5]. It has been determined that the fact of naming an independent school in the statement does not necessarily lead to the conclusion that the LEA is liable to meet the fees but this may be so if that particular school is necessary to meet the child's SENs[6].

Review of statements

LEAs are automatically required to review all statements within 12 months of making the relevant statement or when it was last reviewed[7]. In addition, the parent may request the statement to be amended or for the school named to be changed, and has a right of appeal to the SENT against the decision of the LEA in relation to these matters[8].

Parents' rights or children's rights?

As elsewhere in education law, a striking feature of the special educational needs regime is the emphasis on the substantive and procedural rights of *parents*[9] and the almost total lack of corresponding rights for the *child* despite the rather obvious point that the entire issue of special needs is about the child and what special educational provision should be made for him. Harris puts this down largely to the 'consumer' culture in education which has depended on 'the provision of parental rights of choice, information, representation and redress while the independent interests of children have generally not been recognised'[10]. The

1 Education Act 1996, s 325.
2 Ibid, s 326(1).
3 Ibid, Sch 27, para 11.
4 Ibid, Sch 27, para 5.
5 See, for example, the recent decision of the Court of Appeal in *R v East Sussex County Council ex parte T* [1998] ELR 80.
6 *R v London Borough of Hackney ex parte GC* [1996] ELR 142 and *Staffordshire County Council v J and J* [1996] ELR 418.
7 Education (Special Educational Needs) Regulations 1994, SI 1994/1047.
8 Education Act 1996, s 326 and Sch 27, paras 8 and 10.
9 'Parent' for these purposes incudes a foster-parent who does not have parental responsibility. See *Fairpo v Humberside County Council* [1995] 1 All ER 183.
10 N Harris *Special Educational Needs and Access to Justice* (Jordans, 1997) at pp 4–5.

most obvious omission is the absence of an independent right of appeal and there
has been judicial confirmation that the child has no right to be a party to a
parental appeal to the SENT or thereafter to the High Court[1]. At present, the
child's participation in the process is dependent on the guidance given in the
Code of Practice. This merely advises that the child's views be taken into account
to an extent commensurate with his age and understanding[2]. It remains to be seen
whether the Labour Government will amend the legislation to confer more
substantial rights on the child since the current position arguably infringes Article
12 of the United Nations Convention[3].

CHILDREN ACCOMMODATED IN INDEPENDENT SCHOOLS, LEA SCHOOLS AND OTHER ESTABLISHMENTS

The Children Act 1989 contains a number of provisions which are designed to
ensure proper protection of the welfare of children who are accommodated away
from home for long periods. We are principally concerned here with children at
independent boarding-schools, but the Act also applies to children accommodated by LEAs in special schools, and by health authorities in, for example,
long-stay hospitals. It is convenient to discuss all the relevant provisions here.

Children accommodated in health and educational establishments

Section 85 of the Children Act 1989 protects children accommodated for more
than three consecutive months by health authorities or LEAs. There was concern
about the large numbers of children in long-term accommodation who often had
little or no contact with their families. There was also concern that the system for
reviewing their position and looking after their welfare needs was too haphazard.
Accordingly, the Children Act requires local authorities' social services departments to safeguard their welfare.

Where a health authority, Special Health Authority, National Health Service
Trust or LEA now effects a placement intended to last for at least this period, the
accommodating authority has a statutory duty to notify the 'responsible authority'
of the placement and of when it ceases to accommodate the child[4]. The
responsible authority is that in which the child was ordinarily resident before the
placement or, where there was no ordinary residence, the authority where the
accommodation is situated[5]. On receipt of notification, the local authority must
take such steps as are reasonably practicable to determine whether the child's
welfare is adequately safeguarded and promoted in his present accommodation.
It must also consider the extent to which (if at all) it should exercise any of its
functions under the Children Act with respect to the child[6].

Corresponding provisions under s 86 relate to children accommodated for
similar periods in private residential care homes, nursing homes and mental

1 *R v Special Educational Needs Tribunal and the City of Westminster* [1996] ELR 228.
2 Code of Practice, para 1.120.
3 See Chapter 2 above.
4 Children Act 1989, s 85(1) and (2).
5 Ibid, s 85(3).
6 Ibid, s 85(4).

nursing homes[7]. Failure to notify the local authority of the child's accommodation is, again, an offence. The authority has powers of entry and it is an offence to obstruct its entry intentionally[1]. When children leave any of the above kinds of accommodation, the local authority has duties regarding their after-care[2].

Children accommodated in independent schools

In the period leading up to the Children Act 1989 there had been considerable media coverage of certain instances of sexual abuse of children in independent boarding-schools. These incidents highlighted the lack of statutory responsibility for the *welfare*, as opposed to the educational, needs of these children. The only existing duties of inspection were vested in HM Inspectorate of Schools and these were restricted to educational and other standards at schools such as the state of the school premises. In keeping with the provisions regarding long-term accommodation of children in State-maintained schools and health establishments, the Children Act imposes similar duties on social services departments to satisfy themselves as to the *social*, as opposed to educational, welfare of children at these schools. Local authorities must now be proactive, and not merely reactive to those allegations of abuse which might come to their attention. The law is contained in s 87 of the Children Act, and the Inspection of Premises, Children and Records (Independent Schools) Regulations 1991. There is also a special volume of the *Guidance* on the Children Act devoted to independent schools[3].

The proprietor of an independent school which provides accommodation for a child, or anyone who is responsible for running it, must now safeguard and promote the welfare of the child[4]. The duty does not apply to those schools which accommodate less than 50 pupils, since these qualify either as children's homes or as residential care homes and are governed by the provisions applying to those homes[5]. The local authority within whose area the school is situated must take reasonable steps to determine whether the child's welfare is being adequately safeguarded and promoted[6]. Where it is of the view that those running the school have failed to discharge the welfare duty properly, it must notify the Secretary of State with a view to enabling 'notice of complaint' action to be taken under s 469 of the 1996 Act. If the breach is serious enough, this could lead to closure or removal of the school from the register of independent schools. Again, there are powers of entry and inspection and offences relating to the intentional obstruction of anyone exercising them[7]. In the case of a genuine emergency, it would be possible to seek an emergency protection order[8].

The *Guidance* and the regulations contain a great deal of information about what is expected of independent schools in discharging the welfare duty and what is expected of those inspecting the schools. Particular emphasis is laid on vigilance

---

1   See *The Children Act 1989 Guidance and Regulations Vol 4 Residential Care* (HMSO, 1991).
2   Children Act 1989, s 86(6).
3   Ibid, s 24 and see Chapter 10 above.
4   *The Children Act 1989 Guidance and Regulations Vol 5 Independent Schools* (HMSO, 1991).
5   Children Act 1989, s 87(1).
6   Ibid, s 87(2).
7   Ibid, s 87(3).
8   Ibid, s 87(5)–(9).
9   See Chapter 12 above.

in the initial selection of staff and on providing the children with clear and accessible avenues of complaint[1].

THE SCHOOL STANDARDS AND FRAMEWORK ACT 1998

The Labour Government's School Standards and Framework Act 1998 received Royal Assent in July 1998. It seeks to give effect to a number of the Government's proposals set out in the White Paper *Excellence in Schools*[2] published in July 1997. It is only possible here to set out some of the key elements in the Government's strategy for education and to draw attention to some of the more important sections of the Act, especially those which affect the issues discussed earlier in this chapter.

The cornerstone of the Government's policy is to create 'a greater awareness across society of the importance of education and increased expectations of what can be achieved'. The chief aim of the legislation will be to increase standards of performance. This approach will be underpinned by six principles as follows:

(1) Education will be at the heart of Government.

(2) Policies will be designed to benefit the many, not just the few.

(3) The focus will be on standards, not structures.

(4) Intervention will be in inverse proportion to success.

(5) There will be zero tolerance of underperformance.

(6) Government will work in partnership with all those committed to raising standards.

Among the more important sections which are designed to put these principles into practice are the following:

(1) Sections 1–4 set limits to the maximum size of infant classes in maintained schools and require LEAs and schools to comply with such limits.

(2) Sections 5 and 6 place LEAs under a duty to exercise their functions with a view to promoting high standards of education for pupils of school age in their area and to prepare an education development plan which states their proposals for developing the provision of education for children in their area.

(3) Sections 10 and 11 provide for the creation of Education Action Zones and an Education Action Forum to lead each zone. The zones will enable clusters of schools to work together for the express purpose of raising standards.

(4) Sections 14–19 set out the powers of intervention which LEAs and the Secretary of State are to have in relation to schools causing concern because their standards are unacceptably low or at risk.

---

1 See *The Children Act 1989 Guidance and Regulations Vol 5 Independent Schools* (HMSO, 1991) at ch 3.

2 DFEE (Cm 3681) (7 July 1997).

(5) Section 20 sets out the new framework and categories of school. The existing categories of maintained and grant-maintained schools will be abolished and replaced by community, foundation and voluntary schools and community and foundation special schools[1].

(6) Sections 36–44 are concerned with school government. Section 36 and Schs 9, 10 and 11 provide for changes to the constitution of school governing bodies to provide, inter alia, for additional parent governors. Under ss 38 and 39, governing bodies will be placed under new duties to conduct the school with a view to promoting high standards of educational achievement and to establish complaints procedures. The annual parents' meeting (under previous legislation to be required by articles of government) is now placed on a direct statutory footing by s 43.

(7) Sections 61–62 are concerned with discipline. Section 61 requires the governing body and head teacher of every maintained school to make and publicise a policy for the promotion of good discipline.

(8) Sections 84–109 are concerned with school admissions procedures. In particular, s 99 prohibits any maintained school from operating admission arrangements which select pupils by ability or aptitude unless it is a grammar school or its arrangements fall within the limited forms of selection which are permitted under ss 100–103[2].

(9) Sections 110–111 require governing bodies to adopt, in consultation with parents, a 'home–school agreement', having regard to any guidance issued by the Secretary of State[3].

(10) Section 127 provides for the Secretary of State to issue a code of practice for securing effective relationships between LEAs and maintained schools, which LEAs, governing bodies and head teachers must have regard to, particularly in relation to promoting high standards of education in schools.

---

1   The new categories follow the policy statement *Diversity and Excellence* issued in June 1995. For a full explanation of the reasoning behind the new framework, see the White Paper (above) at ch 7.

2   This part of the Act is designed to put an end to the admissions practice of partial selection by academic ability which had begun to cause concern in some areas. Under guidance issued in June 1996 by the former Conservative Government, schools were permitted to select up to 15% of their pupils by general academic ability. The Labour Government's view is that selection by ability should be limited to priority being given to children who demonstrate aptitude for a specialism which exists in individual schools. See the White Paper (above) at para 33.

3   See above.

Chapter 17

CHILDREN IN THE INTERNATIONAL COMMUNITY

INTRODUCTION

The movement to recognise and protect children's rights has an important international as well as national dimension. In this chapter we look at the attempts which have been made to establish international standards and co-operation between States to uphold the rights of children, whether as persons possessing human rights which apply to everyone, or specifically as children.

The most significant international Convention asserting the rights of children is undoubtedly the United Nations Convention on the Rights of the Child. Since this is now widely regarded as a fundamental source of children law, it was discussed in Chapter 2 alongside the Children Act 1989 – the principal source of domestic children law. The reader should therefore read this chapter in conjunction with Chapter 2. Reference should also be made to Chapter 7, in which there was a discussion of the Hague Convention on the Protection of Children and Co-operation in Respect of Inter-Country Adoption alongside the principles of domestic adoption law.

We begin by tracing briefly the history of the international children's rights movement. This is followed by three sections dealing respectively with the international Child Abduction Conventions, the Hague Protection of Children Convention 1996 and the European Convention on the Exercise of Children's Rights 1996[1]. All these Conventions have in common the feature that they are specifically concerned with the protection of children's rights or interests. The chapter concludes with a section on the European Convention on Human Rights and Fundamental Freedoms about to be incorporated into English law by the Human Rights Bill 1998. The issues which arise under this Convention are rather different since here the question is how far the human rights of adults extend to children and how effective the Convention can be in upholding these rights – especially where they may be thought to conflict with adult rights.

THE INTERNATIONAL CHILDREN'S RIGHTS MOVEMENT

There are really two aspects to the protection of children's rights at the international level. The first is the extension to children of those human rights which everyone possesses as a human being. The second is the development of special safeguards for children 'beyond those granted as human rights to adults

---

1 For an excellent and informative evaluation of the significance of international law generally and, more specifically of the different kinds of international instruments, in the development of domestic family law (including many major areas affecting children), see G Douglas 'The significance of international law for the development of family law in England and Wales' in C Bridge (ed) *Family Law Towards the Millennium: Essays for PM Bromley* (Butterworths, 1997) at ch 3. For a useful account of European law affecting the family, a much neglected area, see C Hamilton and K Standley *Family Law in Europe* (Butterworths, 1995) at ch 17.

because of their physical and mental immaturity and consequent dependence and vulnerability'[1]. International law has frequently singled out particular groups and their need for special protection, two of the more obvious examples being civilians in time of war, and refugees. The case of warfare neatly illustrates both the generalised protection of children, along with adults, and also their special protection[2]. While the Geneva Conventions of 1949 generally protect the civilian population (of which children are a part) and individual civilians (which children undoubtedly are), they also contain certain specific Articles which prioritise the needs of children. Thus, for example, the fourth Geneva Convention of 1949 provides, inter alia, that:

> 'Children shall be the object of special respect and shall be protected against any form of indecent assault. The parties to the conflict shall take all feasible measures in order that children who have not attained the age of fifteen years do not take a direct part in hostilities and, in particular, they shall refrain from recruiting them into their armed forces ...'[3]

The primary focus here will be on this special recognition of children in international law but we must also refer to the debate about whether the more humanitarian aspects of international law apply in their entirety *by implication* to children. Here, reference will be made, in passing, to the jurisprudence of the US Supreme Court and the European Court of Human Rights – both of which lend support to the notion that, in general, fundamental rights enjoyed by adults also extend to children.

The Declaration of Geneva 1924

International recognition of the claims of children dates back to the early part of the twentieth century and the work of such organisations as the International Committee of the Red Cross, the League of Nations and the International Labour Organisation[4]. In 1924 the Fifth Assembly of the League of Nations adopted the First Declaration of the Rights of the Child which became known as the Declaration of Geneva. The Declaration went beyond the earlier, more specific, concerns about the working conditions of children and the problem of slavery. It constituted a more general charter of child welfare dealing with such matters as material and spiritual development, shelter, food, medical aid, relief from distress and protection against exploitation[5]. Yet the Declaration was limited, both in its concentration on welfare needs and in its lack of binding effect. It has been described as an essentially aspirational document, not requiring, but inviting

---

1   These two strands of protection are brought out particularly well in the seminal article, D Hodgson 'The Historical Development and "Internationalisation" of the Children's Rights Movement' (1992) 6 Aust J Fam Law 252. We draw heavily on this excellent article which should be compulsory reading for anyone with an interest in the position of children under international law. See also G Van Bueren *The International Law on the Rights of the Child* (Martinus Nijhoff, 1995) at chs 1 and 2.

2   See 'Children and the Laws of War' (1989) *Childright* at p 19. See also G Van Bueren (above) at ch 12.

3   Article 77, Protocol 1. And see now Article 38 of the United Nations Convention on the Rights of the Child 1989.

4   D Hodgson 'The Historical Development and "Internationalisation" of the Children's Rights Movement' (1992) 6 Aust J Fam Law 252 at pp 259 et seq.

5   Earlier Conventions dealing with these specific concerns were the Minimum Age (Industry) Convention 1919 and the International Convention for the Suppression of Traffic in Women and Children 1921.

States which were members of the League of Nations to be guided by its principles in the work of child welfare[1]. It was left to individual States to determine whether, and if so how, to implement its ideals.

Post-war developments

In the period immediately following World War II, several important international humanitarian Conventions and Declarations were adopted. These were, for the most part, aimed at improving international standards of treatment for *all* human beings and not just children. The two most significant were the drawing up of the Charter of the United Nations in 1945[2], and the unanimous adoption by the General Assembly of the Universal Declaration of Human Rights in 1948[3]. This is now generally accepted as the most authoritative statement of the main human rights and fundamental freedoms flowing from the UN Charter. It was noted earlier[4] that, inter alia, the Declaration explicitly recognises the right to education. Another provision also provides:

'Motherhood and childhood are entitled to special care and assistance. All children, whether born in or out of wedlock, shall enjoy the same social protection.'[5]

Beyond this, the Declaration did not expressly mention children, and it is a matter of interpretation how far its other provisions apply to adults and children alike.

The Declaration of the Rights of the Child 1959

There was, at this time, a gathering feeling that the special claims of children required wider, more comprehensive, recognition. This came about in 1959 with the Second Declaration of the Rights of the Child ('the 1959 Declaration')[6]. While the First Declaration (the Geneva Declaration) had focused rather narrowly on the material needs of children following World War I, the second looked more broadly at the claims and entitlements of children across a range of areas including housing, education, recreation, nutrition, medical services and social security. One commentator's assessment of the place of the 1959 Declaration in the internationalisation of children's rights is that it 'reaffirmed and expanded the provisions of the Declaration of Geneva, and applied generally to children in a more specific way the provisions of the Universal Declaration of Human Rights. Unlike the Universal Declaration, however, the 1959 Declaration [was] devoted almost exclusively to economic, social and cultural rights, omitting such important civil rights as life and liberty, criminal due process, and freedom from cruel, inhuman or degrading treatment or punishment'[7]. The 1959 Declaration, therefore, while much wider in its scope than what had gone before it, fell short of

---

1   D Hodgson (above) at p 261. Indeed, the Declaration itself boldly proclaimed that 'Mankind owes to the child the best that it has to give ...'.
2   The Charter does not specifically mention children at any point.
3   Resolution 217A (III), 10 December 1948.
4   See Chapter 16 above.
5   Article 25(2).
6   Resolution 1386 (XIV) adopted 20 Nov 1959. See D Hodgson 'The Historical Development and "Internationalisation" of the Children's Rights Movement' (1992) 6 Aust J Fam Law 252 at pp 265 et seq.
7   Ibid at p 266.

being comprehensive and, furthermore, did not create binding legal obligations on States which were parties to it[1]. This had to wait 30 years for the adoption of the United Nations Convention on the Rights of the Child in 1989[2]. The true value of the 1959 Declaration was to establish many of the generally accepted international norms of treatment for children which could then be translated into binding legal obligations on States in the 1989 Convention.

The debate about general application

Between 1959 and 1989 the focus of debate was on whether the general human rights instruments emanating from the United Nations and elsewhere[3] could be applied to children. Those provisions which directly referred to children clearly did apply to children, but the notion gathered ground that most of those which did not specifically refer to children also applied to them as human beings[4].

Meanwhile in the USA, the Supreme Court from the 1960s had begun to accept that the fundamental rights enshrined in the Bill of Rights, as constituted by the various amendments to the US Constitution, were, in principle, available also to children, although their application might be qualified in some cases[5]. The breakthrough came in 1967 when, in _Re Gault_, the court said that 'neither the Fourteenth Amendment nor the Bill of Rights is for adults alone'[6]. This decision was followed by a plethora of decisions extending to children protections enjoyed by adults under the US Constitution[7]. In Europe also, the European Commission and Court of Human Rights made a number of significant decisions protecting the fundamental rights of children under Articles of the European Convention which did not mention children as such[8].

The immediate background to the UN Convention on the Rights of the Child was that the General Assembly designated 1979 as the 'International Year of the Child'[9]. As one of its contributions to this, the Polish Government produced a draft text for a UN Convention, the purpose of which was to translate the principles of the 1959 Declaration into international law. The intention was to create internationally binding legal obligations and also to extend the coverage of international protections beyond social welfare needs to the more extensive human rights guaranteed to adults. The original Polish draft, which mirrored the

---

1   Unless, that is, it could be said to have acquired the status of customary international law.
2   See Chapter 2 above.
3   Debate focused particularly on the so-called 'twin' covenants of 1966 – the International Covenant on Civil and Political Rights and the International Covenant on Economic, Social and Cultural Rights. See D Hodgson (above) at pp 269 et seq.
4   But international lawyers were not in complete agreement on this. See D Hodgson (above) at pp 271 et seq.
5   For an excellent collection of materials on the early constitutional breakthroughs for children in the United States, see W Wadlington, CH Whitebread and SM Davis _Children in the Legal System_ (Foundation Press, 1983) at ch II.
6   387 US 1, 13 (1967).
7   Such as freedom of speech in _Tinker v Des Moines Independent Community School District_ 393 US 503 (1969) and the right to a hearing in school discipline cases where suspension was at stake in _Goss v Lopez_ 419 US 565 (1975). It is unlikely that English disciplinary procedures in the educational context would be regarded as constitutional in the United States. See Chapter 16 above.
8   We discuss the European Convention at p 598 below.
9   See D Hodgson (above) at pp 275 et seq.

1959 Declaration, was rejected, but in its place, the General Assembly adopted a more wide-ranging document which had been 10 years in the making and which followed extensive consultation. Its adoption on 20 November 1989 was timed to coincide with the thirtieth anniversary of the 1959 Declaration.

We discussed the substance of the UN Convention in Chapter 2 and now turn our attention to several other important international Conventions which have as their aim the special protection of children. We look first at the two principal Conventions designed to prevent international child abduction and to secure the return of children wrongfully abducted. Secondly, we describe the recent Hague Protection of Children Convention which aims to secure co-operation between States in respect of other protective action required for children. Thirdly, we examine the European Convention on the Exercise of Children's Rights 1996 which is concerned with the procedural or participatory rights of children in family proceedings. We conclude by reviewing some of the case-law under the European Convention on Human Rights and speculate on the implications of its impending incorporation into English law.

THE ABDUCTION CONVENTIONS

Better transport communications across the world have contributed to the growing problem of international child abduction[1]. The English law reports are now replete with cases involving the 'snatching' of children, usually, but not invariably, by one parent from the other, either to or from England[2]. We consider here the legal mechanisms for attempting to prevent the unlawful removal of children from England and the law and procedures which govern attempts to recover abducted children. We also look at the jurisprudence of the English courts when considering requests for the return of children snatched *to* England. This provides some insight into what might be expected of a foreign court in the converse situation of a child taken *from* England[3]. Two international Conventions of 1980, the Hague Convention on the Civil Aspects of International Child Abduction ('the Hague Convention') and the European Convention on Recognition and Enforcement of Decisions Concerning Custody of Children and Restoration of Custody of Children ('the European Convention'), regulate the return of children from those States which are parties to the respective

---

1   See, generally, *Bromley's Family Law* (8th edn) (Butterworths, 1992) at ch 15; and SM Cretney and JM Masson *Principles of Family Law* (6th edn) (Sweet & Maxwell, 1997) at ch 22. See also G Van Bueren *The Best Interests of the Child: International Cooperation on Child Abduction* (Queen Mary and Westfield College, London, 1993). A particularly helpful article is D McClean 'International child abduction – some recent trends' [1997] CFLQ 387.

2   McClean (above) notes, however, that the statistics reveal an important change in the pattern of abductions in recent years. Contrary to the public image of abduction by a 'non-custodial' father, two-thirds of abductions are now carried out by the mother who is usually also the primary carer of the children. See further the remarks of Hale J in *S v H (Abduction: Access Rights)* [1997] 1 FLR 971 at 977.

3   For a discussion of the workings of the Hague Convention in the English courts, see CS Bruch 'Child Abduction and the English Courts' in A Bainham, DS Pearl and R Pickford (eds) *Frontiers of Family Law* (2nd edn) (John Wiley & Sons, 1995) at p 52; and see also CS Bruch 'International Child Abduction Cases: Experience Under the 1980 Hague Convention' in J Eekelaar and P Sarcevic (eds) *Parenthood in Modern Society: Legal and Social Issues for the Twenty-First Century* (Martinus Nijhoff, 1993).

Conventions. Both Conventions were implemented in the UK by the Child Abduction and Custody Act 1985. It is therefore necessary to examine not only the position of children taken to a country which is party to either Convention (and those brought to England from such a country) but also the situation of those children taken to or from countries which are not party to either Convention. We also look briefly at abduction *within* the different parts of the UK, a matter regulated by the Family Law Act 1986.

Preventing abduction

It is axiomatic that prevention is better than cure. Where a child is successfully removed from England, it may be difficult even to establish his whereabouts and more difficult still to secure his return. All available means should therefore be utilised to prevent removal in the first place. The matter is complicated by the fact that the Hague Convention can only operate where there has been a *wrongful* taking and, especially since the Children Act 1989, there may be some ambiguity about whether one parent is acting wrongfully in taking a child abroad[1]. Nevertheless, the general principles and procedures of the criminal and civil law can be stated with some confidence.

The criminal law

Under s 1 of the Child Abduction Act 1984 it is an offence for anyone 'connected with a child' to take or send a child under the age of 16 years out of the UK without the appropriate consent[2]. This is the consent of each person who is the child's mother, father (assuming in the case of the unmarried father that he has acquired parental responsibility), guardian, or anyone with a residence order or the leave of the court. There are limited defences available[3]. An exception applies where a residence order is in force – anyone with this may unilaterally remove a child for a period of up to one month[4]. Thus, apart from this provision, in the usual case where there is no court order in existence, it is a criminal offence for *one* parent to take a child out of the country without the consent of the other[5]. In the case of unmarried parents (assuming the father has not taken steps to acquire parental responsibility[6]), the mother has authority to act alone. A parent may also commit the common law offence of kidnapping[7], or false imprisonment[8] in removing the child without the appropriate consent, although these charges should not be

---

1 See pp 583 et seq.
2 It is also an offence under the Child Abduction Act 1984, s 2 for anyone who does *not* have parental responsibility or 'custody' of a child to remove a child aged under 16, or keep him, out of the lawful control of the person entitled to lawful control. It is a defence to show that the person concerned acted with lawful authority or had a reasonable excuse and there is a special defence which can be relied on by the unmarried father or by someone who believes that he is the child's father. This chapter is concerned only with international abductions and the detailed provisions of s 2 are beyond the scope of the present discussion.
3 Child Abduction Act 1984, s 1(5).
4 Section 13(2) of the Children Act.
5 It is not entirely clear whether a positive consent is required or whether an absence of objection on the part of the other parent would suffice. The latter seems more practicable, especially in view of the defences in s 1(5) of the Child Abduction Act 1984.
6 See Chapter 5 above.
7 *R v D* [1984] AC 778.
8 *R v Rahman* (1985) 81 Cr App R 349.

brought where the facts upon which they are grounded would constitute the statutory offence[1].

Since child abduction is a criminal offence, the assistance of the police may be sought to prevent its commission. In an emergency, when an imminent removal is suspected, informing the police is the best short-term action to take. The police have power to arrest anyone they reasonably suspect of attempting to take a child out of the UK. More importantly, they can effect a 'port stop' through their computerised 'All Ports Warning System'. The effect of a port stop is that immigration officers at all ports and airports will hold the name of the child at risk on an index and will thereafter seek to assist the police in preventing the child's removal. Under a Practice Direction[2] the police will not automatically institute a port alert. They must be convinced that the risk of removal is real and imminent, ie within 24 to 48 hours. In order to enable them to act, the police should be given full particulars about the child, the alleged abductor and travel plans where these are known. The child's name will remain on the stop list for four weeks. After this, a renewed complaint will become necessary if continuing protection is sought. Where the 'child' is aged 16 years or over, the Child Abduction Act 1984 does not apply and a court order is required. But in view of the increased legal autonomy of this age group, it is doubtful how often it will be appropriate to intervene in what may be a joint decision by parent and child to leave the country[3].

The civil law

Passport control

One effective way of stopping the child from travelling abroad is to prevent the issue of a passport or secure the surrender of an existing one. The written consent of a parent or guardian is required before the Passport Agency will either add the child's name to a relation's passport or issue a separate one to the child. This normally allows a parent to act independently, consistent with the broad scheme under the Children Act[4], but this principle will be dislodged where a residence order is held by a parent who makes an objection. Apart from this, where a court order has been obtained specifically restraining the removal of the child from the UK, the court may require the surrender of any existing passport either issued to the child or containing particulars of the child[5]. The court will notify the Passport Agency of the order for surrender of any existing passport issued to the child or containing particulars of the child[6].

Private court orders

A number of options exist for obtaining orders in the civil courts which have the effect of restraining a child's removal from the jurisdiction. One is to ward the

---

1   *R v C (Kidnapping: Abduction)* [1991] 2 FLR 252.
2   *Practice Direction (Child: Removal from Jurisdiction)* [1986] 1 All ER 983.
3   Although Cretney and Masson note that a child of this age could be kidnapped where he is not consenting to leave the country. See SM Cretney and JM Masson *Principles of Family Law* (6th edn) (Sweet & Maxwell, 1997) at p 752.
4   See Chapter 2 above. See also the leaflet of the UK Passport Agency, the contents of which are set out at [1994] Fam Law 651.
5   Family Law Act 1986, s 37.
6   It will do so in order to prevent the re-issue of the passport.

child, since wardship has, as one of its immediate effects, an automatic prohibition on removing the ward from the jurisdiction[1]. A cheaper and more likely alternative since the Children Act may be to seek a s 8 order. A residence order will regulate where the child is to live and it will be incompatible with its terms for the *non-residential* parent to take the child abroad even when exercising contact or otherwise discharging parental responsibility[2]. It will also empower the *residential* parent to take the child abroad for up to one month without the non-residential parent's knowledge or consent. Thus, the court should be wary of granting a residence order to a parent if there is the slightest suspicion that that parent might use the apparently innocuous 'holiday provision' as a cloak for a permanent abduction[3]. However, the residence order is more likely to be invoked as a device *against* abduction rather than a vehicle for it, and it is established that a short-term residence order may be granted in exceptional cases ex parte[4]. Perhaps the most appropriate order will be the prohibited steps order, the specific purpose of which can be to restrain removal[5]. As a practical matter, it would still be necessary to instigate a port alert to enforce s 8 orders, but the existence of the orders should certainly secure the ready co-operation of the police.

Parents, especially at the time of divorce, should be alive to the necessity of making formal applications for s 8 orders where there is the slightest risk of abduction. It should be remembered that s 1(5) of the Children Act (the 'no order' principle) is, rightly or wrongly, likely to be interpreted by many courts as creating a legal presumption against court orders. In a large majority of cases, there will, therefore, be no order, unless one is specifically sought. Even where it is, the onus will be on the applicant to show that it is necessary. Yet there is now sufficient ambiguity about the authority of parents under the Children Act that the wisest course will be to seek an order whenever there is a hint that one parent may, at some future point, try to take the child abroad. Thus, as Bruch advises[6], residence orders should always be sought 'if there have been threats of abduction, or if the parents come from different countries or either has strong foreign connections (such as lengthy vacations, a second residence, extended family or employment opportunities abroad)'.

Other reasons why civil procedures may be advantageous[7] are that: they may act as a deterrent to abduction; they may secure official assistance in tracing the child; breach of the order will constitute contempt of court and may be punished as such; and passport control, as we have seen, will be facilitated.

---

1   Although this is now qualified by the Family Law Act 1986, s 38 as regards removal to another part of the UK.

2   Section 2(8) of the Children Act precludes the exercise of parental responsibility in a way which is incompatible with a court order.

3   The danger of the provision being used for a disguised abduction was acknowledged during the debates on the Children Bill, but it was the view of Sir Nicholas Lyell (the then Solicitor-General) that the law should reflect 'normal and reasonable' behaviour. In other words, such cases would be vastly outnumbered by those of parents taking bona fide holidays, and the law should reflect this.

4   *Re B (A Minor) (Residence Order: Ex Parte)* [1992] 2 FLR 1.

5   As in *Re D (A Minor) (Child: Removal from Jurisdiction)* [1992] 1 All ER 892.

6   CS Bruch 'Child Abduction and the English Courts' in A Bainham, DS Pearl and R Pickford (eds) *Frontiers of Family Law* (2nd edn) (John Wiley & Sons, 1995) at p 55.

7   See the discussion in *Bromley's Family Law* (8th edn) (Butterworths, 1992) at pp 485–486.

Leave to take children out of the jurisdiction

Where a parent who is the child's primary carer (usually but not invariably the mother) wishes to emigrate from the UK, or at least leave for an extended period of time, with the child the appropriate course of action will be to apply to the court for leave to take the child out of the jurisdiction. Often the courts have had to grapple with a conflict of interest between the mother who wishes to make a new life abroad, with or without a new partner, and the father who wishes to maintain a realistic relationship with the child. The earlier decisions tended to support the mother's plan, certainly if it was properly thought out and reasonable[1]. Later decisions, while still attaching considerable importance to the genuineness and reasonableness of the mother's proposals, have also shown a greater awareness of the need to take into account the potentially drastic effect of emigration on the child's relationship with the father[2].

The Court of Appeal's decision in *Re T (Removal from Jurisdiction)*[3] perhaps best illustrates the kind of balance which the courts have attempted to strike in these cases. Here, following divorce, the mother began a relationship with a man from France and applied for leave to take the three-year-old child of the family there[4]. The child lived with his mother but had overnight weekly contact with the paternal grandparents. The father was suspicious that the mother's proposal was designed to terminate his contact with the child and he countered by seeking a residence order. The mother hinted that she might go to France anyway but later made it clear that she would not go without the child. The judge refused leave on the basis that the proposal was ill-considered, ill-prepared and contrary to the child's interest and made a residence order in favour of the father.

Allowing the mother's appeal against the residence order, the Court of Appeal held that mothers who were generally competent mothers should not be at risk of losing primary care where they made an unsuccessful attempt to obtain leave to take the child out of the jurisdiction. The judge had been entitled to refuse leave on welfare grounds but ought not to have altered the child's residence as a consequence and without seeking the advice of the court welfare officer. There had been a failure to realise that the father's application for a residence order was a purely defensive ploy designed to protect his contact arrangements. The appropriate order was a residence order for the mother with reasonable contact

---

1 See particularly the pre-Children Act decision of the Court of Appeal in *Lonslow v Hennig (formerly Lonslow)* [1986] 2 FLR 378 where the mother was allowed to emigrate to New Zealand with the children. The Court of Appeal confirmed in *H v H (Residence Order: Leave to Remove from Jurisdiction)* [1995] 1 FLR 529 that the Children Act has not altered the underlying factors which govern applications for leave.

2 See, for example, *Re K (A Minor) (Removal from Jurisdiction)* [1992] 2 FLR 98 where the mother was refused leave to take a young child to the United States. Her plan to pursue post-graduate education there was considered by the court to be ill-thought out and Thorpe J emphasised the very grave importance of the continuation and development of the relationship between the father and child.

3 [1996] 2 FLR 352.

4 For another case involving France in which the court concluded that, paradoxically, the children's relationship with the father would be better safeguarded by granting the mother leave than by refusing it, see *Re B (Minors) (Removal from Jurisdiction)* [1994] Fam Law 11.

for the father and grandparents, the effect of which was to preserve the status quo[1].

Recovery of children

Action under the Hague Convention

The Hague Convention has been widely ratified by countries as far apart as Europe, the Western Hemisphere, Australasia and the Middle East, and remains under consideration in other States[2]. It has a global dimension obviously lacking in the case of the European Convention, which is confined to certain countries within Europe. It is wider, also, in that it may be invoked even where there is no prior court order, whereas the European Convention is confined in its operation to the enforcement of court orders. Beyond these distinctions, the two Conventions have similar aims which are to return abducted children promptly to their home countries so that any dispute as to their care is determined *there* and the alleged abductor is denied any tactical advantage from the abduction. In this way, it is also hoped to deter other such removals. As a general proposition, there will be a heavy presumption in favour of returning the child, and only to a limited extent will the court be able or prepared to investigate the merits of disputes over residence or upbringing[3]. Otherwise, the very purpose of the Conventions would be frustrated, but in exceptional cases return of the child may be successfully resisted. Increasingly, it has come to be appreciated that there is a tension between the dual objectives of securing the welfare of the child while upholding the integrity of the system. It must be the case that the best interests of individual children are occasionally sacrificed in the more general interests of the wider class of children in the international community. Since both Conventions are based on reciprocity between nations, the principles apply equally whether the child is taken from, or brought to, England.

Procedural matters – how is the Hague Convention invoked?

The Hague Convention may be invoked in relation to any child under the age of 16 years, habitually resident in one contracting State, who has been wrongfully

---

1   But see now the decision of the Court of Appeal in *Re H (Application to Remove from Jurisdiction)* [1998] 1 FLR 848 in which a father who had been very involved with the care of the child nevertheless failed to prevent the mother from obtaining leave to take the child to Alabama. The mother had by this time married an American and the court held that there had to be some compelling reason to justify a court preventing the primary carer from taking a reasonable decision to live outside the jurisdiction.

2   The list of countries which have ratified the Convention is a growing one. An accessible and reasonably up-to-date list of these countries, together with a list of the countries which have signed or ratified the European Convention, is published at the back of each issue of *Family Law* and is updated from statutory instruments amending the Child Abduction and Custody (Parties to Conventions) Order 1986, SI 1986/1159. See also M Everall 'Child Abduction after the Hague Convention' [1990] Fam Law 169; and 'The Hague Convention: The Children Act and other recent developments' [1992] Fam Law 164. For an informative commentary on French practice under the Hague Convention, see A Cornec 'The Hague Convention on Abduction and Beyond: Conflicting Aims, Different Solutions – the French Practice' [1993] Fam Law 148. See also D McClean and K Beevers 'International child abduction – back to common law principles' [1995] CFLQ 128.

3   But undertakings may be required of the aggrieved parent as a condition of the child's return. See particularly *C v C (Minor: Abduction: Rights of Custody Abroad)* [1989] 1 WLR 654. See also

removed to or retained in another contracting State[1]. The applicant seeking return of a child will probably begin by applying to the 'Central Authority' for the country of the child's habitual residence. Both the Hague and European Conventions require each contracting State to set up a Central Authority to undertake responsibility for the administration and handling of child abduction cases. It is the task of the Central Authority to receive applications, collect all relevant information and institute the necessary action, perhaps including judicial proceedings, for recovery of the child. The Central Authority for England and Wales is the Lord Chancellor's Department[2], although work is often delegated by it to private firms of solicitors. In practice, the Department will instruct a solicitor to act for the applicant who will then file an application in the High Court, which has exclusive jurisdiction in these cases[3]. As an alternative, the applicant could decide to approach the foreign Central Authority direct, or even institute proceedings in that country. However, at least as far as removals *from* England are concerned, there are distinct advantages in going through the Lord Chancellor's Department. As well as obtaining the expert assistance of the staff, legal aid will be granted, without regard to the usual means and merits test[4]. The court will then, subject to qualifications, order the child's immediate return to his place of habitual residence, if it finds that the child's removal or retention violated the custody rights of the applicant[5]. It must be emphasised that the circumstances in which the court will refuse to order the return of the child are narrowly defined, and generally restrictively interpreted, since it is an aim of the Hague Convention to prevent the domestic courts of the 'receiving' State from entering into the merits of the matter.

What is a wrongful removal or retention?
The Hague Convention can only be activated where the removal or retention was 'wrongful'. In order to establish this, it must be shown that, according to the law of the child's habitual residence[6], the actions were in breach of rights of custody attributed to a person, an institution or any other body *and* that, at the time of the removal or detention, those rights were actually exercised jointly or alone, or would have been but for the removal or retention[7]. It is *not* necessary for the applicant to hold a court order (as under the European Convention), although

---

Re O (Child Abduction: Undertakings) [1994] 2 FLR 349 and *Re M (Abduction: Undertakings)* [1995] 1 FLR 1021. For a critique of the practice of accepting undertakings, see D McClean 'International child abduction – some recent trends' [1997] CFLQ 387 at pp 392–395.

1 Article 4. As to the meaning of the child's habitual residence, see P Stone 'The habitual residence of a child' (1992) 4 JCL 170.
2 The Child Abduction Unit, Lord Chancellor's Department, 81 Chancery Lane, London WC2A 1DD. Tel: 0171 911 7047.
3 Child Abduction and Custody Act 1985, s 4.
4 For further discussion, see CS Bruch 'Child Abduction and the English Courts' in A Bainham, DS Pearl and R Pickford (eds) *Frontiers of Family Law* (2nd edn) (John Wiley & Sons, 1995) at pp 53–54.
5 Article 3. In *Re N (Child Abduction) (Habitual Residence)* [1993] 2 FLR 124, the Court of Appeal said that proceedings under the Hague Convention are neither adversarial nor inquisitorial but sui generis. The court has a statutory duty to apply the Convention if the necessary facts are present and, in so doing, it is concerned not only with the interests of the child but also with those of abducted children more generally.
6 See P Stone 'The habitual residence of a child' (1992) 4 JCL 170.
7 Article 3.

clearly the existence of a court order in the applicant's favour, especially a residence order, will help[1].

The question of the child's habitual residence may cause difficulties, where the family has lived in more than one jurisdiction in the recent past[2]. This is a question of fact to be determined by the court. The crucial question will be what the child's habitual residence was *immediately before* the alleged wrongful removal or retention[3]. The issue of what is wrongful will often be straightforward, but can be difficult in some cases, and the Children Act may have produced some added complications[4]. The action must be in breach of 'custody' rights[5] which for the purposes of English law usually means 'parental responsibility', but, as we have seen[6], parental responsibility may, because of its durability, be held by more than one person or institution jointly, each of which may prima facie be acting lawfully in taking independent action in relation to the child[7]. The matter is complicated further in that in some cases the courts have found a breach of 'custody' rights where the left-behind parent or carer does *not* possess parental responsibility. We discuss these cases below. We need to distinguish those cases in which there is a court order from those where there is none.

Where there is a court order

Where a court order is in existence, the position ought to be clear, since the order will usually make plain where the child is to live and what degree of contact or involvement parents or others are to have with the child. Thus, if the mother has a residence order in her favour, it will be incompatible with that order for the father to take the child abroad[8]. This would be a clear breach of the mother's 'custody' rights, despite the fact that, for many purposes other than residence, parental responsibility continues to be shared by *both* parents. But what if the mother, armed with the residence order, herself takes the child out of the country? She is entitled under the order to do so, unilaterally, for up to one month, but what is the position if she then *retains* the child abroad for an extended period, perhaps indefinitely? The question is whether that retention is unlawful, given that the initial removal was lawful. The better view, advanced by Bruch[9], is that it is unlawful, since the mother's right to remove the child was a temporary one. The habitual residence of the child would thus remain in England and, according to English law, the retention beyond one month would be wrongful. However, the matter is not wholly free from doubt[10]. Bruch points out that the way around this

---

1 Because of the ambiguities surrounding the concept of wrongfulness as it applies to parental responsibility.

2 See the review of cases under the Hague Convention by P Stone (above), especially at pp 171–172, and the House of Lords decisions in *Re J (A Minor) (Abduction: Custody Rights)* [1990] 2 AC 562 and *Re S (A Minor) (Custody: Habitual Residence)* [1997] 4 All ER 251.

3 *Re S (A Minor) (Abduction)* [1991] 2 FLR 1.

4 CS Bruch 'Child Abduction and the English Courts' in A Bainham, DS Pearl and R Pickford (eds) *Frontiers of Family Law* (2nd edn) (John Wiley & Sons, 1995) at p 55.

5 For a case in which grandparents were found to have joint custodial rights, see *Re O (Child Abduction: Custody Rights)* [1997] 2 FLR 702.

6 At Chapters 2 and 4 above.

7 In particular, there is generally no duty to consult the other parent before taking action.

8 Section 2(8) of the Children Act.

9 See CS Bruch (above) at pp 54 et seq.

10 This is because the House of Lords decision in *Re J (A Minor) (Abduction: Custody Rights)* [1990] 2 AC 562 might suggest that the removal of a child by a parent who is entitled to do so and who

problem is for the residence order itself to deal expressly with the question of trips abroad, if this appears to be in issue. The point is that the one-month rule will be subject to any express conditions inserted in the court's order. Thus, a s 8 order might prohibit the child's removal by either parent, unless specific consent requirements, court approval or other conditions are satisfied[1]. Even where a 'joint residence order' is granted[2] Bruch argues that 'wrongfulness can be established, inter alia, by acts that are inconsistent with the periods in which the order provides that the child is to live in the respective households'[3].

Where there is no court order
The position may be less clear where there is no court order. It cannot be emphasised strongly enough that this will be so in the overwhelming majority of cases and, in accordance with the 'no order' principle in the Children Act[4], it will also be the usual position following divorce. The 'custody' rights which arise by operation of law are, therefore, crucial. The position of *unmarried* parents will usually be straightforward. Assuming that the father has not acquired parental responsibility by agreement or court order, the mother will be solely entitled to it. She may, therefore, take the child abroad unilaterally for as long as she wishes. The father will generally have no 'custody' rights capable of being breached, as held in the case of *Re J (A Minor) (Abduction: Custody Rights)*[5]. The matter was, however, complicated by the decision of the Court of Appeal in *Re B (A Minor) (Abduction)*[6] in which the father, together with the maternal grandmother, had de facto care of the child before the child was abducted. The majority (Peter Gibson LJ dissenting) drew a distinction between strict legal rights and de facto or 'inchoate' rights and held that the factual care of the child could give rise to 'rights of custody' within the meaning of the Convention. This was, however, an unusual case in which the mother's behaviour was particularly reprehensible and it is clear that mere contact, however extensive, is not sufficient to establish 'rights of custody'[7]. In the vast majority of cases outside marriage the mother will be the primary carer.

The difficult legal questions which can arise where an unmarried father without parental responsibility is seeking return of a child have been the subject of a detailed Practice Note issued by the Lord Chancellor's Child Abduction Unit

---

has no intention to return brings about a change in the child's habitual residence. On the other hand, the loss of one habitual residence does not necessarily mean that a new one has been acquired. It is thus possible for a child to have no habitual residence at some point in time. See *Re M (Minors) (Residence Order: Jurisdiction)* [1993] 1 FLR 495. For another case in which wrongfulness was not established because the child could not be said to be habitually resident in the State (Canada) from which the removal took place, see *Re R (Wardship: Child Abduction) (No 2)* [1993] 1 FLR 249.
1 The court has a general power to attach conditions to s 8 orders under s 11(7) of the Children Act. For a case illustrating these principles in the 'holiday' context, see *Re D (A Minor) (Child: Removal from Jurisdiction)* [1992] 1 WLR 315.
2 Section 11(4).
3 CS Bruch (above) at p 55.
4 Section 1(5).
5 [1990] 2 AC 562. A case, in fact, decided under Western Australian law, but the principles would be the same under English law.
6 [1994] 2 FLR 249.
7 See, particularly, the decision of the Court of Appeal in *Re B (Abduction) (Rights of Custody)* [1997] 2 FLR 594.

which also reviews the state of the authorities[1]. Where the father *has* acquired parental responsibility, the position will be identical to that relating to married parents[2], but it is in relation to married parents that there are some uncertainties. What then amounts to a wrongful taking by a parent who has joint parental responsibility but there has been no court order? Again, wrongfulness must be determined by the statutes and case-law[3] in the country of the child's habitual residence, which in England means the Children Act 1989 and the Child Abduction Act 1984. Section 1 of the Child Abduction Act 1984 makes it a criminal offence for one parent to remove a child without the consent of the other but, perhaps significantly for present purposes, there are a number of defences available. Under s 1(5), no offence is committed where the child is removed:

(1) in the belief that the other person (parent for the present purposes) has consented or would have done had he been aware of all the relevant circumstances; or

(2) after taking all reasonable steps to communicate with the other person, the accused had been unable to do so; or

(3) the other person has unreasonably refused to consent.

While the former Lord Chancellor[4] and certain commentators[5] appeared to think that the regime of the Children Act would not make it more difficult to establish a wrongful taking or retention, others were more doubtful[6]. It is, to say the least, unfortunate that the question of wrongfulness under the civil law would appear to turn on what may be implied from the existence of a criminal offence, itself qualified by defences which are grounded in the nebulous notion of reasonableness. Also, it may not be very easy at all to establish a wrongful *retention* if the initial removal was reasonable under s 1(5) of the Child Abduction Act 1984[7]. Again, the answer would appear to be to obtain a residence or prohibited steps order in advance, but there are practical difficulties with this. First, child abductors are not in the habit of giving notice of their intention to snatch a child,

---

1   *Practice Note (Hague Convention: Applications by Fathers Without Parental Responsibility)* [1998] 1 FLR 491. See also now the helpful judgment of Hale J in *Re W; Re B (Child Abduction: Unmarried Father)* [1998] 2 FLR 146 in which she gives guidance as to the circumstances in which unmarried parents should be advised that removal by the mother of a child who is habitually resident in England or Wales will be wrongful under the Hague Convention. These are where:
   (a) the father has parental responsibility either by agreement or court order; or
   (b) there is a court order in force prohibiting removal; or
   (c) there are relevant proceedings pending in a court in England and Wales; or
   (d) the father is currently the primary carer for the child, at least if the mother has delegated such care to him.
   The case is also a good illustration of the practical circumstances in which unmarried fathers may, or may not, establish a wrongful taking.
2   The father may also have 'custody rights' where he has interim care and control of the child in wardship proceedings. See *Re S (Abduction: Hague and European Conventions)* [1997] 1 FLR 958.
3   Central authorities are authorised under the Hague Convention to provide the court with information on the custody law of the child's habitual residence.
4   See the reference in CS Bruch (above) at p 59, to the Lord Chancellor's speech on 12 October 1991.
5   M Everall 'Child Abduction after the Hague Convention' [1990] Fam Law 169.
6   CS Bruch (above).
7   On the distinction between removal and retention, see the House of Lords decision in *Re H (Minors) (Abduction: Custody Rights); Re S (Minors) (Abduction: Custody Rights)* [1991] 2 AC 476.

and applying for an order really depends on being forewarned. Secondly, s 1(5) of the Children Act militates against the granting of orders unless it can be positively demonstrated that they are necessary. Thus, unless there is clear evidence of the risk, the court may simply refuse to make an order. This is one instance in which the courts, notwithstanding the general thinking in the Children Act should, perhaps, be more ready to make orders.

Wrongfulness may also be established where the taking contravened the defendant's own rights (in the sense that he exceeded them)[1], or those of an institution (such as a local authority where the child is in care, or the court where a child is a ward of court)[2]. Ignorance of the wrongfulness of the removal has been held to be no defence[3]. Finally, one of the objects of the Hague Convention is 'to ensure that ... rights of access under the law of one Contracting State are effectively respected in the other Contracting States'[4], and Central Authorities are required 'to make arrangements for organizing or securing the effective exercise of rights of access'[5]. In the English context this, of course, now means contact. However, the Court of Appeal has held that the duties of the Central Authority under Article 21 are of an *executive* rather than judicial nature, creating no rights in private law which a parent can directly enforce[6].

The Hague Convention has proved to be rather ineffectual in the enforcement of rights of access largely because a mere right of access does not amount to 'custody rights' within the meaning of the Convention. Thus, removal of a child is not a wrongful taking merely because it frustrates the access rights of the aggrieved parent[7]. It may be that this is one area in which the Hague Protection of Children Convention 1996 may have a significant role to play[8].

When should the child's return be ordered?

As has been seen, the court is generally precluded under the Hague Convention from becoming embroiled in the merits of rights to custody[9]. The general rule under Article 12 is that, provided the application is brought within 12 months of the removal, the court must order return of the child. This is subject to a number of limited exceptions under Article 13, although, even where one of these is established, the court retains its discretion to order a return under Article 18.

---

1   *Re H (A Minor) (Abduction)* [1990] 2 FLR 439.
2   *Re J (A Minor: Abduction: Ward of Court)* [1989] Fam 85. See also *B v B (Abduction)* [1993] 1 FLR 238.
3   *C v C (Minors) (Child Abduction)* [1992] 1 FLR 163.
4   Article 1.
5   Article 7(f).
6   *Re G (A Minor) (Hague Convention: Access)* [1993] 1 FLR 669 and *Practice Note (Child Abduction Unit – Lord Chancellor's Department)* [1993] 1 FLR 804. This makes it plain that Article 21 confers no jurisdiction to determine matters relating to access, or to recognise or enforce foreign access orders. It merely provides for executive co-operation in the enforcement of such recognition as national law allows. Thus, the Central Authority should discharge its duty by providing the applicant with solicitors who may act on his behalf in applying for legal aid and instituting proceedings in the High Court under s 8 of the Children Act.
7   See *S v H (Abduction: Access Rights)* [1997] 1 FLR 971.
8   This certainly seems to be the view of A-M Hutchinson and MH Bennett in 'The Hague Child Protection Convention 1996' [1998] Fam Law 35 at p 38. (See further below.) See also NV Lowe 'Problems relating to access disputes under the Hague Convention on International Child Abduction' (1994) 8 IJLF 374.
9   Article 16.

Consent or acquiescence

The court may refuse to return a child where 'the person, institution or other body having care of the person of a child was not actually exercising the custody rights at the time of removal or retention, or had consented to or subsequently acquiesced in the removal or retention'[1].

Most of the reported cases on Article 13(a) have been concerned with the concept of acquiescence which we discuss below. So far as the notion of consent is concerned, it has been held that consent may be oral and need not be in writing but must be positive and unequivocal[2].

The notion of acquiescence has caused considerable difficulty[3]. It can be active, where some step is taken by the aggrieved parent which is thought to be inconsistent with insistence on summary return of the child, or it may be passive, as where the aggrieved parent allows time to pass by without any words or actions indicating such insistence.

The leading authority is now the decision of the House of Lords in *Re H (Minors) (Abduction: Acquiescence)*[4], where the parties were Orthodox Jews living in Israel. The mother brought the children to England without the father's consent and, initially, he sought relief through the Rabbinical courts in Israel in accordance with his religion. Only when the mother did not comply with a summons issued by the Beth Din did the father, with the approval of the court, take action under the Hague Convention. The Court of Appeal, which had found for the mother, attempted to draw a distinction between the nature of the test to be applied where the alleged acquiescence was passive and that where it was active. It held that only in the case of passive acquiescence could account be taken of the subjective attitude of the aggrieved parent.

The House of Lords rejected any such distinction, holding that under the Hague Convention the concept of acquiescence was always concerned with the subjective state of mind of the wronged parent whether or not any positive action had been taken by that parent. Since acquiescence was a question of fact, this subjective intention could be inferred from the outward and visible acts of the wronged parent. The burden of proof was on the abducting parent to show acquiescence. In this case, there was nothing inconsistent in the father pursuing remedies in the courts of his habitual residence, whether religious or civil, and having subsequent recourse to the Hague Convention.

Grave risk of harm or intolerable situation

The court may also refuse to order the child's return where 'there is a grave risk that his or her return would expose the child to physical or psychological harm or otherwise place the child in an intolerable situation'[5]. Here, the courts have been at pains to stress that it is not just *any* danger which will trigger the defence. They

---

1   Article 13(a).
2   *Re K (Abduction: Consent)* [1997] 2 FLR 212. See also *Re B (Abduction: Article 13 Defence)* [1997] 2 FLR 573.
3   See, for example, *Re A and Another (Minors: Abduction)* [1991] 2 FLR 241; *Re F (A Minor) (Child Abduction)* [1992] 1 FLR 548; *Re AZ (A Minor) (Abduction: Acquiescence)* [1993] 1 FLR 682; *Re S (Minors) (Abduction: Acquiescence)* [1994] 1 FLR 819 and *Re R (Child Abduction: Acquiescence)* [1995] 1 FLR 716. The latest reported cases are *P v P (Abduction: Acquiescence)* [1998] Fam Law 512, *Re D (Abduction: Acquiescence)* [1998] 2 FLR 335, and *Re S (Abduction: Acquiescence)* [1998] 2 FLR 115.
4   [1997] 1 FLR 872.
5   Article 13(b).

do not have carte blanche to apply the welfare principle as they have in ordinary domestic cases. It must be shown that the risk is a serious one and the harm envisaged must be weighty and not trivial[1]. The court will refuse to listen to the argument of the parent who has effected the removal that it would place the child in danger to allow him to return *unaccompanied*. This would be to allow that parent to profit from his wrongdoing. Instead, the court will accept that a degree of discomfort to the child is bound to be involved in a return and will leave it to the parent to decide whether he wishes to return with the child. In practice, parents often do return with children, perhaps with the financial support of the parent left behind[2]. Occasionally, however, the defence has succeeded where there has been a history of abuse or violence giving rise to a wholly understandable fear of returning on the part of the children and/or the parent[3] and in one case where there was a dislike and fear of the maternal grandmother who was seeking the child's return[4].

The child's wishes

Article 13 of the Hague Convention also provides that the child's return may be refused where the court 'finds that the child objects to being returned and has attained an age and degree of maturity at which it is appropriate to take account of its views'.

It is plain that the views, even of a *Gillick*-competent child, will be accorded less weight than in domestic proceedings[5] again on the principle that to do otherwise would frustrate the principal aim of the Hague Convention – to secure that the substantive issues are determined in the place of the child's habitual residence[6]. Despite this, there is evidence from several reported cases that the courts are prepared to listen to a child's objections, in appropriate circumstances[7], but will not allow the child's wishes to determine the matter[8]. Exceptionally, the court may allow children to be separately represented in proceedings under the Convention[9]. It is clear that something more than just a preference on the part of the child will be required to forestall an order for his return: a mere assertion will not suffice[10]. However, where the child's views accord with the court's own view of his

---

1   See, for example, *Re C (A Minor) (Abduction)* [1989] 1 FLR 403; *B v B (Abduction)* [1993] 1 FLR 238; *Re L (Child Abduction: Psychological Harm)* [1993] 2 FLR 401 and *N v N (Abduction: Article 13 Defence)* [1995] 1 FLR 107.

2   CS Bruch (above) at p 62, notes that this is common where the abducting parent has alleged abuse or other difficult home circumstances and the petitioner is prepared to offer undertakings to alleviate the court's concern. See, for example, *Re O (Child Abduction: Undertakings)* [1994] 2 FLR 349.

3   See *Re F (Child Abduction: Risk if Returned)* [1995] 2 FLR 31 and *Re G (Abduction: Psychological Harm)* [1995] 1 FLR 64.

4   *The Ontario Court v M and M (Abduction: Children's Objections)* [1997] 1 FLR 475.

5   Where they must be taken into account as the first item in the statutory checklist. See s 1(3)(a) of the Children Act and Chapter 4 above.

6   The court may, thus, not be prepared to adjourn proceedings for the purpose of ascertaining the views of the child. See *P v P (Minors) (Child Abduction)* [1992] 1 FLR 155.

7   For a review of some of the earlier cases, see T Sachs 'The Views of the Child in Abduction Cases: *Re R* and *S v S*' (1993) 5 JCL 43.

8   *Re S (Minors) (Abduction: Custody Rights)* [1994] 1 FLR 819.

9   *Re S (Abduction: Children: Separate Representation)* [1997] 1 FLR 486.

10 See *P v P* (above). See also *Re HB (Abduction: Children's Objections)* [1997] 1 FLR 392 and *Re K (Abduction: Child's Objections)* [1995] 1 FLR 997. For recent cases in which the courts upheld the

best interests, the court may be prepared to attach greater significance to them[1]. It has been held that, where the court, taking into account the views of two children aged nine and seven respectively, decided not to return them, this may also justify failing to return a younger sibling, too young to express his own views[2].

Absence for more than a year

It has been noted that the principle of the child's return is mandatory (but for the exceptions) where the application is brought within a year of the removal. Where the absence of the child has lasted in excess of a year, the Hague Convention still requires the child's return 'unless it is demonstrated that the child is now settled in its new environment'[3]. The strength of the status quo principle in domestic proceedings has been commented upon[4]. This is displaced in the case of wrongful takings, but there comes a point when the possible harm and disruption to the child of a further move must be taken into account, whatever the rights and wrongs of the original behaviour. Even here, however, the delay may be attributable to the child having been secreted by the abducting parent or may be the result of inadequate or incorrect legal advice being given to the applicant[5].

Violation of human rights and fundamental freedoms

A final defence is that the child's return would be contrary to the fundamental principles of the requested State regarding protection of human rights and fundamental freedoms. As yet, little or no use appears to have been made of the provision. Bruch attributes this, possibly, to the democratic reforms in Eastern Europe and the absence of cases yet raising issues of gender-based or religiously based custody laws[6].

Action under the European Convention

When may the European Convention be invoked?

The European Convention is utilised less than the Hague Convention since it applies only as between certain European countries, and then only if the applicant has a court order in his favour. This is because the European Convention[7] applies only to 'improper removals', which are defined as those which involve removal across international boundaries in breach of decisions relating to custody. These are defined widely enough to embrace orders for residence or contact[8]. The European Convention is really, therefore, about the reciprocal enforcement of court orders in contracting States and, to that extent, it is similar in nature to the Family Law Act 1986 which does the same in relation to orders in different parts of the UK[9]. The Central Authorities perform similar functions under this

---

objections of the children, see *Re B (Abduction: Children's Objections)* [1998] 1 FLR 667 and *The Ontario Court v M and M (Abduction: Children's Objections)* (above).

1   As in *Re R (A Minor) (Abduction)* [1992] 1 FLR 105 and *S v S (Child Abduction: Child's View)* [1992] 2 FLR 492.
2   *B v K (Child Abduction)* [1993] Fam Law 17.
3   Article 12. The applicant must, however, act expeditiously in the proceedings, which may otherwise be struck out. See *Re G (Abduction: Striking Out Application)* [1995] 2 FLR 410.
4   See Chapter 4 above.
5   Examples given by CS Bruch (above) at p 63.
6   Ibid.
7   Article 1.
8   Article 1(c).
9   See p 592 below.

Convention. The Convention[1] requires the Central Authority in the country of the child's original residence, on receiving a proper application, to act without delay to secure the recognition and enforcement of the custody order. The order must be registered in a court of the contracting State to which the child has been removed. Thereupon, *that* court will have the same powers of enforcement as if it had made the original order[2], and this will enable it to order return of the child.

Can registration be refused?
In limited circumstances, a court may refuse to register an order. The court cannot reopen the merits of the original order, but it may refuse to register or enforce the order if the proceedings were defective, if the order is incompatible with another order which has already been recognised or if the child or defendant has insufficient connection with the State in which it was made[3]. These are matters principally relating to procedural impropriety. Of greater substance is Article 10, which allows a refusal to register 'where it is found by reason of a change of circumstances including the passage of time but not including a mere change in the residence of the child after an improper removal, the effects of the original decision are manifestly no longer in accordance with the welfare of the child'. This, in essence, means that the decision is no longer consistent with the welfare principle[4]. The effect would seem to be to allow the courts to consider the merits of cases more readily than they can under the Hague Convention. Article 8 provides for the virtual mandatory registration of orders, where the application is made within six months of the child's removal, but a number of countries, including the UK, have entered a reservation to this Article[5]. Where registration is refused, other applications can, nonetheless, be made which will be heard on their merits[6].

Despite the more restricted operation of the European Convention, Bromley and Lowe[7] have instanced two situations in which an applicant, having a choice between the two Conventions, might invoke it. The first is where the removal took place *before* implementation of the European Convention by one of the contracting States involved. This is because the European Convention has been held to have retrospective operation, whereas the Hague Convention has not[8]. The second is where the child is taken to a contracting State which has implemented Article 8. Here, an order for the return of the child is a virtual certainty if the application is made within six months of the removal. In practice, they note that there is likely to be little difference, since an order for return under the Hague Convention is also very likely in the circumstances. In any event, where

1 Article 5.
2 Child Abduction and Custody Act 1985, s 18.
3 Articles 9 and 10, and see *Re M (Child Abduction) (European Convention)* [1994] 1 FLR 551.
4 See, for example, *F v F (Minors) (Custody: Foreign Order)* [1989] Fam 1; *Re G (A Minor) (Child Abduction: Enforcement)* [1990] 2 FLR 325; and *Re R (Abduction: Hague and European Conventions)* [1997] 1 FLR 663.
5 The effect is that registration may be refused even where the application is made within six months of the child's removal under the terms of Article 10.
6 Child Abduction and Custody Act 1985, s 20(1).
7 *Bromley's Family Law* (8th edn) (Butterworths, 1992) at p 494.
8 *Re H (Minors) (Abduction: Custody Rights); Re S (Minors) (Abduction: Custody Rights)* [1991] 2 AC 476. Cf *Re L (Child Abduction: European Convention)* [1992] 2 FLR 178.

an application is brought under both Conventions, the Hague Convention has precedence.

Non-Convention countries

Although the Hague Convention has been widely ratified, and further ratifications are expected, there are still many countries which fall outside it. In these cases, the prospects for recovery of abducted children may be bleak[1]. The picture world-wide can only be improved by the process of further ratifications. The options for a parent of a child abducted to a non-Convention country are very limited. They boil down to trying to secure the extradition of the abductor, if an extradition treaty exists between the two countries concerned, or trying to pursue civil proceedings in the country to which the child has been taken. In the case of children taken *to* England, the most likely proceedings are wardship or, possibly now, an application for a s 8 order. The foreign element and probable complexity in this type of case militates towards wardship[2]. Some parents, in desperation, have, in the past, resorted to extra-legal means such as attempting to snatch the child back, with or without the assistance of private investigators.

Abductions between different parts of the UK

This section is concerned with abductions *within* the UK from one of its constituent jurisdictions to another, ie between England and Wales, Scotland and Northern Ireland[3]. Under the Family Law Act 1986, 'Part I orders' made in one of these jurisdictions are recognised and enforceable in both of the others as if made there[4]. This is with a view to avoiding conflicts of jurisdiction between courts in different parts of the UK[5]. The Family Law Act 1986 applies to orders relating to

---

1 But where the English courts do become seised of the matter they are liable to order the return of the child, on principles similar to those which are applied under the Conventions. See, for example, *Re F (Minor: Abduction: Jurisdiction)* [1991] Fam 25. Cf *C v C (Abduction: Jurisdiction)* [1993] Fam Law 185 in which Cazalet J applied the principles of the Hague Convention in *refusing* the return of a three-year-old child to Brazil. The decision was based primarily on the delay which would be occasioned (over a year) if the case were to be heard in the Brazilian courts. Although the courts will try to act in accordance with the spirit of the Convention, the Court of Appeal has emphasised that the issue of the return of the child in non-Convention cases is governed by the welfare principle. See *Re P (A Minor) (Child Abduction: Non-Convention Country)* [1997] 1 FLR 780. In this case the court refused to order the return of the child to India on the basis that the mother would suffer psychological harm which would affect her ability to care for the child if ordered to return there. See also *Re JA (Child Abduction: Non-Convention Country)* [1998] 1 FLR 231 where the Court of Appeal held that it would be an abdication of responsibility for the High Court to surrender the determination of its ward's future to a foreign court (in this case the United Arab Emirates) whose regime might be inimical to the child's welfare.

2 See the discussion in *Bromley's Family Law* (above) at p 487.

3 See Law Com Report No 138 *Custody of Children – Jurisdiction and Enforcement within the United Kingdom* upon which the legislation was based.

4 Family Law Act 1986, s 25.

5 For an example of a conflict of jurisdiction, see *T v T (Custody: Jurisdiction)* [1992] 1 FLR 43. Courts in one jurisdiction will consider themselves bound by the principle of comity and will not, in effect, purport to act as a Court of Appeal where, for example, an interim order has been made in another jurisdiction. For a post-Children Act decision involving conflicts of jurisdiction between England and Scotland, turning on the correct habitual residence of the child, see *Re M (Minors) (Residence Order: Jurisdiction)* [1993] 1 FLR 495 and the commentary by G Douglas at [1993] Fam Law 285. See also *S v S (Custody: Jurisdiction)* [1995] 1 FLR 155 and *M v M (Abduction: England and Scotland)* [1997] 2 FLR 263.

children under 16 years of age but, since the Children Act, there will, in any event, be few English orders relating to children over this age.

The procedure is that the holder of the order applies to the court in the jurisdiction to which the child has been taken. In England and Wales and Northern Ireland this is the High Court, and in Scotland it is the Court of Session[1]. Registration is achieved by sending to the appropriate court a certified copy of the order. Once the order has been registered, the registering court can enforce it[2]. An interested party may intervene in enforcement proceedings and ask that the application be stayed or dismissed. The grounds for doing so are limited to such cases as where the original court lacked jurisdiction to make the order, or the circumstances have changed such that a variation of the order is justified[3].

The Family Law Act 1986 applies only to moves between different parts of the UK and not to moves within *one* of its constituent parts. Thus, it could not be invoked where, for example, a child is moved from London to Swansea, Inverness to Glasgow or Coleraine to Belfast. In such cases, there will be no potential conflict of jurisdiction and, with regard to moves within England and Wales, an application would need to be made for a s 8 order to be granted and enforced. Since parental responsibility is shared between married parents, and it may be exercised independently, moves like this are not unlawful, however distressing they may be to the parent who is left behind. The answer will be to obtain a residence order and enforce it.

THE HAGUE CHILD PROTECTION CONVENTION 1996

The full title of the Hague Child Protection Convention is the Hague Convention on Jurisdiction, Applicable Law, Recognition, Enforcement and Co-operation in Respect of Parental Responsibility and Measures for the Protection of Children[4]. It is a revised and modified version of the little-known and little-used Hague Convention on the Protection of Minors 1961[5]. It would not be an exaggeration to say that few family lawyers had even heard of the 1961 Convention and even fewer knew anything about it[6]. This is not perhaps surprising since both the 1961 and the 1996 Conventions are more the territory of private international lawyers than they are of family lawyers. The Child Protection Convention is concerned with the classic conflicts issues of jurisdiction, applicable law, recognition and enforcement, as its full title makes clear. It is not concerned with substantive rights and,

---

1 Family Law Act 1986, s 32(1).
2 Ibid, s 29.
3 Ibid, ss 30 and 31.
4 For a concise and helpful discussion of the Convention, see A-M Hutchinson and MH Bennett 'The Hague Child Protection Convention 1996' [1998] Fam Law 35 and G Van Bueren 'Annual Review of International Family Law' in A Bainham (ed) *The International Survey of Family Law 1996* (Martinus Nijhoff, 1998) at pp 7–10.
5 The full title of which was the Convention on the Power of the Authorities and the Law Applicable in Respect of the Protection of Minors. The 1961 Convention was something of a flop having been ratified by just 11 States, all of which were European.
6 As the author discovered in appearing for the International Society of Family Law at The Hague.

was fierce resistance at the Hague to the incorporation of any such rights in the Convention[1].

It must also be appreciated that the 1996 Convention is a 'sister' Convention to two other Conventions emanating from the Hague Conference on Private International Law. These are the Hague Child Abduction Convention[2] and the Hague Convention on Inter-Country Adoption[3]. This is important for two reasons. The first is that the Child Protection Convention is not directly concerned with these two great international problems of child abduction and inter-country adoption since they are governed by other Conventions. The second is that efforts have been made to avoid clashes between the respective Conventions so that, for example, the Child Protection Convention should not operate in a way which contradicts the fundamental principles under the Abduction Convention governing the return of children wrongfully removed[4]. So far as substantive rights are concerned, the point should also be made that action taken under the 1996 Convention should be consistent with the rights enshrined in the United Nations Convention on the Rights of the Child.

What is the Convention about?

If the 1996 Convention is not about substantive rights and not (at least not directly) about abduction or inter-country adoption, the reader may legitimately wonder exactly what it *is* about. The objects of the Convention are set out in Article 1, and in Article 3 there is a non-exhaustive list of matters in relation to which contracting States may take *protective measures*. This is followed by a list of matters specified in Article 4 which are excluded from the scope of the Convention.

Objects of the Convention

Article 1 describes the objects of the Convention which include determining the State with jurisdiction to take protective measures; the law to be applied; the applicable law governing parental responsibility; providing for the recognition and enforcement of the protective measures taken in all contracting States to achieve the purposes of the Convention.

The Convention in principle applies to both protection of the child's person and the child's property and 'child' for these purposes includes persons 'from the moment of their birth until they reach the age of 18 years'[5]. Attempts at The Hague to include the 'unborn child' were resisted.

---

1 One of the more vivid impressions made on the author in the course of the proceedings of the Hague Conference on Private International Law.
2 Discussed at pp 582 et seq above.
3 See Chapter 7.
4 The matter is governed by Article 7, the general principle (subject to limited exceptions) being that the State from which the child has been removed, which will normally be that of the child's habitual residence, should retain the welfare jurisdiction and hence the jurisdiction to take protective measures under the 1996 Convention. See further A-M Hutchinson and MH Bennett (above) at pp 36–37.
5 Article 2. The 1996 Convention uses the term 'child' rather than 'minor' which was the term used in the 1961 Convention.

Included matters

It is clear from Article 3 that, inter alia, States may take protective measures in relation to the attribution, delegation, exercise and termination of parental responsibility; custody rights (which include residence and access issues); guardianship; foster-care or institutional care including the provision of care by Kafala (a form of Islamic guardianship) or care in an analogous institution; supervision by a public authority of the care of a child and the administration, conservation and disposal of a child's property.

Excluded matters

Article 4 contains an exhaustive list of matters which are outside the scope of the Convention. These are establishing or contesting a parent–child relationship; measures relating to adoption; the child's name; emancipation; maintenance; trusts and succession; public educational and health measures and penal and immigration matters.

It has been suggested[1] that these exclusions fall essentially into three categories:

(1) matters which of themselves cannot be said to be protective of the child;
(2) matters which touch on general public law; and
(3) matters already covered by other Conventions.

General principles under the Convention

The central principal in the operation of the Convention is Article 5. This provides that 'the judicial or administrative authorities of the contracting State of the habitual residence of the child have jurisdiction to take measures directed to the protection of the child's person or property'. Thus, the normal rule is that the child's habitual residence will dictate jurisdiction. It should, however, be borne in mind that this may change where the child leaves one country and establishes a new habitual residence in another.

The test of habitual residence could cause difficulty in the case of inter-nationally displaced children and refugees who 'have severed links with their former State of habitual residence' but 'their situation is too precarious to have established a new State of habitual residence'[2]. The Convention in these circumstances allows the State in whose territory the child now is to take protective measures. In a number of other respects, the Convention allows for flexibility in jurisdictional matters and encourages co-operation between States. Thus, it is possible for the State of the child's habitual residence to relinquish jurisdiction in favour of another State where it considers this appropriate[3], and it is also possible for that other State to request this as being in the child's best interests[4]. In all *urgent* cases, the authority of the State in whose territory the child is present has jurisdiction to take 'any necessary measures of protection'[5]. Finally, there are limited exceptions which allow a State which is not that of the child's habitual residence, but which is exercising a divorce jurisdiction, to take measures of protection[6].

---

1   A-M Hutchinson and MH Bennett (above) at p 36.
2   G Van Bueren (above) at p 9.
3   Article 8.
4   Article 9.
5   Article 11.
6   Article 10.

Co-operation between States

A primary feature of the Convention is to avoid conflicts of jurisdiction and secure co-operation between States in taking necessary measures to protect children. To this end, and in keeping with other Hague Conventions, States are obliged to designate a Central Authority with responsibility for the discharge of their functions under the Convention. Only time will tell whether the Convention is more effective than its predecessor in achieving these aims.

THE EUROPEAN CONVENTION ON THE EXERCISE OF CHILDREN'S RIGHTS 1996

The European Convention on the Exercise of Children's Rights is, as its title suggests, not concerned with creating substantive rights for children but with the practical implementation of their rights[1]. The Convention is the response of the Council of Europe to the perceived need for an instrument to supplement the United Nations Convention on the Rights of the Child, Article 4 of which requires States parties to 'undertake all appropriate legislative, administrative and other measures for the implementation of the rights recognized in [that] Convention'[2].

The object of the 1996 Convention is set out in Article 1(2) and is:

'... in the best interests of children, to promote their rights, to grant them procedural rights and to facilitate the exercise of these rights by ensuring that children are, themselves or through other persons or bodies, informed and allowed to participate in the proceedings affecting them before a judicial authority.'

The subject matter of the Convention is therefore procedural rights. It is about the participation of children in family proceedings affecting them – in short, their right to be heard – and it builds upon Article 12(2) of the United Nations Convention[3].

Scope of the Convention

The Convention, in common with the Child Protection Convention discussed above, applies to children under the age of 18[4]. It is concerned with 'family proceedings' before a judicial authority which, for these purposes, includes an administrative authority having equivalent powers. The Convention contains no definition of 'family proceedings' but it is made explicit that the expression includes 'those involving the exercise of parental responsibilities, in particular,

---

1 For commentary on the Convention, see M Freeman *The Moral Status of Children* (Martinus Nijhoff, 1997) at pp 57–59; G Van Bueren 'Annual Review of International Family Law' in A Bainham (ed) *The International Survey of Family Law 1995* (Martinus Nijhoff, 1997) at pp 5–8; and M Killerby 'The Draft European Convention on the Exercise of Children's Rights' (1995) *International Journal of Children's Rights* 127.

2 For a more detailed discussion of the initiatives of the Council of Europe in the area of children's rights, see J Fortin *Children's Rights and the Developing Law* (Butterworths, 1998) at pp 56–58.

3 Article 12(2) provides:
   '... the child shall in particular be provided the opportunity to be heard in any judicial and administrative proceedings affecting the child either directly, or through a representative or an appropriate body, in a manner consistent with the procedural rules of national law.'

4 Article 1(1).

residence and access to children'[1]. Each State is required to specify at least three types of family proceedings before a judicial authority to which the Convention is to apply[2]. As Freeman has rightly pointed out, at the current time it would be much easier for English law to comply with the Convention's requirements in those family proceedings in which care or adoption issues arise than in relation to the more 'private' family proceedings such as divorce or freestanding applications for residence or contact[3]. But, as we have seen, there is some prospect following the enactment of the Family Law Act 1996 that children's rights of representation in certain kinds of private family proceedings may be improved[4].

What then are the requirements of the Convention? The key provisions are Articles 3 and 4. Article 3 gives to the child 'considered by internal law as having sufficient understanding' the rights:

(a) to receive all relevant information;
(b) to be consulted and express his or her views; and
(c) to be informed of the possible consequences of his or her wishes and the possible consequences of any decision.

Article 4 relates to separate representation of children in cases of conflicts of interest which preclude the 'holders of parental responsibilities' from representing the children themselves. It provides that, in these circumstances, the child concerned 'shall have the right to apply in person or through other persons or bodies for a special representative'[5]. Other principles under the Convention strike a chord with English family legislation. There is, for example, a duty on the part of judicial authorities 'to act speedily to avoid any unnecessary delay and procedures [must] be available to ensure that their decisions are rapidly enforced'[6]. In urgent cases, judicial authorities are to have power to take decisions which are immediately enforceable and to act of their own motion in 'serious cases' where the welfare of the child is in danger[7]. There is encouragement of mediation, as in the English Family Law Act 1996, but as Freeman comments, the Convention curiously 'does not extend the procedural rights just listed to this method of dispute resolution'[8]. The position of children in the mediation process remains a matter of considerable uncertainty[9]. A Standing Committee has been established to keep under review problems relating to the Convention, to consider any relevant questions concerning its interpretation or implementation, to propose amendments and to provide advice and assistance to the national bodies having functions under the Convention[10].

---

1 Article 1(3).
2 Article 1(4).
3 M Freeman *The Moral Status of Children* (above) at p 58.
4 See Chapters 4 and 13.
5 Under Article 4(2), States are free to limit this right to children who are considered by internal law to have sufficient understanding.
6 Article 7. Cf the 'no-delay' principle under the Children Act 1989 discussed in Chapter 2.
7 Articles 7 and 8.
8 Article 13 and M Freeman (above) at p 58.
9 See Chapter 4 above.
10 Articles 16 et seq.

Assessment of the Convention

The Convention has not had an enthusiastic reception from commentators who have been quick to draw attention to its limitations. Van Bueren regrets that more was not done to encourage States 'to begin to develop innovative methods of child participation in family proceedings' and thinks some of the language used in the Convention to be unduly restrictive[1]. Freeman describes it as a 'weak document' and thinks it 'toothless' when compared with the European Convention on Human Rights[2]. At the same time, there is general acknowledgement that the Convention has a symbolic significance in drawing the attention of States to the procedural rights of children and in recognising that without effective remedies the assertion of rights may be little more than empty rhetoric.

THE EUROPEAN CONVENTION ON HUMAN RIGHTS

All of the above Conventions were concerned specifically with children. We conclude by examining the European Convention on Human Rights which, in contrast, was originally drafted with adults in mind. Here, the central issue is the extent to which the fundamental rights and freedoms guaranteed by the Convention have application to children and can be enforced on their behalf.

The European Convention is about to be incorporated into English domestic law under the Human Rights Bill 1998. What exactly this will mean for English law generally, and for family law in particular, will remain a matter of speculation for some time[3]. What is certain is that so-called 'Convention rights'[4] will be directly enforceable in the English courts, thereby circumventing the long and convoluted procedure which has hitherto had to be followed where a violation of the Convention is alleged. At present, it is necessary for individuals to petition the European Commission having first exhausted domestic procedures. Where a child is a ward of court it has been held by Johnson J in *Re M (Petition to European Commission of Human Rights)*[5] that the leave of the court is not required to bring a petition to Europe. In this case it was held to be inappropriate for the child's carer to bring the petition on his behalf (since there was a conflict of interest between them) and it was left to the Official Solicitor to decide whether such a petition should be brought and, if so, to bring it on the boy's behalf. Where a settlement is not achieved at this stage, the case is referred to the European Court of Human Rights sitting in Strasbourg. All this can take years and the time-scale in children cases can have a dramatic impact[6]. There is no better illustration of this than the

---

1 G Van Beuren 'Annual Review of International Family Law' (above).
2 M Freeman (above) at p 39.
3 For a useful article looking at the issue from a family law perspective, see G Kingscote 'Incorporation of the European Convention on Human Rights' [1998] Fam Law 195. See also J Fortin *Children's Rights and the Developing Law* (Butterworths, 1998) at pp 49–56. The Bill followed the Government's White Paper *Rights Brought Home: The Human Rights Bill* (Home Office) (Cm 3782).
4 'Convention rights' under cl 1 of the Bill are essentially the 'rights and fundamental freedoms' set out in the Convention and protocols to it.
5 [1997] 1 FLR 755.
6 It will be recalled that the 'no delay' principle in children cases is enshrined in English domestic law and we noted above that it is also embodied in the European Convention on the Exercise of Children's Rights.

case of *Hokkanen v Finland*[1], where Mr Hokkanen had been attempting to secure the return of his young daughter, or at least contact with her, from the maternal grandparents – his wife having died when the child was just two years old. His futile attempts to obtain redress in the Finnish legal and welfare system culminated after almost a decade in a final judgment of the European Court in 1994. By this time, the little girl of the original dispute was approaching her teens and had made up her own mind that she was unwilling to see her father.

Now, under the Human Rights Bill, it will be possible for a person who claims that a 'public authority' (which includes a court or tribunal)[2] has acted in a way which is incompatible with his Convention rights to bring proceedings against that authority directly in the English courts[3]. It is also the case that domestic courts and tribunals, in arriving at their decisions, will be required to take into account the judgments, decisions and opinions of the European Court and Commission 'so far as, in the opinion of the court or tribunal, it is relevant to the proceedings in which the question has arisen'[4]. In short, English courts will be required to apply the large amount of jurisprudence which has been, and will continue to be, generated under the European Convention. Will this make any difference? The historical record suggests that incorporation may have a substantial effect on the further development of the notion of 'family life' and its protection against unwarranted State interference – but whether it will also lead to greater awareness and enforcement of the independent rights of children is more speculative.

The family and the European Convention

The most important Article under the European Convention in the context of family issues is Article 8[5]. This provides:

'1.   Everyone has the right to respect for his private and family life, his home and his correspondence.

2.   There shall be no interference by a public authority with the exercise of this right except such as is necessary in a democratic society in the interests of national security, public safety or the economic well-being of the country, for the prevention of disorder or crime, for the protection of health or morals, or for the protection of the rights and freedoms of others.'

Other Articles may, in certain cases, have a relevance to the family or children, such as Article 3, which prohibits torture or inhuman or degrading treatment, Article 12, which enshrines the right to marry and found a family and, perhaps most importantly, Article 14, which is often relied on in conjunction with Article 8. This provides:

'The enjoyment of the rights and freedoms set forth in this Convention shall be secured without discrimination on any ground such as sex, race, colour, language, religion, political or other opinion, national or social origin, association with a national minority, property, birth or other status.'

---

1   [1996] 1 FLR 289.
2   Clause 6 which defines 'public authority' to include 'a court or tribunal' and 'any person certain of whose functions are of a public nature'.
3   Clause 7.
4   Clause 2.
5   For a very useful collection of materials, see M Janis, R Kay and A Bradley *European Human Rights Law: Text and Materials* (Oxford, Clarendon Press, 1995) especially at ch 7 which is devoted to the case-law under Article 8.

There is no question that important changes to English family law have for some years been forced by petitions to Europe, irrespective of the lack of incorporation of the Convention. Among the more important changes have been the abolition of corporal punishment in State schools[1], the creation of better procedural rights for parents in relation to public child care proceedings[2], and disclosure of confidential records relating to children in care[3] or documents relating to proceedings in which it is sought to take a child into care[4]. Other important cases have not directly involved the UK but have certainly had implications for the state of the law here. Developments in relation to the legal position of the 'unmarried family' should be singled out in this respect. Belgium[5] and the Republic of Ireland[6] have, for example, both fallen foul of the Convention in failing to give adequate recognition to the principle that 'family life' can be constituted outside marriage, can arise from the moment of a child's birth and can give rise to *positive* obligations on the part of States to foster it, as well as the more obvious negative obligations not to interfere with it.

The majority of these cases have resulted from the alleged violation of *parents'* rights by the State but some have, at the same time, found violations of the rights of the *children* concerned. This is easy enough for the European Court to find where the parent–child relationship is conceived as a mutual one in which 'the family', consisting of parents and children, are united in opposition to what the State has done, or is trying to do. It is perhaps stating the obvious that, however offensive it may have been to the philosophical convictions of parents to have their children beaten in Scottish schools, it was every bit as offensive to the children who would be on the receiving end! The real test under the Convention is whether it can be effective in upholding the *independent* rights of children when these are set against the interests of adult society and especially where there is a conflict of interest between parent and child. It is to this vexed question that we now turn.

Children and the European Convention

There are perhaps two broad issues which may have to be confronted in the coming years regarding the application of the Convention to children.

The first issue is whether the differential treatment of children and adults by the State can be justified and, if so, to what extent. It will be recalled that Article 14, inter alia, prohibits discrimination on the basis of 'birth or *other status*'[7]. Could 'childhood' or 'minority' be regarded as falling within the term 'other status'? If so, the onus would be on the State to justify the different application of laws to children and adults. The legal disabilities that attach to minority[8] would, for example, need to be kept under review and it is not difficult to imagine challenges

---

1   Following *Campbell and Cozans v United Kingdom* (1982) 4 EHRR 293. See also *Tyrer v United Kingdom* (1979–80) 2 EHRR 1.
2   Influenced in part by *W, O, B and R v United Kingdom* (1987) 10 EHRR 29 and *R v United Kingdom* [1988] 2 FLR 445.
3   *Gaskin v United Kingdom* (1989) 12 EHRR 36.
4   *McMichael v United Kingdom* (1995) Series A, No 307 which concerned procedures under the Scottish 'children's hearings' system.
5   *Marckx v Belgium* (1979) 2 EHRR 330.
6   *Johnston v Ireland* (1986) 9 EHRR 203 and *Keegan v Ireland* (1994) 18 EHRR 342.
7   Emphasis added.
8   See Chapter 3.

under the Convention to the kinds of paternalistic interventions in relation to adolescents which we have seen in recent years[1]. It may well be that greater State paternalism or protectionism is justified towards children than towards adults but the starting point in future may have to be that children are persons with fundamental rights and the burden will be squarely on those who seek to interfere with these rights. If the jurisprudence under the European Convention does develop along these lines it will only, in a sense, reflect what the United States Supreme Court has been doing under the United States Constitution for several decades[2].

The second issue, to which we have already alluded, is also one which would be immediately familiar to American jurists but which has only been approached at the most rudimentary level, if at all, thus far under the European Convention. This is the question of a possible clash of fundamental rights between parents (or other adults) and children. There has been just a flavour of this in the European Court's decisions, especially in the recent ruling in *X, Y and Z v The United Kingdom*[3].

The issues here revolved around the birth certificate of a child, Z. X was a post-operative female-to-male transsexual who had cohabited with his female partner, Y since 1979. They received together licensed treatment and Z was conceived by artificial insemination with donor sperm. X acknowledged himself as the father of Z within the meaning of the Human Fertilisation and Embryology Act 1990. But the Registrar-General refused to allow X to be registered as the father, taking the view that only a biological *male* could be so registered. Z's birth was thus registered with the part of the register relating to paternity left blank but with Z bearing X's surname. X, Y and Z alleged a violation of their rights to family life under Article 8 together with discrimination contrary to Article 14.

The majority found no violation taking into account the wide margin of appreciation enjoyed by States. There was no common European standard about granting parental rights to transsexuals or about the manner in which the social relationship between a social father and a child conceived with donor sperm should be recognised. We are not concerned here with the detailed reasoning in the majority and minority opinions nor with the specific arguments about the rights of transsexuals under the Convention[4]. What is of interest is the apparent disagreement between Judge Pettiti and Judge Foighel about the potential conflict of interest between the social father, X, and the child, Z.

This was a joint petition by all three applicants but Judge Pettiti was clearly concerned that the process might have compromised the *independent* interests of the child. He found it necessary to deliver a separate opinion to urge that the

---

1 See Chapters 3 and 8.
2 See particularly *Re Gault* 387 US 1, in which the Supreme Court acknowledged that 'neither the Fourteenth Amendment nor the Bill of Rights is for adults alone'. See also *Tinker v Des Moines Independent Community School District* 393 US 503 (1969) which was concerned with children's rights to freedom of speech and *Goss v Lopez* 419 US 565 (1975) which was concerned with the right to a hearing in school discipline cases. Perhaps the case which best illustrates the issue of the differential treatment of children and adults is *Ginsberg v New York* 390 US 629 (1968) where it was held that prohibitions on the sale of obscene materials to minors could be constitutional but that they might be unconstitutional if imposed on adults.
3 (1997) 24 EHRR 143, and for commentary, see A Bainham 'Sex, Gender and Fatherhood: Does Biology Really Matter?' (1997) CLJ 512 and C Lind 'Perceptions of sex in the legal determination of fatherhood' [1997] CFLQ 401.
4 These are pursued further in the above notes.

independent interests of Z should have been given more weight, perhaps even to the extent of Z being separately represented. In contrast, Judge Foighel appeared to see the issues entirely from the perspective of the adult transsexual's rights and went out of his way to say that this was 'not primarily a case concerning the welfare of a child'. It is submitted that Judge Pettiti was quite correct to postulate a potential conflict of interest between X and Z or between X and Y on the one hand, and Z on the other. While it is possible to see immediately why X and Y would want X recognised as the legal father (since he was performing the social role of father), it is not obvious that this would have been in Z's interest. As the majority pointed out, X was not prevented from acting as social father to Z and this could be cemented by a joint residence order which would allow him to share parental responsibility with Y. Admittedly, there may be some inconsistency between this stance and the rules relating to the attribution of legal fatherhood under s 28 of the Human Fertilisation and Embryology Act 1990[1]. The point here is that if X had been a biological *male* from birth there would have been no question that he could have been registered as Z's father even though he was clearly not the genetic father. But the fact remains, from the perspective of Convention rights, that it might have been argued on Z's behalf that the child's rights of identity demanded the opportunity for Z, sooner or later, to attempt to ascertain the biological truth and that the registration of X as father could have impeded this.

Suppose, in crude terms, that Z could have been regarded as having a fundamental right to knowledge of his biological origins and suppose also that X and Y could be said to have fundamental rights to respect for their family life which, prima facie, required the State to allow X to be registered as the father. We would then have a clash of Convention rights and it would be necessary for one right to be given precedence over the other. It is surely not difficult with some imagination to visualise potential clashes like this across a range of issues once the idea of children's Convention rights takes root. The parent, it might be argued, has a fundamental right to decide whether the child should receive religious or sex education but, say the advocates of children's rights, children have a fundamental right to receive information in these areas[2]. Parents have Convention rights to liberty and could not possibly be compelled to have contact with their children. Really, say the advocates of children's rights, do children not have Convention rights to contact with their parents? It would be possible to go on and postulate a whole raft of issues on which the Convention rights of adults and children could conflict. It may well be that with the incorporation of the Convention we will increasingly see arguments that these conflicts should be resolved, as issues of fundamental rights, in favour of children. The only certainty is that the development of the modern law affecting children in the twenty-first century is not going to be a boring process.

---

1   As to which, see Chapter 3.
2   For English law on these questions, see Chapter 16.

INDEX